Rays of Truth — Crystals of Light

Information and Guidance for the Golden Age

Dr. Fred Bell

Rays of Truth — Crystals of Light
Information and Guidance for the Golden Age
by
Dr. Fred Bell

Published in 1999
Copyright © Dr. Fred Bell 1998

Cover Artist: Jim Zar

Published by

Medicine Bear Publishing
P.O. Bx 1075
Blue Hill, ME 0461

ISBN# 1-891850-11-3
Library of Congress CCN# 99-070036

FOREWORD

Each generation has its avant garde, whether in the arts or in the sciences. These individuals are noted for their tendency toward bold thinking and an intense belief in their ability to foresee what lies ahead for their society, their people, their loved ones. Once they have focused on their unique vision, they must next possess the courage to pursue it regardless of how strange their quest may seem to the great masses of their fellows who stand idly by in amazement or confusion. And what is more, these visionaries must achieve their dream regardless of personal consequences, for they are pledged to serve the greater good.

These extraordinary men and women are the truthseekers, those who dare challenge the prejudices of their time, those who seek tirelessly to shine a light into darkness and to bring a death to ignorance. Such a person is Dr. Fred Bell.

Dr. Bell's *Rays of Truth — Crystals of Light* ; *Information and Guidance for the Golden Age* is, as he warns, not a book for beginners. It is filled with remarkable concepts that may seem beyond comprehension, almost beyond belief. But the rewards in accepting the challenge to apply oneself to a careful reading and study of this book will lie beyond the reader's present imagination.

It is important that our species must always be able to tolerate our avant garde, our visionaries, our truthseekers, for we may all one day be able to benefit from their visions.

> — Brad Steiger, Co-author
> *The Promise*
> *The Chosen*
> *The Fellowship*

Table of Contents

Part II

*Healing the Body and Soul —
A Journey to Wholeness!*

Part III
The Soul, Energy and Light

Part IV

The Future is Now!

Prophecies are for the weak
who have lost their way
in ignorance
and sought history
from a ship of fools
who likewise lost their course
and admitted defeat.
So live in the now
and create your own reality
rather than riding in the wake
of another
and give our prophets
some time to sleep!

DISCLAIMER

This is not a book for beginners. On its pages will be found information that is candid, direct and written without regard to race, religion or belief. It is only for those who have eyes to see, ears to hear and voices to teach the children of the New Age. If you feel offended, threatened or uncomfortable, the author makes no apologies, for your time has passed and your contribution recorded. Make way for those who know.

The philosophy of the Piscean Age was "I believe." This book is an exclusive for the New Age or Aquarian Age. Here there are not philosophies. Simply, "I know."

The Piscean Age has left the children of the New Age with a world full of pollution, paranoia and stagnation. In short, the human race went downhill after the teachings of Jesus Christ! Great religions were built by weak people that could not grasp the meaning of the teachings of our Lord. But alas! The New Age children know Christ, profess nothing and live the teachings, because they are all incarnations of the Master and seek no recognition but demand truth if you want their friendship. And if not, then dear readers—cast your fate to the winds called mariah!

—Dr. Fred Bell
February 17, 1985

INTRODUCTION

This day has been long in coming. Some people know me as a scientist, others as a writer, or contactee or musician-artist. I know myself to be one thing — a student. Eternally a student of the crafts of God whose universe prevails in all of us.

When I wrote Death of Ignorance in 1979 I was motivated to share from experiencing the changes of my life in those glorious days as the New Age began on Earth. I do not like to write books. I wrote for Rockwell, NASA and many different groups during my early days on Earth. Then I was classified as a scientist- technical writer. Now I am a student-observational writer.

I have spent a lot of time with Patrick Moraz, the true Mozart of the 21st century. He is one of the most disciplined writer-composers I have ever met. Along with Brad Steiger these men have inspired me to put the pen to the paper. Brad taught me about confidence in expressing in words my adventures into the unknown. Patrick showed me a way to orchestrate the penmanship into living sound.

My wife Frauke has been a prime motivation to bring forth the story of the struggle within the human race, the balance of female-male, negative-positive energy, a balance necessary for the coming age. Semjase and the Pleiadeans have been so patient to educate my emotional body into this present age. An event occurred Friday morning on November 22, 1991 at 3:00 a.m., that was to change the course of human events.

What happened in Laguna Beach in the early hours of the morning? Why in Laguna Beach, California? And, why should Fred Bell be the witness? It is very simple. In this book the story, the event and everything that led up to it will be told.

The Andromedans changed the course of human events, divine intervention and as you shall soon see, will effect everyone in the human race. The stage has been re-set and the curtain lifts. Behold we have arrived!

The first thing that would come to mind is where and why? In order to transact such an event a location must be chosen somewhere on Earth. If the time were rolled back, say some one hundred years, Laguna Beach could have been viewed as a group of mountains overlooking the Pacific shoreline. Stretching for miles in both directions, these mountaintops offer a perfect perch for observing ships sailing far out to sea or in the sky.

The Indians, American or otherwise, often chose a vortex point for their initiations and ceremonies. If these locations are proven over time to be effective as a point of invocation, then they would eventually be deemed sacred.

The exact spot that I live in is located on an old volcanic, sacred mountain. The Indians who lived here centuries ago were long since displaced by the white man. But their energies still remain.

When we first moved onto this mountain we had one of the few houses that had been built at that time. I immediately began re-energizing this site with the help of several Tibetan masters. One thing I noticed was that whenever a ceremony took place, especially back in the 1970's, what few neighbors we had acted differently afterward. Some immediately moved away, others became more friendly. Directly to the north of us was a vacant lot and to the south a house that always remained empty. Whenever someone moved in to the southern house they lasted only a short time before moving away again.

There was a tall eucalyptus tree in our back yard, and one day the wind blew it over and we found several gold nuggets attached to its roots. Located on a volcano that is extinct with tons of quartz and gold deposits, lends great energy to the vortex. We had the City of Laguna assess the gold ore and found it to be 3 ounces per ton, fairly rich, although mining is prohibited on this mountain, which I think is a good thing.

When the Pleiadeans began to visit this site they told me it was easy to communicate with me because the vortex lent its energy to their propulsion systems and area blank-out screens. However, the Pleiadeans never fully connected to the grid. The Andromedans did.

In the winter of 1981 I added a program to this grid when I built and operated the T-700 time travel transposer. My experiments in time were exciting and I will share them in later chapters, but activating the T-700 raised the vortex beyond the present time and created side effects!

First, the weather frequencies of Southern California were affected, causing several hurricane-like storms to come into Southern California and leave record rains. Houses slid off the mountains here and in Malibu, California. This made the news for over three months. You can check that with the newspaper reports that are on file.

The second effect was a vortex deep in the Earth which causes plants and trees to grow in strange ways. We have a large pine tree growing in the back yard that was a sapling at that time in 1981. Today as a full-grown tree it looks like the grass, swirled in a clockwise manner as shown in the photos of landing tracks taken by Billy Meier in Switzerland of the Pleiadean ships. This effect is caused when you insert or delete event information into the DNA of any living thing.

When Sherrie Hanson Steiger had the Fire Starr experience (recounted in *The Fellowship* by Brad Steiger, Doubleday Bantam Books) she was taken into a separate time continuum and transported aboard a spaceship. There is a space of concentrated energy coming from the Earth's core that physically exists about 18 feet above the hilltop here, located in our livingroom, which is on the third floor of our house. The floor of the livingroom is exactly 18 feet above the ground. In October, 1991 Sacha Sai Baba materialized in the same exact spot when he visited our house. He is also sending pictures to us and these pictures hang in the livingroom by the vortex.

Over the years people from all over the world have been here and visited this very spot. Literally thousands of people have been here for one experience or another. Several of the Pleiadean systems that we have developed were tested for the first time in this vortex!

When we did weather control experimentation in 1981 we had another interesting experience. Our porch next to the livingroom looks out over the Pacific Ocean, and on a clear day the view extends over 100 miles. That April, when the great storms of the Pacific were breaking up, I placed four Pleiadean irradiators side-by-side and aimed them out over the ocean into a cloud bank that was about 2,000 feet high and 5 miles away. visibility under the cloud line was good — you could see the ocean water.

I connected one of the Tesla Earth Resonant ion generators to the base of the Irradiators, which is called a Mega Orb. Then I put a resonant charge on the entire system. A few people present, including myself, felt a rush of energy as the system charged to a potential of 50,000 volts. The house had to act as a ground and I felt the house losing its ground contact with the Earth. This was only possible because I was not using a DC or direct ground but a floating ground. This allowed the system to float slightly away from the frequency of the normal ground and establish a potential directly by scalar frequencies into the clouds.

When the potential balanced with the clouds, it caused the clouds to release four lightning bolts (one for each Pleiadean Irradiator transmitter) directly into the ocean below. Some of my neighbors happened to be watching these same clouds and saw the same four bolts in unison explode into the water. The explosion temporarily released tension but it soon built again. This time the frequency changed and the potential increased. The house began to glow slightly and creak. Again four lightning bolts exploded from the cloud, this time striking the shoreline closer to us.

The procedure increased again in frequency and I felt the hair on my arms begin to stand up. The tension was almost unbearable. Again, four lightning bolts came from the clouds and this time striking the back of the roof of the observers below me, blowing a large hole into it.

Now the tension really began to build and part of the house began to disappear. Suddenly I realized that the fourth strike was going to be directly into the Irradiators so I kicked them over and shut off the generator. Later on, I conducted a seminar in my livingroom, and guess who were present? — the people whose house had lost its roof! Karma and energy give great lessons and work in strange ways.

As you study the opening drawings, Rays of Truth — Crystals of Light will unfold its mysteries and you will learn the secrets that have long awaited their discovery by the rightful inheritors.

Dr. Fred W. Bell
December, 1997

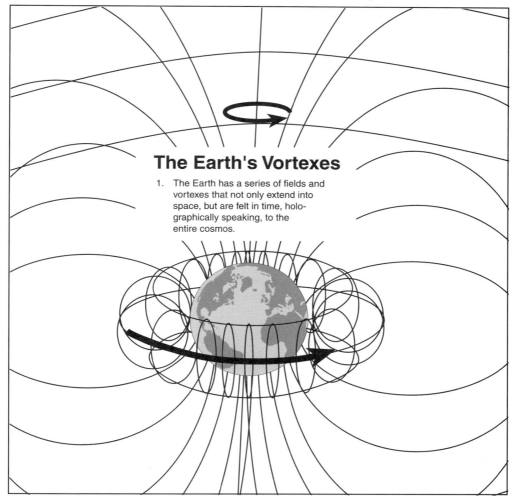

The Earth's Vortexes

1. The Earth has a series of fields and vortexes that not only extend into space, but are felt in time, holographically speaking, to the entire cosmos.

Quartz and gold both have piezoelectric effects, and in combination can, under certain astrological conditions, resonate in similar frequencies as does the Bermuda Triangle. When the astrological conditions were "set" on November 22, 1991 at 3:00 a.m., PST, the Andromedans were able to enter into the core of the Earth, which is also the center or nucleus of the astral plane.

The outer perimeter of the astral plane for Earth residents is fixed near the orbit of the moon. This is called the ring pass not, and no human will be reborn beyond its field until they have evolved beyond its frequencies of consciousness.

Everyone knows the moon has a direct effect on humans, animals, the earth and consciousness. Its gravity affects the surface tension of water which is found in all living things and, of course, our seas are alive. Likewise, the molten core of the Earth is active, and there is tremendous interaction between fire and water. Add in earth and air and you begin to receive a picture. This action of the four elements occurs in space and occurs in time. The Andromedans changed the course of these actions via the different fields shown graphically here, and thus they altered human events. The Pleiadeans set the stage in 1971, but the Andromedans made the movie; a holographic movie, I might add.

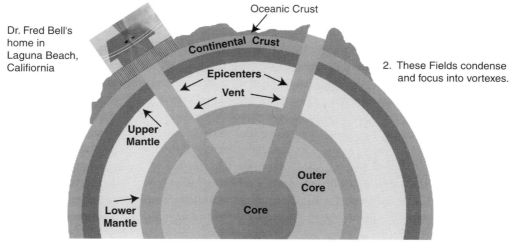

Oceanic Crust

Dr. Fred Bell's home in Laguna Beach, Califiornia

2. These Fields condense and focus into vortexes.

Continental Crust

Epicenters

Vent

Upper Mantle

Outer Core

Core

Lower Mantle

Beginning of a Vortex

Dr. Fred Bell's House

Cap of Crater Top

Vents

3. In Laguna Beach there are many caves connected to the old vent system.

Epicenter Line to Molten Core

Magma Chamber

Volcanic Crater— The Vortex and the Mountain

The Vortex and Field Generators

4. These fields can be harnessed by Pleiadean Technology.
    (Dr. Fred Bell's livingroom positioned on top of an old, extinct volcano)

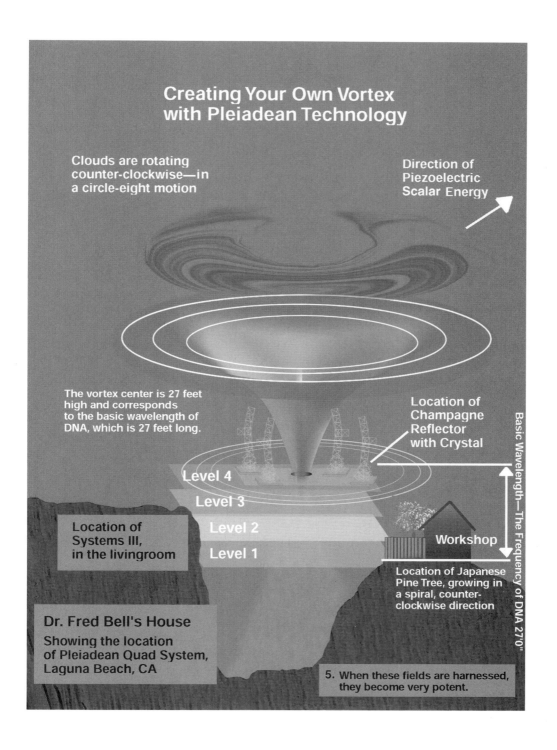

Creating Your Own Vortex with Pleiadean Technology

Clouds are rotating counter-clockwise—in a circle-eight motion

Direction of Piezoelectric Scalar Energy

The vortex center is 27 feet high and corresponds to the basic wavelength of DNA, which is 27 feet long.

Location of Champagne Reflector with Crystal

Level 4
Level 3
Level 2
Level 1

Location of Systems III, in the livingroom

Workshop

Location of Japanese Pine Tree, growing in a spiral, counter-clockwise direction

Basic Wavelength—The Frequency of DNA 270"

Dr. Fred Bell's House

Showing the location of Pleiadean Quad System, Laguna Beach, CA

5. When these fields are harnessed, they become very potent.

Basic Quad System Energy Form

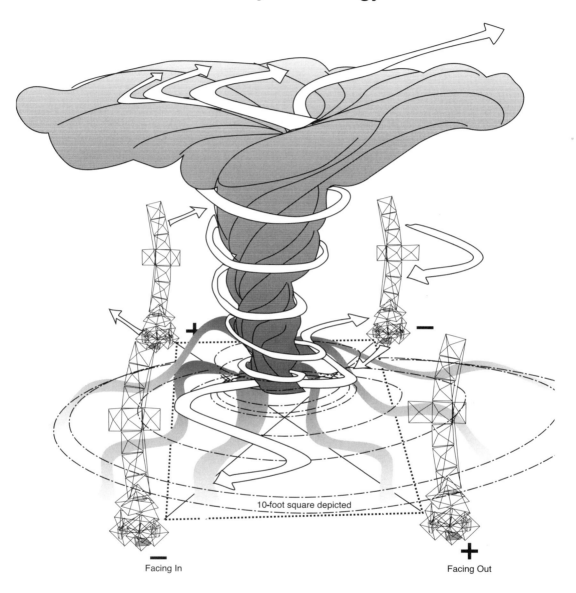

10-foot square depicted

Facing In

Facing Out

6. Under proper astrological conditions, these harnessed energies are felt worldwide.

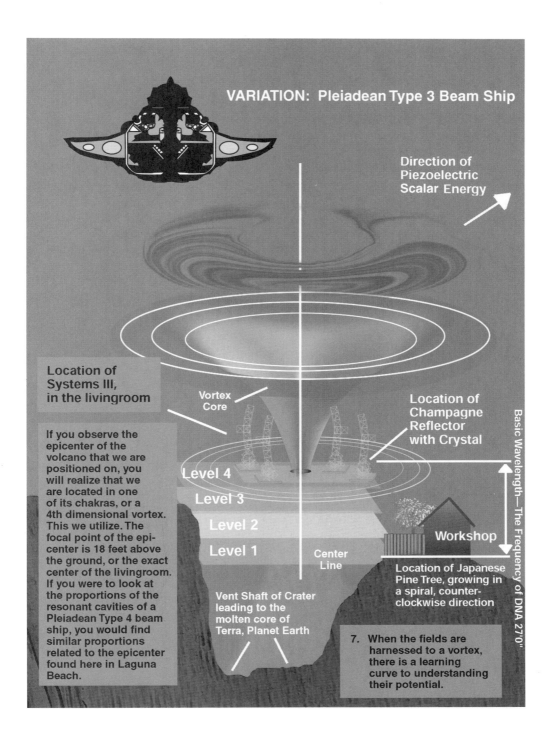

VARIATION: Pleiadean Type 3 Beam Ship

Direction of Piezoelectric Scalar Energy

Location of Systems III, in the livingroom

Vortex Core

Location of Champagne Reflector with Crystal

If you observe the epicenter of the volcano that we are positioned on, you will realize that we are located in one of its chakras, or a 4th dimensional vortex. This we utilize. The focal point of the epicenter is 18 feet above the ground, or the exact center of the livingroom. If you were to look at the proportions of the resonant cavities of a Pleiadean Type 4 beam ship, you would find similar proportions related to the epicenter found here in Laguna Beach.

Level 4
Level 3
Level 2
Level 1

Center Line

Workshop

Basic Wavelength—The Frequency of DNA 27'0"

Vent Shaft of Crater leading to the molten core of Terra, Planet Earth

Location of Japanese Pine Tree, growing in a spiral, counter-clockwise direction

7. When the fields are harnessed to a vortex, there is a learning curve to understanding their potential.

Quad System Energy Field

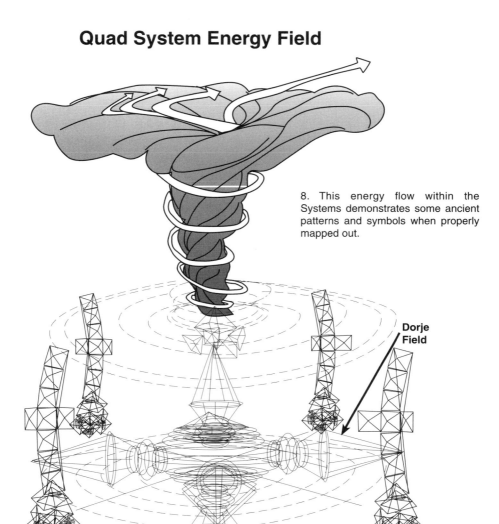

8. This energy flow within the Systems demonstrates some ancient patterns and symbols when properly mapped out.

Dorje Field

Now in the livingroom we are inside of a lens. It is highly focused by the Quad System that surrounds it. Behind the lens is the Earth chakra system, in fornt is the future. The Earth has major and minor chakras. The lens can focus into this system anywhere we desire. Just as the human chakra systems can be reached by specially appointed combinations of sound, light, colors and minerals, so can the Earth's chakra points be individually accessed. Each chakra of the Earth has a specified consciousness that connects it to a point in time and space throughout the galaxy. Each Quad System can be tuned — and one important factor is sound. Each of our Pleiadean sound albums has a Pleiadean harmonic timbre factor.

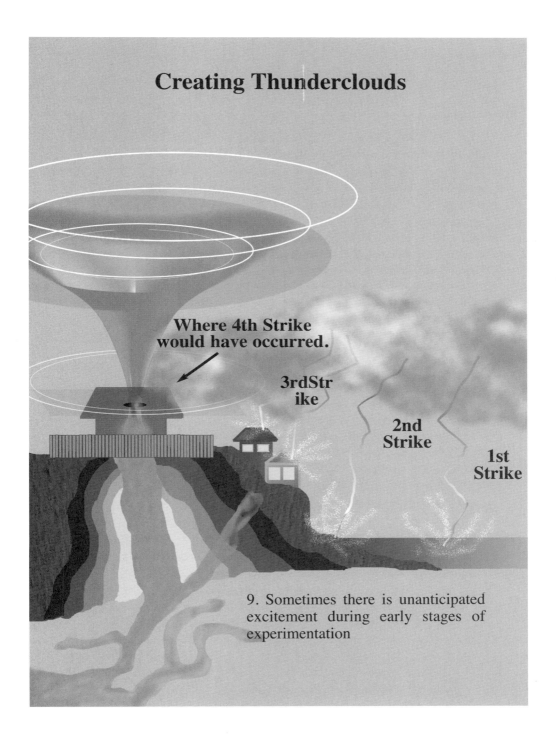

Creating Thunderclouds

Where 4th Strike would have occurred.

3rdStr ike

2nd Strike

1st Strike

9. Sometimes there is unanticipated excitement during early stages of experimentation

Part I
Reality or Illusion?

Chapter 1

Who is Really in Charge?
An Example...

Storms, floods, high wind and tornadoes are wreaking havoc upon American soil.

Droughts in Hawaii, where delicate and rare species critically depend upon the natural balance of fast-disappearing rain forests, and droughts in other rain-dependent countries, are raging woe upon this planet.

Caused in part by the El Niño phenomenon, soon to be followed by the La Niña pattern, these disasters are the legacy of man's ignorance in discharging massive quantities of hydrocarbons and ill considerations of disposing toxic wastes back into our rapidly deteriorating planetary ecosphere.

This roust of disruption is rapidly absorbing our daily lives and stealing away our critically needed leisure time!

What does it take to get your attention? Another teen suicide or schoolyard shooting?

Or, maybe you will ignore all of this in favor of a winning lottery ticket. Where is humanity going?

Do you accept tragedy to others as a form of entertainment, or do you as a human being, a person — one with a voice that will cry out to make a difference, if not for reasons of your own, then for the sake of a better soil for tomorrow's children — want to make a difference and prevent it?

You can become a caring contributor to a better humanity that will make a stand, and exercise choices and execute ideas that will reinstate our global environment back into a friendly world that we older generations were born into and took for granted.

There is help standing by. Powerful beings are in the wings, waiting for the familiar cry that will resonate through the halls of time and give us a commanding edge to right that which is wrong, balance that which is askew, comfort that which is in pain, heal where sickness lies, and educate in halls of ignorance and bring light into the darkness of man's future. I've been involved with government-funded science projects ever since I began working at the University of Michigan when I was just a teenager. I served in the Air Force, tracking bogies traveling at speeds and along flight paths far beyond the technology we had then, or even today. I also worked later at NASA on many programs, including manned Apollo flights to the moon. As a contactee, I have studied in-depth the extraterrestrial phenomenon, including abductions and the continuing government coverup. I've pioneered many alternative science applications, including modern pyramid technology, and served as a formulation consultant for top nutrition engineering developers. These subjects and more I have lectured upon as a National Health Federation representative and personally around the world.

There have been several books written about my work and experiences: Dulce, currently selling in Japan; The Fellowship by Brad Steiger, which sold worldwide, published by Doubleday and Bantam Books Press. The Promise is another paperback book currently published in English, Japanese and German. I could go on, but I think my point has been made: what I say here has validity, is verifiable, and worthy of your time and interest. I would recommend that once you involve yourself within the information presented within this book, you let yourself enjoy and share it with your friends. This is about sharing, and sharing is important.

Subjects covered throughout this book include the Federal Government's Global 2000 Report, economics, foreign stresses, the extraterrestrial coverup, alien technology, both good and bad, abductions, space and time travel; and I am also going to explain ways that you can become involved with our expanding global problems and make a difference. We're also going to learn how to change your life, elevate your consciousness, in the ever-present era of this heavily stressful environment in which we live.

THE CARTER ADMINISTRATION'S GLOBAL 2000 REPORT

The Global 2000 Report was sponsored by the Carter Administration with the cooperation of 44 different nations and subsequently researched and assembled by 19 different federal agencies. It was then released during the Reagan administration. I attained a whole new level of understanding of this incredible document when I started studying the extraterrestrial condition that exists today between the governments of the different countries and peoples of the world and incorporated my own contacts with the Pleiadeans and the Andromedans. Finally, information from covert operational material provided further on in this book gave deeper insights into the relevancy of this government publication. I'm going to share with you now some of the highlights of The Global 2000 Report.

THE AIR WE BREATHE

The Global 2000 Report reports that the carbon dioxide levels have doubled in this century, almost 25 to 30 percent of what they were a few years ago. Now, what does this mean? Higher carbon dioxide levels mean the body has a decreased amount of oxygen available to it, and consciousness begins to suffer. Carbon dioxide is a waste product we exhale for assimilation by plants, while we require oxygen to supercharge and give energy to our cells. I don't think we want to turn into plants, but our brains will be no better than vegetation if we don't do something about our present environmental conditions to adjust our own human biosystems to this change. Look around—society is not functioning properly. You ask someone to perform a task and they inevitably either forget or give a reply a month later.

Simply put: sea level recordings of atmospheric oxygen content are DOWN from what they were 20 years ago. Current readings are equivalent to what was recorded two decades ago at 1200 to 2500 feet above sea level. Think about that. The higher the altitude, the less oxygen there is in the atmosphere. You huff and puff doing things you wouldn't think twice about doing at the altitude you are currently adjusted to. Expand that concept over time and you'll realize that you don't have to travel up a mountain or take a ride in an airplane to experience this phenomenon, you can get the same effect just by living longer, because as the carbon dioxide levels continue to rise, the oxygen readings will continue to drop. Everywhere. Just imagine that the mountain-top oxygen levels and performance envelopes are coming down to the ocean levels to really picture the dilemma.

We are breathing less oxygen and that hurts our brain

The main area affected is the brain. Total oxygen deprivation kills quickly, partial oxygen deprivation kills slowly. The human brain, most active during sleep, selectively curbs vital functions proportional to the amount of oxygen and nutrients it receives. We will study the phenomenon of the brain as we continue into this discourse on deeper and deeper levels.

Later chapters on nutritional systems propose corrective actions, but for now realize that your body is receiving far less oxygen and far more carbon dioxide than it was 10 to 15 years ago!

GLOBAL WEATHER CHANGES

Have you noticed major changes in the weather worldwide: prolonged droughts in the tropics, traumatic floods in arid regions? Overall, does it seem hotter to you? Carbon dioxide is denser than oxygen, creating the "greenhouse effect," where sunlight is trapped in the atmosphere and held until the heat is dissipated. The Earth, as you know, is heated by the "greenhouse effect." With the increasing levels of carbon dioxide caused by fossil fuel technologies releasing tons of vaporous hydrocarbons, the atmosphere is becoming denser, holding more heat and water vapor, interfering with global weather patterns and ocean currents. The recent incidents of three El Niño episodes, the last being the most intense ever recorded, in the past 10 years is potent evidence of this worldwide, man-created effect.

MASS SPECIES EXTINCTION

A few years ago we discovered that we have just as much of a problem with alkaline rain as we do with acid rain. When acid/alkaline rain runs off, where does it go? It seeps into the water tables, affecting, or I should say INFECTING, lakes, forests, streams and rivers. This in turn has precipitated accelerated species extinction. The Global 2000 Report reveals that by 1981 we had already lost close to 2,000,000 species of birds and animals and insects, and further predicts that by the year 2000, 10 to 20 million more species could become extinct. This represents approximately 20% of the life on earth. This is something to think about, because we are going to have to take responsibility for the human race and its rapid degradation of spiritual, ethical and moral values!

THE COMING FAMINE

Species extinction is not limited to animal life; consider the destruction of varietal stocks, our food staples of wheat, corn, potatoes and so on. Our disregard for the impact man-made pollution has on the planet has come back to haunt us! Bite into a tomato, or an ear of fresh corn—it doesn't have the taste it used to have! The living enzymes that provide flavor have been horribly damaged by this more hostile environment.

A contributor to these less-than-favorable growing conditions is another major change in our atmosphere: the depleted ozone layer. It allows too much ultraviolet light to penetrate the outer levels of the atmosphere and bombard the surface of our planet. One effect of the increased ultraviolet radiation is a tendency for our crops to ripen from the inside out, similar to what a microwave oven does, destroying vital food enzymes.

Another contributor has already been mentioned: acid and alkaline rain. For example, acid rain causes oranges and grapefruits to taste bitter by pushing the potential hydrogen, pH, up into top acidic range. You may have noticed oranges and grapefruits taste much more acidic than in the past. This condition and others like it can be rectified; there are technologies available that can repair this destructive soil condition.

HINTS AT A SOLUTION

We researched the pyramid structure and discovered it has the tendency to bring the pH of a plant or animal back within healthy pH levels again. So with the creative use of pyramids, we are able to "re-process" foods before we consume them. Look for this subject in upcoming chapters! There are ways of skirting some of the existing problems we now face, but we must realize the deleterious effects upon our bodies if we choose to ignore our present environmental conditions.

WE PAY WITH OUR HEALTH

The depleted ozone layer is also causing us serious immune system problems. What is the first symptom the body suffers as a result of ozone depletion? Skin cancer is a common answer that comes to mind, but not so. The first thing that sunlight, without the full protection of the ozone layer, affects in the human body is the immune system!

The immune system is responsible for maintaining and keeping the body alive and well so it can excel. If your body is constantly spending life energy trying to rebuild the immune system, you shift into a survival mode and can no longer *EXCEL*. Diseases such as herpes and candida are both symptoms of major breakdowns in the immune system, facilitated by overexposure to ultraviolet radiation and other unhealthful elements that penetrate our damaged ozone protection. AIDS, Acquired Immune Deficiency Syndrome, is a result of further degradation of the immune system. It doesn't take a wise person to look back and see what diseases in our society were precipitated by the gradual depletion of the ozone layer.

DELIBERATE MISINFORMATION

Our society has been led to believe that fluorocarbons, spray cans, leaking refrigerators, and PCBs were causing the depletion of the ozone layer. This is one of the stupidest things

4

ever presented to the gullible public. Even The Global 2000 Report finally admits, in Volume One, that the problem with the ozone layer is actually caused by high-flying jet aircraft, but also states that this shouldn't be made public, because of the tremendous amount of income derived worldwide by the Trilateral, oil companies and other huge organizations that really run our planet from the commercial jet trade. They don't want you to know the damage caused by jet aircraft because changing shipping methods and reducing air travel would severely affect their profit margins. Think about it. A large 747 ready to take off sits there with 100,000 pounds of fuel. It's going to fly continent-to-continent for over eight hours at an altitude of over 35,000 feet with jet engines emitting a pollution-filled exhaust of over 5000 degrees fahrenheit. Tell me that isn't going to do more damage to the ozone layer versus, say, a fluorocarbon molecule from a spray paint can in your garage!

Jets emit exhaust that's 5,000 degress + fahrenheit all the hours they are flying

LOSS OF OXYGEN-PRODUCING HABITATS

The Global 2000 Report also documents another environmental tragedy: the deforestation and desertification of this planet. Sixty percent of Earth's oxygen comes from an algae that lives on the surface of the ocean down to a depth of approximately 75 feet. This algae is rapidly being killed off by large ocean-going ships exhausting tons of hydrocarbons, radiation pouring into the oceans, and other man-made pollutants. The remaining 40% of our oxygen comes from plants and forests. The great movement to raise consciousness about our rainforest areas stems from many valid causes, including the desire to continue breathing oxygen. We are stripping the earth of forest by an area the size of California every year — California is almost 800 miles long and nearly 200 miles wide, a huge surface area — and when we do this, we are not replacing this lost, oxygen-giving forest! There are alternative crops, alternative ways of agriculture we could use to help remedy these problems.

Why do we need to use the land beneath the rainforest? Why are we cutting the forests down? For the most part, the rainforests are being systematically stripped from the surface of the earth on behalf of our ever-increasing beef industry.

FEEDING THE MASSES

Take a look at a hamburger from one of your local fast food places, or anywhere, actually. A quarter pound hamburger represents 55 square feet of rainforest being destroyed. The burning of these 55 square feet, which is how they clear the land to use it, causes 500 pounds of carbon to be released into the atmosphere. Reducing the amount of beef in our protein-rich diets could have profound results. For example, if 1000 people ate a meat-free diet just for two weeks, they would save 150,000 pounds of grain, plus many thousands of square feet of rainforest. This would feed 40,000 children for 8 days. That's something to consider, and that's just one statistic of many, many others.

Hemp root grown to produce paper would use 3/4 less land area than we use by making paper from trees. This would save oxygen!

ALTERNATIVE CROPS

There's a currently controversial way we can reverse this process of depleting our oxygen while increasing our carbon dioxide levels. An interesting article in High Times magazine, April 1990 issue stated that in 1916, the U.S. Department of Agriculture Bulletin predicted that once a harvesting machine was developed, cannabis would again become

America's largest agricultural industry. Some 22 years later, Popular Mechanics introduced a new generation of investors to just such a device.

When we talk about cannabis, we are not talking about the part of a marijuana plant harvested for THC; we are talking about the root of hemp. Hemp has been used for practical purposes all over the world for years; it was one of the largest crops in America for a number of years, until the more politically power-crazy cartels were established. Before this system began its negative inauguration, the hemp was an international product.

Furthermore, in 1916 the U.S. Department of Agriculture wrote a special Bulletin #404 which reported that one acre of cannabis hemp in annual rotation over a 20-year period would produce as much pulp for paper as 4.1 acres of trees over the same 20-year period. This process would use only 1/5th to 1/7th as much sulphur-based acid to break down the gluite liganen that binds the fibers of the pulp. Liganen must be broken down to make pulp paper. Hemp is only 4% liganen, while trees are 18-30% liganen. Thus hemp provides four times as much pulp at five to seven times less pollution. Five to seven times less pollution. And yet, today it is totally illegal, as it has been for the past half century.

WHO CONTROLS THE DRUGS?

Once corrupted systems were instituted, the drug money had to be controlled by different governments. If any government truly wanted to stop the drug trade, all they would have to do would be to go directly into the different countries where these drugs are produced and destroy the crops. We know where they are. If the United States could invade the Middle East and reshape the destiny of the oil coming out of the Kuwait oil fields, then these other smaller countries that have problems with their hemp, cocaine and heroin growth are easily subject to international action. You won't see that happening, because these powerful cartels need the illicit money. It remains underground, hidden away from people.

CHEMICAL TOXINS CONCENTRATE AT THE TOP OF THE FOOD CHAIN

A non-vegetarian mother's milk is very high in DDT due to our use of pesticides

You'll find frightening references in The Global 2000 Report about the misuse of insecticides and pesticides. It reports that sprayed crops are hurt and damaged, then fed to livestock which is later slaughtered and fed to us. The effect of this progressive concentration of toxins can be found in chemical analysis of a new mother's milk. It is so high in DDT that if you bottled it and shipped it across the state line the FDA could confiscate it! In comparison, a vegetarian mother has 1/5th the amount of DDT in her milk as one who consumes dairy products. Look at the illnesses many children are now born with! One formula I developed was a special protein powder for children in the process of switching to solid foods. Most food stores carry nothing but sugar-filled transitional liquid foods for children, continuing the senseless process of feeding ourselves toxic substances.

SUPER SPECIES DEVELOPMENT

The Global 2000 Report also mentioned that some insects are thriving on the DDT. If you go to Hawaii, you'll notice the cockroaches are bigger there than they are in many other places in the world. When I first went to Hawaii in the 1960's I saw small cockroaches. For years now the farmers have been spraying deadly toxins on crops such as sugar cane, pineapple, coconuts and dates. Certain pests have died, but many have become increasingly resistant to the assault, and the roaches have thrived! In addition, native birds that consume the super roaches die from the insects' high concentration of poisons.

DESTROYING OUR DNA

Radiation is another concern. We are creating radioactive wastes, accumulated from nuclear reactors that generate power, plutonium reactors that produce power, and many ignorant countries testing nuclear arms. This radioactive material has to settle somewhere. It has a half-billion-year half-life, longer than the recorded history of man or anything else on this planet. The Global 2000 Report tags disposal and storage as a critical problem, not only to the environment, but to us. We are definitely going to have problems with the people who live near or handle the radioactive materials and wastes as they lose coherency, or higher consciousness, due to molecular and DNA damage. This manner of damage to the body affects our very consciousness right down to the cellular level, another topic I will cover in length in coming chapters.

COVERUPS!!!

In this book I'm going to present evidence of a secret government coverup and other aspects of The Global 2000 Report that are even more unpleasant. This is all necessary so that you have a well-rounded understanding of why it's important to get environmentally involved and how to make a difference, if not for your own sake, then maybe for the sake of someone you love, or your own children.

I encourage you to pursue and document for your own edification more of this information from The Global 2000 Report. This brief discourse has mostly come from Volume One; there are five volumes. If you want to purchase a copy and read these facts for yourself, in California, you can go to Room 2039 in the Federal Building, 300 N. Los Angeles Street, Los Angeles, California 90012, telephone number 213-688-5841.

If you are in Washington, D.C. you can go right to the Pentagon, Main Concourse, South End, Washington DC 20301, telephone number 703-557-1821.

In the Colorado area, go to Room 117, Federal Building, 1961 Stout Street, Denver, Colorado 80294, telephone number 303-837-3964.

If you are out in Texas, go to 45 College Center, 9319 Gulf Freeway, Houston, Texas 77017, telephone number 713-226-5453.

In Washington, you can go to Room 194, Federal Building, 915 Second Avenue, Seattle, Washington 98174, telephone number 206-442-4710.

What I have put forth here is just a gleaning of the information contained in this book. I look forward to sharing this information and offering solutions to you. At times you may experience a sense of "overwhelm," but just relax and let it in. The background information I supply helps support the corrective actions I propose. You can always go back over those chapters that challenge you, and I have supplied numerous illustrations to help get my points across. My goal is to open you up to the possibilities, and the promise of an expanded and better future.

The changes we've been discussing began around 1920 and 1925 when the "big family" stepped in to run this country. We're part of a long-term plan. Our conflicts in the Middle East were planned a long time ago because the people who control the money have the consciousness to make their control effective for long periods.

DENYING AN OBVIOUS SOLUTION

33 out of every 40 hours you work goes to pay for the energy costs of goods and services, based on our current energy sources

Hemp-pulp paper potential depended upon the invention and engineering of new machines for stripping the hemp and hemp hurds. This would also lower the cost of and demand for lumber for housing, while at the same time reoxygenate our planet. If the 1916 hemp pulp paper process were legal today, it could replace about 70% of all wood pulp paper such as computer printout paper, corrugated boxes and paper bags. Pulp paper made from rags is machined from 60% to 100% hemp fibers, is stronger and more flexible than paper made from wood pulp, and is a less expensive and more ecological paper choice. In the book *Solar Gap,* 1980, *Science Digest,* and *Omni Magazine,* the Alliance for Survival, the Green Party of West Germany, put the total figures of our energy costs at 80% of the total dollar expenses of living for each human being. In validation, 82% of the total value of all issues traded on the New York Stock Exchange and other world stock exchanges are tied directly to energy supply companies–Exxon, Shell, Mobil, Edison, etc.; oil wells; coal mines; transportation; pipeline companies; oil shipping and delivery companies; refineries; and retail sales. Americans, who represent only 5% of the world's population, in their drive for more net worth and productivity, consume 25% to 40% of the world's energy output. The hidden cost to the environment cannot be measured. Eighty-two percent of your dollar, which translates roughly into 33 of every 40 hours you work, goes to pay for the energy cost of goods and services. One way or another, transportation, heating, cooking, lighting are all energy-based products you purchase. Our current possible energy sources also supply about 80% of all solid and air-borne solutions, which slowly poison the planet.

THE COST OF DOING BUSINESS

The U.S. EPA Report, 1983 and 1989, focused largely on the world's catastrophic condition from carbon dioxide, a byproduct of using fossil fuels. The cheapest substitute for these expensive and wasteful energy methods is not wind or solar panels, nuclear, geothermal or the like, but Biomass. The world's most efficient solar source has been created, and it's a plant. One of the the early oil barons, Nelson Rockefeller of Standard Oil, had a lot to do with the election and support of the presidency of Eisenhower, and before him, Truman. We'll get into that when we discuss the UFO coverup.

By the year 2,000 the U.S. will have burned up 80% of its petroleum resources!

These oil people were very powerful and they had great vision, not only of possessing great wealth at the time, but possessing the wealth of the future and eventually controlling the world. Nothing has really changed from the times of the kings and the queens to now, it's just a little bit more refined.

The early oil barons were aware in the 20's of the possibilities of Henry Ford's methanol scheme. Henry Ford had 40 acres of hemp for methanol production on his estate; he even grew marijuana after 1937 to prove the cheapness of methanol. Paranoia kept the oil prices incredibly low — between a dollar and four dollars a barrel. (There are 42 gallons in an oil barrel.) This price was kept low for almost 50 years until 1970. So low in fact that no other energy source could compete with oil, and once there was the lack of competition, the price jumped to $40 a barrel. And now here we are in Iraq trying to control the oil market. Suddenly, for whatever reason, we are now in the era where oil is not only prohibitively expensive, but embargoes are threatened by foreign powers, i.e., OPEC, Libya, Iran, etc., to virtually hold the U.S. hostage. That's how dependent we are on foreign sources of polluting petroleum products.

Biomass conversion to fuel should begin immediately to stop the planetary pollution and make us energy independent. By the year 2000 the U.S. will have burned 80% of its petroleum resources, while our coal reserves may last 100 years or so longer. But coal has serious drawbacks. High sulphur coal is responsible for killing almost 50,000 Americans and up to 10,000 Canadians per year by producing acid rain.

Fuel is not synonymous with petroleum, so let's not think about it in those terms. And new hemp Biomass systems can create millions of new jobs we need right now. We could create a healthy economy in the 90's and 2000's. We should wake up. These old jobs of the 90's and the 80's and the 70's no longer suffice because they're destructive jobs. They can no longer provide the income we need, and if we're going to go from survival mode to excellence, we do have to change.

What new energy sources can we use that won't hurt the Earth and us?

Hemp Biomass can replace every type of fossil fuel energy product. When hemp is grown for Biomass as a renewable energy crop, carbon dioxide is absorbed by the living plants, which in turn release much-needed oxygen. Biomass conversion utilizing the same cracking technology employed by the petroleum industry will make charcoal to replace coal. Charcoal contains no sulphur, whereas coal is full of sulphur. That's what makes it so bad for us.

The gases that remain after the charcoal and fuel oils are extracted from hemp can be used for fueling cars, generators, power plants, etc. Imagine replacing all these nuclear reactors with the fuel that comes from the hemp process! This Biomass cracking process can produce a methanol or charcoal fuel, as well as the basic chemicals of industry: acetone, ethyl acetate, tar pitch and creosote. The Ford Motor Company successfully operated a Biomass cracking plant in the 1930's in Iron Mountain, Michigan, using trees. Hemp was too costly at that time, due to the labor costs of land harvesting.

Throughout history, hemp seed was made into fuel oil. Hemp seeds are 30% oil by volume. This oil makes high-grade diesel fuel and aircraft engine and precision machine oil. The genie's lamp burned hemp seed oil, as did Abraham the Prophet's lamp and Abraham Lincoln's lamp. Only whale oil came near hemp seed oil in popularity as a fuel. When Rudolph Diesel invented his diesel engine, he intended to fuel it with a variety of fuels, especially vegetable and seed oil.

Hemp is 77% cellulose, the basic industrial raw material used in the production of chemicals, plastic and fibers. Depending upon which U.S. agricultural report is correct, an acre of full grown hemp plants can substantially provide from 4 to 50 or even 100 times the cellulose found in corn stalks or sugar cane — the planet's next highest annual cellulose plant. In most places the hemp can be harvested twice a year, and in warm areas, such as Southern California, Texas and Florida, it can be a year-round crop. Hemp has a short growing season and can be planted after food crops have been harvested.

An independent semi-rural network of efficient and autonomous farmers will become the chief economic player in the production of energy in this country. The United States government pays in cash or in "kind" for farmers to refrain, listen to this, to refrain from growing on 89 million acres of rich farm land each year, called the "soil bank." Ten million

Running America without oil

acres of hemp would be the equivalent of 500 million to 1 billion acres of corn. Hemp fuel derivatives, along with the recycling of paper, would be enough to virtually run America without oil, except as petroleum fertilizer. And 10 million to 89 million acres of hemp and other woody annual Biomass planted on this restricted, unplanted, fallow farm land, or soil bank, would make energy a whole new ball game and be a real attempt at doing something to save the earth.

THE OBVIOUS OPPONENTS

The Catch 22 is obvious with the energy companies. They own most of the petrochemicals, pharmaceuticals, liquor and tobacco companies, and are intertwined with the insurance companies and banks that own them in such a way as to make untangling the various interlocking dictates of aristocracies a Herculean task for even the most dedicated researcher. Many politicians now in power, according to the press, are bought and paid for by the energy companies. And the U.S. Government is the "arm," i.e., the CIA, The Company, Robert Ludlem, the Bush-Quail administration, which was uniquely tied to the oil; as well as newspapers and pharmaceuticals. The world struggle for money is actually a struggle for energy, as it is through energy that we may produce food, shelter, transportation, environment and entertainment. It is this struggle which often erupts into open war.

It may not be that if we remove the cause, the conflict will also be removed, but the possibility is strong enough that we must try. Ultimately the world has no other rational environmental choice but to give up fossil fuel. At that point we could tell OPEC "goodbye" forever. The national balance of payments deficit would pass by the wayside and personal energy bills could be cut as much as 50%, perhaps as much as 90% with Biomass from hemp as recycled waste. No more elderly or poor people will be freezing to death.

Interestingly enough, there is an article partially in here, too, that states, "the arrival of newly imported hemp, cotton blended clothing from China in 1989 signaled the beginning of the new era for the rapidly changing world of fashion. Joint venturing hempery in the hemp colony in the imports of shirts and shirts in the Stonewear™ (registered trademark label) can be found in a number of retail outlets and ordered through the mail. Public distaste for the cruelty of using furs and leather, along with the search for comfortable natural fabrics to replace synthetics, and fashion society's ever changing trends it takes, all offer a great opportunity to reinvigorate the domestic textile manufacturing retail trade."

WE CAN EAT IT, TOO

Hemp seed can be made to taste like chicken, made into tofu, costing less than using soybeans

Hemp seed can be processed, too, and it's many times cheaper. It also contains all the essential 8 amino acids. Hemp seed extracts, like soybeans, can be made to taste like chicken, meat, steak, or pork. It can be used to make Tofu, curd and margarine at less cost than that of soybeans. Hemp seed can be pressed for a vegetable oil leaving a high protein seed cake as a byproduct. Sprouting any seed improves its nutritional value, and hemp can be sprouted and used like any other seed sprout for salads or cooking. Hemp is a favorite bird seed because of its nourishing oily content. The report also talks about birds living 20% to 30% longer in hemp seed studies. Furthermore, recent studies indicate the depletion of the ozone layer threatens to reduce the world's soy production by a substantial amount, up to 30% to 50%, depending on the density fluctuation of the ozone shield. But hemp, on the other hand, resists the damage caused by increased ultraviolet radiation and actually flourishes in it by producing more cannabinoids, which provide protection from ultraviolet light.

Australia survived two prolonged famines in the l9th century using nothing but marijuana seeds for protein and marijuana leaves for roughage. It's no wonder that Central and South America hate the U.S. and want us out. They see us as ignorant killers. For years our government demanded that Paraguay poison their land—land farmers had grown cannabis on by law since 1654 when Prince Philip of Spain had ordered it grown throughout the Empire to provide food, sail, rope, towels, sheets and shirts, as well as providing the people a most important folk medicine for fever, childbirth, epilepsy, and poultices for rheumatoid arthritis. There were more than 10 million acres of seed-laden cannabis hemp growing wild in the U.S. prior to 1937, feeding hundreds of millions of birds as their favorite and most necessary food, until our government began its policy of total eradication of this primary link in the food chain. Oblivious to these inherent biocide dangers, our government continued to escalate these programs of extinction unabated, both here and abroad, at the insistence of the DEA. DuPont has created new strains of grain, such as wheat that will grow only with their petrochemical fertilizers. Their intention is to eradicate the surviving natural wheat and rice seeds in the name of their personal corporate profits, leaving the planet and all humans solely at their corporate mercy for their hybrid strain, which must have their petrochemical fertilizers and pesticides. Corn is already so hybridized that it is not expected to last 50 years without human cultivation.

Hemp seeds put down as much as 10 to 12-inch roots in only 30 days, compared to a 1-inch root put down by rye or barley grass presently used by the U.S. Government. Southern California, Utah, and other states used cannabis routinely to break up compacted, overworked soil, until about 1915. Up until that time it was America's largest agriculture crop, and we didn't have drug problems in those days.

These varieties of hemp plants that we're talking about are not the kind that people smoke. The people who grow marijuana for profit prefer specially hybrid plants that concentrate THC on the bud. For our energy-related purposes, we're focusing more or less on the leaves and the stalks, the overall material of the plant itself. They're more like rope; they contain more cellulose and fiber. Realize that Biomass crops put a huge amount of oxygen back into the atmosphere and can reproduce themselves almost four times as fast as trees. They are great for areas where the soil is eroded because their quick-growing roots go quite deep, holding the topsoil. According to The Global 2000 Report, we are seeing an area the size of the State of Maine turned into desert every year.

Replenish the Earth's oxygen

Chapter 2

Uncovering 40 Years of U.F.O.
and Extraterrestrial Coverup

There was a Government Report that I read not too long ago dealing with the Star Wars project, the shooting of a billion-watt laser into space from the area of Sandia Labs and Los Alamos Labs in New Mexico. When they shoot a laser beam of a billion watts or so into the atmosphere, tremendous heat is generated. This heat upsets the delicate trade winds that are in the area above the level of the laser beam. It's like going out into the ocean and setting up a boiling pot, boiling millions of gallons of water in the middle of a major current. The heat and pressure divert the natural wind currents. Shooting the laser beam in the atmosphere on a continual basis creates a similar effect in our skies, changing wind patterns and therefore weather.

As you study this presentation, remember, one person does make a difference. During the years I've worked at the National Health Federation I've seen great changes in our society. When the establishment tried to take away our vitamins, the NHF defended Americans' freedom to choose the way they take care of themselves. Small groups of people well-armed with information make tremendous changes!

To continue on, I want to paint a scenario here. Near the end of World War II, Truman allowed the nuclear bombs to drop on Japan, and of course this caused paranoia in the world community. Conflict continued between the Dr. Tellers group and the people down in Los Alamos, New Mexico. A whole new underground facility had been put in there. Russia now also had the nuclear bomb, so the world focused on Russia as the next possible aggressor. In Germany they evacuated the caves in Peenemünde where Werner von Braun had worked. An interesting side note to the end of the war was that the Russians and the Germans decided to divide up the spoils of what technology they found. The Russians took the hydrazine pump and parts of the V-2 and the V-3. The pumps, the actual hardware of the V-3, were fully operational. The Americans, on the other hand, got most of the plans, and hardly any of the technicians. So when the space race developed back in the 50's and Sputnik went up, America, if you remember correctly, had to play catch up.

Werner von Braun was a prisoner of war in a compound in White Sands, New Mexico, and he didn't like that very much. So, when the American government pulled him out of captivity and put him back to work again, he still had an attitude about being in captivity. Werner told us that it would be awhile before we could match the Russian payload orbits because they had the actual hardware and he wasn't the designer of the hydrazine pump. And the technicians that designed the pump were already in Russia. So we had made a mistake by not taking the hardware.

At the same time the Germans themselves had already developed some saucer type craft. Rudolph Schriever designed the Schriever-Habermohl Model 1 and 2, units that used a

The Coanda Design

13

rocket-type engine with a series of vanes rotated by the engine, called a coanda design, which was originally developed in Canada. The coanda design creates airflow with tremendous lift. These craft were circular, wobbly, they weren't stable, but they did fly. They were capable of going about 1500 miles an hour vertically. These designs were test flown during 1941 and 1942. I'll quote something from a book called *The UFO Crash at Aztec,* by Wendell Stevens, which I'll be covering later.

"The Model 2 embodied some of these changes (the stability in the rim, etc.). The size had been increased to accommodate two pilots lying in a prone position, and the engine compartment as well as the fuel-carrying capacity had been increased. This model, also using airplane-like rudders, has a steering assist mechanism for stabilization. Speeds between 1,000 and 2,000 kilometers per hour were recorded; that's between about 600 and 1200 miles per hour. The problem with wheel balancing had been solved and the wing screw or wing propeller arrangement worked to satisfaction. The Germans called it a vertical pull propeller. As soon as the desired altitude was reached, the propeller blades were adjusted to a flat angle and now the pull of the propeller became a carrying propeller, very similar to the principle of the helicopter."

The Model 3 was the final model, some experts refer to it as the Bellouzo Schriever-Miethe discs. This version was produced in various sizes up to 225 feet diameter. Actual speeds recorded were over 2000 kph. Conventional rocket motor speeds from about 2000 to 4000 kph were anticipated. Then Victor Schauberger of Austria came out with a flameless and explosionless implosion motor which powered another type of ship which used a similar airfoil moving system. This became an antigravity prototype.

BOGIES CAUGHT ON RADAR

When I was in the Air Force I worked on the Early Warning Radar. We had one type of radar, we'll refer to as the ANFPS-35, which was a 5 million watt radar set. It's very powerful. In comparison, conventional World War II radios were hundreds of thousands of watts. I also worked on an ANFPS-26, a classified radar, in the late 50's, early 60's. These radar systems were developed in the late 40's and tested at Sandia Labs near Almagordo, at Los Alamos, and they scanned radar beams up and down the desert area of New Mexico. *Some aliens that happened to be in the area at the time got caught in these large radar beams, and as we later discovered, we overloaded their plutonium reactors.* They then reached a critical mass causing a core meltdown, which caused a heat flash within the ship. This flash would act like a shock wave on the crew, knocking them unconscious, which would bring the ship down; in some cases intact.

Major Change on Earth

One crash occurred March 25, 1948. I'll share a little bit with you, because Colonel Wendell Stevens, a retired Air Force Colonel, has documented this one well:

"On March 25, 1948, an unidentified flying object was detected
and picked up on your scopes from strategically located radar units
in the southwestern part of the United States."

One of the radars was a high-powered experimental installation situated high on a mountaintop in the Four Corners area. This is an area where Utah, Arizona, New Mexico and Colorado border each other. All of our sites where I was stationed were on mountaintops. "The beam that emanated from this unit adversely affected the central control system of the flying object, for immediately it seemed to go out of control. It fluttered and wobbled side-to-side and appeared to head toward the ground. Contact with the object was attempted by radio with no response."

"Immediately the Air Defense Command (ADC) was notified and local military units were activated. Experienced with this sort of bogey image, the Director of the high-powered radar site wired a special message to General George T. Marshall and the Secretary of State that an identified flying object was about to crash somewhere in the Four Corners area. Marshall immediately called an impromptu meeting with the Joint Chiefs of Staff, the National Security Council and the President. They were connected to a direct voice-to-voice communication with the top secret radar station."

All of the the radar stations in had what was called a "hot phone" that would put us into either NORAD Headquarters or a direct line to the White House or the Pentagon, depending upon which type of radar installation we were on.

Marshall ordered the ADC and other associated military units to stay on standby until ordered directly by him to take action. He then contacted the MJ-12 group, later known as the Committee of 12 and/or the "special group." He then placed a special unit of Army counterintelligence, the Interplanetary Phenomenon Unit, IPU, or the Scientific and Technical Branch, on Red Alert. When I was stationed on the radar bases, we had many forms of alert; Yellow Alert, which means at any point you could go to Red Alert. During Yellow Alert we were confined to our quarters or close to the installation; we were not allowed to leave, but we were not at our work or battle stations. When we went to Red Alert, we were at battle stations, on the radar, on alert for anything.

Two previous crashes occurred before this Aztec crash. You can still go up there today and see where it went down. There are marks still on some of the trees. The farmer that owned the land and his family were kept inside of his house, told it was a matter of national security, during the time they were collecting all the material. Big trucks came in to haul off the pieces during the night. The IPU operated out of Camp Hale, Colorado, and had the unique purpose of collection and delivery of crash and/or disabled flying saucers to designated secret points. By means of triangulation based upon information from the three separate radar units, the proposed crash sites were calculated to be in the vicinity of Aztec, New Mexico. The information was immediately radioed to General Marshall, who in turn relayed it to the IPU Commander of Camp Hale. A scout team was immediately dispatched by helicopter from Camp Hale to the Aztec area. Within a few hours, the IPU scout unit sighted the object at the top of the rocky plateau in a very rugged area about 12 miles northeast of Aztec. The object appeared to be circular in shape, domed at the top, and nearly 100 feet in diameter. The scout commander radioed back to the IPU headquarters at Camp Hale, "We have a flying saucer on the ground about 12 miles northeast of Aztec."

He gave the exact map coordinates. The IPU commander relayed the message to General Marshall.

The people who went up on the recovery team were: Dr. John Von Neuman, Dr. J. Robert Oppenheimer, Dr. Vannever Bush (Dr. Vannever Bush was the team leader), Dr. Detlen Wulf Bronk, Dr. Lloyd Von Berkner, Dr. Jerome C. Hunsaker and Dr. Carl A. Heiland. All were on the investigative recovery team on this particular incident. This was quoted on page 27 and 28 of *The UFO Crash at Aztec* by Wendell Stevens. I'm just going to quote one more thing before I put the book aside. This is an FBI memo dated March 22, 1950, secured from the FBI under the Freedom of Information Act by Dr. Bruce S. Macabee.

OFFICE MEMORANDUM
United States Government
TO: Director of the FBI
FROM: Guy Hottel, SAC (Strategic Air Command) - Washington
SUBJECT: Flying Saucers Information Concerning

An investigator for the Air Force stated that "The three so-called flying saucers have been recovered from New Mexico. They were described as being circular in shape with raised centers approximately 30 feet in diameter each. Each one was occupied by three bodies of human shape, but only 3 feet tall, dressed in metallic cloth, of very fine texture. Each body was bandaged in a manner similar to the black-out suits used by speed flier and test pilots. According to Mr. X, our informant, the saucers were found in New Mexico due to the fact that the government has a very high powered radar setup in that area, and it is believed the radar interfered with the controlling mechanisms of the saucers."

"No further evaluation was attempted by X concerning the above. Later on we found out that J. Edgar Hoover was a member of the Majestic 12."

Colonel Wendell Stevens, by the way, can be contacted directly in Tucson, Arizona, where he lives. There is one thing that I want to say: is that the nations of the world may someday have to unite. The next war will could well be an interplanetary war if humanity is continually held back from expanding into free energy technologies and more universal concepts.

"The nations of the earth must someday make a common front against attack by people of other planets." Gen. Douglas MacArthur was quoted as saying this in the New York Times, October 9, 1955, and I believe everyone knows who General MacArthur was. He wasn't the type of individual who would make erroneous statements to feed his ego or to get recognition. The man was well recognized because of his Pacific Theater activities in World War II.

After the 1948 crash in Hart Canyon in Aztec, New Mexico, our government became very concerned. Another crash occurred on February 13, 1948, on the Mesa near Aztec, and between the two crashes 17 alien bodies were recovered. Of even greater significance was the discovery of a large number of human body parts stored within both of these vehicles, as was found in a ship that went down in Canada, too.

Why was the CIA formed?

Immediately after the crashes began in early 1947, the government began to clamp down. A special group of America's top scientists were organized under the name of "Project Sign" in December, 1947 to study the phenomenon. The whole nasty business was contained within a shroud of secrecy. Project Sign evolved into Project Grudge in December, 1948.

At that time United States Air Force and the Central Intelligence Agency exercised complete control over the alien secret. *One of the reasons he CIA was formed by Presidential Executive Order first as the Central Intelligence Group was for the express purpose of dealing with the alien presence.* Later the National Security Act was passed establishing it as the Central Intelligence Agency. A similar coverup was happening in England at that time, too.

Then on December 9, 1947, Truman approved the issuance of NSC-4. This was called the Coordination of Foreign Intelligence Measure, done at the urging of the Secretary Marshall, Secretary of State Forrestal, Patterson, and the Director of the State Department's Policy Planning Staff, a man by the name of Kennan. Later Directive NSC-10 and NSC-10-2 superseded NSC-4, then NSC- 4A expanded covert abilities even further. The Office of Policy Coordination (OPC) was charged to carry out an extended program of covert activities.

The NSC 10-2 established a study panel which met secretly and was made up of scientific minds of the day. This study panel was not the MJ-12; I want to emphasize that. Another memo, NSC-10-5, further outlined the duties of the study panel. These NSC memos and the secret Executive Order set the stage for the creation of MJ-12, which would happen about 4 years later.

COVERING UP THE PRESENCE OF ALIENS

Now here's where the spiritual part started to happen. The Secretary of Defense, James Forrestal, began to object to the secrecy. He was an idealistic and religious man who believed that the public should be told. ***When he began to talk to the leaders of opposition party and Congress about the alien problem, he was asked to resign by President Truman.*** He expressed his fears to many people and rightfully believed that he was being watched. This was interpreted by those who were ignorant of the facts as paranoia. Forrestal later was said to have suffered a mental breakdown and was admitted to the Bethesda Naval Hospital. They were afraid Forrestal would talk again. Somewhere around May 22, 1949, agents of the CIA tied a sheet around his neck, fastened it to a fixture in his room and threw Forrestal out the window. The sheet tore and he plummeted to his death and they called this, of course, suicide. He was one of the first victims of this coverup to pay with his life. This was just the beginning.

> **Secretary of Defense thrown out the window**

In 1949, a live alien was recovered from the Roswell crash. They named him EBE. The name, suggested by Dr. Vannever Bush, stood for Extraterrestrial Biological Entity. EBE had a tendency to lie. For over a year EBE would give only the desired answers to the questions asked. During the second year of captivity he began to open up, revealing startling information.

> **Earth's call to space for help**

In 1951 EBE became ill. Medical personnel had been unable to determine the cause of his sickness and had no background from which to draw. EBE's system was chlorophyll based, using a process similar to plants. A botanist by the name of Dr. Guillermo Mendoza was brought in to try to help EBE recover. Dr. Mendoza worked with EBE until about 1952 when the alien died. Upon EBE's death, Dr. Mendoza became our first expert on alien biology. In a futile attempt to save EBE and to gain favor with this technologically superior alien race, the United States began to broadcast a call for help in early 1952 using big radio satellite dishes. The broadcast unfortunately went unanswered.

President Truman then created the super secret National Security Agency by secret Executive Order on December 4, 1952. His primary purpose was to decipher the alien communications and language, such as the unusual markings they found in and on the downed space ships. This urgent task was a continuation of the earlier effort and was code named Sigma. The secondary purpose of NSA was to monitor all communication emissions from any and all devices worldwide to gather intelligence, both human and alien, and to contain the secret of the alien presence. Project Sigma was successful. The NSA group also maintains communications with the Lunar base and other secret space programs. ***By Executive Order, the NSA is exempt from all laws which do not specifically name the NSA in the text of the law as being subject to that law.***

> **The National Security Agency's unquestionable authority**

In 1953 President Eisenhower came into the White House, and he continued on with Truman's work, including informing the Soviet Union of the developing alien problem. And

17

as you see in today's news, the superpowers are now uniting, and one of the primary motivations is the aliens.

Eisenhower knew that he had to deal with the alien problem without revealing it to Congress. Early in 1953 he turned to his friend and fellow member of the Council on Foreign Relations, Nelson Rockefeller, for help. Together they created MJ-12. Asking Rockefeller for help with the alien problem was the biggest mistake Eisenhower ever made for the future of the United States, and most probably all of humanity. Within one week of Eisenhower's election, he appointed Nelson Rockefeller Chairman of a Presidential Advisory Committee responsible for the reorganization of our government. Rockefeller was responsible for planning a re-organization of the government. New Deal programs went into one single cabinet position called the Department of Health, Education & Welfare, a department that participated in the *Global 2000 Report*. When Congress approved the new cabinet position in April, 1953, Nelson was named to the post of Under Secretary to Oveta Culp Hobby.

INDEPENDENCE DAY - 1953

Negotiating with aliens — project Plato

In 1953 astronomers discovered large objects in space moving toward Earth. First believed to be asteroids, later evidence proved the objects to be spaceships. Project Sigma intercepted the alien radio communications. Several huge ships reached the earth and assumed a high equatorial orbit, their actual intent unknown.

Project Sigma, and now a new project, Plato, through radio communication using the computer binary language, was able to arrange a landing which resulted in a face-to-face contact with alien beings from another planet. Project Plato was tasked with establishing a diplomatic relationship with the race of space aliens.

During this same time Semjase's predecessors to this world, the Pleiadians, also made contact with the government. One of these meetings took place at Muroc Field (now Edwards Air Force Base). The Grays landed three ships and left one behind for us to study after the deal was made. The Pleiadians also came, but instead of giving us technology, told us our technology exceeded our spirituality; we needed to grow spiritually first. They offered help, but the government didn't want to go for the Pleiadian deal simply because the Pleiadians were not going to give us any more technology. The Grays agreed to give us technology, so we chose them.

U.S. chooses the wrong alien race

Later in 1954, the race of long-nosed Gray aliens which had been orbiting the earth landed at Holloman Air Force Base, and a basic agreement was reached with them, too. They said they came from Betelgeuse, a red star in the Constellation of Orion. This star is the largest one known to man — over two million times larger than our sun! They control the smaller Grays, which come from Zeta Reticuli III. The long-nosed Grays are more friendly, but they do control the smaller Grays, who commit abductions and the mutilations.

President Eisenhower met with the aliens and signed a formal treaty between the Alien Nation and the United States of America. Then we received our first ambassador from outer space. His name and title was His Omnipotent Highness Krill. In the American tradition for disdain for royal titles, he was called Original Hostage Krill. The alien flag is known as a Trilateral Insignia. It is displayed on their craft and worn on their uniforms.

Both of these landings and the second meeting were filmed. These films still exist today! The treaty, negotiated by the long-nosed Grays and our secret government, stated that the aliens should not interfere in our affairs and we would not interfere in theirs. We would keep their presence on earth a secret. They would furnish us with advanced technology and help us in our technological development. They would not make any treaty with any other earth nation, which they did end up doing, by the way. They could abduct humans on a limited and periodic basis for the purpose of medical examination and monitoring of our development, with the stipulation that the humans would not be harmed, would be returned to their point of abduction, and that the humans would have no memory of the event.

Also, the alien nation would furnish MJ-12 a list of all human contacts and abductions on a regularly scheduled basis. It was further agreed that each nation would receive the ambassador of the other as long as the treaty remained in force. The Alien Nation and the United States would exchange 16 personnel each. The alien guests would remain on earth and the human guests would travel to the alien point of origin for a specified period of time and then return. It was also agreed that the bases would be constructed underground for the use of the Alien Nation, plus two more bases would be constructed for the joint use of the Alien Nation and the United States government. Technology exchanges would take place on the jointly occupied bases. This is a total violation of our Constitutional rights. These alien bases would be constructed under Indian reservations in Utah, Colorado, New Mexico and Arizona. One was built in Nevada in the area known as S-4, located approximately seven miles south of the western border of Area 51, known as "Dreamland." All alien areas are under complete control of the Naval Department Bureau of Ships; all personnel who work in these complexes are on the Navy payroll. Construction of these bases was done by the "Sea Bee's." Progress was slow until large amounts of money were made available in 1957.

Dream-land

Then Project Red Light was formed to test fly alien craft. All Dreamland personnel required a "Q" Clearance. It is interesting to note Q Clearance requires Presidential approval. I had a Secret Clearance when I was in the Air Force and afterward, but a Q Clearance the President doesn't even have, although he approves it. *That means the President is not allowed to go to Area 51.*

President not allowed in area 51

President Eisenhower continued on with President Truman's work. This included keeping our allies, including the Soviet Union informed of the developing alien problem since the Roswell recovery. In today's news you see all the big nations now uniting, primarily because of the alien presence. Eisenhower knew that he had to address the alien problem, but he did know he did not want to reveal the secret to Congress. Early in 1953 he turned to his friend and fellow member of the Council on Foreign Relations, Nelson Rockefeller, for help.

AREA 51, AKA "DREAMLAND"

The Army was asked to form a secret organization to furnish security to all alien projects. This organization became the National Reconnaissance Organization based at Fort Carson, Colorado. Specific teams retained to secure the operation were called "Delta." Our footage shows three spaceships in test flight, shot from one of the shops in a building in downtown Las Vegas. On a clear day you can use a telephoto lens to see the controversial Area 51. Back in the 70's the Air Force suddenly annexed all of the private land around Area 51 without even asking the local ranchers. A great protest was made about this, but the ranchers lost their power, their land, and were paid minimal sums of money. This was an attempt to encompass Area 51 with restricted, Air Force owned property to prevent unwanted observation.

Amazing information about Area 51 continues to surface. A second project, code named Snowbird, was formed to explain away any sightings of the "Red Light" crafts that were being tested. In the course of Snowbird, crafts by conventional means were shown to the press several different times. This disinformation was designed to satisfy the curious while protecting the true research that was taking place.

A secret White House underground group, code named Alternative II, began underground construction. Funding was obtained during Eisenhower's time under the guise of construction and maintenance of sites for the President to be taken to in case of a military attack. This tactic was stretched to the maximum. The money was authorized by the Appropriations Committee which allocated it to the Department of Defense as a Top Secret item in the Army construction program. They could designate it Top Secret because it was associated with creating secret safe havens for the President. Monies were transferred for "landscaping" to the Top Secret fund to a location in Palm Beach, Florida that belongs to the Coast Guard, called Peanut Island. The island is adjacent to the property which is owned by Joseph Kennedy, Bobby and John Kennedy's father.

Meanwhile, Nelson Rockefeller changed positions again. This time he took C.D. Jackson's old position, previously called *Special Assignment for Psychological Strategy*. With Nelson's deployment the name was changed to Special Assistant for Cold War Strategy. This position evolved over ten years to the position that Henry Kissinger was ultimately to hold under President Nixon. Officially Rockefeller was to give advice and assistance to the development of increased understanding and cooperation among all peoples. This official description was a smokescreen; secretly he was the Presidential coordinator for the intelligence community. In this new post Rockefeller reported directly and only to the President. He attended meetings of the Cabinet and Council of Foreign Economic Policy and the National Security Council, which was the highest policy-making group in the government.

THE ESTABLISHMENT OF THE MAJORITY 12

By secret Executive Memorandum, NSC 5410, Eisenhower had preceded NSC 5412-1 in 1954 to establish a permanent committee, not the ad hoc, that we'll discuss later. This created the Majority 12, or MJ-12. Their purpose was to oversee and conduct all covert activities associated with the alien connection. The first Majority 12 members were: Nelson Rockefeller, Director of the Central Intelligence Agency; Allan Welsh Dulles; Secretary of State John Foster Dulles; Secretary of Defense Charles E. Wilson; the Chairman of the Joint Chiefs of Staff, Admiral Arthur W. Radford; the Director of the Federal Bureau of Investigation, J. Edgar Hoover; and six men from the Executive Committee on the Council on Foreign Relations, known as the Wise Men. The Council on Foreign Relations also had a lot to do with putting together the *Global 2000 Report* to which I referred earlier.

MJ-12 members were also members of another secret society of scholars that called themselves the Jason Society, or the Jason Scholars, who recruited members from the "Skull and Bones" and the "Scroll and Key" societies from Harvard and Yale.

The Trilateral Commission true source

A few more people were brought in this group and they were later initiated into the Jason Society. They were all members of the Council on Foreign Relations and at that time were known as the Eastern Establishment. This should give you a clue as to the far-reaching and serious nature of these most secret college societies. The Jason Society is alive and well to today, but now includes members of the Trilateral Commission as well. The Trilateralists existed secretly several years before 1973 when they became well known. The Trilateral Commission originated from the alien flag known as the Trilateral Insignia, a symbol you'll find on all Gray ships. The Majority 12 was to survive right up to the present day. Under Eisenhower and Kennedy it was erroneously called the "5412 Committee," or more correctly, the "Special Group." In the Johnson Administration, it became known as the "303 Committee" because the name 5412 had been compromised in the Book, "The Secret Government." Under Nixon, Ford and Carter it was called the 40 Committee and under Reagan it became the "PI 40 Committee."

By 1955 it became obvious that the aliens had deceived Eisenhower and broken the treaty. Mutilated humans and mutilated animals were found all across the U.S. The last mutilated humans that I know of were found in 1979; mutilated animals continue to be discovered today. It was believed that the aliens were not submitting a complete list of human contacts and abductees to the MJ-12 and that all the abductees had not been returned. The aliens were suspected of interacting with the Soviet Union and manipulating masses of people through secret societies, witchcraft, magic, the occult, religion and other ways. After several Air Force combat aerial engagements with the alien craft, it also became apparent that our weapons were no match against them. As a matter of fact, in one encounter a pilot went after an alien ship, the alien shot a beam at him, and the pilot was suddenly suspended in space with no airplane around him. Two pilots experienced this; the first one got killed, but the second one survived to tell the story.

> **Suddenly suspended in space**

The aliens began using implants to track their subjects. At my workshops and seminars I display actual x-rays and CAT scans of implants. I have medical reports from credible doctors and radiology labs at places like University of San Diego and the University of Southern California in Los Angeles. These major university medical centers are finding not just a few, but hundreds of people with implants. Nobody at this time supposedly knew the true nature of the implants. By Secret Executive Memorandum, NSC 5411 in 1954, President Eisenhower commissioned a study group to discover the truth about the aliens. The study group began a series of regular meetings in 1954 called the Quantico meetings because they occurred at the Quantico Marine Base. The group included 35 members of the Council on Foreign Relations and the Jason Society. Dr. Edward Teller was invited to participate. Dr. Zbigniew Brzezinski was the study director for the first 18 months. Dr. Henry Kissinger was chosen as the group study director for the second 18 months in November, 1955. Nelson Rockefeller was a frequent visitor during the study.

1955 was the beginning of Dr. Henry Kissinger's ever-increasing involvement in the alien connection. The study group was publicly closed in the latter months of 1956 and Henry Kissinger published what was officially termed "The Results in 1957 as Nuclear Weapons and Foreign Policy," by Henry A. Kissinger, published for the Council on Foreign Relations by Harper Brothers, New York. In truth, the manuscript had already been 80% written while Kissinger was at Harvard. The study group continued, veiled in secrecy. A clue to the seriousness Kissinger attached to the study can be found in statements made by his wife and friends. Many of them said Henry would leave home early each morning and return late each night without speaking to anyone or responding to anyone.

The revelations of the alien presence and actions during the study must have been a great shock to Henry Kissinger. He was definitely out of character during the time surrounding these meetings. He would never again be effective in this matter, despite the seriousness of any subsequent event. On many occasions he would work late into the night after having already put in a full day. This behavior eventually led to his divorce. A major finding of this study was that the public could not be told the truth. It would most certainly cause national panic, economic disaster, collapse of religious structure, and anarchy. Thus the secrecy continued.

> **Kissinger shocked**

21

GROSS EXPERIMENTATION BY THE ALIEN PRESENCE

One of the major findings was that aliens were using humans and animals for a source of glandular secretions, enzymes, hormonal secretions, blood, and in horrible genetic experiments. The aliens explained these actions as necessary to their survival. They say that their genetic structure had deteriorated and that they were no longer able to reproduce. If they were unable to improve their genetic structure, their race would soon cease to exist. We looked upon their explanations with extreme suspicion, since our weapons were literally useless against the aliens. MJ-12 decided to continue friendly diplomatic relations with them until such time as we were able to develop the technology which would enable us to challenge them on a military level. Overtures would soon be made to the Soviet Union and other nations to join forces for the survival of humanity. The process of world unification became more noticeable in 1988 as the superpowers publicly drew closer.

We conducted defense research via projects Joshua and Excalibur, developed at Los Alamos Labs. ***Joshua, a weapon captured from the Germans, was capable of shattering a 4" thick armor plate at a range of 2 miles using low frequency sound waves.*** It was believed that this weapon would be effective against the alien craft. This weapon was developed further, as I recall, in 1978 by a company called Ling Tempco Vaught in Anaheim, California. When I worked in the aerospace industry at NASA, Ling was famous for its "shaker table." We would put partially assembled space vehicles on the table and simulate the shaking and vibration of a rocket motor, testing parts of the spacecraft. The table contains a speaker-like assembly, except it is huge, powered by a low frequency generator or oscillator with several tons of spacecraft connected to it.

Excalibur was a weapon carried by a missile not to exceed 30,000 feet above ground level. It would be dropped by another missile or a high flying jet at 30,000 feet would not deviate from a designated target by more than 50 meters, would penetrate 1000 meters into the turf or hard-packed soil, and carry a 1 megaton warhead. This was intended for use in destroying the aliens in their underground bases. Joshua was developed successfully, but never used. Excalibur was not pushed until recent years and now there is unprecedented effort to develop this weapon. In the spring of 1990 I was in Dulce, New Mexico with a film crew, R&D Productions. Jim Delatosso, Paul Shephard, a couple of other people and I heard a rumor from Los Alamos Labs that this weapon was almost used at the Jicarilla Indian Reservation in Dulce, New Mexico. Geronimo was a descendent of this well-known Indian tribe. In 1986 a joint alien-terrestrial technology spacecraft, a plutonium powered Delta range bomber, crashed, spilling dangerous amounts of plutonium near the Navajo River north of the Indian reservation. Pollution flowed into the different lakes used by the Indians. The government covered the site with camouflage nets to conceal it from orbiting spy satellites. ***Russia has a satellite in orbit right over Area 51 and Dulce, New Mexico.***

Paul Benowitz from Thunder Corporation in Albuquerque, New Mexico, was flying over the area and and saw four flying saucers on the ground. He was photographing the ships' maneuvers when he came across the wreckage of the Delta bomber. Over a period of two weeks they covered it up and gradually began to remove it. Later when Paul wrote his Senator, the Air Force took him into custody and debriefed him of this whole incident. This is just one of many incidents that we could get into.

The events of the Fatima in the early part of the century were scrutinized by our government. One suspicion was an alien manipulation. An intelligence operation was put into motion to

Excalibur

penetrate the secrecy that surrounds the event. The U.S. utilized its Vatican moles that had been recruited and nurtured during WWII and soon obtained the entire Vatican Study, which included the Prophecy. This Prophecy stated that if man did not turn from evil and place himself at the feet of Christ, the planet would self-destruct, and the events described in the Book of Revelation would indeed come to pass. It stated that a child would be born who would unite the world with a plan for world peace and false religion beginning in 1992. By 1995 the people would discern that he was evil and was indeed the Antichrist. World War III would begin in the Middle East in 1995 with an invasion of Israel by United Arab Nations, using conventional weapons which would culminate in a nuclear holocaust in the year 1999. Between 1991 and 2003, most of the life on this planet would suffer horribly and die as a result. The return of Christ would occur in the year 2011.

When the aliens were confronted with this finding they confirmed that it was true. The aliens explained that they had created and manipulated the human race through religion, Satanism, witchcraft, magic and the occult. They further stated that they were capable of time travel and the events described in the Prophecy would indeed come to pass. Later the exploitation of alien technology by the U.S. and the Soviet Union utilizing time travel confirmed The Prophecy. These aliens showed a hologram they claimed was the actual Crucifixion of Christ, which the government filmed. The government did not know whether to believe them or not. ***Were they using religions to manipulate us?*** Or were they indeed the source of our religion?

I also researched time travel, and later on I will explain how it is possible. One thing I learned about time travel is the fact that time in the future does not exist. All that exists is a series of possibilities and probabilities and this was used by the aliens to manipulate the minds of the governmental people. When I went for my first trip forward in time, it was only a few milliseconds, just enough to phase out of dimension. I realized on my next trip, when I went a little bit further forward in time, that there was no existence. There is an echo in the past, but the energy of space and time is in the present.

The Pleiadians also have demonstrated to Billy Meier and several others, including myself, this time-viewing technique, something like a holographic television set. However, you can manipulate it, and if the government is stupid enough to believe that these negative aliens created us in the first place, then they truly have no spirituality. These are the kind of people that control our Secret Government, people who would sell the human race out, people who have what I would call a "dead soul" because they are capable of being befuddled by about anything that's high tech.

Future U.S. statements on Gray Aliens' technology

The real spiritual kingdom exists beyond a holographic projector. The Pleiadians oftentimes in their ships for entertainment will look into the past. For example, one time I was shown a shipwreck in a holographic projector. It was viewable because it happened on Earth, stored in the akashic record. The Crucifixion of Christ can also be shown in that way, but it's not something that The Grays created, it's there for anyone to see. Understand there are going to be some strong statements coming out, possibly even by the government, in the future about what they have seen or witnessed as to The Gray's technology. Recognize what the interpretation was.

Suppose you took a small child into a room without his parents and showed him a television screen playing a video of his parents. You tell the child, "Well, look, there's your parents, they're inside the TV set." The child might believe you. A mature adult knows it is nothing more than a magnetic impression on a videotape that is being projected through an electronic beam out to the front of the picture tube. The more you understand the technology, the harder it is to be be fooled.

Alternatives 1, 2 and 3

By now the Secret Government was starting to panic. By secret Executive Order of President Eisenhower, the Jason Scholars, whom we talked about earlier, were ordered to study the projected effects of the nuclear holocaust. The Prophecy predicted and made recommendations. The Jason Society made three recommendations called Alternatives 1, 2 and 3. *Alternative 1 was to use nuclear devices* to blast holes in the stratosphere to allow excess heat and pollution to escape into space. Along with that, we would change human cultures from that of exploitation into environmental protection. Of the three, this to me was totally stupid, due to the inherent, destructive nature of man and the incredible damage a nuclear explosion itself would create.

Under-ground cities — in case of nuclear holocast

Alternative 2 was a plan to build a vast network of underground cities and tunnels in which a select representation of all cultures and occupations would survive and carry on the human race. It is ironic how history repeats itself. In South America, an Alternative 2 situation occurred several thousand years ago. A past civilization was hassled by a predecessor group of the Grays. If you go down to South America you'll find caverns that go hundreds of miles underground. With entrances that are 20 feet x 20 feet square, perfectly symmetrical, they were built by past civilizations, and extend all the way up into New Mexico and beneath the ocean. Many of our scientists have seen this. So it was quite easy to use some of these underground structures. That's exactly what they did. The Jason Scholars decided a select few would go underground and the rest of population would have to stay up on the surface of the planet. It just gets stupider and stupider, but these are the type of plans they came up with.

Moon and Mars space colonies: Adam and Eve

Alternative 3 was to exploit the alien and conventional technology in order to establish colonies in outer space. This was not easy to confirm, but the plan also included the taking of human slaves for manual labor. The moon, code named Adam, would be the object of primary interest, followed by the planet Mars, code named Eve, a delaying action.

All three alternatives included birth control, sterilization and the introduction of the deadly microbes to control and slow the growth of the earth's population. AIDS and Ebola are only one result of these plans. There were others. It was decided that the population must be reduced and controlled, that it would be in the best interest of the human race to rid ourselves of the undesirable elements of our society. The joint U.S. and Soviet leadership dismissed Alternative 1, but ordered work to begin on Alternative 2 and Alternative 3.

The most important issue facing all of humanity today is the crisis of deception and lies perpetrated by the handful of people in power in the world. How can we as a species make responsible choices and awaken to higher realities when our govenments are hiding and repressing the truth about space, UFO's and alternative energies?

Chapter 3

The Haig-Kissinger Depopulation Policy—Fact or Myth?

Now at this point in time let us study what is called Volume 3 of the *Global 2000 Report* to the President. Remember, this was put together by 19 different Federal Agencies. We've reviewed the Department of Health, Education & Welfare being involved in this alien coverup, about the aliens wanting to be here and use part of the human race, and we've talked about the Council on Foreign Relations and Kissinger. The next phase of this study begins on page 85, Volume 3 of the *Global 2000 Report*.

Some of you are going to believe this, and some will assume that I'm wrong and check it out for themselves. I've given you some key numbers for the different Government Printing Offices, where these reports can be obtained. In the very beginning of this book I talked about the current destruction of the earth by population problems, pollution, etc. Now we'll just step right into Volume 3, which projects the future solutions. This part of the chapter is entitled, "Predictions for the Next One Hundred Years."

"The most realistic assumptions that can be made about the future course of fertility is that the birthrate will fall even more rapidly than it has in the recent past in all countries that have high birthrates. In countries where birthrates have not yet begun to decline, this process will begin soon. Those countries where birthrate declines have already gained momentum will see progressive declines. The falling birthrate will continue until it reaches levels where the population growth and the economic well-being have been brought into a more desirable balance. This may include 'negative growth.'

"The trend of fertility decline in Europe and the United States tended to be a gentle, almost linear downward drift over two centuries, with vicissitudes introduced by wars, economic booms, depressions and internal political upheaval. Although demographers have not discussed this problem yet, most of their population projections assume that a fertility decline curve will be linear. They assume that the trend of fertility in developing countries, once the decline sets in, will also follow a linear path. The usual assumption is that the specified rate of decline would begin at the base date of some future designated date and continue at a fixed rate until some terminal date. Both the theory of social change and empirical evidence from the countries where such declines have taken place suggested this is a proper assumption. It is proposed here that the shape of the fertility decline curve during the next century will follow that of a reverse "S." This curve has four phases:

a) slow take-off acceleration
b) rapid mid-period of descent or replacement levels
c) rapid deceleration and decline to low replacement levels
d) return to replacement levels after a period of below replacement fertility.

"The factors that determine the shape of this curve are not demographic, but sociological. Based on research of the diffusion of many innovations, the process of change can be divided into five periods:

1. 'The Pioneer Phase' in which a few daring persons take risk and adopt
2. An 'Early Adoptive Phase' in which a more sophisticated, change-oriented individual joins the pioneers in increasing numbers, realizing that the risk is small in comparison to the reward.
3. A 'Mass Adoptive Phase' in which a great bulk of the population joins in the adoption understanding that the risks are small in comparison with the reward.
4. A 'Late Adopter Phase' in which a more conservative segment of the society follows the lead and the majority adopts.
5. Then the last 'Laggard Phase' in which the most reactionary, distressful and inflexible members gradually conform to what has become a universal practice.

Why don't we just go ahead and call it what it is: clones?

"It is believed that the pattern of fertility decline, even more than innovations, will confirm the sequence because adoption of family planning involves both social and medical risks in the minds of the pioneers and the early adopters. It may be expected to have a slow take-off, with increasing acceleration as more people adopt. Once it becomes accepted normal activity, the phase of mass adoption may be expected. As the supply of potential adopters diminishes, then only those who have opposed family planning on extreme religious, political, moral and unjustified medical basis remain, the pace of decline may be expected to decelerate."

Aids population control program

Remember, 19 Federal Agencies put this together. I hope that those of you reading this material realize what this means. This is controlled genocide. "We believe that the major determinant of the rate of decline in the future will therefore be on the level of the fertility itself. This results in very close relationship between the birthrate and the portion of couples who practice contraception." The AIDS population control program is already in place and has spread to married couples and innocent children. Contraceptives are being pushed out there on television all the way down to the high schools. I was at a high school the other night and they were teaching it in a class. It's just exactly what was spelled out here, and this report was put together before the AIDS scare, back in the70's. AIDS became known in the 80's. This report was already out in 1981. What's going on here is powerful!

"As the birth rates fall to lower levels, the greater percentage of the public practices contraception. The following is an estimate of the proportion of fertile couples at reproductive age, who must be practicing contraception in order to lower the birthrate at each of the levels to be specified...."

And I have this chart here that goes into crude birthrate and then it goes down to receptives, meaning people using contraception. I hate to bore you with all this. I have been hoping that those of you who don't believe me will go out and read this for yourself, but I'll skip down through another paragraph or two and read toward the end.

"As the replacement level is approached, meaning roughly three-fourths of the couples that are contracepting, only the most conservative, firmly pro-natalist segments remain, along with a couple just starting off their families. The pressures to reduce fertility have begun to diminish. Consequently the pace of fertility decline may be expected to decrease. If the population has exceeded its resources, and there is genuine and severe overpopulation, we may expect birthrates to decline below the replacement level and to remain there for a sustained period of time until population growth has not only been brought to zero, but until the absolute population decline is reduced to an amount more consistent with life-sustaining resources."

Now let's look at that phrase "life-sustaining resources." We aren't going to have any life-sustaining resources if we continue on using fossil fuels, etc. The Pleiadians pointed this out a long time ago, but the government did not want to look at this.

"We have hypothesized due to the rapid pace of modernization, religious, public and political resistance to family planning and inadequate communications that give the public advance warning, most of the developing countries will be severely overpopulated by the time they begin to approach the replacement level of fertility. It is our prediction, therefore, that we will proceed immediately and directly to substantial and sustained below replacement fertility. They may remain in this state for a full quarter or half century until their numbers and resources are in balance so that they can enjoy an improved standard of living. We predict that much of the twenty-first century will be at one of replacement level, or below replacement level fertility throughout the world, including most if not all the present high birthrate countries of Asia, Latin America and Africa."

And look at these countries. All of them have starving people in them — all of them. The people in control are relying on them to starve themselves right out of the picture.

Now I'm quoting the *Executive Intelligence Review*, a magazine out of Washington, DC., March 10, 1981:

"In the past year, 13,000 people in El Salvador have been killed in the civil war that has threatened the country. To the U.S. State Department and Office of Population Affairs, that's not enough. To accomplish what the State Department deems adequate population control, the Civil War would have to be greatly expanded, according to Thomas Ferguson, the Latin American Case Officer for the LPA. El Salvador was targeted for population control and war in the 1980 Population Report published by the National Security Council."

I heartily suggest you obtain a subscription to this factual magazine. The National Security Council put MJ-12 together, designed the UFO coverup! Now we read that El Salvador was targeted for population control and war in an April 1980 Population Report published by the National Security Council.

"El Salvador is an example of a country with a serious population and political problem. The birthrate has remained unchanged in recent years, aggravates population density, which is already the highest on the mainland Latin America. Latin America was one of the areas that was mentioned in the population report whose population control program exists on paper. It has not been pursued with strong commitment and contraceptives remain unavailable.

'The population program did not work,' OPA's Ferguson said this week. Infrastructure was not there to support it. There were just too many damn people. If you want to control a country you have to keep the population down. Too many people breed social unrest and communism. Something has to be done,' the OPA Official said. The birthrate he reported as 33.3%, one of the highest in the world. 'This population,' he complained, 'would double in 21 years. Civil war can help reduce the population, but would have to be greatly expanded.'"

Now the Vietnamese lesson.

" 'In making sure that the population falls in El Salvador,' Ferguson said, 'the OPA has learned a lot from its experience in Vietnam. We studied the thing. The area was overpopulated and a problem. We thought that war would lower the overpopulation and we were wrong.'"

According to Ferguson, the population in Vietnam increased during the war despite United States' use of defoliation and combat strategies that encouraged civilian casualties.

" 'To reduce population quickly,' said Ferguson, 'you have to put all the males into fighting and kill significant numbers of fertile, childbearing age females.'"

Isn't that scenario just about to be painted again with the Iraq situation, the recruiters are being shown nightly on television running out getting young American males? This is the plan, this is the program. He criticized the current civil war in El Salvador.

" 'You are killing a small number of males and not enough fertile females to do the job on the population.'"

Kill More Females, he's saying. If the war went 30 to 40 years like this, we, Ferguson and others involved with the OPA and the NSC group (remember, that's the National Security Council), might get something finished. Once again, let me remind you we mentioned them back in the 50's when they were formed, and what did they do? They were part of the alien cover-up, keeping it from the American people. You're starting to get the connection, I hope.

"We have a network in place of co-thinkers in the government," said the OPA case officer. "We keep going no matter who is in the White House."

But Ferguson reports that the White House does not really understand what they are saying, and that the President thinks that the population policy means how do we speed up population increase.

" 'As long as no one says differently,' said Ferguson, 'we will continue to do our jobs.'"

UNDERGROUND CITIES AND GOVERNMENT-SANCTIONED DRUG TRAFFICKING

I'm going to jump right from Ferguson to the Rand Corporation. Remember the big scandal in Los Angeles? The Rand Corporation made the news almost as big as Watergate nearly all summer. The Rand Corporation hosted a deep underground construction symposium. In the symposium report, machines are pictured and described that could bore a tunnel 45' in diameter at the rate of 5' per hour. It also displays pictures of used tunnels and underground vaults containing what appear to be complex facilities and possibly even cities. When Jim Delatosso and I went to Dulce, New Mexico, we took ultrasound equipment. In that area exist what are called great lava tubes. In Hawaii, people for sport go for miles underground in little rubber innertubes through the complete darkness. However, you can go hundreds of miles if you want to, even in the Hawaiian Islands, through wet and dry tubes. *The underground tubes in Dulce extend all up and down through New Mexico and the lower part of Colorado continuing all the way down into Mexico,* but they don't have water in them anymore. They are the perfect place for the Sea Bee's to go in under the Rand auspices with their special equipment. We took measurements under Dulce with the ultrasound equipment and found caverns large enough to hold cities.

The ruling powers decided that one means of funding the alien connection, and other black projects, was to corner the illegal drug market. A young, ambitious member of the Council on Foreign relations was approached. His name was George Bush, who at that time was the President and CEO of Zapata Oil, based in Texas. Zapata Oil was experimenting with the new technology of offshore drilling. It was correctly thought that the drugs could be shipped from South America to the offshore platforms by fishing boats where it could then be taken ashore by normal transportation used for supplies and personnel. By this method no customs or law enforcement agency would subject the cargo to search. The plan worked better than anyone had thought and has been expanded worldwide. Now there are many additional methods of bringing illegal drugs into the country. It must always be remembered, though, that this began during the time that George Bush was working with the CIA." The CIA now controls all the world's illegal drug markets.

Black Projects Funds

I'm not putting George Bush down; I think he's done a fine job. But you've got to realize that the presidents of this country since the Eisenhower Administration have not been given much information regarding the cooperation of the NSC, the MJ-12 and the alien question. If we wanted to stop drugs from coming into this country we could legalize them. I don't think the establishment wants to legalize dope like they almost did in Holland and England, because a lot of tobacco companies would suffer. Marijuana would be preferred over tobacco. So what they did was put on a sham of trying to keep dope from being smuggled into the country.

RAMBO VS. THE DRUG LORDS

How many of you out there are familiar with Rambo? The Rambo character was modeled after a Lt. Col. James (Bo) Gritz. He is America's most decorated Green Beret Commander. He commanded the U.S. Special Forces in Latin America and served as a Chief of Congressional Relations in the Pentagon. He recently brought back a signed offer from General Khun-Sa, overlord of the Golden Triangle, that would eradicate the production of 90% of the heroin that flows into the free world. Bo has been behind Communist lines 10 times since 1982 in search of U.S. soldiers missing-in-action. Accounting for America's MIAs and recovering our servicemen still abandoned in Communist Asian prisons is an important project for his group, which is called Center for Action. The first time he went in there, Khun-Sa didn't want him in there. Khun-Sa was hooked up with the CIA which bought his product. Khun-Sa was Bo's adversary, but Gritz was so efficient rescuing the MIAs Khun-Sa used for slaves, that Khun-Sa decided to join him and reveal his true feelings about the heroin situation. This is happening with a lot of the powerful druglords today. They realize they've created a negative karma for themselves and they want to turn this around. Khun-Sa sent a videotape, which is also available, and a letter to the United States government saying that if we would assist him, he would switch over from growing poppies, ending the heroin supply.

If you want to get more involved with this, you can get hold of the Center for Action at P. O. Box 9, Boulder City, Nevada 89005. Their phone number is (702) 293-3100, and their fax number is (702) 293-6616. They also are involved with a proposed amendment to the United States Constitution called the "Survival Amendment," something I'm not going to get into because I'm trying to stay out of the politics of these things the best I can. I discuss the political side of it so that people will be out there encouraged to protect their personal bodies and prepare for this next wave of negative energy that's coming to this planet.

It's very important that agencies that are trying to help us out, and people like Bill Gritz, are recognized and supported. That's why I give out these phone numbers and encourage you to get hold of these people independently. This tax reform, by the way, was first proposed by President Thomas Jefferson some years ago.

We're on the subject of drugs — I'm going to read a paragraph or so in the next chapter.

Chapter 4

Wars & Famine: Global Genocide
MJ-12 Involvement - JFK's Fatal Discovery

This is from the *Center for Action* newsletter:

"We are in the midst of a heroin hurricane. The Center for Action has a plan to eradicate opium and therefore heroin from the most prolific growing area in the world, Burma's Golden Triangle. General Khun-Sa is the key. The United States is considering paying layout money for a crop substitution program. The others reported that the Prime Minster of Laos is working with Khun-Sa to establish heroin refineries and coffee crop deals in his own country.

"Why don't they deal directly with the man behind these operations, Khun-Sa? He has submitted the most reasonable cotton crop substitution plan to date and he controls the vast majority of the Golden Triangle's opium and heroin. In addition, he has promised to reveal to all the U.S. government officials who have been his best customers for the past 15 years. Write to your Senators and Representatives and demand that they test Khun-Sa and his proposal. The cause is not hopeless and you are not helpless. A resolution very similar to the enclosed was overwhelmingly passed by the Alaska State Legislature. Use this model and light a fire under your own City Council and State government. This is our country, the greatest nation on earth. It's our job to keep it that way."

I'll read one more statement here. It has some statistics in it you can write to your Senator with. Also, if you want to contact the Center for Action, you can reach them at 711 Yucca St., Boulder City, Nevada (702) 293-3100:

"Dear Senator, I share your concern over what illegal narcotics are doing to destroy America. Heroin sells for more than a million dollars a pound on our big city streets." [It then doubles, triples and quadruples as it is distributed.] Recently figures show for every dollar used to procure drugs, the users are stealing $7 worth of goods. We are all suffering financially because of drug abuse. America is on the verge of overdose and I want to help you rid our nation of this plague.
I have attached a copy of a proposal from General Khun-Sa, Overlord of Burma's infamous Golden Triangle. The U.S. Drug Enforcement Administration estimates that 300,000 tons of opiates will enter the free world in 1990 from this area alone. This

31

proposal is an offer to eradicate every ounce. I want to see America drug-free. Billions of tax dollars are being consumed allegedly waging a war on drugs, yet look at history. In 1986, 600 tons of Southeast Asian opiates flowed into the free world. The amount increased in 1987 to 900 tons, in 1988 to 1200 tons. National media has reported that national heroin production in 1989 reached 2,400 metric tons. We seem to be moving backwards. The more money we pour into the war, the more drugs are available for consumption. I read where our Chief of U.S. Customs, William Von Raab resigned out of protest because the Executive Branch of our government is not doing all it should do to keep out drugs. I not only want to fight, I want us to win the war. I believe Khun-Sa's proposal is a move in the right direction. We need to test him for at least one year. We can't lose any more than we already are, and we may be able to help eliminate most of the world's heroin.

"Understand me, I don't believe that we should just buy up the drugs from the suppliers and keep them from being distributed. Khun-Sa's plan does not offer that. He says in the enclosed statement that he will eradicate heroin by uprooting the opium poppies. In return he says in the enclosed statement that he will go through a crop substitution plan, he will legitimize his economy and he needs diplomatic help to share the area's rich natural resources. He would also like us to stop giving the Socialist Burmese Agent Orange, which is obviously not being sprayed on opium, but is being used as a means of controlling our resources of the area. I request that you take a close look at this proposal. I want you to actively support this plan unless you have a better one. I request that you do not ask the U.S. State Department for a reply but you go to your U.S. fellow Senators for a solution. Our war on drugs must be waged by Americans, not Democrats or Republicans."

That is a model letter, which leads me to something else. Remember the malathion spraying here in the U.S.? Malathion is chemically similar to Agent Orange. ***What else are they spraying us with?***

Chemicals to alter us

Remember I mentioned the Ad Hoc part of the Secret Government? They authorized a company called Evergreen to buy and fly malathion helicopters, not to spray flies, but people. Do you really believe something that eats the paint off your car is not going to harm human beings? In Japan, for example, they did tests and studies on the long-term genetic effects of malathion. Some of the first side-effects discovered involved genetic problems in the reproduction system. Evergreen is under the auspices of Ad Hoc. Ad Hoc is under the Foreign Affairs Committee, which is part of the UFO cover-up.

I'm going to cite another source and I hope you don't think I'm just reading this presentation to you. I'm not. ***I'm giving you resources so you can prove me wrong.*** I encourage you to try. When we get further along, I'll show you how to protect yourself against the effects of these evilly-laid plans, you'll know where the foundation for the evil came from. It's not something that I created to justify my ideas by showing you that somebody else created the danger, then tell you how to address it. And if you don't acknowledge it, you're going to become a drug addict, an alcoholic, broke or just depressed; you're going to have genetic side effects, be sprayed with malathion, have breathing difficulties from fouled air, and so on. We're trying to prevent that, so I apologize for this reading, but I think it's very important.

This is a Special Report from the EIR *(Executive Intelligence Review)* March 1981. The EIR is a good publication that comes out of Washington, DC. If you want to read your own EIR Reports, I recommend you contact this group yourself and deal with them directly at (202)

628-0029. Lonnie Wilkes wrote:

"Investigations by the EIR have uncovered a planning apparatus operating outside the control of the White House, whose sole purpose is reducing the population by 2 billion people through war, famine, disease and any other means necessary."

I call this the beginning of the DNA Wars. Remember I told you that the Grays had human body parts in their spacecraft, and that the government made a deal with them with full knowledge of this atrocity? ***The Secret Government also violated our Constitutional rights by signing treaties with Alien Nations without informing the public.*** Our government received advanced genetic science which they used against us via Agent Orange and other delivery systems. They have and will continue to release gene-altering chemicals into our water and food supplies.

The DNA wars

Microbes are used to deliver death, too. This is from the Chicago Tribune, Sunday, August 5, 1990, entitled "Children's Palestine Syndrome Baffles Texas Doctors," Temple, Texas, AP Wire Services:

"Since March, physicians throughout Texas have reported 149 cases of a mysterious new illness called Palestine Syndrome. The malady mostly strikes children and is characterized by a high fever and temporary arthritis.

"Dr. Jeffrey Dunn, a physician at the Scott White Memorial Hospital, who first identified the illness, said last week that experts still know little of its origins and are uncertain of how or if it can be prevented or cured. 'It has not been fatal and victims recover completely,' Dunn said, 'but patients have been hospitalized for as long as 6 months.'

" 'We have no idea whether it's increasing and we're not being swamped with cases,' said Jeffrey Taylor with the Texas Department of Health. 'There are some new ones that had onset in July and we're following up on those. The illness was named after a town about mid-way between Dallas and Houston where it was first encountered in March. Although the ailment is named for Palestine, so far only four confirmed cases came from there,' Taylor said. They have identified cases in 34 Texas counties, most in the north-central and eastern section of the state. Scott White Memorial Hospital spokesman Charlene Lee said the hospital has received inquiries about the Palestine Syndrome from other sections of the country."

The article continues, saying most of the confirmed cases have been in children under the age of 15. This is an example of just one of the many genetically engineered diseases that have been developed.

Back into the EIR Report, the first paragraph that I read said that we have uncovered a planning apparatus to depopulate the world. So I shall continue on now.

"This apparatus which includes various levels of the government is determining U.S. foreign policy."

Here we are back to the Iraq situation, and every other political hot spot, like El Salvador, the so called "Arc of Christ" in the Persian Gulf, other locations in Latin America, Southeast Asia and Africa.

"The goal of U.S. foreign policy is population reduction. The targeted agency for the operation is the National Security Council, Ad Hoc Group on Population Policy," which we discussed previously. It's policy planning group is the United States Department Office of Population Affairs established in 1975 by, guess who?, Henry Kissinger. The group drafted the Carter Administration Global 2000 document which calls for global population reduction. The same apparatus is conducting the civil wars in El Salvador.

" 'Behind all our work, we must reduce population levels,' said Thomas Ferguson, the Latin America Case Officer for the United States Office of Population Affairs. 'Either they, the government, do it our way through nice clean methods, or they will get the kind of mess that we have in El Salvador, or in Iran, or in Beirut. Population is a political problem. Once population is out of control, it requires authoritarian government, even fascism, to reduce it. The professionals,' said Ferguson, [I wonder who the professionals are], 'aren't interested in lowering population for humanitarian reasons [oh, that sounds nice]. We look at resources and environmental constraints. We look at the strategic needs and we say that this country must lower its population or else we will have trouble.' "

So steps are taken. El Salvador is one example where our failure to lower population by simple means created the basis for a National Security crisis. What happened to Saddam Hussein? He was antagonized into invading Kuwait. A long time ago Kuwait used to belong to Iraq. Saddam went to the State Department before he made his move, but they didn't pay any attention to him.

" 'So wars are somewhat ways to reduce population,' " the OPA official added.

The quickest way to reduce population is through famine and disease. Per the EIR Special Report, The Haig Kissinger Depopulation Policy, it reads:

"In 1975, OPA was brought under a reorganized State Department Bureau of Oceans, Environment and Scientific Affairs, a body created by Henry Kissinger. The agency was assigned to carry out the directives of the NSC, the National Security Council. [You'll remember I told you previously that the NSC was formed in the first place to cover Alien Intelligence.] According to the NSC spokesman, Kissinger initiated both groups after discussion with leaders of the Club of Rome during the 1974 population conferences in Bucharest and Rome. The Club of Rome, controlled by Europe's black nobility, is the primary formation agency for the genocidal reduction of world population levels. The Ad Hoc group was given high priority by the Carter Administration through the intervention of the National Security advisor, Dr. Zbigniew and the Secretaries of State Cyrus Vance and Edmund Muskie.

"According to the OPA expert Ferguson, 'Kissinger initiated a full about-face on U.S. development policy toward the Third World for a long time. They listened to arguments from the Third World leaders that said the best contraceptive was economic development. So we pushed the development program and we helped create a population time bomb. We are letting people breed like flies without allowing for natural causes to keep population down. We raised the birth survival rates, extended lifespans by lowering death rates, and did nothing about lowering birth rates. The policy is finished. Population reduction control is now our primary policy objective. And then you have some development.' " [I'm not going to publish the whole thing, you get the idea.]

Let's talk some more about the U.S. Space Program. The official space program was supported by President Kennedy. When we were working at Rockwell we used to hear great speeches about going into outer space. In his inaugural address, he mandated that the United States put a man on the moon before the end of the decade. At this point Russia had just put the first Sputnik in orbit. Although innocent in its conception, this mandate enabled those in charge to funnel vast amounts of money into Black Projects and conceal the real space program from the American people. NASA was the perpetrator of the fake space program with the Apollos and the current space shuttle. The real space program continued on over at Area 51.

A similar program in the Soviet Union served the same purpose. In fact, a joint Alien, United States and Soviet Union base already existed on the moon at the very moment President Kennedy spoke the words. On May 22, 1962, a space probe landed on Mars confirming the existence of an environment which could support life. There have been many secret and covert launches space technology towards Mars ever since the 1976 Viking mission and who knows what a select few inside NASA and the Russian Space Program have uncovered about our mysterious twin planet.

MYSTERIES ON MARS

And this now brings me up to another associate in the field and the work. Richard C. Hoagland wrote a book called *The Monuments of Mars –The City on the Edge of Forever.* He'd been involved in something that happened back at NASA. A group of NASA people were looking at some frames from the Viking probe. Frame number 35A72 showed *a face on the surface of Mars* that resembled the Egyptian Sphinx. Semjase had told me about this and about some old cities on Mars before this discovery was made. Eventually Richard obtained a copy of the frame and began to exploit it. NASA denied the face interpretation, of course, saying it was some strange formation. However, the Russians picked up on it and thought it was a great discovery. They studied the pictures and decided there definitely was a city. NASA was publicly embarrassed, so some real serious studies got started. A budget was approved for the next Mars discovery satellite to include an orbit pattern that would facilitate close-up work on this supposedly ancient city. I highly recommend reading the book. Contact: North Atlantic Books, 2800 Woolsey Street, Berkeley, CA 94705. Richard's audio tape series comes with a complete explanation. Contact: Enhanced Audio Systems, 1900 Powell Street, Suite 1135, Emeryville, CA 94608. This is yet another fascinating item for you to research.

Discover for yourself some of the phenomenal things that are going on. I haven't even gotten to the pyramids underneath the sea and some of Charles Berlitz's work yet, but that's coming. See for yourself the pyramids on Mars; I highly recommend the audio tape and book that I mentioned. Now, back to President Kennedy.

KENNEDY ISSUES ULTIMATUM

At some point President Kennedy discovered portions of the truth concerning the drugs and the aliens. He issued an ultimatum in 1963 to the MJ-12. President Kennedy assured them that if they did not clean up the drug problem, he would. He informed MJ -12 that he intended to reveal the presence of aliens to the American people within the following year and to plan to implement his decision. President Kennedy was not a member of the Council on Foreign Relations, and knew nothing about Alternative 2 or Alternative 3. Internationally, the operations were supervised by an Executive Committee known as the Policy Committee. In the United States they were supervised by the MJ-12 and in the Soviet Union by its sister organization. President Kennedy's decision struck fear into the hearts of those in charge. His assassination was ordered by the Policy Committee and the order was carried out by agents of MJ-12 out in Dallas.

Kenedy killed by MJ-12 agents

The Warren Commission was a farce; the Council on Foreign Relations members made up the majority of its panel. They succeeded in snowing the American people. Many other patriots who attempted to reveal the Alien secret have also been murdered throughout the intervening years.

I'm going to share something with you on the metaphysical level at this point in time. This was something that I learned through my guides about Kennedy and Lincoln.

President Lincoln was assassinated 100 years before Kennedy was assassinated, in about 1861.

Lincoln was elected in 1860.
Kennedy was elected in 1960, exactly 100 years later.
There are 7 letters in each name.
Both Presidents were killed on a Friday.
Both were killed in the presence of their wives.
Both were directly concerned with Civil Rights.
Both Presidents had legality of elections contested.
Kennedy's secretary Lincoln warned him not to go to Dallas.
Lincoln's secretary Kennedy warned him not to go to the theater.
Both of their successors were named Johnson; Andrew Johnson, Lyndon Johnson.
Each name contains 13 letters.
Both served in the U.S. Senate.
Both were Southern Democrats.
Lyndon Johnson was born in 1908.
Andrew Johnson was born in 1808.
Booth and Oswald were both Southerners favoring unpopular ideas.
Oswald shot Kennedy in a warehouse and hid in a theater.
Booth shot Lincoln in a theater and hid in a warehouse.
Booth and Oswald were murdered before the trial could be arranged.
Lincoln and Kennedy in death were carried on the same caisson.
Booth and Oswald were born 100 years apart.
Lee Harvey Oswald, John Wilkes Booth, each name had 15 letters.

More than a coincidence, I would say.

Chapter 5

The Real Beginning of America

A curse was put on the United States because we had gone into Africa for slaves. The United States is a metaphysical country, going all the way back to the Revolutionary War. My great-great-grandfather was Ethan Allen, who was part of the group that initiated the Revolution. The beginning of that historic war is interesting. I'm going to tie in complex metaphysical connections.

Back about the time we were getting ready to go to war and start the American Revolution, everything was put on hold. The Continental Congress was meeting, but no one would sign the Declaration of Independence; George Washington was camped at Valley Forge, but he wouldn't fight; the British were looking at all the aristocrats and saying, "Ah-hah-hah, you guys ought to get up and fight a little bit here." Nobody would do it. It was a stalemate.

While they were hemming and hawing around in the Continental Congress building, a stranger appeared, even though the room was sealed off. He was up on the balcony of the Congress Hall in Boston. He gave a powerful speech and said, "Sign that document." The identity of this mysterious stranger who materialized was later discovered to be Count Saint Germaine, the Great White Master. That's when John Hancock put his giant signature on the paper, he was so motivated by this stranger's speech. Almost at the same moment while this speech was being delivered, two people were having a discussion up in the Lexington-Concord area further north.

Colonel Parker, who was in charge of the militia, asked Ethan Allen, "When's this war going to start?"

Ethan Allen said, "Colonel Parker, well soon. In order for this war to start God-damn it, somebody's got to die." With that speech, Colonel Parker ordered the execution of the 50 British Regulars that crossed the Lexington-Concord Bridge. So the shooting started. The interesting connections to this lifetime is that I started a company called Health Energy Science and I had a partner whose name was Wes Parker. He'd won the World Series for the Dodgers in 1973. He and I discussed this one day and he said, "You know what, Fred, your great-great-grandfather and mine served alongside each other."

Simultaneously, the shooting started at the Lexington-Concord Bridge and the Congressional document was signed in Boston. Then Ethan Allen, with eight of his Minutemen, went with a party up north to Fort Ticonderoga, a fort commanded by General Delaplace. They sneaked into the fort when most of the 800 British who were stationed there slept, went directly into the General's quarters, stuck a musket into his mouth and said, "Surrender the fort or we're going to shoot you." General Delaplace surrendered Fort Ticonderoga to these nine people. Ethan Allen then sent a runner to George Washington to notify him that war had started and Fort Ticonderoga had been conquered.

George Washington received this news at the same time he learned that the Declaration of Independence had been signed. He immediately went off to war.

Later on in the war Ethan Allen was captured and sent to England where he had to face King George III. The King sentenced him to the gallows for treason. Ethan Allen, being the 7-foot-tall giant that he was, stood up before King George and said, "Fine, kill me as fast as you can because I am going to come back and haunt you and your family for generations to come."

This intimidated King George, so he sent Ethan Allen back to America to be traded off in a prisoner exchange. Ethan Allen died long after the war was over. He died from pneumonia as an old man, cursing because his health had failed. For him to live as long as he did in those days was quite interesting.

The spiritual energy of America sustained itself on into Lincoln's time and Kennedy's time. In Lincoln's time, the Africans practiced Black Magic. They put a curse on us for five generations starting with President Lincoln. This curse terminated with President Reagan, who was shot but not killed. If you look at the records, every 20 years from Abraham Lincoln's time until Ronald Reagan, a president has mysteriously or otherwise died in office. Just look at the comparison between Abraham Lincoln and John F. Kennedy. It wasn't just a coincidence, it was something that was highly guided.

Lincoln was a good person, but someone good had to be sacrificed to dissolve the bad. Lincoln was helping the Africans out by getting them free of slavery but still he had to take on a messianic conflict just like Christ did; it was part of the purification process.

Chapter 6

The Secrets Almost Exposed,
The Cost of our Constitutional Freedoms,
& Torture in Our Prisons

Looking back into the era of the United States' initial space exploration and moon landings, every launch was accompanied by an alien craft. Moon Base Lunar was sighted and filmed by the Apollo astronauts. Domes, spires, tall round structures which looked like silos, huge T-shaped landing vehicles, which left stitch-like tracks in the lunar surface and were extremely large, as well as alien craft, appear in photographs.

Fred Steckling, a member of the Jordan Dansky Foundation, wrote an interesting book called *Aliens on the Moon*. His pictures, taken with a high-powered telescope, show objects taking off and landing on the moon. You can reach him at: P. O. Box 1722, Vista, CA 92083. I recommend you get a copy of his book about the astonishing evidence of bases on the moon.

Bases on the Moon

You can learn more about the bases on the moon and the NASA farce by reading *Alternative 3* or watching the video. "Bob Grodin" landed on the moon and found a city up there. Many of the Apollo astronauts were severely shaken by their experiences on the moon; their subsequent statements and the rest of their lives reflect the depth of the revelation and the effect of the secrecy requirements that followed. This secrecy was incredible, even when I was back at NASA. Alan Holt wrote a synopsis on a saucer spacecraft-type engine we were proposing. But nobody wanted to see it. We couldn't talk about our work for ten years after we left NASA because of what they called the "grace period." The astronauts were ordered to remain silent or suffer extreme penalty (death), which was termed "an expediency." One astronaut, given the pseudonym of "Bob Grodin," actually did talk to British producers to expose Alternative 3. There is a tape I've seen of that interview, but right now it's kept in confidence.

The interview revealed that Grodin escaped into alcoholism because of what he had seen on the moon. After trying unsuccessfully to keep it buried, he began to talk about it, even though he was scared to death. "Bob Grodin" committed suicide in 1978. There is much to this astronaut coverup program that people who have been in space aren't talking about. Since we've been working with the aliens, we have come into possession of a technology beyond our wildest dreams. If you view the Area 51 videotape footage that is available today, you will be astounded by the maneuvers that ship is doing.

The Aurora

A craft named Aurora, a replacement for the SR71, exists at Area 51, and makes regular trips into space. It is a one-stage spaceship called a TAV (Trans Atmospheric Vehicle). It has conventional engines in it, another stage that has ram jets, then another stage with a scram jet. I've seen the technology because my friends worked with some of the major aerospace companies that developed it. It can take off from the ground using a seven-mile runway, go into a high orbit, return on its own power and land on the same runway. We currently have and fly atomic-powered alien craft at Area S4 in Nevada, which is next door to Area 51. Our pilots have made interplanetary voyages in these craft and have been to the Moon, Mars and other planets.

THE REAL SPACE PROGRAM

We have been lied to about the true nature of the moon, the planets Mars and Venus, and the real state of technology that we possess today. The SR71 was the stealth craft that we'd heard about in the news. They released the information about the time the ship was retired in 1990. The craft was retired because it was shot at by a Russian Scalar V-Beam, cutting off a two-foot wing section. V-Beam technology involves the tensile effect from scalar waves. Remember the time the Japanese airline pilot was flying a 747 in Alaska a few years back? He saw and flew through what looked like an atomic bomb going off, but there was no shock wave. That's a V-Beam.

When the SR71 was retired, we activated the Aurora. And beyond the Aurora, we go into the Delta craft, which is like the one that crashed in 1986 at Dulce, New Mexico, discussed by Paul Benowitz. Beyond that are the disc-shaped ships. We have drawings of the propulsion systems, although I'm not presenting them here.

In 1969 a confrontation broke out between the human scientists and aliens at the Dulce underground base. The aliens took many of our scientists hostage. Delta Forces were sent in to free them, but were no match against the alien weapons. Sixty-six of our people were killed during this action. As a result we withdrew from all joint projects for at least two years, until a reconciliation eventually took place and we once again began to interact. Today the alien alliance continues.

1969: Alien-Human "Mini war" 66 die

This fatal confrontation resulted in the release of 25 sheets of information known as the Dulce Papers, filtered out and circulated by some of the people that survived. Rumors that came from those papers are now being confirmed. And if you doubt me about Dulce, go up there and have your own experience.

It's been hard work to keep the alien connection a secret. When the Watergate scandal broke, President Nixon had intended to ride out the storm, confident that he could not be impeached. MJ-12, however, had a different idea. The intelligence committee rightfully concluded that an impeachment trial would open up the files and bare the awful secrets to the public eye. Nixon was ordered to resign. He refused and so the first military coup ever to take place in the United States was perpetuated. The Joint Chiefs of Staff sent a top secret message to all commanders of U.S. Armed Forces which stated, "Upon receipt of this message, you will no longer carry out any orders from the White House. Acknowledge receipt." The message was sent a full five days before Nixon conceded and announced publicly he would resign.

White House no longer in authority

Everybody thought the UFO situation would be revealed. Once again, Nelson Rockefeller headed up the commission investigating the intelligence community. As a member on the Council on Foreign Relations he was in a perfect position to maintain the secrecy. Then later Senator Church, another prominent member of the Council on Foreign Relations, conducted the famous Church Hearings; again the coverup prevailed. When the Iran Contra hearings came along, we thought this time some truth would come out. Look how cleverly they covered that up! As a matter of fact, the United States Attorney did not prosecute Oliver North, they hired an independent outside law firm. Remember, when subpoenaed for the real records they said this was an issue of national security. And it's hard to even begin to comprehend the financial empires that have been established by these groups. The amount of money that's hidden is beyond anything you can imagine. Look at J. Henry Schroeder Banking Corporation, the Schroeder Trust Company, Schroeder Limited-London, Herbert Wag Holdings Limited, J. Henry Schroeder, Wag & Helmut Lag Holdings Limited, Schroeder Gerbeter & Co in Germany, Schroeder Munchmeyer Hongst & Co, Castle Bank and its holding companies, The Asian Development Bank and the Nugan, Hand, octopus of banks and holding companies.

OUR SECRET GOVERNMENT

A contingency plan was formulated by MJ-12 to throw anyone off the trail who should come too close to the truth. The plan is known as Majestic 12, released by some people in the UFO movement. I'm sure some of you are familiar with it. It was supposedly perpetrated by what was called the Eisenhower Briefing Document. The credibility of that document is in question as it lists Executive Order number as 92,447, a number that does not exist and will not exist for quite a long time at the present rate of progression. For example, Truman's Executive Orders were in the 9000 range, Eisenhower's in the 10,000 range, Ford was up to the 11,000's. Reagan only got into the 12,000's. Nobody got into 92,000. Executive Orders are numbered consecutively no matter who occupies the White House, for reasons of continuity, record-keeping, and to prevent confusion.

The Executive Order is only one of several fatal flaws contained within the document. The plan so far has thrown the entire research community off the trail for several years and resulted in wanton and wasteless expenditure of money looking for information that does not exist.

One of the worst contingency plans that has been well-implemented is at work right now. For many years drugs have been imported and sold to people, mainly the foreign minorities. Social welfare programs were put into place to create a dependent, non-working element of our society. Then the social welfare programs were cut, even removed, to develop a large criminal class that did not exist in the 50's and 60's. Look at the crime rate. The Secret Government encouraged the manufacture and import of deadly military firearms for the criminal element to use. You can get Uzis and AR15s at pawn shops. You can get the BAR, the Browning Automatic Rifle. This was intended to foster a feeling of insecurity that will lead the American people to voluntarily disarm themselves by passing laws against firearms. Wasn't that an issue back in 1988, '89 & '90? Incidents were to be staged to speed up the process. By using drugs, hypnosis and a process called Orion on mental patients, the CIA inculcated a desire in these people to open fire on school yards and thus expand the anti-gun lobby. We are already well into this operation that is working exactly as planned.

Systematic "voluntary" civilian disarmment

Due to the wave of crime sweeping the nation, the Secret Government will convince the American people that a state of anarchy exists within the major cities, building their case nightly on TV and daily in the newspapers. When you study this as I have, you can discern planted information about UFOs and the like and which agencies are behind it. NASA, for example, has what I call the class cover-up act, people like Carl Sagan and all these people working on the SETI program. The SETI program, which is another document put out by the Government Office Printing Bookstore, covers the research of what data was supposedly extracted from space, which, they state, is absolutely nothing, by radio telescopes. *If there is absolutely nothing detected by the radio telescope, why are we spending billions of dollars to expand the radio telescope program to listen to space?* The discrepancies go on and on.

The Secret Government will work to properly mold public opinion. Then, at the appropriate time, state that a terrorist group armed with a nuclear weapon has entered the United States and plans to detonate this device in one of our cities. I discovered this in the early 90's, and they are already suggesting that this is about to happen right now. The government will then suspend the Constitution and declare martial law. Then the secret army of implanted humans and all dissidents, which translates into anyone they choose, will be rounded up and will be placed in concentration camps which already exist throughout the country.

F.E.M.A. when we lose all our constitutional freedoms

One weekend, a couple of amendments passed through the House and Senate. HR 5210, which is public law #100-690, the Omnibus Drug Bill dissolves the Fourth Amendment Right to proper search and seizure. Once martial law is declared, the government can do whatever it wants. The parent bill, HR 4079, gives the President the right to activate the National Emergency Group, which is called FEMA, Federal Emergency Management Agency, any moment there is a terrorist threat. Like the Drug Bill, when this act is invoked we lose our Constitutional rights and the government can do whatever it wants to do. Now they can move right in and take over, put people in these mile-square concentration camps they've already built throughout the country.

And who do you think they are going to incarcerate? The people that are "resisting." Suppose the government tells us a "terrorist group" is going to be in San Francisco. HR 4079 is invoked; all citizens lose their Constitutional rights; they come in and remove the people that they want out, and they throw them into these camps.

Then suddenly the terrorists are "caught," but the people aren't released from the camps. This is where we truly lose our Constitutional rights. The entire operation I just described, code named Red 84, was rehearsed by the government and the military in 1984 and went off without a hitch. ***When these events have transpired, the Secret Government and /or the Alien takeover will be complete.*** Your freedom will never be returned to you and you will live in slavery for the remainder of your life. We'd better do something about this and become more aware of the problems that are going on. I think that any cursory investigation will show that the Council on Foreign Relations and the Trilateral Commission control the major foundations that fund these Black Box projects; all of the major media and publishing interests are controlled by these same groups; the largest banks, all the major corporations, the upper echelons of the government, and many other vital interests. They are also trying to inaugurate the credit card system into this plan. That's why you can call an 800 number and get a credit line even if you have bad credit or a bankruptcy. They want to get you on their registers so they can begin to control you. This is all part of the big program. It even talks about it in the Bible, the Mark of the Beast.

Here is a little article entitled "Prescription for Torture" by a convict writer, Danny M. Martin, discussing drug experimentation performed on prisoners. The experimenters turn the test cases loose in society and see what they'll do. I'll give you an example of that in a minute. It reads:

"On Tuesday, February 27th, the U.S. Supreme Court rekindled the convict's worst nightmare. The court, by a vote of 6 to 3, gave prison officials sweeping power to force convicts to take psychotropic drugs against their will. The ruling may have

44

played well on the street, but it cast a dread over the feelings of many of us convicts. To those of us who watch convicts be plied with drugs that made them total zombies, the decision was maddening. It is true that some convicts need to be medicated, but we have seen others, who don't need the drugs, being forced to take them by incompetent and tyrannical bureaucrats.

"Justice Anthony M. Kennedy, writing for the majority, said, 'Given the requirements of the prison environment, the State may treat a prison inmate who has a serious mental illness with anti-psychotic drugs against his will. If the inmate is dangerous to himself and others, then treatment is in the inmate's best medical interest.' "

A little further on in the article, it states:

"The drugs we are talking about are sometimes used in here as an exquisite form of long-term torture. Some of these mind and body-paralyzing chemicals are Prolixin, Dartal and Thorazine. They are brand names for a class of major tranquilizers based on the drug phenothiazine, which is widely prescribed for schizophrenia and other severe mental illnesses. Such is the power of these drugs that I have seen men do things under their influence that almost defied description. One man on anti-psychotic drugs at the Lompoc Penitentiary climbed a row of deadly razor sharp wire, oblivious to the danger, and got hung up in the wire about half-way up. A guard fired a warning shot. The convict was then hauled off the wire by other guards. He was so high that he wasn't even aware that he was being cut. Another convict who comes to mind is murderer Gary Gilmore, subject of the Norman Mailer book, "The Executioner's Song." Gilmore was once strapped to a bunk in the Oregon State Prison for five weeks during the early 1970's and injected with massive doses of Prolixin, according to another convict. A man who was there at the time told me that after the ordeal Gilmore completely lost his sense of humor and became extremely morbid. All this was several years before the savage murders for which he was ultimately executed.

I just want to say that the man who wrote this article, Danny M. Martin, a convicted bank robber who has written frequently for Sunday Punch, is currently at the Federal Correctional Institution in Phoenix where he was transferred after writing an article about rising tensions at the Lompoc Penitentiary in California.

Now in the next phase of this we're going to start talking about the mind-body-spirit relationship of the human body. We'll reveal what I have learned from the good extraterrestrials. I have explained to you about the negative side so that I can get it out of the way. I really want to take off and have some fun.

I've also covered the *Global 2000 Report* and what it means for us. I've shown you which agencies compiled the 2000 Report, where it originated; we've seen the political intertwining of agencies; we've discussed the malathion spraying, we've mentioned the depopulation policy and how it intertwines with the UFO and extraterrestrial coverup, how the alien intelligence has used human body parts to further their research as well as using them for food; and of course our Secret Government, seeing as how they are all tied together.

It's easy to see how they are powerful enough to plot the demise of any portion of our population. Also, we've talked a little bit about the health aspects of it and once you understand what you're dealing with it, then it's easy to reverse the energy.

It's not just the dark side of the forces that are here; the Brothers of Light, the friendly extraterrestrials and several others are here. But we have to begin to help ourselves. Their help will be of no value to us if we're not aware — first of all, how the game is being played, where the borders of the game are and who the players are. And up until now I've found that most people I've spoken to in the health fields and New Age fields and different areas really aren't aware of the overall ramifications and do not have a clear view of what is going on. I won't refer back so much specifically to the same material as I will to other things that have to do with these different agencies, other policies that I haven't mentioned.

Friendly beings are here too

And now if you have any questions, I would advise you, before going on from here, to go back and review this material a time or two. It doesn't hurt to be well-informed because the further we get into it, the more sense it's going to make.

I hope that I've given you enough information, such as the location and centers of the Global 2000 offices; documents to refer to; the name of the EIR phone number in Washington, D.C. where you can get more information; or you can even subscribe to some of the publications I mentioned. There are plenty of groups and agencies of people like ourselves banded together to find out more and who want to do something about it.

In the following chapters we're going to study three or four different bodies of energy. The physical body, which we're well aware of, has to do with biochemistry.

We're going to delve deeply into vitamins and nutrition and related information. We're also going to be dealing with the body that directs your physical body, which is called the etheric body. The etheric body is visible through different kinds of dyes. It is an ultramagnetic field that hovers or moves about the physical body. Then, of course, we're going to get into the astral body, which is the emotional body, which is interdimensional. It moves beyond the speed of light and directs the energy down to the etheric body through the planes. And we're going to go through the doorways of these different bodies from one to the other.

Moving beyond the speed of light

Part II

Healing the Body and Soul —
A Journey to Wholeness!

Chapter 7

The Beginning of True Longevity

Suppose I had ten patients and they all had sore throats. If I treated all 10 of them with one means — biochemical, antibiotic, vitamin, nutritional—I might only get a positive response out of two or three people.

To treat a sore throat, I could address the electric-etheric levels in the body. Negative ionization taking place within the cell structure causes biochemical changes, so manipulation of that electrical process can affect you at the cellular level. I would probably get a 50% response. Electrical precursation interacts with the astral and higher etheric levels. A series of parameters are set up on the electrical etheric level or what can be called the astral level, the emotional level, to cause changes on the biochemical level. The electrical precursation devices that work on these levels are items such as Super Receptors, the carefully engineered pyramid structures that we have developed over the years, and the bigger grid structures that we'll get into further on.

Electrical precursation devices can affect mental as well as biochemical processes. People who have been abducted by the negative aliens, the Grays, often don't have memory of the experience. When they are finally hypnotized or something triggers the body, their memories are awakened. Memory recall is another area that electrical precursation can address.

Also intertwined with this concept is the theory of life extension. We used to live longer. Life extension and immortality have been pursued by the human race since time began. The Egyptians developed a remarkable method that preserved their bodies for centuries. After embalming the corpse with tannic acid, they placed it inside a pyramid field, utilizing its dehydration without the interference of bacteria effect on the body. If you hang a bunch of flowers upside down inside a pyramid and let them dry out in there, the pyramid's protective field will prevent bacterial decay. After a few weeks you'll have a perfectly preserved, very bright floral bouquet that you can spray a little clear lacquer on and would last for 200 or 300 years.

Ponce de Leon discovered and named Florida after looking for the Fountain of Youth in 1513, almost 500 years ago. Today pilgrims search different lands to find the answer. I know that many of my friends also have traveled as far away as Tibet in search of truth and ever-lasting life. Betty Lee Morales spent many years in Tibet with the long-lived Hunzikuts. Apricot kernels, which contain laetrile, are an important part of their diet, which we'll get into a little later on.

There are stories of a chosen few who have successfully added a few years to their terrestrial lives. Methusala, for example, supposedly lived to about 650 years back in 600 B.C. In more recent times, Count Ragowsky, who is known as Count Saint Germaine of Transylvania, lived over 200 years in a middle-aged body during the time of Marie Antoinette.

Some known centurians

Madam Dalamar kept a diary of his activities which is in a British museum today in London. Saint Germaine had been documented by several reliable sources to have been active in the European politics in 1710 to 1860, which is a pretty good long lifespan for a politician.

The famous author, Madam Blavatsky, wrote of an eastern gentleman, Mahatma Moria, who was a Rajput prince. He was over 200 years old when she met him in 1851 with Queen Victoria of England. During the ensuing 40 years she spent with the prince he never appeared to age. More recently, 500 year-old Robizar Tarz maintains the appearance of a 40 year-old. He is even said to have formulated some of the many exotic vitamins that combined the use of spirulina, herbs, enzymes and amino acids that are on the market today.

DNA AND LONGEVITY

One of my music albums, called *Atlantis Rising,* begins "Under water a long time ago with the DNA wars"; DNA wars were something that started back when the Black Priests of Atlantis had sold out to the negative extraterrestrials known as the Grays. Today we repeat what happened 12,000 years ago. The human race sold itself out for more advanced technology and ended up with a long-term effect on the human body—shortened lifespans. My newest extraterrestrial contact I'm working with now, Leeara, is teaching us how to stop our DNA from de-spiraling and to start winding up instead, giving us a chance to regain our longevity. We might get another 40 or 50 years out of the bodies we have now if we start using these techniques. But we're going to re-adjust the vibratory and DNA structure to pass on longevity to our children, who might then live to be 200 years old, and their children 300 years old.

The soul reincarnates and we can access this continuity of consciousness. I still remember my past life, the one immediately before this one. I've got tremendous memory of it. This gift is something we all can attain. You have to earn it, but it becomes easier to access the memories. By increasing our own longevity and that of our children and our children's children, we'll in turn come back as one of our children's children with memory of this whole experience. This will enhance the whole human race. That's what makes these studies so important.

Most of society's ideals are based on greed and resultant insecurity, and as a result we live in total contradiction to nature, or what is natural. The Pleiadians live differently. They don't have freeways and trains and cars roaring through their lives. They seek perfect harmony with their surrounding universe. When this balance of body, soul and spirit is achieved by perfect synthesis, we are truly immortal. But today our bodies exist on the bare minimums. We're just trying to survive. Our minds quest for perfect thought; our souls and spirits only wish for a perfect union of a perfect brotherhood of one man, one woman or one child. That's all we're trying to do is just survive and keep our families together. So we've got to go inside ourselves and go beyond that. And that's what we're going to attempt to do now.

THE NATURE OF THE AURA

Let's begin with the human aura. Our aura is a summation of fields that exist around the human body and changes all the time. The human aura is polarized, with a north and south pole. You can imagine the human being as a vertical magnet. The north pole is in the top part of the body in the third ventricle of the brain. The south pole is concentrated around the base of the spine. Imagine if you took an electrical wire about 5 feet long and attached it to a battery, one end to the positive pole, one end to the negative pole. Immediately an electric current would flow through the wire; there would be electricity moving through the wire along this circuit. At right angles to this would be electromagnetic energy.

This electromagnetic field collapses when you disconnect the power source, the battery. When you reconnect the wire to opposite poles of the battery, you've reversed the polarity of the field. The current now flows in the opposite direction, the magnetic field is polarized in the opposite direction. So you now have a reverse magnetic field. The body is the same way.

You can imagine there are 72,000 different wires extending from the base of the brain down through the spinal cord, distributing themselves all throughout the muscles. This electrical field conductor of the body is the nervous system, 100% electrical. The brain, which I'll talk about in awhile, produces electricity that through different galvanic actions, reactions and responses of emotions and thoughts in the brain, transmits different frequencies and vibratory energies. The aura field is the end result of a magnetic field repeating itself down 72,000 major wires in the body. And along with it there are many thousands of smaller nerve circuits that create many smaller, more minute magnetic fields. That's why it's important to realize that magnetic fields do have an effect on the human body.

> **7200 "body wires" in your batery**

The time it takes to disconnect the batteries and reconnect in the opposite direction is called the switching time, or polarizing time. If you were switching or reversing polarity more quickly, say 60 times per second, you would have a field going through the wire at 60 cycles per second, 60 cycles of a building and collapsing of the field. This is alternating current (AC) because you are alternating fields through the magnetic polarity switching action of the battery through the wire. The brain works the same way. To "think" we constantly switch positive and negative in the brain at a rate determined by your thought process. This can be a harmonious rate or this can be a disharmonious rate, depending on the family of frequencies or family of time characteristics that we switch with.

The musical note "A" vibrates at 440 cycles per second, a harmonious vibratory switch. If you switch at a lower frequency, for example, 8.2 hertz, you are switching with the frequency of gravity. If your frequency of switching in the brain is 3.2 hertz, you are switching with the frequency of blood. There are a whole series of characteristic curvatures of frequency switchings within the human brain which has to do with the frequency of the vibratory energy of the human aura, or the magnetic switching frequency around the human body. So the aura is somewhat complex.

> **What is your brain's vibratory frequency?**

You can categorize switching frequencies into three different nervous systems. The lower, more pragmatic switching frequencies are nearly DC (direct current) which means no switching at all. Low frequency current switches directions all the way up to about 18 hertz, which is the frequency of muscle operation. You can think of these as the beta, alpha, delta, and theta frequencies. If you're switching down around 2 or 3 hertz, you're in a very deep meditative state, switching into other dimensions, even though your brain is on a physical plane. These characteristics can be noted at three different nervous networks.

The first nervous network to look at would be the autonomic nervous network. The autonomic nervous network controls your breathing, heartbeat, and other functions you don't think about. If you have a deficiency in that area, basic body functions will suffer. The body is 5% mineral. That 5% mineral content controls 95% of your body functions. We assimilate essential minerals like iron, copper and calcium through our diet. Long ago my co-workers and I developed and continue developing special formulations of minerals to supplement the diet.

Chapter 8

The Secrets of Super Formulation

Chelated iron is more usable by the body than just an ordinary iron supplement because of its special magnetic properties. When you ingest minerals into the body, they are distributed to all the brain synapses and the nervous system. You could say that the minerals are working on three different levels of vibration or octaves; the body is using three very distinctive behavioral characteristics. The first category we've already discussed—the autonomic, or self-governing nervous system. The primary minerals needed there in addition to iron would be calcium, magnesium, copper, zinc, and manganese. These minerals become hemoglobin in the blood, bones, and basic cellular structure. The second range of minerals is the mid-spectrum of the mineral kingdom. These are said to be reflected in nature and literally echo, or ring, throughout the body. This band of vibrations works through the sympathetic nervous system, responsible for the sensations of hunger, pain, excitement, as well as just governing the regulatory functions of our bodies. Thought itself is influenced by these minerals. Thoughts such as "Hello," "It's a nice day," or "I need to go to the store."

Chromium, silver and nickel are in the reflective category. Now one thing I'd like to note is that chromium is probably one of the most reflective of all mid-range minerals. You see it everywhere on cars, at least you used to before they started using plastics in automobiles, along on the bumpers, silvered mirrors, front grill. Chromium stimulates the activity of enzymes involved in the metabolism of glucose for energy, and the synthesis of fatty acids and cholesterol. Chromium also appears to increase the effectiveness of insulin, thereby facilitating the transport of glucose to the cell. A glucose tolerance factor test determines whether you're hypoglycemic or not. Without GTF, glucose tolerance factor, chromium insulin cannot effectively control the metabolism of carbohydrates resulting from elevated levels of circulating insulin, the temporary abnormal high levels of blood sugar followed by reactive hypoglycemia. As the body becomes more depleted by this imbalance, diabetes eventually develops. In fact, many of the early diabetes cases are characterized by excessive levels of insulin and low levels of GTF Chromium. When you are in a diseased condition, the first vitamin you're usually deficient in is Vitamin A, along with Vitamin C. The primary mineral you're missing is chromium. So in the treatment of disease the first thing you want to do is put chromium back in the body. This is crucial due to the reflective energy principle: the body can't properly digest proteins without a reflective reverse of energy. We'll cover this later on when I explain the pre-nuclear devices, including the Super Receptor. In the blood, chromium competes with iron in the transport of protein. Chromium is also involved in the synthesis of protein through its binding action with the RNA molecules.

Reflevtive energy principle

The next nervous system operates at a high frequency. The high frequency minerals are usually referred to as trace minerals, rare earth such as vanadium, gold and titanium. These minerals, too, are also found in your nerves. The nervous network that correlates with these minerals is called the parasympathetic nervous network, sometimes we call the vagus nerve, the psychic aerial. These minerals work when you have thoughts of God, ecstacy, clear meditation, which we're going to do later on, calmness, psychic or intuitive flashes and when you experience a oneness with the universe. Trace minerals ensure a perfect timing in the uptake absorption and release of hormones and neurohormones in the receptor and receptive sites in the human brain. In general, they fine-tune our systems for greater utilization of all body chemistry which gives us the most precise attunement and harmony with our present surroundings, whether we accept or reject them or where we are in the present moment. When we find ourselves rejecting where we are, trace minerals will help us remain calm until we analyze what we must do and transmute the present moment into something more desirable.

MINERALS REQUIRED FOR HIGHER CONSCIOUSNESS

Just remember this if you really want to appreciate the importance of minerals: When you finally pass on to higher existence, your body returns to the earth. The mineral kingdom acts as a neurotransmitter, not only to the DNA helix in man, but also to the DNA helix or equivalent in all things composed of matter on the material planes. The akashic records, the history of all actions of man, nature and true functioning of all things that have been in the past, are registered in the mineral kingdom. Through practices of exercise and meditation, coupled with proper nutrition, it is possible to know all things spontaneously as you live a life of self-respect. Minerals are also responsible for the proper switching speeds of synaptic vessels located in the receptor/effector sites in the brain of any animal, including humans, that have any sort of brain. This is true down even in the basic cell. In the center of all cells is a portion called the nuclear membrane which specifically guides all actions of growth and reproduction within the cell itself. Our soils have long been stripped of their mineral content and, once removed, it literally take centuries to replenish and restore a fine natural mineral balance. Vegetables and plants can only contain minerals when they are present in the soil.

This is nature's way of chelating minerals. We harvest our minerals and grow plants in our specially enriched soils and we harvest those plants, then put those plants into the vitamins themselves. The proper amount of mineral supplementation is now very necessary. Those of you who are going into any kind of a life extension or consciousness raising will need to accentuate heavily on trace minerals as they have a reversing affect on the despiraling of DNA.

Great mineral formulas

Now there are many types of trace minerals available. One that we have been working on is turbocharged ion mineral which was specially developed for us by John Anderson at Integrated Health. In this remarkable formulas we use ginseng, which I'm going to cover presently. Also, in our formulas we use trace minerals that came from the Great Salt Lake. We include supplements which contain minerals from a 2000-year-old fossil bed located in the northern part of the United States. We checked them with auraphotography and saw a huge electrical field around them. We use a deionized water process, which means that the ionization potential of the mineral itself is maintained in the liquid solution it is dispensed in. Sometimes people actually get shocked when they drink our minerals because they are so powerful. We also use an octahedral charging device to enhance female energy and balance negative ionization, which we call the charged negative ion, versus the regular ion, a very important distinction when you assimilate minerals for superconscious work. People training to be ET contactees, developing superconsciousness, telepathy, and channeling should know they'll be depending upon the parasympathetic nervous network and need to have it fully fueled.

And our environment, which is high-stress, high-radiation, high in pollution of every sort, constantly depletes us of these minerals. Most people can't get what they need in their normal food intake.

ENERGY TRANSFER

All of these minerals have to be present in the brain to synapse or fire off the intelligence charges that generate these electrical fields, hence your aura. The human aura reflects your personality, what's happening in your body and your life. If you're eating nutritionless foods and breathing poisoned air, your aura frequency is going to be relatively low. Let's return to the battery and wire. The wire, if you will remember, generates a magnetic field because it's hooked up to the positive and negative terminals of the battery, creating an electrical circuit. If we place this charged wire near an uncharged wire, the field from the "hot" or charged wire will energize the "dead" wire via the property of mutual induction.

Minerals fire off intelligence charges

The magnetic field present in the "hot" wire is invisible to the human eye, but quite measurable with standard, electronic instruments. It transfers energy over to the "dead" wire, which now has its own magnetic field. Running a magnetic field through a piece of iron will generate an electrical current. This is the process of mutual induction. By this same process energy transfers from person to person. One human being with a very powerful, positive aura field can charge someone's lesser aural field up and balance the life-force energies out. That's why people are attracted to others with powerful energy, positive or negative. Your negative field could attract another negatively-oriented person. What I'm saying here then is that the personality has an influence on other personalities, eventually establishing a group personality, or consciousness. I develop a very positive group personality during my seminars. When participants first arrive at the seminar, their aura fields have been polarized by all their different living circumstances and locations. Sometimes people come from all over the world to attend. So I have a composite of people when the seminar begins, everybody a bit confused, apprehensive, curious. There's energy bouncing off the walls. The first thing we do is balance our aura fields to bring everybody to the same frequency. We establish a group vibratory level. This then makes everybody a lot more receptive to their own internal guidance. We reveal or externalize this internal guidance into the seminar, and away we go. And this is the way everybody learns. They are learning things that they already know by receiving positive reinforcement, plus then I'm able to direct them into even higher levels of understanding.

Group consciousness, group vibratory levels, occur in the cities. San Francisco's environment, it's geophysical location, polarizes in relationship to the magnetic field of the Earth, interfering or interacting with the magnetic field of the human. Unfortunately, the magnetic field of the Earth and the people here affects us in a negative way. It used to be positive, but because there are more people thinking negatively on this planet than there are thinking positively, we now have to overcome the planetary aura frequency. Our negative state causes a problem in our solar system. If the Earth's polarity is being influenced by negative people, or what I call growth-resistant people, then the whole solar system feels it because the solar system, all the different planets and objects, have their own auric fields, or magnetic fields of varying magnitudes. Now the Earth has switched out of true positive polarity, out of response to the natural rhythm of the solar system, galaxy, and universe. This is a problem that causes earthquakes, the feedback that comes from other planets. Feedback from the other planets can actually trigger earthquakes! Therefore, if the Earth's aura became more

Each city has its own group consciousness

positive and synchronous with the aura fields of the other planets that adjoin it, then we would have fewer earthquakes and other natural disasters. Since the San Francisco environment and people living in it generate auric fields with a magnetic component, San Francisco's energy aura field is different from the city of Los Angeles. The city of New York exudes a different feeling from Los Angeles or San Francisco.

This is how aura fields work. The group vibratory levels of all of the cities add up to a composite of conflicting personality differences comprising the auric field of the United States. Different nations create their unique auric fields. So you have the national field of the Soviet Union, the Middle East, South America, and the summation of all these fields, then, gives you the summation of the auric field of the Earth.

As I said earlier, the Earth's summation field is produced by all these negative societies where we still have wars, famine, and human tragedy. When man becomes 100% peaceful within himself, and projects that onto his neighbor, man and then the planet will become peaceful and the planet's peace will be felt in the solar system, there will be galactic peace, and pretty soon we will have harmony all over the world.

So, getting in touch with yourself and getting in touch with the aura field is very, very important. Also within these auric fields that we talk about, the summations of this auric fields, are other intelligences at work. If you were to take all of the human beings in the United States and put them into a national energy field, you end up with a galvanized field that an angel can dominate or populate. So angels from the astral plane assume this energy field and work within it. Good angels or bad, whichever polarity happens to be there at the time, it doesn't matter. There are large entities that superimpose themselves and align themselves with these auric fields and have an influence. So the idea of meditation is to purify the negative energies and cause the overall aura field that you put out to become positive, which then automatically pushes away any negative entities that are influencing the total fields. This is the realm the extraterrestrial entities work within. The study of aura fields is incredibly important and will be constantly referring back to different aspects of this during this treatise.

> **Earth's summation field — we all create it!**

CHANGING TIMES, CHANGING FORMULAS

By now you're starting to realize the incredible importance of minerals in the body. Now in the formulas ... one of the reasons that I got into formulations was because I was taking other people's vitamins and found that vitamins were not being formulated for the times. A formula for the 50's might not be a very good source of nutrition for the 60's or 70's simply because maybe in the 50's there were higher levels of nutrition in foods than there were in the 60's and 70's. Pollution factors such as asbestos poisoning rise and fall. The asbestos threat was deeper in the 60's than it was in the 70's because people became aware of it and took steps to combat it. Whereas in the 80's and 90's we're exposed to too much probably ultraviolet, necessitating an increased level of Vitamin A in the system. Ultraviolet and infrared stress the immune system. Vitamin A combats that stressor. Back in the 50's and 60's the problem with ultraviolet wasn't nearly as severe. These are the considerations that are made in formulating a vitamin supplement.

Today we never use iodine or salt in our vitamins because we find there's far too much iodine and salt already in the food that people eat. You can't avoid it. Even if you're a vegetarian, you're going to run into these problems. Chelated minerals have an electrically-charged (therefore magnetic) barrier built around them to facilitate absorption during digestion. Two magnets, side by side, repel each other if they are aligned north-north and south-south. Turn one around and match the poles north-south and south-north, and they attract. That's what chelation achieves.

The intestinal walls, or the villi, where our nutrients are absorbed, are negatively charged. Most of your minerals are absorbed in the last section of the small intestine and the first section of the large intestine. The large intestine can accumulate materials and chemicals that prevent adequate absorption. So I recommend a good program of enemas, even colon therapy sometimes, for people. We recommend the kava coffee for enemas because its de-acidified, not decaffeinated. The caffeine admitted anally stimulates the liver. It doesn't go through your digestive tract, so it's effect is different from drinking it. It cleanses by inducing bile production. If you do enemas, you should also put friendly bacteria, like acidophilus, back into your body. This should be followed by ingesting fiber such as psyllium seed. All ingredients are readily available at health food stores.

The friendly bacteria help you raise your assimilation of vitamins. When positively charged metallic minerals are ingested, a predominant percentage of particles are attracted by the negatively-charged membranes of the intestinal lining. There they are bound with only a relatively small amount passing through into the blood stream. The result is that the absorption of most of these metallic minerals is inefficient. The minerals you've paid for and ingested pass unabsorbed by the intestine and are excreted.

CHELATION AIDS ABSORPTION

Iron is estimated to be absorbed at less than 1% to 4% efficiency. Chelating agents bound to the iron tend to neutralize the positive charge. The neutralized metallic mineral is neither attracted nor repelled by the intestinal membrane wall. The neutral chelate thus passes through into the bloodstream. This is a simplified explanation.

Women have come to me with iron deficiencies who were already taking extra iron. and it's not helping them. They weren't assimilating enough to satisfy the needs of their red blood cells. Red blood cells also need plenty of oxygen, so we use Vitamin E. The life of the red blood cell is 90 days. When your body replaces the old cells, the new cells are again iron deficient. To get around this problem we increased the available oxygen by raising the level of Vitamin E in special formulas.

Manganese is another important mineral in the body. It works with the B Complex vitamins to overcome laziness, sterility and general weakness. It also combines with a mineral, phosphorous, to build strong bones. Much of the body's manganese is found in the liver. Our bodies need manganese for proper enzymatic function to digest food and extract vital nutrients for overall body utilization. Manganese is also important in the utilization of thiamin, biotin, choline and Vitamin C.

Properly prepared vitamin formulations are synergistic. They incorporate a time-release factor that influences certain vitamins to combine at the right time to get the maximum effect, whereas if they're all going in the system at once some vitamins combat with one another. You wouldn't take Vitamin E and Vitamin C together because one would suppress the other and you wouldn't get the benefit of either one of them. And Vitamin A taken by itself in some forms will putrefy in the large intestine. So its important to really understand effective use of vitamin and mineral supplementation.

Calcium is probably one of the most abundant minerals in the body. About 99% of the calcium in the body is deposited in the bones and teeth. People don't realize that calcium is essential to the heart. Some heart problems can be caused by a calcium deficiency. If you get muscle cramps and spasms you could have a calcium deficiency; when the body runs out of calcium, it leaches it out of your bones.

As a result, we put Vitamin D, the "sunlight vitamin," in our formulas. Normally you can't absorb calcium without large amounts of Vitamin D. Vitamin D is manufactured by the body when exposed to sunlight, 15 i.u. per square inch of skin. But the ozone layer is allowing too much ultraviolet through to the surface of the Earth. It has undermined our ability to make Vitamin D. So it is important to assimilate the Vitamin D and the calcium together. Once again, in our formula we use these two in combination.

Manganese is another mineral that works with the B Complex, and the immune system, to help overcome different ailments and strengthen nerves. We also use sodium, potassium and phosphorous in a powerful combination. Humans have 72,000 "wires" starting at the base of the brain and extending through the body. When these wires conduct electricity, they have little amplifiers regularly spaced along the "lines of transmission." These little amplifiers are like little pumping stations. Imagine oil being pumped across the U.S. After a certain length of pipe it would need an additional push because it would start to get too much back pressure in the pipes, so we use pumping stations. Nerve impulses work the same way. These little pushing stations are called Nodes of Ranvier named after a Frenchman who discovered them back in the 19th century, and they have an amplifier effect to push the electric signal on through. If they become weakened, the electrical impulses go through the body too slowly, and the body becomes slothful.

WE NEED ZINC!

Zinc is an essential trace mineral occurring in the body in larger amounts than any other trace element except iron. The human body contains approximately 1.8 grams of zinc compared to 5 grams of iron. Generally, people are always zinc deficient. We've included zinc in the metal alloy of a product we have developed called the Super Receptor. We did quite a bit of experimentation back in the 80's when I was working with Harold Keith at Zenith Advanced Health Systems. We would wear a bar of zinc and discovered that if you are deficient, your body will actually assimilate zinc from the bar. It weighed less and less per day. We also found that some people who wear the Gold-plated Nuclear Receptor will assimilate zinc right through the heavy gold plating. The back of the receptor turns a gray color. And remember, the Receptor itself is a very active device, not something that's always cosmetically pleasing to look at even if the original design was.

Nerve pump stations — They are your electric impulses

The absorption and utilization of vitamins, especially the B Complex, requires zinc. Zinc is a constituent of insulin, which governs the utilization of sugars. Zinc is important for the sense of taste and smell. People who smoke cigarettes are vastly deficient in zinc. That's why they have to put so much salt and pepper and seasonings on their food, because their zinc is so low they've lost the enzymes that allow them to enjoy the sense of taste. It's also good for repairing tissues after you have a burn; it is necessary in the immune system to help protect against infection. It helps repair the DNA and RNA, correcting the harmful effects of x-rays and radiation.

Zinc helps prevent reduced cross-linking of biological macro molecules producing

58

wrinkling, stretch marks and aging. Zinc and Vitamin E are necessary for the health of the reproductive system in both males and females. It is being especially required for the male prostate gland which concentrates zinc 2000% over levels present in blood serum. Prostaglandin production, which chemically regulates hormones and hormone function, also requires large amounts of zinc. And we need Potassium along with the zinc. It's an essential mineral found in the inner cellular fluid and crucial to the body. It helps regulate the water balance. People trying to lose weight need to take more potassium.

Zinc is also a constituent of the male reproductive flow, which is a slight suggestion of its power. A lot of people who are impotent are low on zinc. It helps the storage of glucagon and energy-producing substances, combines with phosphorous to aid in respiration, and also sparks vitamin action. Zinc works through the lymphatic system to help tissue restoration, the intake of oxygen and the expulsion of carbon dioxide and toxic waste. If you're low on zinc, your lymphatic system starts to back up, causing some serious problems. Zinc is also a component of 25 different enzyme systems in digestion and metabolization and helps control carbon dioxide levels in the body and the processing of alcohol. The switch from galvanized plumbing to copper introduces too much copper into the body and promotes zinc deficiency.

Too Much Copper

Copper is necessary in the formation and maintenance of hemoglobin, but we have removed it from our formulas because we have found that people in America have too much copper in their systems already. Excessive copper can cause genetic defects in the reproductive cycle of human beings and increase the chances of your children being born with leukemia. If you check with the City of Hope in Duarte, California, you'll find that the number of children with leukemia goes up every year, as does copper in our bloodstreams. Adults don't realize that by taking copper-free supplements and filtering their water they can eliminate some serious defect problems down the line.

The low frequency minerals band

When you drink soda pop or cola, your body produces ethanol in the brain. Almost a quart of alcohol is produced some days by people drinking and eating a lot of sweets. The sugar is breaking down into alcohol. Compound sugar is a 12 carbon atom. It breaks down to a 9 carbon atom on the way to becoming a 6 carbon atom which the body can utilize in insulin formations. The 9 carbon atom state is an alcohol form. That's why people get a "sugar" reaction. We've found that children who are given plenty of sweets in their adolescent period have a tendency to become alcoholics in their late teens.

We've been discussing the low frequency band of minerals. The autonomic nervous system is relying on your body to have an abundance of these different minerals available, and if they're not, you're going to have gradual organ and systemic failures and they're going to affect your personality and your overall energy field.

Vitamin A

What's the first sign of a Vitamin A deficiency? The immune system breaking down is the first symptom as well as the improper assimilation of protein. There were scandals about Vitamin A. You can bet it is a critical vitamin when the pharmaceutical drug cartels don't want it out there. Vitamin B6 and A were targets of a scare. And there's only been one case of a Vitamin A, called vitamintosis, or overdosing, of Vitamin A ever documented. A person was taking 450,000 mg a day of it in an oil form, which is hard to assimilate. We use it in a palmitate form and a beta carotene form. These two different forms are water soluble, immediately available to the bloodstream without even going into the liver. Vitamin A is incredible for fighting infections. An anti-cancer agent, it's been found in tests to cause remission in squamous and basal cell carcinomas. It promotes good, healthy hair and skin. Even the loss of hair sometimes can be traced back to Vitamin A. I might also add that Zinc also works with Vitamin A to keep the hair production up to a maximum.

We use almost 1.5 mg of octocosanol in one formula, which is important because it gets oxygen to the heart, all the cells, and works well with B15. We use B15 in our formula in a form called NN Demethel Glycine, which we get from Japan. We have to combine NN Demethel Glycine with magnesium to produce the B15 in the body.

Like I said earlier, it is better to do things in synergistic ways. Vitamin E and octocosanol, when combined together, double and triple their effectiveness. We use selenium, a high frequency, one-way anti-conductor. If a nerve pulse travels from your head down to your foot, telling your foot to move from point A to point B, and your body is toxic along the nerve passageways, you're going to get what's called "feedback." You'll experience resistance, or have a coordination reflex which is caused by this resistance. To overcome this resistance, ingredients like selenium and germanium both work together to rectify the current and keep it moving in one direction. So therefore when you combine Vitamin E and octocosanol, you amplify all the benefits. They are all working to oxygenate and keep the electricity moving in one direction. You receive a cumulative effect that's just incredible. We've found that oil of primrose amplifies it even more. So we use all of these in one synergistic combination.

VITAMIN B COMPLEX

WE have been developing a B complex is quite unique. First we use B1, thiamine, which is an important vitamin for cell oxidation, memory, and it strengthens the heart. We call B2 the old "yellow vitamin," riboflavin. It metabolizes as a protein, which then allows nitrogen in adults to be metabolized and utilized more efficiently. This is quite important for vegetarians. You can't become a vegetarian, fruitarian or breatharian overnight. It takes awhile. A meat-eater has taken years to condition his body to be able to assimilate protein from meat, whereas a breatharian would be able to get it directly from nitrogen, like St. Teresa did. The air, you remember, is 69% nitrogen. It takes 90 days to reproduce a single series of red blood cells. It takes 6 months to reproduce many of the skin and other cells in the body, 7 years to reproduce a complete set of bone structure. So to go through one cycle of complete reproduction of the body takes 7 years. If you're switching from a meat to a vegetarian state, it might take you as long as 7 years to do this properly and allow your hormone structures to rebalance.

Supplements should include nitrilicides. Vitamin manufacturers often fail to put nitrilicides, the full complement of B's from B12 to B17, in their foods. A long time ago these wouldn't have been as necessary in the human diet, but now we eat lifeless, over-processed food. Our grains have been stripped, shredded, pressed and heat treated, so what's left? Most of the nutrition is the outer side of the kernel close to where it was exposed to the sun. As a result of this poor nutrition your body can retain carcinogens like nitrites, food preservatives, insecticides and other chemicals. We provide B17 in our formulas by using an almond brand of laetrile. Many people are not aware of the fact that there's cyanide in B17. The enzyme rodinase, present in normal cells, protects each cell from the harmful effects of this cyanide.

Cancer cells lack this enzyme, which is why laetrile, or B17, has been used to treat cancer, and as a preventive. When B17 passes into a cell that does not have the enzyme rodinase, cyanide is released from the vitamin, killing the cell.

If you poured a carbonated soft drink on the floor or on a piece of plastic, it could eat a hole right through it in time. There are acids present in the body stronger than this! So the body makes some powerful acids and antitoxins that it uses to fight other toxins. This is a normal condition in the balanced body as long as your body is balanced and it has a tendency to correct itself. A lot of people don't realize this. Earnest Kreb worked with the Russians on B15 experiments. They found B15 protected people from heart attacks and super-oxygenated the blood. B12 is another sensitive, nerve-oriented vitamin. If you don't have enough B12, you can quickly develop paranoia. Some vegetarians who don't have enough B12 in their diet often have a tendency to criticize people that aren't vegetarian. They think they are spiritually elevated because they're not eating meat, nor having to kill to live. Their energies are not properly directed in true, spiritual consciousness. You have to do what's good for you, and let other people do what's good for them. If you want to have a positive discussion about your beliefs, that's fine. But to readily condemn somebody for where they are because of a particular practice, is wrong.

This emotionality can oftentimes be traced back to the deficiency of B12, which is the beginning of the nitrilicide family. B6 is another vitamin that we experimented with in our formulas, called peroxidine. B6 is good. It works on the immune system as an emotional buffer to the astral plane. If your emotional body gets disoriented, disease may develop in your physical body. B6 is like a doorway B vitamin that will help prevent this from occurring. It also works well with B3, niacin and niacinamide, to eliminate the effects of herpes in the body. Herpes is often considered a nervous disorder in the body first before it becomes a physical disorder. Niacin is one of my favorite holistic prescriptions because of its versatility. Your body tends to trap bad proteins, called antigens, especially if you are exposed to ELF or power transformers, etc. Your system is not going to get a full set of genetic instructions any more, which I'll discuss when we get into the Super Receptor, so therefore you'll start metabolizing proteins that are bad for you.

ELF makes you trap bad proteins

WHAT IS A NIACIN FLUSH?

Proteins that you shouldn't digest end up stored in the mast cells of the body. When you put niacin or B3 in the body, you get a histamine reaction to these particulants. The body releases histamines into the tissues to restrict blood veins slightly, raising your blood pressure and the toxin level in your blood, turning your skin red. This B3 "flush" is a healthy way for your body to free trapped energy and toxins. I take extra niacin, as much as a couple grams, every single day to keep my antigen or antiprotein level low. You can use niacin to test for food allergies.

Eat only simple foods, which then clear out your body, and increase your niacin dosage until you reach a couple of grams a day with no flushes, then start experimenting with different food groups. Don't eat any of the food you want to test for a week or two, and during that time maintain a bland diet. Then eat the food you want to test. Wait four or five hours to let the food assimilate into the body, then take niacin. If you flush, you know that food is toxic to your body; you are not assimilating it properly.

Testing food allergies

Niacin, along with Vitamin C, is also helpful in reducing or eliminating smoking problems. The body absorbs nicotine from tobacco smoke to help in the assimilation of lysine and arginine. These substances forms a hormone called vasopressin, which is usually stored in the pituitary gland. Exposure to negative ionization or even meditative thoughts that are euphoric, can stimulate secretion of vasopressin, causing the body to feel a sense of well-being. Smoking introduces nicotine rapidly into the bloodstream and has a tendency to feel good for a moment or two, a positive "rush," you might say. The body soon starts craving nicotine. You can get the same good feeling by taking straight niacin over a period of time! Not only do you get the same good feeling, you don't get it as a temporary 15 or 20 second rush like you do smoking a cigarette. You feel it all the time. But the body will try to cheat. Nicotine can be assimilated in 15 seconds, whereas niacin takes 4 or 5 minutes. The body decides–hey, I don't want to wait 4 or 5 minutes, I want quick-fix nicotine every day for my euphoria.

As a result you end up with a bad habit. The body is lazy. To get rid of this dependency, start taking large amounts of niacin over a period of time, get through the flushing sensation, and continue to smoke. Don't even bother to stop smoking. And just continue taking niacin. It doesn't work like antibuse does when you try to keep alcohol out of your system. It works harmoniously with the nicotine, and gradually the niacin, nicotinic acid, will displace the nicotine. One day you'll light your cigarette up and realize it made you feel bad shortly after you felt good. Return to that 15-second period before you smoked the cigarette and say — hey wait a minute, I'm getting more pleasure now from not smoking and taking niacin. And then you've gotten rid of the habit. It will work true with cocaine, heroin and some other drugs, too, although when I worked with cocaine free-base addicted individuals, I found there were some other complications that a protein powder I developed, helped to address. But for smoking, just increasing your niacin dosage really helps a lot.

So we put 50 mg of niacin in the formulas we've created, and also 50 mg of niacinamide, which is a weaker form of it, to try to eliminate the flushing many people get. There's not enough in the formula to kick the nicotine habit. You have to take some extra.

FOLIC ACID AND LECITHIN

Folic acid, which helps the DNA, is another important component of our vitamin formulas. The name is derived from foliage, or greenery. Folic acid works well with biotin and with choline, both of which are in the formula. They work together to form acetylcholine, which is an important neurohormone in the body. The nervous system is also strengthened. Often times folic acid has helped in the treatment of schizophrenia, along with slippery elm bark, which we also put in the formula, not as a medicine, but to strengthen the nervous system. When your nervous system starts to stress out or break down, you need these small, bio-chemical constituents readily available in the form of vitamins and nutrition, or you will experience a gradual running down of the system. We have tried a PC (phospitidyl-choline) lecithin form, which is also important, because lecithin is a part of the sheath that insulates your nerve fibers. If your nerves were to touch each other, as in a short circuit, you could get "cross talk" such as tinnitus or ringing in the ear. Keep large amounts of lecithin in your body and reduce the tendency to short circuit internally. Your hearing, memory and the way you feel in general will be better. PC lecithin is much more usable than the normal form of lecithin, and more expensive. Many ingredients for good formulas are expensive. I don't believe in being cheap about your health. Many people don't want to spend the money. They will spend more money on their car or their dog than their own health. And you've got to realize that you've got to respect your own health because you're the one that earns the money. You've got to stay healthy to go out in the world and work away all day long, or all week long, so that you can have a nice dog or a nice car.

We've tried inositol also, which is important, along with para aminobenzoic acid, popularly called PABA. These are considered vitamins within vitamins. They are complete complexes. PC lecithin, inositol and PABA have all been found to be life extenders. Animals and people who have taken these vitamins in studies seem to live longer.

Let's examine the vitamins that are necessary for the human aura field and for the human consciousness to function properly. I often get asked how much additional supplementation should one take? What are some of the general rules to follow?

WHICH VITAMINS REALLY WORK?

First of all, we pretty much need everything. For example, we have 50 times less vitamin E in our meals today than we did 50 years ago. Another question that people ask me is: can I take too much of something? No, not really. You might end up getting what we call "expensive urine." When your body has more of a particular nutrient than it needs, it's going to excrete it via the urine. It's better to be urinating off a few excess vitamins than going to the hospital because you've had a stroke, disease, heart problem or brain damage or whatever because you didn't take enough.

Today we all need vitamin E

In the U.S., the American Academy of Sciences set some general nutritional rules relating to vitamin measurements and the amounts of vitamins we need to consume on a daily basis. The standards of vitamin measurement fall into 2 categories: activity-based and quantity-based. The activity-based measurements are the international units (IU) and the U.S. Pharmacopoeia Units (USP). Now normally you'll see the IU on the vitamin formulas and the USP on drugs. But you will see USP on vitamins A, D and E. The reason for this measurement is the strength of the raw material used may vary by weight because of different compositions of vitamin substances. Vitamin E from a liquid source versus a solid source are two examples that I can give now. The quality-based measurements are used when vitamin sources are standard strength and it is expressed by weight. This will normally begin in grams, "g," milligrams, "mg," and micrograms, "mcg." Most vitamins are measured in milligrams. Vitamin B12 and octocosanol are among the few vitamins more often measured in micrograms.

Next come dosages. First of which is the MDR, which is what we call the minimum daily requirement.

Chapter 9

Vitamins: Types and Dosages

The MDR has not been established for all vitamins as research is still going on. I have found that established MDRs in most cases are barely enough to keep most people alive, let alone well and vital. We all want to have energy. Originally established by the Food & Drug Administration in 1941, the MDRs are now considered obsolete and have been replaced by the RDA, the recommended daily allowance. However, the RDA is still too minimal and now megavitamin or orthomolecular nutrition is gaining nutrition popularity and prominence. As a result, many labels reflect 1000 times or more the RDA amounts.

As we study the label, I'm going to draw for you a mental picture so that you can follow all these things that we're going to talk about such as components, or building blocks, that work synergistically with each other.

Health's building blocks

So first of all, in your mental picture, see a series of squares (see figure 9-1). The first square at the top and left-hand corner of the page we'll call minerals. Put in that little square "Minerals comprise 5% of the body and control 95% of metabolic functions." Draw a little box below the mineral box for enzymes. Enzymes are little chemical units of energy that are necessary for the body to assimilate minerals and vitamins and maintain proper pH factor, meaning potential hydrogen. The body is made up of oxygen, hydrogen, nitrogen and carbon. One of the important points to consider is potential hydrogen.

Visualize an electron spinning around a proton. Energy arrives from another plane, the astral plane. It comes roaring in and animates the electron to spin around the hydrogen atom, giving us energy. If this energy coming in is out of balance, meaning there's too much energy coming from one plane or the other, you get what we call an acid or alkaline shift.

The sun affects the polarity, therefore the behavior, of the hydrogen atom. Rainbows of light and sound, called the "music of the spheres," generate within the hydrogen atom. In the morning, when the sun comes up, the red energy at one end of the rainbow is shining directly down on the proton, the nucleus of the atom, and the violet wavelength, which is at the other end of the rainbow, touches the electron's orbit. Now, just imagine the Earth as the proton nucleus and the moon as the electron in orbit. As the sun sets, the electron polarity of the hydrogen atom reverses. The violet energy is now going into the nucleus, and the red part of the rainbow is going into the electron.

Daily reverse of electron polarity

Your body and consciousness become adjusted to this shift as it occurs in your particular locality. The 180 degree shift, called a polarity shift of the hydrogen atom, deeply affects your consciousness. At night, for example, you have one set of thoughts and during the morning when you get up you have another set of thoughts, you think differently. The reason you think differently is because this hydrogen atom is reversing polarity. Your thoughts have to be processed through the metabolic functions of the brain to come to consciousness, thus are subject to the effects of the polarity shift.

If you flew from the USA to Europe, it would take you a week or two to adjust to the change in energy, and you would call that jet lag. Any great distance from where your body is used to being located and what rhythm it allows itself to establish would be a major change in the consciousness of your body systems. But if you had some magical way of aligning the polarity of the hydrogen atom back with the entire synthesis of the body systems, this jet lag could be eliminated.

Imagine what the astronauts had to go through when they went to the moon! They had to adjust for even greater change. Pleiadian cosmonauts have to adjust for 500 light years from their native world to destinations like Earth. And this is why it is necessary to understand the body on all levels.This nutritional information is essential and important for you to be able to understand the synergy of the body. Biosystems, electrical systems, ethereal systems, astral systems, emotional/spiritual systems, they all have to work together.

The pH scale on the chemical level goes from 0 to approximately 14. Acid rain, for example, occurs in a pH of about 1 to about 5.75; alkaline rain occurs from about 10 to 14. The body prefers a pH of approximately about 5.5 to 7.5. Any foods or substances that you put in your body, juices or liquids that are out of this range require the body to use extra energy from the hydrogen atom for metabolization, causing a depletion of energy rather than an increase of energy.

Remember, the body is comprised of oxygen, hydrogen, nitrogen and carbon. These elements combine to form atoms; atoms then form molecules. The molecules then go on to form cells. The cells reproduce at a rate of about 50 million per second in a healthy individual. The cells form organs, the organs form the organism, the organism is the body, and that's the consciousness. Consciousness then develops into other forms such as group, city, nation and so on. The pH level of hydrogen and its assimilation into the body begins the small changes that become great changes, almost cataclysmic at some point in time.

Return to your mental picture of the boxes, the mineral box and the enzyme box. Now we're going down to the next box, vitamin. Vitamins are units of light energies contained in a chemical form, a substance form. There are seven basic vibratory frequencies in vitamins. These vitamins combine, forming proteins, which combine and form hormones. When we get to the hormone level, we are at the first unit of biochemistry that possesses consciousness.

Some of the supplement we've experimented with contain two amino acids, lysine and arginine. Why do we use lysine and arginine? If the hormones in the body possess consciousness, like vasopressin that gives euphoria and thinking process, and if we realize that the hormones are built with protein building blocks, and the proteins are made of amino acids, our protein sources are lysine and arginine. These two amino acids combined with niacin produce vasopressin.

Lysine and arginine are oftentimes leaked out of the body under environmental, physiologically and psychological stress. So the vitamin formula mentioned here is also an anti-stress supplement as well as a life extension formula. I used to take vitamins individually. If you don't take them in their right order every day, they don't do anything good for you at all.

Most vitamins that you take will tell you on the label you must take them with food. We have found that it is better to take them on an empty stomach to fully assimilate them. Usually the ones that have to be taken with food are incomplete as a protein, or on the enzyme level, so therefore your body has to rob from the food or from the body in order to metabolize the vitamin. To me, this is not a proper course of nutrition in the vitamin form.

Pyradyne DNA & Hormone Chart

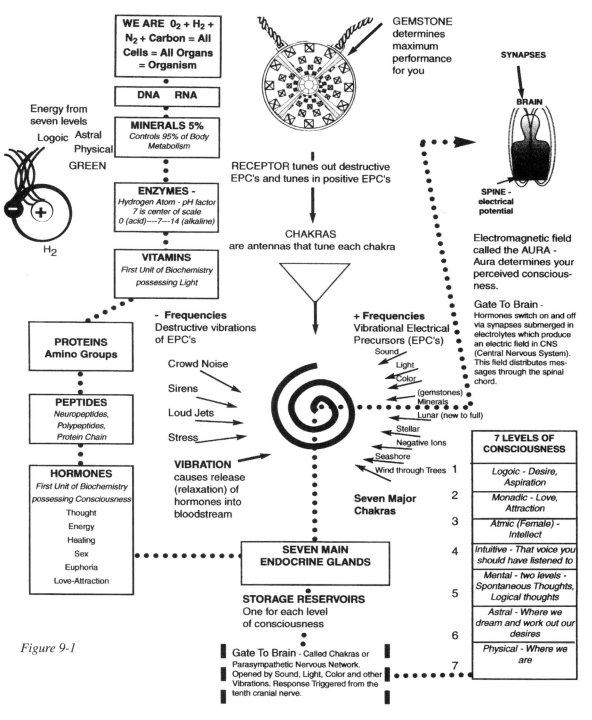

WE ARE O_2 + H_2 + N_2 + Carbon = All Cells = All Organs = Organism

DNA   RNA

MINERALS 5%
Controls 95% of Body Metabolism

ENZYMES -
Hydrogen Atom - pH factor 7 is center of scale 0 (acid)----7---14 (alkaline)

VITAMINS
First Unit of Biochemistry possessing Light

Energy from seven levels
Logoic   Astral
Physical
GREEN

H_2

GEMSTONE determines maximum performance for you

RECEPTOR tunes out destructive EPC's and tunes in positive EPC's

CHAKRAS
are antennas that tune each chakra

SYNAPSES

BRAIN

SPINE - electrical potential

Electromagnetic field called the AURA - Aura determines your perceived consciousness.

Gate To Brain - Hormones switch on and off via synapses submerged in electrolytes which produce an electric field in CNS (Central Nervous System). This field distributes messages through the spinal chord.

PROTEINS
Amino Groups

PEPTIDES
Neuropeptides, Polypeptides, Protein Chain

HORMONES
First Unit of Biochemistry possessing Consciousness
Thought
Energy
Healing
Sex
Euphoria
Love-Attraction

- Frequencies
Destructive vibrations of EPC's

Crowd Noise
Sirens
Loud Jets
Stress

VIBRATION
causes release (relaxation) of hormones into bloodstream

+ Frequencies
Vibrational Electrical Precursors (EPC's)
Sound
Light
Color
(gemstones)
Minerals
Lunar (new to full)
Stellar
Negative Ions
Seashore
Wind through Trees

Seven Major Chakras

SEVEN MAIN ENDOCRINE GLANDS

STORAGE RESERVOIRS
One for each level of consciousness

Gate To Brain - Called Chakras or Parasympathetic Nervous Network. Opened by Sound, Light, Color and other Vibrations. Response Triggered from the tenth cranial nerve.

7 LEVELS OF CONSCIOUSNESS
Logoic - Desire, Aspiration
Monadic - Love, Attraction
Atmic (Female) - Intellect
Intuitive - That voice you should have listened to
Mental - two levels - Spontaneous Thoughts, Logical thoughts
Astral - Where we dream and work out our desires
Physical - Where we are

1
2
3
4
5
6
7

Figure 9-1

ADDITIONAL SYNERGISTIC SUPPLEMENTATION

Other components of well balanced formulas and their synergistic actions must be carefully chosen to assist the body as it combats environmental factors such as smog, heavy metals, and pesticides. These formulas must be created for the times. It is necessary to put things back in the body to overcome the stress reaction and resultant depressed immune system.

We have tried 150 mg of spirulina plankton in our formulas. There are 35 species of algae belonging to the botanical classification of spirulina, some of which are not suitable for use as a food and have low nutritional content. But others have enormous potential for feeding the world. The purpose for including spirulina in our formulas is to facilitate the assimilation of the rest of the amino acids that are present in the formula. Blue-green algae developed on the earth over three billion years ago. Some taxonomists distinguish the blue-green algae from other algae by placing them in a special class of nuclear plants. Nuclear plants are those which are borderline between plants and animals. Some spirulina are close in structure to the first living things which appeared on the earth, and since their primary waste product is oxygen, they, along with the other algae, is responsible for the very air that we breathe.

Remember I mentioned that the Global 2000 Report states that 40% of our atmosphere comes from trees, which we're destroying at the rate of the size of the state of California annually. And I also made mention that we should use a form of hemp plant to replenish the oxygen because it will give us a quicker rejuvenation. Looking at all the pollution that's going into the oceans, we're destroying nature's ability to produce the other 60% of the air that we breathe, which is in the form of spirulina plankton.

As I said before, amino acids are basic building blocks of the body. Of the 22 amino acids that you require, only 14 can be manufactured by the body. The other essential amino acids must be derived daily from the foods you eat. They must also be available to the body simultaneously in the proper ration or they cannot be properly utilized. The cell walls of most vegetables are composed of cellulose, not digestible by humans. Spirulina cellulose is composed of mucopolysaccharides which are complex sugars, easily digestible, thus freeing considerable energy. Digestibility tests have shown spirulina to be 83 to 95% digestible. The usable protein in spirulina, therefore, because of its digestibility and amino acid balance, is about 90%, the highest of any protein other than casein, and that, by the way, is the standard by which all protein assimilation is scientifically evaluated.

For a comparison, an 8 ounce steak is only 22% protein and 15% of which is usable by the body. So that 8 ounce steak is about 1.8 ounces of protein, whereas only .27 ounces, or 7.6 grams, are actually usable protein. When we take niacin to get the flushing reaction, a lot of times we're releasing trapped antigens because the steak and the chicken that we eat today are so full of all kinds of different hormones used to make the animals grow faster and bigger.

Spirulina, on the other hand, is 70% protein, 90% digestible and provides 5 ounces, 140 grams of usable protein in each 8 ounces. That is 18 times more protein than a steak, with a little, if any, waste. The body's easy assimilation of spirulina protein facilitates the assimilation of the entire vitamin formula. Also spirulina has chlorophyll in it, another essential that assists in the development of healthy red blood cells in the body. The carbohydrates found in spirulina provide energy in several different forms, including a rare sugar known as rhamnose. Rhamnose is more biologically active than other sugars because it combines more readily with other nutrients. Sucrose, which is a major ingredient in processed food, is a notorious upsetter of your body blood sugar balance, usually a cause of the pancreas breakdown, hypoglycemia and diabetes.

THE BENEFICIAL HERBS

We have also tried peppermint leaf in our formula as a digestive enzyme. All the mints are said to strengthen the stomach and improve digestion, and the pleasant aroma is soothing and invigorating. Peppermint is used against liver complaints, flatulence, nausea, sea sickness, vomiting, chills, colic, fever, dizziness, dysentery, cholera, influenza, and heart problems. Its also useful in cases of convulsions and spasms in infants, and nervous headaches. So naturally it will work in certain supplements. We also try wintergreen leaf, which acts as a mild stimulant and helps expel worms and is also a great digestive aid, as well as rice bran, another B complex source. By the way, all the B complexes we use are derived from bran and not from yeast, because yeast eventually causes unfriendly bacteria and fungus to accumulate in the body. Yeast infections such as candida flourish in the increased ultraviolet exposure we're getting right now, so it's necessary to put the healthier sources of B complexes in your body.

Steak vs. spirulina protein

Herbs work well in certain formulas and can be good for many different things. One is sarsaparilla, which contains a whole protein and normal forms of testosterone, progesterone and cortin, which increase sexual power. Sarsaparilla is a good maintenance for the female organs. It helps eliminate depression and fatigue. Sarsaparilla is also high in sulphur, which is an invaluable constituent of the amino acid cystine. Sulphur is found in other herbs such as cayenne pepper. When I was studying herbs under the late Dr. Christopher he taught me one of the most important herbs was capsicum, or cayenne. I totally agree with him because it has a tendency to clean the body from the inside out, which is very important. Yellow dock is a very good iron source, and we often use slippery elm bark as a common herb.

Another good herb we use is the acerola cherry, or Barbados cherry, a high source of vitamin C. Every single cell in the body benefits when you have vitamin C, which helps bind the cells together to prevent invasion of hostile organisms like viruses and bacteria. Muscle aches and cramps are improved by vitamin C; it helps your immune system protect you from colds and seasonal viruses. There are so many things written on vitamin C, but the main thing is to take the vitamin C into your body that will work for you.

Protection from colds

Previously we found that people who already had colds did not experience significant symptom relief from the ascorbic acid form of vitamin C. It was pretty hard on the stomach and could also cause sores in the mouth because it would deplete certain B complexes, allowing the formation of canker sores and herpes. The newer form of vitamin C eliminates that. We also learned that if you used vitamin C in a salt form, often listed as an ascorbate, it had a tendency to cause the body to accumulate salt. When they came along with this new vitamin C which we're now talking about, it was pretty much the answer to the C problems. And we immediately rearranged our formula again. It's always getting updated.

We have a bioflavonoid complex to go with it, which consists of citrine and hesperidin and different herbs like that, which also increases the energy of the body.

We also use almond bran, too. Bran is 14% of the kernel, which is part of the grain. Almond bran is extremely high in B vitamins, iron and the complete protein. Butternut is another herb that we use. Its root is useful to establish and maintain enzyme activities, and it's the "anti-ash" answer. Ash foods are dairy products, meats, milk, chicken; animals that are raised on processed chemicals, hormones and junk foods. When your body breaks ash foods down, it creates toxic byproducts. We call this toxic waste antigens, what you "flush" when you take niacin in large amounts. The butternut root helps to break down the toxins and keep the body clean.

Other important herbal components of good vitamin formulations include: comfrey root, which is high in calcium, potassium, phosphorous and trace minerals. It also has a large amount of lysine and B12. Dandelion root is an excellent tonic which increases the action of the pancreas, the liver, spleen and kidneys, and helps the secretion of bile. My favorites that I use are Fo Ti, ginseng and gotu cola. Ginseng has its special charges that I mentioned before. Both Fo Ti and gotu cola stimulate electricity in the brain. They have saponins in them which increase the electrochemical action in the brain. These electrolytes give the brain the ability to become the battery for the body so the body can function. We also use parsley, which helps eliminate gas.

DHEA AND LIFE EXTENSION

One of my favorite formulations utilizes DHEA, dehydroepiandrosterone. There have been so many articles written about DHEA. For example: Saturday, January 15, 1983, *San Jose Mercury News*: "Is DHEA the ultimate wonder drug? If Ponce De Leon were alive today he might be wearing a white lab coat working in Temple University here. In the laboratory of the university cell research center, Dr. Arthur B. Schwartz is experimenting with a mysterious white powder that has enabled mice to live 50% longer than normal. The stuff, known as DHEA, has raised hopes among Schwartz and other scientists that dramatic gains in life expectancy might someday be possible in humans." And it goes on and explains a little bit more about it.

Another article, reprinted from *Diabetes*, Volume 31, No. 9, September 1982: "The Journal of American Diabetes Association, says DHEA causes the pancreas to work much more efficiently. It also mentions weight control. And we found that DHEA had been removed from a lot of pharmaceutical registers even though it was discovered back in the 1800's, simply because it would cause in humans an increase in lifespan which would be a threatening aspect to the social security programs established by the different world's populations. The last pharmaceutical register to remove it was England in 1935.

I worked with some doctors and scientists in DHEA studies. We found that DHEA is the fastest-depleting hormone in the body, past 18 years old. So in other words, in adolescents and children, the DHEA is still present, so when they eat they have a better chance than older people do of processing food into pure energy instead of fat. We require DHEA to break down the carbohydrates, the sugars, of the body. Since we have diminished amounts of it as we age, we have a tendency to gain weight. Adding DHEA to the diet seems to reverse this problem.

So we tried it in a certain formula, and it's been a great success. We knew the Food and Drug Administration probably would not condone the use of it in the Mexican yam form. We looked for other sources, beginning in Asian countries like Japan, because the population there has a lower occurrence of obesity. Sure enough, we found certain kinds of commonly consumed shellfish contain DHEA. The Japanese, however, weren't outliving the Americans even though they were staying thin because we found they were putting 60 grams of salt in their diet per day. If they reduced their sodium intake, I'm sure that you would see the Japanese and the Asians living a lot longer than they do because their diet is rich in DHEA.

I want to mention more about ginseng. A quote from *Ginseng, Eleutherococcus and other Adaptagons* by Elessor, 1979: It says,

> "Examination of clinical studies relating to stress — Ginseng's greatest
> contribution to man's health is the ability to reduce stress levels."

And when we go into this higher state of consciousness, I might add, it's very important to realize that stress is what holds you back. It shuts doors that can't be opened when you want to go into the fourth dimension. You've got to be able to process stress. You can't get rid of it. You've have to process it, and you need the high frequency minerals and the high frequency actions of herbs like Fo Ti, gotu cola, and especially ginseng, to process this energy.

PROCESSING STRESS

Wherever the source, the process of stress is the same. The reaction involves three principal organs: the hypothalamus, pituitary and thyroid. Ginseng aids in balancing the hypothalamus electrical center formed in the brain and its connections to the stomach, thyroid, pituitary, and adrenal glands. The hypothalamus receives notice of stress from higher parts of the brain that monitor the body. It responds by secreting to the bloodstream substances, neurohormones, that are transported to the pituitary. The function of the pituitary is to regulate all other endocrine glands. The neurohormones from the hypothalamus stimulate the pituitary to send instructions to the adrenal glands by means of a chemical messenger, or hormone, called ACTH, which is adrenocorticotropin. ACTH is released into the bloodstream and carried to the adrenal glands.

The pituitary is called the tropic hormone center, and these hormones, tropic hormones. Many of the Pleiadian Systems that we have been working on key these tropic hormones down to the other endocrine glands, producing higher vibratory consciousness levels, by the use of lasers and crystals, etc. In response, the adrenal cortex, the outer area of the gland, secretes hormones called cortico steroids, which mobilize the body's carbohydrate, protein and fat metabolism systems. Ginseng has been found to increase and act as a tonic to this whole entire operation because any form of stress that you receive has a tendency to upset the whole delicate process of the sensitivity of the tropic hormones, meaning the pituitary is sensitized to the smog, just as well as it is to the ringing of a beautiful soft bell. So by lubricating or protecting it with the ginseng, we're able to protect it and make it function much better.

Those are some of the reasons why it's so important to understand the benefits of the biological therapies. The biochemicals that hold leagues of energy fields dealing with biochemistry have to be studied, understood and utilized, and it's always good to have this strong base of information about the DNA and the cells created by the proper nutritional assimilation in the quest to higher consciousness.

Chapter 10

The Science of The Pyramids— Success Related to Health

In this next phase we're going to discuss the Pleiadian pyramids — what they do for you and how you can benefit from them.

Pyramid technology began probably hundreds of centuries ago. It got its first real push into modern society in the 1920's, when Karl Derbal of Czechoslovakia received a patent for the Pyramids used as a razor blade sharpener.

Then Russian soldiers were seen wearing them in 1973 on the Manchurian border to increase their energy under the intense conditions of desert heat and winds. Desert winds known as the Sharau, Chinook, Mistral, the Fuehn or the Santa Anas produce a positive ion condition in the body that brings on depression, anxiety and indecision to those exposed. In effect, it is another free radical condition.

Then another development occurred in the 1940's to 50's. Wilhelm Reich discovered the Orgone effect which, when applied to pyramid technologies, greatly enhanced the multi-purpose healing and detoxification capabilities of pyramid technology.

ANCIENT FORMS AND MODERN TECHNOLOGY

When we make pyramids for human use, we use alternate layers of gold, copper and silver, which are "active" metals, within layers of nickel, which is "passive" in nature. This speeds up the *Bio-Plasmic Life Force* that is the essence of pyramid power.

The semiconductor industry uses a similar technology in their applications of "substrate layering" of transistors and integrated circuits, the devices that provide the "pulse" of our modern televisions, radios, computers and other electronic devices that we depend upon in our daily lives.

A form of aura photography exists today that shows us directly how our life forces, our "Bio-Plasmic energies," are progressing. Developed in the early 20th century by a famous Russian scientist, S.D. Kirlian, Kirlian photography is used today world wide to document the existence of these energies. We have used it progressively in not only demonstrating our Pyramids and Nuclear Receptors, but also in measuring the life force energies of our nutritional products.

When we first started using pyramids in 1974, we used to make a science kit. People could buy two solutions of brine shrimp in the science kit, with a wooden pyramid, a compass and a little solution bin. They would grow the shrimp eggs at home, one group under the pyramid, which has been aligned to the north, the other control group of shrimp ten feet or more away from the first group. After about 6 to 8 weeks, the control group which was placed away from the pyramid would die. And this is significant in the fact that brine shrimp are very similar to the human single cell. Brine shrimp kept under the pyramid would live one or two years.

Why is this? Pyramids block the effect of negative energies and radio frequencies. When WLW first went on the air years ago in Cincinnati, Ohio, they had 500,000 watts of power. They destroyed all the vegetation around the transmitter; everybody got sick. In 1929 the FCC stepped in and made their first ruling against American broadcasters by determining that the maximum transmitter power would be 50,000 watts. That should give you an idea of how potentially dangerous radio and other emissions can be.

That's why we also developed the large pyramid to sleep in, along with the orb and the capstone. We make a 6 foot pyramid for a small bed, an 8 foot pyramid for a queen size, and a 10 foot for a king size bed. I've been sleeping in these pyramids for years. I have three children that were born at home in them, with few labor pains for the mother during delivery. Those children are growing up very healthy. The pyramids are very useful. Defrosting vegetables in them helps to bring the taste back. If you put the pyramid over orange juice or grapefruit juice it will change the taste from bitter to sweet. For those of you who eat meat, and you want to tenderize your meat, defrost it under a pyramid, or if it's fresh, put it under the pyramid for 20 minutes before you serve it. A bouquet of flowers you want to preserve can be hung upside down under the pyramid for a couple of weeks, and all the sap and resins will go down into the flower, preserving its original luster. The pyramid allows the flower to dry out without the interference of bacteria, which will normally cause decaying and shriveling. And after two weeks put the flowers right side up, spray with them with some lacquer and enjoy them for a hundred years.

Some people say wearing pyramids could shrivel your head or shrink your brain. This simply is not true. Pyramids have a tendency to cleanse your brain, but all the pyramid does **Pyramid** when it is over something that's alive is keep it vibrating on its normal rate. When you put **uses** milk under a pyramid, it turns into cheese without getting rotten or smelling bad after a week or two, because the pyramid allows the friendly bacteria to work with the milk while eliminating unfriendly bacteria. It's great to keep a pyramid over your vitamins to maintain full potency longer. There's a million different household uses. A lot of people water their plants with pyramid water. You can put 4 one quart bottles under our 12 inch Vitamid overnight and then water the plants the next day with them. It keeps the mealy bugs out–it's amazing.

Specially-engineered pyramids were the first ones developed to be worn on the head. We developed a tyoe of gold pyramid in the early seventies when I was working with Pyramid Power Five, because we were tired of having to align the pyramids to the north to make them work properly. So I did some research and found the gold molecule happened to be a pyramid shape. By using gold and plating the pyramid in layers, like nickel and copper, we had developed orgone plating, active and passive layers that act like substrate layers in a transistor. The electron or the energy field moves from a negative to a positive to a negative field because the active and passive metals increase or amplify the orgone-pyramid affect. If you want a term for the pyramid effect, in fact, you could call it bioplasmic force, or chi or a lot of different things. It's an etheric energy that when perceived by living cells tells the cells what to do. It is also a source of Electrical Precursing energies, EPC's.

Electrical Precursation is the energy that in the end controls the consciousness of all individual cells. It has basic polarities in that electrical precursation is either stressful or healing (see figure 10-1).

The body, although biochemical in its nature, is also electrical. Electricity controls each and every step of our cellular and organismal growth. A healthy individual will reproduce cells at the rate of 50 million per second. At this high reproduction rate, the entire red blood cellular system reproduces itself within 90 days. The entire body, including all bones and brain cells, reproduces completely every seven years. The integrity of this activity starts with the part of the cell known as the DNA (deoxyribonucleic acid).

Guiding all of this electrical, biochemical and cellular activity is a super intelligence within the heart of the DNA itself, called the Nuclear Membrane (NB), which interprets tiny command signals called Electrical Precursor Energies (EPC's) (see figure 10-2).

EPC's are themselves energies of consciousness that free flow from the astral plane to the physical plane. Initially, to our waking consciousness, they are felt as basic emotions. The astral (Greek word meaning "starry") plane is often referred to by the Eastern cultures as the emotional plane, or center, where all emotions come from.

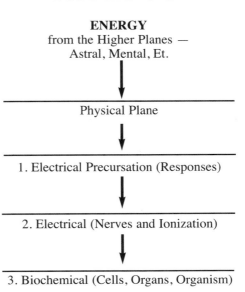

THREE LEVELS OF BODY RESPONSE

ENERGY
from the Higher Planes —
Astral, Mental, Et.

Physical Plane

1. Electrical Precursation (Responses)

2. Electrical (Nerves and Ionization)

3. Biochemical (Cells, Organs, Organism)

Figure 10-1

EPC's have not only energy to sustain life force, but also polarity. They can work for you, or against you! So, as our society begins to embrace conquest of space, time and the stars, likewise it must begin to realize that subtle forces, such as EPC's, can no longer be regarded as subtle, but instead, should be recognizedas being of the same magnitude as what we eat, drink and breath into our bodies!

EPC's are "felt" by the body as good or bad feelings, thus giving them a polarity. They, in turn, stimulate good or bad eicosanoids (pronounced eye-kah-sah-noids), which are the body's super hormones. For those of you not familiar with hormones, they are the first units of biochemistry that possess total consciousness. There are seven levels of consciousness (see figure 10-3).

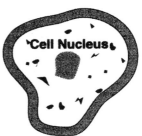

Cell Nucleus

Figure 10-2

1. Logoic	—	**Oneness**
2. Monadic	—	**Duality**
3. Atmic	—	**Intelligence**
4. Intuitive	—	**Sensing**
5. Mental	—	**Knowledge**
6. Astral	—	**Emotional**
7. Physical	—	**Existence**

Figure 10-3

Sensory Organ	**Stimuli**
Nose	Smell
Eyes	Light/Vision
Ears	Sound
Mouth/Enzyme	Taste
Skin	Temperature/Sensation
Chakras (sensing area around endocrines)	Psychic Vibrations from the planets andSpace
Hypothalamus (group of chakras	Psychic Vibrations
Head, Throat, Stomach	Intuitions, Balance, Third Eye

Figure 10-4

TYING IT ALL TOGETHER

Within the body are seven glands, called endocrine glands, one for each level of consciousness. Connecting them to all of the other organs are 14 "energy conduits" called meridians. The energy they conduct via the 14 meridians is called Bio Plasmic Force in Western terminology, and "Qi" (pronounced chee) in the Eastern cultures.

The seven endocrine glands each correspond to one of the seven levels of consciousness. Surrounding each endocrine gland is a ganglia (group) of nerves originating from the parasympathetic nervous system (see figure 10-4).

This pathway, part of the 14 meridians, receives stimulus from the outside world. Some of the stimuli are received by the five senses, and other stimuli are received from the surrounding environment, and some stimuli come from deep within the cosmos itself (see figure 10-5).

In theory, the stimulation perceived by one or more of the above routes triggers the release of hormones to the brain. The brain interprets these messengers and via synaptic activity begins modulating switches, called effector and receptor sites, on and off at a rate that produces thought activity within the brain.

Positive Electrical Precursors

1. Negative Ions Seashore, moutains, wind through the pines, Ion generators, etc.	Low Beta State	Feelings of well being, Euphoria, proper cell reproduction, anti-aging
2. Sounds of Nature Wind through the trees, waves crashing (pink noise, Pleiadian sound concepts	Low Beta State Low Alpha State Low Theta Delta	Complete healing total euphoria tremendous creativity feelings of love
3. Electrical Precursation Devices Pyramids, Nuclear Receptors (a pyramid device) Laser light into Quartz Crystals	immediate Alpha, followed by gradual Theta	Healing, euphoria increased energy, deep meditation, super creativity, increased physical abilities, removal of tension, loss of pain

Figure 10-5

Chart of Negative Electrical Precursation

Negative Precursors	Short Term Effect	Long Term Effect
1. Loud Crowd Noise	High Beta State	Tension, Sleeplessness, Depression
2. Sirens	High Beta State	Tension, Sleeplessness, Panic, Depression
3. Jet Aircraft	Extra High Beta State	Tension, Sleeplessness, Panic, Depression
4. Autobahns/Freeways	High/Extra High Beta State	Tension, Sleeplessness, Panic, Pre-mature Aging, Depression, Suicide
5. Job Stress	Low to High Beta State	Tension, Sleeplessness, Panic, Pre-mature Aging, Depression, Suicide
6. Positive Ions	Highest Beta State	Tension, Sleeplessness, Panic, Pre-mature Aging, Depression, Suicide, Death

Figure 10-6

As these thoughts begin to match the stimuli from the chakra (endocrine) centers, a wave of consciousness is felt as the awareness passes electronically via the aura throughout the entire body. In short, we become animated! It is within this animation process that the pyramids and the Nuclear Receptor function (see figure 10-6).

The first pyramid headgear we created was what we called the Pyradome. At first no one was wearing pyramids on their heads. Back in the early 70's, Dr. Gary Coutoure, a Newport Beach, California naturopath and chiropractor, did some testing with the Pyramids and his own specially developed area of alternative science. He was an early pioneer of *Touch for Health,* or as it was later called, applied kinesiology.

Applied kinesiology was developed in 1965 when Dr. George Goodheart discovered the test used in kinesiology to determine relative muscle strength and tone over the range of movement of the joints could also reveal the balance of energy in each of the body's systems: digestive, circulatory, respiratory, etc.

He found that there is a relationship between the 14 Qi (pronounced "chee") meridians used in acupuncture and the specific muscle groups located within the body. *Touch for Health* allows us to check for out-of-balance conditions created by stress, (now called the science of Electrical Precursation: EPC's) or vitamin/mineral deficiencies. This was later refined by Dr. John Thei of Pasadena, California and Dr. Coutoure was one of his early students.

DR. COUTOURE'S DISCOVERY

Gary found that when he was supposed to be testing for vitamin deficiencies and he put a pyramid over that particular spot on the test point, testing would indicate the person now had that vitamin in their body, regardless of which vitamin you were deficient in. We also found in later tests that if you wore a pyramid your body would digest and assimilate vitamins about 500% more efficiently. That means if you took one gram of vitamin C, your body would have thought that you had taken five. The Ester C that we've put in all our products is already five times more effective that other vitamin C forms. So, if you take five grams your body

Wearing pyramids and vitamin assimilation

thinks you've got 25 grams! It completely saturates the body with healthy vibratory frequencies that cause the cells to bind properly. This series of events eventually led to people wearing pyramids on their heads on a daily basis.

Pyramids are fun to experiment with. We found that wearing the gold pyramid that we created could put you in the alpha state. Everyone experiences the alpha state regularly, but when you can't get into the alpha state, severe headaches may result. Wearing the pyramid induced the alpha state, and the headache would disappear. We also found that if people were uptight and angry, it would help them relax and mellow out. One of the greatest drug addicts at that time back in the 1970's was the American housewife on valium. This was a great place to introduce the pyramids; getting rid of valium and putting people under the pyramid, I thought, was a lot better than drugs. One of the things that really hurt me was to see the liver damage valium caused.

I wondered if using copper in the pyramid would benefit people with arthritis just as copper bracelets. We went ahead and plated the pyramid, copper over gold; I had Gary test it, and it didn't work. We didn't know what we were doing to the pyramids in this different plating process. Our concept seemed reasonable, but did not produce the expected results. So I took 100 copper and gold pyramids home and stacked them under an 8 foot pyramid and let them sit. After 6 to 8 weeks went by I noticed spots on the pyramids, big spots.They looked like they had freckles. What had happened was that the energy of the pyramid field had eaten through the copper and exposed the gold down below, yet there was still a lot of copper on the areas where it hadn't been eaten through, so they were speckled, gold and copper. It had established some sort of a breathing pattern all by itself, breathing chi energy. So I took one back to Dr. Gary Coutoure and asked him to test it to see if it worked now on people. And he tested it and it worked very well. He said, "What did you do to these things?" And I said,"I didn't do anything, they did it to themselves." So it was an accidental discovery.

THE PLEIADIAN INTEREST

There were a series of accidental discoveries that led us to the Pleiadians influencing what we were doing. Even though I was having contact with Semjase back in the early 70's, we weren't discussing science. It was more about us and souls and what relationship I'd had with her in the past life and my relationship with the Pleiadians. But they were watching our pyramid technology develop. I know they were watching it very carefully, and they got active in 1979 when they gave us the first design of the Irradiator, which I'll get into later.

The Irradiator

So anyway, we started marketing copper pyramids to increase people's energy. We didn't treat diseases with them because legally we couldn't. But we noticed the swelling would go down on some people that had arthritis. The way that the medical profession deals with this problem is administering cortisone shots which stimulate the cortico steroids and adrenal glands. When you stimulate the adrenals artificially with these hormones, they quit working on their own. The Japanese idea of having them wear the copper bracelet on the left-hand and right-hand side activated the blood and stimulated the body a little bit, but not as much as the pyramids.

Then we went on a little bit further with our studies and decided, well, this physical energy could occur from wearing the Firedome, why not stimulate the brain to increase the mental energy as well as the physical energy. We now could relax people with the Pyradome, increase energy with the Firedome, what about a Raydome to promote mental acuity? We tried

BLOOD FLOW CHART

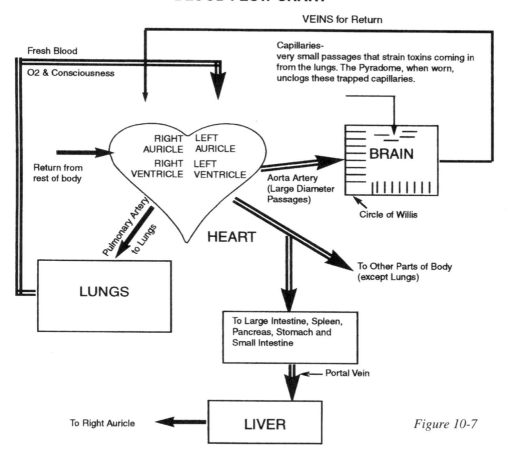

Figure 10-7

different silver metals. None of them seemed to work properly with our process that we had developed at that time. Then we created the heating process. When you buy the pyramids you'll see areas changed by heat. And that's another accident, too. The processing to create the spotted pyramids took 6 or more weeks. I was standing over a stove cooking, trying to figure out what to do to speed the process, when the pyramid on my head fell into the fire and was scorched. The fire burned a holed through the outer layers of metal, and we had our heating process. It's more sophisticated and refined now, but the fact is the hot flame showed us that one metal can burn through another on the pyramid shape.

So we began a host of new experiences with the electroplaters. We tried rhodium and all kinds of different silver metals, but the one metal we didn't try was silver. I probably should have tried it first, but I never even thought of it. One of the workers at the plating shop suggested I just try plain silver. The other silver metals we couldn't burn through with the heating process to make the orgone layers breathe. So we tried the silver and put it in our heating process and it worked perfectly, becoming our Raydome, which I was real happy to have. And when you wear the Raydome it works through the hypothalamus network. I do want to say sometimes when you wear the Firedome or the Raydome or the Powerdome, which we developed later, you'll get headaches. The reason is worth examining carefully.

The brain collects toxins over the years. When you breathe air in through your nose it goes down into your lungs, then it goes from the lungs into the blood, and from the blood into the left atrium of the heart, through carotid artery and back up into the brain.

POWERDOME DETOXIFICATION

The Powerdomes are by far the most potent detoxifiers, especially for the brain. People with a weak or toxic physio-etheric body relationship "feel" the effects of the Powerdome quite quickly. However, the first sensation may be a headache. Unlike the user-friendly Pyradome that eliminates headaches, the Powerdome has been known to cause them. This is because the Silver Powerdome detoxifies the brain rather quickly.

Once the process is over, the brain begins to function as it did when we were younger. Most people find that not only do they have a greater attention span, but also improved memory and, in some cases, better balance.

To better understand how the Powerdome is accomplishing this, let us take a look at the brain and its circulatory components, including the heart. Circulation starts at the heart. Fresh blood originates in the heart as it returns from the lungs via the pulmonary (lung) arteries. The arteries branch outward from the heart with blood that has been cleansed by the liver and oxygenated by the lungs. From the arteries (large vessels), the blood moves into smaller vessels, called arterioles, which in turn open into a closed, meshed network of capillaries. Then the blood, depleted of oxygen and other vital nutrition for the cells, is collected and returned to the heart via a series of larger vessels, called veins.

The human heart is divided by a septum into two halves, right and left, each being further constricted into two cavities, the upper of these two being termed the auricle, and the lower the ventricle. The heart, therefore, consists of four chambers or cavities, two forming the right half and two forming the left half. The two chambers on the right are called the right auricle and the right ventricle, and the two on the left are referred to as the left auricle and ventricle, respectively. The right half of the heart contains venous, or impure, blood. From the cavity of the left ventricle, the pure blood is carried into a large artery called the aorta, which it flows through to the brain and other parts of the body, with the exception of the lungs. We will return to this junction momentarily, but first, let's continue with the functioning of the heart (see figure 10-7).

As blood moves through the body from the heart via the capillaries, it gives up oxygen and nutrition necessary for proper cell growth and function. In short, blood cells transport consciousness to the entire body. But, as it makes this capillary passage, it picks up carbon dioxide and waste materials until it becomes unconscious and impure, venous blood. This impure or venous blood is then collected by the veins and returned to the right auricle of the heart. From this cavity, the impure blood is conveyed through the pulmonary arteries to the lungs. In the capillaries of the lungs, it again becomes charged with oxygen, arterialized, and then it is carried to the left auricle by the pulmonary veins. From this cavity, it passes into that of the left ventricle, from which the cycle begins again.

The course of blood from the left ventricle through the body to generally the right side of the heart consist of the greater "systemic" circulation, while the passage of blood from the right ventricle through the left side of the heart is called the lesser or "pulmonary" circulation. However, the blood returning from the spleen, pancreas, stomach, small intestines and a greater part of the large intestines does not travel directly from these organs to the heart. Instead, it is collected into a large vein, called the portal vein, by which it is carried to the liver.

The blood then returns to the heart via the hepatic veins.

A Pyramid helps to cleanse the blood and detoxify all body parts, especially in all areas of the brain. The brain develops toxicity very early in childhood. It's a gradual process, often discounted as "aging," but it can be reversed.

Looking back at our heart chart, you will notice that the blood becomes charged with oxygen (prana) through the right ventricle, to the pulmonary artery, to the left auricle, which are all large, arterial passageways. Then it carries fresh prana into the left ventricle, via the aorta, and on into the brain to be distributed throughout the brain.

Then, let us take notice that all of the arteries feeding into the brain are very large in diameter. But, once the blood reaches the brain, it is forced quickly into narrow capillaries. The arteries are sometimes one quarter of an inch (one centimeter) in diameter, but the capillaries are only a millionth of an inch (micrometer) in diameter.

Cleansing the blood

Now, let us backtrack to a look at the structure of blood. Blood is composed of hemoglobin, which is made up of hemes. One heme has four octahedrons (pyramid shapes) of iron and is surrounded by hundreds of enzymes. The iron molecules are stacked in line, forming two alpha and two beta chains (see figure 10-8). These hemes are stacked in the blood like wafers. NOTE: for in-depth explanation, see Dr. Bell's book *Death of Ignorance*, Chapter VII, "Blood, The True Elixir of Life and Prodigy of Spirit."

In short, the red blood cell is very complex. This invites it to be vulnerable to all sorts of smoke, gases, fumes and toxins floating in the air. So, when the blood comes from the heart into the brain via the large arteries and then goes into the very small capillaries, the capillaries strain or filter out all of the poisons. There they lodge, permanently, in the brain.

As time passes, the brain fills up with these chemicals and the aging process greatly accelerates. The cerebellum is located at the base of the brain, and this is the first place adversely affected. The cerebellum is responsible for the intelligence of physical balance; and, as it becomes toxic, you gradually lose your ability to physically balance yourself. Remember when you were a child and played hopscotch? You had to "hop" around on one foot. Try it now and see if you can still do it. If you have been wearing a Powerdome for over a year, chances are you still can!

As we progressively age, our brain continues to accumulate toxins in the areas around the capillaries. By the time you are in your mid thirties, the mid brain becomes affected. Now we develop allergies, poor digestion (causing bloating), gain weight, and experience general sluggishness. Then, in their 60's and 70's, some people began to get forgetful and senile. All attributed to aging. Wrong, wrong, wrong! This can be reversed by detoxification of the brain.

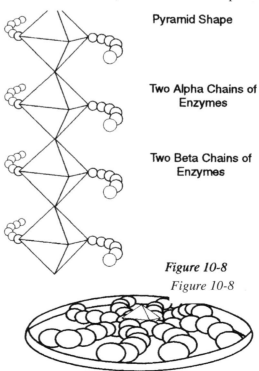

Pyramid Shape

Two Alpha Chains of Enzymes

Two Beta Chains of Enzymes

Figure 10-8

Figure 10-8

81

WHY THE POWERDOME WORKS

Because the Powerdome is a Pyramid that "resonates" with the iron atom in hemoglobin, it sets up a vibration that begins to unclog these delicate capillaries and reverse the "aging process."

However, there are some consequences. Many people experience headaches, as mentioned before. But this time, it is a friendly headache. When this occurs, take the Powerdome off your head, drink some water, and take some vitamin C.

"Why," you may ask, "did I get a headache? What is a 'friendly' headache? I thought all headaches were bad!"

Not so. Look back at the Blood Flow chart.

You will notice that as the blood returns from the brain to the right auricle, it goes back through the left ventricle to the spleen, pancreas and other organs, into the portal vein, into the liver, then back again to the heart. The years of stored toxins that the capillaries in the brain are giving up, have to leave the body somehow. They do, directly through the liver! But the liver can only detoxify so fast, and when it is overworked, it sends "signals" to the brain via the nerves to stop this poison. The brain interprets this message as a "friendly" headache, so remove the Pyramid, stop the detox effect, and let the liver play catch up.

You will find that the instant you remove the Powerdome, the headache disappears! Once you repeat this process several times, the headaches will stop and you will only be too happy you went through this detoxification process.

The arteries coming into the brain are very large, but as soon as the they reach the brain, they narrow; the arteries go from 1/4 of an inch in size down to a millionth of an inch. This establishes a filtering effect. The filtering effect traps toxins into the brain starting at the cerebellum, which is the bottom of the cortex of the brain, which is your balance center. Ever notice that you can't stand on one foot and jump or close your eyes and turn around on one foot like you could when you were a kid? This is because the base of the brain is blocked with toxins and this blockage moves forward to mid brain and starts affecting endocrine function, digestion, allergies, and a variety of other symptoms including mental sluggishness.

Eventually we discovered that when you wear the pyramid, it detoxifies this area of the brain. Sometimes we're detoxifying too fast and the liver can't handle it. If the liver can't handle it, it says "okay, I've got a headache coming," meaning that it tells your head that it's going to hurt so that you stop what you're doing. Take the pyramid off and the headache goes away or within a few minutes. Drink water, take some vitamin C, whatever that you would normally do to cleanse your body and strengthen it. In a few minutes the headache is completely gone. Wait an hour or two, and put the pyramid back on and go through the process all over again. Eventually you won't get a headache and you'll feel a lot lighter, and most people notice that their memory increases and they start remembering events from their childhood and things they had forgotten.

THE BODY - A NATURAL ANTENNA

Also, let us understand that the hypothalamus is an aerial that picks up and receives vibration and stimuli. When you tune a radio to listen to different stations, you can hear good, soothing music, maybe noisy static, or even distressing news or a talk radio show. However, you have control as to what you listen to.

The body, as it moves through the situations of life, is also the same way. You can control the "effects" of the situations that are presented. That doesn't mean that you always have control of what the situation "is," but you have control over what the situation "does" to your physical health and well being.

Example: You are driving leisurely down a highway, listening to your favorite music on a Sunday afternoon. It's a warm, sunny day, and your mood is quite up and happy. Suddenly, as you turn a corner, you come upon a serious traffic accident. You stop to lend assistance to the several people that are injured. A little later, after the ambulance leaves and you are back on your way again, you probably will be emotionally affected.

This is where the proper balance of the hypothalamus can have a tremendous effect.

1.   You can reflect back on the accident and feel sorry for everyone, (grief), begin to worry that you too may have an accident, (paranoia), and in general, consider your Sunday, maybe even the entire weekend, ruined (extreme stress). From these thoughts, grief, paranoia, and stress, you can now allow this to run your vitality down, which will trigger your immune system, and soon you are sick.

2.   OR, you can be thankful that you were there to help these unfortunate souls in a time of need (service to mankind), realize that the accident was a karmic event for all parties involved, which includes you because you were there (wisdom), and give a silent prayer for the victims' speedy recoveries (compassion). Then you can release the entire incident as a fact of balance and return to your normal happy state for the rest of the day. Because you have helped others, your immune system will have become strengthened and your vitality greater.

Both of these examples are a result of "conditioning" of the emotional brain/mind.

"HOW CAN THE SUPER RECEPTOR HELP STRENGTHEN THE HYPOTHALAMUS?"

As stated before, the hypothalamus is an aerial. It is an integration of the sympathetic and parasympathetic nervous systems. It starts in the third ventricle of the brain, which is the north pole of the human aura. Also located within the third ventricle are the pineal gland (emotional spiritual control) and the pituitary gland (physical body control). The emotional brain/mind extends down to the solar plexus (seat of compassion) and terminates at the base of the spine, which is the south pole of the aura (seat of creativity and reproduction). It is electrical in physical nature, and emotional in astral nature.

Because it is a physical complement to the entire aura system, it is highly susceptible to electrical precursing energies that control all of the body electrical and finally physical conditions!

The Raydome helps the wearer develop super concentration powers from a detached point-of-view. Most people wearing it reported a gradual loss of appetite, which is controlled by the hypothalamus, and its also tied in with a specific chakra which affects the pineal, pituitary and thyroid bodies, and balances them. Chakras, by the way, are the etheric counterparts of the physical endocrine system and they're interrelated by small nerves that are very

The Raydome

sensitive to certain electrical vibratory frequencies. Our bodies are electrical-chemical in nature. and when we feel energized it's because we have a large amount of cumulative electricity in us. When you feel tired it's because the electricity is depleted. The body needs to recharge. I remember once Linus Pauling, a Nobel Prize winner, demonstrated this by connecting a 25 watt light bulb to a person who lit it for over five minutes.

Now looking back at the hypothalamus, which is one of the first areas affected by the Raydome, or the Powerdome, which is a titanium version of the Raydome. It's a part of the prosencephalon of the forebrain ang contains a number of nerve nuclei which control the activities of visceral interactive organs, such as the metabolism of sugar and fats, water balance and regulation, and the secretions of endocrine glands. It is the center for integrating the sympathetic and parasympathetic activities.The hypothalamus is often called the emotional mind, and so you can see we need to properly understand this vital center in order to maintain a balance in mental and emotional attitudes. With all the carbon monoxide out there, it's especially hard to do that. That's why I won't even drive a car anymore without wearing a pyramid of some sort on my head.

The hypothalamus operates on the spiritual side, too. As in the higher nature, will is the impelling power, so in the lower nature desire becomes the impelling power. Will power is a creative motivating force that drives us into experiences, which lead us to maturity. Desire is will disowned, the captive slave to matter, no longer self-determined, but taking us away from our goals on its own glamorous sidetrack. When will is feeble, our whole nature is feeble. The effective force, that which we have accomplished, is measured by will power to complete a job. I'll discuss that as we go into our meditation section. Jobs are started but not finished because of diversion. You pick the one that feels the best. One's not better than the other, only the fact of evolution. There's a truth underlying the popular phrase, "The greater the sinner, the greater the saint." The mediocre person can be neither greatly good nor greatly bad. There's not enough of him for more than petty virtues or petty vices. The strengths of desire nature in us is a measure of our desire to progress, the measure of motor energy whereby we press onwards into accomplishment.

MIND, ENERGY AND BODY CONNECTED

Now in physical terms, activation of the cortico thalamic tract, the brain cortex, pancreas and connecting nerves, and maintenance of their dominance over the hypothalamus leads to the transmutation of all desire into will. This means functions through meditation directed into our consciousness from our highest centers.

Now let's just take a quick look at this. When pleasure has been experienced and has passed, desire arises to experience it again, this in fact implies memory, which is a function of mind. If the sensation is unpleasant, we are forced to think about the comparison and this is the first indication of reason. If we have an exceptionally good experience, the mind plans, schemes and drags the body into action in order to satisfy the cravings of desire. And similarly, in an unpleasant experience, the body strives to avoid reoccurrence. Such is a relation of desire to thought, the mind in its early stages is a slave to desire, then maturity makes us aware, the desire is curbed and we thus are forced to think before we react. Emotion is not a simple or primary state of consciousness, but a compound made up of interaction of two aspects of self, desire and intellect. The play of intellect upon desire gives birth to emotion. It is a child of both and shows the same characteristic of its father, intellect, as well as its mother, desire. These are simply permanent moves of right emotion.

So you can see as we recognize our weaknesses they can be corrected. The path of recognition takes us out of frustration. This is what the body is always going through and we found that empirically the Raydome and the Powerdome have a tendency to balance out electrically, biochemically and on etheric level the different centers of the body which then causes a mellowing effect on the overall higher accomplishment rate.

A few years later we developed the titanium pyramid. Titanium was almost unaffordable at one time because it was so expensive, but has become more affordable. It's still an expensive pyramid, but it's well worth the investment. The things that were real interesting about the titanium Powerdome is the fact that if you were to look at its etheric structure, as well as its molecular structure, you'll find it has a kind of cross-shaped energy to it. If you look back at the books written by Leadbeater, back around the 1930's, and Annie Besant, they have the occult meditation on the titanium structure and it has a cross "cristos" energy to it. Also in my ealier (1979) book, *Death of Ignorance*, I have a photograph of water being blessed by Reverend Eardley of Oxford, England, and you'll see in the picture when the water was blessed, the molecular structure picked up a crystal-type shaped energy similar to the shape energy of titanium. Titanium is really amazing. And we don't really understand all that it does, but even when it's used as a metal in an automobile engine, it never wears out. It has its own natural elastic nature to it. In the pyramid it has a healing vibration that's second to nothing next to gold, and it amplifies the effects of gold.

Titanium's energy shape

Another interesting experiment with pyramids occurred when I was at Pyramid Power Five. We were growing plants in darkened rooms, plants that outgrew the control plants that were put in normal light. Some observers believed it was due to the fact that the pyramid makes them grow bigger and better. I felt that the pyramid protects them from harmful elements and allows them to grow naturally. Pyramids emit the same energy as sunlight because they have the vitality globule present.

UNEXPLAINABLE RESULTS

Years ago an investigation at a prominent university in Russia documented a strange phenomenon. When a subject exerts a force with his arms or legs, his efficiency increases if he takes a deep breath. It is natural for all of us to do just this, take a deep breath before we lift something heavy. At first the Russians thought that holding the breath braced the muscles against the thorax, creating a firmer foundation on which the levers of the arm can function more efficiently when they lift. But the experimentation showed that the same increase of efficiency occurred when the legs were used. The phenomena has never been explained in scientific rationale. Oxygen itself cannot possibly play a part because it takes some 10 seconds for oxygen breathed in to reach the muscles of the arm and even longer for the same gases to reach the legs. This is evidenced in the fact that many athletes hold their breathe when they run the 100 meter race. The oxygen from any air breathed in would arrive too late for the use of the legs. In fact, I have heard athletes say that they seem to do better if they take a deep breath and hold it during the race. If oxygen is not responsible for the increase in efficiency in taking a deep breath before exertion, what is?

ENERGIZING WITH PRANA

Prana is an energy as yet undiscovered by science. But science is ready to discover it now in the laboratories of the nuclear physics labs. Prana stems from the first subplane of all the major planes. And it's found not only in physical world, but it exists in even more subtle forms in the astral and mental worlds. So prana is active at all seven levels of consciousness. As a matter of fact, it is the animating effect of the human form – each level of consciousness has a constituent of prana that combines by interweaving down onto the physical plane into one vitality globule. Because it originates on the first of the seven subplanes of which gases, liquids and solids are the lower three, prana is especially related to the material of that substance, which we call the ultimate physical atom.

Prana is an energy which extends into our planet from the sun itself; a high, powerful energy. If you were to look at old Egyptian drawings of the sun and it's rays, you would notice at the ends of the rays are little hands. This symbolized that when you stand in the warmth of the sun you feel heat on the outside of the body. This external warmth triggers an internal reaction of the cells within, causing them to liberate prana or vitality from within their own atomic constitution! This "life," i.e. prana, really comes from within each of the seven planes of life and is catalyzed into vitalization!

Thus, without the sun, we cannot continuously sustain life. There is a "battery of reserve" built into our DNA, but without the sun it will run dry and we would lose our ability to "express our energies" on this, our physical plane. When athletes hold their breath, they're holding their prana into the spleen; the spleen uses the prana. If you were to gaze up on a sunny day, you would see the ultimate physical atom, or the vitality globule, like specks that dart around — you look around the perimeter of a cloud or something or near the sun, and you'll see these things. The vitality globule is composed of the seven ultimate physical atoms. And they are linked together with the energy of prana to form a radiating, light admitting, vitality-ingrowing vortex. They are called the anu.

PRANA CHARGING THE ANU

Mr. Leadbeater, whom I previously mentioned, described in detail in his brilliant classics, *The Hidden Side of Things,* (which is a very good book), and *The Occult Chemistry,* how prana emitted by the sun enters into our atmosphere from higher dimensions. It is the energy from the second aspect, or heart of the sun, and it is therefore evolutionary in the sense that it is spiritually motivating as well as vitality inducing to all forms that use it. When an anu is filled to capacity it begins to glow. An anu is the vitality globule itself, and it is charged with prana, prana being a constituency of the seven levels of consciousness that are filtering through us from the sun. The sunlight is filtered from higher dimensions. Even though we can draw on the energy directly through a pyramid or the carbon atom in the body, the sun does it quite naturally because it is a catalyst for both!

Where an anu of the second ray of love emerges, the ray itself is the energy of the solar logos. It attracts, by means of its inherent enhanced magnetic qualities, six other anu to form the vitality globule. It is in this state it becomes attached to an oxygen molecule and may be drawn to the body with the act of breathing or directly into the body through the spleen chakra, which like other chakras, lies on the surface of the physical etheric body. A logos is the Tibetan way of expressing personification of a deity through a stellar object. Some people are not actually able to use that as well as others because they're not pulling their energy off the sun. These people who can't use the spleen chakra yet will not get the full benefit of the pyramid when they wear it on their head. They're not going to feel it right away. Some people come right up to the booth, seminar or lecture or wherever we're demonstrating the pyramids and immediately feel the effects, even more so than I usually do, and it took me awhile. Other people can't feel anything even though it's working on them slowly and subtly. This has to do with the development of the physioetheric body.

Chapter 11

Absorption of Vital Energy —
Studies on the Effectiveness of the Pyramid

Some people are not actually able to use the spleen chakra as well as others because they are not developed in that area. They are only able to receive their energy from the Sun. These people who can't use the spleen chakra won't get the full benefit of the pyramid when they wear it on their head. They're not going to feel it right away. When we are at a health show, seminars or lectures, some people come up to the booth, try on the pyramid, and immediately feel the effect of the pyramid. Other people can't feel anything even though it is working on them slowly and subtly. That has to do with the development of the physio-etheric body. The vitality globule, amplified by the pyramid structure, vitalizes the etheric structure of the physical body.

In digestion we break food down to into constituent molecules. The molecules are absorbed through the wall of the intestine into the blood. They are circulated through the body around the cells of various organs like the kidney, liver, and muscles, etc. Food molecules are absorbed from the blood through a form of combustion that converts them into the various forms of energy used to drive all cell processes. To release this energy, oxygen must be present. This is known as internal respiration, an energy-releasing mechanism in which glucose is transformed in the presence of oxygen. The release of this energy sustains the physical tissues. Prana released from the vitality globule sustains the etheric organs. This is really the etheric counterpart to what occurs physically during internal respiration. The storage of energy in the glucose molecule is the esoteric counterpart to the storage of energy in the vitality globule.

Six atoms of carbon, twelve atoms of hydrogen and six atoms of oxygen bond together to make a glucose molecule. The same thing occurs in the green leaves of plants using chlorophyll in the process called photosynthesis, a bonding of glucose molecules with light energy, or photons. Vitality globules are most predominant during the hours of about six in the morning until around eleven o'clock in the morning. They are the least predominant in the hours of about two o'clock in the morning until about four in the morning, and this is the time that you have the largest number of natural deaths. Amplify this phenomenon by the reduced light, therefore reduced availability of vitality globules, of the winter months and an even higher number of natural deaths occur in that time period.

Meditation, of course, brings in immense energy from the higher levels down to the etheric body, which makes you more efficient. It facilitates more efficient assimilation of prana by all body structures at all levels: mental, astral, physical, etheric and so on. Vitality globules also enter plants in great quantities. Leaves absorb them through the stomata openings along their edges into the spongy mesophile, where open air pockets lie in opposition to the spongy cells that store the glucose made in photosynthesis. When the plant draws on this glucose, prana that is released from the vitality globules flows with the glucose sap throughout the plant.

APPLICATIONS OF THE PYRAMID

This information is important because it lays the foundation for our discussion about the seven levels of consciousness, the additional sub-planes, and how energy enters the body through the hydrogen atom. Hydrogen, oxygen and carbon are combining in this process. The body is made of oxygen, hydrogen, nitrogen and carbon. The pyramid is the shape of the carbon molecule and carbon atom when it is forming. The shape has to be perfect. For example, if a person not wearing a pyramid is stressed, breathing harmful gases into the system, the perfect shape is distorted. Then the ability to hold onto oxygen, hydrogen and nitrogen is impaired, and the body starts to become less efficient. When we place a pyramid on this stressed-out person, or do muscle testing with the subject wearing a pyramid and/or a receptor, the body tests stronger while the person being tested is exposed to the poisons used for testing because the pyramid is inducing an energy field by resonance into the carbon atom of the body, causing it to overcome the negative effects of the test-given poison or poisons.

Pyramid shape is same as carbon atom

We can even test you right over the phone for different types of pyramids and nuclear receptors. If you test as needing a receptor with a blue stone, you have a heart or circulation weakness. We have you visualize different colors and test yourself, and you will find at one point you are going to become stronger, because the body knows more than you do. When your ego finally confronts what the body needs, the body responds; more on that later.

During the intense disciplines and studies with over 300 students learning psychokinesis conducted with Dr. Lawrence Kennedy, a leading psychokinesis researcher, we noticed a series of patterns occurred time and time again concerning the effects of the head-dome pyramids that we have created. Students wore the pyramids to accelerate their learning psychokinesis. We found that the actual conscious effort of channeling to bend a piece of metal, using mental energies, was amplified by the respective pyramid worn. People who want to learn how to become contactees and channelers and learn psychokinesis will go beyond that in their personal growth, too.

First-time Raydome wearers often find, after several hours of wear, that their mental capabilities are greatly expanded, their energy is very high, but they sometimes suffer from a headache. This immediately disappears when the Raydome is removed and the Pyradome is placed on the head. A second phenomenon we noticed was recurring: when the student wore a Raydome or Firedome until bedtime, the student would have trouble falling to sleep and lay wide awake all night wondering what to do with all this extra energy.

WHAT WAS MISSING?

After a period of time, these students didn't get the same mental lift from the pyramid. We took a look at where this mental lift was coming from, and as I mentioned earlier, it came from the secretion of a hormone called vasopressin which the Raydome and the Powerdome stimulate. The increased rate of vasopressin production depleted the body's hormonal resources, just as breathing smog does. That's why people can't get their mental energies together when they are driving or have been in automobile traffic. We looked at what vasopressin is made of. The French manufactured a drug called Diapid which they

90

sold in the U.S. by prescription, but, once again, putting a hormone into your system in its intact form is not beneficial. The idea is to put the ingredients of the hormone into the body and let the body manufacture it. The body can't manufacture it even with the proper ingredients if the environment isn't right for it. The environmental or etheric conditioning around the organs affects the process through the endocrine system. Wearing the Raydome promotes the proper environment within the system. Irradiators, which I'll cover later, also help give the system energy. But you still need the raw constituents.

The raw constituents in the case of vasopressin would be an enzyme, B3, or niacin, B3, B6, peroxidine, which is necessary, and two aminos, lysine and arginine. These are necessary to bond and create vasopressin. So when you take the Excel Plus formula, which is designed specifically for the Raydome, Pyradome or the Firedome, you can be sure that you have created the proper environment. You've put in the constituents necessary to create the hormone you need. We added lysine and arginine to the diets of those who had reported diminished results from the pyramids, and they experienced renewed and increased benefits of the pyramids once again. That's how we recognized yet another need for diet supplementation.

Getting back to those who experienced sleeplessness and headaches: these are not negative effects, but rather a failure of each of the persons to evaluate the various effects the different head gear were designed to produce. Let me explain.

WE NEED NEGATIVE IONS

Our feelings are determined on a physical level by the quality of the air we breathe, the type of people we associate with and the types of food we consume. When we take a breathe of air (prana, which I talked about earlier as the vitality globule), we are breathing either positive or negative ions, depending on the quality of air. Negative ions build cells in the body. We can't produce a single cell in the body without the presence of negative ions. The average person reproduces their cell structures at the rate of 50 million cells per second. If you're driving in heavy traffic, breathing in toxic fumes, then you are reproducing your cell structures at less than 50 million cells per second. If you've got a negative ionizer in the car, or you are wearing the pyramid, or you're on some powerful nutrition that complements the pyramid or the ionizers, then your cells can reproduce normally. Positive ions cause feelings of depression, short attention span, irritability, fear, paranoia and anxiety, and often bring disease conditions that are psychotic in nature. The air that we consumed was once mostly negative ions. Today it is two-thirds positive ions.

Long-term breathing of positive ions, such as what you inhale in traffic, creates long-term genetic damage. Negative ions, on the other hand, can create a feeling of euphoria, promote healthy cell building and consciousness in your structure, and create a system whereby your body can start genetically mutating forward in a positive way and facilitate moving into altered states. For example, when J.Z. Knight, a well-known New Age author, first starting wearing the pyramid, she was just an ordinary housewife. After she wore it for a short period of time she was channeling Ramtha. She could have eventually become a channeller without the pyramid, but it would have taken a period of two or three hundred years because the environment is so bad. So the pyramid was necessary to help her body make the change it was striving to reach on its own.

Think about the freeway shootings in Southern California. People drive the freeways for several years and their hormone structures go negatively destructive. They can no longer manufacture vasopressin, so when they get into a stressful situation and react violently, it's because they can't process the body signals properly. Negative ions enter the body through the breath and charge the red blood cells in the lungs. The Pyradome, Raydome, Firedome or Powerdome worn on the head produce a negative ion effect within the body, even in the presence of polluted air, because the air is influenced by the pyramid force field as it enters into the body. Another important fact that is often overlooked is that ionized air has a strong influence on our feelings and attitudes. We consume 2,500 gallons of air a day – that's a lot of air. Do you want your air to come from the tail pipe of a car or through a negative ionizer or a pyramid? It's your choice.

THE EFFECTS OF POSITIVE IONS

Imagine how hard your conscious mind has to work to overcome the negative effects of the positive ions we take in with each breath of air. People could say, "Well, my mind could handle that." Well, sure it can, for a certain period of time. Your mind is using up 80% of your energy, and if you have to mentally overcome smog you won't be able to think after a while. The American Medical Association has published statistics that one out of two Americans living today will contract cancer. Guess where cancer most often occurs? In the lungs. Next trouble spot on the list is the large intestine, broken down and cancerous from eating junk foods loaded with chemicals, preservatives and insecticides. These are two major eruption sites of cancer.

Our feelings are deeply connected with our endocrine system. There are seven major endocrine glands in the body which differ from other glands as they secrete hormones directly into the bloodstream. You have got to have pure blood. I am assuming that you are exercising, you are using good vitamin formulas, etc., because the quantity of hormones secreted into your bloodstream is measured in parts per million. If your blood isn't clean enough, I don't care what kind of a pyramid you are wearing, it's not going to help you. So you have to keep the blood clean. If the arterial system is functioning correctly, hormones reach the brain 15 seconds after they are secreted. Remember, I explained earlier that hormones are the first units of biochemistry possessing consciousness. Love, or energy feelings, are felt via the thymus hormone; concentration, which we just mentioned, is controlled by the pituitary hormone, vasopressin. For our sexual arousal, credit the gonad hormone. Negative feelings are usually only produced by one hormone, serotonin. Serotonin is also referred to as the "death hormone" so you want to keep it balanced and not active. Serotonin keeps children emotionally shielded when they come into this world. Serotonin mutes consciousness under stress. This is necessary for young children because their aura fields are so open. In an adult, serotonin mutes vital body functions and puts the body down; this is called death.

Children are not really ready for the world when they arrive here; it's too bad. Like I say in many of my lectures, we should celebrate the birth of children arriving, not have a big celebration or funeral when people die. People who die from illness should not be buried but cremated because the Earth's aura field becomes polluted. It's like putting bad drugs or bad vitamins or bad nutrition into your system when you already sick. It's the wrong thing to do. So we want to keep serotonin, which comes from the pineal gland, balanced. When you breathe smog your serotonin level becomes unbalanced. People who have been breathing positive ions, or pollution, are found to have serotonin distributed all over their brain, which is bad.

HOW WE PROCESS IONS

When we breath, air containing positive or negative ions enters the bloodstream through the walls of a little membrane that is called the villi. There it mixes with the red blood cells and becomes hemoglobin. Hemoglobin consists of iron and seven hundred different amino acids along with small traces of copper. (As most people have too much copper, be careful if you are taking vitamins that have copper in them.) The iron picks up electrical charges, positive or negative, depending on the quality of the air consumed. This charge is carried in the blood through to the heart. It goes from the heart via the carotid artery to the brain. The basic law of electricity that applies to physical action also applies to metabolism in that like charges repel and unlike charges attract. So when negatively-charged red blood cells arrive in the brain they circulate through the Circle of Willis in the cerebellum. Assuming you have negative ions in the brain, positive energy is therefore attracted from outside the body to neutralize the brain discharges. During this neutralization, you have a feeling of consciousness and a positive mood swing or euphoria.

Restating briefly, when you breathe in a negative charge, it goes into the brain, puts a negative charge on the brain's aura field, and attracts a positive outside energy which is felt as euphoria.

If, however, you inhale positive ions which flow to the brain going through the Circle of Willis, you attract negative energy from the outside. Once again, you experience a discharge with feelings of consciousness, but the resultant feeling is of depression, fear, anxiety, paranoia, claustrophobia, asthma and related things. Another interesting phenomenon noted by research scientists is that positive ions isolate iron, the electrical carrier from the red blood cells, thus creating the feeling of suffocation. A lot of people feel claustrophobic at times when the hot winds blow or a room is stuffy. When you breathe positive ions, you literally suffocate from the inside out. This drops the protective electrical barrier and the person is now open to disease.

Thus you begin to realize why people are wearing pyramids. They may look strange at first, but so did extended bumpers on automobiles. They both serve a very necessary purpose in today's times of poor air and stress. A second thing that our pyramids do is stimulate the secretion of hormones, depending on which dome is being worn. This effect is determined by the metals used, which I already discussed earlier. When you first wear these pyramids, you may get a headache from the toxic build-up your system releases. The body, of course, wants to go back to its natural state. Pyramid resonance vibrates the colon and the cerebellum, causing them to discharge toxins back into the bloodstream, which is normal. The liver, the major cleansing organ, picks up these toxins and makes them ready to be discharged from the body. But the liver gets overloaded, thus causing a headache. The liver sends a signal directly to the carotid arteries, which allows blood pressure to rise in the head. High blood pressure in the head causes the vessels in the Circle of Willis network to press against the cranial cavity, producing a headache due to the circulation blockage. This is the body's way of telling us that we are working our liver too hard.

Things to remember about pyramid headgear:
1. The pyramid headgear detoxifies the brain.
2. The pyramid headgear balances your electrical energy.
3. The pyramid headgear raises the vibrational frequency of blood, strengthening your immune system.

4. The pyramid headgear helps eliminate autotoxicity. Autotoxification occurs when irritated areas of your colon are exposed to germs from layers of fecal material, and you poison yourself again.
5. The pyramid headgear helps you develop the higher, clairvoyant, spiritual powers that we all possess which have been suppressed by these toxins.

Once you have your higher power/higher mind operating in conjunction with the lower mind, keep wearing the pyramid. If you don't, the body will return to a toxic condition since we live in this polluted environment. So I recommend that you continue wearing your pyramid headgear even if you gone past the point of detoxifying. It is a very necessary starting point in developing your ability to achieve altered states, etc. Then the Pleiadian Systems will take you to a level far beyond that.

I received a phone call several years ago about two o'clock in the morning from a gentleman school teacher, Sky Lewis, who lived in San Luis Obispo.

"Dr. Bell," he said. "We have amazing thing to report here. We have a student, Stan Alms, who has been treated for over a year for dyslexia. He also has a problem with grand mal seizures, and he was on a medicated mineral treatment by a medical professional. We put the pyramid on his head just for an experiment, and he wore it for over a month, and as of two weeks ago, all of a sudden he didn't have seizures anymore."

As he was developing the ability to write, he wrote me a little testimonial which read:

"Dr. Bell, I thank you for bringing the Raydome. I thank you for letting me use the Pyradome. I'm glad Mr. Lewis ordered these products. I do not know how they work. I like them very much."

This was one of our first testimonials. This event occurred in the seventies when we were collecting data about how our equipment worked. We realized that the pyramid on the child's head had increased the electrical potential in his brain, probably like charging a battery. You know that when you try to start your car with a battery that is not fully charged, it won't start, or maybe just barely turn over but without enough electricity to make the spark plugs spark. Evidently, the medications he had been taking were not strong enough to prevent seizures, but as soon as the pyramid helped release some of the toxins that were in his brain, which then increased the electrical potential of the brain, the medication worked and the child no longer had seizures.

I've scores of testimonials. Here's another; Dated May 23, 1977, this was from Dr. Howard White, Clinical Psychologist. He works in a U. S. Veterans Administration hospital in Washington Square, New York.

"Dear Dr. Bell,

"This letter is to relate some of the preliminary findings of some of the informal research that I have been conducting with your products called the Pyradome and the Firedome, particularly the former in as much as they are the only products distributed by your company with which I have sufficient familiarity. Considering both limited duration and informality of investigation, the statements made in the letter might be best considered my opinions based upon a subjective impression, clinical intuition, and statements made by subjects. That is, they are not statements based upon replication of procedures under controlled conditions.

"First I will report personal experiences with the Pyradome and Firedome. Thus far the latter device has been tested on myself only. Sensations experienced while wearing the Firedome differed remarkably from those experienced while wearing the Pyradome. The Firedome was subjectively experienced as an energizer. There seemed to be mood elevation and an increase in general physical energy and muscular strength. These effects were accomplished by a direct sensation of warmth in the solar plexus area. The increase in muscular strength is particularly noteworthy in the lower extremities in as much as I am still affected by both compression and the corrective spinal surgery. [He evidently has had some spinal surgery from an accident.] The Pyradome was subjectively experienced as an alpha-like state accompanied by relaxation. [Remember, I said earlier it would put you in an alpha state.] I have used this device on my feet and I have found that it provides significant alleviation of the symptoms of specificity. [He had a foot circulation problem, a sensation problem, because of the damage done to his spine previously, and I guess it helped bring feeling back into his feet.] Well, on my feet and other parts of the body I experienced electric-like sensations comparable to my experience during acupuncture. I have also found that acupuncture treatments, per say, seem more effective when combined with the use of the Pyradome.

"The experience reported by other subjects wearing the Pyradome have been quite uniform and reliable. Their experiences have shown some quantitative variability depending on such factors as previous practice of meditative techniques. Those that have meditated reported that the usual effects of meditation are greatly enhanced by the Pyradome. These effects, such as deep relaxation and feelings of well-being, were achieved more quickly and were generally more pronounced. Those who did not practice meditation, nevertheless, seemed to experience similar sensations of those who did and perhaps to a lesser degree. This alpha-like state occurred first usage and within a matter of minutes. In some cases effects were noticed almost immediately.

"I believe that I have sampled a great many of the more highly sophisticated pyramid energy devices currently being distributed by major companies. Based upon experiences with myself and subjects, it is my opinion that the two devices which have been discussed in this letter have been more helpful than any other devices which were sampled when used in the areas and manner employed by myself. The fact that one need not orient these devices to the magnetic north is a major convenience. It should be emphasized these devices are not toys. They appear to serve as a channel or focus for electromagnetic energy. Unlike most other devices which utilize some energies, they prove to be potentially helpful when used properly. The converse would also appear to be true.

"If, as many quantum physicists believe, the universe is composed of energy and the human consciousness itself is a form of energy capable of influencing other energy, any given individual level of consciousness would seem to be crucial in regard to the vicissitudes of how these pyramids energize. For example, if one is ruled by his basic desires, his consciousness may focus pyramid energies largely in these areas. However, if one has the will to move up into higher self awareness, it is possible in his consciousness he may direct pyramid energy to facilitate that action. It is my opinion this warrants further investigation.

" Yours truly, Dr. Howard White"

This is one of many different letters that we have received over a period of time.

THE NUCLEAR RECEPTOR TEST

Now we will begin discussion of the nuclear receptor, which in itself is quite an exciting piece. One of the things that people enjoy about my lecture demonstrations is when I test an attendee in front of the audience. I have them extend their right arm straight forward. Then I press down on it to check the level of strength of the pectoral muscles. They reveal the condition of the adrenal cortex, which measures electricity and energy, coming from the solar plexus area of the body. Then I have them sniff a highly toxic form of glue and have the audience smell it as well when I open the lid. Immediately the subject tests weak. Then I place one of the receptors around the subject's neck, have the subject breathe the glue again, and usually the subject will test much stronger with the receptor on and breathing the glue than with no glue at all and the receptor off.

So here we have demonstrated that a person can breathe toxic fumes and become stronger. I don't recommend you do this as a practice, it is pretty dangerous, but what I am saying is that the receptor's energy has allowed the body's energy to process the effects of the glue very efficiently. This is kind of an overkill. Some people I test on sugar or a pack of cigarettes, but we feel that the glue test is more effective because you can really smell the acetone and other noxious elements in the material. These are a lot more toxic than the normal fumes you would breathe going down a freeway. If this device is allowing you to process them and you still become stronger and feel better in their presence, it obviously is doing something for your body.

HOW THE RECEPTOR WORKS

For you to understand what it does to your body, we would have to look at a whole host of different things. Basically the first thing that we are looking at is the fact that the body wants, once again, oxygen, hydrogen, nitrogen and carbon. Red blood cells are made up of a carbon atom type octahedral pyramid-shape which is the same as our pyramid. In this case it's not a carbon atom, but an iron atom, which sustains the octahedral pyramid shape. When the body is breathing in poison, the poison distorts the octahedron or eight-sided pyramid shape inside each and every cell, including the red blood cells. The oxygen, hydrogen, nitrogen and carbon are linked at the iron atom, which creates two alpha chains and two beta chains in the blood. These chains can't maintain their symmetry and integrity when influenced by the glue. When we put the receptor on the body, the chains can maintain integrity even though the glue is still present. The glue originally pushed the cellular geometry out of place. When it returns to its normal geometric shape, it begins to process or handle all these kinds of poisons that are going through it. God created these geometric shapes, and if you acknowledge the geometric progression in the body, these shapes and how they work, your body becomes very strong at the physical, spiritual, etheric, mental and astral level.

Chapter 12

DNA — The Beginning

The master molecule of all bodily functions is DNA, deoxyribonucleic acid. This complex material contains the blueprints that specify the way your body is built and repaired, your eye color, hair color, blood and tissue type, and focuses on how well your immune system performs.

Consciousness also enters the body via the DNA. But, put briefly as said before, there are seven levels of consciousness. Correspondingly, there are many types of vitamins and enzymes. But they all fall within a family of seven basic functions that persist throughout the body. Also, the endocrine system, which regulates all bodily functions, consists of seven glands, one for each level of consciousness.

The DNA blueprints specify the variety of ways that your body con interact with the environment. Mankind possesses a wide degree of these responses. RNA, ribonucleic acid, is a closely related molecule made up from DNA that assembles proteins from amino acids and guides enzymes into a further combination of neuropeptides and polypeptides that become hormones. Hormones can be considered the first complete unit of human biochemistry that possess complete consciousness. Just as there are seven levels of consciousness, so are there seven sets of hormones contained within the seven endocrine glands.

When our planet was first formed, electricity in the primal form of lightning struck our atmosphere, forming in conjunction with sunlight, the four basic amino acids: adenine, guanine, thiamine and cytosine. These in turn became the sugars and phosphates present in every DNA (deoxyribonucleic acid) structure in the body. These in turn utilize the basic molecules of oxygen, hydrogen, nitrogen and carbon to combine together and build the body at the rate of 50 million cells per second.

THE NATURE OF DNA

The DNA of each cell contains coded instructions that tell the cell how to rebuild itself, maintain itself, and of course reproduce itself correctly. The DNA is rubbery and pliable, and it is never still. It vibrates in resonance with brain signals and even outside influences. DNA is polarized with positive and negative ends like a bar magnet. An upside-down pyramid placed on a subject's head will cause him or her to muscle test weak compared to the same person tested with the pyramid properly placed. This variant between strong and weak would make it appear as though the pyramid had a negative effect on the body when it is upside-down on the head, but that's not true. It converts energy to the female or negative aspect of the yin and yang. Most people are not conditioned to handle properly the negative aspect of the positive energy, so the energy penetrates quickly into the mind, since mental energy is the female energy. The positive, male energy is the physical energy. Energy moving via the aura into the mental level is drawn from the physical and therefore can weaken the physical body.

It shouldn't be this way; our energies should be balanced. Many of the devices that we have designed from extraterrestrial science have facilitated the return of this balance. Healthy DNA reproduces healthy cells and aids the body to naturally overcome and eliminate harmful invasion of these different kinds of negative electromagnetic energies, toxic chemicals and microbes that attack our bodies every day.

EMFs affect our DNA

There are so many different negative things that come into our body with the potential to damage our DNA. It has also been found that even weak natural electromagnetic fields can affect various organisms. All this indicates the necessity for a fundamentally new approach to the problem of biological action of electromagnetic fields and for the need to reconsider the question of the possible role of electromagnetic fields in the vital activities of organisms. This is the type of research I have been active in for many years. The electronic field plays a vast part in the proper balance and activity of the body's physical and etheric systems.

DNA is the first order of biochemistry to interface between the electromagnetic fields and body chemistry. The etheric fields are directing the energy; they are the intelligence of the DNA. It's as though the DNA is the brain and the etheric fields are the mind. Etheric fields and the astral plane are the threshold of consciousness to the physical plane, encompassed within the science of electrical precursation, EPC. This is the area the receptors work within.

The pyramids we created were developed somewhat by science and somewhat by chance, after many mistakes and without direct aid from the extraterrestrials, although they were watching us. When I came in contact with Semjase in 1971, we began work with the receptor. We learned about both the right-side up and upside-down fields of the pyramid. The receptor uses the pyramid energy as a parabolic dish with 154 pyramids, some upside-down, some right-side up.

Let's take some of this more esoteric information and relate it to physical conditions. In cancer, for example, a dreaded disease, some of the conditions that allow for the development of malignant cells are:

1. The body being profoundly deficient in B complex vitamins, usually due to stress and a high input of negative EPCs. This, in turn, causes runaway estrogen levels in both men and women. Estrogen controls protein deposits in the body, and runaway estrogen means runaway protein which in turn forms tumors. Protein accumulates in opportune places in the body, which blocks cellular oxygen consumption and traps carbon dioxide, which cancers thrive upon. (This paragraph references Dr. Harold Manner, Loyola University of Chicago, who wrote several books which are available in health food stores on this subject.)

2. The second thing that we find in cancer is the loose binding of collagen and consequently a lowering of cellular adhesion due to the continuous lack of vitamin C. This is one of the reasons why Ester C is so important in good vitamin formulas. For some of the references on vitamin C, I would recommend reading the works of Nobel prize winner Linus Pauling, formerly a professor in chemistry at Stanford University.

3. Certain viruses can increase your risk of contracting cancer by altering the DNA.

4. Low voltage across the cell skin composition has been researched by NASA, the U. S. National Administration of Aero Space. I didn't personally work with the research on cancer but we have periodicals called "NASA Tech Briefs" that actually anybody can get, and one described applying a negative ionizer directly to the center of a tumor inside the skin, causing a reduction in the size of the tumor.

5. Excess base pairs turning within the DNA double helix, as referenced by Dr. Gianni Dotto of Italy.

Most of the external physical factors which have been implicated in the evolution of life are of an electromagnetic nature. It has now been established that throughout the viewable geological period, the biosphere has been a region of electromagnetic fields and radiation of all the frequencies known to us—from slow, periodic variations of the earth's magnetic and electric fields, to gamma rays.

It is fundamentally possible on the basis of general considerations that any of the ranges of the electromagnetic spectrum could have played some role in the evolution of life and are involved in the vital processes of organisms. This has already been demonstrated for a considerable region of the spectrum; for electromagnetic radiations in the infrared to ultraviolet range (photobiology) and from x-rays (radiobiology).

The situation is different with the vast remaining region of the spectrum, which includes electromagnetic fields of superhigh, ultrahigh, high, low and infralow frequencies. Experimental investigations and theoretical considerations suggest that electromagnetic fields can have a significant biological action only when their intensity is fairly high and that such action can be due to only one process: conversion of the electromagnetic energy to heat or vice versa, which then leads to cellular activity.

There is an increasing amount of reliable experimental data which indicates that electromagnetic fields can have non-thermal effects, and that living organisms of diverse species, from unicellular organisms to man, are extremely sensitive to electromagnetic fields.

Finally, it has been found that very weak natural electromagnetic fields can affect organisms of various species. All this indicates the necessity for a fundamentally new approach to the problem of the biological action of electromagnetic fields and for the need to reconsider the question of the possible role of electromagnetic fields in the vital activity of organisms.

THE DNA INTERFACE

Good health or conditions of disease in the body, which is made up of cells, relies on more than just proper biochemical arrangements. The electronic fields play a vast part in proper balance and activity; and the DNA is the first order of biochemistry to interface between EMF (electromagnetic fields) and body chemistry.

Some of the conditions that can lead to cancer, a dreaded disease of malignant cells, are:

1. The body is depleted vastly of the B complex vitamins, usually because of stress. This in turn causes runaway estrogen levels in both males and females. Estrogen controls protein deposits in the body, so runaway estrogen means runaway protein, protein that can form tumors (protein deposits) throughout the body. The domino effect of system degeneration continues as the formation of tumors block cellular

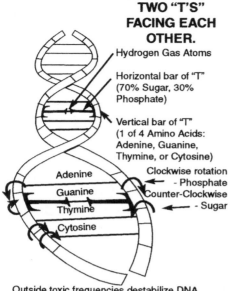

TWO "T'S" FACING EACH OTHER.

Hydrogen Gas Atoms

Horizontal bar of "T" (70% Sugar, 30% Phosphate)

Vertical bar of "T" (1 of 4 Amino Acids: Adenine, Guanine, Thymine, or Cytosine)

Adenine

Guanine

Thymine

Cytosine

Clockwise rotation — Phosphate
Counter-Clockwise — Sugar

Outside toxic frequencies destabilize DNA. These frequencies include powerline frequencies, ELF (Extremely Low Frequency), and radioactive waves.

Unless DNA is protected, it produces toxic cells and wastes in the body.

Good nutrition from Pyradyne and Electrical Precursing Devices, such as the Nuclear Receptor, help the DNA remain positive.

figure 12-1

oxygen consumption and traps C02 (carbon dioxide) instead of allowing the natural body processes to excrete it. Cancerous cells thrive upon carbon dioxide. (Reference: Dr. Harold W. Manner, Ph.D., Loyola University, Chicago, Illinois.)

2. The loose binding of collagen and consequent lowering of cellular adhesion due to a continuous lack of vitamin C. (Reference: Linus Pauling, Professor of Chemistry, Stanford University, CA.)

3. Viral infections. (Reference: Sloan Kettering, New York.)

4. Low negative voltage across cell skin cone. (Reference: NASA.)

5. Excess base pairs per turn on DNA double helix. (Reference: Dr. Gianni Dotto, Italy.)

6. Alteration of DNA code due to certain virus types. (Reference: Temin.)

MORE ON DNA

DNA, besides directing the cells on a maintenance level, also is a major factor in the aging process. To understand the human aging process, let us now examine the structure and the function of the DNA. (see figure 12-1)

Imagine a flexible ladder one meter (39 inches) long, composed of 6 billion steps. Each step has the form of two capital T's facing each other. The horizontal line of the T has 70% of its length made of sugar and 30% of phosphates. The vertical line is of a different composition: adenine, guanine, thiamine or cytosine. At the vertical ends of the T there are atoms of hydrogen. Hydrogen, the first element on the atomic chart, is composed of one proton and one electron. This is where pH, or potential hydrogen factor becomes important, right here in the DNA. It is the ultimate destination of the food we eat, and the pH balance is critical.

At the end of the phosphate rod, the orbital electrons spin clockwise, whereas at the end of the sugar rod they spin counter-clockwise. The electrons in the hydrogen atoms at the end of adenine and thymine spin clockwise. The electrons in the hydrogen atoms at the end of guanine and cytosine spin counter-clockwise. This type of "T" is called a base or nucleotide. (see figure 12-2)

This harmony of vertical and horizontal counter-opposing forces creates an eddy of

100

currents within the cell which gives it mota-tional growth. The pattern is much like the whirlpool formed, rotating in a clockwise direction, when a bathtub drains north of the equator. Consequently, the same whirlpool always rotates counter-clockwise south of the equator, illustrating the correlating effect of the Earth as a giant gene composed of DNA.

The DNA is then formed by 12 billion nucleotides facing each other and connected in a straight line to form the double helix, DNA (deoxyribonucleic acid). This is the genetic code, of which every one of the 6.3 trillion cells of the human body has at least one.

To form a new cell, the DNA must repeat or reproduce itself. This is accomplished by splitting the ladder along the middle of the step and reforming two absolutely identical strands of DNA, sequentially perfect. Another set of 12 billion nucleotides are necessary to do this.

A VIRUS IS A CRYSTAL — HIGHLY SENSITIVE AND RESONANT

Inside the cell nucleus, there are con-stantly at least eight different types of virus; four RNA types (negative charge), and four DNA types (positive charge). Every pair of virus (one RNA and one DNA type) attract each other to form a "bipole." They do so first to protect themselves against any external magnetic disturbance, and second, to accu-mulate energy in the following manner:

Inactive viruses are crystal forms, but in active status, such as inside the cell nucleus, they reveal one RNA or DNA core covered

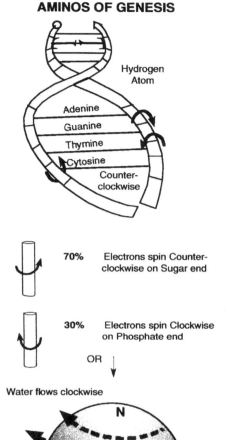

THE FIRST BASIC AMINO OF LIFE

AMINOS OF GENESIS

Hydrogen Atom

Adenine
Guanine
Thymine
Cytosine
Counter-clockwise

70% Electrons spin Counter-clockwise on Sugar end

30% Electrons spin Clockwise on Phosphate end

OR

Water flows clockwise

N

EARTH'S EQUATOR

S   Water flows counter-clockwise

figure 12-2

with protein. Of course, even in active status they still maintain all the properties of a crystal, and as a crystal, they are very sensitive to the high frequency sounds.

Under sound frequencies of up to five megacycles, the two viruses continuously strain against each other and produce energy due to the piezoelectric effect (the same principle is used in the energy conversion effect of the supersonic generator). In the ultrahigh sound fre-quency over five megacycles, an isolated inactive virus can be excited to alter the transition temperatures or Curies point and disintegrate (Ruben). The human DNA (like Yogi antenna,

101

one meter long) is tuned to any radio emission between 375-385 megacycles.

Furthermore, the DNA is under the constant influence of charged ions traveling through the nervous system and acting as a modulation frequency. The combined action of the two physical phenomena force the DNA to emit a high frequency sound in the range of 1.9 - 5.0 megacycles in order to detect, by returning echo, what type of protein is missing in the cell. These sound frequencies are not only necessary to the DNA in scanning the type of RNA to produce, but also to maintain active the virus in bipole form by means of the "strain effect."

A virus can be excited electromagnetically and caused to deteriorate

To control the energy level from the piezoelectric effect, the RNA-type virus covers itself with phosphate and the DNA-type virus with sugar. In forming this special type of coating, the virus, like any living organism, produces waste. These wastes—adenine, guanine, thymine or cytosine—are accumulated in the center of the rod just formed according to the type of virus bipole. The process to make the coating is accomplished at the expense of the electrical charge accumulated by the piezoelectric effect. At the end of the charge, to remain active, the group of viruses removes the coating that now is in the form of a capital "T" and exposes itself to the high frequency sound produced by the DNA, and the process starts all over again.

Due to the described phenomena, the DNA has always enough bases available to produce RNA strains, and to reproduce itself. Now, let's go back to the flexible ladder composed of 6 billion steps. Suppose we twist this strange ladder so many times to have only a few steps for every turn of the coil so formed. (These steps are called "base pairs per turn.") Since every base has different polarity according to the code formed by passed generations, the DNA can be compared to the multi-polarity rotor of an alternator. In the alternator, the speed is inversely proportional to the number of poles and the output power is directly proportional to the energy applied. At every electrical impulse flowing through the nervous system, the more base pairs per turn, the less degree the DNA has to move, and less energy is required to make it vibrate. Then there are the controlling factors for the DNA to reproduce itself and create a new cell:

1. The kinetic energy of the electron in the H bonds
2. The number of the base pair per turn in the double helix (DNA)
3. Energy and the frequency of charged ions traveling along the nervous system; i.e., the DNA of the embryo cell in the mother's womb has 46 base pairs per turn; the kinetic energy of the electrons is weak, charged ions coming from the mother's body are strong. Result: the DNA produces one cell per second. After 6 weeks of pregnancy, the DNA in the cell of the embryo has 34 base pairs per turn; the kinetic energy of the electrons in the H bonds increases, the charged ions from the mother are unchanged; the DNA produces one cell every minute, and so on.... By the time the fetus is in the 10th lunar month, the single DNA (half from the mother, half from the father) has already reproduced itself more than 6 trillion times.

As you age, the base pairs per turn in your DNA decrease like a spring unwinding

When the baby is born, the slowing process of reproduction increases. At the age of two, the DNA winds again to have 22 base pairs per turn, 14 at the age of 21 and 10 at the age of 35. From the age of 35 to 55, the 10 base pairs per turn in the DNA do not change. By this time, the kinetic energy of the electron in the H bond and the energy of the charged ion become very weak and the DNA stops reproducing itself and the aging process begins.

HOW DOES DNA COMMUNICATE?

At this point, it is necessary to clarify one important factor that is the basic secret of life creation. Without explaining the working principle of this secret, we will never understand the vital importance of the homogeneity and orientation of the magnetic field in the human body. All the 6.3 trillion DNA of the human body are absolutely identical, all are tuned to the same resonance frequency, all have exactly the same genetic code sequence. Yet, the 6.3 trillion cells in the human body, where each DNA strand is enclosed, are all different, and each one of these cells fits exactly the proper place and functionality in the human system. How is this possible?

The human DNA, as mentioned before, is approximately 39" long (1 meter), and has 6 billion steps formed by 12 billion bases. The entire length of the DNA is necessary to maintain and transmit from generation to generation the entire genetic code. Yet only a portion of the DNA (a different portion in every cell) is used to create a specific cell. How is this accomplished?

Suppose we have a thread one meter long. On this thread, we string 46 nylon light beads 1/2 inch long. Let us now insert this strange chain into the center of an electrostatic tube with bipole orientation. After a few seconds, all the nylon beads will be charged with the same electrostatic energy, and they will repel each other, leaving an interspace between them. They will repel each other, but not with the same force. The interspace between the beads located near the north side of the electrostatic charge will be shorter gradually toward the opposite polarity of the tube, where the interspace will be longer. Now the only part of the thread we see is the one not hidden by the beads. (See DNA Formation illustration on next page.)

Let's now call the thread DNA and the 46 beads chromosomes. Since the chromosomes act as a shield, the only portion of the DNA that controls a specific cell is the one of the interspace between the chromosomes, which for every cell has a different length according to different magnetic intensity, polarity and orientation in the human body. Each chromosome encloses 1,250 DNA lengths (genes), and each gene is formed of 100,000 base pairs (micro-genes). Of the total 6 billion steps of the ladder (DNA), only 250 million are really controlling the cell life.

> Cancer can be caused by the wrong interspace sequence of chromosomes

The chromosomes appear immediately after the DNA is formed and they disappear when the cell is complete and just before the DNA is ready to repeat itself, to reappear again, only in the new DNA. If the chromosomes of the new DNA, due to the phenomena previously explained, have the wrong interspace sequence, it is quite possible that the DNA will produce an errant cell, i.e., in the neck it could produce a cell suited for the kidneys. This can also be called cancer.

The right sequence is the key of our DNA — a magical and mysterious process that scientists are just beginning to glimpse. One thing is quite certain. If we work with our DNA to build stronger genes, then not only can we live a more harmonious and productive life, but we can transmit this enlightened gene and DNA activity into a healthier, future generation.

Chapter 13

pH, EPCs and
the Anti-Aging Process

PROTEIN

Protein is the most plentiful substance in the body next to water. It is a vital part of all body tissues. Protein is needed for the formation of hormones, which are the sources of our feelings. Protein helps balance the body's pH and water levels. Enzymes, substances necessary for basic life functions, and antibodies, which help fight foreign substances in the body, are also formed from protein. In addition, protein is important in the formation of milk during lactation and the process of blood clotting.

As well as being the major source of building material for the body, protein may be used as a source of heat and energy, providing four calories per gram of protein. However, this energy function is spared when sufficient fats and carbohydrates are present in the diet. Excess protein that is not used for building tissue or energy can be converted by the liver and stored as fat in the body tissues.

AMINO ACIDS

During digestion, the large molecules of proteins are decomposed into simpler units called "amino acids." Amino acids are necessary for the synthesis of body proteins and many other tissue constituents. They are the units from which proteins are constructed and are the end products of protein digestion.

The body requires approximately 22 amino acids in a specific pattern to make human protein. All but eight of these amino acids can be produced in the adult body. The eight that can't be produced are called "essential amino acids" because they must be supplied in the diet. In order for the body to properly synthesize protein, all the essential amino acids must be present simultaneously and in the proper proportions. If just one essential amino acid is missing, even temporarily, protein synthesis will fall to a very low level or stop altogether. The result is that all amino acids are reduced in the same proportion as the amino acid that is low or missing.

The eight essential amino acids that the body can't manufacture and therefore depends upon are: tryptophan, leucine, lysine, methionine, phenylalanine, isoleucine, valine and threonine. In a progressive and health buildng formula, all of these essential eight amino acids mus be present.

Foods containing protein may or may not contain all the essential amino acids. when a food contains all the essential amino acids, it is termed "complete protein." Foods that lack or are extremely low in any one of the essential amino acids are called "incomplete protein." Most meats and dairy products are complete-protein foods, while most vegetables and fruits are incomplete-protein foods. To obtain a complete-protein meal from incomplete proteins, one must combine foods carefully so that those weak in an essential amino acid will be balanced by those adequate in the same amino acid.

MINIMUM REQUIREMENTS

The minimum daily protein requirement, the smallest amino acid intake that can maintain optimum growth and good health in humans, is difficult to determine. Protein requirements differ according the the nutritional status, body size and activity of the individual. Dietary calculations are usually based on the National Research Council's Recommended Dietary Allowances. The protein recommendations are considered to cover individual variations among most persons living in the United States under usual environmental stress. The National Research Council recommends that 0.42 grams of protein per day be consumed for each pound of body weight. To figure out individual protein requirements, simply divide body weight by two, and the result will indicate the approximate number of grams of protein required each day.

PROTEIN AND VEGETARIANISM

Vegetarianism is essentially eating a meatless diet. This can cause in some individuals protein deficiencies, as well as mineral and B12 deficiencies. Ovo-lacto vegetarians eat animal by-products such as cheese, milk and eggs, but exclude all flesh foods such as meat, poultry and fish. Lacto vegetarians eat cheese and drink milk, but exclude eggs. Vegans eat no milk or animal-related foods.

Because most of the formulas we have been working on are all natural and organic in most cases, they are excellent for all diets as they contain no animal by-products.

CARBOHYDRATES

Formula: Carbohydrates + Fats + Protein = Energy!

Fats, protein and carbohydrates are prime energy sources for the body. Their energy potential is listed in calories. A calorie is defined as the amount of heat required to raise the temperature of one gram of water one degree of centigrade at sea level. So, in other words, a calorie is heat energy. Fats yield approximately nine calories per gram, and carbohydrates and proteins yield approximately four calories per gram.

Carbohydrates are the chief source of energy for all body functions and muscular exertion and are necessary to assist in the digestion and assimilation of other foods. Carbohydrates provide us with immediately available calories for energy by producing heat in the body when carbon in the system unites with oxygen in the bloodstream. Carbohydrates also help regulate protein and fat metabolism; fats require carbohydrates for their breakdown within the liver.

The principal carbohydrates present in foods are sugars, starches and cellulose. Simple sugars, such as those in honey and fruits, are very easily digested. Compound sugars, or double sugars, are harder to digest, and in the body, sugar often converts into toxic alcohols during digestion, and should be avoided. Starches require prolonged enzymatic action in order to be broken down into simple sugars (glucose) for digestion. Cellulose, commonly found in the skins of fruits and vegetables, is largely indigestible by humans and contributes little energy value to the diet. It does, however, provide the bulk necessary for intestinal action and helps elimination of toxic waste.

All sugars and starches are converted by the digestive juices to a simple sugar called "glucose." Some of this glucose, or "blood sugar," is used as fuel by tissues of the brain, nervous system and muscles. A small portion of the glucose is converted to glycogen and stored by the liver and muscles; the excess is converted to fat and stored throughout the body as a reserve source of energy. When fat reserves are reconverted to glucose and used for body fuel, weight loss results.

> **Why eat veggies? You need carbohydrates to break down fats in the liver**

ATP, adenosine triphosphate, is the substance which stores energy that is created when the body burns carbohydrates and fats in the citric acid or Krebs Cycle, which is the normal cycle of digestion.

When energy is needed by the body as in a muscular contraction, ATP is broken down to release the stored energy. ATP is the universal biochemical molecule for body energy, much as electricity runs a computer.

THE SUGAR ROLLERCOASTER

Carbohydrate snacks containing sugars and starches provide the body with almost instant energy because they cause a sudden rise in the blood sugar level. However, the blood sugar level drops again rapidly, creating a craving for more sweet food and possibly fatigue, dizziness, nervousness and headache.

Overindulgence in starch and sweet foods may crowd out other essential foods from the diet and can therefore result in nutritional deficiency as well as in poor health, hypoglycemia and tooth decay. Foods high in refined carbohydrates are usually low in vitamins, minerals and cellulose. Such foods as white flour, white sugar and polished rice are lacking in the B vitamins and other nutrients. Excessive consumption of these foods will perpetuate any vitamin B deficiency an individual may have. If the B vitamins are absent, carbohydrate combustion can't take place, and indigestion, symptoms of heartburn and nausea can result. Research continues as to whether or not such problems as diabetes, heart disease, high blood pressure, anemia, kidney disorders and cancer can be linked to an overabundance of refined carbohydrate foods in the diet.

Carbohydrates can be manufactured in the body from some amino acids and the glycerol component of fats; therefore the National Research Council lists no specific requirement for carbohydrates in the diet.

Differences in basal metabolism, amount of activity, size and weight will influence the amount of carbohydrates the body needs to get from an outside source. However, a total lack of carbohydrates may produce ketosis, loss of energy, depression and breakdown of essential body protein.

FATS – LIPIDS – OILS

Fats or lipids are the highest form of concentrated energy in our diets. When oxidized, they contain more than twice the number of calories per gram than proteins and carbohydrates. A gram of fat yields nine calories to the body.

In addition to providing energy, fats act as carriers for the fat-soluble vitamins, A, D, E and K. By aiding in the absorption of vitamin D, fats help make calcium available to body tissue, particularly to the bones and teeth. Fats are also important for the conversion of carotene to vitamin A. Fat deposits surround, protect and hold in place organs, such as the kidneys, heart and liver. A layer of fat insulates the body from environmental temperature changes and preserves body heat. This layer also rounds out the contours of the body. Fats prolong the process of digestion by slowing down the stomach's secretions of hydrochloric acid. Thus fats create a longer-lasting sensation of fullness after a meal.

Fats differ from oils in that they are solid at body temperature, while oils are liquid at the same temperature.

Fatty acids give fats different flavors and textures. The two types of fatty acids are saturated and unsaturated. Saturated fatty acids are those that are usually hard at room temperature and which, except for coconut oils, come primarily from animal sources. Unsaturated fatty acids, including polyunsaturates, are usually liquid at room temperature and are derived from vegetable, nut or seed sources, such as corn, safflowers, sunflowers and olives. Vegetable shortenings and margarines have undergone a process called "hydrogenation" in which unsaturated oils are converted to a more solid form of fat. Other sources of fat are milk products, eggs and cheese.

FAT WE NEED

There are three "essential" fatty acids: linoleic, arachodonic and *eicosapentaenoic* acid, collectively known as vitamin F. They are termed "essential" because the body can't produce them. They are unsaturated fatty acids necessary for normal growth and healthy blood, arteries and nerves. Also, they keep the skin and other tissues youthful and healthy by preventing dryness and scaliness. Essential fatty acids may be necessary for the transport and breakdown of cholesterol.

Cholesterol, necessary for good health, is a lipid. It is a normal component of most body tissues, especially those of the brain and nervous system, liver and blood. It is needed to form sex and adrenal hormones, vitamin D, and bile, which is needed for the digestion of fats. Cholesterol also seems to play a part in lubricating the skin.

Although a cholesterol deficiency is unlikely to occur, abnormal amounts of cholesterol may be stored throughout the body if fats are eaten excessively. Research continues as to the relationship of increased cholesterol storage to the development of arteriosclerosis.

Excessive fat in the diet, of course, makes us too fat. You should regulate your caloric intake to maintain a proper weight/height balance. In addition to obesity, excessive fat intake will cause abnormally slow digestion and absorption, resulting in indigestion. If a lack of carbohydrates is accompanied by a lack of water in the diet, or if there is a kidney malfunction, fats can't be completely metabolized and may become toxic to the body.

The U.S. National Research Council sets no Recommended Dietary Allowance for fats because of the widely varying fat content of the diet among individuals. Linoleic acid, however, should provide about 2 percent of the calories in the diet. Vegetable fats, such as corn, safflower and soybean oils, are high in linoleic acid. Nutritionists suggest that an intake of fat providing 25 to 30 percent of the total calories consumed daily is compatible with good health.

LIPIDS AND OILS – A CLOSER LOOK

As it is probably obvious to you, unsaturated fats and oils that are liquid at body temperature are far better for you than those that are release of ATP (adenosine triphosphate), the universal energy storage molecule! So to be safe and healthy, we need to be careful of what we consume.

Lipos means "fat." The lipolytic substance of correct lipids causes saturated fats to dissolve again. These types of fats are very necessary for good health. Often people begin a "low fat" diet to lose weight and find that they either "gain" weight because of the carbohydrate cravings, or simply don't lose weight. In dieting, you need to stay in a zone of properly balanced caloric intake, which would be approximately 40% carbohydrates, 30% protein, and 30% fat. And this must be the "proper" fat.

Flax seed and borage oils can reduce toxic effects of saturated fats

Flax Seed and Borage Oil Formulas are a critical form of life-giving fat-complexes, that when taken properly, will reduce the toxic effects of saturated fats within the body and help you to lose weight, or gain weight, as you balance your body's biochemistry into the proper zone.

Proper fat taken into the body is "electron rich," highly unsaturated fat. To better understand fat, let us break it down.

WHAT IS FAT?

Fat consists of glycerine. Glycerine has three "arms." A chain of fatty acids is attached to each arm. This chain of fatty acids has, in butter, for example, 4 links to it; that of coconut butter and palm nut oil, 14 or 16 links.

We all eat butter at one time or another, but these naturally occurring saturated fats can't be turned into energy by the body without the presence of essential fatty acids!

What is saturated fat? Upon analyzing fatty substances we come to fatty acid chains with 18 links not so firmly attached to each other. The chain is "loose," and it absorbs water (what most of our body is comprised of) more easily. In the same way, these looser fatty acids with their weak, unsaturated connections, form protein associations very easily. The fatty acids become water soluble through this association with protein.

Olive oil is an example of an unsaturated fat, but olive oil has itself only one unsaturated connection in the fat chain. This fat is not harmful, but what we really need is highly unsaturated fats. The moment two unsaturated double links occur together in a fatty acid chain, the effects are multiplied, and in the highly unsaturated fats, the so-called linoleic acids, a field of electrons is generated, a veritable electrical charge which can be quickly conducted off into the body, thus causing a recharging of the living substance, especially of the brain and nerves.

Our body composition is determined on three levels (see figure 13-1):

1. Electrical Precursing – The science of the balance of stress and relaxation (covered further on in the Pyradyne Manual)
2. Electrical – Proton/Electron relationship between all atoms, molecules, cells and organs in the body, which is itself an organ
3. Biochemical – The result of all atoms, molecules, cells and organisms taken via the mouth and processed through the citric acid or Krebs cycle

Each step is as important as the next step. Oils are a main bridge from the electrical body to the physical and visa versa.

One of the problems with the food industry is the processing and handling that our precious food endures. When fats are oxidized before our ingesting them, they lose their electrical charge and, to compensate, "steal" vitality from the body! This directly affects the ability of the blood to pick up carbon dioxide from the cells and leave oxygen to vitalize them. In other words, the respiratory function of the breath itself is greatly shortened, and often symptoms occur, such as dizziness after a meal, or when you are tired. In some cases, a person can asphyxiate despite being given oxygen, even in a hospital. The lack of highly unsaturated fatty acids paralyzes vital functions and most store-bought foods induce this condition on various levels if left unchecked! Many people are so low in unsaturated fats that their food has to be pumped through the body three or four times by the heart just to maintain a clear consciousness! This is why you should consider taking Flax Seed and Borage Oils.

There is also a life-giving electrical side to essential, highly unsaturated fatty acids.

In growing cells we find a dipolarity between the electrically positive nucleus and the electrically negative cell membrane with its highly unsaturated fatty acids. When a cell divides (a process that occurs in the body at the rate of 50 million per second), the surface area of the cell is larger and must, of necessity, contain enough molecular material in this surface with fatty acids to reproduce a complete, healthy new cell. If there are saturated fats present, this process is hindered and energy, oxygen and electrons are stolen from the over-all body! If this condition is left unchecked, the DNA master clock is sent off frequency, and the body aging process is accelerated.

The difference is quite noticeable from one person to another. It usually is presented with a statement such as "Boy, she sure looks young for her age!" or "He is only 30? He looks twice that age."

Let us explore this dipolarity further.

PHOTONS AND PRANA — LIFE FORCE

Our bodies are composed of hydrogen, oxygen, nitrogen and carbon. When discussing unsaturated fats, we are dealing with the relationship of oxygen (prana life force) and hydrogen (consciousness).

Many of the best, highly unsaturated fats come from seed oils such as flaxseed, linseed or pumpkin seed. These seeds store energy or photons from the sun. That is why you'll often see these oils stored or sold in black or dark containers. This keeps the photon energy inside the container until it can be released into your body. If, for example, you left flaxseed oil out in the sunlight, it would oxidize and give away its photons back to the sun. To be of benefit, photons need to be kept active.

All cells consist of protons and electrons (see figure 13-2). When these protons and electrons, as in the example of hydrogen, are combined with other, heavier atoms such as oxygen, which also contains protons and electrons, electromagnetic waves are released at the time of the reaction. These magnetic waves attract photons (activating life force energy to the body!), and the life force of the sun is felt in a personal radiance. Highly unsaturated fats provide this "photon ambience" to the reaction. The result is complete oxidation at the cell site with a resulting release of ATP (adenosine triphosphate), the universal energy storage molecule!

110

THERE ARE 3 BALANCE POINTS TO KEEP YOUR BODY, HEALTH AND ENERGY IN THE PROPER "ZONE."

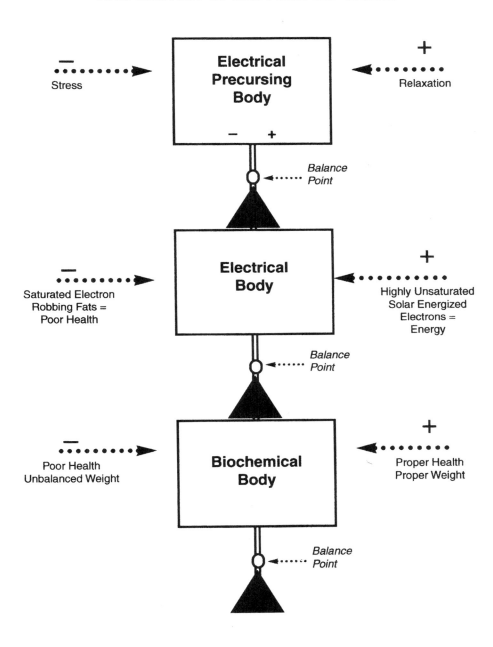

Figure 13-1

111

If the body has a higher ratio of saturated fats, then when oxygen is delivered, it can't be electrically connected, and the body produces instead free radicals, or toxic by-products!

An electrical charge in motion produces a magnetic field. When, as in cell reproduction, these charges are moved away from each other, electromagnetic waves are produced.

When the sun shines on the leafy canopy of a tree and is absorbed through the leaves via photosynthesis, movement occurs in the electrical charge of the electrons. A magnetic field is also brought about when the water in a tree rises. When we walk in a forest, this field charges our aura field and amplifies our energies with a solar (photon) charged electron. When blood circulates throughout our bodies, it causes a movement of the electrical charge in the magnetic fields on the surface lipids of the red blood corpuscles, which then cause rapid induction and reinduction of the solar life force energy.

With each heartbeat, a dose of the body's own electron-rich, highly unsaturated fats from the lymph system, together with lymph fluid, enters the blood vessels

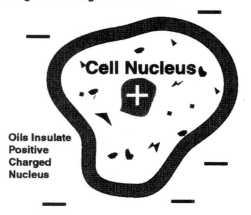

Negative Charge on Cell Wall

Cell Nucleus

Oils Insulate
Positive
Charged
Nucleus

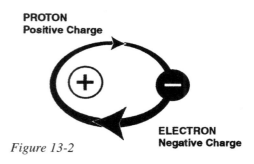

PROTON
Positive Charge

ELECTRON
Negative Charge

Figure 13-2

and thereby into the heart. This action contributes to the human electromagnetic aura, and when transmitted to others, gives a loving, healing bio-force. Many ancient races used trees to help them send their thoughts over long distances to communicate with others.

So, you can see in this brief discussion on lipids and oils, that they are vastly important to proper health, balance and our electromagnetic nature.

For further reading on the exciting subject, I recommend a book entitled *Flax Oil* as a reference to flax oil as a true aid against heart infarction, cancer, and other diseases. (FeHe Als Wahre Hilfe Gegen Deteriousklerose Herzinfrokt Krebs by Dr. Johann Budwig, Vancouver, BC: Apple Publishing ©1994. Telephone 604-325-2888).

Cells have a positive charge in the nucleus and a negative charge on the cell wall. (see figures 13-3 and 13-4)

The essential fatty acids (oils) protect the cell by providing electrical insulation between the cell nucleus and cell wall. If the body receives too many saturated fats, this insulation is damaged, resulting in a damaged cell. Too many damaged cells lead to disease, because the lymphatic system can't remove damaged cells fast enough, and the aura begins to collapse.

This relationship is much like a proton, with a positive charge, and an electron, with a negative charge.

Too many positive ions cause failure of the electron to remain attracted to the proton. The

Photon Interchange

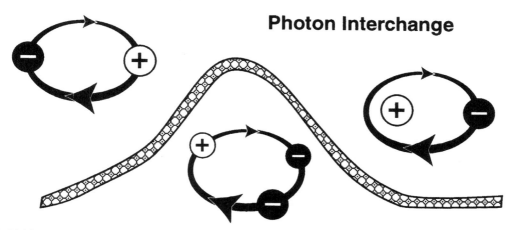

In highly unsaturated fats, photons are exchanged with cell motion vibratory energy into the consciousness and the body.

Proper fats act as a DNA antenna tuned to life frequency.

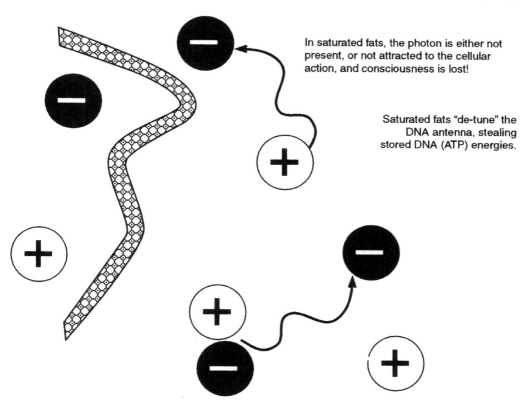

In saturated fats, the photon is either not present, or not attracted to the cellular action, and consciousness is lost!

Saturated fats "de-tune" the DNA antenna, stealing stored DNA (ATP) energies.

Figure 13-3

result: a free electron, which can become a "free radical." Remember that cells are macro constructions of micro systems of protons and electrons. Thus, essential oils provide healthy proton/electron balance. This, in turn, makes a healthy aura, as the aura is on one level "electrical cellular" or cellular electrical.

In the building action of the aging process, outside forces begin to work in opposition to the internal forces and this slows down the growing process and increases the aging process. Imagine, for example, this harmony of vertical and horizontal counter-opposing forces creating eddy currents within the cell which gives it motional growth.

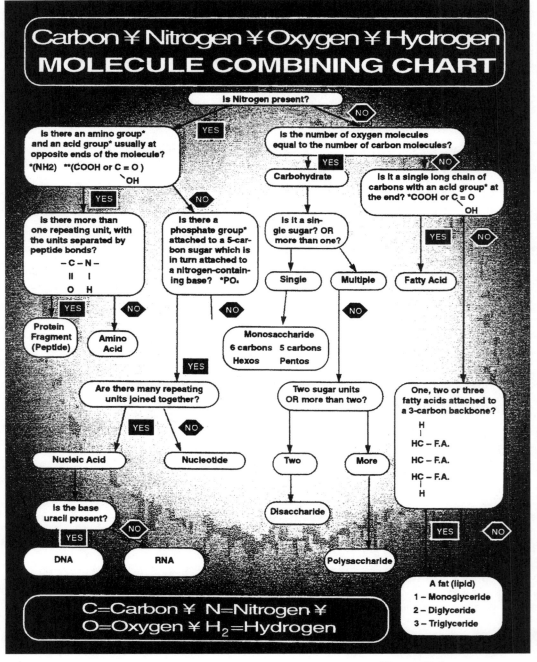

Figure 13-4

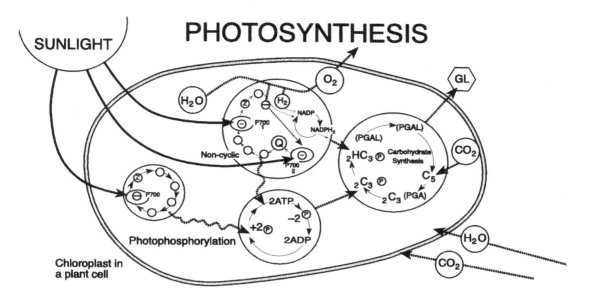

PHOTOSYNTHESIS

Light energy picked up by CHLOROPHYLL is stored for future use in the chemical bonds of GLUCOSE molecules via PHOTOPHOSPHO-RYLATION and CARBOHYDRATE SYNTHE-SIS.

PHOTOPHOSPHORYLATION: There are two types: clycic and non-cyclic. **In cyclic**, photons of light energize two electrons in a special form of chlorophyll "a" known as "P 700" and these electrons are then pulled away from P 700 by a powerful electron receptor known as "Z". Z then passes these electrons down a series of molecules known as cytochromes which act as an energy gradient to slowly lower the electrons back to their normal energy levels. In the process the energy released is used to add a phosphate (P) group to ADP (adenosine di-phosphate) in order to form energy-rich ATP (adenosine tri-phosphate), the energy carrier for all biological processes. **In non-cyclic,** after Z has pulled the electrons from the P 700 in one "photosystem", it passes them on to NADP (nicotinamide adenine dinucleotide) which, once it becomes energized, pulls two hydrogen protons (H+) away from an H_2O molecule to form $NADPH_2$.

In the meantime there is a second excited "photosystem" involved which passes two P 700 electrons to an electron carrier "Q" which then passes them down a cytochrome chain back to the first "photosystem" as replacements for its missing electrons. Electron replacements for the second "photosystem" come from the H_2O which has last two (H+) to NADP. The remaining O_2 is then passed out of the system and eventually exhaled by the plant.

CARBOHYDRATE SYNTHESIS: CO_2 combines with a 5-carbon sugar (ribulose) to form a 6-carbon molecule which is then energized by ATP and combined with the hydrogen from $NADPH_2$ to form two 3-carbon molecules of PGAL (Phosphoglyceraldehyde). Most of this PGAL is then recycled back into 5-carbon ribulose, but some of it is used to synthesize a complex 6-carbon carbohydrate known as GLUCOSE. GLUCOSE is used by animal and human cells as a source of energy in a process known as RESPIRATION.

Figure 13-5

Cellular Respiration

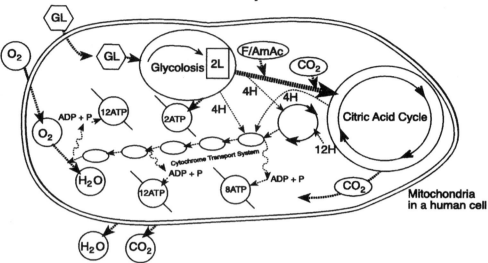

Light energy stored in one molecule of GLU-COSE is released through GLYCOLYSIS, the CITRIC ACID CYCLE and the CYTOCHROME TRANSPORT SYSTEM to charge up 34 ATP molecules. GLYCOLY-SIS: A 6-carbon molecule of glucose is bro-ken down into two 3-carbon molecules of LACTATE. In the process, energy is released by charging up 2 ADP molecules into high-energy ATP molecules and 4 electrons are donated to a cytochrome transport chain.

CITRIC ACID CYCLE: Next, each lactate molecule is combined with fats, CO_2 and amino acid before entering the citric acid cycle. During this stage four more electrons are passed on to the cytochrome chain. Next, this combination enters a continuing cycle of reactions in which it is changed into citric acid and then broken down from a complex carbon compound into CO_2. During this cycle 16 more electrons (H) are freed and passed on to the cytochrome system.

CYTOCHROME ELECTRON TRANSFER SYSTEM:
Electrons freed during previous steps are passed down a chain of electronc carriers called cytochromes. As they proceed down this energy gradient, they drive the phos-phorylation of 32 "discharged" ADP mole-cules into 32 "charged" ATP molecules (oxidative phosphorylation). At the end of the chain these electrons (H) are combined with O_2 to form water (H_2O).

Figure 13-6

116

Chapter 14

Color/Crystal Frequency and DNA
ELF's Destructive Cause:
A Brief Review

At this point you may want to review some of the material we have covered. You'll get a basic overview of what we have been addressing.

There are four basic amino acids. These four basic amino acids are formed by electrical fields and they form all life on earth as we know it. The four basic amino acids bond to become nucleotides which form figure eights made up of substructures of horizontal T's like this I– and vertical lines. The T's are made of sugar and phosphates and the vertical lines are made of hydrogen atom-based amino acids. So these combinations form all of the different 12 billion nucleotides in the DNA. When you bring in a counter-opposing force, even though this is a condensed vibratory frequency, damage is caused.

These 12 billion nucleotides are facing each other and connected with a straight line to form a double helix form the genetic code, the DNA, that is in every one of the approximately 6.3 trillion cells in the human body. To form a new cell, the DNA must repeat itself. This is accomplished by splitting the ladder along the middle of the step and reforming two absolutely identical DNA strands in the same the sequence. To form two new complete DNA structures, another 12 billion nucleotides are necessary. Beside the cell nucleus there are constantly at least eight different types of virus, four RNA types with a negative charge and four DNA types with a positive charge. Every pair of virus, one RNA and one DNA type, attract each other to form a bipole. They do so first to protect themselves against any electromagnetic disturbance, and second to accumulate energy in the following manner.

Inactive viruses are in crystalline form, but in the active status such as inside the cell nucleus they reveal one RNA or DNA core covered with protein. Of course, even in the active status they still maintain all the properties of a crystal and, such as the crystal, are very sensitive to high frequency sound. This is why when we use quartz that many people carry around in their pockets. Quartz has a healing effect on DNA that reverses the effects of radiation and other things that adversely affect DNA. In the Receptor we use different kinds of crystals and gemstones because everybody's DNA responds according to their particular needs.

Let's say there is a DNA problem in the thyroid. Green frequency crystals focus sound vibrations at the thyroid DNA helix. A person who is overweight, underweight or has an energy imbalance between the upper and lower parts of the body needs some green energy. We put an emerald in that person's Receptor. Energy is trapped on the dish of the Receptor and processed into a form of life force that the body can use, moving through the green stone and passing behind through the hole in the center of the dish. Then the wearer receives an increase in the green frequencies. If a person had a heart problem, we would increase the blue frequencies using a sapphire. Someone low in the red frequency area would use garnets or rubies, and so on.

Below frequencies of five megahertz, or megacycles, the RNA and DNA type viruses continuously electronically balance each other and produce energy due to the piezoelectric effect. The same principle is used in the energy conversions of ultrasonic cleaners. In the ultra high sound frequencies, over 5 megahertz, an isolated inactive virus can be excited through altered transition temperatures or Curie point and disintegrated. The human DNA is like a yogi antenna, we call it the yogi antenna that is one meter long, and it is tuned to radio frequencies between 375 to 385 megahertz. So if you were to unwind this DNA you would end up with an antenna. The frequency of Citizen's Band radio is 27 megahertz. One wave length is approximately 27 feet long. A 9-foot-long and a 3-foot-long antenna are used to monitor the frequencies. If you divide 27 by 9 you end up with a shorter wave length, which means that when you get up to 375 to 385 megahertz, you need a 3-foot-long antenna to tune in. This happens to be the length of the DNA if you unwound it and held it up and stretched it into a rod-like radio aerial.

The reason the antenna length is critical to a receiver is because the antenna is tuned a frequency based on the cycle of the one revolution of the wave from positive current to negative current, ebb and flow, which would rise and fall across a given point in a medium, giving a particular energy transmission, making it resonate. If the wire the length of the antenna isn't resonating to the frequency of the incoming wave, the antenna is not going to absorb or accumulate the energy at a greater amount than it would if the antenna were the proper ratio to wavelength. DNA cellular frequencies work this way all through the body, but there are different parts in the brain that receive different vibratory levels, different frequencies, which they respond to by sending transmissions through the endocrine system.

The endocrine system consists of seven different endocrine glands. All have nerves that are wrapped in sheaths the length of these nerves which determine the frequencies to which they respond. You could look at the frequency response of the body as a rainbow, starting with red at the top of the head and ending with violet at the base of the spine. This is only a static explanation of this condition. During the day, the frequency points change, which I will explain later, but for purposes of basic understanding of how the body works, look at this antenna system as starting out with red at the head and violet at the base of the spine. Each color corresponds to a note; each note is a frequency. Now look at the body as a different series of frequencies at each endocrine gland, a rainbow, with every endocrine gland receiving one of those color gemstone frequencies, it begins to become a lot simpler. The Receptor uses seven different colors of crystal to tune into and amplify or correct these frequencies.

Off-color stones like pink tourmaline combine different areas. It is not a primary vibratory generating source to the body but a secondary which is used to elevate two or three primaries. Once the person goes through the therapies of balancing their color frequencies, which in turn balances their electromagnetic etheric frequencies, then the body moves from an existence mode to an excelling mode. To realize the excelling mode, we combine different color stones. For example, pink, violet, blue and red affect three different organs in the body. We have charts that have been drawn up that you can request. The body takes about a year of therapeutic processing before it goes into the secondary process of raising up its energy and vibratory frequencies to reach safe inter-dimensional consciousness and the altered states. If you prematurely try to raise the body frequency and go into the altered state, your DNA cell

Your DNA is like a three foot antenna

Receptors tune your frequencies with the 7 differrent colors of crystal

118

antenna stores the energy instead of resonating, and as a result you become ungrounded and develop feedback problems of great magnitude which are very unpleasant. So this is not a good idea.

In the body we have different frequency centers, like the thyroid center and the heart center, with different lengths of nerves wrapped around them that respond to different vibratory levels, and these vibratory response levels of length are, once again, corresponding to sound frequencies. We want to "tune" our antenna to the different frequencies to get the most out of the energy available. Once again, if you had a Citizen's Band transmitter in your home and wanted to transmit to a Citizen's Band receiver in your car, a 50-foot antenna would not be as effective as a nine-foot antenna because a nine-foot antenna would be a frequency that corresponds to one of the octaves or wavelengths of the basic wave which is 27 feet long.

If you were wanting to transmit 60 cycles per second, the wavelength would be 1,200 miles long. 60 cycles is a much slower frequency and takes, therefore, a longer period of time to switch from positive to negative to create an electromagnetic wave. A Citizen's Band transmits at 27 million cycles per second. Because the human body runs at a multitude of different frequencies, we have to take into consideration the correct frequencies of our trans-mitting and receiving devices, in radionics equipment and scalar wave equipment.

The pyramid, because of the way it is shaped, becomes an all-wave frequency antenna. Meaning that you can't look at the size of the basic pyramid as a length of the wire and measure it like you would an antenna. Look at the focal point of the antenna within the pyramid, the apex, as the zero point, and the base as the the endpoint. This occurs on all four triangular faces of the pyramid. The pyramid receives and transmits an infinite number of radio and other fre-quencies that all correspond to the different points in the human body. The perfect, "fifty-two degree"-angle pyramids emit no frequencies that are not harmonious in some way to the body. However, because there are infinite numbers of harmonious vibrations present in the pyramid, it becomes necessary to direct the pyramids' center frequencies to the center frequencies in the body which is done in the pyramid by the different kinds of plating materials used, and in the Receptors by the different kinds of gemstone materials that are used. Furthermore, the DNA is under a constant influence of charged ions traveling through the nervous system acting as the central modulation frequency. We covered that earlier when we discussed the three basic nervous systems in the body and the need for trace minerals. The combined action of the pyramid and Receptor, forces the DNA to emit a high frequency sound in the range of 1.92 megahertz in order to detect by returning echo what type of protein is missing in a cell.

Basically, when the body absorbs protein and it has arrived at the site in the body where it is needed, the DNA pattern is already present in the body. This is why when you ingest protein in the body it is necessary to have eight essential amino acids present. The body cannot manufacture some of these amino acids, so they have to be put in directly. That is one of the progressive qualities about the the formulas we are working with. We use herbs like sarsaparilla and amino acid protein sources like spirulina plankton. When you take these for-mulas on an empty stomach, you receive a full load of the necessary positive DNA building blocks for your body to recombine with the rest of the ingredients in the vitamins for maximum assimilation. Proteins that are already in the body seek newly absorbed proteins to combine with. These already established proteins transmit a 1.92 megahertz pulse. There is also a 3.58 megahertz process involved, that the new proteins receive. Whenever new proteins arrive into the body, such as when you eat a tomato, the existing eight essential amino acids provide electrical frequencies to be transmitted to them from already present DNA.

Before you eat protein, you need the 8 essential amino acids already in your body

119

The eight essential amino acids provide sub-frequencies which add up to 3.58 megahertz. This is transmitted to the tomato and the frequency of the tomato protein combines with the 3.58 megahertz transmission by a process called "heterodyning." This heterodyning provides a return echo which goes back to the eight essential aminos. The returning echo determines whether or not the protein will be absorbed. If the echo response is right, the proteins split and they become transfer RNA. The RNA then connect with the incoming messenger RNA, reconnect to the DNA, split, combine, split, combine, and so on, and this causes the ladder to grow. The half of ladder of DNA joins another, the two ladders join to form a nucleotide, and of course there are 12 billion nucleotides in one small amount of DNA.

ELF, extremely low frequency, seriously affects this delicate replication process. It was developed during World War II for submarine communication. It was soon discovered that the people working around these transmitters got quite sick. Russia, and America too, began to figure out they could cause great damage by transmitting ELF waves deliberately.

ELF waves fool your body. When proteins attempt to bond via the echo transmitting pulse/return echo technique, ELF fools your body and causes you to assimilate proteins that your body should normally excrete. For example, proteins would come in (from animals fed on hormones and steroids) which your body should reject, but it doesn't, it accepts them, which causes genetic problems. When you take a small maintenance amount of niacin, these antigens won't remain in the body and will be passed harmlessly through.

Chapter 15

DNA / RNA Links to Life Extension

Remember, at the age of two, we have 22 base pairs per turn in our DNA. That is reduced to 14 by age 21, 10 by age 35 and 6 by age 55. After 55, the number of base pairs per turn stays the same. By this time the kinetic of the electron in the H bond and the energy of the charged ion become very weak, and the DNA stops reproducing itself, and the aging process begins.

> **Our DNA is de-spiralling**

DNA is despiraling at a fairly fixed rate, and at the same time there is an increase of flow of the production of serotonin in the body, which is what we call the "death hormone." Pleiadian DNA unwinds over a longer period of time, so their aging process is much slower. They live approximately 10 years for every one year that we live, and this could be reversed if we take the stress out of our environment and start using the devices that they have given us to slow down the aging process. When we use DHEA, in special formulas, along with the Nuclear Receptor, to slow down the despiraling process, we employ an anti-aging technology that bears experimentation and examination.

A bat, for example, navigates by radar: transmitting and receiving an electric field such as radar. With radar, an electronic pulse detects a target and sends a return echo. A bat uses radar to detect and avoid obstacles. The same process occurs in the body. The body is generating a series of frequencies between 1.2 megahertz and 3.58 megahertz. If it gets the proper reflection, it accepts an ingested protein. If it gets the improper one, it rejects it. Each protein, depending on how hard the body has to work to assimilate it, gives the body a certain amount of nuclear energy. When this nuclear energy is distorted because of ELF fields and other negative or harmful EPCs in our environment, over a period of time the overall body of information starts to say, "I can't fight this all the time, I want to withdraw from the physical," and of course, then, the aging process starts.

The technology and science the extraterrestrials have given us can start reversing the aging process. We might not make a tremendous dent in our own lifespans by practicing these techniques, but we might extend ourselves 20, 30 or 40 more years in this lifetime. The new information is recorded in our DNA, so when we reproduce with other people that are practicing this form of life extension, our children will have the tendency to live maybe 60 or 70 years longer, and if they practice these techniques, their children might live another 100 years, and maybe in two or three generations, our lifespans will climb to 300 to 400 years again.

Also—remember that all of the DNA in the 6.3 trillion cells of the human body are absolutely identical. All are tuned to the same resonant frequency. They all have the exact same genetic sequence code. DNA strands are all the same length, so they are all tuned to the same frequency. That's what I am trying to impress upon you, they are the same length.

Like a musical instrument, the sound produced by the DNA within its own scanning system, has different harmonies according to the chromosome gaps or inner space. We have produced a couple musical albums where we have actually reproduced this sound.

Now let us review a few things here. First of all, we said earlier that the human body has seven basic frequencies. These seven different frequencies correspond to the seven different endocrine glands. We are now breaking down why the body has to be addressed at the cellular level. Even though we have seven different frequencies from the body, the body responds to only one frequency. In our music we blend the timbre structure because when we go into the fourth dimension with our consciousness, we also have to take our cells into the fourth dimension. Addressing the cells only with sound of a piano would not be enough if we were using the sound attribute, to go with the color attribute, to go with the gem attribute. We have to address the cell frequencies and the sub-cell frequencies with these different timbres.

Instruments in the past that were not electronic, like the flute, would slightly address that, but moreso the older Indian instruments such as the sitar. The sitar is quite capable of generating interdimensional musical tonalities, but not as well as modern day synthesizers. We created our microtonalities of these different tone frequencies on our synthesizers by analyzing the Pleiadian spaceship sounds, using the harmonics in groups of frequencies that we found in the resonances and timbres of the Pleiadian spaceships, then amplified upon those characteristics.

Now I'm going to repeat myself just one more time to make sure this is getting simple. This is very important, and that is why I keep emphasizing that the body is made up of many different frequencies. These frequencies are divided into seven sub-frequencies, but basically the body's DNA receives at one frequency and then breaks it down into sub-frequencies. All DNA receives energy on a frequency of 350 - 420 megahertz. This requires an antenna approximately three feet long. Each and every single cell of the body has an antenna. The antenna is sensitive in certain areas. As an example, one set of cells might use two-thirds of the antenna. The basic frequency is transmitted and received at 100%, but the cell does not use 100%. Maybe it is a thyroid cell and uses only 60%, or a heart cell that uses 50%. So we have a series of filters within the cells that utilize or amplify that particular part of the frequency. These filters we could refer to as chromosomes. They dampen out the energies that are not needed and bring in the energies that are. Then, as energy enters the cell itself, it is further amplified and broken down by a finer series of filters, which are even tinier bits of information, the genes. The sound frequency energy is broken down 1,250 times further than at the previous level, the chromosome. Then the gene breaks it down 100,000 times, and these are microgenes. So we end up with a ratio of 46 because there are 46 chromosomes from the very beginning. The 46 is divided down into the 1,250, then the 1,250 breaks down to the 100,000. Now we want to amplify that 46/1,250/100,000 and break it down with sound. Sound will help. In the 46 divisions of the frequency band, we can break down the musical scale into sevenths per division. In music we can descend or ascend three octaves from middle C.

Now we have covered seven vibratory frequencies. So we could use A, B, C, D, E, F, G as sound therapy addressing any body process, such as the energizing process or the reproduction process of cells in the body, to increase cellular output. If we wanted to work with the stomach or solar plexus area, or the adrenals, we use the musical note D which energizes that area. But now let's say we want to amplify areas of the cells within the adrenal gland, the liver and the kidneys. We'd have to subdivide microtonally a division of 1,250 parts. So now we would transmit more than the basic notes; we have to transmit sub-components of the notes. This is where we use timbres, which break sound frequencies down to the level of the 100,000 base pairs, which would be a subdivision of one of the 1,250 tones.

Hopefully I am beginning to communicate this well enough so you can understand this a little bit better. Furthermore, like the musical instrument, the sound produced by the DNA and its scanning system has different harmonics according to the chromosomes' spacing. Man, at this point in time, is doing everything humanly possible to accelerate the DNA unwinding or aging process, so that the aging within the cells is increased. And we should be doing the opposite! It's silly. All forms of microwave radiation should be avoided, and this is impossible, because every moment we are being dosed by radio, TV, radar, aircraft, satellite short wave, a whole host of surveillance and communication radio frequencies, and they do nothing good for the body. So what can you do? Well, you can do a lot of things. A whole new technology has been created to reverse the negative effects. Remember what I said earlier: start with the basics such as herbs – ginseng, Fo Ti, gotu cola, etc. – and begin to cleanse the blood.

The Nuclear Receptor helps this process through a multitude of ways. One of the metals in it is cadmium, which absorbs radiation from the body. Because microwaves neutralize the trace minerals or high frequency minerals in our body, it is necessary to ingest the herbs that have the high frequency trace minerals.

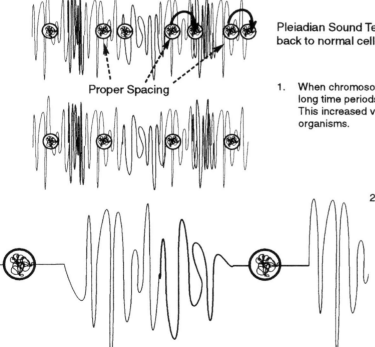

Proper Spacing

Pleiadian Sound Techniqes place chromosomes back to normal cell frequencies.

1. When chromosome spacing remains constant over long time periods, cell life and durability increases. This increased vitality extends lifespan in living organisms.

2. The timbre in Pleiadian sound corresponds to deep and hidden primal creative frequencies that are the building blocks to the eternal structure of creation. The frequency of the gases within a star, for example, corresponds to a stellar DNA frequency.

    Remember, creation stems from the stars and the lifespan of a star is tremendous in comparison to the human lifespan.

Figure 15-1

123

Chapter 16

ELF Fields Harming You

Another thing I want to refer to is a book that I recommend that everybody read. It's called *The Biological Effects of Electric and Magnetic Fields of Extremely Low Frequency,* by Sheppard and Eisenbud. It was presented by the Institute of Environmental Medicine and the New York University Medical Center and was published by New York University Press. This publication not only clearly outlines what I am explaining, but also examines the Russian weather control and negative energy transmission experiments that are currently going on which will definitely damage the human race.

I just can't emphasize enough that it is necessary for people to know about all the negative effects of ELF and other phenomena that we are being affected by and at the same time, I am trying to emphasize how the body works so you can further understand, with greater clarity, what we are presenting

I'd like to quote a part of the book I referred to, *The Biological Effects of Electric and Magnetic Fields of Extremely Low Frequency,* by Sheppard and Eisenbud.

"I want to give you an idea what this book acknowledges. First of all, this study should not have been possible without a postdoctoral fellowship granted to Dr. Sheppard by the National Institute of Environmental Health Sciences and the NIEHS Center Program Grant which provided many forms of institutional support. We are also grateful for the assistance provided by the American Electric Power Service Corporation."

The introduction begins:

Until one century ago, human exposure to external electric and magnetic fields was limited to natural fields arising from atmosphere, electricity and geomagnetism. However, within all organisms are endogenous electric fields and currents that play a role in complex mechanisms of psychological controls such as neuromuscular activity, tissue growth and repair, glandular secretion and cell membrane function. Because of the role of the electric fields in current flow, there are so many psychological processes. It is not surprisingly that questions have arisen concerning possible effects on biological systems exposed to artificially produced electric fields such as those in the transmission and use of electrical energy."

Now we are talking about transmitters and power lines, too.

"Apart from the question of possible human effects is the question of behavioral and or influences of lower animals and plants. There is convincing evidence of field responses in some animal species. Certain birds are responsive to the orientation of the Earth's magnetic field. And in the case of the some fish, electric fields are used for the protection of prey, navigation, and communication. This report is the review of the existing scientific literature on the effects of electrical magnetic fields from zero to about 300 hertz which spans the frequencies on which the electrical power is generated, transmitted and used."

Skipping a paragraph, it continues,

"Second, the subject of the effects with both frequency fields have recently attracted attention because of the possibility of deleterious effects on humans and lower life forms. The major source of environmental exposure is the electrical industry, and in addition interest in research is being generated by the Navy's proposed Project Sanguine (more recently known as Sea Farer), a system designed to permit communications with submerged nuclear submarines. The long wave length at which the Sanguine transmitter will operate, 4,000 and 7,000 kilometers," (remember, we talked about that earlier in wavelengths), "requires a large buried antenna, leading to the concern about the ecological effects on a considerable land surface influenced by the antenna currents and fields. In 1968, the Navy sponsored a review of the Extremely Low Frequency, or ELF research, which disclosed such a paucity of relevant research that the Navy undertook its own program of studies. Beginning in 1970 the research has been performed in government and university laboratories and on site at the Sanguine test facility in Wisconsin."

I'm reading from a footnote because I want you to do your own research with this book.

"State of New York Public Service Commission, PSC case numbers 26529, 26559 concern applications by the Power Authority of the State of New York, PASNY, Rochester Gas and Electric Corporation and the Niagara Mohawk Power Corporation to construct and operate a 765,000 volt transmission lines. Cases 26758, 26462 concern an application by a Long Island lighting company to construct and operate 345,000 volt lines. In the 765 KV case, PSC conducted generic rule-making hearings beginning in the winter of 1975. The intervention by the New York State Department of Health, Department of Agriculture and Markets, The Department of Environmental Conservation, and the Attorney General is on the basis of the issues of noise and ozone production as well as the electrostatic, electromagnetic and other induced effects of 765 KV lines and the relationship of all of the foregoing living organisms, including any possible effects on human beings. In the Lilco case, the towns of Huntington and Islip, Suffolk County intervened against a proposed line which would be constructed on existing narrow right-of-way passage through populated areas."

This is a very serious thing.

Now you begin to see why we need to protect ourselves. That is why I say it is important to sleep inside a Pyramid. These studies have been done by a bona fide government agency, more of which I will be quoting here. That's why we have developed a product

126

called the Starr Orb which stops negative energy fields in the human body. That is why we have a product called the Nuclear Receptor to wear on your body to help reduce negative effects. I am going to quote some interesting things from the same book, pages 5-34, Fisher, 1973, chapter entitled, *Effects on the Immunological Ability*.

"The electric field in the range 2400 KV/m were found to have a beneficial effect on mice as measured by their activity rate, liver respiration, and their ability to form antibodies. In contrast, mice which were deprived of any electrostatic fields by being enclosed in a Faraday Cage showed opposite results."

This research was designed to investigate the importance of ambient electrostatic fields to human health. It contains the suggestion that immunological preparedness could be increased by increasing the field as a clinical practice. There are some frequencies that are good for the body.

"The effects on ATP metabolism. In the Soviet Union, there has been some experimentation of frequencies that are somewhat above the ELF range. Two sets of experiments, which demonstrate biological changes, are discussed below on the basis of the English language abstracts on the Russian work. In the first experiment, at seven kilohertz, a pulse of electromagnetic fields demonstrated that morphological changes in a rat's liver were correlated with and proceeded by a change in metabolism. Up to 15 exposures over a six-month period of unspecified field strength disrupted the liver cell metabolism so the ATP content was decreased with a concurrent increase in the associated compounds ADP and AMP which normally are phosphorylated into ATP in the course of cell metabolism. A decline in the synthesis of urea and other biological changes were also reported."

What this means is that by decreasing the ATP, you drop the body's ability to discharge solar energy from the Krebs cycle, and this causes a gradual weakening. So this is what happens when you are near a power line and feel weak. A lot of people get weak around power lines, which are very toxic.

Pages 6-12, referencing Asanova and Rakov in 1966, give a couple of curves on the previous page of electrical fields going on and what it says is that "medical examinations of subjects exposed as above" and it shows these fields and the frequencies "disclose neuropathology in 28 subjects. Disorders occurred while the person was in the field and disappeared quickly after they left the field. Subjective complaints were headaches, sleepiness, sluggishness after work, and sexual weakness developing after eight to ten months of working in a sub-station. Because of the long-term genetic dangers of electric fields, further symptoms developed such as palpitations, chest pains, irritability and poor appetite."

ELF fields can shorten your body's circadian rhythm gradually destroying your body

And finally, page 6-17 from Weaver, 1967, 1968, 1974, *The Effects on Biological Circadian Rhythms*.

"Many body functions – temperature, hormone levels, alertness – vary periodically throughout the day within a period of about 24 hours, the means of which organisms, including man, maintain a regularity that is not yet understood. [This last thing we know, this is what the extraterrestrials are teaching us how to understand.] Recently, the hypothesis is that the Circadian clock results from interactions between organisms and an electromagnetic environment have been given increasing attention. The circadian rhythms of human subjects were investigated during long-term exposures to an external electrical field of 2.5 volts per meter at a 10 hertz introduced into the shielded room. Experiments lasting 3 to 4 weeks in an isolated chamber involved two factors: the influence of natural electromagnetic fields determined by the comparison of subjects in the shielded and non-shielded rooms, and the effect of an artificial electric field, 10 hertz, introduced into the shielded room. The investigator measured the times of waking, sleeping, degree of activity, motion, body temperatures and the electrolyte activity by urinalysis and administered several tests. The subjects exempted no perception of the acquired field but the field did have the effect of shortening the Circadian period by 1 hour after 9 days of continuous exposure to the field."

When you shorten the length of your Circadian rhythm, you shorten the normal biological response times to reproduce cells in the body. Therefore, by exposing yourself to the electrical fields, you are shortening the life process, because the cell does not have enough time to go through a complete mitosis period, which in the case of all the blood cells in the body is 90 days, so therefore you get an incomplete set of genetic instructions to cells themselves, which causes gradual destruction to the body.

"A statistical correlation was found between admission to a psychiatric hospital and changes in the geomagnetic field." This is still on pages 6-18. "Data were gathered from seven hospitals in the same area over a period of four years and correlated to the geomagnetic field data taken by the Coast and Geodetic Survey. The authors comment upon the well-known fact that correlation does not imply a causal relationship, and concludes with their impressions that: 'In view of the diversity of the two variables under their investigation and grosses in the measures, the present investigations offer correlation of a surprising magnitude.' " Meaning that even though they only have a short amount of data in, they got some surprising results.

There is also a reference to an experiment with animals indicating higher rates of cancer induction for mice in grounded cages as to compared with mice in cages insulated from the ground. And then it goes into dowsing. "Experiments on the phenomenon of dowsing imply a link between curious human activities in the presence of geomagnetic anomalies. One thinks that the dowser holding a fork rod walked over land and determined where the underground water is. However, the dowsing phenomenon is not limited to the determination of water, nor does it seem to require a special rod. The dowsing reaction expressed as the turning of the extended forearms can occur under diverse circumstances when the arms are extended with or without a rod."

Tromp, pages 6-26, in 1968 remarks, "It is doubtful whether as much investigation and discussion have been bestowed on any other subject with the lack of positive evidence with the reality of the observed fact. If substantiated, dowsing is related to our interest in the perception of magnetic fields. Experiments which demonstrate the psychological changes which occur within the dowser entering the dowsing zone show marked changes in skin potential and in the DC level of the electrocardiogram. Using soil resistivity as a measure of subsoil geological discontinuities, Tromp demonstrates that the dowsing zone correlates with geologic discontinuity indicated by regions of lowered soil resistivity. Laboratory experiments found some dowsers could sense magnetic field gradients lower than .1 gauss per meter. Some of the references in this chapter would be:

128

1. Beischer, D.E., 1965, Biomagnetics Ann., N.Y. Academy of Sciences, Number 134, 154;

2. Brown F.A. 1972, The Clocks' Tiny Biological Rhythms, The American Scientific Volume 60-756.

3. Koneg, H.L., 1974, Behavioral Changes in Human Subjects Associated with ELF Electric Fields and ELF and VLF Electromagnetic Field Effects, M. Persinger Edition. Plium Press New York, p. 81.

There are so many references in this book to other major scientific publications. So now you begin to see why the Nuclear Receptor is so important.

Part III

The Soul, Energy and Light

Chapter 17

Cellular and Stellar Interactivity, Galactic Consciousness

As we explain how our Systems change the vibratory frequencies of your entire house and workplace, you are going to understand the importance of working with these devices, given to us to use by our extraterrestrial friends. Realize, on the other hand, the negative extraterrestrials, the Grays, are fully aware of all of this, and they're generating negativity all of the time to harm us. That is why forums to explore these matters continue on an on-going basis, gaining popularity each day.

Let's examine meditation and inter-dimensional analysis. But first, I want to take a step back again and basically paint another picture here about extraterrestrial scientists. In our terrestrial science, people are taught to evaluate everything from a mental standpoint. I've learned from extraterrestrials, like Semjase, that we have to include feelings, too, within our evaluation process.

Let me give a brief background history as to the basic function and origin of our great planet Earth. The Earth is part of a great cycle, with changes occurring in the skies, the ground and the great inner core. Man, of course, out of ignorance has interfered with natural laws of planetary and universal change. And this interference now poses a major threat to the existence of life itself in all the domains of the nature, the mineral, the vegetable, human and animal.

Just imagine that we are flying a 747 across one continent to another. Suppose we're flying at 30,000 feet, completely contained within the cabin environment. Someone smokes a cigar, another person spills paint. It becomes uncomfortable to live in this increasingly polluted environment. It's so bad you can't think clearly, you can't sleep, you can't meditate because you are fighting all the toxins and fumes.

What's happening on that plane is exactly what is happening on the Earth.

Let's look at the physical structure of the Earth as it is now. The Earth contains an inner core surrounded by an outer core, a lower mantel, an upper mantel and a basalt crust which is proportionately very thin compared to the interior layers. The Earth's outer layer is mostly granite on the land and sediment under the sea. I look at it as a cell on a macro-cosmic level. The skin of the Earth is the crust which is thin and delicate, just as our skin is thin and delicate. Similarly, when its surface is punctured, it too, like our body, is subject to infection. Did you know that neither the Pleiadians nor the Andromedans mine their home planets? They mine asteroids. We have already mined our home planet, and we have done a lot of damage to it because of greed. Normally, if a human suffers a surface wound, white blood cells, leucocytes, combat infection. When the body is healthy and balanced, the infection threat stops at the outset. The Earth, too, has a natural defense mechanism which we are slowly hindering, setting ourselves up for total racial annihilation. Think about the hydrogen and atomic bombs and how powerful those are and how they affect the Earth as a being.

By now it should be evident that even the most minute electrical changes can, in time, cause a change in the world situation. Remember we established the cell as an organism, the organism generating the aura field, the aura field connecting to the population, the population and the community into the nation, the nation into the world. I cannot put enough emphasis on the importance of maintaining balance in our daily activities, because you are the expression of your thoughts. Your body is an expression of what you put into it. Whether it be the air you breathe, the food you eat or the love you give and receive. Meditation is also recommended as part of mental balance and toning, just as exercise is important for muscular toning.

I'm sure you have seen pictures of the Milky Way Galaxy and Andromeda, and if you look at a galaxy on its side, you'll notice a cyclic pattern that looks like hemoglobin. An iron atom, of course, forms a pyramid-shaped molecule at the foundation of hemoglobin. The hemoglobin, with the action of negative ions and oxygen, transports life into the body and picks up wastes and gases. Then the waste products, including carbon dioxide, are ingested by hemoglobin in the blood and exhaled, and absorbed by chlorophyll in plants and converted back into oxygen in the plant. So the hemoglobin creates food for the plant cell, and the plant creates oxygen for the human cell – this is one cycle. And of course, this cell cycle that oscillates back and forth in the body, in other words in the action of the red blood cells passing off carbon dioxide and receiving up oxygen, has a frequency. That is the Bohr Effect. Galaxies such as our Milky Way support the carbon cycle process and supply the light necessary for that process. In return, our actions feed the mental energies back via black holes to the source of creation, the influence within the higher realms. We are going to explore the higher realms. But there is a process in the supporting of life where energy is fed out of a galaxy and into the higher realms. (see figure 17-1)

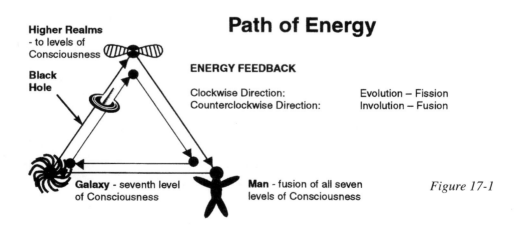

Path of Energy

Higher Realms
- to levels of
Consciousness

**Black
Hole**

ENERGY FEEDBACK

Clockwise Direction: Evolution – Fission
Counterclockwise Direction: Involution – Fusion

Galaxy - seventh level
of Consciousness

Man - fusion of all seven
levels of Consciousness

Figure 17-1

Another interesting cell I would like to mention is the acetabularia. This is a very symbolic-looking cell. It is considered a giant, algae-forming cell from tropical seas. It consists of a root-like holdfast and a long, cylindrical stalk. At its sexual maturity it turns into a cup-like cap. The nucleus is found in the holdfast, as far away from the cap as possible. To give you an idea, just imagine at its sexual maturity that it is like the shape of a mushroom. The top of the mushroom opens up, and if you are looking at the mushroom coming out of the ground and are standing directly over it, the shape of the top of it will look like a galaxy.

So in the mushroom cap you are looking down on the energy that is moving like the galaxy itself. Look down the stem of the "galaxy." Where it goes into the ground is called the holdfast, which is where the nucleus is. The nucleus of the cell is at the base, the ground, and the energy part is at the very top. As it reaches its prophase stage of mitosis division, the nucleus divides down at the bottom part and the pro nuclei swim up into the cap where they become the pronuclei of sex cells. They are released upon maturity to swim away in search of partners (see figure 17-2).

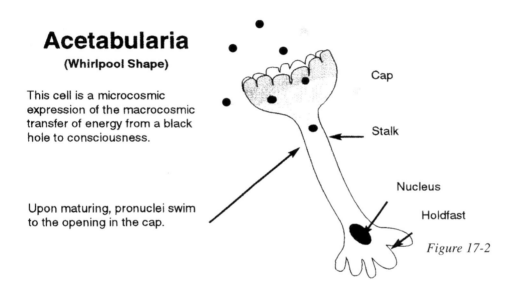

Acetabularia
(Whirlpool Shape)

This cell is a microcosmic expression of the macrocosmic transfer of energy from a black hole to consciousness.

Upon maturing, pronuclei swim to the opening in the cap.

Cap

Stalk

Nucleus

Holdfast

Figure 17-2

The pronuclei swim up to the cap, the top of the mushroom and swim away into the ocean. They reproduce at the base or stem of the mushroom, still floating in the ocean, then the pronuclei swim up the stock in the cap where they are whirled off to reproduce other cells.

Just as the acetabularia can be found in the salt water, so can a black hole be found in the "sea" of space. The black hole, with a similar shape of the acetabularia, has a stem called "space-time singularity." Its purpose is a complete reverse of the acetabularia cell. Composed of a collapsing or spent star, it attracts matter and energy via accelerated gravity into its bell-shaped intake, and transmits this energy and matter into the fourth dimension of time and beyond through its long stem. Gradually, as the energies from the black hole neutralize themselves, the hole evaporates (see figure 17-3).

So just imagine, once again, this cell like a mushroom floating in the ocean. Its nucleus is at the stem, the very bottom. Energy moves up to the very top, leaves the cell and seeks the bottom of another cell in order to reproduce. A black hole does just the opposite. It is another "mushroom" in space, with everything coming in from the top, going down through

Nature's Grand Scale of Life
Fusion to Fission and Back Again

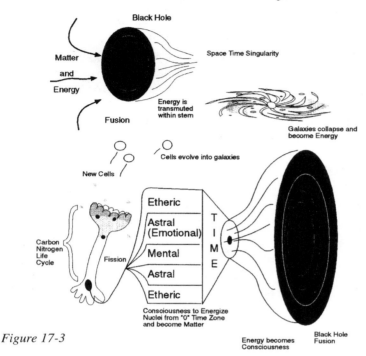

Just as the Acetabularia can be found in a sea of salt water, so can a Black Hole be found in the sea of space

The Black Hole, with a similar shape as the Acetabularia, has a stem called a space time singularity. Its purpose is the complete reverse of the Acetabularia Cell.

Composed of a collapsing or spent star, it attracts matter and energy via its accelerating gravity into its bell-shaped intake and transmutes this energy and matter to the fourth dimension of time and beyond through its long stem. Gradually, as the energies within a Black Hole neutralize themselves, the hole evaporates.

Figure 17-3

the stem, and disappearing off into another dimension. The dimension that it moves into eventually becomes consciousness. And this becomes the etheric, the physical, the astral, the mental and other higher levels. Seven different dimensions are reached through the base of the space-time singularity until the energy finally evaporates.

Once this energy evaporates into space and time, it remanifests itself into the cell. So energy and matter cycle through this huge, powerful black hole, through the space-time singularity at its base, over to the base of a cell. The energy could even manifest at the base of the acetabularia cell. This energy perpetuates in the form of intelligence converted into the cell which reproduces itself in the sea. And of course, when these kinds of cells reproduce, they create our atmosphere. Many different algae, for example, such as spirulina, create our oxygen atmosphere. The oxygen is breathed in by man who gives off carbon dioxide that goes back into the cell, continuing the cycle. So there is an actual feedback between black hole and space time singularities and cells. You start to get the bigger picture.

The largest cell known is the ostrich egg, which contains a large quantity of yolk nourishment for the developing bird. Neither the white of the bird's egg nor its shell is counted as part of the cell because these structures are non-living materials secreted by the walls of the mother bird's oviduct. An average cell measures about ten micrometers, or one twenty-five hundredths of an inch in diameter.

Now let's consider the shape of the typical animal cell. In the center is the nucleus,

136

Path Of Energy Fission Fusion/Consciousness

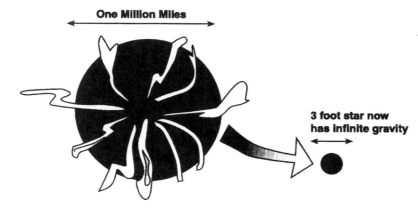

One Million Miles

3 foot star now has infinite gravity

1. A star burns out, collapses, and its own gravity reduces its size from a one million mile gaseous body to a cold rock the size of a basket ball.

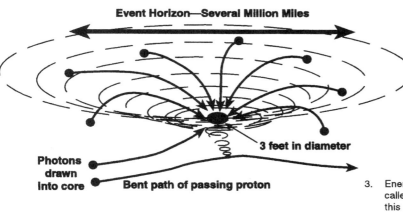

Event Horizon—Several Million Miles

3 feet in diameter

Photons drawn into core

Bent path of passing proton

2. This condensation from 1×10^{6} miles or more to 3 feet condenses gravity, creating an event horizon millions of miles wide, with the collapsed star as its nucleus. Light is pulled in if it comes too close. If it is able to pass by, it is deflected. This is part of the basis for the theory of relativity.

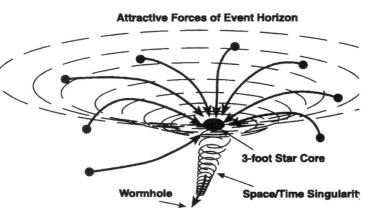

Attractive Forces of Event Horizon

3-foot Star Core

Wormhole

Space/Time Singularit

3. Energy begins to focus in a path that is called a space time singularity. Around this singularity path a "worm hole" is formed. This dissipates the immense gravity into the 4th dimension and beyond, and particles of fusion begin to fission into other dimensions of the seven levels of consciousness. This energy sort of restocks the shelves of the seven levels, ending at the logic plane. The logic plane then expels these particles back down to the physical plane. As they arrive there they potentize the living cells of the 3-D world. After they energize the physical plane, density is created. The reverse force of density is called gravity. The oscillating cycle between DNA animation and gravity is a rhythm known as time.

Figure 17-4

137

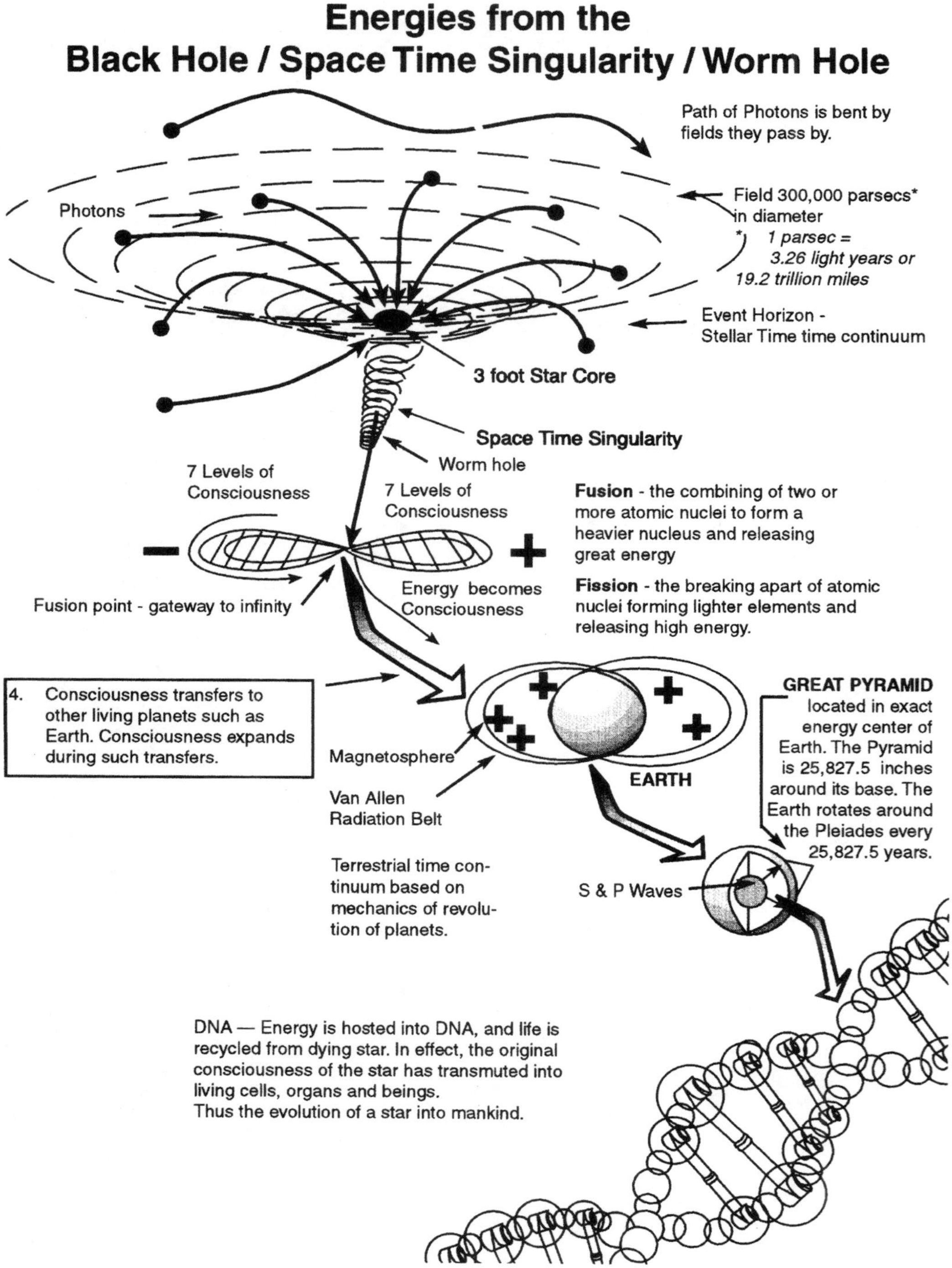

Energies from the
Black Hole / Space Time Singularity / Worm Hole

Path of Photons is bent by fields they pass by.

Photons

Field 300,000 parsecs* in diameter

*) 1 parsec = 3.26 light years or 19.2 trillion miles

Event Horizon - Stellar Time time continuum

3 foot Star Core

Space Time Singularity

Worm hole

7 Levels of Consciousness

7 Levels of Consciousness

Fusion - the combining of two or more atomic nuclei to form a heavier nucleus and releasing great energy

— +

Fusion point - gateway to infinity

Energy becomes Consciousness

Fission - the breaking apart of atomic nuclei forming lighter elements and releasing high energy.

4. Consciousness transfers to other living planets such as Earth. Consciousness expands during such transfers.

Magnetosphere

Van Allen Radiation Belt

Terrestrial time continuum based on mechanics of revolution of planets.

EARTH

S & P Waves

GREAT PYRAMID located in exact energy center of Earth. The Pyramid is 25,827.5 inches around its base. The Earth rotates around the Pleiades every 25,827.5 years.

DNA — Energy is hosted into DNA, and life is recycled from dying star. In effect, the original consciousness of the star has transmuted into living cells, organs and beings. Thus the evolution of a star into mankind.

Figure 17-5

138

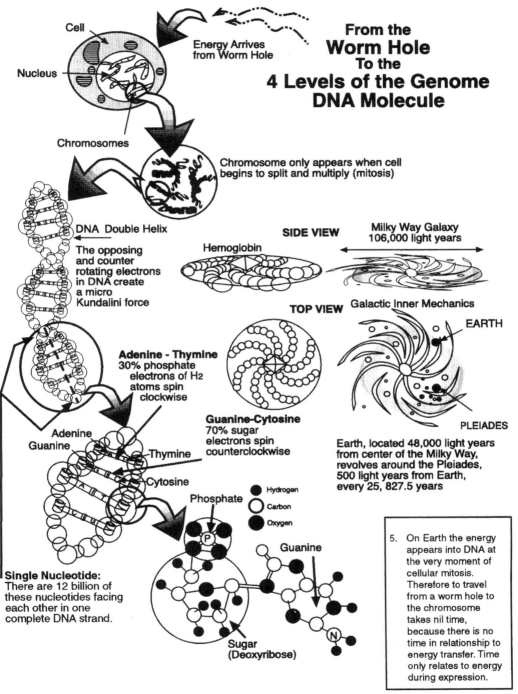

Figure 17-6

whose functions have already been mentioned. Around the cell nucleus is the cellular membrane made of cytoplasm. Remember, we reviewed DNA, how it electrically interacts and interworks in different vibratory frequencies and how the antenna, the "DNA antenna," is wound up in the nucleus. We covered how a particular cell is connected to a particular antenna which has a series of frequencies, and then sub-frequencies that operate depending on the kind of cell. The parts of the cells include the lysosome, which contains the digestive enzymes; and the endoplasmic reticulum, or ER, which transports nutrients through the cell. It's like the cell's freeway system or the correspondent of our veins. Then we have the centrioles which surround the nucleus itself. They have a function in mitosis. There is the cellular membrane, the cell wall itself, which regulates the entrance and exit of materials and energies.Then there is the cytoplasm, then the nuclear membrane, and in the center, the nucleus. The mitochondria, the powerhouse of the cell, store the energy for the cell. And then we have a thing called the Golgi apparatus which packages the protein for the cell. (see figure 17-7)

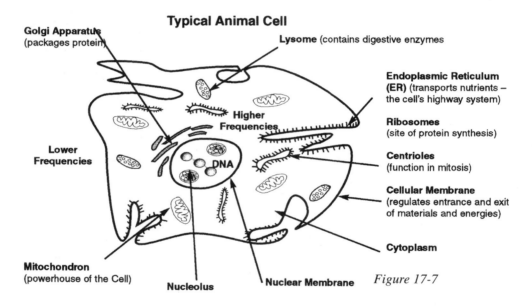

Typical Animal Cell

Golgi Apparatus (packages protein)

Lysome (contains digestive enzymes

Endoplasmic Reticulum (ER) (transports nutrients – the cell's highway system)

Ribosomes (site of protein synthesis)

Centrioles (function in mitosis)

Cellular Membrane (regulates entrance and exit of materials and energies)

Cytoplasm

Lower Frequencies

Higher Frequencies

DNA

Mitochondron (powerhouse of the Cell)

Nucleolus

Nuclear Membrane

Figure 17-7

DNA is like a star in the center of a cell whose pure rays turn to ash and firmament in the outer walls of the cell. Likewise do the frequencies of a cell start higher in the center and progressively lower to the outer perimeter.

So the cell itself is like a smaller version of the human body. If you start looking at the chain which I laid out earlier of minerals, enzymes, vitamins, proteins, polypeptides and finally hormones, you start to see a cell is nothing more than a micro-version of the whole chain of how the body works in the first place.

Let's turn our attention to the Earth. Let's look at the Earth as a solar cell on a macro level. First of all, there are belts around the surface of the Earth. We have the inner core which we mentioned earlier. Now let's look at the outer belts of the Earth. We mentioned the two mantles, the crust, and the inner core. The thin layer that supports life on the surface of the Earth is the troposphere. The mesosphere is the next layer of the atmosphere. The ozone layer occurs at the lower level of the mesosphere right above the troposphere. Then we move up in to the stratosphere, then to the thermosphere, then the magnetosphere, or the Van Allen radiation belt, which is further out yet. The ionosphere is in between the stratosphere and the exosphere at around 400 miles above the surface of the Earth. The metallic inner core of the Earth is estimated to be about 800 miles across in diameter and the lower mantle is approximately 2,600 miles across or 1,300 miles on each side of the center and the upper mantle is about 1,800 miles beyond the lower mantle on either side. The crust is about 5 miles thick. So you can begin to see how the planet is put together. (see figures 17-8 & 17-9)

The Earth and its Spheres

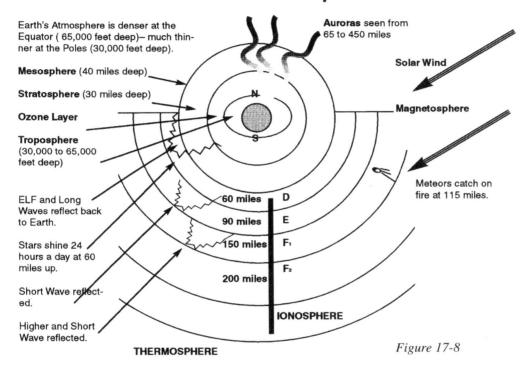

Earth's Atmosphere is denser at the Equator (65,000 feet deep)– much thinner at the Poles (30,000 feet deep).

Mesosphere (40 miles deep)

Stratosphere (30 miles deep)

Ozone Layer

Troposphere (30,000 to 65,000 feet deep)

ELF and Long Waves reflect back to Earth.

Stars shine 24 hours a day at 60 miles up.

Short Wave reflected.

Higher and Short Wave reflected.

THERMOSPHERE

Auroras seen from 65 to 450 miles

Solar Wind

Magnetosphere

Meteors catch on fire at 115 miles.

60 miles D
90 miles E
150 miles F₁
200 miles F₂

IONOSPHERE

Figure 17-8

To grasp the overall magnitude of the concept of life, I found that if you study the basic components of each living thing in the game of life and our relationship to these respective parts, then a general outline of the divine game begins to emerge. Next, look at the basic rules of motion and the limitations of time.

The concept of time will begin to orchestrate itself in the subconscious mind, giving you a greater understanding of the basic flow and interworking of all things. The most important thing, however, is that you begin to realize you are a part in the overall scheme of things. This is what Einstein called the General Theory of Relativity. The cell, like the Earth, has a core; we call this the nuclear membrane and the nucleus. The nucleus is the actual center of the cell that is surrounded by the nuclear inflow, which is interpreted by a tunnel system called the endoplasmic reticulum, the highway of tiny tunnels or pores that permits a passage of molecules between the cytoplasm, which is the outer layer, and the nucleus. Within the nucleus are manufactured the genes from a substance called deoxyribonucleic acid, coded in a specific linear order which becomes the chromosome. The genes are chemically coded within the DNA and contain the intelligence to order the correct formation of the amino acids. This consciousness comes from the six higher planes.

The Currents and the Core

Our huge Solar Cell, Earth, has a metal core (nucleus). This maintains a temperature of around 7000° F which is in constant motion opposite the surface rotation. This counter rotation sets up a delicate frictional barrier that is semi-solid and 1800 miles thick, composed of heavy silicate rock that is brought to the surface by volcanic eruptions.

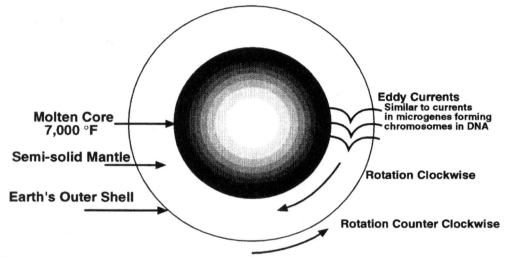

Most of the Earth's uranium, thorium and potassium are in the outer crust but the mantle does contain some radioactive elements. As the Earth gives off heat to space, convection currents from its central core are set in motion via volcanic action and herein lies a delicate balance that man has begun to interfere with. On a similar level, man has begun to interfere with his own cellular growth, by introducing many toxic imbalances.

Figure 17-9

Amino acids form protein. And these proteins form the balance of the cell itself. To further simplify the chromosome-gene relationship, think of the chromosomes as a chemical "cook-book" and the gene as the individual recipe. In a human, each and every cell contains 46 identical chromosomes. Cell division, or mitosis, takes place when the DNA duplicates itself and two complete sets of chromosomes are formed.

We have covered vibration and radar, how they work in transformation, how the Nuclear Receptor helps cellular division take place correctly, and about how ELF equipment has a tendency to disrupt accurate cellular division and cause the cell to combine with things that it shouldn't. All cells have organs just as the body has organs, perfect component functions within the whole. If you want more information, see the cell chapter in the my book *Death of Ignorance.* More information on consciousness interaction and the seven planes will be the topic of my next book, ***Restoration.***

Now let's look at a solar macro cell. Draw a picture in your mind . . . the sun on the left side, shining energy into space, and in orbit around the sun is the Earth, surrounded by a positive charge, the magnetosphere, containing the Van Allen radiation belt. Imagine that energy is moving from the sun onto the Earth. All the energy coming from the sun toward the Earth would be called the solar wind. Velocity carries the solar wind around the Earth and behind it into Earth's shadow. Call this area independent time, where time has a tendency to change to its different phenomena, different frequencies.

In respect to the inner core and outer core of the Earth, the Earth has to process energy as it goes through its 24-hour revolution. Two kinds of seismic waves are released: the S wave and the P wave. The S wave moves down from the crust of the Earth, partially into the core of the Earth, and bounces back up to the surface again in an S shape. Imagine a big ball, and inside the ball is something moving to the inner edge of the ball and then falling back down toward the center and going back up to the edge and falling back down.

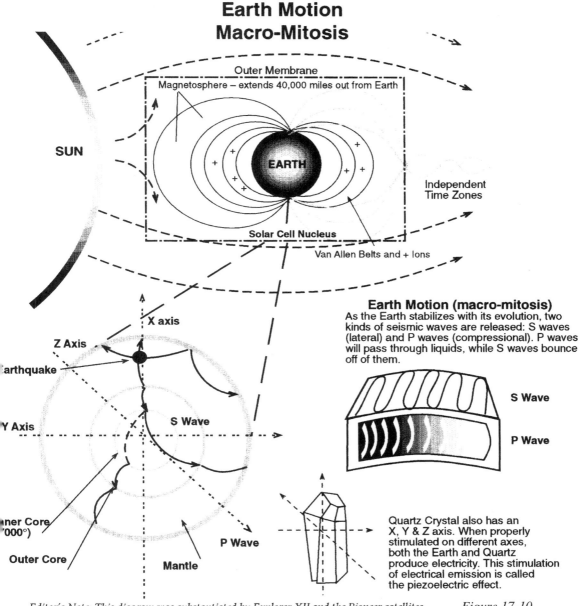

Earth Motion Macro-Mitosis

Outer Membrane
Magnetosphere – extends 40,000 miles out from Earth
SUN
EARTH
Independent Time Zones
Solar Cell Nucleus
Van Allen Belts and + Ions

Earth Motion (macro-mitosis)
As the Earth stabilizes with its evolution, two kinds of seismic waves are released: S waves (lateral) and P waves (compressional). P waves will pass through liquids, while S waves bounce off of them.

S Wave
P Wave

X axis
Z Axis
Earthquake
Y Axis
S Wave
Inner Core '000°)
Outer Core
Mantle
P Wave

Quartz Crystal also has an X, Y & Z axis. When properly stimulated on different axes, both the Earth and Quartz produce electricity. This stimulation of electrical emission is called the piezoelectric effect.

Editor's Note: This diagram was substantiated by Explorer XII and the Pioneer satellites. *Figure 17-10*

P waves, on the other hand, go all the way down to the center and come all the way back up. They are more direct, more penetrating. The S waves are lateral and they bounce around, where the P waves are almost straight, like the FM-type signal. They pass through liquids that S waves would bounce off of. That's why S waves will bounce around off the bottom of the ocean. Another more recent finding is that the Earth is like a giant crystal. Crystals have an x, y and z axis. Each is a lattice structure. Each lattice will have a different resistance to pressure, further explaining the velocity differences in S and P waves! (see figure 17-8)

The metal core of the Earth maintains a temperature of 7,000 degrees Fahrenheit, and is in constant opposite of the surface motion in rotation. This counter rotation sets up a delicate frictional barrier. It helps produce the Earth's magnetic field. Outside the core is the mantle, semi-solid and 1,800 miles thick. It is composed of heavy silica rock which is brought to the surface by a volcanic eruption. The Earth rotates West to East, while the core rotates East to West, producing a magnetic field. Magnetic fields are also present around human beings; that is part of the aura. By mutual induction, attraction or repulsion, energy is increased or influenced by the Earth's magnetic field. At night when you go to sleep, for example, you are charging off the Earth's magnetic field. At the same time, you are discharging negative energy into the Earth's magnetic field, and it's going to be affected. If the effect is too great, it is going to put stress on the Earth. And of course, the Earth's magnetic field interacts with the different magnetic fields of the other heavenly bodies in the solar system.

After awhile, the Earth's magnetic field gets too negative because of too many negative people in it. We explored the evolution of people's interacting energies. One person becomes a single individual, the personality, the personality of the town, city, and then in the nation and the whole world. As the energy gets too negative, it creates a friction which disrupts the P waves and the S waves, which then causes an earthquake. Man can control earthquakes if he learns how they are created in the first place.

Most of the Earth's uranium, thorium and potassium are in the outer crust. But the mantle does contain some radioactive elements. As the Earth gives off heat in space, convection currents from the central, hot core are set in motion via the volcanic action and herein lies a delicate balance that man has begun to interfere with. On a similar level man has begun to interfere with his own cellular growth by introducing many toxic imbalances.

Now you may ask yourself - just where did we go astray to interfere with the delicate balance of nature? A hundred years ago, or when? Let's just trace back in history for a few seconds and you can come to your own conclusion.

Five billion years ago, the Earth's original atmosphere was probably composed of hydrogen and compounds such as water and ammonia and the carbon-containing substance called methane. Today Jupiter has a similar atmosphere because it is further away from the sun. Eventually, however, scientists believe that as the sun ages and becomes much hotter, Jupiter will receive only 127th the amount of the increased sunlight as the Earth will, and Jupiter may develop a similar atmosphere to what the Earth has now. Of course, by then the Earth's atmosphere will have changed again also. I make this statement only to show that there is a constant growth within the solar system, as well as of our own personal environment.

Semjase has told me that if we destroy the Earth, we would remain in astral bodies, waiting for another Earth-like incarnation cycle to begin. We would need another Earth condition to come back to and finish up our racial dharma. Therefore, the people that weren't free of the solar karma, the solar system, couldn't evolve beyond the "Ring Pass Not" of our solar system. We would be stuck in astral plane limbo until a habitable planet could be made possible. She had pointed out that Jupiter would be the next planet, but we would have to wait millions of years before we could come back to incarnate on the "new" Earth to work out physical plane conditions so that we could be free of that lower karma and move into other dimensions, other times and other spaces.

In 1952, Stanley Miller, a graduate chemist, constructed an early hypothetical atmosphere of water vapor, hydrogen and ammonia and methane. He then exposed this to a lightning bolt of 60,000 volts. The gases were contained within a sealed flask and the electricity discharge caused precipitation of water at the bottom. After a week of exposure, the condensed waters at the bottom contained the four basic amino acids found in DNA—adenine, thiamine, guanine and cytosine. This action is called by science "spontaneous generation."

As the primordial Earth evolves further, the surface temperatures begins to drop. Vast electrical storms ravage the gaseous atmosphere, bringing about a condensation of some 200 million, billion tons of water above the planet's surface. That is about a tenth of today's water. Yet no oceans existed. Planet Venus is in a similar condition today with most of her water still suspended in vaporous state above her surface. During this post-deluge period, the skies are probably a vivid greenish-blue. The following rains lasted for one million years after that, a whole million years of rain. During this period in the continuum, the Earth is constantly reversing its polarity. This means that instead of the top of the compass needle pointing to the north as it does, now it would have pointed to the south.
(see figure 17-9)

The Earth, as far as its normal cycle, reverses polarity every 400,000 years, which accounts for the vast electrical changes. The Earth cycles back and forth with its polarity, just like the brain does when it is switching electrical energy, just like my earlier example of the long wire attached to a positive terminal and a negative terminal and we switched it positive negative. The Earth has switched polarity at least ten times in the last four million years, and this cycle has repeated itself at least for 72 million years. The Earth's poles shift geographically and magnetically, usually a few inches a year, going back to 700 million B.C., when the north pole was in Arizona, then the Pre-Cambrian

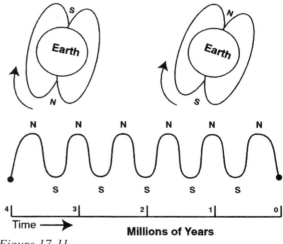

Figure 17-11

Sea. As the Earth's magnetic field literally rolls through space end over end, it moves in complete harmony with the sun's magnetic field. The area in space where the two interact is called the magnetosphere. (see figure 17-10)

The fact that the Earth is a super organism or a super cell should rapidly become more apparent as evolution unfolds even further. As the internal motions continued, the semi-solid and the outer motions, gaseous and plasmic, reacted during the rain period, and the surface was covered with 300 million cubic miles of water, three hundred cubic miles of which evaporate every day to rain and circulate planet-wide. Every 3,000 years, every drop of water in the sea has recirculated through the atmosphere and land. Every 2 million years, all of the water on Earth, through photosynthesis, circulates through all animals and vegetable cells. Oxygen that is not bound up in water completes its cycle through our bodies and through plants in 2,000 years. Carbon dioxide takes only 300 years to circulate, and that is progressively decreasing as man's lungs, chimneys and exhaust put forth more each year. This is really bad.

The Earth As a Slow Motor

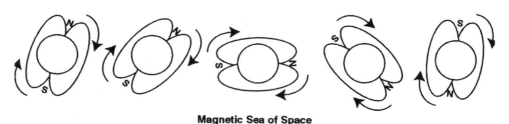

Magnetic Sea of Space

The Earth's magnetic field literally rolls through space end over end as it moves in complete harmony with the sun's magnetic fields. The area in space where the two interact is called the magnetosphere.

Figure 17-12

Evolution continued as lakes form through the separation in the land, minerals and the ocean. Then came proteins, developed in still lake bottoms, and the long chains of molecules. From this developed enzymes to speed up chemical actions and flat molecules to carry red blood cell pigment, hemoglobin, and green plant pigment, chlorophyll. And realize also that the oxygen production increased through spirulina. Spirulina also has a similar constituent as our blood. Then photosynthesis became a large-scale phenomenon, increasing the consumption of carbon dioxide, and so plants began to surface everywhere. Millions of tons of oxygen, a byproduct of photosynthesis, "poisoned" the air. In a few thousand years the air was about 20% oxygen. Today it's down to about 17%. As soon the new oxygen-dependent animal cells were formed, the great carbon cycle came into balance. Then came the specialist cells to various agents of large animals, the Pliocene era, and then finally man.

Man was then super impregnated with extraterrestrial races, and super humans evolved, coming back and forth on the planet. Now we are just getting to the beginning of the picture. Let me just give you a couple of examples where we ruin this beautiful, grand scheme of things.

The overall consciousness of man began to evolve during the Industrial Revolution of the late 1800s. A source of energy was needed to propel our machines. Wood and coal for steam power was the first source man sought, because it was readily available. Now realize that this is only one cycle, as we go around the Pleiades every 25,827.5 years. There have been many times the human race has evolved and fallen down, evolved and fallen down. Earlier societies used free energy sources and did not use fossil fuel, but as a greater portion of our present society became dependent on the sources of energy, great entrepreneurs such as J.P. Morgan and the Rockefellers quickly moved in and began to control the fossil fuel industry on all levels. Atmospheric pollution was, in fact, the problem at the turn of the century as the Londoners coined the term "smog" of smoke and fog. I find it quite interesting that a lot of people don't realize how long smog has been around.

Great inventors and masterminds of today were still alive during this period, men such as Nikola Tesla, Michael Faraday, Gustav Eiffel (who built the Eiffel Tower), Albert Einstein,

146

Voltaire and others. Being men of great vision, they saw the impending doom of the byproducts of their progeny and immediately set out to develop alternative forms of energy sources,
including free energy solar power and advanced wind machines.

Chapter 18

Free Energy Coverup
and the Tragic Price

They were quickly suppressed, however, by the establishment of cartels, who through large banking agencies, such as Chase Manhattan Bank of New York or the Rockefeller family, control all the development money needed to further the progress in these new realms. And, of course, you've got to remember the classic argument that took place between the Nikola Tesla and J. Pierpont Morgan, back in the late 30's.

Nikola Tesla said he had developed a use and equipment for free energy, and all people needed to do was have an antenna in their house to receive this energy from a master power station. No longer would we have to generate electricity with toxin-producing processes like burning fossil fuels. Now we could use the Earth's magnetic field with ERG equipment (Earth Resonant Generators).

J. Pierpont Morgan said, "No, we don't want to do that, because we can't charge for it. Once we have the initial installation we're out of business." And, of course, you know the rest.

The fallout from our decision to create energy by polluting processes is that our cells became unable to breathe properly, starved for nutrients, and full of poisons. They began to genetically mutate in the wrong direction, developing a whole new host of diseases that target the human body. This, of course, gave birth to another cartel, which we call the physicians and drug firms. Administration of hard drugs to cover up symptoms of the increasing environmental toxicity produced a mental stress factor which sent people everywhere looking for quick relief, a quick way out, thus creating the mass practice of psychiatry and psychology. A great number of cults began to appear as street drug users began their protests against sociological pressures.

Let's just take a quick look at air pollution on a grand, karmic scale. Millions of years ago, during the Pliocene Age, the surface temperature of the Earth was much higher than it is today. Life forms had reached gigantic proportions. Dinosaurs and heavy vegetation were everywhere. Vegetation was huge in those days. Leaves could be half the size of a house. But at that time, the Earth's surface was quite unstable as there were no inner shock absorbers built into the lower levels of the Earth's crust. The core and the mantle layers of the planet were quite active, as if life itself had to be adaptable between the core and the surface. And so Nature, knowing that Man was on the way, began to prepare the Earth's surface.

Earthquakes and volcanic eruptions occurred everywhere. The entire surface of the Earth was transferred deep into the interior of the planet. Now subject to great pressure, animal life and plant life decayed and formed massive crude oil deposits deep below. These oil deposits became a perfect shock absorber for the surface against the then superactive lower mantles. Even an automobile rides better with shock absorbers, which of course are filled with oil. Think about it! Then Man came along and drained the shock-absorbing oil from the Earth. Now we must realize that the earlier races that existed during this time of earthquakes were nomadic, hunters for food that had to move around constantly. Consciousness couldn't evolve when Man was on the run. You need to sit still to meditate and contemplate on where you are, and who you are, and the earlier races couldn't do that because they were in constant turmoil from the massive Earthquakes of the earlier times.

Oil drilling destroys Earth's shock absorption

Geologists, however, began to notice that the land became unstable around oil fields and suggestions were made to replace the oil cavities with water. A very poor choice, I should say. Try to replace the oil in your car's shock absorbers and engine with water and see what happens. How long will the engine run? How comfortable will the shock absorbers be? The core of the dilemma was that this dinosaur death was removed from its grave in the Earth by mechanical means in the name of progress and spread and dissipated into our precious atmosphere. I'm not against progress, but blind progress in the face of facts is what I call greed. The oxygen-carbon cycle of plants and man calls not for fossil fuel as a means to an end.

Then tragedies from smog began. One of the first was in 1948, in Donora, Pennsylvania, population 14,000 people; 6,000 people got sick from the atmosphere. The worst of tragedies occurred in Meuse River Valley, Belgium back in 1930's. Thousands of people got sick; 60 people died from poisoned air. This was the beginning of man-made smog. When it rained, airborne pollutants washed down into the water supplies. In Japan they started wearing oxygen masks outdoors, and on, and on. So you begin to see what has been happening here. It's really sad.

While I'm on this subject, I just want to mention the ozone layer briefly for a second here. The top of the troposphere, we mentioned it earlier, its called the troposphere, and above it is a relatively still zone called the mesosphere. Convection currents rarely rise into it, so it gets small amounts of heat from below and it contains very little water vapor. Remember that our atmosphere is heated by the Greenhouse Effect. And the mesosphere is where the sun's rays reflect from the surface of the Earth and are then trapped in our atmosphere. The mesosphere's important constituent is a small amount of ozone, an active form of oxygen, whose molecule is written as O_3, made up of ordinary oxygen (O_2) that had been broken down by ultraviolet light. Ozone is violently poisonous, but in the mesosphere, it filters the sun's light. It absorbs a kind of ultraviolet radiation that would kill (basically, it would be like being in a microwave if we didn't have it) all of the Earth's contemporary organisms if unprotected, by destroying the vital nucleic acids in the cells. Remember I mentioned the 12 billion nucleic acids in the cells. The ultraviolet just cooks them. Ozone is only found in trace amounts in the atmosphere, equivalent to 1/100,000th of an inch of surface pressure; without it all life on Earth as we would know it would die. Of course we've already learned about the destruction of the ozone layer, the high flying jet aircraft and how the establishment is trying to blame refrigeration chemicals. But that's not the problem at all. High flying jet aircraft are controlled by another major cartel.

In summation of this last topic, we defined how most of the external physical factors which have been implicated in the evolution of life are of the electromagnetic nature. It has now been established, as I've pointed out earlier, that throughout the renewable geological period the biosphere has been a region of electromagnetic fields of radiations of all frequencies known to us, from slow periodic variations of the Earth's magnetic field and electric fields, to gamma rays. It is fundamentally possible, I've found, on the basis of general considerations that many of the ranges in the electromagnetic spectrum have played some role in the evolution of life and are involved in the vital processes of organisms. This has been demonstrated, for a considerable region of the spectrum for electromagnetic radiations in the infrared to ultraviolet range, which is photobiology, and from x-rays, which is radiobiology. This is not true for the vast regions of the spectrum remaining, which include ultramagnetic fields of the superhigh, ultrahigh, high and ultralow frequencies.

I pointed out definite examples in the last chapter, especially from the book entitled *The Biological Effects of Magnetic Fields of Extremely Low Frequency,* that showed that experimental investigations in theoretical considerations suggest that these fields have a significant biological action. And I emphasize significant. The effects are seen especially when their intensity is fairly high, and such action can be due to only one process, conversion of electromagnetic energy to heat, or vice-versa, because when electromagnetic energy hits the body it starts to heat the body up in different areas internally, and chemical reactions do respond to heat. There is an increasing amount of experimental data that indicates man-made electromagnetic fields have deleterious effects, and thus living organisms of diverse species peculiar to the inner cellular organisms of man are extremely sensitive to electromagnetic fields. It has also been found that weak, natural, ultramagnetic fields can affect the organisms of various species. All this indicates the necessity for a fundamentally new approach to the problem we've got to look at now.

> **Extremely low frequency fields have a definite biological action**

Facts about HAARP

- **Injecting high-frequency radio energy** into the ionosphere to create huge, extremely low frequency (ELF) virtual antennas used deep beneath the surface of the ground by collecting and analyzing reflected ELF waves beamed down from above.
- **Heating regions** of the lower and upper ionosphere to form virtual "lenses" and "mirrors" that can reflect a broad range of radio frequencies far over the horizon to detect stealthy cruise missiles and aircraft.
- **Generating ELF radio waves in the ionosphere** to communicate across large distances with deeply submerged submarines and, patent documents filed during an earlier research effort that evolved into the HAARP program outline further military applications of ionospheric-heating technology:
- **Creating a "full global shield"** that would destroy ballistic missiles by overheating their electronic guidance systems as they fly through a powerful radio-energy field.
- **Distinguishing nuclear warheads from decoys** by sensing their elemental composition.
- **Manipulating weather.**

THE HAARP PROJECT

One of the newest follies that is Pentagon sponsored is a radio physics project called the High Frequency Active Aural Research Program, or HAARP as it is often referred to.

A project of true notoriety, it is man's latest effort to interfere not only with the ozone layer but also almost all phases of the Earth's delicate biosphere and electrosphere. In short, it is the ultimate ELF nightmare.

A 1990 Internal Government document revealed some of the following facts about HAARP (see chart below). To see what a nuisance this system is, let us examine how it works and what it is (see figure 18-1). The location here is a drawing showing the earth's atmosphere.

Although electromagnetic disturbances anywhere in the vast atmosphere of the Earth affect the delicate etheric surroundings of our planet, areas of the ionosphere located 500 miles from the Earth's surface are critical because this is the area that interfaces with the magnetic (solar) wind that emanates from the Sun that all human beings have as part of their physical body and etheric levels. They are called respectively the chemical reflective and light ether bodies.

The second ether, the reflective, is the one that is affected by the ionosphere as this is in often considered the reflective ether of the Earth on the macro scale. Just as man has a physical body consisting of solid, liquid and gaseous bodies, so does the Earth have comparative, similar bodies. It is via man's etheric body that allows him to receive the vital forces that the Earth provides to vitalize his physical and spiritual bodies.

The Earth sends signals to the Sun that are combinations of messages from man's physical, emotional and spiritual bodies via the Earth's ionic and etheric bodies. The Sun

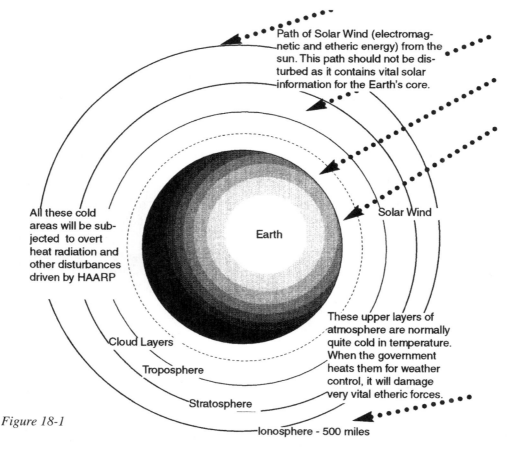

Figure 18-1

receives those signals, processes them and sends them back.

The HAARP project is ignorantly and blatantly interfering with this two-way signalling system. A lot of the return signals from the Sun come via the solar winds, especially vital information to be processed at the Earth's core. As a result of HAARP type projects, and there are others on the drawing board, the seismic and volcanic activities have already begun to increase on the Earth's surface and in the core.

At the heart of HAARP is a large array of 360 antennas that are called the Ionospheric Research Instruments, IRI.

"The IRI is designed to temporarily modify 30-mile diameter patches of the upper atmosphere by exciting, or "heating," their constituent electrons and ions with focused beams of powerful, high-frequency radio energy. A household analogy would be a microwave oven, which heats dinner by exciting the food's water molecules with microwave energy.

"Such an ELF antenna can emit waves penetrating as deeply; several kilometers into the ground, depending on the geological makeup and subsurface water conditions in a targeted area. Aircraft or satellites stationed overhead would then collect the reflected ELF waves and relay them to computers at a processing station, where subsurface inhomogeneities that trace underground weapons facilities can be imaged. North Korea and Iraq, where buried nuclear weapons labs are believed to exist, would be prime candidates for earth-penetrating tomography surveillance.

"Virtual lenses and mirrors will be generated in the ionosphere.... By precisely warming a patch of the lower ionosphere, the IRI reduces its density relative to the surrounding atmosphere. An 'ionospheric lens' thus formed can in turn focus a radio beam into the upper ionosphere (see figure 18-2).

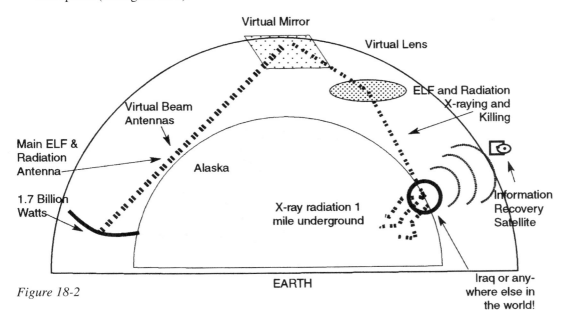

Figure 18-2

"Next, the focused radio beam excites a patch of the upper ionosphere to form a virtual mirror. Finally, a radio-communication signal broadcast by the IRI, focused through the lens and reflect from the mirror, can be directed far over the horizon.

"Virtual lenses and mirrors could also be used to scan a blanket of very low frequency (VLF) radio waves transmitted by an over-the-horizon radar. Although they reflect little VLF

153

energy, stealth aircraft can appear from above as 'holes in the blanket,' thus betraying their position.

"Proprietary phased-array, transmitting, steering, and pulsing techniques built into the IRI will permit rapid aiming of the radio-frequency beam in any direction, and at angles as low as 30 degrees above the horizon. This 'oblique heating' ability enables HAARP to form virtual lenses or mirrors at distances of more than 1,000 miles from the transmitter.

"The full global shield is an exotic proposal for an Earth-encompassing shell of high-speed electrons and ions that would be generated by a much more powerful version of HAARP. Any missile or warhead passing through the protective shell would explode."

It is rumored that the full global shield is already in place to stop unfriendly ET's as they visit or invade Earth. When you see objects preceded by a green flash , such as what has been reported to have appeared across several states, it is rumored that large objects made of beryllium, possibly the mother ships of the Grays, are being neutralized by the full global shield. Beryllium gives off a green flash when it is overheated or melted down, possibly, as it does when the protective shield that guards the ship against the air friction of atmospheric entry, is distorted by the HAARP rays.

"Or, a 'soft-kill' weapon system using ELF waves produced by HAARP heating could be used to overload power-distribution grids and destroy unshielded microelectronics using electromagnetic pulse energy similar to that released by a high-altitude nuclear explosion.

HAARP could destroy nukes in flight

"Real nuclear warheads and decoys, or the constituent materials of unfamiliar satellites, could be remotely distinguished in flight by bathing them in accelerated electrons. Analyzing the electromagnetic signal returns would reveal their elemental composition.

"Weather manipulation may be possible by building an ionospheric heater a thousand-fold more powerful than HAARP. Differential heating of areas of the atmosphere could induce local weather conditions, such as floods or droughts, useful to the military. Smooth seas might suddenly be raked by treacherous squalls, creating or denying a tactical advantage.

"Speculation and controversy surround the question of whether HAARP's 1.7 gigawatts (1.7 billion watts) of effective radiated power in the 2.8- to 10 mhz frequency range might cause lasting damage to the Earth's upper atmosphere. By comparison, the energy level is more than 3,000 times greater than the biggest commercial AM radio transmitters."

and manipulate the weather in war

If you are concerned about this, then consider an Air Force 440 page HAARP Environmental Report that states:

"...that the normally upward-directed IRI transmissions can raise the internal body temperature of nearby people; ignite road flares in the trunks of cars; detonate aerial munitions that use electronic fuses; and scamble aircraft communications, navigation and flight control systems."

The HAARP is only the tip of the iceberg of the Earth's Destruction programs our government is putting in place over the next century!

154

Chapter 19

Old Problems & New Science

In the last century bear in mind Baron Von Richenhoff from Germany conducted immense research on the effect of the applied field to amplified currents across dissimilar surfaces. Later in the century, his work was followed up by Wilhelm Rickenhaus and Townsend Brown. At the turn of the century, Michael Faraday did work on isolating organisms and their respective fields. His work was followed by Nikola Tesla, and by the 1940's Thomas Colsen and Fred Hart, (they, by the way, were the founders of the National Health Federation), had built a device called the "de-polar ray" that brought about almost instantaneous healing of certain ailments of the human body. Colsen and Hart primarily were working at that time with arthritis and a 44 megahertz infrared device. We're going to explore that more when we discuss the X-1 healing machine. These were the roots of the X-1.

And, of course, the first proven electronic cure for cancer was brought about by Gianni Dotto, a University of Milan graduate in the 1950s. This device was called the Dotto Ring, operating on the same thermomagnetic effect that the Earth's magnetic aura is created by, which is called the SeeBeck Effect, where you use two dissimilar metals, one of copper and one of nickel, put a DC current through it, and create a magnetic field with no polarity. The human aura is a magnetic field with no polarity. Most magnetic fields have a plus and a minus, and when you alternate them you have current, so there is a difference between Earth's magnetic field and a normal one. Dotto's work was paralleled by Professor Gerald L. Willis and Dr. Robert E. Ziph, Ph.D., both of the University of Dayton in Ohio.

For years, orthodox medicine has approached disorderly conditions strictly on a metabolic level using herbs, liniments, tonics, drugs, fine extracts of alkalines and acids from herbs, and a whole field of inorganic creations, such as aspirin, acetomenaphin and ibuprofen to alter the biochemical systems within our bodies. Some of the methods discovered and used were highly effective, others were pure and simple scams to raid the consumers' pocketbook. Today everyone is confused because technology on a biochemical level has been corrupted by greed and ignorance, something we always have to work through.

In the 70s, the New Age appeared and everyone had a solution. Greed disguised itself and slowly slipped into the holistic health movement to begin its worldwide crusade. Vitamin companies, if you remember, began to appear right and left on all sides. Each one had the miracle ingredient: DMSO, procaine extracts and products such as Geravital, human placenta shots, proclaimed by the greedy as a solution for the needy. To further confuse the intellect, which was now seeking hard to reverse the aging process, great seers of greed began to bring miracle cures from the East to the West and take discoveries of the West to the East from where all the Gurus were coming from. Religious crusades, as in the Medieval times began to appear, except greed was educated and ignorance was not. The great religious movements sprung up at a close parallel to the already corrupted holistic health movement. In the name of Spirit, ignorant men, women and children now, in almost a fever, sought out the Reverend Moons, the Jim Joneses, as the answer to eternal peace and salvation. On a quieter note, the calmer, distressed citizens put even greater emphasis on the traditional religions. Since theirs were the beliefs that stood the test of time over a few centuries, they argued, they must be on the right path for this eternal peace, yet everyone still had a personal savior. Still is the puzzle yet to come, to put the final seal of approval on everything holistic and spiritual.

Well, here we are approaching the twenty-first century, and guess what? Things haven't changed that much. Children are dying more painful deaths at earlier ages. Leukemia in children, for example, is on the increase. I mentioned why – when adults ingest too much copper, they unbalance their red and white blood cell counts, and their children have a tendency to be born with leukemia. Check with the City of Hope in Duarte, California. The medical profession is introducing, of course, stronger drugs to calm us more quickly because our nervous breakdowns are more intense, more frequent. The religious factions are condemning everyone and everything that defies their dictates. The family, which is the most powerful unit of energy in the whole universe, has divided itself like nuclear fission in atomic reaction, and those not caught in the middle are either on strike or protesting. Occasionally a ray of light does appear in the darkness only to illuminate the way for terrorist threats.

What do I say is the answer to all this? I'll give you a few clues about some of the philosophies that you might look into that might help. First of all, realize that energy seeks its own balance. You attract to you what you express, which is why I emphasize so much about the human aura and the condition of your environment, where you sleep and eat. Your body is an expression of your thoughts. Many times in relationships people don't want to face the problems. But what you don't like in others that you love, is most often your predominant trait. So its very important, I think, to recognize faults in others because they may be the foundation for some faults in ourselves and from that point on recognize and work with these faults.

And another thing our society does is judge everyone. Don't judge anyone unless you've walked a mile in their moccasins, as the Indians say. Another one of my favorites is "condemnation without experimentation is the height of ignorance." Don't destroy people's thoughts or ideas until they have actually been tested. And Christ had a good one when he said, "May he who is without sin cast the first stone." And, of course, you attract to yourself what you express, which is a perfect example of energy seeking its own balance.

As far as a healthy relationship with time, I've always said, "Time is a lady, treat it with respect," and "Patience is a virtue, not a gift." Many people don't realize that you've got to work for patience, it just doesn't come. And of course, the one hard rule to live by is, "Love your neighbor like you do yourself." These are some of the basic things that are necessary in our personality systems that need attention, often time, before we attempt the higher solutions.

The extraterrestrials are teaching us a lot, and I think you have to work through those basic things to get in touch with yourself before you really pursue the higher realms. And on top of all the negative things that are going on, there are a lot of positive things, and it's really important to start focusing more on the positive things, but at the same time when you're making this focus, be sure that you realize what the negative energies are all about and that they're very much there. You have to guard yourself. This is why it's so important to keep yourself low-key, balanced, think things out, and explore this new science. I think it will help, but I don't want to suggest anything or any solution at this point in time. Everybody has to find their own way. Scott Wolf in his introduction has stated some of the things that I'm reviewing right now. I hope some of this will make a difference and work for you. I realize there are a lot of things out there that don't work, and we're trying to show you why our things do. There are a lot of other things that do work out there, too. But that's why I'm going into such great depth in the scientific principle and the philosophical and psychological elements, because I think it all has to correlate and work together.

Now we're moving further into the spiritual side of it and I'm going to quote a little bit about a few things from a book I wrote, ***The Death of Ignorance***. I did this in 1979. I think it's appropriate at this point in time, before we get too heavy in the spiritual and meditation and music, to cover a few more things here because it's very important to understand some of the old Eastern philosophies, as well as Western. The Eastern philosophic sciences came from the Brahmans and Indians of Tibet, and the Brahmans were taught by the Rishis, and the Rishis were a group of Pleiadians. ***On The Fellowship the Sound***, the musical album, there is a poem called "Heritage"on the second side, the story of the Rishis and the Pleiadians. Now let's begin to start quoting from ***The Death of Ignorance***:

"Let us now begin studying energies as they are in the universe, as they are in you, and as they work together in us. All master souls are tested by other master souls when they are in the mental plane, but the results only become real when they are demonstrable on the physical plane in everyday life—and these truths must be understood by others. As many gather a truth brought on by a master, a new level of consciousness is said to be brought into mass consciousness.

"Mass consciousness is grown in steps and becomes real when it is accepted by the masses. We have seven levels of consciousness: Logoic, Monadic, Atmic (Female), Intuitive, Mental, Astral and Physical. Each level has sub-planes. The physical has seven sub-planes:

1. Solid–world of physical solids, Earth, metal, etc.
2. Liquid–world of water, lakes and oceans
3. Gas–world of heat, steam and vapors
4. Ionic–world of electrical behavior, aura fields, physio-electrical gases relationships
5. Third Ether–medium of conscious interactions with ionic fields
6. Second Ether–medium of high, free beings, angels and other semi-physio-etheric beings (still part of physical plane)
7. First Ether–world of light merging with consciousness in process of becoming dense physical

"The world is yet to realize any of this. Energy follows thought, thought provokes action, action yields habit, habit breeds society and tradition. Within society we have Karma, that which passes between two individuals, and Dharma, that which passes between three or more people.

Dhama exists between three or more people

"People will become more responsible as they work out their Dharma. Dharma is what creates racial tension. The only solution is education and acceptance of Karmic teaching by the masses, because energy on the physical plane is stored in the actions, proper and improper, of the masses."

Imagine we are back 8,000 years ago, sitting in a cave. I am your teacher. I am teaching sub-levels of consciousness on the physical plane. I mention that the physical plane has solids. Everyone agrees, because they can see with the eyes of their consciousness the times, trees, mountains, and rocks, all physical.

Now I mention liquids. Everyone, once again, agrees. There are lakes, streams, oceans, and, of course, the rains.

Then I mention gases. No one agrees whether they can "see" gases with their present mass consciousness "eyes." Beyond current understanding, no one in the entire world at this time believes in "gases."

So I put some liquid (water) in a clay pot and proceed to boil it with fire (still physical to them, because it burns). Soon they see "steam," a form of gas, and become believers. Then they all leave the cave of the teacher and go to the caves of others worldwide and teach about "gases." Soon gases become accepted on a mass level, and the consciousness of the world could be said to be elevated.

Today, it is no different. The classroom now demonstrates the ionic and third etheric sub-levels of the physical and the world, as a result, begins to accept auras, super-physical consciousness and the possibilities of greater beings, such as angels living upon the higher orders of reality, yet having direct interface with all of us in the here and now.

There is another example of a teacher bringing a message.

Back in 1861, a Tibetan Sage named Babaji called a railroad worker, Lahiri Mahasaya, to his mountain cave. This was the first lesson given to the world in this time of Kriya Yoga, which today is practiced worldwide by millions. It's greatest message is how to read time through the present; understanding the implications of actions that are happening before our very eyes, precisely at the moment they are happening!

Then he went back to his home in India and educated a man named Sri Yukteswar, who in turn taught Paramahansa Yogananda. In 1927, Paramahansa Yogananda booked passage on the Star of India, the first ship to arrive in America from India after WWI. Yogananda was the first Yogi to be received by an American president, Calvin Coolidge. Paramahansa Yogananda proceeded to spread the Kriya teachings, write seven books, and open a large center of learning all over the world. He even taught in his passing on to the other side.

Yoganada's body remained normal 80 days after his death!

"On March 7, 1952, Paramahansa Yogananda gathered together over eight hundred people at the Forest Lawn Cemetery in Los Angeles, California. Among his guests were California's Lieutenant Governor Goodwin Knight, Binay R.Sen, then Ambassador to us from India, and many other prominent people."

Paramahansa Yogananda gave a farewell speech, and left his body on stage to the world! His body was stored in a crypt and remained at normal body temperature for 80 days. He had demonstrated the conscious exit of the body, a new level of understanding for the masses of the world. This has inspired millions of people to study his techniques at the SRF Foundation which he created for those who are interested.

"In order to teach life principles from an unbroken lineage of masters, of which Christ and his Disciples are part, there existed before Christ's time esoteric schools of thought. Most true esoteric schools test their Initiates to a stress test, whereby the Initiate can show others he has conquered the greatest lie in the universe, which of course is death."

The American Indians did this with their finest braves when they went to the top of the sacred mountain, got within a semicircle of rocks and allowed rattlesnakes to strike them again and again. (I'm sure a lot of you saw the Billy Jack movie.) The amount of curare released from one bite would destroy the form of the average person in about an hour by paralyzing the Central Nervous System (CNS), thus driving the consciousness out of their form onto what is called the astral plane. Once the CNS is paralyzed, circulation stops and oxygen cannot circulate to carry the grounding energies that are vital to the conscious mind and material body to manifest in balance with the material world. So you lose form, and uneducated beings in the material world view this as death, but a free soul knows that the consciousness of the

158

deceased is moved into a higher plane. Most Indian braves, however, survived the ordeal because they had wise teachers. A teacher's wisdom may be gazed upon by the progress and achievement of the students.

"In the Egyptian Mystery Schools, the same task was administered in the bottom of the great pyramids in a place called Chamber of the Ordeal. The Initiate entered a pyramid from an underground passageway located between it and the Sphinx. Before the Initiate could be admitted into the upper section of the pyramid, he was given a poisonous extract from a mushroom and spent seven days and nights with the Ordeal of Soul on the lower astral planes. These bands of energy in physical existence are under the Earth's surface where a consciousness manifests itself into the second etheric and into the lower astral plane. [These are the bands that are in this chamber and we'll get more into the chambers of the pyramid later on.] Modern theology is very much aware of this space and terms such spaces as Hell, Hades, Purgatory, Home of the Unrested Soul, etc. These names have been coined to express a lower feeling brought on by the misuse of the life force.

"When the initiate had conquered the passions of life by realizing the penalties involved and realizing further that God is all forgiving, he began to rise higher into the pyramid itself, into the Queen's Chamber. Here he experienced his second birth, or realized life in greater abundance. The time spent in this part of the pyramid was only three days, and then he moved upward into the King's Chamber. Before entering the sarcophagus in the King's Chamber, he went through the outer room called the Room of Triple Veils, where he learned the lesson of maya, false deceptor of the illusion, which traps us by our five senses until our sixth sense opens and frees us. Before the Initiate can realize his quest for freedom (resurrection of the spirit), he has to crawl on his hands and knees through a small passageway that leads to the King's Chamber. Here he learns that he must humble himself before he becomes exalted and 'one who exalts himself first shall be humbled.' Upon reaching the King's chamber, he has spent nine days in the pyramid, seven days below underground, two in the pyramid itself and the third day reaches the King's Chamber and understands what Christ meant when he said, 'In three days I shall build again this temple.' "

The reason the Initiate had this experience in the pyramid is because the pyramid shape itself is a representation of all of the seven levels of consciousness, and where you are located within the pyramid structure determines which level is to be experienced. The total time the Initiate spent was ten days. The first seven days signified God building creation and man attempting to destroy it through ignorance, and the last three days signify rebuilding of the temple: mind, body and spirit; so that he shall dwell in the house of the Lord forever. Now I'm not trying to get religious or anything quoting *The Death of Ignorance*. This is a spiritual input and has no connotation about a person's particular belief system. What we're doing is just quoting the facts of how things happen at a particular time and space and what this really meant.

Now it's interesting to note that he spent seven of these days below ground and three above, for a total of ten days. Christ himself was the last of the great Initiates to be initiated in the great pyramid. The teacher, master of ceremonies, or the keeper of the pyramid was called the Hierophant and it was he who handed down to the Master of Jesus the title of the Christ. This great Hierophant was called in the Bible the 'Ancient of the days.' The pyramid, in those days, was part of the magic city of Heliopolis, which was the last mystery school Christ attended before taking up his ministry when he was 29 years old. Strangely enough, just as this was Christ's last school, so it was that he was the last Initiate to take initiation in the pyramid. When Jesus left for Israel, the pyramid was sealed off and it's passageway was blocked, and the entrance to the sphinx was hidden away. The theologians of that time called it a 'Bible sealed in stone,' to be opened again only by divine appointment.

The Christ principle is in our own nature

"Today, 2,000 years later, we are beginning to realize that the Christ principle is in our own nature, and we take initiation not in a chamber inside a pyramid, but face the ordeal in life itself by taking responsibility for our actions, and forgive the irresponsible actions of others, which is sometimes quite hard to do, especially for those who are quite ignorant, by showing them a better way. Thus begins a birth of Christ within the hearts of all of us.

"A few years ago, when I was active in my studies with the Tibetans, they asked me to go through the sacred ritual in the desert, as had the American Indians a century before me. The poison they selected was strychnine and I agreed, with a little apprehension, to do this in the upper Mohave Desert in a very sacred place. It took me a year and seven days of preparation for the experience. I was ready for the ordeal, which lasted three days. During the ordeal I had to use every bit of knowledge and wisdom I had accumulated to survive and return. Sometimes I ran, sometimes I prayed, sometimes I did intensive Yogi breathing exercises. My entire life ran before me, past lives ran, future experiences here, and other worlds of consciousness became apparent. Late in the second day I knew I was winning the battle for return to civilization in my present form, and I began to experience a tremendous high, and also began to realize this entire life existence is all energy moving from one place to another, and God gave us total freedom to move this energy any way we desire. When I returned from the desert I knew I had conquered fear and was and will eternally be thankful to all my beautiful teachers for those divine moments of truth. To show my gratitude, I vowed to serve God by educating others not so fortunate as to have had the direct experience as I had. I will present these different energies as I experienced them in the metaphors for correctness to the modern school of thought that worked for me. You may see things differently, and that's what I would encourage, because beauty gains its essence in individual experience and reality becomes more real when we share our different viewpoints."

THE LOGOS

"The names 'God' and 'Logos' connote a divine being, omnipresent as the Universal Energizing Power, Indwelling Life and Directing Intelligence within all substance, all beings and all things, separate from none. This being is manifest through our solar system as Divine law, power, wisdom, love and Truth, beauty, justice and order." Justice and order deal with the sciences, terrestrial and extraterrestrial, they all come together at one point.

"The Solar Logos is regarded as immanent within and transcendent beyond His System, of which he is the threefold 'Creator,' sustainer and regenerator of all worlds and the spiritual parent of all beings. [This statement deals with understanding we are all cells in the greater being.] Whether as a principle or being, God has been conceived in many aspects and as playing many roles, ancient Egyptian, Hellenic, Hebrew, Hindu, and Christian cosmogonies represent Him as bringing His worlds into existence by means of the creative power of sound [I wrote this in *The Death of Ignorance* in 1979, and now today we use sound combined with laser light to create this consciousness.] Then God spake and in six creative epochs, or 'days,' each followed by a period of quiescence or 'night,' all worlds, all kingdoms of Nature and all beings came into existence. As a result of this outpouring of creative energy as sound, forms appeared expressive of the divine creative Intent, embodiments of divine life and vehicles for divine intelligence. Thus God may be conceived as a celestial composer, divine musician, perpetually composing and performing his creative symphony, with its central theme and

160

myriad variations.

"God has also been poetically and mystically described as divine Dancer. Nature, with all its varied, rhythmic motions, including the cyclic swing of planets around the sun, terrestrial changes, the flow of rivers, waterfalls and streams, the ceaseless movement of the ocean waves, the swaying of the trees and flowers, the ever-changing forms of fire and flame. The motions of electrons around their nuclei, is conceived, notably in Hinduism, as part of the great dance of the supreme by which all things are created and sustained.

"A man's idea of God is the image of blinding light that he sees reflected in the concave mirror of his own soul, and yet it is not in very truth God, but only His reflection. His glory is there, but it is the light of his own spirit that man sees, and it is all he can bear to look upon. The clearer the mirror, the brighter will be the Divine image. But the external world cannot be witnessed in the same moment. In the ecstatic Yogis, in the illuminated seer, the spirit will shine like the noon-day sun; in the debased victim of earthly attraction, the radiance has disappeared, for the mirror is obscured with stains of matter.

"From these concepts of deity there emerges inevitability the idea of divine purpose, a great plan. That plan is assumed throughout *The Death of Ignorance* to be evolution, but not of form alone. The word 'evolution' is herein used to connote a process which is dual in operation, spiritual as well as material, and directed rather than purely natural or 'blind.'" There is a freedom, and this is what a lot of people have trouble understanding, there's this freedom between what is ordained and what is preordained in their lives and what control they have.

"This process is understood to consist of a continuous development of form accompanied by a complementary and parallel unfolding of consciousness within the form.

"Although man cannot completely know the evolutionary plan from his superiors, sages and spiritual teachers, throughout the ages he learns that the motive is to awaken and bring to fulfillment that which is latent, seed-like, germinal. Divine will, divine wisdom, divine intellect and divine beauty are latent in all seeds, macrocosmic and microcosmic. The apparent purpose for which the universe comes into existence is to change the potentialities into actively manifested powers.

"On Earth, for example, for each of the kingdoms of nature there is a standard or ideal which is dual, as is the evolutionary process. The ideal for consciousness in the mineral kingdom is a physical awareness, and for form, hardness and beauty. For plant consciousness the ideal is sensitivity, capacity to feel, and for the plant form, beauty. For animal consciousness it is self-consciousness of feeling and thought, and for animal form it is beauty. For man the evolutionary goal is the complete unfoldment and expression of his inherent divine powers–will to omnipotence, wisdom to omnipresence, and intellect to omniscience. In the perfect man or adept, these powers are expressed in a fully conscious unity, and therefore in perfect cooperation with the Creator in honor of the fulfillment of His plan."

Basically I believe we should all strive for the Adept stage, the Master stage. And what is necessary to fulfill this self-mastery is the temple or a body that can realize the full awakening potential of our inherent spirit that we all possess. No one has a greater spirit than anyone else. Some are just more developed, more conscious, in the physical life than others. The extraterrestrial sciences truly assist us in this area by allowing our body the flexibility to pursue its normal path into this higher consciousness. But unfortunately the environment is so badly polluted that it detracts from the Divine plan preordained for all of us.

"If we consider the Logos as The Musician and the continuous process of creation as the performance of a great symphony [remember music is considered a universal language],

> Creation...
> the per-
> formance
> of a great
> symphony!

then this, 'The great work,' He conceived and developed in earlier creative 'Days,' and perchance perfected it in the silence and darkness of the intermediate, creative 'Night.' When once there is to be light, He 'speaks' by the power of his 'Word' all things into being. This first expression of the 'motif' of the new universe is 'heard' or responded to by virgin matter, and the planes of nature with their forms and inhabitants gradually appear. Into these, the logos pours forth perpetually His Life that they may live, this being his continuous sacrifice, his everlasting obligation."

So it is in essence of the Spirit of this greater Entity, the universe, the galaxies, that their aura fields keep our physical bodies and spiritual bodies alive. When we delve further into the ET meditations, and the science part of it, you'll get in touch with the actual different divisions or categories of this Power itself. Right now I'm just presenting an overview.

"The Logos or Verbum is, in reality, no word or voice of any being; it is Pure will expressive of the presumed purpose of intent of the Divine Father-Mother in bringing forth the Universe. It is the irresistible, all pervasive, inherent impulse to self-expression, expansion (hence the name of Brahma from the Sanskrit word, birth, to expand and grow), and fullness, which reigns at the heart of all Nature and all creation from the highest to the lowest. It is the will to fullness which 'sounds forth' at that cosmic moment when the divine ideation is first emanated as will-light from the absolute." And you're going to find that out in our meditation in a little bit.

"Throughout the Cosmic days and years to follow, that will-light calls into existence the sun, planets, and beings in obedience to law. Level after level and plane after plane of increasing density come into existence and gradually embody and show forth the will-light. Monads flash forth their rays, beings are emanated and inhabit the planes. Deeper and deeper penetrates the Cosmic will-thought-Word, awakening the sleeping substance, forcing its atoms to answer, to embody, echo, or resound the cosmic word. The light shines forth from the center to illumine the darkness and render visible the heretofore invisible robes in which the All-Mother is enwrapped.

"The universal 'word' when uttered becomes manifest as myriads of chords, each a coherent self-existent sound with its force and light manifestations." Remember, we mentioned how light and sound work together? And how they work via a basic frequency in the body? Everybody has a central frequency which is determined by the length of the DNA, which is 39.5 inches, and the individual parts of the body use individual notes whose sound manifests this power into the oneness, the beingness that we all are.

"Each chord appears as a relatively changeless, abstract form, Archetype or divine idea, in the higher worlds of the plants. These archetypes in their turn sound their 'word,' 'relaying' into the lower worlds the primal word-Force. Magnetic fields are set up therein, matter is drawn into them and, with the aid of the Gods, is molded into evolving forms. These forms, vivified by divine life, become the abode of intelligences, which is the Monads, and the mineral, plant, animal, human and super-human phases of development."

And the extraterrestrials, by the way, are very respectful of nature. The Pleiadians, for example, look at horticulture as the way of life closest to God, and even though they have this tremendously long lifespan, they have done amazing things with horticulture and raising of plants. In their spare time, they all have gardens that they work. Their spaceships—some of which have hulls grown like huge mushroom-shaped plants—they inject with a resin before they harvest them, which makes them hard like steel, light as aluminum, which they then can use as a spaceship fuselage or hull. I remember when Leo Fender and Fender Music Instruments of Fullerton, California, one time used to inject trees with a certain dye which causes the trees to grow with a color within the woodgrain. Later he would harvest the trees, and within the rings of the trees would be the different colors from the different dyes. They used them to make the most beautiful veneers for the guitars, calling them the "wildwood" series.

Pleiadians do similar things in nature; they can color woods before they are ever harvested and they can cause things to grow into specific, usable shapes. And then they can increase the density of this naturally growing organism from a soft plant solid to hardness many times that of steel by injecting certain kinds of resins at the right moment.

"As a result of the experience in the forms, these intelligences, assisted by the Gods, gradually unfold their intimate innate faculties and powers until the degree of development set both for them and for the forms has been attained. The Gods are thus conceived both as builders of form and assistants in the evolution of consciousness.

"When this standard has been reached by all beings and, in obedience to the law of cycles, the time limit of objective manifestation has been attained, the whole solar system is withdrawn into subjective state. In this condition it remains until under the same cyclic law it reappears and the process of development or ascent is continued from the point reached at the close of the preceding period of objective manifestation. Occult philosophy sees this process as continuing indefinitely, there being no limit to the evolutionary possibilities. This orderly progression has no conceivable beginning and no imaginable end."

What we're stating is that the universe is not silent, and creation is not in the linear time-frame that it appears to be. The universe and the galaxies are solid and present one minute, then disappear into nothing the next minute, and then a second later they resolidify again, and so on. There's a "day" and "night" period in the entire existence of the universe, yourself and everything else around. And when you start to realize this, you begin to get free of the illusion, because you can start to tune into these moments of non-manifestation, and recognize your power. How do you think that Yogis, for example, become invisible, or Christ was able to demonstrate walking through a wall? This is possible by realization and working through it, but to the ego or the imagination that is not aware of the fact that creation is rising and falling, or you could say in another term, "Breathing," there is no awareness of these freedoms, these motions that one can move into. Even some powerful magicians and illusion artists get in touch with this energy field, which is like a day and a night, day and a night, happening millions of times per second, an actual vibration. Your heart has a vibratory rate; everything in the universe has a vibratory rate. Gravity has one, and when you discover what the vibratory rate is, you can operate outside its vibratory principles and become free of it.

> **Everything has a vibratory rate**

"From the solar Gods it passes through to their lesser brothers, rank upon rank, until it reaches the physical worlds. There, with the assistance of nature spirits, it throws matter into shapes conceived by the creative mind. [I am referring to creative energies when I say "it".] The capacity of sound to produce forms may perhaps find support from sonorous figures which can be formed by the vibrations of substance emitting a musical tone. Geometrical figures are, for example, formed by sand on a plate of glass or metal when the bow of a violin is drawn along the edge. Ernst Florens Friedrich Chladni (1756-1827), a German physicist, produced geometrical acoustical figures which were formed by the nodal lines in a sound-actuated vibrating plate, made visible by sprinkling sand on the plate—where it settles is on the lines of least resistance. Jules A. Lissajous, a French scientist, produced figures formed by curves due to the combination of two simple harmonic motions. They are commonly exhibited by the successive reflections of a beam of light from the prongs of two tuning forks, or by the mechanical tracing of the resultant motion of two pendulums as in a harmonograph, or by means of Wheatstone's rods. Lissajous also produced figures given by a horizontal and a vertical tuning fork vibrating simultaneously. These figures differ when the forks used are either in unison or at varying differences of phase or notes apart. If the capacity of physical sound to produce forms may also be attributed to sonorous, creative energy or word force emitted at super physical levels, then the Logos Doctrine finds some scientific support."

You can try to create geomectric forms

The experiment just described looks like this: use a 12-inch by 12-inch piece of glass or mirror. Place the glass or mirror flat on top of a one-inch diameter wooden pedestal on a table, so that the base of the wood is glued onto the table top, or fastened to it with a vise, and the top supports the center of the square foot piece of glass. Then sprinkle sand on it, and vibrate the glass on its edge by moving up and down with a violin bow, and you'll observe different geometric shapes forming. This brings us to the Fibonacci series, in which you'll see the mathematical order of the pyramids. This vibrating energy field starts to form and define shapes which then you recognize, if you'll look around, in a snail shell and other surprising places. You'll begin to see that there is a compelling natural order to all things, which I think is crucial to understand.

The extraterrestrials, in their teachings on their own planet (you'll remember I mentioned that the Pleiadians go to school for almost 120 of our years), teach about how energy fields around different objects work, and they get in touch with these concepts by the time they're in their teens, which is about 115 to 120 terran years old. The Pleiadians have begun an understanding of nature herself, and man, of course, lost his ability to deal with nature a long time ago when he fell from the grace of God.

A pyramid is the final shape energy assumes before it forms cells

Discussing the pyramid shape itself – the pyramid is a collector of all these different forces we've outlined, forces that originate from different planes of existence. We consider the pyramid as the final shape that the energy assumes before it builds and connects to other atoms that form molecules that form cells. And from an intellectual point-of-view, you could define pyramid energy as a progressive energy transfer through geometric focusing and dynamic electrical amplification over a measured plane of coordinates. This defined into simple lay terms means that the pyramid shape is one of the four building blocks of man and the surrounding universe.

If you were to look at a Nuclear Receptor we've been developing, you would notice on the face of the Receptor a pattern that is formed by not only the positioning, but also the size of the different pyramids. This arrangement conforms to what science calls the Fibonacci (Phi) Curve.

If you were to look at a single pyramid, such as one found in the Super Receptor or a Headgear Pyramid, or even the Great Pyramid in Egypt, you would discover a couple of interesting facts:

1. If the ratio of the height of the pyramid to its apex is compared to the radius of a circle, then divided into the distance around the Pyramid's base, the result is pi (π).

2. If you wound a coil around the pyramid starting at the top and continuing to its base, the ratio of the length of the coil as it varies from turn to turn would define Phi, or the Fibonacci Series. Named after Leonardo Bigollo Fibonacci (circa 1179), this series of numbers defines the natural order of growth from cells to the order of petals on a rose. The numbers progress 1, 2, 3, 5, 8, 13, 21, etc. the arrangement and sizes of the Pyramids on the Receptor face also are placed according to the Fibonacci Series.

164

The series is unique in the fact that its value, written as "Phi" can be determined. The Phi equals 1/2 of the square root of five over two. A Fibonacci series of numbers is determined in the following manner:

Each succeeding number is determined by the sum of the two preceding numbers, beginning with the lowest whole number. Thus:

$$1 + 2 = 3,$$
$$2 + 3 = 5,$$
$$3 + 5 = 8,$$
$$5 + 8 = 13,$$
$$8 + 13 = 21,$$
$$21 + 13 = 34,$$

and so on. And all of these succeeding terms then define a pattern, for example, leaves on a plant, kernels on a pine cone, or buds on a pineapple. We find there are two things occurring: The leaves, kernels and buds all rotate around the central axis in a clockwise and counter-clockwise direction, and the numbers of leaves in any one direction is always different from the distribution in the other direction. The difference is always according to the Fibonacci number system. For example, if one pine cone contains 21 kernels in the clockwise direction, there could be 34 in the counterclockwise direction. A sunflower may have 21 kernels in a clockwise direction and 55 in the other direction. These ratios are also incorporated as Phi in dimensions of all living things.

Even if you look at Leonardo da Vinci's work, which I discuss in *Death of Ignorance*, you'll see the divine section of man being defined. The human spine also can be developed into these periods of energy starting at the base of the spine and working up. The mathematics of the vertebrae going up the spine correspond to the number of spokes in a Chakra, and the Chakra, if you remember, goes in opposite directions, and starts to form the same series. The Great Pyramid is the only structure known that incorporates the ratio of Phi into one building. This makes it all the more unique as the ratios of Phi are not supposed to have been known when the pyramid was supposed to have been constructed.

The Great Pyramid: only known structure to incorporate the ratio of PHI into one building

Pi (π) is a magical, mystical, unending number: 1.618033989. This number so fascinated the artists during the Renaissance that they spent most of their time exploring endless possibilities and utilizing its ratios in their paintings and sculpting. Modern architects have been found it to be a very pleasing ratio in building design. So this gives you the concept of Pi (π).

Besides Pi (π), the measurement of the circumference of a circle can also be found in the pyramid. Now this is something I should mention, too, because people often confuse two things together when we talk about pi. Don't get pi, designating the ratio of the circumference of a circle to its diameter, 3.1415926..., mixed up with Phi. If you have a six-foot base pyramid, the apex will be two-thirds the base length above the surface of the ground plane of the pyramid. People become confused and think a ten-foot base pyramid is ten feet tall. No, a ten-foot pyramid is about seven feet tall. If you multiply this height by two, and divide the answer into the entire base circumference, your solution will be the mathematical unit called pi. This is used to compute the diameter of the circle. The number is always 3.1415926... and can never be rounded out. This means a true circle cannot exist in one plane, energy or consequence.

What are the implications of this? **The pyramid mathematically forms a circle, but this circle mathematically never comes to an end.** We're actually forming a spiral, so the force spiraling around the pyramid is being defined by Phi, larger at the bottom and smaller at the top. Mathematically, it is vibrating. The Phi series, which predicts the number of units in each row of a pine cone or other natural spiral, where a row will have 35 and the next one will have 54 kernels, is mathematically progressive; so the pyramid structure is a vibrating form that's mathematically progressive. It's fascinating to put the mathematics together and connect them with the fact that **the pyramid is the shape of the carbon atom in the red blood cell, the iron atom in the body.** When you begin to comprehend the incredible functionality of the pyramid structure in the human body itself, all the pieces of the puzzle start to fall together.

In this next phase, written by Scott Wolf, Scott will discuss more spiritual aspects and other points as well.

Chapter 20

Spirituality, Vedic Science, and the Aura as Light Emanating from the Soul

by Dr. Bell's friend, Scott Wolf

I'm going to describe to you the ancient signs of neuro-life illumination and its relation to the UFO extraterrestrial phenomena. This science has been taught directly to me by aural sound vibration from the ancient masters of the Sanskrit Vedas, the oldest body of knowledge on the Earth's planet. The Vedas were originally not written down until approximately 10,000 years ago in the Sanskrit language. It was revealed in the language of the Gods, and originally the knowledge was passed in a strictly disciplined succession from guru to disciple, telepathically. Now in the modern UFO phenomena, we find this happening quite frequently, where people report a telepathic communication, and indeed some of the reports that we hear about extraterrestrials being captured by the government, report extraterrestrials communicating telepathically by putting people in a trance and then speaking through them.

This was particularly the case with Lt. Col. Robert Friend, who was head of the *Project Blue Book*, the government's secret project, when he was visited by the three beings, Krill, Alamar and Afa. He described in a tape that in 1952 a woman from Maine had said that she had received telepathic communication from aliens. Of course at that time, Project Blue Book was checking out any potentially serious UFO phenomena. They met with the woman in an abandoned warehouse just near the Capitol building in Washington, DC. The woman went into a trance and started revealing highly technological information that she couldn't have possibly known. Later, the extraterrestrial speaking through her told her they were willing to transmit the information through one of the lieutenant colonels who was present. One of the colonels volunteered and immediately went into a trance through the power of the extraterrestrials. With his Adam's apple moving up and down, he rapidly began to describe highly technological information.

Later, they asked if they could see a UFO as proof these were beings that were claiming to be from Uranus on an intergalactic mission. The group moved to the window and saw a UFO hovering right outside. The building, like I mentioned, was an abandoned warehouse between the Capitol Building in Washington, DC and this area. The area had been blanked out on the radar, and there was no signal that they could receive, because they had checked right on the spot there.

Going back to the office they discussed this incident with Lt. Col. Robert Friend, who, as I mentioned, was head of Project Blue Book, and again one of the lieutenants went into a

> **Telepathic incident experienced by head of project blue book**

trance and received telepathic information. So, by incidents like these that we have documented evidence of occurring, and the spoken testimony of Lt. Robert Friend and others, we know that telepathic information is being transmitted by the extraterrestrials. So, the ancient Vedic Signs of neuro-life illumination were originally given in a telepathic way in a strict disciplined session from guru to disciple.

True ecstasy is the sought-after goal of each conscious unit in creation. Everything that we see around us is a conscious unit of creation. They experience growth, maintenance and eventually death, and the presence of the soul inside of each conscious unit gives it its life form. A close examination of each motivated action from every unit of consciousness beyond the normal survival functions, such as in the case of humans and animals: eating, sleeping, procreating, and defense, shows that ecstasy via the nervous system as the feeling function of the body is the true motivating factor of existence. Why perform the repetitiveness of life, be it work, recreation, romance or parenting or whatever it is a person does, with all their con-comitant struggles to various degrees, without the vital result of true ecstasy and happiness? If we can oblige ourselves sufficiently to do at least a preliminary study of the following proposed argument regarding natural ecstasy, then we will do ourselves a great favor and service.

Now please try to understand that when I describe ecstasy here, I am not talking about ordinarily what often is interpreted as ecstasy, such as sexual ecstasy. However, I will be talking about the vital centers of the body and how they are connected with these life energies that are associated with sexuality and orgasm. I am speaking of ecstasy, or what is known in Sanskrit as ananda, in a higher level of understanding that transcends the lower functions of the lower Chakra centers. Because of society's total lack of experience in combination with its actual taboo against ecstasy, it's no great surprise that the amount of available literature describing, and henceforth arguing for ecstasy, is very limited. Society, as a conforming unit of suffering, or at best a complacent tolerance for standard life joys, such as sports, recreation, family, resists true esoteric ecstasy because of the overall lack of proper teaching facilities and also because of the soul's eternal influence of the deluded potency, which is otherwise known as Maya, a separation, the curtain, the known life, the doubt and the contraction that is in all of us. The general stimulus of the world and, indeed, the self-inflicted cloud of denial of our very real and ecstatic nature as consciousness, has thwarted the plans of all but the greatest of seekers.

To project ourselves beyond the hopes of non-illuminated life, non-ecstatic existence, will be the truly human goal of life, to feel the full force of charm and the sweetness released to the soul rather than to merely exist in economic development, population increasing and various types of recreation. In its natural condition, it must now become the priority goal of existence rather than mere existence in search of an "answer" to satisfy our insatiable mind and intellect. The mind and intellect are constantly seeking to satisfy themselves in a world of infinite expansion. But true ecstasy, true happiness, true satisfaction comes not by adding or pasting on an additional form of intellectual stimulation, but in merely realizing our living action condition as ecstasy.

In the ancient Vedas, the soul, or the being living within the body, is described as Saht Chit Ananda. Now for those of you who have not studied this course from my book, *The Death of Ignorance*, there the beginning course in that book called, "UFO Extraterrestrial Cultures and World Governments." Please read that book first before proceeding and do the experiment inside of the book that I give about perceiving yourself as illumination, as the being behind the body, the mind and the ego. First do that and read that section in the book before moving further. What I am going to describe further is how to connect with that ecstasy and how to experience yourself as ecstasy.

There is a verse from the Bhagavadgita, which is the primary scripture of the ancient Vedas, that is spoken directly by the Supreme Personality of God. He says, "In order to enter into mysteries of Yoga and the Universe, you must become my friend as well as my devotee." So God is saying, "Become my friend, become devoted to me and I will allow you to enter into the mysteries of the Universe."

Now the astounding thing about this verse is that we often think of the environment as perhaps a cold, mysterious, large, black, infinite universe with billions of stars and galaxies, and possibly, for those of you who are just beginning to study this subject, extraterrestrial cultures, but in the ancient times many of these extraterrestrial beings were known to come to Earth and participate in Earthly activity, and they are described elaborately in the Vedas. The ancient flying machines that are described in the Vedas go back 10,000 years ago, when they were first recorded in the the Vemonic Asastra as being shown part of the Remayan and some of the other ancient scriptures. I'll be describing some of these later.

I'm describing the teachings of the Neuro Life Illuminations from the Vedas because this is a very ancient Earth science that has been on this planet for a long, long time. We don't want you to feel like you're being assaulted with too much information that is so intergalactic that it doesn't ring home for you. What we cover here must be something that you can apply in your life and help you become more connected with your own inner ecstasy. Now, the process of life illumination is so beautiful because it takes who and what you are now and helps you to understand that your existence as individual spirit or soul is made up of what the Veda describes as "Sat Chit Ananda," which is knowledge, eternity and ecstacy, or blissfulness. The Vedas also refer to ecstacy or bliss as the food for Sat and Chit, which is knowledge, and feelings of eternity, which are usually brought up during periods of meditation or periods where there is a lot of elation in your life. But Ananda is the living condition and it is experienced neurologically through the nervous system.

> Flying machines— Yemanas— described in ancient Indian literature (The Vedas)

You see, we are so conditioned to experience ourselves in a limited way, a way that is possibly full of pain or problems or dilemmas, that we never get a glimpse beyond the state where dilemmas don't exist. We see ourselves as the primal energy/force of ecstasy living behind the dilemmas, behind the dramas that keep us back from feeling our total unity and our real self in connection with the universe.

Now if you take a drop of water, for example, out of the ocean, and you put it under a microscope, you will find that that drop has all the same chemical constituents as the entire ocean. The chemical constituents of water are there, and salt, and other trace elements are in the drop just as they are in the entire ocean. So similarly, the individual soul, the Ghiva spirit particle which is Sat Chit Ananda Ghiva as described in the ancient Sanskrit, is a drop of the infinite ocean of Godhead or the Supreme Being, the Supreme universal form of God, and these individual drops, by examining themselves, can discover that we are indeed ecstacy in our original condition, and we always were ecstacy and we always are ecstacy. By connecting with this, we will be able to outshine all the lower dramas and all the lower dilemmas that plague the psycho-physical form, or the body/mind.

> Outshine all the lower dramas

There is a verse from the Sermon Baghavatan, spoken by the Sage Vidhivihas, describing at the conclusion of this great scripture a message to humanity, which is:

"The Baghavatan is considered by all great saints, Yogis and spiritual masters of the Vedic Disaplix Succession, the Sampra Dias, to be the essential conclusive wisdom of Vedic thought and aspiration."

In this verse, which is indeed the concluding revelation, it is indicated that to enter the highest plane of reality, we must become submissive to God as the highest being whose spiritual form and abode transcends all of our limited conceptions and powers of knowledge.

Often we give credit to our own mind as being capable of perceiving the highest limits of thought and wisdom, assuming that somehow, by our own limited experience, we can analyze all the things that are presented before us in their entirety. Of course, the foolishness of this idea becomes obvious when we consider how even though we put so much emphasis on our own limited sense perception, we are constantly experiencing the futility and limits of those senses. For example, right now, if the sun and the moon weren't present, the public electrical source failed, and there were no candles or flashlights, you wouldn't even be able to read. So you would see that the limits of your auditory, visual and other sensory capabilities would limit you automatically just by being in the psycho-physical form, which is the body. So although we stress seeing something as proof of its existence, we are constantly reminded of the finite limits of our physical senses. The mind, according to the Vedas, is considered to be the sixth sense, and it also has similar limitations. And so, to prepare ourselves for the path of the Neuro Life Illumination Yoga, we must first learn that to understand our limits of perception is the beginning of transcending our limits of perception.

Believe it or not, this understanding will actually lead us to a higher awareness in the future. To simply sit down and admit, "Yes, I, as an unlimited spirit/soul, as a Ghiva Atma, I have an unlimited capacity, but I am sitting in a body and a mind. I am sitting in this body and mind which have limited sensory capacity, limited auditory capacity, and limited visual capacity." Often when I am lecturing around the world on the UFO phenomena, people say, "Have you seen a UFO before?" And it's easy for me to say yes, because I indeed have. I have seen physical UFOs – in one case one of them followed me out to the forest up in the Sequoias in Northern California. It was quite an amazing experience.

Often people say, "Well, I liked your lecture, I see the documents you are presenting. It all looks pretty good, but unless I see one, I won't believe it." Well, of course, it's only natural that they say "seeing is believing," but you know in the higher wisdom, believing is also seeing. We have to understand that the ocean of faith is crossed with the boat of knowledge, but we are always on the ocean of faith. We have faith that when we come to a red light that it will turn green, we have faith that the green light will mean that the opposing traffic will stop for us. We put our faith in that. We put our faith in the government, and ultimately we put our faith constantly in our own sensory experience, which, as I've already demonstrated to you, is very limited. So, if we actually ride on the boat of faith of the higher intuition, by understanding that we are in a body that is limited by the senses, including the mind, and limited by the form itself, we will be able to get a clear understanding of who we are as our unlimited self, or the Ghiva Atma, the soul within the body that permeates the whole body.

So this is a proper understanding in preparation to bring us to the path of what I call Nadasingha Yoga, or Neuro Life Illumination. Nadasingha refers to, in ancient India, a Lion God. There is a deity of God in India known as Nadasingha, who exists in the form of a lion, so in this path of Nadasingha Yoga, we've got to bring the Lion God, or the form of the lion power, down into us.

The Lion Power

The Lion God is all that we have right now. All that can protect us is Lion Power, because in the ancient times the Nadasingha appeared out of a pillar to challenge Haranukashipu, a very powerful Yogi who was ruling the universe in a corrupt way for his own personal gratification. He had become so powerful that all the gods from throughout the universe had given him the boon that he had requested, "May I never die in the land, the air, or the sea." So the

170

great God, Nadasingha, burst out of a pillar, laid the Yogi on his lap with his claws, tore open his chest and destroyed the demon, Haranukashipu. This story is symbolic of how the actual power of Nadasingha, or the power of God in the form of a Lion, can enter us to destroy all obstacles, including those which we often present to ourselves through our own action. So this Nadasingha Yoga, or Neuro Life Illumination, can really help us in this.

Next, within the limited jurisdiction of our sensory perception, we come to primal forces that are working to influence us through the senses, and they're known as the modes of natures, or in Sanskrit, the Guddhas. Now the Guddhas function in 3 different ways; the function known as Sahtva Guddha, which is the positive mode of goodness; the Raja Guddha, which is the passion, or inertia, of maintenance; and the Tama Guddha, which is the force of density and ignorance. Often, whenever we do various things, we see how these modes are mixed and influencing

Nadasingha Yoga, the ancient science of transcendental Near Guddha Bakti, where the aspirant transcends the mode of nature in practice and acquires his Baktii, or love, that is described in the Baghavatan verse that we spoke of, is love for God by seeing that he is the greatest being in the world, and that we are part of that universal conception. We must realize that we have limited perception in perceiving him because he is so great and so awesome. He created the whole universe, including all the UFO phenomena, the intergalactic beings and races, all were expansions out of this supreme personality of God and the supreme personality of the universe. Persons associated with this higher mode of Near Guddha Bakti find the lower tendencies begin to drop off, while at the same time they will be able to experience ecstacy, or this Near Guddha Bakti that we are describing. We will see ourselves as a unit of consciousness described in the Baghavatan as Saht Chit Ananda, and ultimately this Saht Chit Ananda feeling, the essence of which I hope you are understanding.

We are ecstacy. We always already were ecstacy from the beginning of creation up through all our forgetfulness of what has been up to now. We hopefully are reuniting and remembering who we really are. To remember is to become again a member of the organization of ecstacy, the life illumination network of ecstacy and to enter into deep intensive practice of this. In another verse, the Supreme Being describes the Vermon, where, "The light surrounding me is coming from the aura of my body. And it is the abode of eternity, happiness and ecstacy."

In this verse from the Ghita, the Supreme Being is describing that he has a body made of spiritual or near-Guddha elements. Similarly, although we are wearing a material body, we also are exhibiting an aura which is the light of our soul, and can be recorded photographically. It is the light from the soul, the Ghiva Atma, seeping through the skin of the body. In a funny way it's just like little kids putting a flashlight in their mouths, or behind an old blanket or sheet, playing monsters. The light shines red when covered by the mouth, and is completely shielded by the cloth. Similarly, this soul inside of our body is light, and of course the more we develop it, the brighter it shines. Through this understanding of Neuro Life Illumination, the light permeates through the nervous system and out through the skin. And that is the aura that we perceive, what we sense when we say we can feel another person's aura. We're feeling the brightness of that person's soul. We can even perceive, with a certain kind of sixth vision or sense, the light coming out of their body through the skin.

Make your soul shine bright

According to the Vedas, the soul, or the Ghiva Atma, although transcendentally situated within the body, lives within the heart, and is experienced through the kundalini electrical system, which was originally transplanted into the body at the time of creation. "God blew the breath of life into our nostrils at the time of creation." This is the Bible's description of the soul and the electrical kundalini system. The breath of life, or the soul, the electrical system, was transplanted exactly at the moment of conception. When the sperm and the ovum connected, God breathed the life into the being and transplanted into the physical body this electrical system, which later develops into a full spinal system that runs the whole body through the neurological system.

The seven energy centers, or poles, are the key awareness centers of the body, rising from the lower chakra areas–the chakra in the groin area, which represents sexual energy, all the way through the pineal gland in the Third Eye, as it is often described, to the Brumurandra Crown Chakra at the top of the head. Yogis of the past would study for literally decades under the strict guidance of a guru, their teacher, and they would be able to push the soul up through these energy centers and out through the top of the head and travel to different planets and astral planes.

Veda Knowledge proven

Ironically, people in America who practice Yoga on a smaller scale, 10 or 20 years or whatever, just a short time, have experiences of being able to astral project. It's quite common in the New Age world for people to discuss astral projection. The thing that excites me about the UFO phenomenon and why I interconnect it with the Veda Knowledge is that the Vedas described many of these locas or astral planets thousands of years ago, including material things, too, that have since been measured by modern astronomy. The Vedas describe travels through different planets by the Yogis. Now we have the extraterrestrial phenomena, where we are actually seeing real proof of beings coming apparently from other worlds and other dimensions to interact with our world here. I feel this validates the reality of the Veda of Knowledge, and this is what I like about it.

Prior to the UFO phenomena becoming well-known, many people believed that the Yoga system was strictly for health or improving your diet, or your sex life or whatever. The true purpose of Yoga is to connect with the universe. However, the general opinion has been that this talk about astral travel and everything is like a fairy tale — just imagination. The presence of the UFO phenomena brings the concept of astral travel third-dimensionally demonstrable. In other words, we can see physical evidence such as photos and videotape of UFOs.

The original science of the Vedas used to be transmitted telepathically, as I mentioned to you before. Then this Age, known as Kali Yuga, started about 5,000 years ago. It is more "dense," so the ancient Vedas had to be written down in Sanskrit so we could have this teaching transmitted. During my course of studies over the last 16 years, I have had personal association with my teachers in the ancient disaplixic sessions, the Sambradis. They have verbally transmitted this teaching to me as we sat in India along the banks of the Gangis, and in the jungles of Puris. I have had the electrical transmission of this ancient Veda teaching brought to me. And I wish to share it with all of those who are interested in this.

From 1980 to 1985 I hosted a very exciting television show, Insights. We had a large number of viewers every week who participated with us as we described the process of transforming our lives into ecstacy through the teaching of the ancient Vedas and through the understanding of the modern UFO phenomenon. We wanted to convey that the universe is genuinely alive and personal, and that this ancient teaching is authentic.

An interesting part of the ancient Vedas is that they describe aerial devices known as Vemanas that were used by beings such as Lord Brahma, Lord Krishna and others to fly to other universes and galaxies. The scholars who were studying the Vedas thought that this must be some kind of myth. I'm going to give you just a brief history of the Vemanas and some of the things

172

that happened with them, so that at least you'll know that the extraterrestrial science of physical, third-dimensional flying craft goes back to ancient times.

A number of literary works contain either references to graphic aerial flight or to the mechanism of the aerial vehicles used in the old ages of India. These works were researched in '68 and later published around 1973 through the International Academy of Sanskrit Research in Maysoru, India, and the Vemonic Asastra were brought to light by various people who were involved in their studies. There were references to vehicles capable of going through the air with living beings on board, either mortals or Gods, as were described in the Vedas. Often the Gods or the Demigods were extraterrestrial beings that were living on earth. There are many references to this. It's found in the written Veda, in the hymns addressed to the twin Ash Vedas, the Rupus and other deities who were considered to be the sons of the architects of the universe.

The stories from the Vedas are a fascinating history of how creation began and how the original Demigods and extraterrestrial beings came to this plane. There were huge jugyas, or sacrifices, made for them. These would attract extraterrestrial beings from the other parts of the galaxies. Two thousand years ago, when Lord Buddha came to the Earth, he stopped all the vedic sacrifices and the Demigods, then the extraterrestrial beings of the really high nature, stopped coming here. Buddha described the Vedas as not important and not necessary. He did that because the Vedas were being used to sacrifice animals without the proper performance of mantras, the Veda invocations. It became a debauchery of animal slaughter and degradation. So Buddha came to refute the Vedas and try to erase their significance for the purpose of establishing his doctrine of Ahimsa, or nonviolence, to try to save the poor animals that were being sacrificed.

Of course when these jugyas, or sacrifices, were stopped, the Demigods and other higher beings from the universe stopped coming to the Earth planet.

When I was in India in 1989, I went to the sacred city of Rendaben, where Krishna actually grew up and lived his past times on Earth. I talked to some very old Holy Men there, and this is a very interesting story for those of you who have followed the UFO phenomenon. You may remember the book, "Chariot of the Gods" by Erich Von Daniken. That was one of the original books that kind of started the whole search into the UFO phenomena and the mysteries around Krishna and Rama and the Vemanas, etc. Well, when I first approached these old Sadus, these old saintly people in Rendaben, I showed them some pictures of UFOs and they said, "Oh, Devaroth." Deva means God and roth means vehicle or carriage. So I described these things and they kind of laughed and they said, "Oh, they come here all the time to the birthplace of Sri Krishna, to feel the energy of the birthplace of Sri Krishna." To them it was a common thing seeing these, what they described as Devaroth. Now Devaroth literally translated means Chariot of the Gods.

They were described as possessing speed faster than the mind. This aerial vehicle was triangular, large, three-tiered (which means three levels), uneven, and was piloted by at least three persons. It had three wheels that were probably withdrawn during flight. In one burst the chariot is said to have three columns. It was generally made of one of the three kinds of metals — gold, silver or iron — but the metal most commonly used was gold, and the Vedic text described it as being for the purpose of making the craft look beautiful. Long rivets were attached to it to close off the layers of the craft and the chariot contained honey or liquid that was served to the beings who would ride in the craft, which moved like a bird in the sky, soaring toward the sun and the moon.

It used to come down to the Earth with a "great sound." The great sounds that are asso-

"Chariot of the Gods"

ciated with these spacecraft are referred to in modern UFO literature just as it is described in the ancient Veda. The "chariot" had three types of "food," or liquid fuel, in three tanks placed above. A fourth vessel was filled with soma rossa. Now soma rossa, believe it or not, is an ancient psychedelic liquid taken from a special plant that is very rare. It grows high in the Himalayas in India. It's practically impossible to find now. The Yogis would take it in ancient rituals after practicing austerity for a long time, and they would travel out of their bodies. According to the Vedas, this soma rossa, this liquid beverage, was available on the Vemana, probably for the purpose of helping the people on it be prepared when the craft would pick up speed or travel to different dimensions, to be able to dematerialize their bodies at a quicker rate.

In describing the Vemana, we have different astounding descriptions of their parts. They had names for all the different parts, and their exact descriptions, which lends credibility to the existence of these objects. I'll just describe a few of them — there are over 50 of them. One part was known as Vispakriyan Dharpana, possibly a telescope-like instrument for viewing various actions of the world. There was a Chakyakarshnantra, which was a "mirror for attracting energy." In other words, there was a mirror-like device that attracted energy, possibly solar energy out of the sky into the Vemana. The Puspini, or Pinjaladarpina, was an instrument for seeing lightning and controlling its effects on the Vemana. The **Vemanas— some types** Viduvadashika was an apparatus with 12 types of electricity flowing through it, something still unknown to modern science. Another object was described as the Pahtikabraka, which was a sheet with a mica-like surface for use in the airplane's internal and external solar power system. And then there was the Ompashmura, which was possibly an exhaust device placed at the junction of the intakes where the solar energy was focused. And then what I think is very interesting is the Stabinayantra, which was an apparatus for arresting motion, like a brake. In other words, these craft, according to Veda, would be flying at rapid speeds and could apply this particular device known as the Stabinayantra, and come to an immediate halt in the middle of the sky.

Those of you who have studied the UFO phenomena at all know this maneuver is often performed by UFOs. So all I know is these descriptions in the ancient Vedas are quite astounding because what they describe is being observed now in the modern UFO experience.

Now consider this if you will. Bombay, September 21, 1952 — an article appeared in the newspaper that described an airplane based on the sutras of the Vemonic Asastra of Maharishi Paradabaj, a manuscript which was recently discovered by the Director of the International Academy of Sanskrit Research. A Vemana was actually flown in Bombay during 1890. This information is contained in a research article in this week's issue of BeBetrada, a leading Maharishi daily paper in Bombay. Now the article was written under the contribution of Sri Lalubi Khansara, who studied the Vemanas for quite some time. He discovered that in 1890 a man named Sri Talpaday first constructed a model of an aircraft in the lines laid down by the Vemonic Asastra. The model was exhibited in an exhibition arranged by the Bombay Art Society in the 1890s. Following its success, Mr. Talpaday constructed a bigger airplane with the help of his wife, who was also a great Sanskrit scholar. He was also assisted by a friend and an architect from the Bombay School of Art. What he had done was to construct this plane based on the descriptions of the Marupsaka and the Pushpataip of Vemanas, which were part of the Vedic knowledge. And the general idea of the plane can be found in the 20th Avaya of the Rhig Veda. That is where the general description was given. I've described to you some of those parts that were in there.

The completed plane was shown to the late Justice Mahadaya Ranundi. He became so impressed, this Chief Justice, this Judge, that he thought he should invite European experts to proceed further. But Mr. Talpaday did not agree to that because he thought it would be a sign of inferiority on their part, and that the Vedic knowledge was sufficient for them to construct it. But apparently the plane made its first and probably its last flight in 1885 in Chupati. Apparently this craft was later flown, according to this, in 1885 and the first flight was witnessed amongst a throng of persons over 100 years later. And this is quite astounding because the plane ascended to a distance of 1500 feet before coming down. And it says that it was equipped with automatic devices for descent when it reached a certain height. So, after the death of his wife in 1917, Mr. Talpaday lost all interest, and later his relatives sold the different pieces. But it was actually demonstrated, and this is documented evidence in India of the actual flying of the Vemana.

A Vemana built and flown

So what we've done now — this will conclude our section on the ancient Vedas, the Vemana, the Nadasingha Yoga and the Neuro Life Illumination. What we've described to you is your personal entrance into this study of Neuro Life Illumination, feeling the presence of the light and the spirit soul within your body, emanating out through the neurological system. This will be of primary importance in understanding your existence as ecstacy and living your life in this full blissfulness. We've also described some of the verses from the ancient Shuman Vhagatan and the Vedas for the purpose of describing the ancient telepathic process and the modern form of speaking sound vibration.

I've given you some ideas of our living condition as ecstacy. Now I want to talk to you about the environment. And I don't mean here, just the environment in terms of defor-estation, air pollution, and so on, which of course are very important and urgent problems, but something a little different, something a little more personal that involves your day-to-day existence. The environment is the key to harmony, ecstacy and higher consciousness.

First of all, there's something that's very important for me to know that you understand clearly. I told you that we have limited sense perception. And the reason it's important to get this concept clear is it opens the door to unlimited thinking. Now you may wonder how, because different tape series and positive motivation seminars focus on becoming unlimited and thinking unlimited, and expanding our thinking. And I completely agree with that. In fact, that's what we want to promote here. But by recognizing your limits, you transcend them. Remember that — by recognizing your limits, you transcend them. How can that be so? By pretending to think you're unlimited, without clearly first understanding your natural limits, you will only be able to go so far, because those natural limits will come back to challenge you later as you attempt to see yourself as an unlimited thinker. So, first, by identifying our limits, we can develop our genuine, unlimited, intergalactic consciousness.

Science has proven that inside of the atom is the swirling energy which ultimately forms atoms, yet they have not yet figured out how the energy goes from being pure energy to physical form. Albert Einstein once was asked to give his definition of matter and he said, "Matter is merely energy in a form that we can perceive by our senses."

Be aware of what you are projecting (creating)

So I have a saying in regard to our living environment and I'd like you to think about it carefully. In fact, it has to do with our electrical environment, the environment that is around us in which we create our thoughts and our own reality. Now I have this posted on my wall because I always want to remind myself of this, because it is a moment-to-moment living reality for ourselves. You may also want to put it in a place where you can read it on a daily basis.

"What we feel, see, hear and project through our neurological system outward towards the present projected environment is the living condition of our reality."

Our living condition is the immediate environment and our whole existence is created by the energetic thought-forms projected out each moment into it. What you are projecting out through your nervous system, toward the current right now, is the environment that is sitting in front of you. That means the people you meet, the work you do, your job, the relationship you have with your family, your kids, all the people who you're close with, your relationship even with yourself, your relationship you have with everything you do, the relationship you have with driving your car, if somebody cuts you off, the relationship you have when you go to get some gas, when you go into the grocery store, everything. What you see, feel, hear and project through your nervous system outward towards the present projected environment, whatever it might be, good or bad, that is the living condition of your reality. It's not something else that you imagine yourself to be or wish you were, but it's exactly what you're projecting out at this time. So take this idea, realize that our living condition is our immediate environment and that our whole existence is created by the energetic thought forms that are projected out each moment into it.

I feel that when people discover the UFO phenomena, and all of our limited concepts of thought in science, government, politics, religion, and education are challenged, there will be a tremendous movement towards some of the thoughts and ideas shared here. And I believe that there will be a revolution in the total thought process, which you can see going on in our world today. Something is about to radically change. I look forward to sharing this whole existence with you and I hope to meet you personally some day.

"What we feel, see, hear and project

through our neurological system outward

towards the present projected environment

is the living condition of our reality."

Chapter 21

A Matter of Time
(Dr. Fred Bell continues)

Now let's discuss time and vibration. If you look at human beings, their sensitivities change to what goes on over a period of time, to different kinds of energies, both dimensional and interdimensional. For example, the Earth and the moon have 30-day, 28-day and 33-day cycles as the moon goes around the Earth. We have tide changes, changes in consciousness, called the circadian rhythm, which corresponds to these cycles.

During this cycle of the month, we have 2 $\frac{1}{2}$ weeks of the full moon and 2 $\frac{1}{2}$ weeks of the new moon. Each day, the tides of the oceans change levels of ascent and descent. No two days are the same with tides. The human body is also mostly water. What changes in correspondence to the Earth tides, in humans, is the surface tension of all of our cells. Because many of our organs are membranes, they change tension by the pressures brought on by the individual surface tension changes within their individual cellular structures. In the case of the seven endocrine glands, there is a direct relationship of surface tension versus vibrational endocrine threshold response. What this means in simple lay terms is that as the moon transits through the sky, it affects the endocrine system in such a way that all of our feelings of consciousness change on a daily basis. Remember, the endocrine gland secretes hormones into our brain due to emotional-vibration responses from both the inner and outer planes of existence. Here is an example I like to give people during my lectures and workshops.

Imagine that you are on a boat, looking out over the ocean. One of your friends walks behind you unnoticed. Suddenly, your friend decides to surprise you and quietly steps behind you, still without you noticing, and blurts out a loud BOO! Usually one of two things will happen:

1. You jump out of your shoes. Because of this surprise, your pulse goes up, your blood pressure can reach 240 over 160, or,
2. You calmly turn around and say "hello."

Why the extremely different responses? Because of the surface tension on the endocrine system, in this case, the adrenals, and their relationship to a particular phase of the moon. This is only one example of an emotional response. There are intellectual and physical responses governed by other organs as well. This is a prime example of the circadian rhythm in action.

In addition, there are big changes that affect the hemoglobin in blood (the pyramid-shaped iron atom) in women, causing menstrual cycles, and other, less noticeable changes. By the way, I might add that men also have "menstrual cycles" the same as women, but because men do not ovulate, the effects are noticeable in other ways. Usually, men are shorter tempered during their respective cycle and also less creative in their thinking.

Moon causes serotonin level changes in us

The moon revolves around the Earth at 2,300 miles per hour, its motion around the Earth causing serotonin level changes in the human being. For example, during the full moon, serotonin levels have a tendency to be higher in the human brain and throughout the human body, and a non-spiritual entity will have a tendency to behave differently from a more spiritual entity because he's more tied into the whims of his physical body and less to the whims of his spiritual body. What this means, then, is that if your chakras aren't tuned into the moon changes, the solar changes, and all the other changes, you're very susceptible to going upside-down to the positive energy point, which is what the bulk of humanity does, as we covered earlier in the aura field presentation. The aura fields are going upside-down in people.

Now as the Earth and the moon go through cyclic changes, the Earth and the moon also revolve around the sun every 365 $\frac{1}{4}$ days. That's why we have a Leap Year every four years. As it revolves around the sun, the Earth goes through summer, winter, spring and fall in the northern and southern latitudes, each being opposite.

There's a vibratory frequency within the Earth itself that's representative of the Christ energy, and as this energy moves about from the North to the South Pole, it vacillates, setting up a spiritual frequency within the Earth, like a pulse or a heartbeat. Remember we explained the Anu earlier, which is in the vitality globule, and during the winter months we have a situation whereby the natural death rate is at the highest, while during the summer death rates drop because another kind of vitality is there. When we have the cycle of the winter, the Christ energy is in the ground and during the summer it is in the air, if you want to look at it in simpler terms.

When this energy is in the ground during the winter, in the northern hemisphere, the trees and other plants sense this, and they go down into the ground to gain the energy of the Christ consciousness from the Earth and re-charge from this energy field. As the spring comes, and as the sap moves back up into the trees and plants, and the leaves open to the solar energy, the Christ consciousness prevails back on the surface. During this time the seed is produced. When it falls off the flowers and all the different trees in the fall, the seed then goes back in the Earth where it is vitalized through the winter by the Christ consciousness. The seed, by the way, of any food is the highest form of energy.

As our solar system revolves around the Pleiades, we address a much larger cycle of energy. In this cycle there are 25,827.5 years. In this great cycle of 25,827.5 years, we have a sub-cycle which divides it by 12, or 2,152.3 years. During the sub-cycle we experience changes — just as the Earth and the moon cause changes in the body over a 30-day period, and the Earth, moon and the sun caused changes in the body over a 365-day period — so do we have changes in the earth, sun, and moon over a 25,827.5-year period, or the procession of the equinox.

There's an old temple in Egypt in the spiritual city of Dendora along the Nile River, and this is called the Temple of Hathor. It's dedicated to the Goddess of love and the stars of Hathor, the Pleiades. In this temple, a marvel of man's beginning can be found. An eons-old carving on the ceiling, intricate in design, a star clock, carved before Christ, celebrates the Pleiades, the vastly greater sun around which our solar system revolves, taking 25,827.5 years to complete the revolution. Called the Procession of the Equinox, this clock of stone survived the Ages.

The 2,152.3-year sub-cycles are called Ages. The Piscean Age we are coming out of; the

Aquarian Age we are going into. Coming out of the Piscean Age, we are coming out of an age where the spiritual tenet of the people was "I believe." They believed, but in order to have a belief system, they had to have an idealism, and so this was the birthplace of religion. The level of soul consciousness changes during these 2,000-year periods. There are 12 levels of souls that enter into our Earth cycles at different points along the Procession of the Equinox, and the level of soul consciousness that entered during the Piscean, or Christ times, was the believer. And because the believer needed a system of belief, many different religions were structured during that time. Of course, there are older religious structures that intertwined through these younger religions. I would say Christianity had its birth 2,000 years ago. Before that, of course, was the Jewish faith and beyond that, the oldest surviving faith, the Brahman faith of Tibet. But looking back during all these different times, the strongest period of belief system has been during last 2,000 years, when we had to have the believers.

In the Aquarian Age, which we're going into now, the level of the soul that's born is of a higher consciousness, **The knower.** These people don't have to have a religion to stand upright in this world, and they don't have to have a five or six-set version of the Global 2000 Report to realize this planet is in trouble. They know by looking around and feeling and sensing. And as a result of that, the knowers, which are known as the Age of Aquarius-type consciousnesses, will move ahead, forge ahead, stand alone if they have to, and change the face of this Earth.

The Aquarian age

When you realize that this evolution is taking place, then you begin to understand that along with the knowers are going to be the extraterrestrial souls. As we cycle from the Pisces to the Aquarius vibration, the chakras in the body change; the vibratory frequency and sensitivities of the bodies change. There are so many different changes. People on the whole are much more susceptible to sound, for example, now than they were 2,000 years ago. Naturally there are many masters that are impregnated within the bowels of the human race that survived these cycles because they're transcendental in nature, meaning that they have moved beyond this planetary stellar/lunar ramification, and feelings, spiritual consciousness and awareness.

Take the cycle of 25,827.5 years and divide that by 52, which corresponds to a one-year cycle of the earth, you come up with 496 years. The Shinto in Japan refers to this number. It also claims to have Vimanas and saucers like Scott Wolf had elaborated on earlier that the Vedas did. Japan was the center of civilization through the Atlantean times, until about 5,000 years ago when China broke off and for some reason they became a smaller civilization as a world power, but you can see they're fast coming back again.

The Shinto Master is said to be born every 496 years, approximately, in Japan. This is one of their high spiritual leaders, much like the Dahli Lama, who takes a centennial reincarnation cycle in Tibet. If you divide that down even further by 52, you end up with 9.5 years, or one decade, and you can see that one decade, a 10-year cycle, falls in the greater cycle, and you always see changes in a 10-year period. Look at how we were in the 60s, in the 50s, in the 40s, and so on. The Native American Hopi tribe, for example, understood this Pleiadian cycle and has its major ceremonies divided into 52-year periods.

Now the Great Pyramid, of course, is riddled with the Pleiadian mystery. Its seven mystical chambers suggest the seven levels of consciousness. And we also noticed that if you took the rotationary period of the earth around the Pleiades, which was 25,827.5 years, and took two times the base diagonals of the Great Pyramid, you would end up with half that period of time, which is 12,913.75 pyramidal inches. So if you marked one pyramid inch per year and went around the entire base of the pyramid, you come up with the exact frequency

The Great Pyramid geometry equals the number of years of the procession of the equinoxes

179

or count of 25,827.5 years, the great age of the cycle of the Procession of the Equinoxes.

The Great Pyramid and the carbon atom resonate together, because they share the same geometric proportion, shape and size, and are related mathematically by Pi and Phi. What are they going to resonate to? The Earth's structure is carbon-based, as are the pyramids, and as we are, and so the carbon atom and the great pyramid resonate to their location and position in space and time. And so it just happens that at this point in space and time we are going into the Aquarian Age, which is the doorway to the Fourth Dimension. Now a lot of us are Piscean, too. We have the Aquarian awareness, but we don't have the consciousness yet and one of the purposes of the Pyradyne product line and the things that I and some of the other New Age-oriented people do is to enlighten consciousness by means of technology, as did the Ancients a long time before us.

Chapter 22

Connecting Ourselves to 4th Dimensional Sound Embodied in Pleiadian Ships . . . Holographic Sound Principles

Some people say, "Well, I can just get into a spaceship and fly away, that would be fine. I realize that technology, so why couldn't I just go home and sit down in a chair and make my body into a spaceship and fly away?" Well, some people can do that. Most of us can't, including many extraterrestrials who rely on an external means of transportation, but at the same time, there exists the principle of acclamation. If your body is not used to or ready for this great change, and you jump into an extraterrestrial spaceship, you're liable to come back after your voyage quite disoriented. If you come back disoriented, like a lot of contactees and abductees have, it's hard to readjust to this life back here on earth. UFO abductees and contactees can go crazy, as did Betty and Barney Hill, for example. Betty survived the ordeal, but Barney didn't. He got ulcers after it happened, and he died a few years later after the experience. He never did adjust to it. It can be a positive experience sometimes. Even though they were picked up by the civilization called the Grays, the Grays did not severely mistreat them at that time, they just indoctrinated them into the ways of what they were about.

When I worked at the NASA facilities with Rockwell, I was adjacent to a program of space medicine whereby the astronauts were conditioned to go into space. Some of the astronauts had trouble staying in their bodies. They were highly powerful athletes. You use 99% of your energy supporting yourself in gravity every single day. When you put yourself out into space for two weeks without a bit of gravity, and you have a powerful, athletic body, as does an astronaut, your energy and consciousness has got to go somewhere. And unless you're strongly anchored into your physical body, as most of them were not, you're going to have an out-of-body experience. Even if you don't have an out-of-body experience, you're going to have a higher vision, a higher awareness of the presence of extraterrestrial vehicles in space, accentuated further by actually being in space.

I'm sure you've heard of the times when some people see an extraterrestrial device or a UFO and others in the same group can't see it. They're all looking in the same direction at the same point in time, but for some, their consciousness is not sensitized yet. I'll give you an example:

Take a look around the room you are in now and observe everything in the room that's brown. See all the brown things that you can in the room. Now, close your eyes, take a deep breath, and say to yourself, "Wait, I want to remember all the things I saw that were blue or green." Keeping your eyes closed, try to remember all of those blue or green items. Now open your eyes and look around, and suddenly, things that are green and blue you will have an awareness of.

This is the awareness, preparing ourselves for this higher space consciousness, which is important for all of us to realize. I'm sure most people would like to have some kind of a spiritual experience. Some of you want to become contactees, some of you probably want to make a big trip, some of you want to maybe build a spaceship, some of you want to use this technology for healing purposes. I'm sure there are a thousand different uses that people have, and motivations for examining the kind of material that we're presenting now.

And now we're coming into the sound phase of this material, the meditation phase. We're going to bring the level of consciousness up still even further. And the reason we're doing so is because at this very moment, we're moving at a thousand miles an hour along the surface of the Earth, and we're moving several thousands of miles an hour with the solar system around the Pleiades and the Pleiades of course, is moving with the Milky Way, and the Milky Way is moving around other celestial references. So you have this grand scale of motion going on continuously with many different, comparing cycles.

We are tuning you into this series of cycles. We have to open the chakras up gradually, while remaining grounded. This began at the beginning of this material, as we explained in depth the great government cover-ups, the good and bad aliens, and more. The ego had to understand those things to relate to where we are now. And where we are now is only the beginning of where we're capable of travelling. That's the fun of holographic sound.

When people ask, "What is that?" I say, "Well, the Andromedans are teaching me holographic sound."

"Oh, is that some form of new microphone, speaker or sound system?"

No — you can use any microphone in holographic sound. What holographic sound is all about is triggering one series of events to another series of events by the timbre, not the chord, but the chord, of course, has to be first. We begin this musical communication with the chord as played by the piano, then go deeper and project more of the subtle timbres by using the sitar, then the incredible impact of the sound of a Pleiadian Ship.

Note: If the publisher has not presented a tape with this book, you can order one free by calling 1-800-729-2603 or outside US 1-714-499-2603.

Listen to the enclosed tape now for Sound #1.

As you listen over and over again to the sound of a Pleiadian ship, you will notice an ever-widening spectrum of sound, a blend of chord and timbre, affecting your psyche. Sound facilitates and can even induce meditation, especially the complex and aligned vibrations of the Pleiadian ship. You start feeling something from it. You connect subconsciously and consciously to the Pleiadian vibratory frequency. This draws you more towards the society of the Pleiadians, because your aura field starts opening up and blockages are removed. These kinds of things truly will happen.

When you start applying our Systems, like our Fire Starr Orb, along with specially designed tapes, lasers, and more, you begin to extend yourself outward and inward. Just about every single individual who has installed a FireStarr Orb, for example, has some kind of an extraterrestrial experience, which could be a sighting, or a direct contact. I can't think of one Pyradyne System that has been installed somewhere in the world that somebody hasn't had a major spiritual experience with. I give all this credit to the Pleiadians and the higher forms.

I take no credit. I was just taking directions from a Pleiadian cosmonaut, religiously trying to understand how she told me to construct these type of devices.

Now listen to Sound #2.

When we play an "A" chord, we're talking to a chakra in the body. The piano doesn't have the timber element in it as does the Pleiadian Ship or the sitar. So if you look at the body, starting with the head, and go all the way down to the base of the spine, what you'll find is a series of chakras, or energy points. The effect of the Nuclear Receptor and its gemstone, say a ruby pituitary, or an emerald for the throat, or a sapphire for the heart, is amplified when you add the proper sound, tuned to a particular chakra vibration. The note "A" tunes into the pineal gland in the body, or the areas of the highest head chakra within the body. The crown chakra is quite different, but here we're referring to the seven basic notes: A, B, C, D, E, F, and G.

These seven basic notes cause different responses. The next power level, or the next energy field, is the note "B."

Listen to Sound #3.

It goes down a little bit further into the body than does the note "A". The note "C"...

Listen to Sound #4.

...resonates to the throat chakra. And so on, down the whole spectrum of the body, the major notes of the octave trigger the different chakras. This is something interesting to know. We begin with F, and a few notes beyond that.

Listen to Sound #5.

When we as a society moved into the era of electronic music, the first changes in electronic music allowed us to take the piano and add a more penetrating timbre to it. An "A" chord played with a little bit of timbre is more moving, a richer sound, achieved without increasing the tempo of the note progressions or chord changes. Just the quality of the sound itself creates the mood.

Listen to Sound #6.

When you go beyond the mood, and actually start playing the piano, you increase the intensity of the message.

Listen to Sound #7

Sound quality differs greatly, depending upon the instrument used to create the tone. I'm a clarinet player, and I have great respect for them and other brass and wind instruments.

Listen to Sound #8.

Two trumpets together sound quite gorgeous. But the trumpet is a sounding instrument. Remember, armies played coronets and bugles going into battle! It's a simple instrument, but when combined with an orchestra or band, it gives a good feeling. I also played guitar. Being an orthodox instrument player, it's wonderful. But still there's something about the Pleiadian ship sound that just never ceases to amaze me and causes me to really want to have more of that energy around me. As a result of that, we've gotten into sound laboratories and created our albums and tapes.

Sometimes, when you first hear our music, it's a little different, maybe a little bit difficult to adjust to. You say you sort of like it, but you're not quite sure what kind of music it is; you've never heard it before. That's fine, because you have blockages, and after you hear the music a little bit more and a little bit more, especially *The Fellowship* album, two or three times, it becomes habit forming. It's not a bad habit, in that it clears you out and relaxes you and gets rid of different kinds of stress.

I remember when my dear friend, Steve Halpern, first came out with the anti-frantic alternative music, for that particular time. It was the very beginning of New Age music. New Age music is still finding its way into the hearts of many people, some of whom are turning to New Age now because most music that you hear on the radio every day doesn't "take" you anywhere. It's repetitive. It sounds good in bars, and I suppose it blends well with drugs, but for a normal person who's trying to excel in something, the music on the radio, for the most part, sounds incomplete. And that's why a lot of the top ten hits are by the older bands that are coming back into focus again because they had a stronger message, or new bands re-recording older songs.

Look at the Moody Blues, for example, the band that I traveled with for a long time as a friend. They have a tremendously powerful sound, even now. The type of music we are introducing with our albums is to today's music such as Roy Orbison or Willy Nelson introduced in yesterday's time period. They all had a new style of music. Even Elvis had a new style of music, and for the first three or four years people weren't sure whether they really liked it or not. When they finally decided they liked it, it had staying power. The pop music you hear today sells because people are subjected to it over and over again. There's no substance or deep, positive effect from it, and when the reality of what the real musical message is sinks in, it disappears off the charts.

The record companies today are struggling because they don't understand what they're doing any more. They concentrated on money and profits and forgot about consciousness. And today, people are seeking consciousness, and that's why this music is so full of consciousness. And this is what I've learned from the Pleiadians and that's why we use their sound techniques in all of our music, including the Rock & Roll album that we recently finished, called *From Andromeda With Love*.

Music that "takes you places"

We don't consider our music to be New Age. We consider our music to be Four Dimensional. Our band Voyager plays live concerts, and I might explain briefly about Voyager. Voyager is a band made up of different members of other bands that you've heard of, sort of a New Age Traveling Wilburys. What we're looking for primarily is talent. And each band member from a larger band that comes in to help Voyager makes the contribution for that particular album. So we might have one musician from one band on one album, and another musician from another band on another album, because it's not about getting out the album, it's about bringing in an individual artist and letting him explore his talents to the fullest. When the artist can

184

explore his talents to the fullest, then he can realize his or her potential. And if you look at the music scene now and successful music, a lot of bands are doing that. A lot of different major artists, like Phil Collins, do solo as well as group projects. Paul McCartney has a band, does work solo, and also performs with other people. The Traveling Wilburys are another example of a collection of highly talented musicians that have gotten together to express a mutual energy, a mutual feeling. So music has finally started to get real, and these are the sounds and bands and combinations that will survive.

Now what I want to do is explore the intricacies of timbre. To create a sound that's very close to the sound of a Pleiadian ship, as far as timbre goes, the instrument I use is a Roland D-50 linear arithmetic synthesizer. Because it's so rich in timbre, or has the capability of being rich in timbre, it makes it an ideal device to use to work on chakra opening and Transcendental Meditation techniques that we use in mass audiences. If I'm just playing a solo concert and I only bring one synthesizer, you can bet that this is the one that I will bring because it has the most power for this particular aspect of what we're doing. Now there are other synthesizers that all have aspects, but this has what you would call the "root vibration" or the root energy field in it.

When we did an analysis of Pleiadian ships with a spectrum analyzer, we found that there was a 1,000 cps main frequency and several sub-cycles underneath it. Some of the cycles that we found were cycles of the musical notes, especially lots of "G's" and "D's", and also a broad range of timbre frequencies that extend down into the blood pressure or blood circulatory frequencies. The heart frequencies that we found in the Pleiadian ship sounds were harmonious to the human body, oftentimes a bit intense, however, to the uneducated body, meaning that they could de-sensitize their chakras before they could understand the sounds.

It is essential that you gradually unwind the negativity and disharmony in your chakra system to allow you to be able to withstand the tremendous power of the Pleiadian ship. When you travel near the speed of light, the energy field goes up. The physical size of the traveller goes down. The energy density goes up. And the material density, of course, goes down when the concentration goes up in energy. You move over to the next dimension, the next plane, and the atoms in the body have to be able to change frequency, especially the hydrogen atom.

> **Near the speed of light, the energy field goes up... and you move over to the next dimension**

This heavier sound might be a familiar sound, and I'm going to move this sound around a little bit as I play it. And this sound, by the way, you won't be able to find anywhere because it's a sound that I created with the use of an Atari computer, and the system of matching the different parameters of the ship versus the parameters of the synthesizer, and it takes literally hundreds of hours, even with the proper computer setup to create these sounds. I create these sounds once I have the basic sound, then I can build actual families or banks off these sounds, which I've done, and that's when I start using multiple synthesizers to show you what happens when we start stacking these sounds, all with 4th-dimensional timbre characteristics.

Listen to Sound #9.

First, I'll play "G," then add "D" and move across the keyboard. As I proceed up the scale, I'm going up the chakras. "D" and "G" address the solar plexus area of the body. Remember, "A" resonates at the top of the body and the "G" note the bottom. So we're also affecting the base of the spine, which is a logical place to begin because we're just introducing you to this practice of sound.

Now when I talk about "A" being at the top of the head and "G" at the base of the spine,

I don't want you to think this is happening all the time. Realize that sound has to enter somewhere in the body. I mean that the sound just isn't hovering down there and just jumps on the body. It doesn't work that way. It goes into the cells first, and the cell group in the frequency of "G" at the base of the spine. Through these cells, naturally, it has to go into the molecules. If it goes into the molecules, it has to go into the atoms. If it goes into the atoms, then we are back at the four basic atoms that compose your body. Yes, believe it or not, an atom is sensitive to sound. It doesn't have to be in your ear or what you feel; the atom feels sound itself.

The hydrogen atom is the most sensitive to sound. Remember, I referred earlier to "the music of the spheres." When an enzyme group is close to the right frequency of the body and vibratory rhythm, the hydrogen atom allows the energy to enter the body. The body, of course, receives the energy as the motion, rotation and frequency of the hydrogen atom. In the morning, as you remember, as the sun rises, the energy comes from the astral plane into the hydrogen atom. It's various frequencies shower the hydrogen atom like a rainbow. The red end of the spectrum rainbow reaches the nucleus of the hydrogen atom, and the other end, which would be violet, is felt strongly by the electron, the outer perimeter revolving particle with a smaller mass. The hydrogen atom is nothing more than a proton and an electron which this rainbow energy animates.

If you look at the hydrogen atom and its distribution of mass, you will learn something more about consciousness. The proton, or center of the hydrogen atom, weighs 1,640 times more than its orbiting electron. Therefore, consciousness will be affected more by the heavier mass of the center than it will be by the lesser mass of its orbiting electron. However, the orbiting electron is moving faster, or vibrating, at a slightly higher frequency. When an object is in motion, its energy increases proportionally to its speed, and its outer mass decreases. It can begin to act as a carrier vehicle for other energies. This is precisely what happens with the hydrogen atom. It carries consciousness into the cells that it becomes a composite of.

> **When moving, an object's energy increases proportionally to its speed and its outer mass decreases!**

In the morning when Red, the ray of will, energizes the hydrogen atom proton, the consciousness of Red (the will) animates our body. Will wakes us up from our astral sleep. It opens our eyes; it starts our day here on Earth. (see figure 22-1)

At the end of the day, the red color has switched over to the electron, and the violet energy is now focused on the proton. Again, our thoughts change. Because the Violet Ray is that of order and magic, we begin to reflect on what has transpired during the day as we begin to enter "night." Of course, there are seven basic colors in the rainbow, and each color corresponds to one of the seven levels of consciousness. Thus, during a 24-hour period each color touches the proton and affects our consciousness to the level of correspondence. There is an exception, however. That is the color green.

Green is a central frequency for hydrogen in that it is not affected by time. If you could imagine looking from the end of a rainbow rather than the customary "side" that we normally see, you can begin to get the real picture. In your mind, imagine the rainbow to be straight rather than curved, and you're looking at the end. Now rotate the end so the rainbow begins to spin on its axis. When this happens, the red is on one end, and the violet is on the other end. Green is in the middle. It doesn't move! It is now the center of the hub. (see figure 22-1)

This is precisely how it behaves in the energy role within the hydrogen atom. It is a female energy, the color of nature, the sign of intellect in our consciousness, represented by the throat chakra, our body's gateway between our head and our heart!

Now later on, when we go into the meditation, we're actually going to go into the hydrogen atom and have the experience, but right now, we're just visualizing it. We're breaking you in slowly. We use these sounds in the upcoming exercise. The meditation will sensitize the hydrogen atom in the body.

Hydrogen Atom 24-Hour Shift

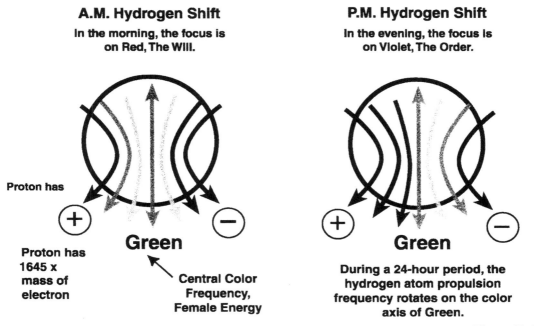

A.M. Hydrogen Shift
**In the morning, the focus is
on Red, The Will.**

P.M. Hydrogen Shift
**In the evening, the focus is
on Violet, The Order.**

Proton has

Green

Green

Proton has
1645 x
mass of
electron

**Central Color
Frequency,
Female Energy**

**During a 24-hour period, the
hydrogen atom propulsion
frequency rotates on the color
axis of Green.**

Figure 22-1

Remember, as the sun appears to move in the sky, (which is the Earth rotating on its axis), the hydrogen atom is changing polarity. That means that the vibrations, the frequencies, the music is changing polarity. When the sun goes down, the violet part of the energy field shifts to the nucleus, the proton, and the red energy focuses on the electron. It's made a 180-degree phase change (see figure 22-2). The only thing that's remained consistent is the center frequency, or note, green, which represents nature. Nature is a green energy field. Consciousness rotates 360 degrees through hydrogen. That's why you think differently in the morning than you do at the middle of the night. And that's why if you transit from L.A. to Germany in twelve hours, it takes you a long time to adjust to the geographical change, because the hydrogen has to repolarize. And this is called, of course, jet lag.

There's one thing about getting up in the morning. You can always count on "A" being at the very base of the head and "G" being at the base of the spine. This is the way it is. And during the day, of course, it shifts. It's like a master re-set button on a computer. If something gets jammed electronically in one of my synthesizers, I push the re-set button, or unplug it and turn it back on again to set all circuits to zero. The same thing can be felt in your body. When you get up in the morning, usually you feel the purest that you're going to feel that day, unless you have a tremendous hangover. And if you have a tremendous hangover, your alignment to your musical sounds versus your body might be off because your body hasn't caught up with itself yet.

24 Hour Shift

During a 24 hour period, the hydrogen atom propulsion frequency
rotates on the color axis of Green.

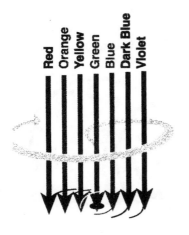

Figure 22-2

To explore this we're going to play "D" and
"G" chords. As we go deeper with the sound, notice
what it does to you. You might just close your eyes and
take a deep breath and listen to this:

Sound #10.

Now I'm sure that did a little bit more than the
previous examples because we did a few other things.
Not only did we add some very powerful root chakra
sounds with great tremendous timbre, but we also bent
their frequencies down to the next note spectrum below
it. So we swept the whole chakra system. And when we
sweep the whole chakra system, and we bend these
notes with note bending techniques, what happens is
you end up sweeping out the entire body, cleaning the
entire body out. Now we'll show you what happens
when you make an actual music sound with the synthesizer using this. We'll put something together where
you actually hear music from it using these sounds.

Listen to Sound #11.

Now what I want to do is have a little bit of fun and go to the next level of the sound.
I'm going to stack more of these same synthesizers together using harmonic characteristics
of the same sound but with different timbre characteristics, so the harmonies are going to be
the same, the notes are going to be the same, but the timbres are going to be different. They're
going to be higher, more refined, lower, more coarse. We're going to show you an entire sweep
of the chakras and at the same time we're going to sweep the timbre frequencies through the
chakras.

Chapter 23

Converting Sound & Scalar Waves

Note: If the publisher has not presented a tape with this book, you can order one free by calling 1-800-729-2603 or outside US 1-714-499-2603.

We're going to review. We've been showing you this family of sound curves, the basic timbres of the synthesizer.

Listen to Sound #12.

Now what we're going to do is add families of timbres from other synthesizers to take the timbre deeper and deeper and deeper into the body until at some point we're going to cross into the 4th dimension. So at least the atoms will be vibrating on the 4th dimension. To build visuals, I suggest fire breathing. We use the laser and the crystal technique where we shoot the laser right through the crystal. Remember, you can always come back to these basic sounds. We demonstratedt his first technique on our *Fellowship* album in the song "Journey, Part 1."

Listen to Sound #13.

I consider myself a musician-student because some of the people that I'm seeing from time to time in my career whoare musicians are just blowing me away, like my friend Patrick Moraz, formerly of the Moody Blues, or Jon Anderson, from Yes, or George Winston. They've dedicated their entire lives to music, 100%. And when you put these Pleiadian tools in their hands, you should hear the sounds of the music that they create. Anyway, during the production of our Fellowship album I discovered I was going through a personal transformation myself, accelerated by the pyramids I was wearing. Remember, I described earlier about the changes the pyramid can precipitate. A lady by the name of J.Z. Knight wore the pyramid for a period of time. Her hormone structure changed, and she started channeling Ramtha and brought a whole new level of education from the Ramtha level, or the Warrior level, the deep spiritual warrior to the Earth.

So I found that by using the pyramid, opening myself up to the channeling energies and letting myself go in that energy, I was able to channel different musicians – and it was an interesting experience. On "Journey, Part 1," from the *Fellowship* album, if you listen to the background, you'll hear a Jim Morrison and the Doors sound coming out of one of my synthesizers. I wasn't even aware of making that sound. It sounds like his entire band is playing with him. I tried to duplicate the technique that I used the night that I recorded it. I just happened to be in the right rhythm that night to channel his energies, and I was thinking about him when I played, but I was never able to channel him again to that degree. So as a result, I was never able to play that song live in concert when we went on one of our concert tours.

In the second album, we used another technique, which I'll describe momentarily, but first, let's demonstrate the technique where we stack sounds and timbres and augment the

hydrogen atom into the 4th dimension. If you're listening to this tape in the morning you're going to get a certain feeling from it, with these sounds, and I guarantee if you listen again to it in the evening, you'll get another set of feelings, and if you try it at midnight you're going to get another set of feelings from it. Because it's going to trigger different energy centers in the body even though the notes are the same.

I am going to start with the one synthesizer we were using before. Then I am going to progressively add synthesizers, going deeper in timbre and deeper in consciousness. The total number of synthesizers I will use will be three.

Listen to Sound #14.

Look how deep the sound went. You can almost hear the other instruments that aren't even present at this point. The music starts to get very deep, very quickly. Now I'm going to add another sound from a different family. We call this sound "distant." You're going to hear the 4th dimension harmonics beyond everything else. And the reason "distant" sounds like it's above and beyond everything else that you've heard so far is because you've opened up your consciousness to a deeper level of meditation, a deeper level of understanding within the human form, the God consciousness in the body. Our sounds are divided into different families. Each family affects consciousness in different ways.

Now when I add this family I'm going to turn it up. I'm not going to change notes for a second until I bring this other sound up, and then you're going to hear it come up.

Listen to Sound #15.

We have another family of sounds that we used on our second album entitled Atlantis Rising which had a different technique, more derivatives from the Pleiadian sound, but with much different timbre characteristics, more of a softer, less-penetrating energy, whereas the first album opens the chakras, the second album elevates you more into them. And the third one will do even more than that. So each album that we produce is designed to take you some-where beyond where you went with the previous album or the previous sound.

Now in this comparison, as we did on the Atlantis album, I begin with the one basic sound that we started with. Then I've got other derivatives on higher octaves, different kinds of timbre sounds, so it's going to sound different now because I've changed the patches.

Listen to Sound #16.

And on and on it goes, and you begin to see that we can go into all different kinds of spaces with this type of sound, this type of technique. And so this is just the beginning.

In the ancient times long before the synthesizers, some races of mankind were able to reach similar vibratory levels and keep those levels alive. For example, during the time of the rotation of the Earth around the Pleiades, we go into what's called the Renaissance period. And this means we have another division of time. We divided it before into 2,100-year periods, calling those Ages. We can look at the basic 25,000-year revolution as two 12,000-year periods, one of darkness, one of light, and we're of course entering into the light age now.

Some types of music were forbidden in the Dark Ages, like during our historically titled Renaissance Period, because some music has a tendency to raise the consciousness. The musicians went underground, like the Masters in the White Brotherhood who live in the Himalayan caves, for instance, Master Koot Hoomi Lal Singh (KH). For those of you who are not familiar with him, he's one of the members of an elite group that helped preserve the consciousness during the darker period of the winter of this greater 12,000-year-on, 12,000-year-off cycle. KH plays the piano and the organ, which he keeps in his home in the Himalayan mountains. Different masters are revealed during the Renaissance time to keep just enough music alive to maintain the flow of consciousness. Richard Wagner was one of these great Renaissance musicians. And, of course, the one comforting thing in Hitler's life was to hear Wagner's music, because it was a very enlightening music, and Hitler had a heavy soul and needed some relaxation. And it took a very heavy timbrel sound such as Wagner produced to relax someone as confused and powerful as Hitler was. So music has its many purposes.

Music hidden during the dark ages

Now the next thing I want to do is demonstrate a few other sounds from times gone by and show you what they do, and how they compare the sounds we just heard. The first thing I'm going to demonstrate is a lower chakra stimulant, called a Rangoon gong.

Listen to Sound #17.

The deep sounds of the Rangoon gong have been around for a long time. They can be 10, 20, even 30 feet across. They can be heard for miles around when played outside. Now I will play more than one gong at a time.

The Rangoon Gong — can be 30 feet across!

Listen to Sound #18.

The multiple gongs sound like "mother" Spaceship, which is a very large vehicle. The energy is very similar to the deep-rooted sound of the mother ship. These different kinds of Tibetan bells possess a penetrating, lingering timbre. They have different combinations of metals in them, which determines the quality of the sound. The hand-held Tibetan bell has more than seven metals in it. It vibrates with sound a lot longer than other sets of bells with fewer metals because of the harmonic frequencies of metals interweaving in the molecular structure. This bell that looks like a school marm's bell mixes well with the lighter bells.

Listen to Sound #19.

The hand bell has more than seven metals in it, and you'll notice it has a deeper tone to it. These harmonic frequencies relate directly to the minerals in the body and how they interact. The lower frequencies resonate to the mineral controlling vehicle, the metabolism, so that the spiritual energies can become deeply rooted into the body. Now remember that trace minerals fire off the synapses in the brain, enabling you to reach super-physical, higher consciousness states. Without the trace minerals in abundance in the body, the body can't develop the hormones that are necessary to produce the feeling that brings the soul, along with its physical body, into a higher consciousness position for any length of time.

When you listen to Tibetan Bells made from precious metals and small amounts of trace minerals, which are, of course, metals themselves, you will probably notice a peculiar "ringing" sound. This distinctive "ringing" sound is not present in normally constructed bells, such as a church bell. The Tibetan Bells often are made with "secret" portions of unknown trace minerals. When they ring, they produce harmonics that bring consciousness to the crown chakra, which is the doorway to the 4th dimension.

What is necessary, of course, is that you are consciously ready to experience the "unconsciousness reality" of the 4th dimension. This means your body needs the elements of the 4th dimension to be present within it to become "conscious" of "unconsciousness!"

Voilá! You need those trace minerals in your system! These activate the 10th cranial nerve and the parasympathetic nervous system, which is the doorway to beyond. But, where do you get trace minerals? They are no longer present in our daily foods. That is why most of society can never reach, in reality, the 4th dimension. This is why the world is trapped in its Dharma, its own wake of racial karma. It's why there is always a war going on somewhere on this Earth, because people can't see the position of eternal happiness, they are spiritually blind.

Mankind clutches to its religion and not the greater truths of life. Mankind, as a whole, desires to step beyond. But without trace mineral activation, mankind lacks the fuel to fire the flame of greater truth. At best, people go to the movies or read a science fiction book about utopian societies. Until we become whole again, and replace those vital substances that no longer are available from food sources, we shall remain fragmented.

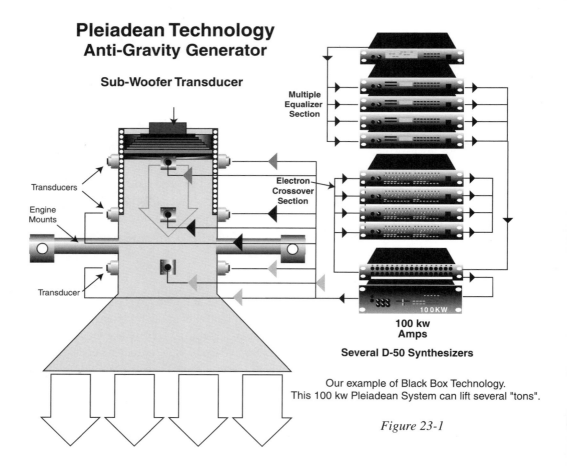

Pleiadean Technology
Anti-Gravity Generator

Sub-Woofer Transducer

Multiple Equalizer Section

Transducers

Engine Mounts

Electron Crossover Section

Transducer

100 kw Amps

Several D-50 Synthesizers

Our example of Black Box Technology.
This 100 kw Pleiadean System can lift several "tons".

Figure 23-1

192

Now you can see why I got into trace mineral formulation! There is so much you can learn from a small little bell! Remember the Universe, Uni-Verse, UNIfied VERSE, came from AUM, the sacred word. Existence came from Light, but Creation came from Sound. Pleiadian Ships are sound-powered and light-separated! Need I emphasize this any more?

Higher quality metal bells obtain these higher resonance frequency sounds so we can reproduce the high frequency spectrum down on the physical plane where you can hear it. So you combine the trace minerals in your diet with the trace mineral sound in the Tibetan bell and you start to see what happens. You can start to draw your own conclusions.

We're going to add another sound that's very mystical and I bet you can guess what it is because you've already heard it. If you said sitar, you're right. This is a very old instrument, almost as old as the Tibetan language itself and came from the Pleiadians. It was brought to the Brahmans by a group called the Rishis! For an acoustical instrument, it has a broad band, multi-timbrel sound to it.

Listen to Sound #20.

Amazing sound. Now we add a few other instruments to it gradually, and you see what happens when the Pleiadian music meets the West.

Listen to Sound #21.

You can just go on and on. It's a lot of fun. And you begin to comprehend and integrate the powerful effects. We add one more lower chakra instrument to ground the whole thing. This, of course, is the tabala.

Listen to Sound #22.

I'm sure by now you've gotten the idea about music. There's just an endless list of possibilities, combinations into infinity, that you can put together. As we say at Pyradyne, "the impossible takes 15 minutes longer."

And I'm not claiming to be the greatest keyboardist in the world. I'm just pushing a few white notes here to let you feel the combination of the instruments. And if you want more, you can listen to our albums. The last piece that I demonstrated, we used on both albums in two, different techniques. The marriage of the sitar with the Pleiadian instruments I used in a song entitled "Heritage" on The *Fellowship* album.

And there are other possibilities of instruments that can accommodate more than one input feeding into the same instrument, and this, of course, causes a playing back and forth of energy fields. Like here we're starting to get into bands of two drummers or two keyboard players or more than one guitar. And there's the interchange, especially in guitar playing, that goes back and forth, sort of a camaraderie that establishes itself after awhile. But imagine — two people playing one instrument that's breath controlled. Not only do they have to feel together, they have to breathe together to sound the instrument properly, because it plays a multiple of harmonics. This instrument exists on the Pleiades, but has not been yet brought to Earth. It is called the "S" curved flute. Two people place themselves opposite each other and look into each other's eyes. After they establish eye contact, they breath into the flute in unison and alternately.

The "S" curved flute on the Pleiades
***
Releases light into the spectrum

This establishes a beautiful rhythm that excites the very ether that carries the sound.

Remember, the physical plane is solid, liquid, gas and ether. The highest ether is that of light, and when excited, it releases light into the visible spectrum. The "S" curved flute can generate the sounds required to do so. As a result, when it is played, it causes light to liquify around the musician and become visible to the audience. I call it a step beyond the laser light show, yet there are no electronics used, only acoustics!

In the song "Heritage" from The *Fellowship* album, the lyrics are about the Rishis being the people that brought the Brahmans knowledge, and in *Atlantis Rising* we use another technique in a song called "The Horizon of Valentina." Here we use the sitar and the D-50 with another set of patches and a different kind of a rhythm. Eastern rhythms use up to a 64th note and have patterns that flutter back and forth, whereas American music has a tendency to be pretty much linear. So there is a difference, and we combine the two music styles to end up with another kind of music style. The linear style of music is fine for one set of moods, and the nonlinear Eastern sound is great, too, but when you combine the two, you open your consciousness to both American and Pleiadian frequencies. And we're just getting into music here in our studios. We have some great expectations for our music department because we're doing more research with sound all the time.

Now another thing that's interesting about these different patches is that they also have harmonics that, when coupled to scalar wave technology, can cause things to happen. When **Black Box** your body is exposed to those sounds, it tries to interpret the 4th dimension and its aspects, **technology** which takes us into scalar waves. A scalar wave is a timeless wave which occupies space with a given direction that can be controlled. But it remains a timeless event, making it different from the normal space-time cycles and frequencies that we have dealt with so far. We receive the sound at our eardrums, and our body converts it into scalar waves, which is an energy form necessary to make the transition off into the astral plane. This effect can be amplified by our System III or quad system.

We have an even more advanced technique where we couple our synthesizers into transducers and use these sounds in their "raw" form to levitate objects and transform matter. This we call our "black box" technology.

Right now we're just playing the music and marketing it in albums because people are not ready for this giant transition that they're going to get when they start energizing sound into the 4th dimension through black box scalar technology, which is up and coming.

So you begin to realize that it gets deeper and more complex, yet simpler, because as you arrive on the physical level into these higher dimensions and these higher states of consciousness through the auspices of sound, it becomes a lot more relaxing and a lot more spontaneous. Remember, the great creator started with the word of creation, primal creation, which is AUM. I'm sure you have heard that before, and, of course, sound has a lot to do with the creation or destruction of any living or even non-living thing. Remember the Walls of Jericho were brought down by a magic horn. So with this kind of knowledge and this consciousness, we want to go deeper and deeper into the next phase of our development.

Consciousness divides itself into seven different vibratory frequencies, corresponding to the seven different notes—A, B, C, D, E, F and G. On the physical plane, consciousness goes down into seven sub-levels: the solid, liquid, gas, and the four different etheric states.

And further up we have the Astral plane, the mental plane, the Buddhic Plane, the Atmic Plane, the Monadic plane and the Logoic or the Divine Plane. And each one of these planes is a vibratory frequency. Each one of these planes could be represented by a light, sound or color. A combination light, sound and color can represent all of them. In the back of the book, *Death of Ignorance*, there is a chart that shows different attributes of energy fields, or consciousness, that coincide with these different planes simultaneously. (See chart on next page.) And we call these Ray I, II, III, IV, V, VI and VII. Ray I would be a red color, whereas Ray VIII would be violet in color. Ray III would be green. And each one has 4th Dimensional Holographic Sound Principles. And each one has an energy and consciousness assigned to it. Each one relates to different geometric shapes, and even different planets. For example, on Ray VII, the Earth and the Moon are very much related. Whereas on Ray I, the Earth and Moon aren't as related as the Sun and Uranus are. So they all have a tendency to interrelate and inter-correlate. When you meditate, this is going to mean a lot more to you, Pleiadian Meditation.

I want to explain it, simply because you probably won't understand it until you feel it. And once you start to feel it, as you meditate, that will be something that you can take with you from this point on through this journey through this lifetime, through this dimension. Because that's the unique, amazing thing about this meditation I learned from Semjase, it allows you to begin to feel the science and the technology. On this planet, on the physical plane here on planet Earth, I find that it's really interesting that all my science teachers required me to use my intellect and mind. In Pleiadian experiments you learn to feel some of the experiments, or the results. And I discovered something about first contact with the Pleiadians: You have a certain set of feelings and emotions that are highly keyed, yet under control, because their emotions are amplified by the contact. And then, secondly, I found that by relating each emotion to a feeling and to a consciousness, I could be guided by my feelings and consciousness, not my thoughts so much, and begin to relate to where energy was coming from and what it really represented. It sort of allowed me to have the inner meaning behind the emotion, and you're going to learn that, too.

When Semjase gave me the gift of this information. I wondered how I was going to bring it to the world, and now I'm finding myself getting this burden off of me, which is a nice burden, and I'm out being able to share it with you.

THE SEVEN RAYS
Correspondences

Figure 23-2

RAY	I	II	III	IV	V	VI	VII
Qualities	Will and Power	Love Wisdom	Active Intelligence	Art and Harmony thru Conflict	Concrete Knowledge Science	Devotion and Idealism	Ceremonial Order and Ritual
Colors	Scarlet White	Indigo	Green	Yellow	Orange	Blue Rose	Violet
Zodiacal Signs	Capricorn Leo Aries	Gemini Virgo Pisces	Libra Capricorn Cancer	Scorpio Saggitarius Taurus	Aquarius Leo Sagittarius	Sagittarius Virgo Pisces	Aries Cancer Capricorn
Planetary Rulers	* Sun **Uranus	*Jupiter **Neptune	*Earth **Saturn	*Mercury **Mercury	*Venus **Venus	*Mars **Jupiter	*Moon **Earth
Foods	Protein	Fats	Carbo-hydrate	Fruit	Vitamins	Water	Mineral **Salts**
Notes	A	B	C	D	E	F	G
Politics	Fascism	Democracy	Socialism	City State	Oligarchy	Theocratic Despotism	Communism
Gases	Nitrogen	Oxygen	Hydrogen Dioxide	Carbon-laden	Ammonia Oxide	Incense	Nitrous
Senses	Sight	Intuition	Hearing	Taste	Concrete Touch	Pain	Smell
Plane	Logoic	Atmic	Mental	Buddhic Intuitive	Monadic	Astral	Physical Etheric
Nervous Equipment	Cerebrum	Mid-brain	Medulla	Cerebellum	Peripheral	Sympathetic	Para-Sympathetic
Endocrines	Pineal	Thymus	Thyroid	Adrenals	Pituitary	Pancreas	Gonads
Nation's Soul	India China	U.K. U.S.A.	South America	Germany Austria	France	Italy Spain	Russia
Nation's Personality	U.K. Germany	Brazil	China France	India Italy	Austria	U.S.A. Russia	Spain
Shapes	Circle	Triangle	Square	Circle Squared	Sphere (lens)	Cube	Pyramid
Chakras	Head	Heart	Throat	Base of the Spine	Brow	Solar Plexus	Sacral
Kingdoms	Shamballa	Hierarchy	Deva	Humanity	Animal	Plant	Mineral
Metal	Silver	Gold	Copper	Nickel	Titanium	Copper	Titanium
Gemstone	Diamond	Lapis Turquoise	Emerald Malachite	Onyx	Opal	Ruby	Amethyst

Chapter 24

Seven Colors, Seven Rays, Seven Levels
Your Ray at Birth: 9 Initiations

In order to really "feel" and understand the seven levels of consciousness, and their relationship to interdimensional travel, a good understanding of the physical human body is quite necessary.

Just as the human body has a highway of nerves and passageways, so does the universe have a system of highways and passages that are interdimensional! Through proper studies you can establish a "road map" of the portals of time and interdimensional travel.

First of all, become familiar with the physical plane and the human body, using pictorial resources such as Gray's Anatomy. The central nervous system's skeletal structure, the muscular structure, all these structures that you see are analogies for other, inter-related, inter-dependent dimensions. We are ourselves in a greater body, part of a greater being, like the Logos, for example. In the seven levels of consciousness, the top level is called the Logoic. When you get through the upcoming meditation, you'll have a greater understanding of it.

Now a long time ago, before the human race was developed or even existed, there was a greater scheme of prevailing space and time. The human race has been around for a tremendously long period of time, but it was not ultimately the species that was created first, because when you access and explore that consciousness, there is no source of creation, nor is there an end to it. It boggles the mind to even become aware of it, but for purposes of this explanation, let's just assume that the solar system is like the Chakra system, or the endocrine gland system, a comparison to our own body.

Now if you remember, I explained earlier that the body is first made of minerals, then enzymes. We discussed the hydrogen atom. We're always referring back to it, the pH factor of the enzyme; in other words, the energy to enter into enzymatic action has to go through an initiation or qualification, and that's what the hydrogen atom does. It qualifies energy to enter the aura's sphere of the human body, to go from enzymes down to vitamins, proteins, hormones; hormones being the first unit of biochemistry that possess consciousness; and the hormones are then stored in the endocrine glands. The endocrine gland then secretes the hormone by vibration into the bloodstream. The hormone goes up into the brain, and the brain responds by vibration, switching on the electrical fields of the body, then the body develops the consciousness for that particular hormone structure, and this is how we function on a conscious level.

The solar system is the same way. There are planets, sacred and non-sacred planets. And these planets act as Chakras, or endocrine glands, and you could say the aura fields of the planets are the electrically sensitive devices that respond to vibratory frequencies which cause the secretion of hormones on a planetary level, which would be more like the human race, or other races of consciousness. In short, we are a species of galactic hormone and this motion within the being of this greater structure is what we experience as our reality, our world.

And ET's experience the same thing. Now for every race of extraterrestrials I've dealt with, there's always been one that they've looked up to. For example, the Pleiadians look up to the Andromedans , they look up to beings of pure light, the beings of pure light look up to somebody else. And finally when you get looking up higher and higher at the hierarchy of someone else, you begin to approach the hierarchy of the planetary or solar Logos.

Galaxies are also beings

The solar Logos encompasses the whole solar system as the being that all the planets are a part of. Then you ascend to cosmic Logi or Logos, with an entire series of solar systems, even a galaxy, as a greater being, and if you don't think of a galaxy as a unit of consciousness, then you're missing the point. What do you think keeps the stars from colliding? It's not spontaneous, and when star systems do come together, that's like two cells colliding in the body and going through a change. It's all part of a grand scheme of things.

And so, when these higher extraterrestrial races like the Andromedans, for example, connect with higher energy fields, or high consciousness, they approach the levels of the people that they encounter, of the solar Logos, the cosmic Logos, and begin to realize the scheme of things and the energy fields within this greater being. And as a result, their propulsion systems are designed around manipulating through these cosmic highways.

Another way you may relate to this concept: Remember the movie The Fantastic Voyage where a medical team and their "submarine" were reduced down to microscopic size and injected into a stroke victim to remove a blood clot? They traveled the human body and had all these incredible experiences in the film. Well, it's very similar to the way reality exists.

Now within that structure are the seven levels of consciousness, and the seven levels of consciousness on the macro or on the micro level, all relate to the same thing. If you look at the chart in the back of the book, *Death of Ignorance*, (or on page 196 of this book), you'll see many correlations outlined. And this particular correlation, of course, has to do with the lower aspects of the seven rays, the seven energy fields, the seven colors of the rainbow.

I mentioned that there are hierarchies, and that as we revolve around the Pleiades, we experience 25,827.5-year cycles during which we have approximately 12,000 some-odd years of darkness, and 12,000 years of light. During this time, different brotherhoods, such as the White Brotherhood, have helped us through different crises, to keep the music alive, the vibratory frequencies alive, the higher consciousness alive. This epic, this consciousness, started on this planet approximately 18 million years ago during what we call the Lemurian Epoch, which is the 3rd root race of our souls. But the soul has different vibratory patterns, as does everything else. During this period of time, 18 million years ago, the planetary Logos, or the beingness of the Earth scheme, one of the seven great spirits before the throne, took a physical incarnation, under the name of Sanat Kumara, ancient of the days and lord of the world. And he came down to this physical planet and has remained here ever since.

Because of the extreme purity of his nature and the fact that He is, from a human standpoint, relatively sinless, and hence incapable of response to things on the dense physical plane, he doesn't take a dense physical body. He takes an etheric body. He is the greatest of all the Avatars, and when He takes the dense etheric body, all the breath, all the energy fields that come into our aura field, the animating forces of our aura fields, permeate his aura field. Therefore, his aura field is called the "ring pass not" of the Earth. You can supersede his energy fields, but you have to become pure enough or free enough to "move into his thoughts," so when He thinks about others, other star systems, other galaxies, or whatever, you can move out into the sphere of influence and then reincarnate on an etheric, physical level into some other being. You have to basically move through his thoughts to get from one place to another, so therefore you have to get as pure as possible to reach into his thoughts and his mind power.

Many would say we're not clear enough, therefore we're stuck in his lower Chakras, so we have to keep incarnating back on the Earth again. And a lot of people don't understand that once you break the karma of having to incarnate on the Earth, that doesn't mean you can't come back.

He is like the guru or the outshining, outpouring force, the influence, of what's called the White Brotherhood, which is located in a specific place called Shamballa. Shamballa is located physically in the middle of the Gobi Desert, in an area called White Island, and consists of etheric matter. When Man has adopted etheric vision, its location will be recognized and reality admitted.

Shamballa: a location of etheric matter

We should be seeing more on the etheric level now. The problem is that there is so much pragmatism on the physical plane, so much pollution, that our etheric vision is clouded. It's like trying to see through a sand storm on the physical plane. One of the things that we developed is the "champagne reflector." It helps man overcome the limitations of the physical plane distortion and see into the second ether. We'll get back to the champagne reflector, the chemical ether and the reflective ether. But right now I want to communicate this concept so you can begin to understand it.

In Aspen, Colorado, near a mountain called Pyramid Peak, near an area called Blue Bells, is another etheric city. I've seen it. Semjase took me on a sojourn at three o'clock in the morning one winter night. I walked through the area and saw the city, which is visible if you have the awareness, the vision, to see it. It's protected by white wolves, which I thought was fascinating.

Another point to keep in mind: We are the expression of energies flowing out from a central source. The pituitary, for example, sends energies out to the thyroid gland and other glands in the body, and when it sends this energy out, the energy then triggers different vibratory responses in the endocrine system, creating an overall field of energy. The same thing goes on in the solar system. The planetary bodies have energy going from one to the other. This action generates the magnetic fields of the different planets. Some are stronger than others; the rotational rates differ in speed, even direction. Venus is Earth's alter ego; it turns opposite to the direction of the Earth's spin. As was stressed earlier in this dissertation, the Earth's feedback field, or the part it plays in the grand scheme of things, is negative. It's "sick" because the Earth's human population, which had been given the freedom to express itself, has violated divine or cosmic principle, and caused the Earth to no longer be coherent.

Some more aware people are tuning into other star systems and the power of what is called the triangles or trines. In the body, for example, we have the alta major center, which is a trine of three Chakras: the crown Chakra, the throat Chakra and the pituitary-pineal gland Chakra. Those three Chakras together consist of the alta major Chakra. The greater being, the "grand man of the heavens," which consists of the local constellations, has a Chakra feedback system which consists of the Earth and its solar system here, Sirius and Pleiades, and also the Great Bear.

Krishna came from the star system Sirius

On Sirius is a lodge called the Blue Lodge, which is a higher aspect of the White Lodge located within the Great White Brotherhood that is stationed on Earth. Some people reporting UFO sightings describe the blue-skinned people that come from Sirius, called the Sirians. The old Hindu bible, the Bhagavadgita, relates the story of the revered, blue-skinned Krishna. He came from Sirius. It's fascinating to see again how ancient, religious information sources corroborate this information.

Sirius acts as a transmitter. Energies flow from greater places than Sirius, such as the Great Bear, the Pleiades, and places even further away. Just pretend this entire galaxy of galaxies, this cosmos, is a greater being, and he's moving energies within himself, just like we transmit energies inside of ourselves, but the energies that he's manipulating are important to us. They have to reach us somehow. Sirius is one of the places that focuses and amplifies; it enhances the influence that produces self-consciousness in man. When you become "self" conscious, aware of yourself, the energy is coming from Sirius. Another kind of energy is emitted from Pleiades. It passes through the Venusian scheme.

These stellar energies pass through the planet Saturn before they reach us here on the physical plane on the Earth. They then have a defined effect upon the causal body and serve to stimulate the heart center. Remember, the Pleiadian Cosmonauts always interrelate to the contactees as communicating from the heart Chakra and through the emotions.

Another kind of energy that comes to us and affects the head center emanates from one of the seven stars of the Great Bear, whose en-souling light holds the same relationship to our planetary Logos as the ego does to the human being. This seven-fold energy differs according to man's greater type, which we will soon explore.

I'm preparing you now for our meditation, to understand the consciousness you will be accessing. There is a consciousness associated with every single ray, and you're going to feel its influence. For example, the Red Ray, Will, which comes from the father, stimulates the pineal gland and has a tendency to give us will-power, to push. And there are paths that emanate from these different energy fields.

The 9 rays of initiation

The first path, which is called the path of Earth Service or Ray, is where Paramahansa Yogananda and Babaji reside. Babaji is free to move out of this Ring Pass Not and go wherever he wants. Why does he stay here? Because he's on a path of Earth service. He's been around the galaxy and around the universe, so he works under the Lord of Consciousness from this area and he's always helping people realize certain levels. He falls into what is called the Lipika Lord category. You can learn about these two beings presented in a book entitled, *Auto Biography of a Yogi*, available in most New Age book stores.

There's a second aspect, which would be the Christ Consciousness, to a degree. It's a path of magnetic work, and people on this path work with the elementals, ideals and public opinions on astral levels, and they have a great influence there.

The Third Ray Path, the Training for Planetary Logi, is the level of energy where you're going to be working in these different planetary schools. For example, if you were on a higher plane, Jupiter would appear to be physical on it's surface, but it's not a habitable planet for the human body, but if you reach a higher level of consciousness, like an etheric level, you'll find there are schools of thought on Jupiter to teach things. On Saturn there are also schools of thought. These thought influences emanate out into the sphere of influence here and cause our bodies to respond to the astrological energy fields. So when you talk about astrology, you are looking at a grid of energy coming from a greater space, out in the cosmos, that comes through this grid.

This grid, of course, is composed of the planetary bodies, and when you take physical birth at a certain point in time you are polarized on this grid, as it was, as the energy flowed on that particular day that you took that incarnation. So you'll have a tendency to have certain characteristics as that day was. There are 12 days in a Sirian week. So you end up with 12

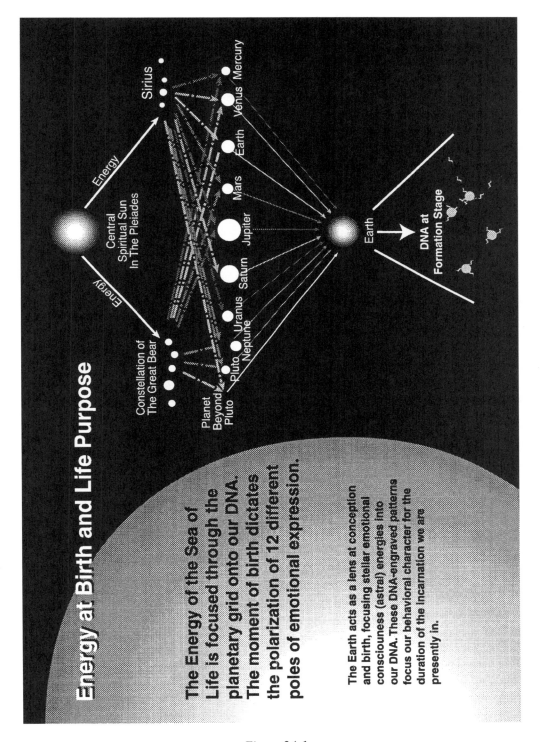

Energy at Birth and Life Purpose

The Energy of the Sea of Life is focused through the planetary grid onto our DNA. The moment of birth dictates the polarization of 12 different poles of emotional expression.

The Earth acts as a lens at conception and birth, focusing stellar emotional consciouness (astral) energies into our DNA. These DNA-engraved patterns focus our behavioral character for the duration of the incarnation we are presently in.

Figure 24-1

different signs, 12 days that have nothing to do with the seven days of our week because of our solar system, the Earth, the moon and its rotationary complex. These 12 days have to do with the complex year of the Great Bear and Sirius and the Pleiades and the higher level of days and nights as we would know it.

So we end up with 12 major influences through seven different planets, which ends up giving us the 12 different polarizations to emotional thought. And that means if you have a different situation presented to you, let's say, 12 different individuals have a situation presented to them, each situation is the same but the individuals are born into the 12 different consecutive birth signs, each person will have a tendency to approach that situation from a different point, that point being polarized on a planetary grid system as they were polarized on when they were born. That gets us into astrology.

It's something that eventually you can transcend after you have worked through astral karma. I consider the planetary logos training as a divine psychology, because when you're working through emotion, you're working through the science of psychology, or reactionary science.

The Fourth Ray path, Sirius, is where many people incarnate because it's the way towards direct incarnation within the Pleiades. This is the path that people travel when they want to be extraterrestrials. They reincarnate on this path because they're already on it anyway, and they are familiar with the different kinds of energy fields. For example, there are seven different energy fields within the Pleiades, so there are seven different types of goals. This is discussed in the Old Testament, Job 38:31, "Canst thou bind the sweet influences of Pleiades, or loose the bands of Orion?"

Then path number five is the Fifth Ray, a complex path, for it necessitates the capacity for the most intricate mathematics and the ability to geometricize in the 4th dimension, as did Einstein. The three-dimensional brain concept is out. You've got to think in the 4th dimension. And this is taken by people who work on the law of vibration, and the law of vibration is profoundly important. Most people born in the Pleiades are on the Fifth Ray.

And the next path is the one the Logos Himself is on, and this is where you're developing into the consciousness where you end up being a Master at some point in time in a particular solar system.

The next path is the path of Absolute Sonship, and it corresponds to a level of subservience, known as Christ Consciousness. The Lipika Lords, for example, such as Babaji, follow this path, and they have an avatar or higher Christ-type consciousness of service. It's a very hard path, but these are beings who are serving the higher being who's above them — that's their purpose. Compare this path to the Sirius path: the Sirius path is for those who say, "I want to go live on this world, and I want to have fun, and I want to enjoy myself, and I want to go where there's no stress and pain." Well, after a while that path gets boring, so some entities come back and say, "Now that I've been away from difficult paths and had this no-stress existence, and I've been in heaven for 12 million years, I want to come back and serve, and help the people who haven't gotten here yet. Well, that's what the path of absolute Sonship is all about.

Once you move into this 4th dimensional concept, you have to be qualified to move through the Ring Pass Not of the Earth and this solar system. But first, there are what I would call "qualifications" or initiations that are necessary in life. And there are 9 different levels of initiation. The first one is birth, which occurs on Ray 7. This is where you wake up to the awareness that consciousness exists, you are something beyond an animal. An animal is conscious, but a human is aware of his own consciousness. You wake up, realize you exist,

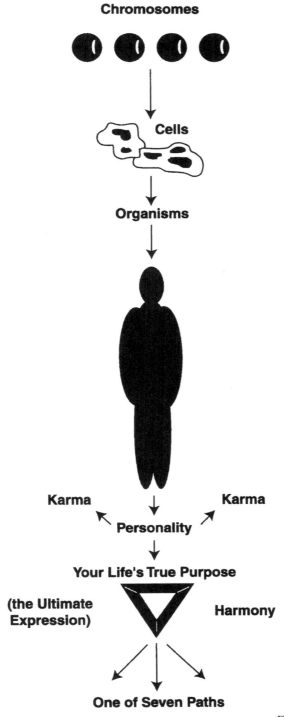

Chromosomes

Cells

Organisms

Karma   **Karma**

Personality

Your Life's True Purpose

(the Ultimate Expression)   **Harmony**

One of Seven Paths

Figure 24-2

that there are other people here, and you start practicing compassion.

The second initiation falls on Ray 6, baptism. You're baptized into the spirit, meaning that you realize you are a Christ being. Christ is not an external being, but within you. While in that consciousness, you start taking on responsibility, and you can pretend that you are the Christ if you have to look at it that way. You don't walk around saying, "I'm Christ." Instead, you live that, you feel it, and you sense it as best you know how, and of course you don't know how at first. You have to learn how, and you have to surrender. That means if someone slaps you in the face, you have to forgive them for it, and that's hard to do. Then turn the other cheek!

Then you go into transfiguration, which uses Ray 5, and is the third initiation. You start to remember past lives. You can do a fire breathing exercise we teach, where you look in your left eye in a mirror and you do fire breathing. Then you fire breathe with another and you can see how you worked with other people in past lives, and you develop a kind of spiritual camaraderie. Remember the most powerful unit of energy is the family unit of energy, and that is developed over a period of time. It doesn't always mean your biological family.

Next you experience the fourth initiation, on Ray 4, which is called renunciation. Typically in life, there comes a time when you've got to renounce relationships, ideals, and dreams. You've got to realize you don't throw pearls before swine. You move away from certain enmeshing situations in order to internalize and build your own power, because these relationships are draining you, and you're not getting your personal best. We fall apart in the astrological aspects of the spiritual body. We may not want to renounce certain friends, but it becomes necessary for their good, too. You might be holding them back, arguing around in an endless loop and that goes nowhere. So you've got to move away from them, renounce them, forget them. Maybe someday you'll come back to them, once you're strong enough, or they are.

You know you don't put a young corn plant that's growing in a field out in the middle of the freeway and expect it to flourish. Whereas a kernel of corn might survive the freeway for a limited amount of time, you know the young shoot won't, because it's not strong enough yet. So you have to work on your own self first, and grow strong.

And then we go on to the fifth initiation, which is revelation, found on Ray 1. This is where you begin to wake up, and certain truths are revealed to you spontaneously.

Soon you wake up to the sixth initiation, which is called decision, Ray 3. And decision is where you decide your path, where you're going to go, your spiritual direction. Am I going to go out to the Pleiades, am I going to come back and work on the Earth. What am I going to do?

As we move up through these initiations, there are fewer and fewer people who qualify on to the next. Eventually a group of people will qualify simultaneously, and will become the beginning of a root race, or a particular cosmic camaraderie of a whole family of energies which have completed an initiation. As the Earth moves around the Pleiades and reaches a peak of that cycle that we talked about, the 12,000 years of darkness and the 12,000 years of light, then obviously you have passed these, at least up to this sixth initiation, and you're able to free yourself of the Ring Pass Not of not only the solar system, but probably some of the cosmos and move on out and do what you want. Every 25,827.5 years, 144,000 souls clear the Ring Pass Not of the solar system. So that's what decision is all about.

The seventh initiation is called resurrection, and this is where you have the power over the physical body to resurrect the full waking consciousness. Continuity of Consciousness, it's called. I remember when I was born I had memory of my past life; I didn't have to guess at it or have a psychic tell me. I remembered it. That level of consciousness is a Ray 2 attribute.

The next initiation is transition, which covers rays 4, 5, 6 and 7. There are very few people now qualified to be at that level. It takes a lot of work to get there, and it's a very slow process. It's far in the distance.

And finally, the last initiation, which is called the refusal, is the level at which someone like Jesus Christ would be. Refusal means you are making a decision for the galaxy and the cosmos to continue on or to take a break and reconstruct itself, create a new sun, a new solar system, etc.

So these are the things that go on as you begin to approach the 4th dimension. I realize the bulk of humanity is potentially qualified to go into the 4th dimension, so it's not that you can't. You need to purify your body, mind and spirit. This allows mankind to release its Dharma that binds it to the physical plane. When everyone "purifies" in this manner, evolution moves at quantum rates. This increased vibration allows cells to reproduce and vibrate at the speed of light. When mankind takes this initiation as a whole, the 4th dimension opens for all. The Andromedans are here to initiate the process. Humans who fail will die physically until the next Renaissance period, 12,000 years from now!

The Earth's population is ready to ascend, but that doesn't necessarily mean we will leave the Earth. The 4th dimension takes us to other worlds, other planes of reality, but we first must master the techniques that allow us to navigate the new universe now opening to us. I've just given you an overview of the initiation process.

I hope you're starting to get a little feel for the Seven Rays and the nine levels of initiation. If one person can grasp this, that's important, but if two people grasp it, then four, then eight, the energy produced grows exponentially. If you were to walk down the street and start explaining the astral plane to everyone, most wouldn't accept it yet, because they don't realize that the dream state occurs on the astral plane. People dream every night, or they're supposed to. A lot of people don't believe they dream. This consciousness must shift if humanity is to step into the 4th dimension.

Chapter 25

The Seven Subplanes of Our Reality

The first step in shifting the awareness is knowledge about where we are on the seven sublevels of the physical plane, and that many people of humanity are still coming up through the seven sublevels. Let me explain:

Energy follows thought, which is what formed and is still forming our present reality. What if I were alive back during the caveman days? I pound a club on the ground, stating that solids exist. Everybody would probably agree because they see the club hit the ground. And I could say liquids exit, too, and demonstrate by pouring water on the ground. Everyone, again, could see the liquid, and agree that water, liquids, exist. To explain the next level on the physical plane, I'd have to get quite creative.

I'd say, "Gases exist." And they'd respond with, "What, gas? That doesn't exist! We can't see it! You're crazy." So I'd say, "Watch."

And I'd go out and fill a big clay pot full of water and start a fire under it, maybe even explain about heat at that point. Soon the water would boil, start forming steam, and the steam would billow around the cave. And I would say, "Look, it's gas." And they'd say, "Wow! Gas." Now the whole group has accepted this new level of consciousness, gas. And, of course, they would go out and they would tell their friends.

Well, their friends think these folks have been in the cave too long. Gas? They're all crazy, a bunch of nuts talking about "gas." Then they see a demonstration of gas given by their newly enlightened friends, they accept that gases exist, and their consciousness grows, too. Soon this has been demonstrated over the world. Now the whole population accepts gas, so this new level of consciousness is said to prevail all over the world — everyone believes in the existence of gas.

The four etheric states that exist beyond solid, liquid, and gas, do exist. Science, through nuclear reactions, cellular/nuclear fission, fusion and all kinds of forms of nuclear physics, has accepted the fact. We can photograph the etheric body through Kirlian photography. So gradually man is starting to accept the fact that the higher etheric levels exist. This awareness moves mass mind to mass consciousness. As we ascend the ladder, the increased awareness becomes more subtle, more refined. Don't look at this consciousness as a bookshelf with many different levels; look at it as one thing within the other, things getting smaller and more fine-tuned.

Etheric levels do exists

Eventually all of humanity is going to realize that the astral plane does exist. And when they realize it, not just become aware of, but integrate it, then we shift to the 4th dimension. You've also got to realize that this is the emotional plane. Another indication that we are heading in that direction is the vast growth of world communication. For example, during the Iraqi war crisis, the CNN network communicated the facts and the feelings about the war, the pain of the deaths of the children, and the deaths of the people on both sides, and the families suffering, much more so than we had been able to communicate during Vietnam or World War II. The Iraqis were watching the same program that we were in America at the same moment in time. We can have one world opinion because of the advanced communication systems we've developed.

And so you realize that the instantaneous response to a situation worldwide is bringing us together, bringing us toward the 4th dimension, and very quickly. I have to admit, that my hat's off to Ted Turner who developed the concept of CNN. Before that, we had different major networks like ABC and NBC, but none of them had an effective international system. And pretty soon we're going to have the intergalactic system; it's on its way. There are a few of us who are contactees now. I'm training more and more people, helping them become contactees, if that is what they want to be. As the physical landings start taking place, the whole world is going to start accepting the extraterrestrial aspect, that we are not alone. So we are moving very fast, and those of us who are out here in the forefront are going to reap the benefits first, and we're going to have a lot of fun, but then we're going to have a responsibility which we're going to have to the people.

We're ready to explore the etheric part of the body and how it works with gravity and so on, but first let's add the next element which I call the study of extraterrestrial sciences, and with the goal of moving toward the higher consciousness, and altering our hormone and bodily structure to be able to receive, interpret and work with this form of consciousness.

The problem with terrestrial science, as we know it, is that there is always somebody talking to you and you listening, and by logic and memory you define what you have heard. You end up supposedly assimilating some truth. And this absorption of truth by logic does nothing for the spiritual development of man, and also I think it is a real problem because it doesn't do anything toward the raising of man's consciousness. For example, you can be as scientific as you want, but we still go to war with our high degree of science.

Why don't we take our high degree of intellect that we have developed at this point in time in this civilization and apply it towards peaceful scientific developments? Why do we always have to parallel it with wartime development? And, of course, you could say, "Well, because the other person is going to." Well, forget the other person. Somebody has to have enough confidence within and set an example for the entire world with no malice or after-thought about doing this. No one is doing this on a mass scale, no nation is leading the technology into these tremendous achievements that are quite possible to us now: healing techniques, interplanetary propulsion, time travel — all these exciting technologies are available right now!

So what we want to do is realize that we have to develop something other than logical science. We have to develop the emotional aspect of the body and bring the emotions in alignment with the physical aspect of the body. In other words, the emotions and the consciousness have to be together with the mind, the intellect. What I learned, when I was becoming a contactee in the early days, was that I used to always try to out-think what Semjase or one of the other ET's were trying to teach me. I would think about it, and think about what was going to be next, and think about what this really meant; and that was a block. You have to go with the emotions, the feelings.

We need to experience the 7 levels of con-sciousness

We've covered the seven levels of consciousness and what they are and where they are located as far as we can understand them. But now, it's time to actually experience them, because if you actually experience the levels of consciousness along with the intellectual understanding of the science, if you add the experience of knowing and relating to some sort of feeling to the actual construction of some idea on the physical plane, the resultant product

208

MEDITATION CHART
FOR
THE SEVEN LEVELS OF
CONSCIOUSNESS

Logoic
Desire, Aspiration

Monadic
Love, Attraction

Atmic (Female)
Intellect

Intuitive
That voice that you should have listened to

Mental-Two Levels
Spontaneous Thoughts
Logical Thoughts

Astral
Where we dream and work out our desires

Figure 25-1   **Physical**
Where we are

will have more integrity than it would if you arrived at it with sterile, unemotional thoughts. The meditation will be on the tape.

In our *Promise* Tape Series we have a musically narrated, sound coordinated section that takes you on a journey through the seven levels. The reason we use these techniques is quite simple. When you work with ordinary science, the methods are mostly mental at first. Then, slowly, you get a feeling for the art of the science by exercising your mentality through experimentation, and gradually this yields a confidence. The old way of trial and error is a time-limited way of approach, and the Western mind soon loses interest in the deep meanings of the experience, due to recent progression in planetary consciousness! (see figure 25-1).

In the extraterrestrial approach we learn the feelings of the parameters of space and time in the form of intuition (which is in itself a parameter). The we can cross the boundary layers of experience almost instantaneously and create results!

The first thing that we need to understand is the effect of time on our consciousness. The greatest influence on group or humanitys' consciousness is the position of all of our heavenly bodies starting with the moon (lunar) to the planets (planetary) extending out to the nearest star (solar) then on out to other galaxies (galactic).

There is often a masculine effect on consciousness (thought) in this lineage, but with the marriage of the female aspect (feeling), it presents a permanent change. On the other side of the coin is the phenomenon known as the parallel universe. Parallel universes co-exist within our universe as well as others. If you were to look at the astral plane or lower spiritual planes just beyond our present dimension and opposite that same dimension in another universe, you would begin to understand parallel universes. Eight of these can co-exist around one time zone or central point of the astral plane (see figure 25-2).

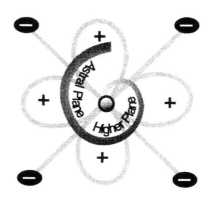

There are eight Parallel Universes to each Universe.

Figure 25-2

209

7 Subplanes of the Physical

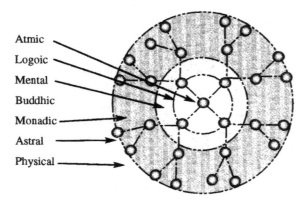

Atmic
Logoic
Mental
Buddhic
Monadic
Astral
Physical

Parallel Universes spread out across the seven levels of consciousness.

figure 25-3

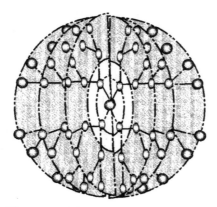

The progression of parallel universes is multidimensional.

figure 25-4

All eight of these universes will, during the period of creation, be expanding. From our perspective these universes are intermingling literally billions of times every second. On a galactic level, they could be said to be eight levels of galactic consciousness existing throughout space as separate cells of co-existing time that all connect in one place of zero time on the logoic plane, the ultimate existence, where all creation emanates from (see figure 25-3).

To see this in your mind's eye, close your eyes and imagine that there is nothing in existence but a black, absolute void where nothing exists, no universe, no sounds, no light and no consciousness.

Suddenly there exists a brilliant white light. From its source, which is so bright that sunlight dims in comparison, extend brilliant rays as far out as you can imagine. This is the logoic plane of the *Father's* energy.

When this reaches your conscious mind it extends into the pineal gland and is felt as the color red. Its activities are felt and experienced as will or desire to manifest motion within the boundaries of space and time. The central bright source is the heart of all creation and the infinite extending rays are the pathways to all of the galaxies and universes aforementioned (see figure 25-4).

Gravity of the soul

If you channel this desire into selfish purpose you become heavier and create not only gravity of the soul but also physical gravity. If you channel this desire into selfless purpose you become lighter, more transparent and freer to move into the more inner planes.

In the Eastern practice of Siddhis, one is to lessen the boundary and when this Siddhi is understood, physical levitation is often a side effect. In my book *Death of Ignorance*, I detail this in Chapter IX, "Bodies of Man or Man of Bodies."

Semjase explained time as gravity in this quote:

"Time is the vibrational exchange rate of Spirit and Matter. Motion is the movement of divine will split by desire! Gravity is the recombination of desire ascending to spirit after its expression through form."

Antigravity, detachment or impartiality is created by mind when it is disciplined to be free of desire, thus free of the time zone on a particular plane of consciousness. However, all time on all the planes is interpenetrable. Each of the seven planes has its own time zone. From our point of view, the higher the plane, the slower the time.

Spiral Galaxy

Figure 25-5

Now that we have seen the logoic plane into our mind's eye, let us focus on the monadic or second plane.

Still being aware of the white light we have created, close your eyes and realize that while you still see the white light, you are also aware of your thoughts and your own individual existence. This ability to self-individualize and be part of creation is the second cause, called the Principle of the Divine Son or Christ Principle.

Blue frenquencies can be sent deep into the DNA to help it

It is represented by the color blue and anchors itself into our beingness through the heart organ and chakra. As opposed to the Will or Desire nature of the Father energy, the heart chakra (monadic plane) gives us the feeling of love. Humanity can continue to exist, and on the higher nature of love, become co-creative with the very nature of God.

When blue is weak at the DNA level, the body becomes weak and insecure. By using, for example, a sapphire gemstone mounted into a device such as the Nuclear Receptor, blue frequencies can be retransmitted deep into the nuclear membrane of the DNA. This is true of all of the different chakras and all colors, three primaries and four secondaries, within the human form.

In the early stages of color-energy transmission it is usually best to transmit one color at a time, even if there are multiple color deficiencies. The reason is quite simple. Too much healing and balancing too quickly overloads the body's toxic drainage system and a resultant healing crisis ensues, making a pleasant experience uncomfortable.

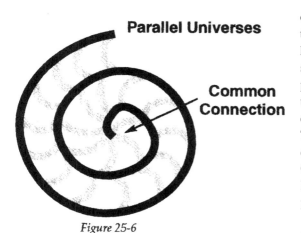

Parallel Universes

Common Connection

Figure 25-6

Another problem that I have observed in Western man is that he tries prematurely to heal others when he is not yet complete within himself. This can lead to a variety of psychically-related diseases in that the healer is not able to release the energies accumulated from others. This is why I am showing here how deeply these seven energies penetrate. Once a realization of service is unilateral, inner understanding becomes possible.

Now that we have seen the first and second cause, let us look at the third.

The essence of the void and essence of the white light and the separation of individuality becomes known as the female aspect, or the Holy Ghost. This is the atmic plane, and is, in fact, a summation of the other two. This atmic plane becomes the source of intellect (female) and later thought. Many seekers fail to realize that basic intelligence is feminine in nature.

The color of expression of the third plane is emerald green and is felt in the body within the throat center via the thyroid gland. Centered between the head (Father) and the heart (Son), the thyroid provides the consciousness of balance and centering in both the male and female of our species. In sound, this balance can be amplified by the musical note "C" on the diatomic scales of music, and often becomes the central chord in a composition.

The emerald is the gem of choice for the atmic plane, and in a nuclear receptor is quite amazing. Once the form experiences true balance, the holographic phase of thoughtforms begins to enter the full waking consciousness. This in turn helps us overcome the desire nature of the emotional (astral) body.

Buddhic plane or tunnel

Following this plane outward we next encounter the buddhic plane or intellect. Here is where the upper three begin to project the essence of creation and life into the lower planes. Sometimes called the tunnel, the buddhic plane forms the focal point of holographic images that become so apparent and familiar to our eyes here on the physical plane.

The color of this ray of energy is yellow, and strikes us directly in the solar plexus or stomach area. Working through the spleen, the pranic or oxygen/anu life force is directed into the bloodstream. Our bodies — via photosynthesis, then the Krebs cycle — become part of the Earth's environmental biosphere. In simple terms, sunlight creates sugars and starches that our bodies metabolize for energy. In turn, we release wastes in the form of carbon that plants recycle into life-giving oxygen, the host to valuable prana. See *Death of Ignorance* for greater details of this process.

The consciousness associated with this particular plane is compassion, feeling others' condition as well as our own. Often referred to as the Ray of Harmony through conflict, in its light we face the problems of others to resolve the confusion within our own nature. The gemstone best used for this ray is yellow citrine, and the musical note falls within the range of "D."

Often certain individuals center their lives on these different levels of consciousness to learn specific lessons. Gautama Buddha (Siddhartha) was one of these individuals who spent most of his life working on compassion, and through this became a master of his own actions.

Figure 25-7

Jesus Christ was considered a master of the Second Ray, love, and often the Manu or Lawgiver of new lands is considered a First Ray Master.

The Fifth Ray or Energy division is often referred to as the Ray of Concrete Science and Knowledge, and is known to us as the Mental Plane.

It has two major divisions: the arupa or spontaneous, and the rupa, or logical, respectively the upper and lower mental planes. Its color is orange, represented by the orange citrine or tourmaline. Its sound is in the "E" range, and it is not centered, but divided into several chakras.

When human beings begin to discover their true mental capacities, they move from the logical side of life to that of one of spontaneous and automatic decision. The orange Ray is one that almost all of the Pleiadians as a race follow. In Tibetan lore the God Agni is the personification of the mental plane. The Rishis (Gods of the Mental Plane) transmitted science, including Sanskrit, to the Brahmans 26,000 years ago. Sanskrit, the world's oldest language, came from the Pleiades. It is language based on the phonics derived from the motion of nature in its pure form. The numonics of Sanskrit are readily found in the Asian languages.

The sixth division of consciousness, the dark blue ray, is often called the Astral (Greek for starry) or Emotional Plane. In psychological or emotional terms, it is called the Ray of Abstractional Devotism. It is the path of the unenlightened soul that leads to the promised land via the way of trial and error. The majority of the human race is fast approaching this plane via sleep, and soon enough in the full waking consciousness. In the last 2000 years (Piscean Age) many souls came in on this ray. They were believers and therefore were afraid to trust in the hereafter. So as to not assume responsibility for their own actions, they created religion to structure their beliefs upon. Such was the call for help so loud, that it awakened the sleeping Christ within us all.

Some rose to the occasion but most fell short. One race went into complete denial when the master Jesus appeared on their doorstep 2000 years ago! As of late, powerful religious groups calling themselves the Illuminati or Golden Ones, rose in political world power, and under the guise of the orchestrated Revelations chapter of the Bible, proudly hailed us to unite in one World Order!

Meanwhile, the Aquarian soul quietly incarnates, ignores religion, and gradually begins to solve the world's problems via being born as the Knower. From an extraterrestrial point of view, this planet is business as usual, because Earth is a birthplane of evolving souls, and often a soul's first human incarnation is here.

But, baby is trying to break his cradle and kill his mother (Earth)! So, this is where the Eternal Babysitters, the Pleiadians and Andromedans and others, got involved. Not all ET's are friendly. However, there are insects, gnomes and bad fairies everywhere. Astral, terrestrial, extraterrestrial—they come in many forms.

It is up to you to choose your game and the Sixth Ray is where it all begins. You make the choices. You have the answers, don't you?

The prime gem of the Sixth Ray is lapis, and the metal silver. Some forms of turquoise also fall into place here.

The final split from the One light is the Seventh Ray — Ceremonial Magic. Led by Count St. Germaine (Master Duhl Kuhl, Tibetan) for the last 1000 years, the Violet Ray puts all things in righteous order. It is the pressure against Karma, forcing the soul upward towards perfection, ever agitating the fools caught in the foray of the sixth ray. It is physically detectable at the base of any pyramid, locked deeply within all of us who possess biological bodies built around the carbon atom.

Final split from the one light

A perfect synthesis of fire and air, it shines potently as amethyst and crosses over at times into tourmaline. Located in the sacral and sexual chakras, it can transform one into a vicious sexual animal or an enlightened master. This always occurs at the most inopportune times because, as I said, the violet ray is the pressure of Karma.

Those who have worn the amethyst receptor often tell the most amazing stories. The musical sound of magic is located in the key of "G."

What I want you to do now is to relax, stand up, stretch your arms, do whatever you have to do to get totally relaxed. Feel your breaths, breathe in, out, in (hold it), out, and do this a few times until you get your body relaxed. When you take a long, slow, deep breath and hold it, it puts oxygen into your system and gives you a tremendous rush, a good feeling. Now what I want you to do is close your eyes, sit back and relax a little bit. I want you to imagine that there is nothing but blackness everywhere you can think of, or see, or feel, just blackness, nonexistence.

There is absolutely nothing in existence at this point in time. You don't exist, the world doesn't exist, there is no such thing as light, your mother doesn't exist, your loved ones don't exist, your kids don't exist, nothing exists at all anywhere. There is absolutely nothing anywhere existing. And your thoughts — I want you to even clear your mind of all thoughts, not even thinking about what you're thinking about. Try to still yourself on every level. I know it is hard, but I want to give you a minute or two now to just think and clear your mind out of everything.

We're going to be using sound. You've already felt the difference sounds can activate within your being. We're going to be using the appropriate sound and note patterns with this meditation so that when we're on a particular level, we experience the corresponding sound at that level. This could be done in the morning, or this could be done late at night, or in the middle of the afternoon. It doesn't matter when you do it.

Now still your mind. Get a very, very quite mind at this point.

That's it, think of absolutely nothing.

Listen to Sound # 23 as you read this next section.

THE LOGOIC PLANE

Imagine one light — time does not exist

I want you to imagine One Light. In the middle of nowhere, in the middle of this darkness, is One Light coming from nowhere. Just suddenly out of nowhere exists One Light, and the energy extends as far as you can imagine. Imagine this One Light, then, to be the energies of the Father. This is the first energy field of existence. Time still doesn't exist yet. Only the Father exists. This is the Father energy, One Light. And the One Light transmits itself down into the body as One light.

You wouldn't be able to relate with this One Light if you didn't feel it in your body somewhere. Now I want you to feel it in the top of you head, just underneath your hairline. Feel it right in that area. It's the pineal gland, where the oneness is. The pineal gland has in it the hormone serotonin. Serotonin is a very powerful hormone, and if it's not balanced properly, it causes the energy to get completely out of control and become very negative. So you want to always have that hormone level balanced. The pineal gland is so sensitive because this One Light is the first source of energy, the first Ray. And it's a White Light. When it reaches the body and the pineal gland, the energy transmits as the color red. Red, then, slows down the flow of serotonin in the body, stimulating the pure energy of red itself, which gives you will power. So the first energy that's coming from the White Light is the Father, created out of emptiness and nonexistence, the first aspect, the first motion of the universe when the universe comes into being and consciousness comes into being. This directly relates to the pineal gland, which then slows down the flow of serotonin, and as a result you build up will-power, desire to accomplish, the desire to go out and motivate, the desire to make a move in some direction. On page 196 of this book is a chart from *Death of Ignorance* showing the respective rays and correspondences. After this meditation, look up Ray 1, where it says "Will," and you will see its different attributes and different energy fields, as well as direct applications to physical realities, even countries, in our world today.

Now that you realize the Father's energy at the top of the head, I want you to suddenly realize that somebody's talking to you. You're being guided through a meditation. Your own thoughts exist as does this White Light, and now, this other presence. When you start to realize that, you say to yourself, "Wait a minute. There's somebody else here. There's more in existence now than just the Creator. I'm here. But I'm different from the Creator because I'm realizing the Creator. I hear somebody's voice."

THE MONADIC PLANE

This energy you are now aware of is that of the son: S-O-N energy. This is love wisdom, Ray 2. This energy doesn't come to the head; it goes directly into the heart and the thymus gland. The thymus gland secretes hormones that regulate the heart, and the heart is also regulated by other areas in the body, such as the pituitary and different heart energy regulation centers. From this, a feeling is born inside you. That feeling is called wisdom, the desire to help or heal someone who's sick, or the love that you have for your mate, or your parents, or your children, or anyone. This is love. It's color is a beautiful blue energy, all permeating.

> One light... our own identity — the Son energy

Now you've seen the One Light. We realize our individual identities. We identify our individuality from the White Light, the separateness of it, and now we've talked about the Son, which is the blue energy, and comes from the heart Chakras and the actions of the heart.

THE ATMIC PLANE

The next energy we're going to realize is a combination of the essence of the White Light. In other words, what are the substances that make up the White Light, the substances of thought? What is the relationship between individual units that we are and God? What is the common thing that makes us all one and the same? The answer to all these questions is very simple: the Holy Ghost, the energy of the Holy Ghost. It's a combination of the first and the second and the third, so the individual White Light coming out of nowhere was the Father, and the separateness of our thoughts and our ability to identify and have this conversation and these feelings is the son, and the whole combination of everything, the intellect, the energy, the colors, the light, the darkness, everything, is made up of the Holy Ghost. Therefore you could say that the one and the three are the same.

The Holy Ghost is one of the two prime energy movers of the universe. The Father is more of a male energy, the son's a male energy, and the Holy Ghost is a female energy. The energy secures itself at the throat Chakra, the thyroid gland, the hormone thyroxine. The energy is expressed as the color green and called active intelligence, or the ability to think. This is thought itself. In the nuclear receptor, for example, a green stone would amplify the action of the thyroid gland. A lot of people don't realize that when they have weight problems, they also have thinking problems. The real problem is the thinking problem, not the weight problem, because they didn't approach the problem correctly. They approached it from the lower plane, the physical plane, and they forgot that the physical plane is only the lowest totem on the totem pole. The body gets directions; it is told what to do. It just doesn't somehow "get" fat or thin without something controlling it.

What directs it is the third Ray, the third energy, active intelligence. The kingdom of nature is keyed up on this energy field. Remember, the hydrogen atom rotates its polarity through the action of the Earth revolving around the sun, and the Earth's rotation itself. This changes its polarity. But green always remains constant.

So we've established three energy centers in the body, three main centers. Now what I want you to do is imagine from this White Light, which has a blue and a green aspect to it, also has a yellow energy field coming from it. (And you'll notice we're describing a rainbow at the same time.) The yellow energy secures itself down into the stomach area, that's the solar plexus, the first of the four lower sublevels of life. We've gone from the first three primary Rays of light to the fourth sublevel. There are seven altogether.

Now looking back at what these levels are, we talked about the first as the White Light, and we felt that White Light, let it permeate our bodies. That's the Logoic Plane, as outlined in the Death of Ignorance. The White Light is the real essence of the Logoic plane, meaning the one source, the Father, the male energy.

Then, of course, the second aspect was the Monadic Plane, where the energies of the son come from, meaning the Christ Son, the separateness, the freedom to be an individual energy. And then number three, which was the active intelligence, was the Atmic plane.

THE BUDDHIC (INTUITIVE) PLANE

And now number four, coming down again, is the intuitive plane. The Ray type, because it's a stomach energy, would be harmony through conflict energy. Now we pointed out that the different masters were related to these different rays. These highly developed individuals had reached a level of consciousness centered more on the rays, and on the energies as they are. And not only our masters, but our entire intergalactic civilizations are centered on the rays, which you'll discover as we progress. The Master centered on the first ray. The will ray, the White Light, is known as the Manu, the law-giver, the power that brings the laws to the society, to help society regulate and live with itself. In the White Brotherhood we have a master called Master Moria, who was known as a very powerful master who, even though he didn't show his compassion like some of the other masters did, he showed his compassion by direct power and confrontation, with basically no room for forgiveness as you would understand it, unless you really understood what his message was.

The second Ray defines our separateness, where we realize each other as individuals. Jesus Christ would be an example of a master on that Ray. Master KH, Koot Hoomi, would also be a good example, or Master DK, Djwhol Khul, who is the higher nature of Count Saint Germaine, and some of these other masters of science. He was in his primary aspect a second Ray master.

On the third Ray, the love, active intelligence ray, would be Master Hilarion and Master Serapis. There was a Venusian Master by the name of Kandrupa, also the energies of Aphrodite fall on the green Ray. And the White Brotherhood is called the Mahachohan, or Lord of Civilization. The cocoa plant, not the drug cocaine, but the cocoa plant itself, is used for spiritual rituals by the Indians in South America and Peru. For literally centuries, even millennia, they have observed this plant as a divine plant, calling the female plant Mama Cocoa, which is very much related to Mahachohan, the White Brotherhood aspect of it.

And now, back into the yellow light — the master of the yellow ray was Guantanama Buddha Siddhartha. He lived his life by approaching conflict and resolving it into harmony.

Christ did that, too, but Buddha processed it. Christ came into situations from a perspective of love and forgiveness, whereas Buddha came in with confrontation. As a matter of fact, the unfortunate thing about Siddhartha was that he left the physical plane by eating some chicken, something he normally didn't eat. He went to a person's home one day, and he didn't want to insult this person, so he ate the chicken when it was served. He couldn't digest it because he had become too refined. He wasn't able to process meat any more. That meant it was probably time for him to leave anyway.

So we know that fourth ray activates itself through the stomach, through the adrenal glands, through the liver, kidney, spleen, and they in turn secrete corticosteroids into the brain, such as norepinephrine. Epinephrine and norepinephrine enter the blood stream and give you a feeling of energy. Another spiritual feeling evoked here would be compassion.

Compassion is the feeling that allows you to feel, when in a confrontation with others, how they feel towards you. In any situation involving another, try to put yourself in their place. Don't force your reality on them. This fourth Ray feeling differs, for example, from a second Ray feeling, in that the second Ray is an "outpouring of love" feeling or a feeling of attraction, versus confrontation and sensitivity.

The Nuclear Receptor we wear also because the different colors of gems mounted correlate to these different consciousnesses. Because the hydrogen atom receives the consciousness to the body, and the Nuclear Receptor is an antenna for any one of the seven colors, or consciousnesses, it is very effective in helping to understand the nature of consciousness itself.

A red (Ruby) receptor amplifies the Father energy. The Blue (Sapphire) Receptor amplifies the second Ray energy; an Emerald (Green) amplifies the Atmic Plane. and so it goes. And of course, Citron, being yellow, will work as the gemstone of choice for the fourth Ray!

THE MENTAL PLANE
(Ray of Concrete Science & Knowledge)

Now we move down into the fifth Ray, the fifth energy field, coming from the one, became the three, became the seven. This is the Ray of concrete science and knowledge; it's orange in color, and very powerful. But it's also, just as the fourth Ray, a mixture. It's not one of the primary colors, but instead a mixture of primary colors. And somebody might say, "We've got the White Light. The White Light wasn't a mixture." But the White Light is a mixture. The sunlight, which is a source of White Light, breaks into seven visible colors when focused through a prism. So the Ray of concrete scientific knowledge is orange. And it, of course, corresponds to the mental plane, which is split, the lower, the arupa, and the upper plane, which is the rupa, according to Tibetan teachings.

You can approach logic in two ways: view a situation from a logistical standpoint and act accordingly, or you can approach it spontaneously and just let it happen. I remember before I was speaking in New Age terms or the new more expanded concepts, the open concepts. I used to start and run businesses. Starting a business logically means to view the process as having to project sales, and then find money to meet the sales projection. And then, of course, when the sales figures were established, try to bring them up higher and require less investment money.

That would never work in the New Age business philosophy. That's why the banking systems are having problems now, as do other businesses, because there is no logistical approach, rather, New Age businesses are spontaneous. They can find their own way. The way you run a business today is to just let it happen, let it have its own mind, don't try to second-guess it or outthink it, just let it happen. This what I'm mean by splitting the mental plane in half. Pleiadians, being a very mental race and a very scientific race, would be more in the orange area of Ray types. Whereas you could say, for example, within the second ether the inhabitants living in Shamballa, the White Island, are more related to the blue energy, because they're more into love, wisdom and the service of the race.

RAY OF ABSTRACT IDEALISM (Astral Plane)

The next ray, which is the sixth Ray, is royal blue. It's called the ray of devotion and idealism. It's a mixture of many different colors in the body, more towards the base of the spine, and encompasses ideals and goals. This Ray of consciousness relates to the astral plane. It's where you go when you dream at night. And which, if you're doing this meditation properly, you are in somewhat even now. It's the place the entire world is moving toward, the 4th dimension. The sixth Ray becomes the doorway to that.

PHYSICAL PLANE (Plane of Magic and Ceremonial Order)

The seventh Ray is the ceremonial order of magic and ritual. Count St. Germaine was the master who did a lot of work with that through the ages. It's color is violet. An interesting point is that when we first discovered the pyramids a long time ago, we used the magic of the pyramid, or the seventh Ray of the pyramid, to share it with the world. It is the energy that when you put a Pyramid over grapefruit juice or orange juice, causes it to go from being bitter to sweet by changing the enzyme value. Changing the enzyme value this way makes the food palatable for the human body without making the body use energy in order to absorb or assimilate it.

Just as in our earlier example, where mass consciousness accepted the existence of gas, so now are we re-accepting the existence of this active principle generated by the Pyramid structure. In 1973, Russian soldiers wore Pyramids on their heads to counter the effects of the positive ions on the desert winds of the areas of Manchuria they were occupying. They also used the Pyramids to sharpen razor blades! All these occurrences interrelate because the Pyramid contains all these different levels of consciousness.

But right now I want you to feel these levels of consciousness, I want you to feel the White Light and realize it's the will, I want you to feel the blue energy, realize that it's the son loving from the heart, and I want you to feel thyroid activation and know that it's active intelligence coming from the Holy Ghost, and I want you to feel your stomach area pulsating with yellow energy and realize that yellow energy is harmony through conflict, tremendous power for passion, forgiveness for others, as we've all been in all spaces at one time or another. Just feel the integration of the science and knowledge going through the body, and the aural language. I want you to feel the devotion of the fifth ray toward completing your life in a positive way. And I want you to respect the magic of the seventh Ray, the violet, the natural order of all things falling together, and get in touch with that order, because that order had to do with these seven Rays that we're exploring.

The music that you're hearing accompanies each one of these levels. The musical notes with the timbres are required, not just the notes themselves

I want you to repeat this exercise, not just do it once and forget about it. I want you to come back to this section of the book, maybe once a day, or once a week, until it becomes natural to you. When you see somebody walking down the street wearing a red dress, you'll think, "That person must have a strong will power." Or when you see somebody driving around with a blue car, you'll think that person could be a caring person. Start to relate to the colors that you see externally, and start to relate to sounds that you hear, and start to relate to the attributes of different kinds of food that correlate to these rays. And start to realize the different shapes associated with these rays, and the gemstones that go to these rays. For example, in the receptor we use an amethyst to express violet. Start relating to this, start feeling it, and then, spontaneously, things are going to open up in your mind, body and spirit, and you're going to start to realize the extraterrestrial science, and you will attain a much higher, greater, inner meaning and understanding of all this.

So now I want you to take a deep breath and prepare to readjust to the outside world. You've just come from an inner experience, and this inner experience is a lot closer to perfection than what you normally experience during the day. So I want you to wake up, open up and stretch, and gradually acclimate yourself back to the physical plane.

Chapter 26

The Four Ethers, Your Etheric Body, and Moving Into Dimensions Beyond

I hope you all enjoyed that meditation. Take your time and read through it and then try it again, before proceeding on. It will help you "feel" the next section.

Now we will study further the etheric body. We've just been through seven bodies of consciousness in our meditation. Now we're going to explore the logoic, monadic, atmic, intuitive, mental, and astral planes, all the way down to the physical body. That's our destination, the physical plane. Everybody says, "I had more fun on the higher planes." That may be so, but we have to understand the upper levels of the physical planes, because if you don't understand them, that's where you're going to stay. You're going to be stuck. And it doesn't mean that you have to be a mental giant, intellectually gifted, to transcend or move into the 4th dimension and through the physical plane. Quite the contrary. It's better if you just feel the understanding of what the higher inner planes are about, and through this feeling, we would move through into the other planes. But the fact is you must develop certain parts of your body in order to get through these other planes of consciousness.

The etheric body interpenetrates every cell of the body. It resembles a golf ball with tiny indentations in it, but the nuclear membrane, which is where the DNA is encased, has a regular pattern of tiny openings. What passes through those holes? Not air, but the etheric body of energy, which is the link up to these higher, inner levels. ***In order to attain higher consciousness and move into the 4th dimension, you need to close the openings with a densified nuclear etheric field.***

Now within the etheric body itself there are several core centers. We've been talking about them already, they're known as chakras. The existence of these chakras has been known for centuries, and they are described in many metaphysical books through the East, particularly in the Hindu sacred writings from the Bhagavadgita. The many different sources of information about chakras can be traced to the original source, the Pleiades.

Chakras arise in the etheric portion of the nerve centers within the spine, but terminate in circular depressions. Via the three different nervous ganglia in the body, which we have previously studied, energy is transmitted along an "electrical wire." Ganglia "wires" extend down from the brain, and within these ganglia are the chemicals sodium, potassium and phosphorous. These are separated by pumping stations known as Nodes of Rainier. Visualize these nerves extending from the brain down through to the feet, with little pumps at different intervals along them, pumping electrical energy.

If we were to go a step further now, and look at the nerves through a microscope, we would see the many cells that make up each nerve, and within each cell you would find a nuclear membrane, or the nucleus of the cell. The nuclear membrane of the cell is peppered with holes through which the etheric body of consciousness passes. This etheric body is energized via the astral plane and other planes of consciousness. It becomes necessary to bring the whole nervous system up to the vibratory level of the command signals that are coming from the astral, then etheric levels into the brain centers of the nuclear membranes within the cell. Concentration of mind energy, our consciousness, fills these holes with etheric substance, because energy follows thought on this level. To clarify that a little more, the mind is the slayer of the real, so don't rely on the mind to give you decisions. Make your decisions from life as it presents the solutions to you. But at the same time, the mind can be used as a great focal lens to bring upon the physical body higher and stronger currents of etheric energy (see figures 26-1 and 26-2).

Your etheric body of consciousness passes through cell holes in the tiniest nucleus in the nerves

The "input" openings of the nuclear membranes in the chakra areas, which receive the higher, inner plane energies, are flared or trumpet-like in shape, like a morning glory. This characteristic is specific to cells located in the chakra center itself. For example, if you examine the entire central nervous system, you'll find most cells exhibit the typical opening in the nuclear membrane like that shown in this illustration (26-1). But when you examine the chakra areas, the nuclear membranes of the cells there look a little different. The golf ball similarity is there, but the openings are flared, because this is the main input for the entire system. These funnels gather energy, which is then concentrated and sent to the DNA of the chakra area cells. Then it is propelled out into the aura field. The chakras accept the input of vibration, vibration then sensitizes the endocrine structure, the endocrine structure then secretes hormones, depending on the stimulus coming from the chakras.

If you find the material overwhelming at this point, you may wish to again review. I constantly do, as we all have a tendency to forget certain things when we move through other levels. The human brain is like a muscle you have to work to keep strong. Don't be embarrassed by having to work the human brain over and over again. If you say, "My neighbor read the book once, and he gets the idea right away, and I have to read it six times," let me tell you something. If the neighbor read it once, and you read it six times, Dr. Fred Bell has read it 25 times. Repetition is the mother of success. I learned that a long time ago. When I read something 20 times, I know it forever. And that's the same for most everyone.

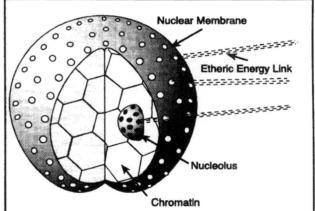

The Brains of the Outfit

The cell's brain, the nucleus, is contained by a pore-pocked membrane through which the nucleus communicates to the surrounding cytoplasm. The nucleolus (of which there may be several) is something of a mystery, but it may be the vital source of nuclear protein. The chromatin material contains all the hereditary information needed for the reproduction of new cells.

figure 26-1

The etheric body interpenetrates the cells of the physical body, and this input of life force energy comes from within the chakras themselves. The chakras deviate from the rest of the etheric body at the point where the etheric body interpenetrates the physical body to convey information and consciousness. Somewhere in the etheric body of man, which interpenetrates all cells, there has to be an input center or centers. The chakras serve this purpose. Where the chakra-assimilated energy is received, its frequency is determined by the frequency of the DNA, which is an interpenetration of energy coming through the etheric level, coming from the higher, inner astral levels. If you wonder where this consciousness starts, in other words what determines what cell becomes a chakra and what cell becomes a regular cell in the body, this occurs on the astral level and this is determined at the moment a woman gets pregnant. Certain commands from the 46 chromosome base of the male/female combination take place. In the consciousness, the numbers of these 46 chromosomes, not being 49 chromosomes or 32 chromosomes, is determined by the locations of the chakra points.

> **The chakras are the input center of your etheric body**

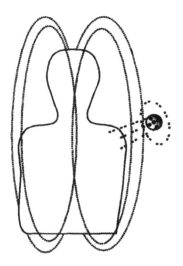

Figure 26-2

The nuclear membrane holds the etheric body to the physical body. Under extreme stress or near death, this bond begins to exit the physical body and move into the etheric body. The "etheric double" as it is called has three higher states. The intermediate state is the second ether where, if a termination occurs, loved ones will greet the newly deceased and then escort them into the astral plane.

During communication with higher beings, the middle state of the second ether acts as a doorway to higher dimensional beings.

The chakra at the base of the spine, at the back of the body, is specialized to absorb a combined chi force known as Kundalini. Kundalini emanates from the Earth and gives life to the organs of the body. This force is just becoming known to mainstream science. The Kundalini force is an energy similar to that generated by a linear accelerator. The brain is a receiver/transmitter of energy. The Kundalini force transmutes the body's resistance to electricity moving from the brain down to the base of the spine. When the Kundalini rises up the spine, it results in the brain using less effort to receive energy from the base of the spine, or vice versa.

> **Kundalini energy emanates from the Earth**

Look at the spine as a freeway. If you're in a car that begins at the base of the spine, and you drive towards the brain, you will be travelling as easily as if you were coasting, when you are in harmony. Whereas, if you're not working with the Kundalini force, you would essentially be driving uphill. Driving uphill takes a lot more energy, and as a result, the cerebrospinal fluid which moves up the base of the spine to the brain only causes the sexual activity of the brain to increase. Whereas, if you're going downhill because the Kundalini is raised, the energy in the brain is tremendously elevated from the sexual to the spiritual, and you become incredibly creative. Developing the Kundalini force enhances, or builds, the spiritual energy, the creative energy of the body. This is great for anyone, from engineers to artists, who wish to transcend linear thought processes.

> **The ether is a pathway for interdimensional life force energies!**

The next chakra center is situated over the spleen. The spleen is a vitalizing center, taking the prana from the vitality globule via the sun, converting it directly into spiritual physical consciousness. In other words, allowing awareness. Prana is split up and distributed to various parts of the body, vitalizing many of the nerve centers and causing the flow of ethers over the physical nerves. The other centers are links by means of which forces from the subtle bodies are expressed through the physical body. The term "ether" that I'm using right here to describe this whirlwind of matter, has just recently been clearly defined by the New Age scientists as a pathway for interdimensional life force energies. However, in the past, metaphysical people, students and clairvoyants have seen the etheric forces by their extended vision and described them in their own terms. That's why there hasn't been validity in the field.

Now we're trying to validate the field by bringing it to you in a scientific manner. Scientists, on the other hand, have discovered the laws governing the phenomena of certain lower ethers and many valuable inventions have resulted. So we know the ethers by their products. New Age science is destined to meet with traditional metaphysical science in this era, as well as extraterrestrial science.

Humans create disharmonic frequencies that transmit to Earth's astral body and disrupt the solar system

Marconi, famed as the inventor of the wireless, or transmissions through the air, is usually regarded as the first to use the etheric forces of electromagnetism in radio transmission, thus opening the door to the vast developments in communication that is so rapidly drawing all peoples of the world into a close-knit human fellowship. Remember the story about the cave? The caveman had to develop the conscious acknowledgment of the existence of solids, then liquid, then steam, or gas. During war in Iraq, for example, the whole world tuned in to Ted Turner's world wide television network. Soon the whole world will come to a mutual understanding. When I say the whole world, I mean a significant majority, but sooner or later, everyone will move into that consciousness.

Just as Man's physical body is contained within his etheric body, so the Earth is enveloped with its own etheric reality. Life could not exist on Earth without this etheric Earth body that allows the inflow of vitality or life force from the sun, solar fire, and universe into the surrounding network of global forces, and finally into man. Mankind, however, is not clear in its existing body. Due to high levels of stress he has created in his environment, he has created disharmonic frequencies that place subtle stress on his electrical precursing, sensing body (etheric). This puts a growth-resistant harmonic upon his astral body, which is transmitted into the etheric/astral body of Earth. Mother Earth then amplifies this harmonic of confusion and sends it to the sun and surrounding solar system.

During certain times of the year, the planets align in close physical order, called the "Jupiter Effect." When this happens, they reject the disharmonious body of Mother Earth. This sends negative waves of emotional or astral energies into the sun, usually during a full moon. Solar flares are evidence of this anger, or disturbance, and impact us in many ways:

1. They send back powerful, astral/emotional destabilizing waves into the Earth's core, which re-centers its frequency alignment to the solar system. Because the Earth's core is a crystal lattice consisting of X, Y, and Z axis minerals, it causes the Earth's surface to destabilize and herein causes earthquakes.

2. Solar flares also have an etheric force called "solar wind." During flaring, this wind upsets our upper atmosphere, causing tremendous weather changes.

3. Solar flares alert extraterrestrial activities, causing their interaction. In most cases, the Andromedans intervene to control the cause. Note: the two most active times for this are March and October. Sightings of UFOs globally peak during these times. Pyradyne, with their Systems Technologies, greatly interacts within these change periods. One person using one Systems III or Quad System can place positive energy back into the Earth's core, greatly relieving the negative impact of these conditions. One person with a properly connected and synchronized System can overcome the negative effects of thousands of negative-energy people. This is a tremendous "assistance" to the friendly ETs, and often people become contactees in the process, usually because they are recognized by the higher, creative forces. Nature is a two-way street: give Her life, and she will comfort you. (see figures 26-3 to 26-9)

Aura Field

Earth's Aura Field is disharmonious because mankind is not yet as a unit producing harmonious auric interchange with the surrounding nature and universe. The bulk of mankind is called the "Growth Resistant Generation" or GRG.

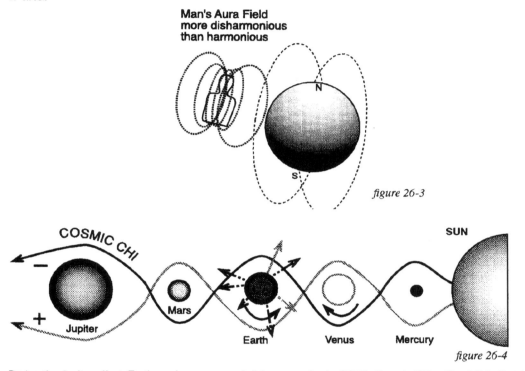

figure 26-3

figure 26-4

During the Jupiter effect, Earth produces waves of disharmony due to GRG's. Cosmic Chi or Kundalini effect is amplified by the Jupiter effect between the planets and the Sun. Unfortunately, the chi is disturbed and sent out of balance as it passes by the Earth. This disturbance is amplified as it moves toward the Sun.

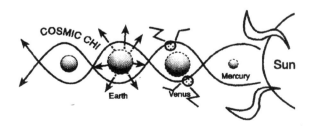

figure 26-5

Then either during the spring or fall equinoxes this energy goes into the Sun. The Sun reacts with increased solar flare activity. This energy is so negative that it hits the Sun and produces a bullet hole effect. This hole then exhausts core gases millions of miles into space.

225

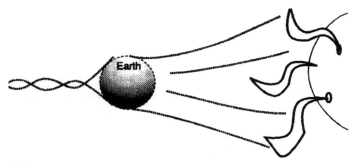

Figure 26-6

The solar flares intensify the solar wind, which reacts with the Earth's molten core. This sets up a negative scalar wave effect. Because the Earth is like a giant crystal, these negative scalar waves move to the surface on the S & P Axis. When they strike the surface, the tectonic plates are shifted, causing a quake action!

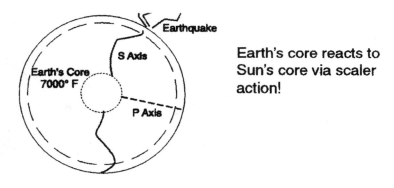

Earth's core reacts to Sun's core via scaler action!

Figure 26-7

Using Pleiadian technology, the Andromedans work through non-infected human beings to stabilize the Earth's core. Non-infected humans are people who express a positive aura field that is in harmony with the universe. Although there are more humam beings on earth that are "Growth Resistant Generation," the Pleiadian technology, along with the fewer harmonious souls using it help even up the odds, making global harmony a future possibility. This assistance to humans and technology is called "Divine Intervention."

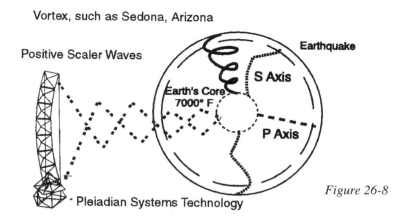

Vortex, such as Sedona, Arizona

Positive Scaler Waves

Earthquake

S Axis

Earth's Core 7000° F

P Axis

Pleiadian Systems Technology

Figure 26-8

As many Systems go into effect worldwide, a networking program is being put into place. This network moves into the arena of "time" and puts into place a "holograph" sychronized by the combined action of the **minds** of the New Age souls.

This shortening of time by a few overcomes the damage created by the ignorant mass or bulk of humanity. If the Earth had to wait for humanity to become enlightened without this assistance, the Earth would long be destroyed, as was the palnet that died earlier in our solar system — the asteroid belt.

Earth's Aura being Holographically repro-grammed. Hologram of balance and harmony to the surrounding universe is multidimensional.
figure 26-9

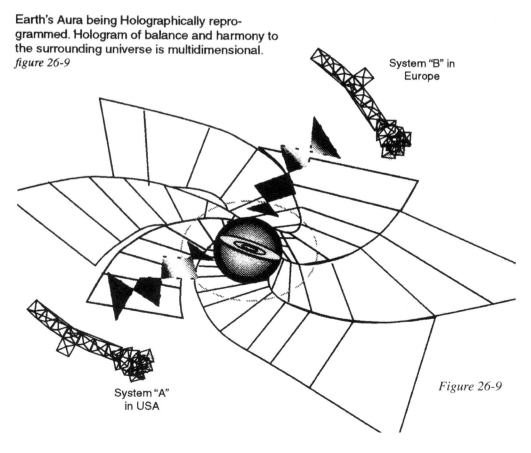

System "B" in Europe

System "A" in USA

Figure 26-9

227

The cultists reverently refer to the universal life force as the Christ consciousness, or the Christ Life, and so do metaphysicians, even the extraterrestrials to a degree. Again, we speak of the world of life spirit, meaning not only one of the planes of spirit matter, but also the exalted state of consciousness in which only one universal life is recognized. The supreme master of human evolution, not life evolution, but human evolution, is Jesus Christ, the world's outstanding example of what the attainment of this universal consciousness can mean. Nobody can deny that fact. By the law of reflection, familiar to all of us, this high plane of universal life is a prototype of the etheric realm and it is a manifold phenomenon. Things visible and tangible in the etheric realm are signs and tokens of great powers resident in the higher realm of life spirit and Christ consciousness. This means that there is a very intimate connection between the Christ Life and the life forces which operate in the twilight realm of matter toward which material science is groping its way. Through mental, moral and physical discipline, according to spiritual law, a new etheric sheath is actually formed within the refined essences of the etheric body. This second etheric structure is the prerequisite to all initiatory development, and that's what we're all trying to accomplish, to initiate ourselves into the next consciousness. Without initiatory forces, the etheric body's progress through higher spiritual planes or states of initiation would be an impossibility.

THE CHEMICAL ETHER

Metaphysical science teaches that the ethers are capable of division into four states or properties by varying degrees of density, each having its own special function. The densest of the four ethers is called the chemical ether because it is the field of activity for the chemical force, biochemistry, which underlies the structure of our material universe, and which is realized by alchemists for transmuting one element into another. It is so nearly material that only a slight expansion of sight is necessary to see it. It's basic color is dark blue, and it is sometimes observed at the base of blue flames, or when the gas is turned very low, or it may have the appearance of thick mist or smoke. And I know in our light shows we often see this energy field, especially when we use the violet (Helium Cadmium) laser.

THE SEVEN SUB-PLANES OF THE PHYSICAL

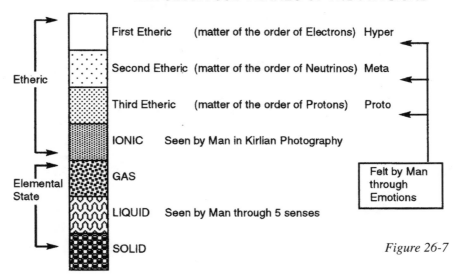

Figure 26-7

Through this ether, the new age chemist may be able to study the activities of chemical forces which he knows now largely through their results and not by direct observation. In the human organism, **this ether seems to take the form of prisms through which the colorless solar energy radiates, assuming a rosy hue.** This does change during the times of day. These prismatic ether atoms seem to be embedded in the center of the physical body atoms.

The chemical ether is a twofold current possessing a positive-negative pole or function. (All spirit or life is dual manifestation, expressing itself as positive-negative or masculine-feminine.) The positive etheric current attracts and builds the physical atoms of the body and the negative current disintegrates and eliminates them. Thus we may describe the chemical ether as a whirlpool of forces that flow new molecules through the positive pole, and push old molecules out through the negative pole. All this has to do with the reproduction of the cell. These molecules have actually been recognized in some instances as pertaining to known substances. To the lay mind, this process suggests that vital electricity converts the body into a kind of ultra-magnet for attracting or holding elements needed in body building, and for rejecting or eliminating those not needed. The flow of life force is correspondent to the turning off and the turning on of a current, alternating current (A/C).

THE LIFE ETHER

The second ether known to the metaphysical sciences is called the life ether because it is concerned with the propagation of the species, whether it be a plant, an animal, or a man. Physical science is eagerly anticipating the day when it can study these forces first-hand, which is just starting now to happen. The time is not too far away before we can start to make measurements, thanks to the biofeedback equipment we're working with now. One of the people I worked with, a scientist who was an American Indian spiritual master, Quentin McConnell, developed a Spectral Analyzer around 1979 which he connected directly to plants. I remember Peter Tompkins was also doing research with plants at the time, and he was fairly impressed with the Analyzer, because it didn't just measure the resistance changes in the leaves like ordinary biochemistry equipment does. This particular equipment would look at the central nervous system of the plant itself. When the plant was acclimated to a human being, we got some amazing results. If you were happy, so was the plant!

> Light ether: motion & color

The life ether is also a positive-negative, and within it the secret of sex will be found. The knowledge of this ether will give to biological science control of the sex of the unborn infants. *Sex hormones are crystallizations of this ether.* Differentiation of the sexes as we know it today will seem very crude and primitive to the future generations. If you have etheric vision, blood is seen coursing through the veins in the form of gas, which reminds one of the legend of certain spirits known in Oriental mythology that are said to have fire in their veins instead of blood. Now *blood, by the way, is a complete crystallization of the life ether*. It brings the spiritual force to the body. Ancient Greeks offered that the veins of their Gods were filled with nectar instead of blood. A hint, again, of the miraculous power stored in the life ether.

> The light ether reaches consciousness as a feeling

The two ethers, chemical and life ethers, surround and interpenetrate the physical form, constituting its matrix. *The chemical ether reveals itself as a blue field, while the color radiation of the life ether is a rosy or orange hue, which varies somewhat according to the species and status of evolution*. But it is always present where life is found. *In the plant kingdom there's a delicate pink-orange,* the color of a certain lotus known in the Orient. In the human kingdom, it is described as the color of the newborn peach blossoms, a deep pink with

229

a suggestion of blue or violet overtones. And as you see more aura fields, while using our equipment regularly, you'll be able to analyze these aura fields, because they open up that consciousness that's normally blocked in most people. Enjoy noticing the many colors people have, and now that you've been through the meditation, you begin to see how the different colors relate to the different levels of consciousness. For example, if we're looking at a peach color, then peach is obviously some offshoot of orange and white, sort of a cream color. White, of course, is the first aspect, the Ray aspect, which we did in our meditation. And the orange part would be more in the solar plexus, so it's a combination of bringing the will down into power, expression in light ether. *The second ether is* also the one that will soon be revealed to mankind as the one that is *the doorway to the astral plane.* Many beings base their existence upon this ether.

THE LIGHT ETHER

Motion and color characterize the planetary light ether. A high degree of spiritual perception is necessary for investigating these ethers, but it doesn't take that much time to develop, if you go slowly. Do the meditation that we did earlier a few more times through. That will really help you, because you begin to see this in your meditation. *The light ether is an ether that sparkles and flashes with all the hues of the rainbow.* It is sensitive to the presence of light, whether it be from the sun or artificial illumines, or whether it beats or pulsates in a wing-like motion while "seeds of light," many, or a few, according to the intensity of light, float about. We would consider this to be possibly the photons of physics, but actually *the photon is the first level of the astral interpenetration of the physical plane. So the light ether is made up of the photon, but the photon itself is consciousness, an intelligence, coming down from the astral plane,* and which we'll cover when we get to lasers. The light ether also has a connection with blood in human beings, as its positive current infuses the blood with heat and controls circulation as well. The negative current operates through the five senses, especially sight, although t*he basic color of the light ether is said to be the beautiful golden effulgence* described as the Christ Ray. It actually displays all the colors of the spectrum.

Remember, the second Ray of the sun is the Christ Ray. Now I'm not trying to be religious, that just happens to be what it's called. Extraterrestrials call it something else, but it means the same thing. Because *this ether is the avenue for sensation, life vitalizing the nerves* as it works and moves through the *parasympathetic nervous system.* The *autonomic nervous system* subconsciously runs bodily functions, and the parasympathetic nervous system is the nervous system in the body that perceives the sensation of feeling. So it's this light ether that is the consciousness. It transmutes the electrical sensation to the etheric sensation in an intriguing interplay. That's when it reaches the consciousness as a feeling.

Let's say you drop a brick on your own foot — you feel pain. You think you felt the pain by the electrical current conducted to the brain, but you wouldn't feel anything until the etheric was galvanized. As soon as the etheric counterpart, what we call the electrical precursing area, or avenue, is open, then you feel the pain. The pain comes through the opening of this energy field. Now realize that when you talk about the Pyramid and the Receptor and these other devices and systems, that these are precursing devices, and this explanation further clarifies why and how they work.

Because this ether is the avenue of sensation, it makes it a channel for sensations which do not ordinarily register in the brain. The eye begins to see colors not usually visible. The ear begins to hear sounds not normally audible.

I'm making a commentary from Chapter IX, "Bodies of Man, or Man of Bodies?," from *Death of Ignorance*, reading and commenting at the same time. Basically, once you've put more of your consciousness and your energy from the electricity towards the galvanization of the etheric levels, your sensitivity goes beyond the electric, which is really important. Even the sense of touch is enhanced so the individual can feel etheric currents, both in his own body and in the atmosphere. Biological electricity is an expression of the negative pole of light ether as biological heat is the expression of its positive pole. Science has already been able to create metals that, when an electric current polarized one way runs through them, get hot, and if polarized the other way, get cold. This science is quickly coming upon us.

> The Blue Light crystal

THE REFLECTIVE ETHER

Most attenuated and refined of all the etheric substances is the fourth or reflective ether, which too is adjacent to the astral plane. Just like the structure of the atom, there are smaller sub-components of existence. We're down to the level of *the last sub-components on the physical plane, which transmute energy from the astral plane.* The substance is clear and luminous, as it is truly a reflector of the eternal truth transcribed upon the Scroll of Ages. It, too, has positive and negative aspects, but *this ether is scarcely physical at all* in any known sense of the word. It is the avenue through which thought makes its impression upon the human brain. Electricity is one level of energy, and then as you get more sensitive, you use the light ether, and then finally the reflecting ether makes this impression on the human brain. It's *the final aspect of the emotional energy fields* that make this touch possible.

The masculine, or positive, aspect of the reflecting ether works through the brain and voluntary nervous system, promoting reason and creative activity. The negative, or female, aspect operates in and through the involuntary nervous system, promoting intuition, feeling. The positive pull of the reflective ether is, therefore, a special channel of the ego; the negative pole that of the Human Race Spirit.

The work of meditation stimulates both aspects of the reflecting ether in the new and higher activity. Before the meditation, we covered the subject of initiation. No ether is more important than this ether in the mysterious labor of initiation. Awaken to it — a new life under the control of individual will — and discover the many new miraculous powers latent therein! This is where you actually become enlightened or aware of beingness and becoming. It's a state of "growing awareness," to look at it in lay terms. The reflecting ether is a negative aspect in the subconscious mind nature of humans. It is the blue light crystal in which the seer reads certain records, but it is not the true memory of nature found in the different sphere, which, of course, would be the Akashic records.

Now that we have observed the four states of ether, remember that all these are part of the physical plane and exist inside of each other. At the fourth state, or ionic state, their compound density is so great that gravity precipitates them, and they become gases which are attracted not only to each other, but also to the Earth. Once impressed inside the atmosphere, they become solids and liquids. From these our bodies and environments are thus fashioned. Let us examine our body energies more closely.

Chapter 27

Chakras and Energy Absorption

The study of the etheric body in its relationship to the physical realms presents us space, time, motion, gravity and magnetism. Here is how gravity comes into our being. And for those of you who are designing antigravity systems, there are some real hints as to some basic principles. Gravity does not work at all like most people think, and it is not related to magnetism. Magnetism is a physical plane of energy. Gravity is a universal fact existing on all planes simultaneously, holding them together in perfect balance. Understanding of gravity is not necessary to overcome its effects. ***Every atom in the body possesses consciousness.*** Consciousness receives its direction from the mind. The mind can think positive, and the consciousness of the atoms spontaneously forms molecules, which begin to form healthy cells. The conscious mind does not have to understand how this process occurs, but only has to think positively about its occurrence.

> **Magnetism exists on the physical plane. Gravity exists throughout all planes at the same time!**

The second thing necessary to know about gravity is the physical plane's rebounding action called karma. It makes us lighter or heavier physically in relation to the Earth's karma by simple definition. It's the old philosophy, "an eye for an eye," "give love and you shall receive love," "serve others and you in turn shall be served," or, as I like to say in my lectures, "energy seeks its own balance."

The third thing to understand about gravity is the action of the will and its purpose for self-achievement. Anyone who seeks to find the principle of antigravity will find it. Some strive for conscious development so they may dominate and use others, while the majority strive to release themselves from the limited bounds of Earthly karma so that they may help others develop more efficiently. Either motive could bring us to the state of levitation, but the one who reaches it for selfish gains will be a slave to it, while the one who accepts it as a step for self-improvement will pass on to higher goals and accomplishments.

The Pyramid works through the etheric double. Every cell in our bodies is permeated with small holes, viewable at magnification of 50,000X on an electronic microscope. This energy, or etheric current, is still invisible, like electricity through a wire, but you can see the etheric passageways through a microscope. These holes in the brain cell, or nucleus, is where the etheric energy passes, giving each cell an etheric brain to control physical growth. The sum total of all these cells forms the etheric brain or body.

Let me elaborate a little bit on that. Just imagine that all the cells in the body have holes in them. All these cells in the body have holes in them and have to be filled with something. We're talking about the nuclear membrane, which I briefly covered earlier. This touching, this connecting energy, is the etheric current and it locks the etheric body down to the physical body. It's where the consciousness comes through, through these holes. And as you densify the etheric, you can lighten the physical. And in Pyramid energy, this is Level 1, or the Path of the Violet Ray, the ceremonial order and magic, depending on who is a relative observer and what level he can perceive, view, recognize, and then maintain and store.

The ability to contain knowledge when exposed to it and realize its existence long enough to recall it again and again is what we call memory. Memory is magnetic. Magnetism has polarities wherein opposite poles attract, and like poles repel each other. A bar magnet is a one-half north pole and half south pole magnet. The midway point, the equator, is a neutral line of attraction or gravity. This fact in the human brain allows thought energy to travel along the magnetic equator and form in the etheric counterpart of its gray matter, and thus gravity can be observed as a holding together or unifying principle, including the human mind as well as the Universal Mind.

This individualization of gravity that we all possess forms our ego, which grows with the passage of time. The invisible part of the physical body is of great importance to us, for it is a vehicle through which streams a vitality which keeps the body alive. And without it as a bridge to convey undulations of thought and feeling from the astral to the visible, dense or physical matter, the ego could make no use of the cells of the brain. It is clearly visible to the clairvoyant as the mass of thickly luminous, violet ray mists interpenetrating the dense part of the body and extending very slightly beyond it.

The life of the physical body is one of perpetual change, and in order to live, it needs constantly to be supplied from three distinct sources. It must have food for its digestion, air for its breathing, and vitality in three forms of absorption. The vitality is essence of force that, when clothed with matter, appears as though it were a highly refined chemical element. It exists upon all the planes, but our business for this moment is to consider the manifestation of the physical world.

Hormones get unbalanced by a lowering of the frequencies of the seven sets of endocrine glands

Although the etheric body penetrates every cell of our body, there are seven energy centers, called chakras, that direct all lower chemical metabolizing processes. Now realize that these seven centers have a lower counterpart, or seven sets of endocrine glands, which secrete seven different sets of hormones in the body. The purpose of the different Receptors and Systems we have been working on is to focus and work with the different metabolizing process centers. And the outer environment of the planet, as you well know, tries to interfere with this metabolizing process. Called a lowering of frequency or a lowering of consciousness, or a dysfunction of these centers, various environmental factors cause incomplete utilization of incomplete hormones.

The chakra or core centers are points of connection through which energy flows from one vehicle or body of man to another. Anyone who possesses a slight degree of clairvoyance may see them in the etheric double when they show themselves as saucer-like depressions or vortices at the surface. The vitality globule works powerfully within the etheric body of man, through the spleen center. The vitality globule is pulled out of the atmosphere and into the body. This concept also correlates to negative ions.

One of the types of negative ion generators that we developed produces a "Vitalized Negative Ion." In other words, it generates the negative ion such that you receive when you're in the sunlight and at the seashore simultaneously, compared to other ion generators that just put out a non-vital negative ion. Most ionizer manufacturers do not understand the difference and are not aware of the proper procedures to make an ionizer effective.

These centers, or chakras, when undeveloped, appear as small circles about 2" in diameter, glowing slightly in the ordinary man. But when awakened and electrified, they are seen as blazing, coruscating whirlpools, much increased in size, resembling suns. We sometimes speak of them as roughly corresponding to certain physical organs. In reality, they show themselves at the surface of the etheric double, which projects slightly beyond the outline of the dense body. If we would imagine ourselves to be looking straight down into a bell or flower of the convolvulus type, we can get some idea of the general appearance of a chakra. The stalk of the flower in each springs from the point of the spine, so another view might show the spine as a central stem from which the flower shoots forth at various intervals, showing the opening of their bells at the surface of the body.

Remember my comparison between the acetabularia cell and the black hole in space? Well, the black hole is a giant macrocosm of the acetabularia. An opening of a black hole in space with a space-time singularity is like the opening of a flower that terminates its base energy back into the fourth dimension, forming a simple kind of cell on another plane. Now all these chakra wheels that we're talking about are perpetually rotating. Visualize seven different wheels on the body that are rotating, and into the hub or open mouth of each, a force from the higher world is always flowing. This is a manifestation of the lifestream issuing from the second aspect of the solar levels, which is called the primary life force. The force is seven-fold in its nature, and all its forms operate in the centers, although one color of the seven primary colors, in each case, usually dominates over the others. Without this inrush of energy, the physical body could not exist. Therefore, the centers are in operation in everyone, although in the underdeveloped person they are usually sluggish in motion, just forming the necessary vortex or force, and no more. In a more involved man they may be glowing and pulsating with life, allowing enormous amounts of energy to pass through them, with the result that there are additional facilities, additional possibilities, open to man. Many times this is experienced as acute sight or sound perception!

The energy that's coming into the chakras emanates from the different seven levels of consciousness described earlier, not directly from outer space or from some unknown external area. It actually flows into the chakras from other dimensions, then diffused into the body, after it's processed at the chakra centers, through the action of the spleen and the blood. We've talked about the golf ball-like characteristic of the nuclear membrane within each cell,

#	English Name	Sanskrit Name	Situation	No.of Spokes or Perm	Color	Frequency in Angstroms *	Musical Note
1.	Root or Basic Chakra	Muladhara	At the base of the spine	4	Violet	3900-4280	G
2.	Spleen or Splenic Chakra		Over the spleen	6	Indigo	4280-4680	F
3.	Navel or Umbilical Chakra	Manipura	at the navel, over the solar plexus	10	Orange	5970-2660	E
4.	Heart or Cardiac Chakra	Anahata	Over the heart	12	Yellow	5770-5970	D
5.	Throat or Laryngeal Chakra	Vishuddha	At the front of throat	16	Green	4920-5770	C
6.	Brow or Frontal Chakra	Ajna	In the space between	96	Red	6220-7700	B
7.	Crown or Coronal Chakra	Sahasrara	On the top of the head	960	White	Full Spectrum	A

Figure 27-1   **CHAKRA TO FREQUENCY CONVERSION CHART**

* One Angstrom unit is equal to 1/10 of a nanometer or one ten-millionth of a millimeter.

which has holes in it, which are proportionally even smaller.

The etheric part of the seven levels energy is disseminated into the nuclear membrane through these tiny openings. This is the vital energy that entered the body through the chakra points. The etheric part is processed through the spleen, and the astral part is processed through the solar plexus center; the heart-type energies, love and attraction, process through the heart area; and the intelligence processes through the throat, and so on. The processing center that they're absorbed through is, once again, called the chakra (see figures 27-2 through 27-6).

The chakra is the processing center for the etheric energies

When the vital energy comes into each chakra center from this inner space, it causes changes at right angles to itself as it enters the physical plane. And that is at the service of the etheric double. Just as a bar magnet thrust into an induction coil produces a current of electricity which flows around the coil at right angles to the axis or the direction of the magnet, secondary forces move in an undulatory circular motion. And the primary force itself, having entered the vortex, radiates from it at right angles. So look at the chakra as a wheel. You're looking at a spoked, covered wagon wheel, flat on your body (for the sake of explanation.) The energy is coming in from where the spokes meet the hub at right angles.

By means of these spokes, the force seems to bind the astral and etheric bodies together as though they were grappling posts. The chakras then turn, but at different rates. If you look at the chakra chart, you'll see that there are only four spokes at the lowest chakra, located at the base of the spine. The energy there is heavy, very coarse, and moves at a slower, longer vibratory wavelength, therefore less intense. The crown or coronal chakra at the top of the head radiates 960 spokes, so there's a much finer energy that's permeating the body there. The heart area has 12 spokes, the throat has 16, the brow or frontal chakra has has 96, the spleen has six. You can see that it takes a much finer energy to

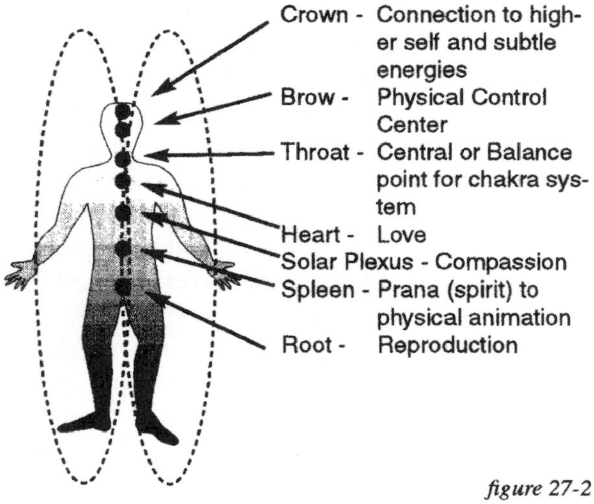

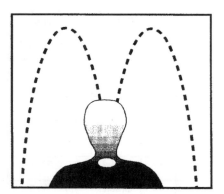

Crown - Connection to higher self and subtle energies
Brow - Physical Control Center
Throat - Central or Balance point for chakra system
Heart - Love
Solar Plexus - Compassion
Spleen - Prana (spirit) to physical animation
Root - Reproduction

figure 27-2

Example of operation of one chakra Throat or Thyroid center (balance)

Thyroxine and other hormones are stored in a capillary gland called the thyroid gland. These hormones control functions such as calcium absorption, body temperature, and are a gateway from brain to all lower body functions.

figure 27-3

236

interpenetrate the 960 spokes in the crown chakra. The gross, pragmatic energy of the base of spine energy would just bounce off the crown chakra. So the body has to assimilate vital energy in the appropriate area. If you punched several holes in a bucket and threw it in a pool of water, all the holes would leak, but the big holes would leak first, and the smaller holes would leak later.

> **The chakra spokes bind the astral and etheric bodies together**

Figure 27-4

The parasympathetic nervous wreath **contracts** by vibration, holding hormones within or **relaxes** and releases hormones from the brain.

Figure 27-5

The contraction or relaxation of the parasympathetic wreath is tuned to subtle frequencies that could be considered harmonics of the musical note "C" and extend up into the region of green, 492-577 angstroms. The number "16" spokes refers to an old vedic measurement of the frequency of DNA that acts as a filter for this band of wave-lengths in the green spectrum. Thus, when stimulated, the DNA resonates the hydrogen atom to chemically combine with O_2, N_2 and carbon to form thyroxine and other compounds on this spectral level. All DNA in all chakras are of a specific frequency to their respective functions.

Figure 27-6

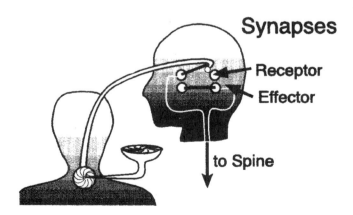

Synapses
Receptor
Effector
to Spine

Once manufactured and stimulated by vibrational stimuli, the hormones flow via the bloodstream into the brain, where in the presence of electrolytes, they release their spectral data across the receptor and effector synapses.

As a review: The vital energies are absorbed into the body by means of these spokes. Each chakra has a different number of these spokes requiring finer and finer energy. Because these spokes are there, these centers have often been poetically described in Oriental books as resembling flowers.

Then we have the secondary forces. Each of these sweep around saucer-like depressions and has its own characteristic wavelength (just as each color of light does) but instead of moving in the straight line characteristic of light, it moves around a relatively large undulation of various sizes, each of which is a multiple of the small wavelengths within it.

These varying wavelengths relate back to the DNA. Even though all DNA is about the same length at birth, 39.5 cm, different strands are attuned to different wavelengths. The energy available at the chakra follows the antennae tuned to it to the various cell nuclei.

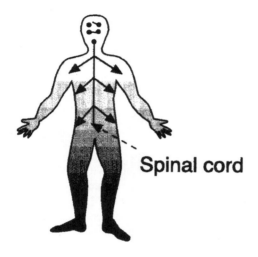

Spinal cord

Figure 27-7

This data then conducts pulsed intelligence (electrical in nature) into the 72,000 major nerves starting at the brain and moving throughout the body.

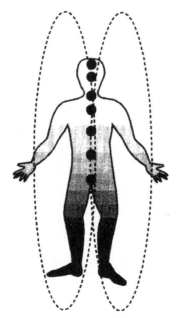

Figure 27-8

As these currents move through the spinal cord, they create motion of sodium potassium and phosphorus ions. This motion creates a field called the "aura" around the body. The auric field stimulates other atoms, ions and other currents within the body, causing a consciousness that relates to all thyroid functions.

Each chakra works in a similar manner, and each is a part of the totality of the human organism.

The difference in the wavelengths distributed are infinitesimal, and probably thousands of them are included in one of these undulations. As the forces rush in around the vortex, these oscillations of different size and color, even sound, cross one another in a basket-weave fashion, producing the flower-like forms to which I've referred. It perhaps is still like the appearance of certain saucers or shallow vases or vases of irridescent glass, such as those made in Venice. All of these undulations or petals have that shimmering, pavonine effect, like Mother-of-Pearl, yet each of them usually has its own predominant color, as covered in the meditation. The colors and sounds of the chakras come from each level of corresponding energy. These energies are also absorbed through all of the hydrogen atoms in the body. This nacreous, silver aspect is likened in Sanskrit works as a gleam of moonlight on water. (see figure 27-8).

AN EXERCISE IN CHAKRA MOTION

Imagine that the body has energy coming into it through spoked wheels. There are four spokes to the wheel at the base of the spine, and 960 spokes to the wheel at the top of the head. The wheel rotates, assimilating energy — the finer energy through the top, and the coarser energy from the lower — and this assimilation and explosion of the energy looks like a flower. At impact with the lower, root chakra, the energy is directed into the four directions, where it gradually dissipates into all the cells whose antennae connect to that region, generating cell reproduction (see figure 27-9).

Now the force of impact of this energy coming into the physical plane causes the cells to grow, and the shock of impact causes the four spokes to rotate like a wheel. The force at impact is called a strike. Realize that the Earth is moving, the sun is rotating, there are many variants as to where the energy is coming in, constantly changing. The area where a strike occurs is called the "struck zone." As the wheel rotates from this energy, it marries or balances a secondary, or nervous energy in the body. This intermingling is much like a weaver's pattern. The central nervous system then begins to pick up this energy as its primary force is released through the chakra centers of the body. That's why it's real important to use the Nuclear Receptors to keep that area open; our environment has a tendency to block this. You could have all kinds of nervous, physical and psychological disorders if this energy is blocked. The entire body then becomes blocked and can't produce the hormones needed. The effect can be traced all the way from consciousness. The hormones store and transmit this vital energy, and the body can store it in the brain to be used at a later time. (see figure 27-10)

If this energy is blocked by an overload of negative EPCs, then the entire etheric body is affected. When two or more etheric zones are blocked, our immune system, which is a consciousness itself and the doorway to our feelings, begins to steal all of the energies stored within the body's storage facilities,

Fats are, of course, necessary for a reserve to back up our immune system. People who have little fat place themselves in jeopardy if they are exposed to a killer virus or bacteria, because they will not have a "reserve" necessary for the body's immune system to convert fats to helper T cells and white blood cells to combat the alien invader.

Likewise, a person with too much fat is in danger, because the immune system is burdened by the energy required to keep the circulation and other vital functions alive.

These chakras naturally divide into 3 groups, the lower, the middle and the higher. They might be called respectively, the physiological, personal and spiritual. The first and second chakras, having few spokes or petals, are principally concerned with receiving into the body two forces at the physical level, one being the serpent-fire from the Earth, and the other the vitality from the sun. The three centers in the middle group — the third, fourth and fifth chakras — are engaged with the forces which reach man through his personality, through the lower astral in the case of the third chakra, the higher astral in the case of the fourth, and from

There are three groups of chakras

239

Desire - Will to highly amplify thought fields

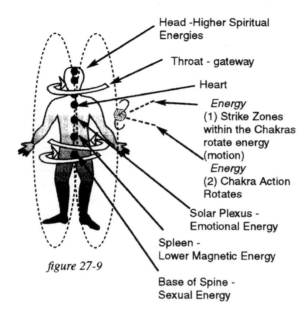

Head -Higher Spiritual Energies

Throat - gateway

Heart

Energy
(1) Strike Zones within the Chakras rotate energy (motion)
Energy
(2) Chakra Action Rotates

Solar Plexus - Emotional Energy

Spleen - Lower Magnetic Energy

Base of Spine - Sexual Energy

figure 27-9

The Aura is a final result of the blending of all chakra energies.

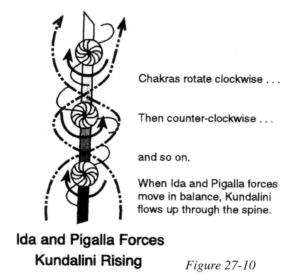

Chakras rotate clockwise . . .

Then counter-clockwise . . .

and so on.

When Ida and Pigalla forces move in balance, Kundalini flows up through the spine.

**Ida and Pigalla Forces
Kundalini Rising**

Figure 27-10

the lower mind for the fifth. All of these centers seem to feed certain ganglia in the body. The higher centers six and seven are at the top of the body, and they stand apart from the rest, each being connected with the pituitary body and pineal gland respectively. They come into action only when a certain amount of spiritual development has taken place.

You are receiving the seven colors of light, but when we start moving towards the white light, you don't really process it properly. It's mostly processed into the violet. And the average man who's processing the violet in has to transmute into the white to reach the higher consciousness.

Imagine, as we continue, that your relative point-of-view is outside yourself looking back, giving you a frontal view of yourself. Every human on this planet is out of balance in one way or another. I'm sure you all realize that, otherwise you would not be interested in this material. So at the exact moment, energy from a balanced universe such as ours strikes our bodies, entering our bodies at the chakra points, it encounters our unbalanced bodies, putting us into an extremely brief moment of temporary shock. When this beautiful energy comes to our body, our body isn't quite ready for it, because we're not perfectly balanced, otherwise we wouldn't be here in the first place. When this energy strikes, we have what we call a "striking energy" creating a small shock. When the internal seven levels of consciousness energy hit the spoke of the wheel, the "shock" only lasts a split second. But a lot happens during the strike-produced "shock."

It's like a spark of light. When the Earth formed, the four amino acids were here, but it took a spark of electricity to strike the life process to create the lifeforms in our body. The four basic amino acids had to be energized. The shock only lasts a split second, but during that shock, life is sustained in our body, and gravity is created.

So, bam!, energy is hitting our bodies right now. Some of the energy balances perfectly, sustaining life in the form, while some of the energy collides with the form, creating "shock waves." This energy is called "strike zone energy" and causes fusion of the three etheric zones, defining physical matter. Then the four levels of solids are created. Although our form is created this way, the spirit enters the chakras first. It's the molding essence. Energy permeates all forms this way and forms patterns. If viewed at various intersections, the strike itself is a fusion pattern and the network of a strike can be visualized macroscopically as one of our pyramid orbs. The orb structures that we make are harmonious to the human body, and they go through the universe receiving a similar energy from different stars on a lower level. One of the destructive problems we presently face is created by man-made electromagnetic distortion. In sending these negative waves to our delicate chakras, man has succeeded in maligning his own chakras. When you use a device such as a pyramid Orb, placed on top of a large, six-foot or larger, portamid, these maligning affects are dissipated and the chakras can function more efficiently and

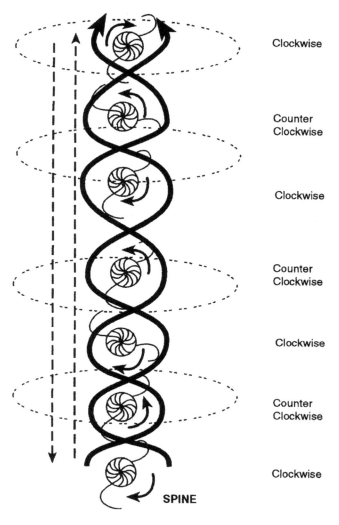

Clockwise

Counter Clockwise

Clockwise

Counter Clockwise

Clockwise

Counter Clockwise

Clockwise

SPINE

Figure 27-11

If all chakras are synchronized and the Kundalini flows, the electrical resistance of nerve passageways becomes less and electrical values increase. When electricity increases, the brain has more energy to radiate through waves into the universe.

Figure 27-12

Brain Synapses — Fast-moving electrons bombard brain and the brain radiates high powered thought waves. These though waves are further amplified in a pyramid system.

Energy is hitting our bodies right now!

241

normally. And if you look at some of the structures, you'll see what this field looks like because the antennae are created in the shape of the field, which makes them resonate into the human body more quickly.

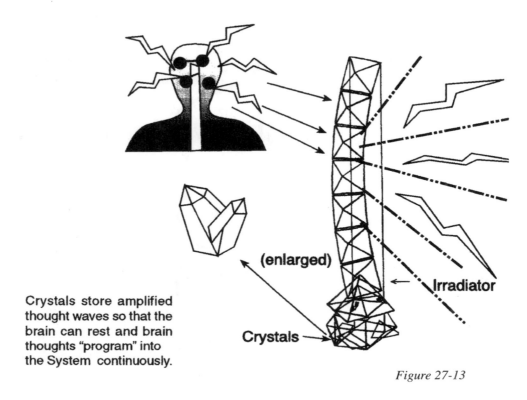

(enlarged)

Crystals

← **Irradiator**

Crystals store amplified
thought waves so that the
brain can rest and brain
thoughts "program" into
the System continuously.

Figure 27-13

**Gravity is
an inter-
change of
energy
between 7
planes of
conscious-
ness**

The angle at which this collision occurs is always like a cross. When this energy comes at right angles, as it should, it creates the shock wave and the absorption wave at the same time. The orb is a framework of the strike and struck zones, forming all form as we know it. It also is the shape of the physical and etheric body relationship. The orb is also a crystal. A crystal is the perfect synthesis of spirit and matter at zero time, as Semjase had told me a long time ago.

Now the energy of spirit is trapped into the form to animate it, it awakens to a spontaneous desire to return to its source once it experiences the form, re-feeling it. If the form is clear and moving with the spirit, it becomes lighter. If it is caught in the desires of the lower nature, energy will be trapped and the form becomes heavier. So, if the spiritual energy were transmitted into sexual energy, it would become so heavy it would cause the form to reproduce. But if it were light, it would cause the person to become enlightened. One is not good or better than the other; it just is a matter of fact. The constant vacillation between the two natures, with the spirit trying to escape from being trapped in the form, constitutes gravity.

Gravity is the interchange of energy from the seven planes of consciousness. It is a mutual force causing a downward thrust of seven energies coming from the upper inward direction of spirit, which we refer to as seven levels. So, in other words, as the energy enters our consciousness via such means as meditation, it actually is absorbed by our bodies, creating gravity. A total synthesis of this energy would turn you into a total light being; or a total non-synthesis of it, a total rejection, would turn you into pure matter.

The struck zone contains some energy that has worked off karma, or "spent" itself. Remember energy is not created or destroyed, only transmuted. This coming and going in the struck zone creates a rhythm, known as time. So the energy is trapped and released in the body, and this action, the process of trapping the higher energy and holding it, creates gravity, and the coming and going of this energy being trapped and released, forms time. This time rhythm synchronizes the "Bohr Effect."

The Bohr Effect is an electrical function of the heart. When you inhale, your body, lungs and blood absorb oxygen. During this cycle, the oxygen travels to the lungs and binds with the amino acid, histidine, which donates a negative charge that enables iron to form a loose bond with oxygen. Just previous to this, the iron atom itself is termed "Ferrous," wherein it has a positive two (+2) valance charge. As soon as it comes into contact with oxygen, it binds the oxygen atom and carries it to the mitochondria of cells where myoglobin (part of the red blood cells) deposits it.

Once the oxygen is deposited in the cells, then the charge on the pyramid-shaped iron molecule changes to a Ferric or positive three (+3) valance, removes the carbon dioxide from the cell, and transports it back out to the lungs for expulsion. Because there is electrical involvement here, the body's electrical system is in full activation.

Working synchronously with this Ferrous, Ferric transition is the electrical action of the heart pump. On the biochemical level, the body is absorbing calcium and converting it to an enzyme, called actin, in the heart. Actin acts as an electrolyte in the electrical body, transmitting a master command signal from the pineal gland which basically says, "Blood, circulate!," "Heart, beat!," "Blood, carry oxygen," "Heart, beat," "Blood, release oxygen," "Heart, beat," "Blood, transport CO_2 to lungs," "Heart, beat," Blood release CO_2 from lungs to outside environment," etc.

This combined orchestration of organs, enzymes and cells is called the Bohr Effect. When you receive negative electrical precursing energies (stress), the process can become somewhat disturbed, resulting in hypertension, claustrophobia and premature aging.

All Time on all planes is interpenetrable!

Time is the vibratory exchange rate of spirit and matter. Motion is the movement of divine will being split by desire. Gravity is the recombination of desire ascending to spirit after its expression through form. Antigravity, detachment or impartiality is created by mind when it is disciplined to be free of desire, thus free of the time zone on a particular plane of consciousness. However, all time on all planes is interpenetrable. Each of the seven planes has its own time zone. From our point-of-view, the higher the plane, the slower the time. So it doesn't hurt for you to go back and review the material presented thus far, and the meditation, and apply some of these principles to your consciousness, and find out what happens.

By the way, spent energy from the physical returning to spirit, is also called the Christ Principle. And I might add something at this point in time. I've had religious people say, "The Pyramid, what's that got to do with Christ? Do people worship that?" And I say, "No, the Pyramid is a principle of matter made flesh. And Christ is the principle of flesh made spirit...different principle." Meaning that the carbon atom is the physical form that contains energy, or your spiritual essence, and when spirit educates itself and learns to become free of physical boundaries, the Christ Principle enacts itself, and the carbon atom is no longer necessary to contain the spiritual essence in physical form.

Struck zone interchange can be seen as a fusion, or as a return of the Kundalini, as spirit releases itself into form, creating time. The law of inertia causes a downward flow, and the effect is the attraction of the physical to physical, (a sort of bonding action). In the highly developed individual, the organized force is in balance and moves out and away from the physical and creates the antigravity state of consciousness. But when the average person's energy hits the physical form, the shock is directed downward. There is no ability present to allow the energy to escape back to spirit again. So most people become gravitated rather than antigravitated. Control of this energy comes from the higher mind, via the upper mental plane. Then the lower mind stands aside and allows the higher mind to reach the astral and physical bodies. The lower mind, in most people, doesn't "stand aside", which leaves them gravity-bound to this planet rather than able to release. And that's why when we developed our pyramid and orb systems; we found that, the higher mind is freed to pass the obstacles presented by the lower mind. They begin to become free of gravity, and levitation becomes possible.

Antigravity consciousness is being reached by people through various Yoga disciplines, and a side affect of levitation is demonstrated. The Yogis called this state of consciousness "Siddhi." People taking advanced courses in Transcendental Meditation actually levitate during public demonstrations. One of our pyramid systems and its balancing antenna enabled me to, in my earlier days on Earth, levitate people in the audience of my seminars. I don't do that any more, because it's not the summation of what we're all about. Just like we don't put the Pyramid over grapefruit juice to show that it turns sweet, as we did in days gone by. Levitation is not the goal of Siddhi, only a side effect. Once a person reaches this consciousness, he seeks a better goal and proceeds onward. Levitation serves no purpose other than giving the seeker a sign that Siddhi has been reached.

We have been describing the vital or etheric body. In superimposing this body over the other states of the body, the nerves become alive, and our body's "telephone system" is put into operation. We now have a physical mechanism for motion in addition to the vitality to produce the motion. Messages can now be sent by the brain to all parts of the denser vehicle. Action can be ordered in a multitude of subconscious operations. But, there is more to us than just vitality. There is a vastly greater person than an automaton moving and acting without a glimmer of understanding about what he or she is really doing. Humans can feel, they can think, hope, and love, and turn his mind to the sacred realm of spiritual aspiration. Action is an end product of all these greater things. An automaton moves, but Humans move with purpose, and that makes all the difference.

Chapter 28

A Brief History of Physics

Our sense of purpose comes from the Will and the seven planes of consciousness that we've already studied. We have a physical mechanism in the vital body which gives life and animation, but the physical body itself is a heartless, senseless thing that we have produced. It has organs of sense, but it cannot use them. It doesn't know the fragrance of flowers, the inspiration brought about by the odor of pines. It has lips and tongue and vocal chords, but it cannot utter a word. Each of its eyes have half a million nerve fibers leading to the brain and several million rods and cones to light impressions from the retina which have been transformed into electrical impulses, but there is no consciousness of the glories that the vision brings. The ears are ready to catch the sound around the ear drum, one of nature's amazing devices, but only vibrations reach the awaiting mechanism, and there is nothing to turn them into sweet cadences of melodious sound that man can contact and respond to with ecstatic joy.

To supply this need, let us go beyond the physical realms to extraterrestrial science, into the collection of vehicles of human consciousness that we have described. We must add a few more so that man can stand up and become complete. Soon we'll explore the human brain on a much deeper level. But for now, we'll look at the astral body.

The astral body

The name "astral" was originally used by medieval alchemists. It signifies "starry" and is supposed to have been applied to the plane just above the physical because of the luminous appearance which is associated with the more rapid rate of vibration. As I stated before, as we ascend the different levels of consciousness, the energy levels go up, and so the vibratory rate goes up. The astral plane is the world of passion, of emotion and sensation, and it is through man's astral vehicle on this planet that all his feelings exhibit themselves to the clairvoyant investigator. **The astral body of man is therefore continually changing in appearance as his emotions change.**

So far we have observed that since **ethers in the threshold of the ordinary perceived physical world are simply a rarified condition of matter,** slight physical development is required for their investigation. In fact, thousands of people who have given no special thought to either psychic or spiritual development have seen and are continually seeing one or more of them without knowing there is anything unusual about the experience. As the Aquarian Age draws near, the number of persons sensitive to the finer ethers, the consciousness in this, is going to increase year by year. An advantage of our Pleiadian systems technology is the fact that they help increase that consciousness, not only on the etheric levels, but also on the astral levels, too. Even now there are cases on record among pioneering scientists where etheric vision is momentarily opened in the course of particular investigations. This was well demonstrated at Sandoz Laboratories in Switzerland with the discovery of lysergic acid (LSD) in the rye mold by Dr. Albert Hoffman.

The etheric region may be designated as the atomic and subatomic areas of the material world, invisible to the human senses in their present state of development. Ether is nonetheless a substance belonging to the physical world, though raised to a higher vibratory octave than physical matter. This being so, it has gradually yielded up to material scientists many mysteries that for centuries have been known only to the metaphysical community.

Now one thing that is really interesting is that **science has advanced to the point where it recognizes that there's a relationship between the experiment and the experimenter.** And if you read Popular Science, Scientific American or any of the magazines or scientific journals, you'll find that they're discovering and naming subatomic particles. For example, they're calling some particles "strange," "charm," "up," and "down." These different particles are further named "beauty," "truth," and "justice," and their names have a psychological influence or attribute. **It is now a recognized fact that there is a relationship between consciousness and particles.** And then when you move into the astral plane, the particles that are on their way out to the physical plane also have characteristics, which haven't truly been named yet—other than being callead "hadrons" and "quarks." Further in on the astral plane where color comes from we reach a particle called "omegons."

I'm sure you remember the meditation that we introduced, experiencing and exploring different levels of consciousness. One of the attributes of that exploration is moving into our psychic systems through the hydrogen atom. If we were to look at the hydrogen atom, for example, we would see that there is a proton as the nucleus, and an electron spinning around it, similar to the Earth and the moon relationship. If we were to examine this a bit deeper, through the discipline of quantum mechanics, we would designate energy levels from the electron down to the proton.

A scientist named Lord Rutherford discovered in 1911 that atoms consist of one or more electrons revolving around a positively-charged nucleus. Later, Neils Bohr added the condition that electrons have certain orbits and that **radiation was the result of electrons jumping from one orbit to another.** This gave birth to the science of quantum mechanics. Max Planck pioneered the subject into the hands of Albert Einstein. This led to the birth of the atomic age in 1942 when the first self-sustaining atomic disintegration was accomplished in a uranium reactor beneath the stands of Stagg Field of the University of Chicago.

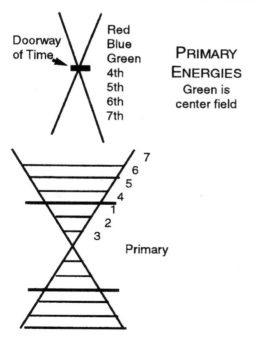

This radiation that is given off is very predominant in the hydrogen atom, which consists of a proton and an electron. This radiation, although harmful in the hands of a nuclear physicist, is, when in perfect harmony, the life force coming from the seven levels of consciousness. In our body systems the hydrogen atom is the one that delivers the most energy to our cells!

figure 28-1

In the early morning hours in the hydrogen atom in the body, the seven levels of consciousness polarize with the color red, the Logoic Plane, releasing energy (radiation) into the pineal gland. If you look at the colors as a rainbow, with violet last, it is releasing physical plane energy into the sexual areas and the base of the spine. The control or mid-color is green, and it is centered in the throat (thyroid) area.

As the sun moves across the sky and evening comes, the violet end of the rainbow shifts to the proton area (nucleus) and the red (Will in consciousness) moves to the base of the spine. As a result of the shifts through the day (180 degrees), and into the night (180 degrees), our entire consciousness and the way we think changes. Our bodies adapt to a particular time versus sun shift, and we become climatized into a consciousness of the area where we live. All of our habits of sleeping and eating and thinking are thus firmly affected.

But, when we relocate suddenly, via a plane trip several miles away, our hydrogen frequency bio-clock is disrupted, and we experience what is called "jet lag." As we age, the hydrogen atom gradually drops down in frequency, and the "jet lag" becomes more noticeable.

> **Jet Lag: when our hydrogen frequency bio-clock is disrupted (slows down in frequency)**

There are many things that we can do to alleviate these types of problems, one of which is the proper usage of a Pleiadian science technology which is implemented in a device called the "Nuclear Receptor."

Imagine, for example, the jet lag that would occur when, rather than switching continents, you switched planets.

This science is called "space medicine," and is studied in our astronaut programs.

Neils Bohr Orbit

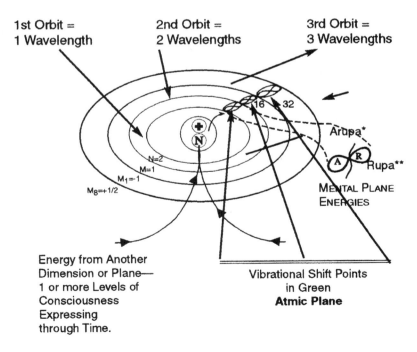

1st Orbit =
1 Wavelength

2nd Orbit =
2 Wavelengths

3rd Orbit =
3 Wavelengths

Arupa*

Rupa**

MENTAL PLANE ENERGIES

16   32

N=2
M=1
M₁=-1
Mg=+1/2

Energy from Another
Dimension or Plane—
1 or more Levels of
Consciousness
Expressing
through Time.

Vibrational Shift Points
in Green
Atmic Plane

*Rupa is spontaneous thought and action.
**Arupa is logic and ordered thought.

figure 28-2

247

Around the nucleus of the atom are shells of electrons. When the shells are complete, electrons form another outer shell. For example, hydrogen is +1 (N) as it has only one electron. Helium is +2 as it has two electrons that complete its outer shell. The hydrogen atom's shell, as it is incomplete, looks for a second electron to complete its shell. If it finds only one extra electron, it becomes complete and becomes helium. As an element gains more shells, it becomes heavier and the next shell level to complete is level M-1 which has eight electrons. Oxygen has only six electrons on level M-1, so it seeks two more electrons to become complete. Therefore oxygen is also active (see figure 28-2).

The next level, M1-1, seeks 16 electrons.

Between each shell level the vibrational level increases light wavelength. The particular wavelength is determined by the type of element involved.

The seven colors of consciousness are responsible for the frequency multiplication. Here consciousness meets math! The rainbow is found in the atom! (see figure 28-2).

As the energies fuse into the nucleus of the atom from the seven levels, fusion in physics occurs. As energies fission from the nucleus to the quantum orbital levels, fission is created.

These are sub-atomic reactions. When scientists speed up the process by energy accelerators, i.e., cyclotrons or linear accelerators, the sub-atomic goes atomic and nuclear reactions realizing huge amounts of energy are created—i.e., nuclear reactors (fission) or H bombs (fusion)!

We've covered the first three etheric states and the ionic, or fourth etheric state on the physical plane. On the astral plane we would find two particles that are known by today's science as the "lepton" and the "hadron."

We experimented on the mental plane because to experience that plane we look at colors and listen to sound. The energy that causes the formation of color originates on the Buddhic plane where the "gluons" and the "omegons" are located. The omegons function through the colors of red, green and blue. The Buddhic plane, you realize, is made up of what? Red, from the Logoic plane, blue, from the Monadic plane, and green, from the Atmic plane, or the plane of intellect. Those three colors together naturally form the Buddhic plane, which is yellow in nature.

UPAs come from the logoic plane

The energy drops down to the fifth plane, which, as was stated, is orange in its overall nature. On the fifth plane we have sound, the musical note E, and we have the quarks, which are colored by the omegons, coming from the Buddhic plane. The substance of the omegons, of course, is going to be the "ultimate physical atoms" which come from the Logoic plane, called the "Ultimate Physical Atoms" (UPAs) or "ultimatom". Each ultimatom is comprised of 49 of the ultimate atoms on the Monadic plane, and 49 ultimotoms combine together to form one unit of energy on the Atmic plane. So we begin to see where the different energy fields, or the 49 fires of Agni (the god of fire), and these terminologies come into being.

If we examine the hydrogen atom again at a particle level, we would find that the proton has two micro-quarks in it, or "U-quarks", as they're called, and one "D-quark." This previously elementary particle, the proton, is now determined to be comprised of three or more separate particles! The electron itself also has different particles in it. Delving further into the proton, we find it has three U-quarks and two D-quarks. Inside the quark, from the standpoint of a physicist, are nine omegons. Inside a neutron, such as that of heavy hydrogen, deuterium, are nine different colors of hadrons. Auras contain sub-atomic particles called leptons. The characteristic names of the quark and hadron are: "isospin", "strangeness", "charm", "bottom" and "top." The book *Extrasensory Perception of Quarks,* written by Stephen Phillips, published by the Theosophical Publishing House in London, England, can give you a more detailed schematic of quantum physics. (see figure 28-3)

Science is now beginning to define "quantum chromodynamics." These drawings, reprinted from *Death of Ignorance*, show energy fields as they build up from the Logoic plane, all the way through the other planes that you have already studied, to form **the first heavy particle.** When the particle is charged by the sun as its energy field comes within the sphere of influence from the infinite, the energy field of these seven levels comes through the aura of the sun, which is like processing a field of a Chakra of a Higher Master or Solar Logos. Then the energy transmutes to the physical plane as vitality globules, or prana, vitalizing the being via the six remaining levels of energy.

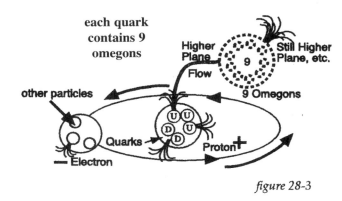

figure 28-3

Reprinted here from *Death of Ignorance* is a chart detailing some of the results achieved around the turn of the century by meditation done by various people in the theosophical group or order, regarding the anu and its relationship with the atom (see figures 28-4 and 28-5). For example, the element hydrogen has one proton in its nucleus, but this single proton was found to be made up of 18 anu atoms, or sub-physical anu. These particles that science has defined, now known as quarks and omegons and leptons, had no scientific names during the early 1900s.

Not knowing that we would later name these particles, they were given the name of "Ultimate Physical Atoms," UPAs. Each UPA was a particle representing a flavor from one of the seven levels of consciousness. When combined, these UPAs formed heavier particles called "Micro Psi Atoms," or MPAs. These MPAs are the structural shape of the atom itself. There are seven structural shapes for atoms. They are:

Seven Shapes of the Atom

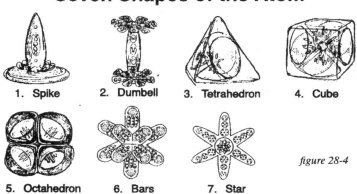

1. Spike
2. Dumbell
3. Tetrahedron
4. Cube
5. Octahedron
6. Bars
7. Star

figure 28-4

1. Spike Group
2. Dumbbell Group
3. Tetrahedron Group
4. Cube Group
5. Octahedron Group (Pyramid)
6. Bars Group
7. Star Group

The Seven Planes

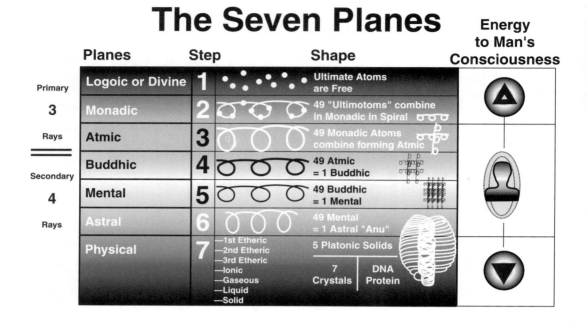

Planes	Step	Shape	
Logoic or Divine	1		Ultimate Atoms are Free
Monadic	2		49 "Ultimotoms" combine in Monadic in Spiral
Atmic	3		49 Monadic Atoms combine forming Atmic
Buddhic	4		49 Atmic = 1 Buddhic
Mental	5		49 Buddhic = 1 Mental
Astral	6		49 Mental = 1 Astral "Anu"
Physical	7	—1st Etheric —2nd Etheric —3rd Etheric —Ionic —Gaseous —Liquid —Solid	5 Platonic Solids 7 Crystals | DNA Protein

Primary **3** Rays

Secondary **4** Rays

Energy to Man's Consciousness

Man's Corresponding Bodies

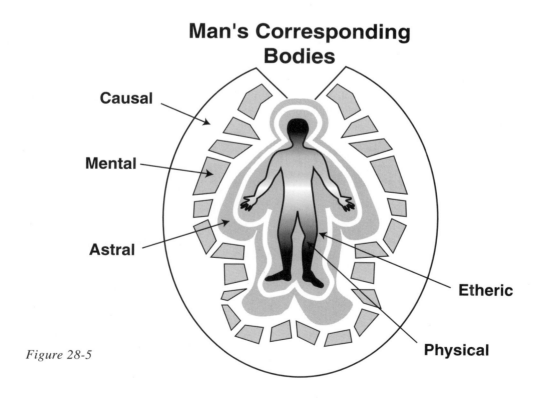

Causal

Mental

Astral

Etheric

Physical

Figure 28-5

250

Energy—Consciousness to the Atom

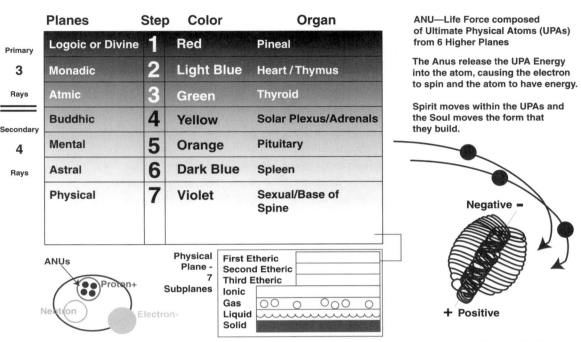

ANU—Life Force composed of Ultimate Physical Atoms (UPAs) from 6 Higher Planes

The Anus release the UPA Energy into the atom, causing the electron to spin and the atom to have energy.

Spirit moves within the UPAs and the Soul moves the form that they build.

Figure 28-6

Each group represents, once again, a level of consciousness. Then, because hydrogen is the simplest element, 18 UPAs were noticed in the nucleus.

When they looked at oxygen, they saw 290 UPAs. Next, hydrogen was divided into oxygen by its UPA number, and the common denominator of 16.11 was deduced. At that time, the atomic number of hydrogen was 1.0080 and oxygen was 15.9994, very close by comparison!

Element	Number of Ultimate Physical Atoms (ANU)	Weight Compared with Hydrogen Taken as 18	Atomic Weight (1974)
Hydrogen	18	1	1.0080
Oxygen	290	16.11	15.9994
Nitrogen	261	14.50	14.0067
Carbon	216	12	12.011
Gold	3546	197	196.9665
Copper	1139	63.277	63.546
Silver	1945	108.055	107.868
Iron	1008	56	55.847
Titanium	864	48	47.90

figure 28-7 reprinted from Death of Ignorance

Then, they looked into carbon, and found 216 UPAs. This, divided by hydrogen's 16.11 UPAs, equaled 12. The atomic weight of carbon is 12.011. Next, they looked at nitrogen, 261 UPAs were found! Divide this by hydrogen and you get 14.50. The atomic weight of nitrogen is 14.0067. This was done with all of the elements in 1895! (See figure 28-7.)

Now that the Ultimate Physical Atoms, made up of energies of the seven levels of consciousness, were mathematically connected to the chart of atomic weights, it was just a matter of time before science caught up and began defining the combinations of these particles as "quarks," "hadrons," "leptons," etc.

So clairvoyants were able to verify from the study by physicists from a metaphysical, meditative point-of-view almost the same correlations, and I would have a tendency to say that the metaphysical way is all the more accurate, and it was done almost 100 years ago. This also correlates to what the extraterrestrials teach us. As it originated from the metaphysical sciences on our own plane, we can deduce an extraterrestrial influence.

Continuing our quotation from *Death of Ignorance*:

"The etheric region may be designated the atomic and subatomic areas of a material world, invisible to the human senses as now developed. Ether is nonetheless a substance born of the physical world, although raised to a higher vibratory octave than physical matter. This being so, it has gradually yielded up to material sciences many mysteries that for centuries have been known only to cultists of metaphysical science. It is quite otherwise with the desire of the astral world. Unlike the region of the ethers, the realm of the desire world is another plane of existence, or beingness. It is not just a finer gradation of matter, actually, it is not material, it is astral. While it flows in and through the physical world, interpenetrating the chemical and etheric regions of the physical and constantly influencing all activities within the sphere, it is of a different nature and subject to laws other than those operating in either the physical world or the higher worlds of mind and spirit."

Earlier I explained to you how the etheric body attaches itself to the physical cells of the body by entering through little holes as an energy field or a plasma. These little holes are in the nuclear membrane of every single cell in anything that exists.

"Students unfamiliar with theosophical terminology will have no difficulty understanding the desire world if they think of it as the world of the heart's desire, or simply as the soul world, for this world or state of consciousness corresponds to what the orthodox theology describes as hell and/or heaven where the spirit abides after physical death." Remember that when two or more people get together, their energy or aura fields interchange, creating the astral plane, and if a person goes out of body, they go into that interchange field. That interchange field could be several people grouped together. They could name that field a religious field, and call it different denominations. So when a person dis-incarnates, he goes into that specific field via these other spirits that are on the physical side of it. The Egyptians created a huge cult using this principle thousands of years ago which survived many dynasties. When that spirit is finished and is in limbo in that specific area, it reincarnates back on the physical level again, and this is the cycle of birth, death, and rebirth that we have to break. When you transcend the cycle, you move out of Earth's auric field. (See figures 26-3, 26-4, 26-9 and 26-10.)

"The orthodox heaven is a place of inconceivable bliss, every heart's desire being fulfilled through God's infinite goodness and love. The metaphysician prefers to give this place, this state of consciousness, another name. It is generally known in Western wisdom as desire, or the astral world. When, in later infancy, a child begins to be conscious of his environment, he at first is not aware of the substance of things. He does not realize that certain solid objects can bruise the body, or that sharp objects will pierce it. Nor does the child sense distance. Even an adult is not able to perceive with his physical senses the atoms compromising the substance of material forms, including his own body.

AURIC AMPLIFICATION

An individual has an individual Aura field.
A single soul would have no personality.

God Head

Figure 28-8

Two or more people interface—then their auras would have personality. The action of personality creates karma over time.

Duality

Figure 28-9

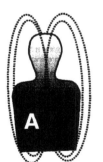  

Three or more people create, via the personality and action, karma and racial dharma. Three or more begin a nation.

Trinity

Figure 28-10

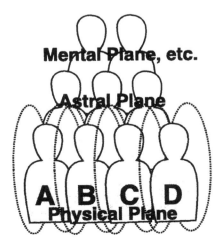

The dharmic action of the aura creates the astral plane. If a person on the physical plane disincarnates, he or she departs temporarily to the astral plane into a world there that was created by idealisms of the remaining beings on the physical plane.

Figure 28-11

253

In a similar way, when first entering the desire world, the untrained clairvoyant sees form but not the nature of the substance of which these forms are composed. This being so, observations recorded are not uniform, some being of clearer seeing and deeper understanding than others. This accounts for the variation in the vision of the church saints, who may have been mystical seers, but not necessarily trained clairvoyants. Consequently, their conclusions are not always collaborated by the findings of the cult sciences that have made a study of that world."

The astral plane is also where the spaceships and flying saucers phase into to move beyond light speeds. **You can call the astral plane the "plane of light," but that plane is an interdimensional consciousness and is not something stretched across an ether to create a span, like a physically measurable distance.** It takes many years for the light we see on the physical plane to reach us from different stars.

"The desire world is composed of what may best be described as 'force matter.' Unlike ether, desire substance is not just a fine gradation of chemical matter. Physical instruments cannot penetrate its secrets. It is the world of life, feeling and emotion. As our bodies and our physiological functions consist of material substance, so our feelings, sensations and emotions become a tangible form in the force matter of the desire world, each type having its own particular form-colorated vibration." We cover all that in the meditation, where we actually feel each emotion and realize its source. Everything beyond that (such as will, love, and thinking, manifest in the astral plane through the sets of emotions, except their source of essence) comes from the higher planes.

"The feeling itself, you might say, of these different emotions, arises on a higher plane. The actual area where it is felt, for example — will — doesn't originate on the astral plane, as you probably know by now. But it is felt on the astral plane. Yet on the plane of origination, will itself is not felt, it is just will. But when it is expressed, it becomes desire. In the morning, after sleep or exiting the astral plane, Will is felt as desire to "wake up" and begin the day—and acting through the pineal gland, it sends a wake-up call throughout the entire body systems, which then begin the physical plane's daily activities.

"The desire world is not a space/time realm. This is the first destination of the scalar wave. Scalar waves do occupy "time," as I have already stated. And, by the way, we've got some beautiful pictures of scalar waves now, too. So people can see them, photograph them. **Perceiving and moving in and out of the 4th dimension is one of the ultimate goals of this presentation.**

"Within the aura of the feeling body is, in fact, the 4th dimensional body. It by nature possess senses far keener than those known to man when in the physical body, as evidenced, for example, by the ecstasy accompanying the soul-transporting experience, known as 'illumination.' The force matter of the desire world is in continuous motion, pulsating in a bright, kaleidoscopic array of ever-changing lights and colors. Its basic substance is soul light, out of which everything is formed." Now I might note that in my travels to astral worlds I have seen their suns, but the worlds themselves are self-illuminating, so there's no dark side.

"Where a soul light is either partially or completely absent, there exists the condition spoken of in the Bible as outer darkness, where there swells unregenerate spirits until purged of the basic elements in their natures. This is the purgatorial region of the Catholic theology, or Hell of the Protestant Orthodoxy. Force matter, our basic soul light, is both positive/ negative, and masculine/feminine in function. The term fire and water is applied to the masculine/female principle respectively, derived from the desire world. For here the masculine quantity is now manifest in fiery, glittery radiations familiar to every seer, while feminine soul qualities are visible as most exquisite colors seen in the clouds of light, having a distinctly watery appearance, a water such as no one on Earth sees with the physical vision. As evolution advances feminine souls, they'll display more of their fiery masculine qualities, while masculine souls will take on the ethereal beauty of the feminine.

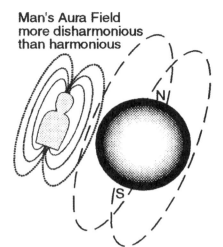

Man's Aura Field more disharmonious than harmonious

The world's auric dharma is created by the summation of its citizens. Unfortunately, today's world is ruled by selfishness and ignorance.

Figure 28-12

Planet Earth, because of dharma, is in conflict with the solar system. This conflict is transmitted to other planetary systems. The citizens of other worlds come here to "repair" the damage, i.e., visits.

Figure 28-13

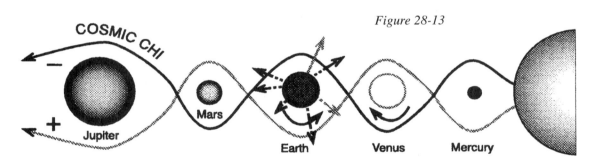

"In our present state of unfoldment, desire is the mainspring of action. It motivates our conduct and thought. Such being the case, angelic beings inhabiting the desire world are of prime importance to our development." Now one thing I might say, even though that I've written that desire is the catalyst that causes things to happen, will is the impelling mode of desire. When you can move past desire and go straight to the willing force, or true passion, you get closer to the true nature of your destiny, and therefore you can achieve your goals with far fewer obstacles often presented in the normal pursuit of the desire path.

"The dominant laws of the desire world are rules of attraction, metamorphosis, and transformation. Of course metamorphosis is most easily seen in the insect kingdom, such as the caterpillar becoming pupa, becoming the butterfly — the first, second and/or third degrees of metamorphosis. Add to these the laws of repulsion — the forces of hate and self-assertion that prevail on the lowest levels of our world. Fairy tales are beautiful illustrations of the ever-changing substance of this realm, where form is not fixed as in the physical world, but constantly metamorphosing.

"The desire world is the home of innumerable beings who operate in diverse, subtle ways to influence man by means of his desires and emotions. These activities are sensed, but the

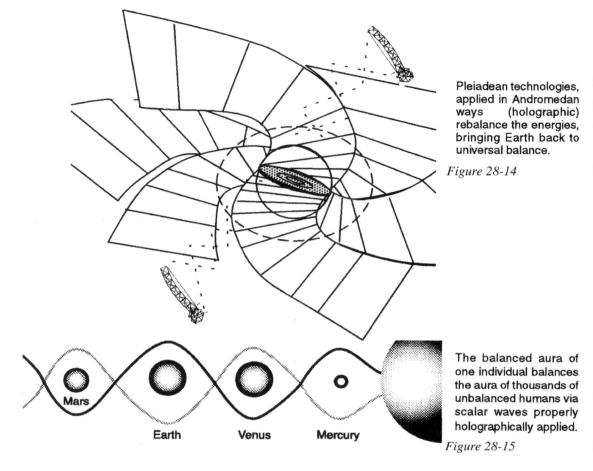

Pleiadean technologies, applied in Andromedan ways (holographic) rebalance the energies, bringing Earth back to universal balance.

Figure 28-14

Mars   Earth   Venus   Mercury

The balanced aura of one individual balances the aura of thousands of unbalanced humans via scalar waves properly holographically applied.

Figure 28-15

presence of these beings is unperceived by the vast majority of the people. To the activities of these denizens of that realm, man owes an inestimable opportunity for growth through experience, by which he is building and increasing moral strength and beauty, and achieving mental beautification. For in our present state of development, the average man's mind is but dimly awakened. As previously stated, the principle element of the desire world is soul light. And the chief function of it, which is transmutation, or metamorphosis, is readily amiable to the power of thought. Both the Archangels, the Hierarchy of Capricorn, and the Angels Hierarchy of the Aquarius are active in the higher heavenly region of the swirl, whereas the Lucifers and Reptilians have charge of the lower purgatorial levels. Their activities, however, are not confined to these levels, but now extend into the heavenly realms as well.

"How the two divisions of the desire world, the higher planes where the force of attraction holds sway, and the lower, where the force of repulsion is dominant, are related to human experiences in the manner in which they operate, are the subject of this lesson. Man is a free agent. He can revel in unbridled passion, low desires; he can elect to live as do the majority by drawing to himself proportionate amounts of high and low desire substance. He can follow the spiritual path as do aspirants, and thereby lay hold of transmuting, transforming powers, having their source in the higher planes of the desire world. In these higher planes is the fountain of life, the fountain of youth, long sought by the medieval alchemists, but entered only by those who gave their all to the quest."

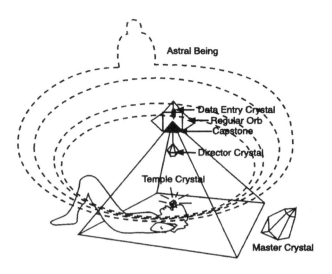

Astral Being
Data Entry Crystal
Regular Orb
Capstone
Director Crystal
Temple Crystal
Master Crystal

Another auric fact is that when someone is on the astral plane (disincarnated), they may need to communicate to a family member on the physical plane, and vice versa. This is done during the REM (rapid eye movement) stage of the sleep cycle.

The Portamid or an equivalent pyramid placed over the sleeping individual ensures sound communication between the dimensions, because the pyramid canopy can block distressing radiation that is everpresent and hazardous to the sleeping individual's "astral" body.

Figure 28-16

Remember, 5% of your body, minerals, controls 95% of your metabolic functions. Your minerals are subject to the elementals and the desires of the elementals that have been returned to the ground. And so, the quicker your body returns to the Earth, the more quickly it and the desire of the summation of all the elementals that compose your body are satisfied. These desires can lead your body into destructive habits to destroy itself so that it can be return quickly back to the earth. That's where the desire of the lower side is expressed. You'll learn about this in the book *Death of Ignorance*, and how you can recognize the characteristics of lower side expression. We want to teach the body not to yield to that desire, but instead to raise the desire up from returning to the Earth. The Earth and the elementals can then transmute into a higher consciousness, rather than the elementals "fearing" this transmutation of the spirit as it occurs through their loaned-out "vehicle." Subjects such as this I discuss in *Death of Ignorance*, but it is not basically the subject of extraterrestrial sciences. This knowledge I acquired along the way on my path of becoming a contactee.

AURAS, NEPTUNE, DOLPHINS AND WHALES

At this point I would like to tell a brief story of planetary auric concern.

One of my early Tibetan teachers was a credentialed Rajput Prince by the name of Mark Sirjou. I met him in 1973. One of his lessons to me was about King Neptune and the greater mammals of the sea, dolphins and whales.

Mark asked me one day, had I ever heard of a being called King Neptune? My answer at the time was, "Yes, he is a mythological being who lives in the sea."

Mark then asked me if I had ever seen him.

"Of course not. Who has?"

He smiled at me and said, "You will someday know the secret of Neptune." Then he asked me, "Why do whales migrate?"

I politely told him I had no idea! Mark then told me that whales migrated along different auric currents of the Earth's field. He also told me that Neptune himself followed them and could be found at the rear of large migratory movements. He also told me that

Whales migrate along the Earth's Auric currents

257

Neptune was a being from the second ether of our planet Neptune, and that whales and dolphins originate from that planet, where they were not in aquatic-mammal type bodies. When they came here to Earth, that was the body of their choosing. The reason they selected this type of body was that if they could swim in the sea, they would have ultimate freedom to roam the planet and help stabilize the psychic ecosystem of the second ether of the Earth, which in turn affects the lower physical plane. Also, remember that 60% of the world's oxygen is produced within the first 60 feet of the ocean's depths.

In addition, dolphins were guardian angels to certain souls who, when at sea, would be under their protection. It's no wonder that sometimes people who are shipwrecked or whose vessel has capsized are rescued by dolphins or whales. These survivors suddenly wake up on the shore, having been delivered there by a dolphin or a whale. Incidentally, I might add that "killer whales" are some of the friendliest water mammals on the planet. They are only hostile to life forms that are hostile to beings that threaten the "greater good" of the survival of the planet Earth!

Mark then told me that King Neptune was a true Neptunian king that gave up his throne on Neptune to come to Earth to protect his royal subjects deep within the world's greatest oceans. He gave his "subjects" "Super Sensory Powers" so they could carry out their guardian missions with greater safety as they can sense danger "psychically" long before it is any harm to them. It's no wonder that dolphins can hear sounds as high as 150,000 cps (hertz) and see well into the astral plane. Whales can sense the intuition of humans at sea miles away from their physical presence. When dolphins move in packs in the ocean, sharks often follow, because they know that dolphins create a safe passage.

This was to me a great lesson, that second etheric beings somehow "watched" over the denizens of the deep.

It was not until 1985 that I gained the real perspective of Mark's message. In 1981, Mark had committed an act of self-immolation and left me alone on this, the physical plane, with his teachings. He had told me at our initial meeting in 1973 that once he was finished imparting certain truths to me, he would leave the physical plane. So by 1985, I knew what he meant. A Rajput imparted truth with a passion, and to make sure that the impartee (me, in this case) got the message, he self-immolated.

I was in Laguna at West Street Beach alone just after sunset. It was late summer, early autumn. That evening I felt like I was walking on a magic, empty beach. I walked alone toward a large rock jetty that reached out into the sea. It was made from large rocks that protruded sharply from some very deep waters. On the west side of the jetty, about 40 feet out from the shore, were two very large grey whales, each about 40 feet long. The nearer whale faced the shore and was gently spouting water out of its blowhole. Just next to the first whale was the second, facing out to sea. Both were gently spouting and appeared quite calm. I was in shock. I had never seen whales near the shore in Laguna Beach, let alone been only a couple of feet from two of them. In awe I reached over from where I was standing on the jetty, and carefully patted the nearest whale on the back. I feel that the one I touched was a female, but I am not an expert on whales. Even at Sea World I had never been anywhere close to a whale. A sense of calm moved across my being. Little did I know that I would need this calm for what would happen next.

The two whales remained there for about one hour, or well after sunset. Then, they began to swim, still in tandem, slowly out to sea. I watched them until they disappeared, and then I walked off the jetty back to the shore west of the jetty. There I sat down and began to ponder the events that had just transpired.

Full darkness was quickly approaching, but there was some visibility out to sea. Suddenly I saw a round object about a quarter mile out in the ocean with two red lights shining from it. I at first thought it might be a lobster buoy that had severed its mooring and was drifting toward the shore.

But, as it came close, I saw to my surprise that it was an object at least three feet across. Then it came closer, and I realized it was a head, a very large head! I sat there on the beach in total amazement. Suddenly it rose above the water, a human-like, giant head with two blazing eyes staring directly at me. Two shoulders appeared, then a giant chest surfaced. This giant being was now less than two hundred feet away. I was sitting about twenty-five feet from the shore. I was looking up at least twenty-five feet in the air at a being that looked human with scaly, dark skin. It was too dark by now to determine its exact color, but gauging the slant of the beach going into the ocean, this creature was at least forty feet tall. As he stood there, looking at me with blazing red eyes, I realized I could not run away. All he would need was three or four steps to be upon me. I was helpless, but I was receiving a powerful lesson from the Sea. He felt very stern and focused, and I then realized that I was face to face with King Neptune. He was standing, waist deep in the mighty Pacific, with waves breaking around his sides. He was very, very physical. Then, after five of the longest minutes of my life, he began to gently back, step by step, into the sea, all the while still facing me. I could see the whales behind him, although it was getting quite dark by now. Soon he was a small object with two faint red points of light. Then he and the whales disappeared. I was stunned. I thought of Mark's teachings and wished I could communicate this experience to Mark, but Mark also was gone to other worlds. I felt very alone.

About three weeks later, my girlfriend at that time, Rowena, my daughter, Alana, and I went to West Street beach for a sunset swim.

Just after sunset, I again saw the head with the two red lights out at sea. To my surprise, both Rowena and Alana saw the distant head. Neptune this time never came close to the shore but remained visible to us for at least twenty minutes after the initial sighting. What was very interesting about this sighting was that we were not alone on the beach. Several other people nearby had stopped their activities and were blankly staring directly at where he was. I knew they could not see him as we did, but they definitely "sensed" that something was out there.

I will never forget the lessons of the sea and the power of the auric field. Someday, others in this world will respect the oneness that auric fields present when in perfect harmony.

Interlude with King Neptune

Chapter 29

Blood — Transmitting Spiritual Information to the Brain

Now, as we move along to the next interrelated phase of the human body, we're going to examine blood. It is the physical life force that circulates through the body, and without it, we wouldn't be in our bodies. The red blood cells in the body reproduce every 90 days, making blood one of the first complete cell structure groups that reproduces itself in the shortest period of time. I referred earlier in the nutrition section to people who become iron deficient or anemic. They start taking iron to compensate for that, but the supplementation doesn't do any good, because they don't also take Vitamin E, which is an antioxidant that holds the oxygen in the blood for a period long enough for the cell to reproduce normally. And if you don't have pantothene, a B vitamin, the body reproduces cells in a period shorter than 90 days, and therefore the iron content fails to stabilize within the body.

There are different types of blood: A, B, AB and O. These are determined by testing a substance called agglutinin in the red blood cells which coagulates or clots when exposed to different types of agglutinogen in the plasma. If you're doing a transfusion, for example, it's important to know the different blood types involved. A transfers to A, type B to B, and type O to O. Type O, by the way, has no agglutinin in it, hence the name "universal donor," just as AB is the "universal acceptor."

One important factor about blood transfusions is often overlooked: the astrological signs of the donor and the recipient. This applies to transplanted organs, too, because if the astrological sign is taken into consideration, the astral energies can be matched that much closer. If you remember from our meditation, the astral precedes the etheric. And the etheric, of course, on this different level, goes into the healing of the body and the acceptance of different changes and elements in a person's body. If the etheric and the astral levels are mismatched, the acceptance on the physical is less likely, and therefore the body may more readily reject the blood transfusion or organ donation.

Different types of antibodies are manufactured in the blood cells. There are the agglutinin, which we just mentioned. They cause clotting or grouping of antigens. The obsonins increase the activity of the eating cells, which are called the phagocytes, which engulf the antigens. Then there are the bacteriocides, which dissolve the antigens, and the antitoxins which neutralize the antigen poisons. The body receives large quantity of antigens from time to time when you eat the wrong kinds of food. And vitamin B3, niacin, helps the body to get rid of them.

Diseases of the blood include leukemia, which is an excessive increase in the white blood cell count, the opposite of granulocytopenia which is a marked decrease in the white blood cells. Polycynthemia is the excess of red blood cells. And, of course, anemia is a problem many people have. That's "oxygen failure." the lack of red blood cells or hemoglobin. Anemia is one of the conditions that causes the brain to retain toxins over a period of years, causing symptoms. (Remember, when a pyramid is worn on the head, the brain discharges the toxins that have built up in it.) Hemophilia, a hereditary disease, is an inability of the blood to clot. People with hemophilia are often called "bleeders." Blood poisoning, which is called septicemia, occurs when bacteria and blood cause local points of infection and congestion. Terminal toxemia is caused by toxic substances. These are the types of blood diseases that respond to and can be prevented by the different kinds of healing energies offered by the extraterrestrial sciences. We can build the entire immune system to where it is so powerful that it is typically not subject to these kinds of infections.

Hemoglobin is composed of four different iron atoms. Imagine them as four pyramids with a top and a bottom, forming the full octahedron, stacked on top of each other, 1-2-3-4. Wrapped around these four octahedrons are two alpha chains and two beta chains, which empower the blood to transfer oxygen to the cells of the body, or to pick up carbon dioxide and bring it out and discharge it into the air for the plant kingdom to absorb. This switching action of picking up oxygen, dropping off oxygen, is called the Bohr Effect. Don't confuse this with the earlier mentioned Neils Bohr and quantum mechanics. That is entirely different. Our meditations feature some rhythms that are very similar to this primal beat. This rhythm is regulated through the pineal gland, and in the death process, the rhythm is slowed down so that the consciousness can start shifting from the physical body to the astral body. The first phase of this shift takes place when the oxygen is no longer capable of moving through the body properly, and the physical consciousness is no longer able to anchor itself to the physical body via the struck zones. The soul-consciousness then starts moving toward the astral plane.

Iron is at the nucleus of the blood. It's ferrous and ferric. If you were to take an iron frying pan, for example, and rub off some of the dark, blackened metal, you would find the shiny, frying pan surface. When the shine has been exposed to air for any length of time, it rusts. Rust occurs when oxygen oxidizes iron, forming iron oxide. The iron is now ferric, with a valence of plus three, which means all of the electrons available in that range to fill that orbital pattern of that particular ring of the combination of oxygen and iron are complete. If you were to rub the surface shiny again, it would again become actively ferrous as it looks for another electron to fill its outer orbits. Once its orbit was filled, it would go from ferrous to ferric again. This is specifically how "rust" or oxidation happens, picking up oxygen when it's in the active stage.

The Bohr effect

Blood enters the lungs in the ferric state (the shiny, active surface), and as soon as it combines with oxygen, it goes into the ferrous state (the blackened, stable surface) and circulates through the body, carrying oxygen. It connects with other cells in the body and switches from the ferrous to the ferric state by leaving the oxygen behind, then returns to the lungs. So blood cells constantly switch from the ferric state, complete with carbon dioxide, back to the ferrous state, where carbon dioxide is discharged, and become active again, looking for more oxygen. This is the vital action of the iron atom in the body, switching from ferric to ferrous in a rhythmic pattern we previously called the Bohr Effect. And as I said earlier, in old age or when the death hormone sounds, this process is interrupted.

We've just explored the mechanical purpose of blood in the body. Of course, blood works at levels other than the mechanical level. The shape of the iron atom itself, for example, is that of a pyramid. A pyramid has seven different levels of energy fields in it (which we discuss during meditation) that enter the red blood cells. When Christ was initiated into the Great Pyramid, he went into the seven different chambers and had seven different experiences as part of the initiation process of the Great Pyramid.

The Great Pyramid itself is so well centered on the face of the Earth that it can't help but be a powerful, complete channel of energy from the higher planes and bring that energy from the inner planes out to the physical planes. For example, if you go into the Queen's Chamber, you're on Ray Two, and you're going to have a Ray Two experience, which is the experience of the Son. If you go up into the King's Chamber, you're going to have a Ray One, or a Father/Will experience, because it's bringing you that level of consciousness.This is the advantage of having something built in the exact geometric center of the Earth. If you were to take all the land masses of the Earth, all the valleys, hills and mountains, from the Marianas Trench to the top of Mount Everest, and average the land masses above and below the sea, you would arrive at the solution of 454 feet. The Great Pyramid is 454-$\frac{1}{2}$ feet tall. The King's Chamber maintains a temperature of 68 degrees Fahrenheit all year around, the best temperature for the outside of the human body for obtaining the highest amount of consciousness, with the least amount of air, oxygen or food requirements.

The Great Pyramid bears strong significance which does not stop at physical comparison of the geometrics of the Earth/Pyramid relationship. It also, as we discussed earlier, relates to the revolution of our solar system around the Pleiades. It also defines just about everything that has to do with the carbon atom. When you're actually in the Great Pyramid, it's possible to experience levels or changes in consciousness similar to

Pyramid/Iron Atom Relationship

Pyramid Shaped Iron atom in Hemoglobin

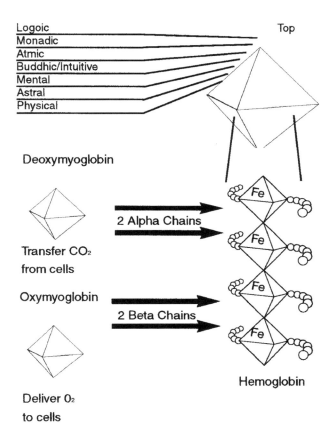

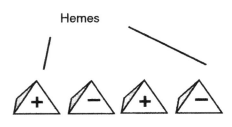

= Deoxymyoglobin shift to oxymyoglobin is a rhythm called the Bohr Effect.

figure 29-1

what Christ went through during his initiations by the Hierophant. If you were to project all of these energy fields from the Great Pyramid into your consciousness, you would find them in your red blood cells, each one of which has four iron atoms, with four positive and four negative energy fields within, creating a perfect synthesis of the seven levels of energy being synthesized right inside the iron atom or the carbon atom in the body. And because the iron atom is shaped like a pyramid in the body, it has the seven levels of consciousness on a small level represented in each and every red blood cell of the body. So as this blood is pumped through the body by the heart, this consciousness is then dissipated through the body, all seven levels, flowing to where the vibratory frequency of the specific cell structure is "tuned" via the DNA.

Each cell calls for the consciousness it needs

Remember when we talked about "tuning up" or resonating to the DNA of the cells? The consciousness carried by the red blood cells is distributed via the iron atom to where the consciousness of the individual body cells "calls" for it. And as a result of that, the blood then becomes the spiritual life-threading force, because if you didn't have these seven levels of energies coming onto the physical plane somewhere, then you could not have any physical plane reality or consciousness. This physical reality arrives within the physical plane and the human being through the action of the red blood cells. Now you can begin to realize that we are weaving a spiritual thread through the body and that's why healthy circulation is so critical, because when blood stops going through the brain, the brain no longer receives spiritual information from the seven levels. When the brain is no longer animated or vitalized from these seven levels, it starts to die. When the brain starts to die, then the rest of the physical body starts to die, and therefore you have a loss of consciousness (see figure 29-1).

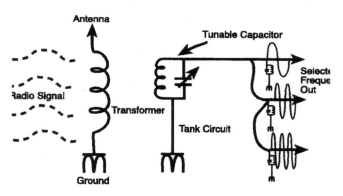

Equivalent to DNA

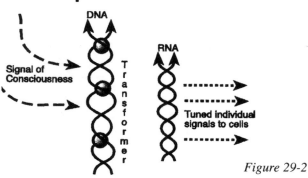

Figure 29-2

Many people don't appreciate the spiritual aspect of blood. Blood typing reveals the different characteristics of that person's body. You can call it "body interface" between the spirit and the form. The body has its temperament, and that's our right to be individuals exercising that right to temperament, as the blood carries much more than physical sustenance to the body.

To summarize: Blood, on the chemical level, transmutes from ferrous to ferric and back again. It is this process red blood cells use to transfer oxygen to your body. The cell releases the oxygen (fuel), bonds to carbon dioxide (waste), carries the waste to the lungs, and discharges it via exhalation. On another level, the pyramid-shaped iron atom deposits seven levels of consciousness through the body, and depending on which cell is attuned to what frequency, that consciousness is amplified, i.e., the consciousness of the sexual organs would be organized more on the 7th Ray of violet, therefore the energy would have a tendency to flow to the 7th Ray or the 7th plane, which is physical reproduction, or 2nd Ray energy, monadic, or attraction, or love, would concentrate in the heart/thymus area of the body. The 3rd Ray (green), atmic, intellect, female energy, would center its activity in the thyroid area. In this manner, all Rays center on one of the seven endocrine/chakra areas of the body, one for each of the seven levels of consciousness.

Remember when we detailed the structure of the DNA, deoxyribonucleic acid? We explained how the DNA in each particular cell, if unwound, would measure 39.5 centimeters. The 46 different chromosomes constructed from DNA are small, active radio transmitters that direct the flow of conscious energies into the more complex, heavier genes. There are 1250 different genes that make up the chromosomes and they, of course, are mechanically tuned by physical location and spacing into the proper wavelength to receive that electrical etheric impulse, that particular vibratory frequency, into the body. This is a 39.5cm long antenna with a resonant trap, or in electronics, a tank circuit at the base, and is tuned to a particular section of the chromosome chain so that it electronically can receive these signals that are brought in through the activities of the iron molecule within the heme of the iron red blood cell (see figure 29-2).

Now, the next way to look at blood in the body is to look at the fact that it is iron! Iron circulating through long arteries, capillaries and veins throughout the body generates a magnetic field. This magnetic field exists side-by-side with the central nervous system, composed of all three different electrical nervous networks: the autonomic, the parasympathetic and the sympathetic nervous systems. Naturally, the nervous system is going to induce its different frequencies of electricity into the red blood cell. The iron in the red blood cell also transforms and carries a magnetic field. This has tremendous significance! The blood carries this magnetic field into the brain, through the different cavities that have been formed by memory programming (which we'll cover more completely later). As the electrical aura fields caused by the central nervous system scans the different cavities in the brain, electrical imprints or blueprints of consciousness transform them into direct memory patterns and direct memory thoughts.

When a child is first born, the child is very curious. The child's higher self and organized consciousness have not been able to descend into the physical form of the child yet, meaning that the child's past memories, higher consciousness, and awareness of things that already are, are not expressible into physical consciousness. The body has not been fabricated and connected yet to this higher realm. What we call a series of growth patterns are established, so that a reconnection is made between the higher self and the lower self. The quality of this connection determines the frequency of the soul and the karma of the individual. And the whole alignment of the soul processing into the form has to do with spiritual growth on this planet.

So the child wants to learn things. The Will, first of all, 1st Ray, is pushed into the child's consciousness. The curious child walks up to, for example, a table and says, "What's that?" And of course the child's fovea centralis, the most acutely perceptive area of our eyes, focuses on the table, burning the identity pattern through the retinal nerves, through the retinal optic passageways, into the gray matter of the brain. The light of reality literally imprints itself on the child's brain, and then the mother or father answers, saying, "That's a table." So now the child hears "table," as well as sees "table." The sound input to the olfactory nerves is a reinforcement to what has been the child's primary consciousness input, vision. Probably the next thing the child will do to reinforce this learning experience is to touch the table. In addition to these three senses: sight, sound and touch, the child may notice the smell of the wax used on the table.

The bottom line is that this three or four-way stimulation of the senses defines this single object. If the child is blind, of course, the primary sense would be audio, and if the child is blind and deaf, then the child would experience by feel, which can take even longer. The focusing process of the mind selects a primary sense to keynote on recognizing this table/ stimulus again. Usually, it's vision. The child now can visually recognize and identify a table. This association is probably going to remain consistent from that point on in the child's life.

Memory Imprint Recognition

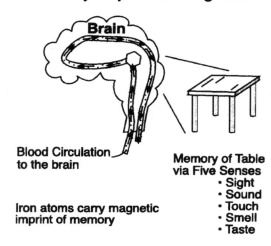

Brain

Blood Circulation to the brain

Iron atoms carry magnetic imprint of memory

Memory of Table via Five Senses
• Sight
• Sound
• Touch
• Smell
• Taste

figure 29-3

In our example we have used many senses to identify an object, the table, but recall has been keynoted to the vision into the gray matter of the brain. Actually, it's like shooting a laser into a piece of plastic. An intense enough beam will burn a hole. This experience has burned an impression of the table into the brain. Not only as a visual impression, but as a multi-sensual impression that the brain can interpret to retransmit back to consciousness when the child recalls the vision of the table, and the sense of the table. The child now has a memory.

Here is where the mechanical part of the blood plays into all this: The gray matter of the brain, which was virgin until that point in time, responded by etching the messages from the senses through the nervous system to the gray matter. And from that point on, any time blood flows to that part of the brain, it will be slightly diverted from its normal path into this little message that's been etched in there, the image of the table. And once again, I specify that the image is not just the image as you would look at it or draw it, but the multi-faceted image the body responds to when it is magnetically "swept" by the thought process. In sweeping I refer to the consciousness searching for analysis across the brain patterns. The table is now recognized on a magnetic level, because iron, as we've said, is already present in the blood, and when it circulates past and is galvanized by electricity generated by the nervous system, the iron is imprinted with a magnetic pattern similar to core memory in a computer (see figure 29-3).

As more and more pattern identity stimuli occur, the brain begins to organize and map the child's entire individual reality process. Thus the character of the environment where a child is raised is tantamount to his or her foundation to what is reality for this lifetime.

Pretty soon the child becomes familiar with all kinds of objects. So, therefore, an area of the brain has been familiarized to these different objects and their identifications. Then the child meets another child. Say they have a little conflict, and one child pushes the other child down. The child that was pushed down gets up and pushes the other child back. The child realizes that this is uncomfortable! But through the stimulus of the unpleasantness, the child learns compassion. The opposite would be that the child, smelling a flower, learns euphoria. Now the child has a complete set of learning experiences and encounters another person. This is a new area of the brain that gets galvanized by thought and experience.

Soon the child has more complete memories of objects, thoughts and experiences, "burned" into two areas of the brain. The area of the brain where all these things are identified — table, chair, and so on — carries a lot of electricity, because it's the first area that has been "carved" out. If the child suffers a head injury that wipes out or damages that part of that area of the gray matter that recalls these objects, the sophistication of the child will determine whether that recollection will be reconstructed in that area or another area of the brain, and the child may have to go through a therapy program to reestablish certain things that were known previous to the injury.

Add to this the interesting factor of time. When someone tells me, "this is a table," I recognize that not only is this a table, but it is a 19th century Victorian table. I can identify the type of wood, the proportion of height to depth, even decide if I like it or not. I am responding with a consortium of time identification and hierarchal identification, finely classifying the object as more than just as a table, but what kind of a table, and who built it. I would automatically think of and link up a whole series of events that took place through human actions to create the table in the first place. And this, of course, is the way human memory works. The linking of thoughts together anchors memories over a period of time and dimension, where the brain is correlating traditional building blocks to interpret the full meaning at that moment that it's exposed. Then we start linking time with the expression of memories. This is a brief explanation, but you understand it has ramifications in that once you realize this process, you can free yourself of that process and move out into a dimension where time is not yet present in the human mind. This is the science of time travel.

How memory works

The child has had sensory input that created experiences the child identifies as memories, stored magnetically in the child's mind. Moving forward, the child begins to project into the future possibilities of different kinds of reactions. Through this series of projections, the child is developing what we call "gut feeling" or intuition, and now that area of the brain is activated. Three areas of the brain are now in play, the intuitive, object identification and the "possible encounter" or personality system.

When these three systems become activated, spontaneously a fourth area of the brain begins projecting out of sheer curiosity, anticipation and character of spirit! Remember, time can be represented by a spiral, it doesn't repeat itself, but like the mystical number defined by the Great Pyramid, pi, it spirals forward. The timeline is not a circle, but a spiral — and consciousness, when sweeping through these three different galvanized areas of the brain, has a natural tendency to start projecting. When this fourth area is activated, a person may become a channeler, a seer, a shaman; someone comfortable in dealing with reality beyond the stimuli of the five physical senses.

The gestalt recognition of this possibility becomes a 4th dimensional reality, or time-less aspect. Time-less means "slowed down" in this area, because as you increase your level of frequency, vibration and consciousness, time begins to slow, but to us in the 3rd dimension, time appears to speed up.

This is the illusion of "Maya" because our soul essence is timeless. Consider the consciousness of the Solar Logos, for example, the one whose Being is our whole solar system, while we're just cells inside of cells in His body. His "nap" could be three billion years for us! We see another fascinating time link here, a concept that dispels us of the paradox of the bulk of humanity's consciousness and frees us, at least time-wise, from the bulk of humanity's problems and forms of ignorance that hold us back in our spiritual upward spiral.

A little bit more about time travel — previously I explained how the spirit enters the body, sending a shock as it enters the Chakras. Some of it spins down into the body and is trapped, while some of the energy is freed to return to spiritual kingdoms. I could probably consolidate this a little bit further, but I feel it's necessary to present it at a certain level that will give you the freedom to put these ideas together for yourself. The way I interpret what I'm explaining to you, the listener, and the way you interpret what I'm saying to you, could vary. If I lock concepts down too quickly and too rigidly, and the configuration becomes too fixed in appearance, I think that you'll lose the freedom to interpret and analyze what I've explained and integrate it for own personal interpretation, what's necessary for your own ego and your own spiritual requirements, to resolve the bottom line.

Chapter 30

The Discovery of Scalar Waves, Pleiadeans & Andromedans, Programming the Systems at Home

Back in 1948 there was a reconnaissance plane flown by the Navy over the verdant Cumberland Valley in Pennsylvania that took pictures of crops that had been blighted by locusts (during the time we had experienced locust plagues). The pictures of these orchards, which were taken from quite a good altitude, were then taken to the Homeotronic Naval Laboratory in Newport, Pennsylvania. They were studied, then put in a black box with some insecticide and given to a farmer whose crops had been photographed. The lab technicians told the farmer to leave the photos in the box all the time and every day at a certain time turn the dial on the black box. After six weeks went by every single insect in the orchard had been destroyed by the combined energy of what was in the black box, the picture and the insecticide.

This was the beginning of what we would call "psionic energy," or scalar wave technology which has become more prevalent today, and is a part of our Pyradyne Systems. T. Galen Hieronymus was the one who had applied for patents. It was his system they were experimenting with back in 1946. Patent #2,482,773 was issued in 1948 (you can call the Patent Office and see yourself!). That is the patent number which our Systems Technology is based upon.

Dr. William Hale at Dow Chemical began research in the 50s with this energy and found that anything that had a cell and consciousness in it broadcast an electronic field. In previous sections of this discourse we discussed the intricacies of that electronic field and the sensitivity of DNA. Dr. Rickenbauch in Germany, during World War II, had done substantial research along these lines, and so by the time that Dr. Hale was conducting research at Dow Chemical, scalar energy was a more recognized phenomenon. It was presented to the U.S. military also, but they weren't really interested in the possibility of a "beam" weapon. The Russians found it quite interesting, though. In 1987, a 747 Japanese jet flew through what appeared to be a hydrogen bomb explosion, but there was no explosion, no heat, no radiation. They sighted it originally near the North Pole, north of Alaska.

Later on we found out this was part of a scalar-based "V-beam" technology.

And so, this energy that killed the insects is something that we work with all the time, only we don't kill with it, we heal with it instead. It can work for either purpose. It's the same energy field that becomes characterized by the soul and enters into the body when conception occurs. Shortly after conception, the nature of the spirit records a particular vibratory pattern in the soul, and this then galvanizes the iron in the fetus of the embryo. The galvanic action of

269

the iron within the red blood cells, which has also already been covered, begins to form the baby's fingerprints by its characteristic energy field.

The Pleiadeans and the Grays, two different types of extraterrestrials, are both aware of this same kind of frequency and identification of the soul. As a result, when a Pleiadean family member's energy field leaves, which means dies or leaves the body, it is easier to find. Whether the Pleiadean incarnates in an Earth-bound body or some other solar system, the family can find him eventually, because they know how to look for the essence of the soul that forms the physical fingerprints. So as the human kingdom can recognize the soul by its fingerprint patterns, the Pleiadeans can recognize the individual soul before a person is born. Contactees are even "found" before they are born on the Earth-physical plane because of the vibratory energy field that the mother has around her!

One thing I want to clarify at this point in time about these "Grays" — many people wonder if they are "good" or "bad." I am certain that they do come here. I've had several contacts with them. They were uncomfortable, because I'm not mentally geared to deal with them; somebody like Whitney Streiber, the author of Communion, is. The first contact I had with them was when I was a child. The second contact occurred about 1980. The energy entered my brain, my consciousness, and it wasn't like a Pleiadean contact. When the Grays called me, the message went around inside my head, and eventually it slowed down after a few days, and I was able to grab the words out of this beam of energy.

What I found out from them was that they are scavengers of energy. The Grays go through the galaxies and they pick up stray or spurious non-harmonic energy and process it into harmonic energy. If you look at their metabolism, you can begin to understand how this is possible. They are like a jellyfish, or a shrimp, or a lobster, or something at the bottom of the sea — they have the same kind of scavenging capability. The Grays have done a lot of bio-breeding and inter-genetic breeding with other beings. They have a group "over-soul," but they don't have an individual soul on the lower levels. One of their motivations for interactions with the human kingdom is to establish a soul that can follow a hereditary reincarnating process as Man, the Pleiadeans, and other humanoid races.

Another thing that is interesting: because the Grays are scavengers, they absorb our "loose"' energy. They were doing this in the Mexico area back in the 40s. Their plutonium reactors in their spaceships were picking up radio frequency and radar energies, and these radio frequency energies overcharged them, causing a flash inside the ship. The flash didn't burn them but brought the ships down intact. The effect was like a miniature hydrogen bomb going off inside the perimeter of the flying vehicle because they had absorbed too much energy from the radiation we were producing from our experimental ANSFPS-35 and ANSFPS-26 radar tests. So their power source systems were characteristically absorbing other kinds of energy.

The Iragans are another group I have worked with. They have a different purpose here — they're the alchemists. They teach humans alchemy. For example, in 1947, Hoffman, who was working at Sandoz Laboratories in Switzerland, discovered lysergic acid in the rye mold and had an out-of-body experience. He put a substance in his body that caused biochemical change. This event evolved humanity's consciousness. It just so happened to be that he was synthesizing something that could be found naturally in the psilocybin mushroom, but science was not aware of that yet. As the Iragans come here to teach humans alchemy to help raise the body frequencies by changing food habits, nutritional habits, and so on, they create what are called elixirs, and these elixirs help the DNA within biochemistry receive the higher vibratory frequency of the human race as it moves on its upward evolution cycle and its ever-constant course around the Pleiades.

The Pleiadeans, on the other hand, come to us when man's emotions are open and receptive to the fact that we are not alone. As the Pleiadeans educate us, higher races like the Andromedans or the Lyrians take their place, races who are more on the mental plane and who don't have to work through the emotional aspects of the human race. So each of these extraterrestrial beings and groups come to us in a different manner of consciousness, each for a different purpose. We've already mentioned several different extraterrestrial types and will continue to refer to them throughout this material.

Now what I would like to do is talk about the Pyramids for a few minutes, give you a quick review before we get into the Systems. The aforementioned patent number is the one that I have developed my Systems under, and the Pyramids, of course, are necessary to get you ready for the Systems and the Receptors. We discussed at great length the Receptors previously, and you may wish to refer back to that section at this time.

The Pyradome was the first Pyramid that we developed and, like so many of our other devices, was developed by accident. As I said earlier, I didn't put Pyramids on people's heads. Dr. Gary Coutoure did in his clinic in Newport Beach, California. He found that the Pyramid caused people to have higher energy fields, and whenever he examined patients by muscle testing or kinesiology, the Pyramid compensated for their weaknesses, i.e., vitamin deficiencies. So if the patient was low in vitamin C, then the Pyramid was put over the test area, and vitamin C would test strong; if the patient was low in vitamin B, then they put the Pyramid over the area on the body where they tested for vitamin B, and they tested strong. And so from that we were able to derive there were seven different vibratory rates inside the Pyramid that corresponded to all the different vitamins that we found. In the 70s when we introduced them, of course, the Pyradome was the greatest seller because the biggest drug addict in those days was the American housewife, strung out of valium, spending many billions of dollars a year. So we introduced the Pyradome as a drug-free tranquilizer.

The Headgear Pyramids weren't developed through perfect calculation and timing; it was all a series of accidents, I would say, a controlled series of accidents. As I mentioned earlier, when we first put the copper on the Pyramid, we were trying to get the Pyramid to stimulate the adrenals. In fact, the Japanese were successful in doing this with their copper bracelets. We failed miserably, and then we noticed that a stack of test Pyramids had, over a period of time, developed little 'holes' in their finish. These holes had burned through the copper, exposing the gold layer below. We muscle tested again.They were now effective as far as stimulating the adrenals! When we developed the Raydome, we tried to use all kinds of exotic plating materials like platinum or rhodium. Finally a plating company employee suggested that we might just try the simplest of the white metals, which was silver, and it worked perfectly. The heat process was also developed accidentally one night, when I dropped a Pyramid on the stove. The stove burned a hole in the outer plating, exposing the inner plating, and our heating process came into fruition.

So it was often a series of accidents that led us to successful discoveries over a period of time (see figure 30-1).

The Pleiadeans started getting seriously involved with my work about 1977. Up until then, our contacts were about who they were, what my soul relationship was, what my purpose on Earth was, the validity of their being here, the validity of my acceptance, my friends meeting them, and other similar topics. In 1977 Semjase surprised me by following us. We were in a motor home, we were traveling across New Mexico near the White Sands testing facility south of Los Alamos, when we noticed there were three ships in the sky following us behind

Pyramid Posing
The Bridge to Mankind
Pyramid

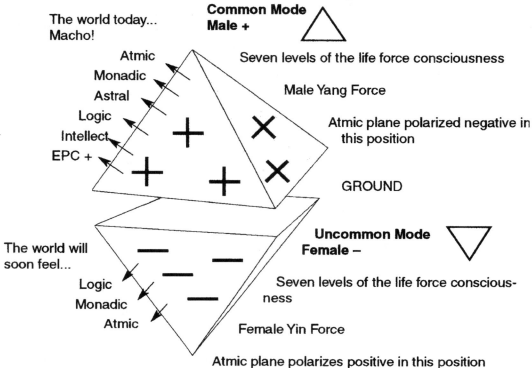

The world today... Macho!

Common Mode Male +

Atmic
Monadic
Astral
Logic
Intellect
EPC +

Seven levels of the life force consciousness

Male Yang Force

Atmic plane polarized negative in this position

GROUND

The world will soon feel...

Uncommon Mode Female –

Logic
Monadic
Atmic

Seven levels of the life force consciousness

Female Yin Force

Atmic plane polarizes positive in this position

And then, the Perfect Synthesis . . .

reticular cloud formations. They transmitted information to me, and the main content was the design of what we now call the Irradiator. And the Irradiator was the first real "scalar wave machine" that we had.

If you were to take a positively positioned Pyramid and place it right side up on your head and perform a muscle test, you would find that you would test very strong. If you were to turn the Pyramid upside down and put it on your head, or have somebody hold it and muscle test, you would probably test very weak. (see figure 30-2). And this is because the energy field of the Pyramid is reversing itself. The

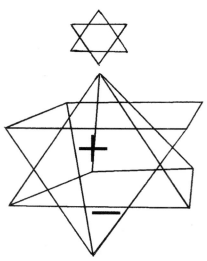

In this position, the forces of the Holy Grail will prevail. Man and woman will soul emote a perfect whole. Ecstacy will be felt by all of those who have trusted within the inner highways.

figure 30-1

pyramid upside down is reversing its polarity into the feminine aspect, or the 3rd Ray, the intellect ray, and therefore the energy from the physical body drops as it transmutes into the mental aspect. This indicates poor energy balance. You should test strong both ways, but we are so overdeveloped in positive energy on the masculine side, and so underdeveloped in the female negative energy, then the human psyche, when confronted with pure amounts of female, or negative energy (negative in this context meaning good), usually tests weak. If you were to take a positively-positioned Pyramid and hold it right side up, and a negatively-positioned Pyramid and hold it upside down, and make a 2-dimensional drawing out of them, superimposing the positive with the negative, you'd have created a model of the Star of David. And so you can see, this implies a synthesis is necessary.

If you were to wear a Pyramid upside down for a great length of time, which you could do, eventually you would become acclimated on a physical plane to the negative energy or the female or intellectual energy of it. And this is also energy to the mind. Then what would happen is that you would probably be able to test positive and strong with the

Muscle Testing with the Pyramid Headgear

1. Standing comfortably, hold your right arm straight out and have another person push down at the hand. Notice the force required to move your arm down.

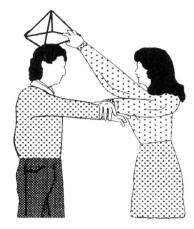

2. Now, place the pyramid, apex up, on your head. Have your companion try to pull your arm down again. Notice how much more force it takes to move you.

3. For comparison, now have your companion hold the pyramid apex pointing down over your head. This last muscle test will be by far the weakest!

figure 30-2

Pyramid upside down over your head. Over the years I've been conditioned in these energies. Therefore I test presently, positive, or strong, under a reversed Pyramid.

So from Semjase's desert transmission we developed the Irradiator. The Irradiator was approximately five feet tall, freestanding, with some Pyramids in the positive position of right side up and some Pyramids that are upside down. And if you were to imagine each one of these Pyramids generating a field out in front of it of opposite polarity, you would see a trapezoid-shaped waveform coming from the Irradiator. This trapezoid wave would repeat itself over, and over, and over again. And this trapezoid wave, of course, is timeless. It's a scalar wave. The trapezoid wave perpetuates itself through space and through time. Later on we where able to photograph the scalar waves using Infra-Red photography.

The Irradiator rests on a device called the Mega Orb. The Mega Orb has a series of octahedral chambers in it, creating positive and negative energy fields. There is a neutral zone

Pyradyne Mega Orb and Irradiator and Associated Components

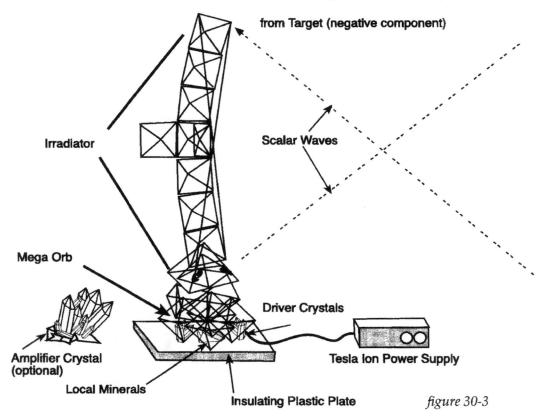

figure 30-3

located in its center that contains programming information. The Irradiator/Mega Orbcombination uses geometric chambers and dynamic positioning to open up portals of space and time.

Within the mixing chambers of the Mega Orb are placed silicon dioxide crystals (quartz), local mineral from the area surrounding the structure (rocks, stones, seashells, etc.), and intelligence gathering data. (Information on this aspect is available to those who wish to work with these devices.) Next, the Mega Orb is placed on a plastic plate to insulate it from the ground. Then a special pulsed D.C. negative ion power supply is attached, which energizes the contents of the mixing chamber. A computer interface is also available for programming this phase (see figure 30-3).

In order to transmit the intelligence into the universe, the irradiator is placed on top of the Mega Orb and acts as a transmitting/receiving antenna. Because scalar waves are timeless, they are transmitted interdimensionally.

Scalar waves transmit across dimensions

The best way to visualize this whole process is to close your eyes and look into your mind. Your mind is infinite in its imagination. The Irradiator /Mega Orb can amplify what your mind creates and thread that creation into this, our present reality. To explain the process would take hours, but you can experience its reality in a few minutes. This is why we have personal training seminars worldwide.

We have pictures of these scalar waves. We developed an exposure technique whereby we use a time exposure at night along with laser techniques to see the scalar waves, but now through infrared film techniques we are actually able to film the scalar waves, even in daylight, at times. These pictures are now available, although I have not yet released them to the public, but are viewed in my slide shows. When I do my seminars you will be seeing them.

Our Systems are programmable, which means that some form of mental clarity, I would say, would be helpful in order to program them. This is another advantage of getting into and understanding the Receptors, having experiences with them to build confidence, so that when you get into Systems work, you will have confidence. The old Systems energy field is based on self-confidence, and you'll need that in the beginning to appreciate the results, since they're often very small and minimal at first, eventually becoming quite profound and obvious to many people.

But in order to achieve that profound state, you have to hold a certain mental clarify and be receptive to observation, to make mental adjustments at the very beginning. Because, as I explained earlier, when the blood passes through the lungs and pumped out via the heart through the carotid artery into the brain, the brain's minute arterial **sizes?** act like a strainer. The brain then retains the accumulated sediment of toxins strained from the blood, impeding blood circulation in the brain. Over a period of years this becomes a severe problem. As the blockage gets into the base of the brain, it causes a balance

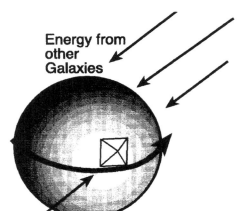

Energy from other Galaxies

Earth rotates at 1000 mph. Orb is on surface of Earth moving 1000 mph. This creates eddy currents as the stellar life forces interact within the orb structure.

figure 30-4

Pyramid - moving at 1000 mph with respect to incoming galactic energy

problem; as it gets toward the mid-brain it causes problems with assimilation and digestion and energy distribution throughout the body; and as it reaches the forebrain it causes senility. Wearing Pyramids (other than the Pyradome) detoxifies the brain tissue, relieves this condition, and gradually opens up the brain again by electrically removing these debris particles. Electrolysis then dissolves them back into the blood and sends them on to the liver (see Chapter 10). Our Pyramids that cause this to happen include the Powerdome and the Raydome. You can only handle or digest so much information at one time in the form of these negative particles. You're liable to get a series of headaches at first. Once you get past this headache syndrome, you'll find that your brain will start working clearly, and because you've gone through this uncomfortable experience, you'll now experience the positive.

It will give you tremendous confidence when you advance to our Systems. If you are wearing the Firedome, Raydome or Powerdome over an extended period of time, especially the Powerdome, which is the most powerful, and you find yourself getting a headache, remove the Pyramid immediately and proceed to drink large amounts of water, and try our Ester C, vitamin C or other Ester C's that are available on the market in the larger doses as mentioned earlier, because this is very effective in helping the liver remove these toxins from the body so the brain can function properly.

Now getting back to the Systems — one of the first areas I find it necessary to thoroughly understand is that of the nature spirits. One of the concepts that the Pleiadeans taught me was the necessity of this. Remember I explained how the Pleiadeans spend so much time in horticulture because they believe that God can be found in nature as well as many other places, and it's very evident that God exists through observation of the nature kingdom.

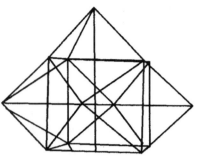

When field arrives from space it combines with the energies of the orb. This amplifies strike and struck zones within the cells or the being within the orb-generated fields.

Pyradyne Orb (use over Portamid)   *figure 30-5*

Nature spirits occur on different vibratory frequencies. One of the really classic examples that Semjase gave me years ago was that of the bee. We all require vegetation. Animals require it, and even if you're a meat-eater, vegetation has to feed the animal that you're going to eat. Without the cooperation of the nature spirits on this planet, especially the devas of the bee kingdom, the Earth would not be able to perpetuate most of the species of plants, therefore we wouldn't be in physical bodies.

Nature spirits have vibratory frequencies

The output frequencies of a single Pyramid, like a Raydome or a Powerdome, exert themselves through the atmosphere and the environment. If you were to graph this on a chart recorder, you would see a P-orbital design pattern, which is in physics one of the paths that electrons take around a proton within a hydrogen atom. A Pyradyne Orb is comprised of many of these patterns, forming a lotus field, because it's a combination of five Pyramids (see figures 30-4 through 30-6).

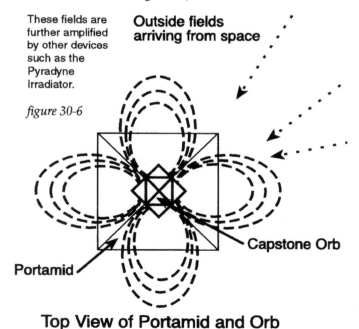

These fields are further amplified by other devices such as the Pyradyne Irradiator.

figure 30-6

Outside fields arriving from space

Capstone Orb

Portamid

Top View of Portamid and Orb

These patterns and fields are created by the fact that the Earth is revolving through space while rotating on its axis at 1,000 miles an hour, but at the same time, it's receiving direct energies from the sun, the moon, other planets, and of course, the stars themselves. The influence from the stars is becoming more apropos to this dissertation because of the tremendous, profound effect on our consciousness via the etheric chakras, via the endocrine glands, via the hormone constructions, etc.

The bee kingdom is an excellent illustration of the active process of scalar waves. Flowering plants, as living beings, generate their own scalar waves, which bees are naturally tuned into. Stamens literally beam the information to the hive, "pollen is now available!" The scalar wave itself exists in a timeless state, but its mere existence generates a vibratory frequency which then resonates at a regularly timed rate.

Even though scalar energy can be timeless, it can be turned off and on during a period of time. So it generates a certain particular vibratory frequency, a particular lotus frequency, that is characteristic of the stamen. The hive operates like a giant antenna system, and over the hive is an angel, an angel that resonates to it at a specific vibratory rate. Angels exist on one of the etheric states, second, third, or first ether, somewhere below the astral plane but visible to most people. The angel has six of seven chakras within its form like a human being does, and a few external ones, but the chakras we're concerned with now are the upper head centers in the angel. When an angel secretes a hormone into its system, it creates a reaction, just like in the human body!

We have six endocrine glands that secrete hormones into our body that catalyze a positive reaction, and the seventh endocrine system in the body which secretes a hormone that shuts down bodily processes, and if left unchecked, creates a death-syndrome hormone. Of course, the gland we're talking about here is pineal gland. An angel's pineal gland is an externalized gland. It's kept active, but it's not physically active. The pineal gland of the angel of a particular hive is the hives' queen bee. Now you begin to understand why the queen bee does all unique things that queen bees do, strange rituals that demonstrate a tremendous intelligence contained within the entire hive. The whole hive is subservient to the queen bee.

The queen bee's vibratory frequency, which is the same as the angels, corresponds to whatever type of flower that the whole hive is polarized to. In other words, there are clover angels, orange angels, alfalfa angels, avocado honey angels, all these different vibratory frequencies. These are, in fact, denizens of the spirit world that live right on the edge of the physical plane, manifesting energy in consciousness for man to exist. A long time ago man knew this, but man does not now exist cooperatively with the nature kingdom. For example, when we detonate a hydrogen bomb or an atomic bomb, think how many bee hives and other nature spirits are destroyed. The aura field of the angel extends out to the farthest perimeter of the particular type of flower to be pollinated.

The polarity of the angel will depend on where the hive is in relationship to the Earth's north and south poles, and the angel will be rotating around the beehive itself. The bees are actually like diodes, like rectifiers. They're able to take the energies of the angel and convert them directly into motional electricity, which then propels their wings.

If a scientist were to show you the amount of wing space it takes to fly an airplane with a fuselage proportional to the weight of the center section of the bee, the bee would weigh 50 times too much or it would require 50 times larger wings or wing areas to get off the ground in the first place by conventional aerodynamics, yet with one fiftieth the wing size required, the bee flies quite well. The bee is able to transmute pure energy from the angel into itself. Now if you were to position a camera 500' high above the beehive with a time lapse exposure, and you were to mark every bee with some very bright paint so you could watch its motion to the flowers and back to the hive, what you would eventually see is an impression of these time motion tracks of these bees coming and going to and from the hive to the flowers and back. You would actually paint an image of the angel on film as it moved around. So you would have to have different sections of time lapses as the angel moved around and breathed and sensed the different flowers at different times of the day.

One of the byproducts of the production of honey is propolis. Propolis, shed by the bee, is representative of a lower frequency part of the angel's presence, and it's great for "drawing" energy. This means that the propolis is used for externally drawing out poisons from the the body, like a poultice on a cut. Honey — a very high source of energy, a pure form of sugar and a six-carbon atom base — doesn't turn into alcohol in your body, as does a 12-carbon atom compound sugar when it dissolves down to nine carbon atoms (alcohol) during the digestion process. It's a natural form of sweetener. The Royal Jelly, which is kept around the queen bee for her food, is the highest essence of the angel frequencies. It should be consumed by humans homeopathically, meaning that it's so pure that to eat large amounts of it could be destructive to the body. You should eat it in moderate amounts, and you should be sensitive to that. In order to really receive it properly, you really should have a fairly clear body.

Propolis has a "drawing out" of energy

Another interesting fact about bees — if they are bothered, or an animal gets in the way, or a human is around, they may sting even at the sacrifice of their own life. They do this when they perceive anything that's interfering with what they're trying to do in their path of service to the angel and the beehive. When a bee stings something, the bee dies. But that doesn't matter to the bee, because he knows that his soul is in the group oversoul auric field of the beehive, and so this essence of the soul is entered back into the hive, and the bee is re-born again somewhere in one of the queens' new eggs. The consciousness of the bee is trained to know that the energy field allows the bee to reincarnate within its hive structure again and again. Bees aren't just spontaneously born somewhere, but within their regional aura field of the bee kingdom; and, of course, the energy level that the bee reaches when he leaves his body is now second etheric and astral energy. The bee now transmits etherically and astrally as scalar energy back into the hive, and is reborn within the angel's aura field.

The interplay between two human aura fields creates the astral plane, and the interplay between many humans in the astral plane creates a religious domain, so you can see the same thing happening in the bee kingdom example. Angels create the 'religion' of each hive, so when the bees reincarnate, they do so back into the same group oversoul. Angels do communicate with each other, and there are prodigy and extensions of angel frequencies. They change and multiply under the auspices of the group oversoul. We will review how angels reproduce or perpetuate their species, but in a future discourse.

Now many insects exist under similar circumstances. Ants are another example — they're scavengers. Ants have a queen ant, or leader. And black ants and red ants are usually at war with one another because they're opposite frequencies. All of the insect kingdom works this way in the higher domains. Flies are less controlled and more at random. The best comparison I can make is to relate flies to the Grays. They're a kind of scavenger, they go around cleaning up things, and they have to go through a metamorphosis, a kind of a time-domain, built-in system in their DNA which changes their structure from egg, to maggot, to pupae, to fly. Some kinds of moths are that way, too. Whereas butterflies, like the monarch species and other higher frequencies, are closer to the angel kingdom. There's a whole hierarchy of different nature spirits that work over the insect kingdom, as there are a hierarchy of different spirits that control an eagle, or a raven, or an owl. These are the energies and spirits that you may communicate with using our Systems. Nature spirits cover a realm not limited to only insects and animals. This angelic consciousness extends right into the mineral kingdom. The mineral kingdom has a vibratory frequency, too, that flows from a huge, overall unit of consciousness. That brings us to the doorway of the crystal kingdom.

We work with the Coleman Brothers in Arkansas, who own and operate the largest crystal mines in North America. We also work with people in South America, and we distribute crystal quartz all over the world. When we're working with our Systems, not only is it important to address the nature spirits on all levels, but its also important to incorporate the mineral spirits and the mineral kingdom, and synchronize them. Because when you start dealing with the higher powers and currents over a long period of time, you can affect thousands of lives. When programming a powerful Quad System, or our Systems III, it becomes necessary to be at harmony with all of the surrounding elements to get the total result that you might be looking for. You are entering nature's own domain here, playing as a god with powerful, primal forces, so you have to be responsible for your own actions as to how you communicate within these different, delicate kingdoms. The quartz we use is of the highest vibratory frequency available, and quartz, as Semjase says, is the perfect synthesis of spirit and matter at zero time.

Chapter 31

Exploring the Power of Crystals

The quartz kingdom should never have been mined on this planet, nor any other mineral for that matter. Normally minerals are mined from other worlds when they're needed on the home world. Pleiadeans don't mine their home world, for example, but Earth-bound man, being greedy, has been mining this planet for a long time. The people of Atlantis were using the quartz crystals for record keepers, monitors and amplifiers, but they weren't bringing them out of the ground. They were able to access them as they lay right in the ground, wherever they were located. That was the beauty of the Atlantean technology.

The quartz kingdom is the home body, or home base, of the Akashic records. So that means that crystals are always growing! As a matter of fact, crystal growth is a one tenth of 1 percent of its weight every 10 years. And of course, humanity is enhancing itself and increasing, so more people are having more and more experiences all the time. This generates residual energy that is collected by silicon dioxide, causing the quartz kingdom to grow and expand as it is resonant via the second ether, the prime domain of the Akashic records.

All the different mineral kingdoms have something to do with the human kingdom. The emerald, for example, has quartz, silicon dioxide, and a good amount of chromium in it, which gives it a green hue. Different gemstones have different forms of minerals in them and, of course, you can

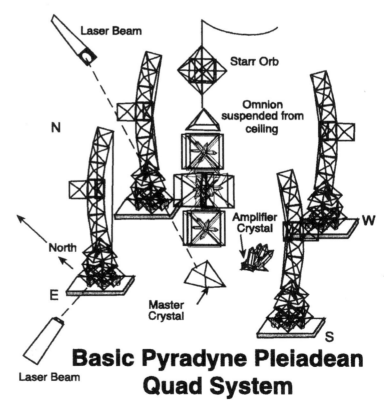

Basic Pyradyne Pleiadean Quad System

figure 31-1

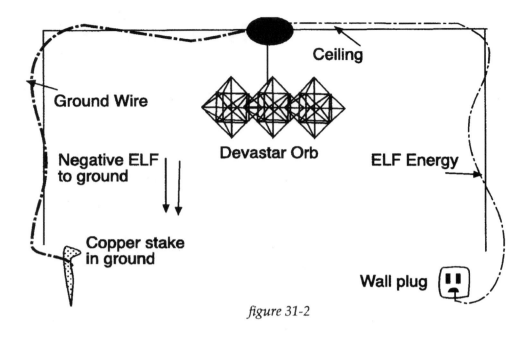

figure 31-2

correlate through that mineral what they actually do in the human body, what thought process is activated by the color frequency of the particular gem or mineral. For example, trace minerals amplify the parasympathetic nervous system, while low frequency minerals activate the autonomic. There is a consciousness in a mineral that tells the body how to utilize that mineral. Just visualize a rainbow and place the colors accordingly.

Remember, I've told you many times that 5% of your body controls 95% of all metabolic function. So it's important to realize that your body is somewhat regulated by your thoughts emanating from the synapsing of the minerals in the brain over a given period of time. Each mineral vibrates at one of seven frequencies. That frequency is amplified in the brain, sent out, and transmitted over the auric field. The auric field responds via the endocrine system, the endocrine system responds by secreting hormones. This is the key to understanding the mineral frequencies. It's a whole inner relation that if you follow it into the external world, can greatly enhance your own biosystem.

Minerals vibrate at a frequency that is amplified in your brain

Collecting quartz is really interesting. We establish a large, single point Master Crystal as a virtual protector, because it will store and lock energy by frequency into all the crystals in your possession. When you start using a device such as one of our Fire Starr Orbs, you start to combine all the energies of your crystals. We place them where they can all start feeding back to one another. We obtain remarkable results when we install Fire Starr Orbs in people's homes, especially when we use another Pleiadean device, the Omnion, in conjunction with it. People then round up their crystals from shelves and drawers and outside their house, crystals they had been collecting for years, and put them all in a specific area. Then they start making them work. This is one of the things that happens when you work with the mineral kingdom. You become conscious of the mineral and gem kingdom, of how it interfaces with the rest of the Pleiadean systems technologies.

I didn't know all this about quartz when I first worked with it a long time ago. We were building the Irradiators, and I was learning how to ground them. Semjase had told me about putting minerals in the base of the Irradiators, but I really didn't understand what it was all about in those earlier days. I still am learning, but I know more than I did then. A friend of mine had sold me a Master Crystal which weighed about 80 pounds. He was a medical doctor, dying of cancer at the time, and he was basically giving me this crystal. His name was Dr. Harvey, and I really didn't know that he was giving me a Master Crystal. And I didn't know he had cancer at the time — but he knew. So $80, which was the price I paid, was a bargain for a crystal worth several thousands of dollars. I brought this big 80-pound crystal home, it sat in the middle of my livingroom. I looked at it for a few days and said, well, wow, it's a nice crystal but what am I supposed to do with it?

And so then my friend Ron Spencer came to visit. He was one of the few people who used and bought Systems from us and knew how to place them in his own clinics better than I could. The first time he bought a System from me, we were visiting in Applegate Valley, Oregon (next door to Richard Bach, author of the book *Jonathan Livingston Seagull*), and Ron had bought several complete Systems at one of my seminars and set them up in his health and biofeedback clinic. So the next day I figured I would organize all of his new Pyradyne equipment and show him how to use it.

He had a large piece of biofeedback equipment that he had brought from Japan and Europe, and he wanted to coordinate his new Systems with it. So the next day I got up bright and early and progressed over to his clinic prepared for a good hard day's work. And to my surprise when I walked in, he had been there the night before and had set everything in place. Not only perfectly, but more than perfectly. He was showing me how to use my own creations!

Anyway, he visited me at home one day several months later and saw the Master Crystal. He must have picked up on the fact that I didn't know what it was, and so he said, "Fred, I'll give you $500 for that piece of quartz over there." And I thought, wow, that's a lot of money. My little greedy brain sat down and calculated a $420 profit—how can I lose on this deal? I said, "Sure, take it." So he wrote me out a check for $500 and left for Applegate Valley with my big Master Crystal, because I didn't think I needed it any more.

Well, after about a week went by, I started noticing the house had some kind of emptiness it didn't have before. Something seemed to be missing, and I couldn't put a finger on what it was. And finally, after about 3 weeks, every time I walked into the livingroom where the crystal had been, I felt a sense of depression. I began to realize that the crystal had something to do with me (who knows from what and when at that time) and that it belonged there. Six weeks went by, and I started thinking I really needed my crystal back to see what was wrong here. About this time Ron called me up and said, "Hey Fred, I'm going to Hawaii. Would you be interested in buying your crystal back?"

I said, "Ron, send that crystal right away, I'm more than interested. You played a trick on me. You tried to teach me something."

He just laughed and said, "I won't ship this crystal, but I'll bring it to you because I'm on my way. I have to go to LAX from Oregon anyway to get over to Hawaii." So he flew down from Oregon with my crystal, and when he brought it up to my livingroom I had five one hundred dollar bills sitting on the diningroom counter just for that crystal to get back into my possession, and I haven't let it go since. That lesson taught me that once you get your Master Crystal, you hold on to it.

You go into a crystal store or a shop in Arkansas, where the crystal mines are, and there's always one crystal there, one of the nicer ones usually, and it's just not for sale. You might ask the proprietor how much he wants for that crystal. He'll say, "We don't have that crystal for sale." You can offer him or her any amount of money, but they won't sell that crystal. These are simple folks who just "know" about crystal intuitively.

So then I learned how to program it, and when I learned how to program it, I programmed it to learn how to get more crystal, and as a result I started attracting more and more crystal around the crystal that I already had. Now also in the process of programming it, I began to collect it. I began to learn that different crystals have different vibratory frequencies, and in working with our Pleiadean and extraterrestrial Systems, they all have a place. Sometimes you have to use your imagination a bit at first, and your intuition to find out where they go, and if you miss the positioning of where this or that crystal goes, you're going to notice it. We have a customer by the name of Mrs. Terry in Hawaii who does spiritual channeling for crystals. She goes out to people's houses worldwide and helps them place their crystals. And sometimes they're moved, and sometimes you have crystals that you shouldn't have, they're not attuned to you, and they work against the other crystals.

**Polariz-
ation of
various
crystals**

The McEarl was an interesting group of crystals that we added to our collection to start working with. It's probably the finest crystal that was ever mined off the surface of the planet. In fact, only between 5,000 and 6,000 pounds of it were ever found, and it was the clearest crystal we've ever seen. We use it in our laser show, and light moves through it forming a perfect rainbow. The crystal possesses a very high vibratory frequency. All of the Arkansas crystal is polarized to the right, meaning that if you were north of the equator and pulled a cork out of your bathtub and watched the water go down, the water would turn clockwise, to the right. If you were south of the equator and pulled the plug out of the bath-tub, it would go counter-clockwise.

South American crystal, which comes from south of the equator, is polarized in the opposite direction. Arkansas crystal has a tendency to have more of a healing vibration. South American crystal has a tendency more towards extraterrestrial and communication vibration, but the two work well together.

**Amethyst
is 7th ray
material**

We use vast amounts of Arkansas crystal in our Systems because it has a tremendous grounding, healing effect, and small amounts of South American crystal because it has an amplifying, penetrating effect. Along with those two types of crystals, we use amethyst, which comes from both South and North America. Amethyst is 7th Ray material because it is violet, and quartz is 1st, 2nd and 3rd Ray material, depending on what kind of quartz it is. And so you'll end up working with four Rays simultaneously when you work with amethyst and quartz. Now when we start adding all the other gems and materials that are available, we start fine-tuning our Systems, as in the case of Systems III or the Quad System. For sources of activating the Mega Orbs and the Quad System, or the Systems III, we find that the amount of gemstone material that's available in a Receptor, for example, is usually adequate to modulate a particular frequency that's necessary to create and build up a scalar wave of a pitch of that type octave. We also use sound with it.

So what I recommend is that first of all, you get a large Master Crystal. Take some time to select your Master Crystal. We always have a selection of them here. Now Master Crystals are also becoming an investment, too. We sold one to a Buddhist temple, which was later named the Shiva Lingum, over in Hawaii, on Kauai, the Garden Island. The crystal was 700 pounds, and the Buddhist master who ran the temple had seen a vision, and he wanted it for his temple. Since then they've built a temple around this crystal, and they've energized it with lasers as we do our Systems crystals, and it's been a very successful energy attraction. People come from all over the world to see it.

Another thing about quartz is that we're not finding many specimens with big points (a specific crystal structure) anymore in the currently known mines. They're starting to get

284

"mined out." People in later generations who want to have these big points for their Systems, I would say, are going to have an awfully difficult time finding an original crystal, because there aren't that many available any more, especially the ones from Arkansas. But we do have a selection of them from weights of a few pounds up to weights of a ton or so. What we call a large crystal now may be 200 or 300 pounds. We're not finding any with clarity or substance over 300 pounds anymore. And the average person obtaining the System we recommend will go with a crystal somewhere between 50 and 175 pounds; 65 seems to be the average weight.

Now the other thing we found is when you work with the Systems, any kind of a pointed crystal that you add to your System that weighs more than the Master Crystal is going generate a conflict between the crystals. The crystals are also sexed in that they have masculine energy and feminine energy. The "tabbies" are the flat, wedge type, and are usually female energy crystals, and the male ones are usually the pointed ones. In my own collection I have a large tabby weighing about 45 or 50 pounds, brought home from Arkansas. It was a gift from the miners. I had spotted it several years before I brought it home. I had been repeatedly talking about it to Ron. I said, "Someday, Ron, I'm going to buy that crystal from you because I like it," because it was an unusual crystal and I was attracted to it. He said, "Someday I'm probably going to give you that crystal." Well one day I brokered a quartz collection in Arkansas for him and he said, "Fred, I think I'm going to give you that crystal today," so I brought it home.

I first put it in the livingroom. I wasn't sure if it was going to harmonize with my Master Crystal or not, so what I did is move it into the bedroom down the hall from where my Master Crystal was. You could see the tabby down the hallway from the livingroom. I felt this tremendous sexual energy between the two. It was real interesting, and other people noticed it, too. They'd say, "There's something funny — I feel this funny feeling." Both crystals had come from Arkansas, and this wedge crystal had come from a different mine, and we oftentimes grade them by the mines. But I had to rise beyond all this grading and valuing and weight system and realize there was a male/female energy going on here.

And so I decided, "Well this Master Crystal obviously is not disliking this new crystal," because I had brought other crystals into the house, put them near my Master Crystal, and it didn't seem to like them. You'd feel nervous when around them. Remember, whatever feeling you sense when you're around your Master Crystal is usually the feeling coming out of that crystal, and it's keying into your body systems and your biosystems through the minerals in your body. So I brought the new crystal from the bedroom and put it about two feet away from my Master Crystal. I had a circle of harmonious crystals around it already that it is attracted to, a group of small, different points ranging from anywhere from maybe five pounds up to maybe 30 pounds. I had reservations against putting a 50 pounder next to a crystal that only weighs 75 pounds. But I did it anyway, and it really seemed to like that, and the rest of the crystals seemed to agree with it.

A few months later while I was playing a concert in Marnau, Germany, located high within the Bavarian Alps using a Fire Starr Orb, I met a young woman. I was playing for about 500 people in this concert hall, using Pleiadean ship sounds and wrap-around sounds of the Roland D-50 synthesizer, and all 500 people were energized on that Fire Starr and chakra frequency. Suddenly we had a group of Pleiadean ships hovering overhead, and people were seeing them through the windows. Then the German Air Force came out and started chasing them, after which the police arrived and cordoned off the town of Marnau. So this was a really exciting evening, and in all this excitement. the young woman, who was also the hostess

> Crystals send energy into your body via the minerals in your body

> Pleiadean ships attracted to fire starr orb in Bavarain Alps

of the group, Frauke Plogg, had become familiar with me and I of her, and we became friends. To make a long story short, she ended up coming to America about a year later and becoming my wife.

One night after we were married, we were sitting in the livingroom talking about how to acquire a Master Crystal, and she was asking me how she could get her Master Crystal, because I had told her the story of how I'd gotten mine. She started looking at that 40-pound wedge crystal next to mine and she said, "Fred, you know what?" And I said, "Yeah, you just found your Master Crystal, and it had attracted itself here even a year before I knew you were coming." And she just said, "I know this is my Master Crystal." She knew it and I knew it at the same time. So that kind of cemented that. Master Crystals come in the funniest ways. Not only did the crystal come before my wife, my wife followed the crystal into the house. It was really a funny situation.

And that's just the beginning of the magic that occurs when you use quartz along with the Systems, the tip of the iceberg. The Systems are incredibly fun to play with when you start to realize how they work.

Now besides the points, we use big clusters and small clusters. They are amplifiers. I always recommend to someone that they try to get hold of a really decent 40, 50, or 60-pound cluster, because it does a tremendous job of breaking up the intensity of a single point energy and dissipating it throughout the Irradiator System into all the subsystems that are involved with the crystals. So I highly recommend this arrangement for most people.

When you use more than one Irradiator, you'll have a Mega Orb at the base of them, with quartz placed in each Irradiator. We usually use a small crystal, assuming now that you have your Master Crystal somewhere, and then put two small (three-, four- or five-pound) points in each of the two chambers that it shows you in the diagrams provided. Then you put a plastic plate underneath each Mega Orb, because the System is now grounded through the quartz itself. Physically you don't want the Mega Orb/Irradiator combination to touch the ground, so it needs to be on a plastic plate. If you're going to use a power supply with your System, you definitely want the Mega Orb on a plastic plate. Then go outside your home and find two local stones per Mega Orb. In Laguna Beach we live on top of a lot of natural quartz and gold. Our house is located over a gold vein. When a tree blew over, we actually found some nuggets that assayed out to three ounces per ton, which is kind of interesting. So we used a couple of those ore samples to represent the local elementals.

The quartz kingdom, with the Akashic records, cues itself into the human mind, the human aura fields, the human consciousness, planet-wide, stellar-wide even, and this combined energy field feeds back into the local area around your house by using the local stones with your crystals. The nice thing about using local stones is cost—they're usually free. Then position the unit, if you're using a single Irradiator, at the foot of your bed. If you're using more than one Irradiator, you would align the bases of them (Mega Orbs) to magnetic north, and if you're using four of them, position them in a large square, each one of the bases aligned north, with two Irradiators pointing into the center, and two Irradiators pointing out to the side (see figure 31-1).

If you're working with a single Irradiator and a Mega Orb and some quartz, and you don't have a Master Crystal, don't be afraid to start using the System without one. Just program the System for one. The arrival of your Master Crystal will ground your System and maximize its power. The second thing that's really important when you're starting out with our Systems is to purchase a Starr Orb right away. They're not very expensive, by the way; some of these things cost hardly anything. The Starr Orb is a series of six Pyramids all facing each other.

Stainless steel ground wires focus the energies coming into the Starr Orb to one point, and that one point feeds a wire that you can affix to a water pipe or run outside your window, down the side of your house or apartment, down into a metal stake in the ground.

Place the stake firmly in the ground. Any time you work with scalar energies you're going to attract some opposing energy forces. This opposite force has to be directed back into the Earth to be rendered harmless and make it harmonious for us. That's what is called "grounding" it, a very important function of the Earth.

When a local dentist, Jack Alpin in Los Angeles, put a Starr Orb up in his clinic, we found that it drew negative energy out of his patients. He had a large dental clinic. When people would walk into his clinic, they would no longer have apprehension, and so he was able to use reduced dosages of painkillers. Plants grow really well inside of Starr Orbs, too. So it makes a very attractive yet functional device if you don't want to tell people what you're really doing with it. Starr Orbs also operate to offset the side effects of ELFs, extremely low frequencies, and other forms of 60-cycle radiation. Remember I covered ELF hazards when I referred to the book, Biological Effects of Electrical and Magnetic Fields of Extremely Low Frequency, in the earlier part of this dissertation? If you have high voltage power lines next your house, you may wish to set up a Starr Orb, or even the Deva Starr. The Deva Starr is a large version of the Starr Orb, and we normally recommend it for high rise buildings. But the Deva Starr is also excellent to use in your home to ground out any extremely negative energies coming in (see figure 31-2).

Some people report they have problems with negative spirits coming in. These are called "mischievous spirits," spirits trapped in limbo between the physical plane and the astral plane. And we find that these devices, especially when integrated with the laser, are helpful with these problems, too, and free the spirit to go on and do its work. Once again, when you're doing this, be sure it's grounded.

Another thing that I want to touch on here is placing large pyramids over the bed. Remember our experiment with the brine shrimp? They far exceeded their lifespan when kept under a properly made pyramid. Well, for the Systems to benefit you the most, it's necessary to put a pyramid over your bed. The pyramid will help you tune into the System because we're all working with pyramid shapes. The shapes resonate to each other, and attract energy between each other. If you're using a single Irradiator and your Irradiator is projecting, for example, the energy of a book or a tape into your aural field at night while you sleep, and it arrives on the astral plane (because the second stage of sleep is the astral plane), then what happens is it will allow the assimilation of this energy to take place much more concurrently.

Tips on placing pyramids over your bed

Many people complain when they first start sleeping under a pyramid. They may feel nervous for the first two or three months, and/or uncomfortable sometimes. They wake up in the middle of the night, in the wee hours of the morning, and find they can't sleep that well. Just as the Headgear will detoxify your brain, the larger pyramid over the bed detoxifies your entire body. This process initially produces a state of nervousness for some, but after about three months of sleeping in the pyramid, you will sleep very well.

Did you ever go to bed at night and, just as you start to fall asleep, notice a jumping sensation?

When you first lie down, a few things begin to happen:

1. Your spine decompresses due to the fact that you are not overcoming gravity, which compresses your spine.

What happens during sleep?

2. This decompression allows higher amounts of electricity to move from the brain to critical organs.

3. When critical organs such as the liver and kidneys receive this energy, they begin to detoxify the entire body at a very high rate.

4. Stimulation of the growth hormone increases, which slows down the aging process.

5. The brain, in order to supply more electricity, uses 80% more energy during sleep.

6. The body removes large amounts of lactic acid from the bloodstream. Lactic acid is created by the muscles working hard to overcome gravity.

These are just a few things that go on during the first critical hours of sleep. So obviously this jumping sensation is a disturbance to vital processes.

When your spine decompresses, as in step one, vital nerve conduits are exposed to various forms of radiation — an airplane flying overhead using radar, a taxicab using a radio telephone, a cellular phone, telecommunication beams, and a whole myriad of electrical signals moving about.

So to protect the sensitive, now exposed nerves, the spinal cord "contracts," giving you the jumping sensation.

When you sleep with a pyramid or a Pyradyne Portamid over your bed, the pyramid shields you from these annoying toxic radio signals. Then what happens is your body can rejuvenate properly and in addition, it can receive the healing currents of the Earth's etheric field (called the anima munde by the Tibetans) of which the Earth's magnetic field is a side effect.

During this first stage of cleansing, healing sleep, our aura field usually extends no more than a few inches beyond the physical body.

Then after a few hours of radiation-free sleep, the 14 prime chi meridians become free of negative psychic and other types of blocking energies.

This then frees the astral body to move 13 feet or more from the physical and our consciousness can enter the astral worlds. As this process engages, our eyelids flutter and we enter what is called Rapid Eye Movement (REM) sleep. It has been medically proven that if this process is repeatedly interrupted, we lose our balance with life and communication. If all of the people in the whole world were to sleep under pyramids, the world would change overnight.

I might emphasize here that if you were to construct your own pyramid for sleeping under, be careful what materials you use!

Avoid aluminum, copper and plastic! They produce toxic positive ion side effects. Use only wood, steel, glass or gold or other natural, non-toxic materials. We use a mildly magnetic steel in our Portamid Systems, topped off with a 24 carat gold-plated capstone. We find that using an open frame pyramid construction with a small gold capstone gives the best results of better, more relaxed sleep, brighter, more colorful dreams, and total elimination of the jumping sensation.

When using our Portamids with other Pyradyne Pleiadean devices such as an Irradiator, Fire Starr or Omnion, we usually place a Pyradyne Orb on the top of the capstone. Within that Orb we place a small, hand-picked crystal, and sometimes we beam this with a special laser.

A lot of programming for future events is possible when sleeping in a Portamid with an Irradiator placed within the 13-foot field that emanates around it during REM sleep.

288

I could give several personal examples wherein I met several beautiful people and had several wonderful experiences using this technique. I personally have slept in a Portamid for over 22 years.

Also, I have had three wonderful daughters, whose mothers went full-term under the Pyramid, and gave birth at home under the same Portamid System. Labor pains were greatly reduced. My third daughter was delivered by myself within the Portamid. Her mother, Rowena, had only one contraction and virtually no pain on delivery. The term "pain of birth" is only for the ignorant, and no woman should suffer at the hands of the inexperienced practitioner. Someday, many more home Pyramid births will occur with resultant healthy, happy children!

> **Pyramid over bed helps with childbirth**

Chapter 32

Color Therapy, Lasers and
The Key to the Fourth Dimension

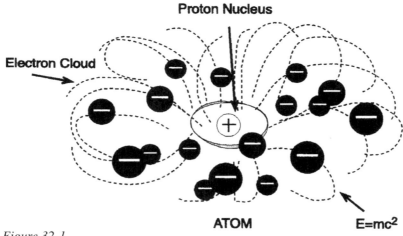

Proton Nucleus

Electron Cloud

$+$

ATOM $E=mc^2$

Figure 32-1

Understanding the values of coherent light in the living organism

1. Energy is required to cause an electron to propel itself around the nucleus of an atom.

   Unfortunately, Humans have become disrespectful of this atomic need common to all of us and through their own misunderstanding created a block in his own energy at the atomic level whereby their cells can't reproduce harmoniously as they once did.

2. So, as their atoms fall in atomic frequency, they turns to drugs, aspirin, cigarettes, crime, herpes, AIDS, producing paranoia, denial, drowsiness and finally through BHT preservatives, their fears. Now with cellular reproduction and unwinding DNA, everything gets old and boring quickly, including sagging eyelids, loose skin and bad breath.

3. There are several simple solutions, such as get some balanced sunlight. So we go to the beach and get skin cancer! Why? Because the ultraviolet level in sunlight is too high!

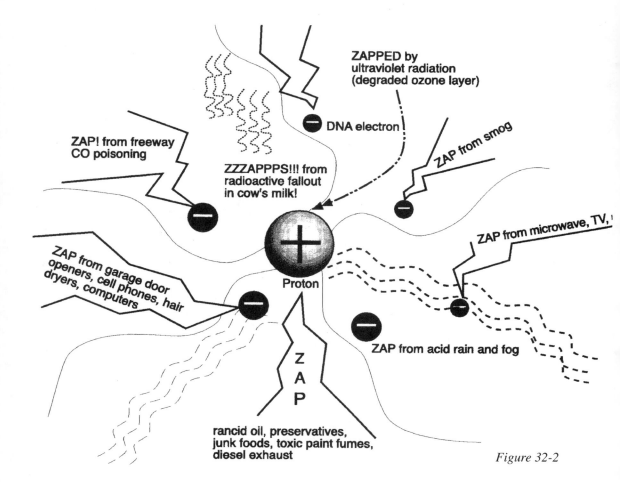

Figure 32-2

No problem. I will go to the health food store and try PABA and vitamin A or many other biochemical remedies.

Go ahead and do so. You have now solved one seventh of your body's cellular energetic needs, and you haven't yet addressed the true nature of the real problem.

Hey, you can't fool me. I know there are other factors. I've been into proactive health for fourteen years. I've read books, attended conventions, visited retreats. I've got an ionizer, a back ease, I run, I eat 50% raw foods, take vitamins, do yoga. My backhand is improving. I met my chiropractor through my acupuncturist at a "Touch for Health" seminar while listening to Steve Halpern's relaxing music the very day after my meeting at the National Health Federation...

Stop!

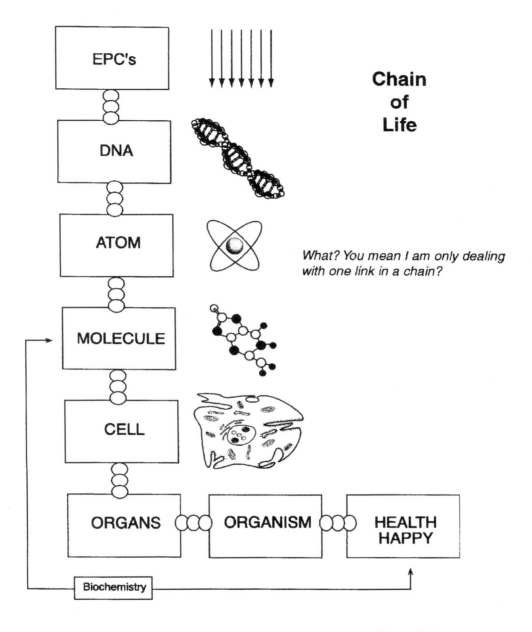

**Chain
of
Life**

*What? You mean I am only dealing
with one link in a chain?*

Figure 32-3

Wrong!
Let go of logic . . .
Toss the Chain explanations . . .
Let's talk Light!
We are light!

Stop thinking . . . Stop trying to have a "clear brain," a good figure and perfect health and learn to receive what has been taken away by negative technologies.

Look:

Vitamins polarize light!
(A, B's, C, LECITHIN)

Minerals store light!
(TRACE, RARE COMPOUNDS)

Enzymes balance light!
(6.5 — PH —8.5)

Cells reproduce in Light!

Oxygen is made by Light!

We see by Light!

Figure 32-4

Now, let us enjoy life through light in a coherent way, and enter the Age of the Universe which is composed of eternal coherent light.

The use of therapeutic light, called ACTINotherapy, has been documented since the earliest writings of mankind. The following are instances you can research yourself.

1. In the Ria Veda, a Sanskrit document circa 1500 BC, Sanitir, a sun god, was worshipped by the Aryans in India. They believed Sanitir was a divine physician who could drive away disease and increase longevity with the power of the sun.

2. Hippocrates (370 - 460 BC) practiced heliotherapy in Aesculapius, which had a roofless gallery facing south with an opening in the sick ward.

3. In 1892, Niels Ryberg Finsen (1860-1904) began the first experiments with light and later became known as the "Father of Actinotherapy." In his treatment of smallpox he used red light to abolish suppuration, lessen scarring and shorten the period of disease.

4. Red light therapy was used even earlier by Henri de Mondeville (1260-1320) in smallpox treatments. Henri had learned these therapies from the Arabians who had in turn learned it from the Chinese.

5. John of Goddesden, physician to Edward II of England, is quoted in the book Compendium Medical (1510): "Then taking scarlet from the bramble bush and completely covering the eruptions or else using another red derived from grain, I thus treated the son of the most noble King of England when he was afflicted with this disease, and I made red everything about the bed, and it was a good cure-all. I cured him without a vestige of pockmarks following."

6. In the 1930s the Europeans were using cold neon red light for tissue stimulation at wavelengths of 650 nanometers (nm). It has since been proven that a healthy cell emits a wavelength of light between 625 and 700 nm. Red lasers used in cell and organ treatment emit a typical frequency of 632 nm. Some physicians use lasers as high as 904 nm, which is the area of near-infrared. As mentioned earlier, the Chinese were probably the first to use red color therapy and they, remember, discovered acupuncture over 5000 years ago. In my earlier studies, Semjase told me that the Chinese were direct descendants of the Atlanteans and in Atlantis, there were highly sophisticated coherent light machines, much like today's lasers.

7. Laser therapy is typically applied directly on the main acupressure points on the 12 main meridians. One to five milliwatt (mw) lasers are used and the time of application is typically 4 to 10 seconds, repeated daily, until a total treatment time of one hour has passed. Stimulation has been found effective as deep as 10 millimeters (mm) beneath the skin at these power levels, when using 5 mw at 632 nm.

8. Laser therapy has been effective in treating not only all diseases via the meridians, but also for severe burns, vaginal infections, skin ulcerations with histological granulation and proliferation, bone fractures, rheumatoid arthritis, herpes zoster and a variety of other irritations.

9. One of the methods of dealing with laser light is that the coherent low-power beam can stimulate the healing energy process via ATP formulation and activation of enzyme activity, leading to restoration of normal properties on the cell-organ-organism levels.

10. Further research has proven that light possessing the seven levels of consciousness enters from the astral plane to our body via the hydrogen atom. We at Pyradyne, therefore, have been using laser light in all seven colors for therapy for a number of years. We virtually have lasers of all colors of the light spectrum, and make them readily available to our clientele.

11. Because the laser acts as a doorway to the 4th dimension (astral or emotional plane), it is essential in a variety of functions, including time travel.

A HISTORY OF THE LASER

The predecessor to the laser was a microwave amplifier called the MASER. First demonstrated by Charles H. Townes, Microwave Amplification by Stimulated Emission of Radiation (MASER) was used to amplify radio waves in 1954. Later the maser was extended to optical frequencies by Schawlow and Townes in 1958, which led to the device now known as the laser. Masers were quite popular in radio telescopes because they could filter out unwanted noise signals from outer space and amplify low-level intelligence signals coming from deep space, depending upon where the telescope was oriented. Frank Drake was the first radio telescope astronomer to use masers successfully. In 1966, he received several intelligently modulated signals from deep space, sent by extraterrestrials; this, of course, soon became deeply classified by our government.

After the 1958 applications of the maser, the laser — Light Amplification by Stimulated Emission of Radiation — was demonstrated by Maiman in 1960 using a ruby crystal. A few months later, Javan and his associates constructed the first helium/neon laser which we currently, after many refinements, use today as our red laser light source.

Lasers have found many industrial applications. Because light is a much higher frequency than microwave, it has a broader spectrum of frequencies, therefore a wider band width. This makes it usable in the communications field. Many cable TV companies are installing laser-powered fiber optics systems to reach their subscribers. From a radiation standpoint, this is better for the general public, as the fiber optics are all subterranean.

Laser surgery is becoming more mainstream as it is a programmable tool and relatively painless for the patient. Lasers are used to make optical measurements for land surveying, measurements of rotation of the Earth, isotope separation measurements, drilling and cutting exact patterns, tracking satellites, three-dimensional imaging (holography) due to precise phasing possibilities, and many other yet unexplored applications.

There are two highly specialized application of lasers I feel will in the near future make themselves more apparent to the general public and will probably find their way into the news media from time to time.

The first is called the Yttrium Aluminum Garnet, $Y3, Al5 O12$, most popularly entitled the YAG laser. Back in the 1960s when I worked at Autonetics, which was then a subsidiary of Rockwell International, we experimented with rare earth laser technologies. One such project was called the "Eyelass" project. Highly classified at the time, it later became part of the "Star Wars" project made well known later by president Ronald Reagan.

Using rare earth neodymium and sometimes europium, it was discovered that a laser made of these materials had a very high rate of efficiency. In fact, low-level solid state lasers, as they are called, can produce upwards of a billion watts of power! Now in comparison, a one-watt laser can ignite a piece of paper at a distance of one mile.

Weapons of continuous power levels greater than thermonuclear bombs are possible with this technology.

I remember reading a government report made public a few years ago that stated that a billion watt laser was being tested in the infrared range (invisible to the naked eye). These tests were conducted at the Los Alamos, New Mexico facility where the radars were developed which I mentioned in previous chapters that caused the crashes of the alien spaceships in the 1940s.

The report stated "that a continuous billion-watt beam was projected into the troposphere and that the heat buildup there was greater than had a nuclear weapon been detonated at the same altitude." It further stated that because it was a continuous beam versus a temporary explosion, it would affect the high altitude winds and cause weather pattern changes!

This report told me two things: (1) that weather control was, in fact, being experimented with, which became quite evident when the Air Force environmental impact report was released on the HAARP project; and (2) the obvious fact put together some scuttlebutt that originated in Dulce, New Mexico, and that was we were afraid of an Alien Invasion and had to have weaponry for this potential emergency!

It is highly probable that solar-powered YAG weapons are in place in space, serviced regularly by the Aurora spacecraft, which I have seen as well as heard, as it created many skyquakes when it returned earthward over our home in Laguna Beach, California.

One incident occurred here in Laguna Beach, California, in the fall of 1993, where an Aurora experienced some technical problems and may have landed at El Toro Marine Base, California.

I sometimes go for a walk on the mountain where we live late at night. On this particular early November evening I was on the side of the mountain at about 2:00 in the morning. Below me was a valley with no population, a military restricted area that aircraft fly through coming from missions out at sea, en route to the El Toro Marine Facility.

The point that I was standing on gave me a view of the flight path wherein aircraft are at almost eye level with me on their approach path to the bases. So, it would not be uncommon for me to look straight out 1000 feet into the cockpit of a jet fighter. In fact, during air shows, I have even looked down at aircraft as they flew by. The air over this valley is military restricted airspace.

I saw three large helicopters approaching me along the valley. This got my attention as the military rarely flies helicopters late at night. Suddenly I noticed a large object moving very slowly behind the choppers. I would estimate it to have been going only 30 to 40 miles per hour, much too slowly for conventionally-powered aircraft of this size. This speed is not even recommended for helicopters, because if they lose power, they don't have enough forward velocity to safely auto-rotate to the ground — especially at night when the ground is only 1000 feet below.

As the object passed by me, it was almost silent and had military (red lights only) lighting. It was stealthy in shape and was approximately 600 feet long, or longer than three Boeing 747s. As it passed by with its black helicopter escort I knew right away there had to be reverse-engineered antigravity propulsion systems on board that were still functioning. My guess was that it had a high-speed power system (what could have been a scramjet system) failure. As it approached from the East and moved past me to the West where the base is located, I got an excellent view of it from the side and a partial top view which I am presenting in the above drawing (see figure 32-5).

Figure 32-5 Possibly the Aurora — definitely a military ship.

About 3 minutes after it disappeared, a formation of nine jets flew by in groups of three at an altitude of approximately 1300 feet, or 300 feet above my head. The reason I believe this was the Aurora was because several friends of mine in engineering in the aerospace industry had recently hinted a strong possibility of its presence. They had mentioned that the SR-71 was out of service because a Russian V-Beam (scalar technology) weapon had removed a two-foot wing section while the SR-71 was high over Russia on surveillance and that the SR-71 was extremely obsolete (1950's technology).

Figure 32-6 Side view at about 1000 yards away.

I am giving these examples of technology versus experience so that you can draw your own conclusions as to what is really going on. As I said earlier, the Aurora is servicing our secret deep-space programs and it's quite known to many that NASA (Never A Straight Answer) is a cover-up WPA (Works Project Administration) for what really goes on. I further know, for a fact, that the ETs known as the Grays use plutonium and beryllium in the construction and operation of their deep-space vehicles. I further believe that the Grays are becoming hostile to our government and that they are occasionally fired upon by our Star Wars weaponry. When their beryllium craft hit our atmosphere out of control, they leave a long green flash, as seen crossing many of the United States, as they burn up in the atmosphere.

One other application of lasers that you still see in the news concerns laser-induced fusion or controlled thermonuclear plasma. Trying to harness the energy of the stars has long been a scientific dream. The nucleus of an atom consists of protons (positive charge) and neutrons (neutral charge). Each particle is approximately the same mass. Neutrons and protons are usually referred to in science as "nucleons." Normally, in an atom, the core consists of more than one nucleon held together by a very strong attractive force. This force is called the binding force and is represented by Einstein's famous theory of relativity: $E = mc_2$, where

$c = -3 \times 10_{10}$ cm/sec (represents the speed of light in free space),

m = mass, and

E = energy.

To us day-to-day folks, this means that if you consumed an atom of water, H_2O, it would be healing to the body. But, if you used an outside force and tried to separate the nucleons within the hydrogen nucleus or break the binding attractive force, not only would tremendous energy be required to do so, but tremendous energy would be released. Lasers can provide that energy, and if this power is focused via a laser, a sustained thermonuclear reaction is possible within a laboratory.

Deuterium is available from natural water and constitutes .015% of the water we drink. It is a source of "deutrons," commonly called "heavy water," and it is used in particle accelerators as a source of deutrons for nuclear exploration.

At the nucleus level, the binding force of a nucleon computes as follows in a fusion process:

$E = mc^2$ as a reference, therefore,

Δ = change

Z and N represent the number of protons and neutrons inside the nucleus of the atom, and their binding energy. Δ will be given by:

$$\Delta = Z_{mp} + N_{mn} - MA)^{c2}$$

where M_n, M_p and M_A represent like masses of the neutron, the proton and the atomic nucleus, respectively. For example, the nucleus of the deuterium atom (deutron) has a mass of 2.0135^{-6} Δmu (1Amu = 1.661×10^{-24} grams) which is equivalent to 931.5 mev. or (931.5 = nine hundred thirty-one and one half million electron-volts).

Since a deutron consists of one proton and one neutron, one obtains:

$\Delta = (1.00728 + 1.00866 - 2.01356 \times 1.661 \times 10^{-24} \times 3 \times 10^2$ erg (erg = energy units – now we commonly use joules instead of ergs)

$= 3.56 \times 10^{-6} \times (1.6 \times 10^{-12})^{-1} \times 10^{-6}$ mev

$= 2.23$ mev or 2,230,000 electron-volts, which represents the binding energy of one deutron. In the above equation we have used 1.0078 Amu and 1.00866 Amu to represent the masses of the proton and neutron respectively.

299

This is a tremendous force for binding one atom. **This is nuclear fusion.** The reason I am citing these energies is so that later on when we cover time travel and laser energy, that you can have an appreciation of the tremendous energy that exists between the planes of consciousness as we accelerate mass (including ourselves) into another dimension.

**Tremen-
dous
energy
between
planes of
conscious-
ness**

While we're here in physics, let's talk about **the atomic process of fission**, which is different from fusion.

The atomic bomb is a fission device that creates enough heat, approximately 100 million degrees Kelvin, to start the above-mentioned fusion process, or in other words, set off a hydrogen bomb. Without an atomic bomb for a detonator, the hydrogen bomb is merely a bunch of readily available household cleaning chemicals.

In the fission process, a loosely bound heavy nucleus splits into two tightly bound lighter nuclei, again resulting in the liberation of energy. For example, when a neutron is absorbed by a thorium $_{92}U^{235}$ nucleus, the $_{92}U^{236}$ (plutonium) nucleus is formed in an excited state (the excitation energy is supplied by the binding energy of the absorbed neutron). This plutonium $_{92}U^{236}$ nucleus may undergo fission (atomic subdivision) to form nuclei of intermedial mass numbers (like $_{56}BA^{140}$, [barium] and $_{36}KR^{93}$ [krypton]); along with these reactions, the energy released is about 200,000 million electron-volts (200 mev).

Using the CO_2 or rare earth laser as a source of heat, and bombarding deuterium tritium pellets, scientists have hoped to produce a laser-induced fusion reactor for power and experimentation. Our use of lasers has been, already mentioned, in the healing field, using red and multi-colored lasers, and as a doorway into the 4th dimension.

Let's take another look at the atomic world.

An atomic system is characterized by discrete energy states, and atoms unstimulated exist in the lowest energy state, which is referred to as a "ground" state. An atom in a lower state may be excited to a higher state through a variety of processes. One example would be a glass of water at room temperature compared to boiling water, or super-heated steam.

Another important process of excitation is through collisions with other particles. Excitation can also occur through the absorption of electromagnetic radiation of proper frequencies. Such a process is known as stimulated absorption. On the other hand, when the atom is in the excited state, it can make a transition to a lower energy state through the emission of electromagnetic radiation; however, in contrast to the absorption process, the emission procedure can occur in two different ways.

First predicted by Albert Einstein in 1917 as a description of thermodynamic equilibrium (active temperature changes to reach a balance of energy), two kinds of emissions — spontaneous and stimulated—describe the balance between atoms and the radiation field of excitation.

In "spontaneous" emission, the atom in the excited state emits radiation, even in the absence of any incidental radiation. Further, the rate of spontaneous emissions is proportional to the number of atoms in the excited state.

The second state of emissions, in which an incident of appropriate frequency triggers an atom in an excited state to emit radiation, is referred to as "stimulated" emission.

The rate of stimulated emission for absorption depends both on the intensity of the external field as well as the number of atoms in the upper state. The net stimulation transition depends upon the difference in the number of atoms excited and atoms in the lower states, which is different from spontaneous emission, which depends only on the population of the excited states.

These types of physics are called "quantum mechanics," and these spontaneous and stimulated emissions were shown by Einstein in 1917 to obtain what is referred to as Planck's

Radiation Law. If you want to go deeper into laser physics, there are references in the Bibliography of this book.

Now, let me show you how we use lasers for our interdimensional and transitional applications.

Lasers, once stimulated by one of the abovementioned processes, emit coherent light. Coherent light is different from "regular" white light in that we can separate the individual colors, amplify those colors and transmit their energy across a given median.

Remember that we are dealing with quantum physics and the behavior of the hydrogen atom. Color, as you know, is one of the animation factors within the hydrogen atom. The hydrogen atom is our source of consciousness. There are seven basic colors: three primary — red, yellow, blue; and four secondary — orange, green, indigo, violet. Each color brings consciousness from a conscious plane. The messenger or doorway is the photon as it arrives here in our three-dimensional world.

The 4th dimension is the gateway to time, and anything moving from here to there changes its mass into a form of energy. Anything coming from a higher plane through the 4th dimension brings energy to mass already here. Mass does not pass through the doorway, only energy does. But energy can maintain its form as it moves upward and inward.

The 4th dimension is timeless

These principles are well adhered to when moving objects beyond light speeds, or moving through time (time travel!). The 4th dimension is timeless, and it is also where mass transmits its form and energy into another time. Once in the new dimension, form gains mass back proportionally to the energy necessary to hold it in the continuum (area) of the higher or other dimension.

An example would be moving up onto a higher (astral) plane, or simply switching to another equal dimension (side continuum or parallel universe). **Gravity also plays an integral part as it is present on all planes. Gravity unites energy into form, providing mass.** In the case of a form moving from the physical plane onto the astral plane, gravity reunites the form upon its conversion of mass into energy during its transition through the doorway or portal of the 4th dimension. Furthermore, the strength of gravity is also proportional to the energy of the mass that holds it together. Although gravity is peculiar to different planes or levels of consciousness, magnetism is not in its present form as we know it here on Earth. The atomic frequencies are higher on the upper planes, therefore currents produced by electron flow that create magnetic fields are non-existent. As a matter of fact, electrons are non-existent on higher planes. What is in their place are more infinite, faster particles that are occasionally observed here on Earth when we conduct extremely high energy nuclear experiments.

As relativity decrees, an object whose velocity is approaching the speed of light decreases in size and increases in time relative to a third-dimensional world observance. As the object reaches the speed of light, its size becomes naught to the third-dimensional world and its time becomes temporarily infinite as its mass converts to energy. **In the case of a spaceship, the ship would disappear to the 3-D observer and appear to an observer stationed in another world located within a different continuum**, or an astral world. Once this transition takes place, the spaceship could remain within the destination world for a period of, for example, one week. After one week in the destination world, the spaceship returns to our 3-D world. Arriving back upon our world, only a few minutes would have passed since the original transition took place (see figure 32-7).

Example of Transition Time Difference in Relation to 3-D and 4-D Observers

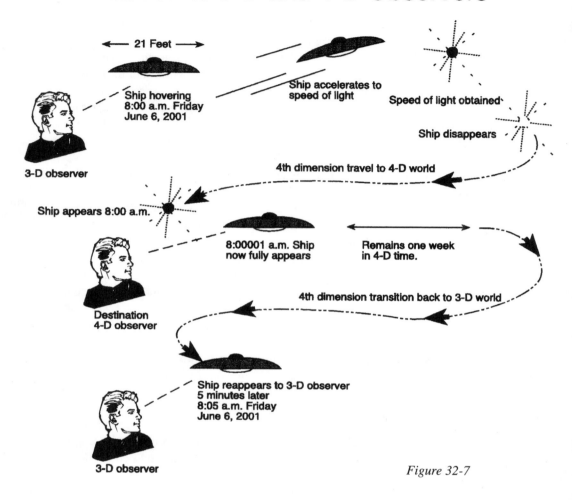

← 21 Feet →

Ship hovering
8:00 a.m. Friday
June 6, 2001

Ship accelerates to
speed of light

Speed of light obtained

Ship disappears

3-D observer

4th dimension travel to 4-D world

Ship appears 8:00 a.m.

8:00001 a.m. Ship
now fully appears

Remains one week
in 4-D time.

4th dimension transition back to 3-D world

Destination
4-D observer

Ship reappears to 3-D observer
5 minutes later
8:05 a.m. Friday
June 6, 2001

3-D observer

Figure 32-7

FORMULA PENDING

As you can see, when an object begins to reach the speed of light, its mass increases and its size decreases to zero in this dimension. Light speed has been determined as the zero point when crossing into the fourth dimension. The speed of light was first approximated in 1675 by Olaus Roemer, a Danish astronomer, when he observed the eclipse of Jupiter's moons from the far side of the Earth's orbit as compared to the near side (see figure 32-8).

Visible light from a particle is called a photon. Within a photon are particles called omegons.

When a photon vibrates, its frequency or wavelength is visible to the naked eye as white light. The modulatory frequency of photons is determined by the omegons within the atomic structure. Omegons are the color characters that bring the colors of the seven levels of consciousness within the astral plane to the physical plane.

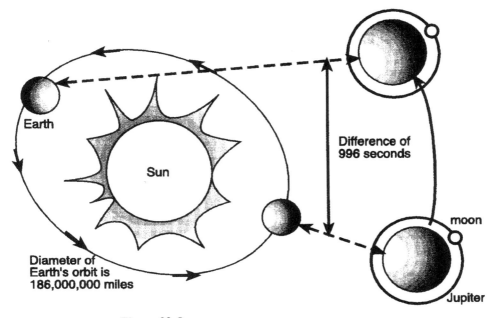

Figure 32-8

Photons are generated on the physical plane when electrons orbiting a proton of an atom "jump" from a higher state of energy to a lower state of energy. Photons, along with the omegons and other particles within them, help stabilize the fast moving electron shells that surround the nucleus of an atom. When these shells are disturbed, then photons are released as heat and light.

In the case of a normal incandescent lamp, the tungsten atoms in the tungsten filament react in a random manner, releasing photons in an unharmonious manner that likewise releases consciousness in a random manner.

As a result, over time the use of regular light bulbs or fluorescent lamps (high in ultra violet) actually moves consciousness away from the 4th dimension and causes a distortion in concentration. A candle, for example, is a much purer light source with no side radiation and is a much better source of healthy, consciousness-raising illumination.

A laser, however, emits light only on one wavelength. Depending upon the color output, the medium within the laser will vary. For example, we use helium and neon to produce a red beam in the 650-690 nm (nanometers) range of the spectrum. If we want a blue green color we use argon for the 514-520 nm and helium-cadmium down to about 442 nm, which produces our highest meditative color, violet. So by controlling the pure coherent color of photon radiation, we can control the effect of consciousness that we want to enter or raise. Remember, in a world of artificial lighting, consciousness becomes artificial, especially after

Electrons jump from higher to lower states of energy (or vice versa)— then photons appear as light within that energy dimension

303

sunset. In the world of lasers we can begin to literally fly into a euphoric reality of living color.

In order to perform laser magic, let us study this further. The three main components of a laser are the active medium, the pumping source, and the optical resonator. The active medium consists of atoms, molecules or ions, usually in a gas or liquid form, or, in the case of the newer compact solid state lasers, gallium arsenide (GaAs) is used.

What is really interesting is that whatever the pumping source is and regardless of the color output, the color green, the central frequency of the hydrogen atom, is the color that the laser medium absorbs to produce the output.

Here is an example of the complete operation of a ruby laser. Our example here will consist of a flash tube random energy source, a ruby rod, the active medium, and two mirrors, one with a 5x coating of silver and one with a 10x coating of silver, which are our optical resonators.

Laser Tube Configuration

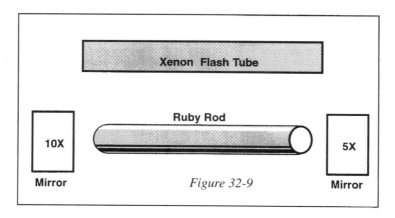

Figure 32-9

1. Using a high voltage power supply, we flash random white light down onto a ruby rod.

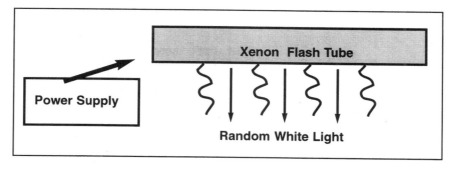

Figure 32-10   **Random White Light going to Ruby Red**

2. Inside the ruby rod the protons and electrons are sitting at rest.

+ = proton
- = electron

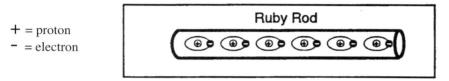

Figure 32-11   **Laser Atoms at rest**

3. Pumping Phase — The atoms absorb only the green (female) energy of the random light, and the electrons are pumped up with energy and move away from the nucleus (proton). As they are pushed away, the atom stretches like a rubber band.

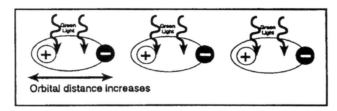

Figure 32-12   **Population Inversion Begins**

4. Population Inversion — You can only stretch a rubber band so far, then it wants to return to its normal state. The electrons then travel back to their original orbits, releasing photons coherently and orderly from the astral plane. If you as an observer were inside the ruby rod, these photons would appear to you as if they came from out of nowhere, much like the spaceship did to the observer in figure 32-3.

5. Now the red photons travel down the tube in phase and harmony as coherent organized light.

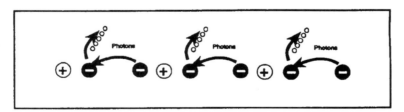

Figure 32-13

6. The two mirrors (optical resonators) reflect the coherent light back and forth between the mirrors, and as the flash tube continues to add more energy, the beam gathers energy and finally penetrates the weaker (5x) mirror. We how have a perfect

source of photon energy with raw 4-D consciousness. When this beam is applied to living cells, it places them in perfect order. When it is applied to crystals, it organizes the lattice structure within the crystal to release information stored in the Akashic records of that particular crystal into our etheric bodies via the second ether. When we access the Akashic records in this manner, all of the Lemurian and Atlantean Science becomes immediately accessible to us.

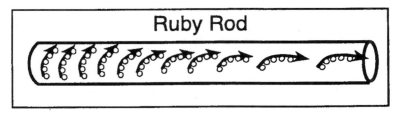

Figure 32-14   **Red Photons travel down tube in phase as Coherent Light**

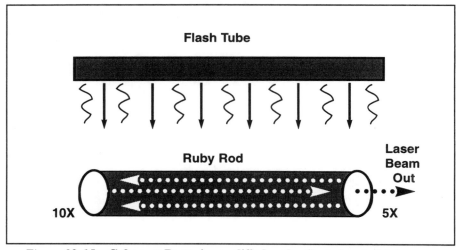

Figure 32-15   **Coherent Beam is amplified and reflected out of tube**

When the crystals are placed within the different Pleiadean structures, the intelligence and character are amplified and transmitted onto the 3-D world. With some of the structures, such as the Fire Starr Orb, the information can be sent on to other dimensions or continuums with other devices such as the Irradiator/Mega Orb combination.

Devices such as the Champagne Reflector are threshold doorways and can move energy either way, in or out, of a dimension. When these devices are compounded in their applications, the effects are greatly amplified, not only on global, but also stellar levels!

There are also mini applications. Because laser light (when observed through a crystal) stabilizes the hydrogen atom as shown in the earlier presented medical applications, carrying a small one milliwatt (1mw) laser and a small crystal in your baggage when you travel is quite feasible. When you arrive at your destination, place the crystal in front of you and shine the laser into it. Then gaze into the crystal and allow the laser-astral haze to fill your vision.

306

As you do so, take a few deep breaths and relax. **You will find that jet lag literally disappears as your pineal gland resets your bioclocks to the location that you are presently visiting.** This is an example of the flying saucers and the interstellar devices that the Pleiadeans and the other races produce. They install field generators that produce a similar or same effect, and they are often seen as laser lights on the outside that help stabilize the metabolism of the occupant on these long, deep space journeys.

How does the laser stabilize the hydrogen atom? Remember, the energy comes in from the higher planes that we experienced in the meditation. And so the energy spreads itself through the hydrogen atom in the form of a rainbow. Violet, in the morning, touches the electron, the outer level, with red at the nucleus, the proton, and green in the center. As the day goes by, this polarity changes. As the sun goes down, the energy coming in from the other dimensions — each and every single Ray we've experienced — is now painting a violet picture on the nucleus of the proton, a red picture on the electron. We've even gone deeper because we found out there were quarks and hadrons inside these atomic particles, and we explored other minute particles which are the essence of light itself. And we begin to see that this interaction of light and consciousness has a dramatic effect on the hydrogen atom.

Part IV

The Future is Now!

Chapter 33

Pleiadean Technology: The Irradiator

One of the first things we focus on is the Pleiadean device known as the Irradiator. Given to us as a gift in 1979 on the desert of New Mexico by Semjase, the Irradiator technology was the very heart of our Systems technology that would be introduced to the world over the next 20 years.

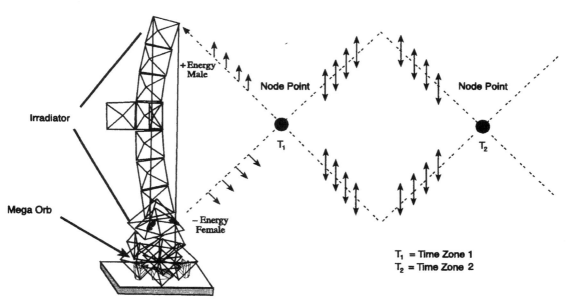

In the previous chapter we discussed the muscle testing of a right-side up pyramid (male) and an upside-down pyramid (female).

figure 33-1

The Irradiator has seven main pyramids in its vertical column (see figure 33-1). If you were to stand in front of it with dowsing equipment, you would experience points called nodes that would be a combination of where the male (yang) and female (yin) points come together. This is where the energy enters into the 4th dimension. The energy coming out of the Irradiator is a trapezoid wave, or scalar wave.

311

If you were to observe a Nuclear Receptor, you would also notice that although smaller and circular, it also has upside-down and right-side up pyramids. (see figure 33-2). In fact, it is like a small Irradiator worn around the neck. The difference is that the energy field of an Irradiator can be changed by the Mega Orb that it is placed upon and focused forward to infinity, whereas the Receptor is focused to its first node point and reflected back through its center to the aura of the wearer. In an Irradiator we control the node points via lasers and gemstones placed in the Mega Orb; and in the Receptor, we use a gemstone on the bridge. Similar technologies, but different applications.

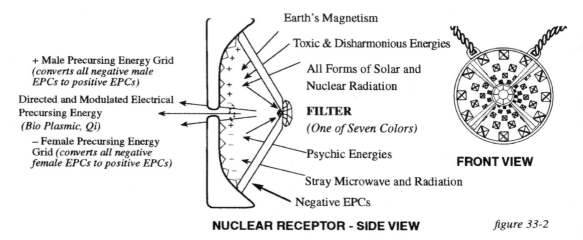

NUCLEAR RECEPTOR - SIDE VIEW   *figure 33-2*

Systems such as these have been used for millennia on this planet, as well as others. There has been a large amount of evidence gathered from underwater findings in both the Atlantic and Pacific oceans. In his book *Atlantis, the Eighth Continent*, explorer and writer Charles Berlitz goes into great detail about the civilizations of Lemuria and its later follower Atlantis. One of the pyramids in the Pacific near Bimini, still emits a green glow that was seen as far back as WWII by pilots on bombing missions to Dachau. The famous Stonehenge in Glastonbury, England, has 12 tall columns that are aligned in a similar manner and resemble our Pyradyne Irradiators.

The technology we are currently leaders in started gaining popularity in America in 1947 when the U.S. Navy began crop control experiments in Norfolk, Virginia. From the Homeotronic labs in the Cumberland Valley came the famous T. Galen Hieronymus and U.S. Patent No. 2,482,773 in 1948. This was a patent on the transmission of Eloptic Energy. As time went on, other names such as Radiestha, Psionic, Bioplasmic, Precursing, Radionic and Etheric energies became quite popular both in scientific and metaphysical circles. Scalar waves became the medium in which these phenomena present themselves to the universe from their respective transmitters.

Scalar waves travel at the speed of thought

Scalar waves travel at the speed of thought, which is, of course, instantaneous. The unique thing about a scalar wave is that the moment the positive component is properly generated, the negative component is received from the target source. Moving in a geometric form known as a trapezoid, they oscillate from earth-resonant frequencies to speeds well beyond that of light. Their targets are always in the subatomic spectrums of the nuclei of the atoms of the objects targeted, or in the case of human and animal targets, they directly affect the neuronic synapses in their respective brains. They can be used to shorten or lengthen the lives of all living targets. They can move objects in and out of a person's possession. They can change the weather or start or stop earthquakes. The greater the focus, the greater the result. The chants of the American Indians, followed by the focus of the medicine wheel, could be used as a rudimentary example of scalar transmission.

A Comment from a Pleiadean:

"When you begin to understand and realize scalar waves, you begin to fathom the ultimate light, love and sound of perfect balance. When working within scalar wave technology for the greater good, you become free of all causes. Remember, a cause is only a moment where goal and purpose meet. Before a goal ends, a purpose (whether it be self-esteem or service to mankind), must discern itself. Then time will engage itself and the unguarded consciousness will uplift itself to a form.

"Scalar waves are a moment of energy that comes from infinity, past, present and future, and that can be felt and realized now—in this moment, of course, only what will always be for you and me.

"The word 'scalar' means to scale or climb in separate moments of time, long enough to realize the progression of unity."

—Semjase, 1980s

The Irradiator works much like a laser in that the energy is raised to a high velocity and projected out of the base in one direction only. Let us briefly review the laser.

The action of the laser (Light Amplification of Stimulated Emissions of Radiation) is similar to the generation of electricity, except that instead of a rotating magnetic field being the source of motion, we use random light as our source of motion. The random light separates itself inside of a medium, and depending upon the medium used (ruby rod, helium argon gas, etc.), filters itself into one frequency. This frequency, being one of the seven primary colors, then leaves the crystal in a high-energy beam.

In the Irradiator, we feed in processed energy from one of the Orb bases, amplify it, focus it into a vertical beam and project it outward in a very tight pattern. One of the secrets in the projection of fohatic force, or scalar waves, over a vast distance via pyramidical structures lies in grounding the apex of the pyramid with the feed wire coming from the Orb column which is placed at the base of the Irradiator (see figure 33-3).

Therefore, it is a perfect marriage made in science when we use the laser in conjunction with the Irradiator. Along with the Irradiator, we use the Mega Orb. The Mega Orb is placed at the base of the Irradiator (see figure 33-4).

The Mega Orb is a second generation orb that will handle multiple numbers of gem-stones and includes a processing chamber where the horizontal eight petal lotus field is polarized vertically and sent directly into the Irradiator column (see figure 33-4). The processing chamber is necessary because the addition of negative ion generators greatly accelerates the speed of the electron cloud formed in the lower chambers. A quartz or diamond crystal is used as a processing gem.

The Mega Orb was especially designed for use only with the Irradiator. Their reason for its conception was that when an ordinary Orb was used, with only one chamber, it severely limited the output capacity of the Irradiator column. The regular Orb can be used by itself for an effect; whereas, the Mega Orb can only be used in conjunction with an

The Pyradome vs. Irradiator Element

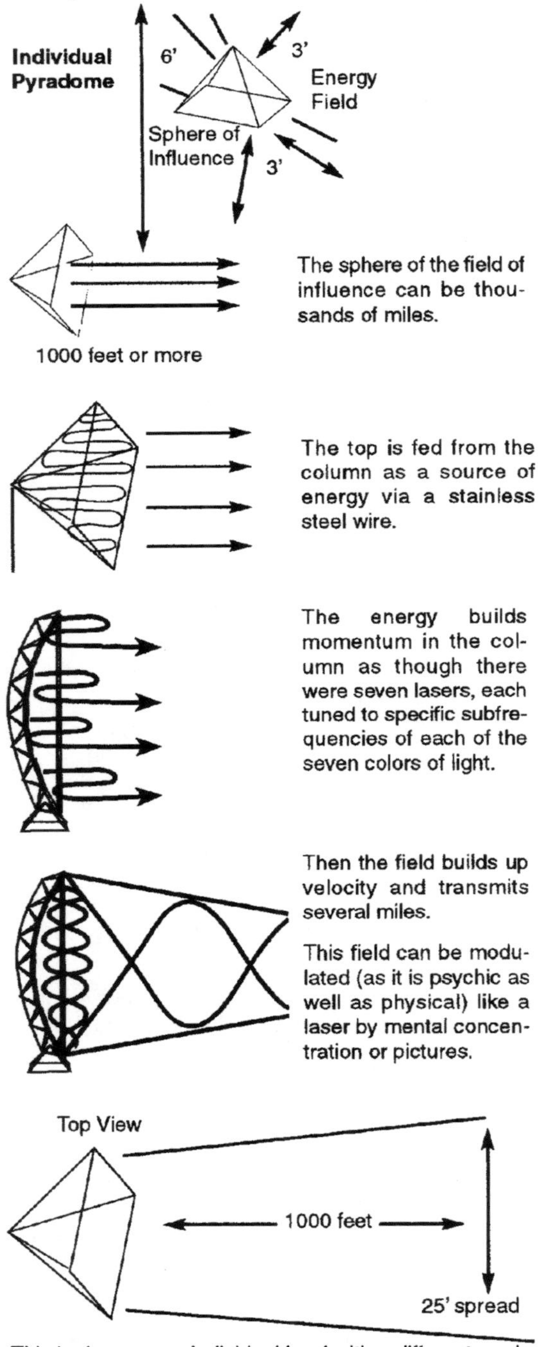

Individual Pyradome

6'

3'

Energy Field

Sphere of Influence

3'

The sphere of the field of influence can be thousands of miles.

1000 feet or more

The top is fed from the column as a source of energy via a stainless steel wire.

The energy builds momentum in the column as though there were seven lasers, each tuned to specific subfrequencies of each of the seven colors of light.

Then the field builds up velocity and transmits several miles.

This field can be modulated (as it is psychic as well as physical) like a laser by mental concentration or pictures.

Top View

1000 feet

25' spread

This is done on an individual level with a different mode of Irradiator usage than the application of Irradiation in Systems III.

figure 33-3

Irradiator column, since all of the stainless steel circuitry is of a closed-loop design.

It is important to understand the field relationships and their basic interactions when dealing with Systems that produce time and space warp capabilities. Without this as a consideration, it would easily be possible to be lost in space and time.

The Orb, when used with the Irradiator, will pulse the field of the Irradiator, forming a diamond shape when viewed from above. The human body responds to this vibration in that transmutation (into the higher DNA frequency octave) becomes possible: Genetic (physical), Electrical (mental) and Siddhic (spiritual). This fact was also implied in ancient texts when humans had magical powers due to the application of the Philosopher's stone (diamond). (See figure 33-5)

In the case of a complete Irradiator System, we place a gemstone or series of stones into the Mega Orb transmission cavity. Then the cavity is excited by the raising of the electron rings in the gemstone by the addition of negative ions (electrons). The rate of transmission is determined by the frequency of the stone used. The human instrument responds to seven different octaves of sound, light and color (see figure 33-6).

Once ionization takes place, the energy — now exact intelligence — is sent up the feed-wire on the back of the Irradiator column and transmitted through space and time by the actual column of the Irradiator itself (see figure 33-7).

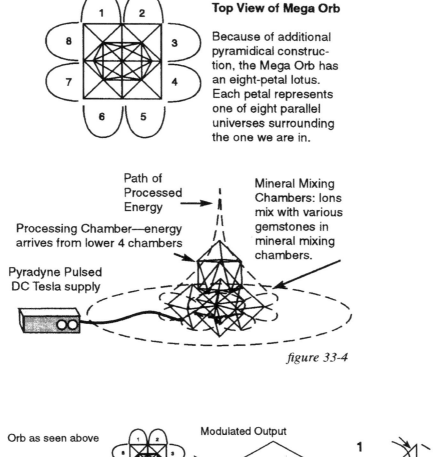

Top View of Mega Orb

Because of additional pyramidical construction, the Mega Orb has an eight-petal lotus. Each petal represents one of eight parallel universes surrounding the one we are in.

Path of Processed Energy →

Mineral Mixing Chambers: Ions mix with various gemstones in mineral mixing chambers.

Processing Chamber—energy arrives from lower 4 chambers

Pyradyne Pulsed DC Tesla supply

figure 33-4

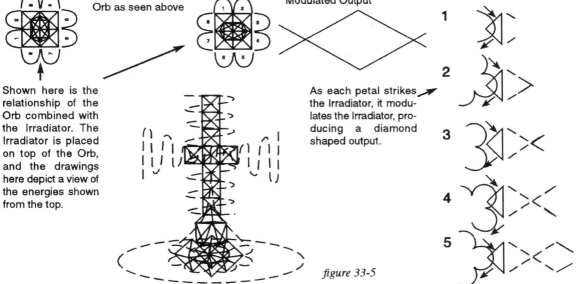

Orb as seen above

Modulated Output

Shown here is the relationship of the Orb combined with the Irradiator. The Irradiator is placed on top of the Orb, and the drawings here depict a view of the energies shown from the top.

As each petal strikes the Irradiator, it modulates the Irradiator, producing a diamond shaped output.

1
2
3
4
5

figure 33-5

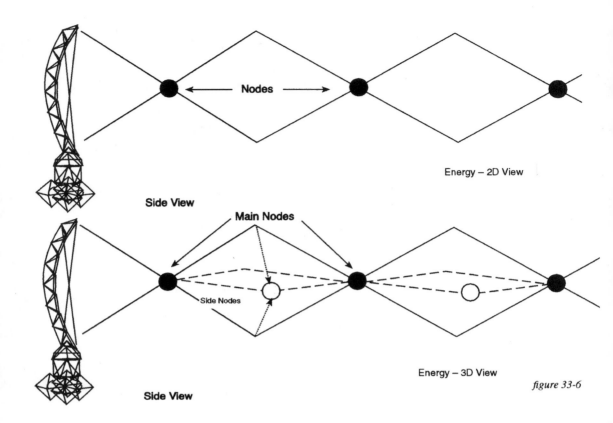

figure 33-6

Notice the arrows signifying the directions of the energy flow. In a normal electrical wave transmission, there is a positive and a negative component of a propagation wave. The interaction between the polarity of negative and positive crests gives the wave its propagational qualities. In the case of an Irradiator System, the wave differs in that one component

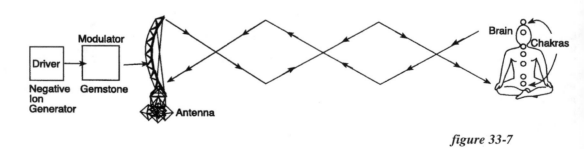

figure 33-7

is sent to the receiver or person and the second component is fed back to the antenna. This completes an interdimensional loop-transmission through the astral plane and thus the term irradiation comes into being. A complete understanding of this is necessary when designing time travel equipment. The distance between crests is signified by T_1, T_2, T_3, etc. This distance changes with the different gemstones used. It is called "peak modulation distance."

On the receiving end, the chakras or nerves of the parasympathetic nervous network respond by stimulating or blocking hormone uptake to the brain. The brain responds at the sympathetic junction of the sensory neurons. Here, through enzymatic action, a release on the transmitter sites takes place at the neurons. The transmitters are either excitatory or inhibitory, depending on the type of transmission released. Such synapses have been distinguished morphologically in the electron microscope; excitatory synapses tend to have round vesicles and inhibitory synapses tend to have flattened vesicles. Thus you can easily see how shape energy in biochemical transmission and reception is extremely critical and effective.

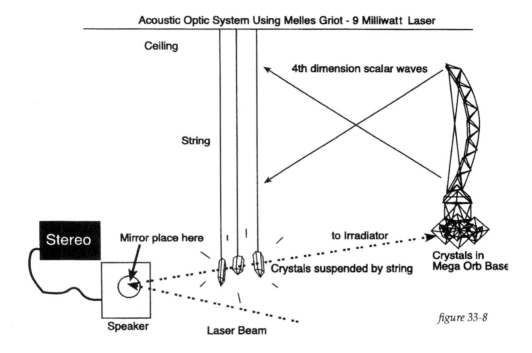

figure 33-8

When setting up a System of any sort we used sound in conjunction with light (see figure 33-8). For this purpose we have recorded several musical albums on tape and CD format. You can refer back to the DNA section to reference Pleiadean sound. Using Semjase's spaceship sound, we recorded a rock opera tape that is 90 minutes long. Called *The Fellowship*, it has all of the sound character necessary for a trip within the Systems III for an astral journey to the Pleiades and back. The Fellowship album is tuned to the 4th dimensional mechani
cs of the human bio systems.

Our second album *Atlantic Rising* uses real dolphin and whale sounds and is excellent for nature journeys. Atlantic Rising is tuned to the resonant frequency of water in human consciousness.

Our third album is on CD and tape, called *Galactic Meditation*. It was performed in conjunction with a Japanese master who uses 19 different metal bowls, three synthesizers and a Pleiadean ship sound. It is as its name connotes — an excellent meditation album. The fourth album was in participation with Steven Halpern, called *Higher Ground*, and is great for meditation, astral travel and sleep. Other music tapes are forthcoming.

As an addition to lasers, we couple a device called a scanner. Scanners synchronize laser light to form various patterns of chakras, mantrum and mandalas within the confines of the System and the respective crystals also being utilized. Scanners are also used to scan various centers located on the body with laser energy so that healing portal openings can occur within the consciousness of the person being scanned. It is not uncommon to open a 4th dimension within a System and greet and meet beings from other dimensions. In addition, the scanners have audio inputs so that beams may be directly synchronized with the music coming from your respective sound system.

For those of you who can't afford a scanner, a simple one can be constructed by gluing a small mirror chip on a speaker cone. When you shine a laser into the mirror while the stereo plays Pleiadean music through that speaker, the resulting pattern output will be a holographic representation of Pleiadean and etheric or 4th-dimensional energy.

There are substantially expensive scanner systems available, expensive because they are computerized. You could use them to write your name, for example, with the laser. Also, we developed an IBM-compatible scanner which programs our Systems.

There are many different accessories you can use with the lasers. Oftentimes I'll tell people that one small laser and a couple of well-placed mirrors and lights can give you a tremendous astral energy effect. For example, you can connect three or four rooms with one laser. Have the mirror laser output going into one mirror, say the farthest optical distance away, maybe 25 feet, and a mirror positioned there. You can buy small cosmetic mirrors that can be glued on the wall with hot glue or even tape. The laser beam strikes the first mirror and then can be directed to the second mirror, which might be another 25 feet away in another room, and then to a 3rd and 4th and 5th mirror. One laser beam can be directed to maybe 15 different places. The effect of this, of course, is to open up the astral energies throughout the entire house or building at a very economical rate. The more mirrors you use, the larger the beam becomes. And at night when this system is activated, it may even be modulated with a little sound through a scanner. It produces a phenomenal overall area of response.

Our Systems are divided into four categories, the first category being cleansing Systems, like the Ion Shower Meditation System, consisting of the Pyramid and Sleeping System. The second category would be the Self-Help System, which I'll cover in a minute. The third category would be what I would call Consciousness Changing Systems, which would be a Quad System, or a Systems III, which you use to program events to happen or not to happen and delve into interdimensional work such as levitation. Then the fourth category system is the Systems that build the telepathic ability, the ET communication Systems, and the Beacon System that involves the Fire Starr, which I'll also cover later.

The first requirement for a basic System is to get rid of the negative energies that the System's going to attract, or the balancing, opposite reaction. This is accomplished with the Starr Orb (see figure 33-9). It's used to negate all negative energy from the System that the System will receive. A wire is attached to the Starr Orb and then connected to a water pipe or metal stake driven deeply into the ground or even the grounding wires in your home or office. Whenever you wish to generate positive energy towards a goal, you will meet resistance. Since resistance is electrical in nature, it can be rectified by the antenna configuration of the Starr Orb. When there is no resistance, then the rest of the System can perform.

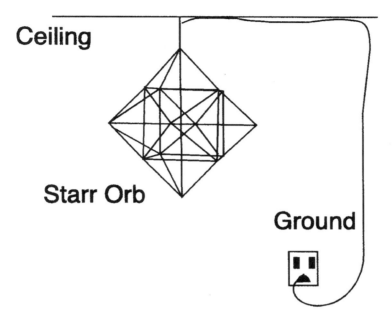

figure 33-9

When connecting the Starr Orb, it is necessary to isolate your electrical sub systems within your house or office. Turn on all of the lights in the room you are checking. Also place something into all of the plugs in the rooms or series of rooms. Next, have someone stay in the room being tested while you go to your central fuse box or circuit breaker. One by one, pull the fuses or breakers and have the observer tell you which group of electrical appliances shut off with each breaker. This isolates each circuit in the house. Make a note of this and connect them individually to your Starr Orb. Obviously if you are doing several rooms, you will need more than one Starr Orb. In larger applications we have a larger device called the Deva Starr (see figure 33-10).

Unlike the other Orbs, the Starr Orb and the Deva Starr can't be modulated. (see figure 33-11). This is because we use stainless steel circuitry in their core network. The properties of stainless steel tend to dampen stray energy vibrations. This means that negative sounds and frequencies such as noisy mufflers, street noise and other acoustical annoyances can be neutralized when combined with pyramidal forms such as the ones in the design of the Starr Orb and the Deva Starr. Random and negative psychic energy can also be neutralized. This type of equipment is in use by different governmental agencies worldwide to protect their high level officials who are relied upon for major decisions that affect people, property and freedoms.

Checking Grounds

1. Turn on all appliances in room.

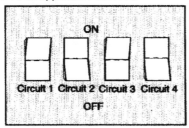

2. At circuit breaker or fuse box, turn off each breaker or fuse. Note which outlet or appliance shuts off. Example: Ceiling lamp may connect to TV on Circuit 1. Table lamp may be on Circuit 2.

3. Connect wire 1 to ceiling lamp and wire 2 to table lamp. Connect both wires to the Starr Orb, which is connected to a grounding stake outside.

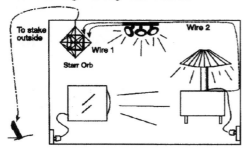

4. Once these two circuits are grounded via the Starr Orb to the outside stake, the room will be free of ELF and ready for Systems installation. Repeat for all other rooms that you want to protect.

figure 33-10

Each Pyradyne Orb has a definite purpose. The Solar Orbs are used as negative ion distributing units. When placed over a desk or work area, the Solar Orb provides a constant source of energy. The regular Orb and the Solar Orb can be modulated (the energy directed into the mental centers for mental activities, physical centers for physical activities, and so on).

The Starr Orb is usually used in small areas such as lobbies, waiting rooms, bedrooms and other such areas where a high level of calming is desired. The Deva Starr is used in large buildings such as high rises, department stores, or auditoriums where hundreds and even thousands of people are subtly affected by the Deva Starr to help them achieve a more harmonious state of being.

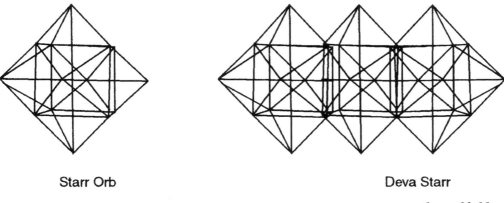

Starr Orb   **Deva Starr**

figure 33-11

The Mega Orb and Irradiator are used to transmit and receive all messages, instructions and intelligence via the scalar wave. The base of the Irradiator, the Mega Orb, is always oriented toward the Earth's magnetic north. I also want to say something about scalar waves. A few people have tried to duplicate our Systems out there because of the results we've achieved, and I want to say that these people do not know what they're doing. Sometimes I wish they did, but they don't. They use the wrong materials, the wrong plating processes and the wrong angles in their pyramids. I don't have an aversion to competition that's real, even though a lot of our things are copyrighted and patented, but I totally detest rip-off people, and there are plenty of them in the New Age Movement, people who claim to have invented things that they haven't, or copy things and have no working knowledge of what they're doing. This only makes it harder for people who are really trying to move ahead.

The Negative Ion Pulse Power Supply is another component of the System. It's used to raise the orbital velocity of the soft electrons (subatomic particles) within the orb structures and the minerals placed within them. We use a Master Crystal and Driver Crystal to connect thought forms within the human mind directly via the Akashic records, through the transmitting and receiving equipment. And, of course, we have the local minerals gathered from the surrounding area of the Systems to allow the interfacing with the local magnetic fields. In some kinds of programming, a link-up is established also with local nature spirits. And we use a plastic insulator plate to electronically insulate the transmitter, the Irradiator Mega Orb column, from the Earth's grounding (see figure 33-12).

The Orb, Capstone and large Pyramid (Portamid) are used to provide a stress-free, radiation-free, interruption-free environment for programming and receiving instructions. A lead glass Director Crystal and a quartz Data Entry Crystal, are used to load the System. Once you get your System set up, the best thing to do is lay down underneath the Pyramid, directly under the Data Entry and Director Crystals, which are suspended above you, under the Capstone of the Orb. Place a smaller lead glass crystal, which is called a Temple Crystal, on your forehead and begin to meditate on your wish or thoughtform that you want to load into the System. The reason that we use leaded crystal at this point is that most people have a significant amount of lead in their body, and for this kind of experience, we find that lead crystal seems to work the best because they'll sense the System feedback pulses. Start to meditate on what you want to release or concentrate on, but don't force it, just relax with the thought of this wish that you want.

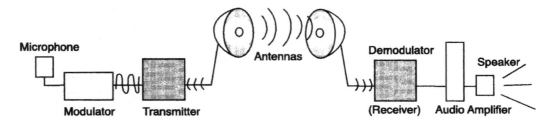

Antenna Systems Second Function

Normal antenna systems consist of a transmitter or receiver and an antenna.

Electrical energy is stored in the transmitter until it reaches peak potential, then it is carried by a co-axial wire or wave guide, depending on the bandwidth, and delivered to the antenna. When it reaches the antenna, it propagates itself off the antenna and is dispersed into the surrounding environment. In its most common usage, radio and TV communications, the intelligence is received as electrical energy and converted back into audio and visual information and then heard on a speaker or seen on a screen.

In the case of the Pyradyne Antenna Systems, the phenomenon is the same but the universe is the transmitter and the human instrument becomes the receiver, or vice versa.

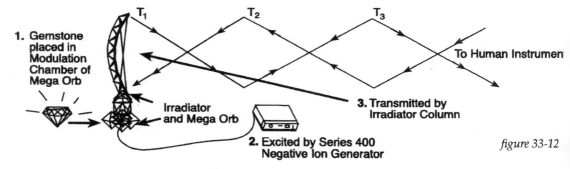

figure 33-12

When a System starts to work, you'll feel a pulsating going on at your forehead at the brow level, where the Temple Crystal is placed. When the pulsing becomes intense, that means the System is loading into the Master crystal and you're getting feedback from the Master Crystal and the Driver Crystal. A feedback system of scalar waves and thoughtforms responding to scalar waves establishes itself. You'll actually feel the pulsating. When the System has received the message and processed it, the Temple Crystal will then fall off your forehead. It's quite an experience to have this actually happen. A lot of people are amazed when the pulsating begins.

Some people can get in the System and feel the energy right away, meaning that the pulsating sensation will start rather instantly and the crystal will roll off their heads. Other people will need half an hour before the phenomenon starts. Some people lay there two or three hours. Other people can do it in 15 seconds; it depends on your conditioning. Don't be discouraged if it doesn't happen for you the first time around. It will happen, it always does. It just takes a little practice. Mainly the practice is to learn how to relax, because once you relax, the System is automatic (see figure 33-13).

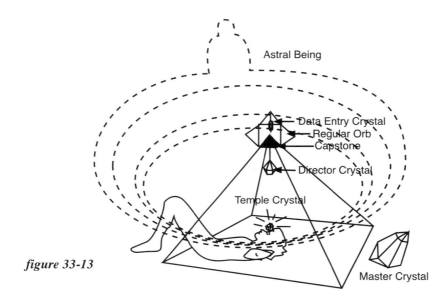

figure 33-13

Some Important Tips About Programming:

Timing is of the utmost importance when programming a system. Never initiate a new program during the full Moon cycle, which is a two week period. This is because the consciousness of the unenlightened is serverely governed by the three cycles of the Moon: a 28-day cycle, a 30-day cycle, and a 33-day cycle.

Light workers who use the systems for the benifit of planetary evolution will be met by resistance during the full Moon by those forms who are in the process of disrupting the planetary forces that are working to bring int he New Age. However, during the new Moon period, these forms are asleep and will offer no resistance. So choose a period of the new Moon to officiate your programs, and if you want to amplify your effort, choose a time daily to meditate in your system.

Once you begin to observe the feedback from your program, you will begin to build a confidence that will eliminate the daily reinforcement program. Some people only address their systems anually, whereas other will go to a cycle of every few months.

To load a program into the system, first set up the basic configuration as to the type of program you desire. Then lie down directly under the Director Crystal and place the Temple Crystal on your forehead. As soon as the energy is strong enough, it will proceed on its own into the system. It is quite common to feel a tingling where the crystal is making the body connection. When the program is loaded into the Master Crystal, the Temple Crystal will fall of its own accord off your forehead.

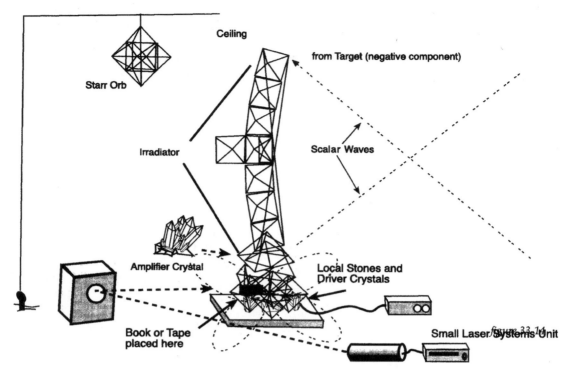

figure 33-14

Some of the projects you can do at this point are, for example, put a book in the System and program to read the book, or you could place a cassette in it and listen to the words on the cassette subconsciously. These are the kinds of things I would imagine that you would do before you go to bed (see figure 33-14).

For the more sophisticated System user we have an IBM computer-based programming device. It uses the Basic programming language and information is typed into the keyboard onto a special program screen. When the "enter" button is depressed, the program goes out of the computer via the printer output port. This then feeds a specially encoded laser/scanner which downloads your Pyradyne System via the Master Crystal. For specific details on this or any aspect of the Pleiadean/Pyradyne Systems —

call: 1-800-729-2603 or outside the USA call: 1-714-499-2603
or visit our website at http:/www.pyradyne.com.

Moon Cycles

We have to take into consideration the moon cycles for programming. When you program for outside events, you only program during the new moon period, which is approximately 2-1/2 weeks of the month. The full moon period, which is the other 2-1/2 weeks of the month, is a very powerful period of agitation on the astral plane, and any kind of energy that's going to block you will be prevalent on the surface of the Earth and in the ether. So you don't want to program or even work with your System that much as far as trying to influence outside events or others during the full moon period, because you'll only meet with blockage, and it's an energy draining experience. So you leave the System alone and it will work itself through these obstacles automatically. During the new moon period you can then reprogram again for what you want.

If you were going to initiate a self-help type of System Program such as the one we just mentioned, you wouldn't have to align the Pyramid to the magnetic north because of the gold Capstone atop its apex. But it would be necessary to align the bottom part of the Mega Orb to the magnetic north.This can be done with a small compass. The Mega Orb has four octahedrons on it, in pairs of two and two and two, so you align one wall of octahedrons to magnetic north, along with the insulating plate and the crystals, of course. If you find that when you align the Mega Orb to the north and the Irradiator is not facing you as you lay in the Pyramid, then swivel the Irradiator on the top of the Mega Orb and position it to face you. And once you've got it facing you, use a little duct or masking tape, or twist ties, and secure it so it doesn't fall off. The Irradiator is designed to swivel on the top of the Mega Orb, but it still has to be secured. The impermanent mounting allows you to position it facing other directions when needed. For example, if you wanted to program for a new car, aim it in the direction of where your car is. Then I usually tell people (for the example of the cars) to place some part of the car in the Irradiator, like the one they want in the System, because it's similar. Take a piece of material, usually a piece of carpet from the car dealer will do, such as a piece of the carpet or other item from the car (one item), and put it in the Irradiator. Turn the Irradiator in the direction of the dealership where the car is located, or wherever this car is.

This process could be done for anything. For healing: put a piece of the sick person's hair into the System and turn it in their direction. Now one of the things that I must emphasize again here is that when you program don't tell any other person what your program is. You can write it down, such as doing your affirmation in handwriting and sealing it in an envelope and putting it in the System. More than one person could use the System simultaneously. The System will handle as many messages as you want it to. But it's necessary that one person doesn't know what the other person's messages are, because as soon as you tell one person what you are doing, whether they encourage you to have this program come true or not, it interferes with the energy field because it has to be a one-on-one field with you in the System. The scalar wave is a very temperamental energy, and the human race is not quite ready yet for joint programming, meaning that you and two or three others would share a program. It's all right to network the System for a joint cause, but not for individual program requirements.

In other words, if you're networking a System, you're working with a group and you're saying to the group, "What we want to do is heal the planet, we're going to send out healing energy to the planet. Maybe we want to work on the environment, we want to send some healing energy out to the animals affected by oil spills." You would individually, without telling the other person how you programmed it, program your System, but you could have conversations saying, "Yes, my System is part of the group, and we're all working together to get this common goal accomplished." That's the type of thing I'm talking about here.

Joint programing— a future possibility

Now when you install a System, when you place the Starr Orb, I always tell people to put the Starr Orb away from the System. It doesn't matter where in the house or building or shed or apartment or office, where you put it, but preferably put it some distance away from the Self-Help System. When you work with the Quad System, it's a little different.

More on Systems Programming

First of all, timing is of the utmost importance in programming a System. Never initiate a new program during the full moon cycle, which is a 2-1/2 week period. This is because the consciousness of the unenlightened is severely governed by the three cycles of the moon. One is the 28-day cycle, one is the 30-day, and one is a 33-day cycle. Light workers who use the Systems for the benefit of planetary evolution will be met with resistance during the full moon by those forms who are in the process of disrupting the planetary forces that are at work to bring in the New Age. However, during the new moon period, these forms are asleep and will offer no resistance whatsoever. So pick a period of the new moon to initiate your programs if you want to amplify your effort. Choose a time daily to meditate in the System. Once you begin to observe the feedback from the program you will begin to build a confidence that will eliminate the daily reinforcement program. Some people only address their Systems annually, whereas others will go to a cycle of every few months.

To load a program into the System, first set up the basic configuration as to the type of program you desire. Then lay down directly under the Director Crystal and place a Temple Crystal directly over the bridge of your nose. Close your eyes and allow your thoughts to be directed into the crystal on your forehead. As soon as the energy is strong, it will proceed on its own into the System. It is quite common to feel a tingling where the crystal is making the body connection. When the program is loaded into the Master Crystal, the Temple Crystal will fall off your forehead of its own accord. If, for example, you were asking for a new car, a positive affirmation would be advisable. Before submitting your thoughts to the System, go to the dealership that has the exact auto you want and remove a small strip of carpet from the car. Put the sample into a nontransparent envelope along with the written request. Place the envelope into the transmitting chamber of the Irradiator and then proceed to use the above-described loading methods.

I thought is was quite amusing when an aerospace engineer came to one of my seminars and bought a System. He wanted to use it to program some real estate transactions. So he opened escrow on a condominium complex in Phoenix, Arizona and he was going to have to come up with about a $10,000 down payment. Well, by programming the System as he went into escrow, he found three people who wanted to rent condominiums in the complex, each to put up a $4,000 deposit, which included a first and last months' rent and the cleaning fees. And so as he closed escrow, he ended up with $12,000 available to him. The man didn't even have to put monies out of his own pocket to get into this building that he wanted. He got the deal and he had some money left over. Even though this was a materialistic use of his System, it's just one example of programming a System. I could give many, but it's not really necessary. The Systems are so effective, and there are so many people that we can network you to when you're ready to purchase a System that already have one and have had results. It's easier for other people to directly explain to you their results.

The next level up in Systems technology is the Quad System. (see figure 33-15). That's the one that's normally used for programming for objects or events. The single Irradiator System is normally used for the programming of self-help and maybe remote healing somewhere. The Quad System is set up in a large square, about 7 or 8 feet from one corner to the other. In each corner of the square you would set up one Irradiator and one Mega Orb on a plastic plate with all the appropriate crystals that are necessary for it. The Mega Orbs are all lined to magnetic north in the Quad System, and then all the bases are wired together with a special high voltage wire that we use that makes it possible for the tesla-powered negative DC power supply to connect all of the units together.

Now once you've learned to use the System and program it with your crystal, you can disconnect the DC generators for many applications. For some applications they are always required. Eventually you won't have to program your System by having the lead glass crystal on your forehead. The way I program mine is to carry a crystal around that I just leave in my pocket; it's a little crystal that I've become very fond of. And when I'm at home during the new moon, I always put it on the Master Crystal, which is inside the System, for it to charge the System. And then I carry it around in my pocket when I go different places for programming purposes. And that crystal will come into your life when you're ready for it, and you're ready to receive it, and you ask for it. It's usually a crystal that comes to you automatically.

Once you've got your bases of your Irradiator set up, you have two options. Naturally the Systems can be programmed during the new moon and left alone during the full moon. So your first option is to have the Omnion and add the Starr Orb and use it in the center of the System, which eliminates the need to rotate the Irradiators back and forth, or you cannot use the Omnion at first and rotate your Irradiators back and forth according to the new moon/full moon.

When you work with a big System like this during the full moon, you need to cancel all the negative energies that are coming into it. Just as you would position the Irradiator towards yourself as you lay in your bed underneath the Pyramid, you would during the new moon cycle position the Irradiators all toward the center of the room. During the full moon period, you would face all four of them out, pointing out to four different directions of the universe.

Every two weeks of changing, rewiring and securing four, big Irradiators gets to be a problem, so the Pleiadeans solved the problem for us in 1982 when Semjase gave us the Omnion design. The Omnion is a large structure that's placed directly in the center of the Quad System, and then two Irradiators are placed facing out and two Irradiators are placed

Basic Quad System
Top View

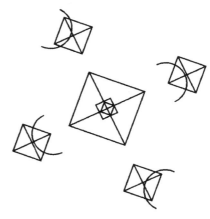

This system utilizes everything shown in previous systems, with the addition of 3 Mega Orbs, 3 Irradiators, and 1 Omnion. Many other accessories may be added. The next System in complexity is the Systems III-2.

**Irradiator
Facing Out**

**Irradiator
Facing In**

figure 33-15

facing in. So, in other words, two are permanently placed facing toward the center of the System, on opposing corners of the square, and the two on the opposite corners of the square are permanently facing out. The Omnion is then connected to a ground wire and suspended directly below the Starr Orb. The Starr Orb is also connected in series with the Omnion and the ground wire to a pulley directly above the center of the System. Then the wire is run outside the house and grounded. For this application it must be grounded into the ground. A water pipe is not going to be sufficient; it has a tendency to be noisy and there's not enough grounding energy. This System requires heavy grounding because it will move heavy energies.

Omnion: doorway to different dimensions

The Omnion acts with our System as a doorway, similar to the laser, to different dimensions. In the Systems III with the seven Irradiators, we suggest you place the Omnion right in the center and move it up and down with the moon cycles. Even though it helps relieve the negative energy that comes through on the master crystal, the Omnion also brings positive energy down from the 4th dimension of the astral plane. We also use it as a radionic transmitting device with the single System. If you're set up with a one Irradiator self-help System, you would mount the Omnion behind the single Irradiator at the exact center point, and you would have the Irradiator point away from the Omnion towards you. So it would be the Omnion hanging, then the Irradiator pointing towards you and then you on your bed where you're sleeping, or a pyramid where you're meditating.

It provides a constant output of energy of even polarity both day and night, so it stabilizes the hydrogen atom frequencies in the body, even though they are switching through their normal phase of the morning to the afternoon to night, to midnight, to the next day. Thus a sound and polarity light shift takes place in the hydrogen atom and it then becomes stabilized.

According to Semjase, this device taps into the powers beyond the parameters of our physical universe. The design was given to me on Christmas Day in 1982. We use several different types of crystal configurations with them now. We use amethyst in the center, we use Arkansas quartz in the top part and the bottom part of it, and sometimes we will use South American quartz in the bottom part and Arkansas quartz in the top. That gives you the clockwise/counterclockwise, or figure eight-type of energy field when it's put into operation. Remember, water goes counterclockwise south of the equator, and any crystal formed in that area orients that same direction because silicon oxide has a high water content. The southern crystal, being formed in water, possesses a counter-rotation polarity field. The two polarities working through amethyst, one positive and one negative, generates a tremendous field into these parameters that are beyond our physical universe.

The Omnion, along with the Starr Orb, is grounded, and during the full moon they are placed directly in the center of the System, preferably quite close to the ground. Then, when the new moon comes into phase. A second pulley is used to swing the Omnion up and out of the way. Now the Omnion and the Starr Orb still remain grounded, but they won't interfere with the System.

We have designed several different types of Omnions. Each has a different purpose. Although the basic 24 karat gold Pyramid configuration is the same, we use many different internal quartz/amethyst gemstone combinations. If you notice in figure 33-16, the majority of the pyramids have all of their apexes facing each other.

The apex of the pyramid has a First Ray energy characteristic. When all of the Pyramids face each other on a horizontal axis, physical plane energy is drawn via the base which is facing outward. Once this energy arrives at the apex, it is transmitted to the inner octahedral structure. The octahedron is a basic doorway to the astral plane, and if you look back at Chapter 28 showing the heme construction of the red blood cell, you will see a similar structure as the geometry of blood transmits the higher six levels into the seventh (physical body). So we can, via geometry and minerals, move energy back and forth onto the astral plane. In the case of blood, its shape brings consciousness into the body as it threads through the veins. Remove blood from the body and no one is home.

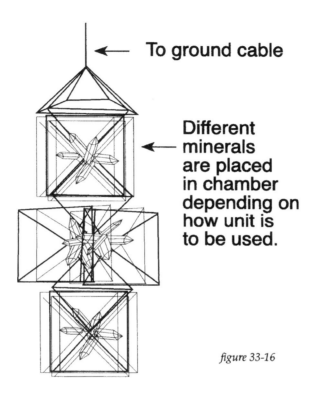

To ground cable

Different minerals are placed in chamber depending on how unit is to be used.

figure 33-16

The same goes for Pleiadean Systems. They breath life into the physical plane and you can control the creation. OR, you can send intelligence back into other planes of creation. In a sense the Systems technology is a first step for mankind to reinherit his God-given powers of creation and control.

With this comes a sense of responsibility. But, we might as well accept it now as later, because as we move in our procession around the equinox we are coming into an age of immortality. No longer can we solve our serious crime problems by execution, because the offender will immediately incarnate back onto the physical plane within the Ring Pass Not of the Earth and Lunar confines, with the same set of problems and a bigger attitude of injustice than before. In other words, our next generation will have harder criminals. The solution is to spend taxpayer dollars and **educate with a passion** our criminal elements into an understanding that crime only hurts criminals and criminals are a part of the whole, the same as saints.

Systems technology, when properly utilized, helps change the **entire thoughtform** into a system of respect, equality and understanding for **all living forms** whose brain it enters.

Chapter 34

Atlantis, Scalar Wave Warfare and the Eternal Struggle Between Good and Evil

Now you may ask, what if someone uses Systems technology for selfish and evil purposes? The answer is that's possible. This has already been done. 12,500 years ago the Atlanteans did just that. During the peak of Atlantean times, the DNA was so well-tuned that mankind had an average lifespan of over 800 years.

Intellect flourished and priesthood was saintly. But as we reached the backside of the equinox, the Dark Forces intervened and great temptation reigned. The Grays appeared and Scalar Wave Wars erupted, causing great destruction.

Because of the misuse of scalar waves, the DNA of humans was affected and lifespans decreased by 90%. The offensive, destructive force released carved huge negative vortexes into the cities that were toppled as the civilization and science of those times became less than history — almost mythical — to the average human brain with its severely limited genetic memories! The famed Bermuda Triangle is one of three such spots still acting as an astral doorway when planetary conditions amplify lunar energies. Poseidon was the principal city of Atlantis. Here were located the ancient mystery schools, spaceports and Hall of Records for Akasha. This bubble of positive existence became a black hole of negativity much like the fall of the Roman empire after the demise of Mark Anthony and Julius Caesar. Strangely enough, the island of Poseidon was located exactly three miles off the coast of Florida near Miami, right in the heart of the Bermuda Triangle.

Today, Miami is still thought of as the drug and crime capital of the world, and as Earth's aura retains more recently incarnated souls, other cities located in other vortexes are fast becoming full of recently executed criminals that have reincarnated back to regain their vengeance and destructive ideals until humanity wakes up and **gets the big picture!**

Let us examine a few details for the Big Picture.

First of all, let us consider the Universe as a precision Swiss watch. We are beings living somewhere inside of this watch, tiny little specks residing like a little gear deep within the highly jeweled, precision works. As the watch ticks away and gears mesh, time is measured by the scale of numerals numbered 1 - 12 with a big hand for minutes of which there are 60, and a small hand for the 12 hours.

Before you go any further, review the chart in Chapter 9, figure 9-1.

In humans, hormones once created form the first unit of biochemistry that possesses consciousness. They are stored in one of seven endocrine glands. There are seven endocrine glands because one is required for each level of consciousness. When any one or more endocrine is stimulated, these hormones go to the brain. The brain, in turn, switches on and off via the synapses, realizing consciousness into the mind, and magnetic and electromagnetic aura are created around us as a necessary side effect so that the mind can use the body to work out its desires or aspirations.

Aside from this biomechanical being are a group of spirits, with both good and bad intentions, both highly realized or highly undeveloped.

These spirits are either trapped in the vicinity or free to roam unlimited, but they all have one thing in common — they need a body to fulfill their passion.

Once inside the body, however, there are several restrictions that will affect their behavior. Here are a few of them:

1. The inherited genetics of the body composition, i.e. birth defects or perfect health and form.

2. The response characteristics of the chakra system that controls the emotional behavioral patterns of the body that the spirit incarnated into.

3. The location of the planet in reference to a particular solar system—where the planet is located.

4. The karmic and dharmic balance that by divine principle will dictate the expression of this particular spirit during its genetically determined longevity.

Minerals vibrate at a frequency that is amplified in your brain

Next, we need to consider the Ring Pass Not of limitations imposed upon our spirit.

As we discussed earlier, the astral plane is where disincarnated spirits reside when on a path to lower world service. It is created by lower world beings. **A Ring Pass Not is a density level that allows enough etheric density, so that a disembodied spirit can create an astral form and existence in an astral world, until he or she can incarnate into the denser physical plane.**

Spirits are limited to the lower astral density levels for in and out-of-body experiences until they can move out of the incarnation cycle and onto less dense astral levels or higher planes of existence. You might think of Earth as a planetary school on a lower density level. Once a spirit leaves low-level spirit lessons, the spirit may move to a higher planetary school such as the one on Venus or Uranus. When the Spirit moves here, you could say that the Ring Pass Not has extended to a planetary level. When planetary level training is complete, the spirit moves to an interstellar density level, and so on. As more schools are completed, the accompanying soul that the spirit acquires becomes permanent and eventually could be thought of as a super soul. Those are the basics.

Now, back to the Swiss watch. Consider our planet and singular moon to be the first two gears in the works of the timepiece. The human spirit acquires its soul here on Earth over an approximate line period of one million years. After about one million years, the soul could be considered a master soul.

Good and evil are still to be balanced, but the soul can now journey out of its first Ring Pass Not limitation into higher, more intricate gears of our watch. The process of evolution is limitless and eventually the soul/spirit becomes one with the watch. But that is later, much later.

Right now our concerns are our little gear spaces in the massive Universe that we reside in — and the bulk of humanity, most souls on Earth, are continually confined within the Ring Pass Not of Earth. Man has once again landed on the moon, so there are those among us who have had their Ring Pass region of their astral body extended to the moon, which is some 230,000 miles away (see figure 34-1).

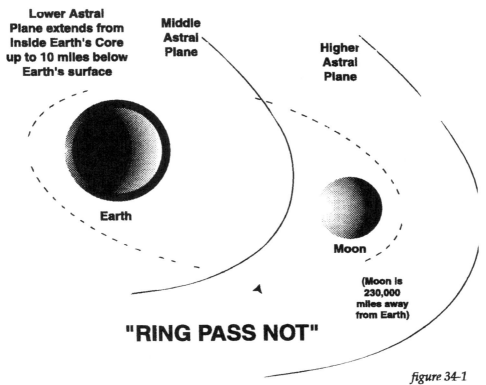

figure 34-1

The bulk of humanity is limited to these regions until the soul is free of this cycle and can move on to other planetary schools.

As mentioned earlier, the moon, as it moves around the Earth at 2,300 mph, creates different rhythms in the water substructure of the human bodies that are living within its sphere of influence. Some of those changes are due to the surface tension of the skin. Other changes are due to emotional changes upon our endocrine system as it hormonally resonates to the lunar seasons. In addition, there are planetary influences, which of course keep astrologers busy. The end result is **a base frequency emitted by the summation of humanity's DNA** that regional souls are accustomed to incarnating into.

Our Earth and moon encircle a larger gear in our watch, called the Sun. As we circle the Sun, DNA has seasonal frequencies that are ever-present in all living species that lead to procreation of nature at springtime, harvesting in the fall, storing in the winter and a variety of behavioral patterns that life on Earth traditionally has become accustomed to. Families tend to gather at Christmas as the spiritual energies reside deep within the bowels of the Earth at wintertime. This induces a collective spirit into our DNA and we celebrate the holidays. Squirrels store their seeds in the autumn and live deep inside their nests during the winter. Bears hibernate in colder regions. The spirit is in the ground. Remember I mentioned earlier that the seed contains the most energy? Well, now the seed is receiving it from life itself. As soon as spring arrives, the plants open their leaves to receive the sun, and our consciousness moves from the etheric levels to the summer outdoors, and we flock to all perimeters of our summer world with great appreciation for nature. Thus you begin to see how DNA traditionally resonates to the times, clocking and checking our bodies and spirits for the appropriate occasions.

But now, let us look at a greater cycle, or deeper into the works of the cosmic Swiss watch.

Our entire solar system moves around our central sun, circling the Pleiades every 25,827.5 years. During this greater rotational period we have sub-cycles of 2152.2 years which prophets, seers and astrologers call "ages." During these ages, due to the vibratory exchange of our DNA to the local stellar surroundings, we exhibit an entire shift in consciousness. When this shift is enacted upon our globe, great millennial changes permanently reside for long periods of time. Entire civilizations rise and fall. Lemuria was a product of this cycle, so was Atlantis, so are we now. As we move from one period to another, the consciousness of the incarnating soul changes. For example, currently we are moving into a higher DNA frequency as the Piscean Age closes and the Aquarian Age opens.

Our solar system rotates around the Pleiades every 25,827.5 years

During the Piscean Age, the incarnating soul was one still bound to the Ring Pass Not of Earth. Thus these souls could be called "believers." They believed in a higher way and constructed great churches, shrines and organized huge religions to support their belief systems, which in turn fed into politics and governments. The church and state were one and went out on quests to conquer other lands, teach natives in small countries their God, and like a great serpent, hold the Earth in the bonds of belief.

Now as our watch runs and gears turn, we encircle the Pleiades and our DNA moves to a higher frequency that allows a different soul to embody itself for work on Earth. The presently incarnating Aquarian soul is often one who is free from the Ring Pass Not of Earth and in many cases free from ring pass nots extending into other galaxies. As these people step in, their consciousness is not "I believe" but "I Know." They don't need a Bible to find God or a Global 2000 Report to know that Earth needs help. Nor will they start new religions.

The plight of government, church and state is not a factor to them, either. They know no bounds, only service to mankind and the greater good. With them they bring the extraterrestrials that will help solve the problems of the world as our problems are now felt deeply into other galaxies. Because as we move into the present position of the equinox, the Earth's frequency is approaching that of a microwave transmitter, and transmits frequencies deep into the cosmos.

At present, as we well know, the humans who control the world are not in proper frequency for the rest of the solar system. This problem can't remain because of negative input into other solar systems (see figure 34-3).

Earth Imbalances Solar System

The world's auric dharma is created by the summation of its citizens. Unfortunately, today's world is ruled by selfishness and ignorance.

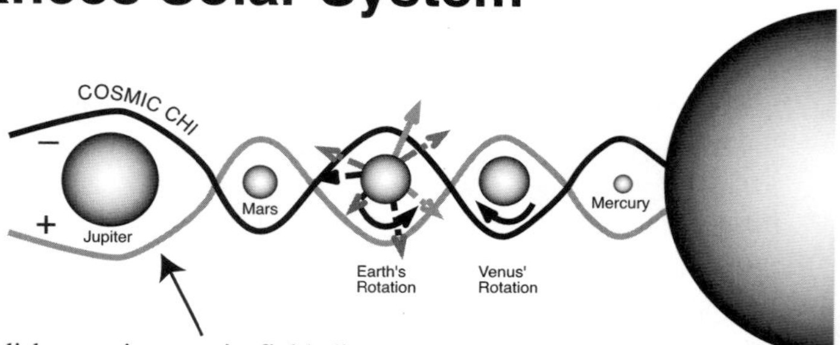

figure 34-2

Earth's disharmonious auric field disrupts the entire solar system with inharmonious frequencies.

Our Universe of Time

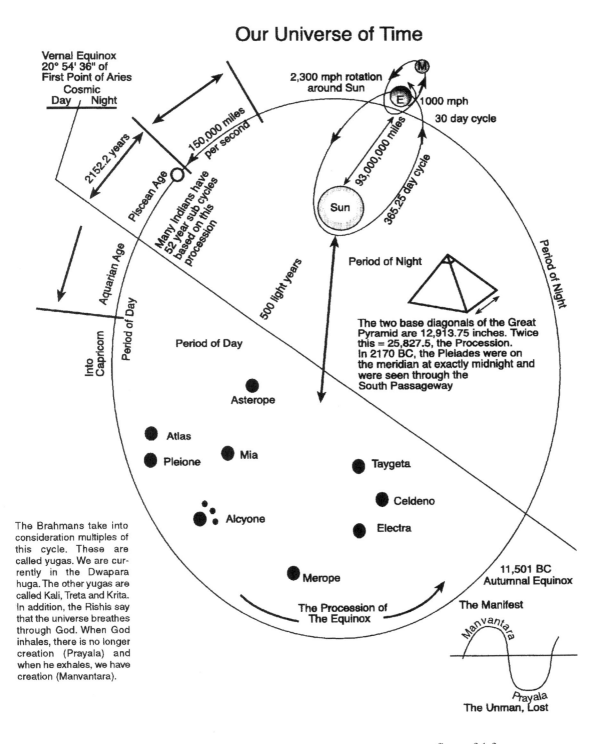

Vernal Equinox
20° 54' 36" of
First Point of Aries
Cosmic
Day / Night

2,300 mph rotation
around Sun

1000 mph

30 day cycle

2152.2 years

150,000 miles
per second

Piscean Age

Many Indians have
52 year sub cycles
based on this
procession

93,000,000 miles

365.25 day cycle

Aquarian Age

Into Capricorn

Period of Day

Period of Day

Period of Night

Period of Night

500 light years

Sun

The two base diagonals of the Great
Pyramid are 12,913.75 inches. Twice
this = 25,827.5, the Procession.
In 2170 BC, the Pleiades were on
the meridian at exactly midnight and
were seen through the
South Passageway

Asterope

Atlas

Pleione

Mia

Taygeta

Celdeno

Alcyone

Electra

The Brahmans take into
consideration multiples of
this cycle. These are
called yugas. We are cur-
rently in the Dwapara
huga. The other yugas are
called Kali, Treta and Krita.
In addition, the Rishis say
that the universe breathes
through God. When God
inhales, there is no longer
creation (Prayala) and
when he exhales, we have
creation (Manvantara).

Merope

11,501 BC
Autumnal Equinox

The Manifest

The Procession of
The Equinox

Manvantara

Prayala
The Unman, Lost

figure 34-3

335

As you notice in our illustration "Our Universe of Time," you can begin to get the clock picture. We are coming from a great dark period of night, where the souls were pretty much in the dark about "reality."

**Tibet —
remote
outpost of
Pleiadean
principles**

During these dark periods or nights, there are a few fully enlightened souls ever present to keep the spark of the truth alive. Seers such as Nostradamus understanding the greater day/night cycles give accurate predictions. Brotherhoods such as the great White Brotherhood keep truth alive and a select few appear through the ages. Of course, the Dark Force Lords exist, too, and often you hear of the destruction of literary works of the higher teachers, such as the burning of the libraries of Alexandria or other important gleams of truth. This is one of the reasons that many rumors exist of the secret hidden documents stored in the Pyramids of Egypt and other places.

The Tibetans, being a remote outpost for higher Pleiadean principles, have many old schools that are thousands of years old. Brought here from the Pleiades by the "Rishis," these documents were sought after by Dark Power groups such as the Chinese and the Third Reich. Many were found, destroyed or hidden.

However, today many of these treasures still remain hidden away by the proper record-keepers until society is ready for the real truth and the big picture.

So as these new souls come into place to set Earth into its rightful position, we will have new terms such as "walkins," ascended masters and a whole myriad of new explanations for entirely new behavioral patterns that will make Freudian psychology look archaic.

Chapter 35

Pleiadean Systems Configuration
for 4th Dimensional Transition

One of the main functions of the Pleiadean Systems technology is to stabilize and sanctify our local environment so that our DNA can focus on this newer, fresher breath of consciousness. As you can see, the Omnion is a major player in our Systems technologies. It can be used with a single Irradiator in a Self-Help System or in combinations of four or more Irradiator Systems.

The next thing we always tell people is that the best place we find to put the Master Crystal is directly below the Omnion in the center of the System, because during the full moon, when the Master Crystal is receiving a lot of negative energy, the Omnion, which also has crystal in it, will be pulling this negative energy out of the Master Crystal so that the Master Crystal can function, cleansing the energies as they come through and putting more positive energies back out. The full moon phase is the time when the Master Crystal has to work very hard at doing its job. During the new moon, the Master Crystal has plenty of excess energy, doesn't need the Omnion per se, so you can pull the Omnion up and out of the way on its pivotal arrangement.

The Master Crystal in the center of the System can be used to program for other crystals that we call Amplifier Crystals. These Amplifier Crystals can be placed in the vicinity around or surrounding the Master Crystal, and eventually you'll find that you have several large crystals similar in size to the Master Crystal—but as I explained previously when I talked about crystals, you don't want them quite as big. The System will automatically attract the kinds of crystals that it wants, and it will reject the crystals that it doesn't want. This takes a period of a year or two, but it's really fun once the process begins this crystal arrangement and rearrangement into your life. It's a great pleasure to watch this process going on.

We'll often have other Amplifier Crystals placed at different points throughout the room, and we have a Pleiadean device called a "choke," which requires some explanation.

If you were to take a carbon atom and accelerate it beyond the speed of light, it would collapse upon itself. Normally a carbon atom is an octahedron, but as it approaches the speed of light, it begins to collapse on itself, forming a Star of David pattern. This looks like two pyramids — one right-side up and one upside-down — almost growing inside each other; and as they collapsed on each other you'll see four different areas in the four corners of the two pyramids forming another set of octahedral triangles, upside-down and right side-up. If you were to observe this from a distance, you would notice four sets of octahedrons

PYRAMIDAL CHOKE

Side View

Top View

Represents Carbon Atom below speed of light

2. Corner Expanding

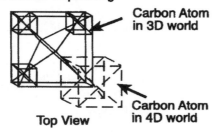

Carbon Atom in 3D world

Carbon Atom in 4D world

Top View

As carbon atom moves toward speed of light, one of four corners moves into another dimension.

This original shape diminishes in size as we approach the speed of light

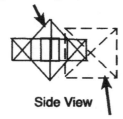

Side View

This shape now forms as carbon atom moves toward speed of light.

figure 35-1

— one forming in each corner — as the central carbon atom collapses. This represents the geometric progression of the interdimensional transition of the carbon atom into the 4th dimension. It actually speeds up in its energy field and forms another shape (see figure 35-1).

At the point that you have these four configurations forming in each one of the four corners, you would choose a direction and send your consciousness into that direction. That would be the plane of dimension that you would move from, because the 4th dimension is a key to the 5th dimension and other different paths and dimensions. Once you have gone into, say, the north quadrant of a collapsing carbon atom, to merge with your consciousness, it would come up in a multiple of the speed of light. It would now be in an astral shape and it would start to collapse and regroup as you went into another multiple of the speed of light and move again in that direction, and in that way it begins to form a scalar process; and you begin to be mechanically moved through the galaxies of space and time.

The total science of a choke can't be unveiled here, but it represents a DNA frequency pattern that holds the atoms and cells in place as you move through multiple light speeds. In our Pleiadean Systems applications, the shape energy is useful for DNA adaptation to higher time frequencies.

If we were to travel in a spaceship from here to another completely different solar system, it might, on the physical plane, take 600 light years to reach; but when the actual physical transition occurs related to the way the fabric of space is contained, this collapsing and building process might move you just slightly to the right or the left and you would cross great distances of space and time. You've gone down inside, the illusion is that you have decreased your energy field to smaller than the size of an atom. In this configuration you become a fabric of something else. And then when the process is reversed, you restructure yourself somewhere else in this fabric and you end up in a universe completely across space from this your present location.

This is why we talk about flat space, negatively curved space and positively curved space. The Pleiadeans developed the device that goes on the Irradiator that represents this configuration. That's why it's called a "time choke" (see figure 35-2). It speeds up or slows down the scalar transiting frequencies, meaning that **scalar waves are timeless and they move through space and time.** You can affect their movement and their distance to the depth of penetration into the fabric of space with this type of choking apparatus. To use the time choke device, you put it in one of the four Irradiators, and then the entire System is geared to work in this manner.

In the Systems III we use seven Irradiators. It is a little bit more difficult and cumbersome, so you'll need a slightly larger area to work in. But, of course, the results are quite a bit different, too. To set it up, place a compass at the center of the room and draw an imaginary circle as far out as you can within the confines of the area in which you wish to set up your Systems III. (Try using masking tape to draw your imaginary lines—you can always pull it up later.) From the center of this circle where you've placed the compass, draw an imaginary north/south line out to the northern edge of the circle. Where this line intersects with the circle is a point referred to as "T-1," and that's where you would place your first Irradiator, facing the center of the room, with its Mega Orb base lined up to magnetic north.

Go back to the center of the room again and put a protractor along this imaginary line at the point where the compass was sitting at the room's exact center, and draw off another imaginary line at 52 degrees, the angle of the pyramid. Where that line intersects the circle becomes T-2, the place for your second Irradiator. Draw another imaginary line **52 degrees** off that

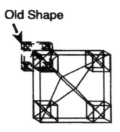

Old Shape

3. Corner now becomes predominant.

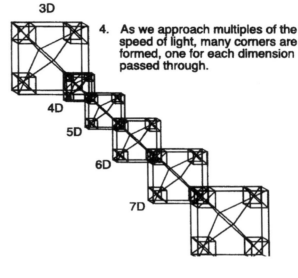

3D

4D

5D

6D

7D

4. As we approach multiples of the speed of light, many corners are formed, one for each dimension passed through.

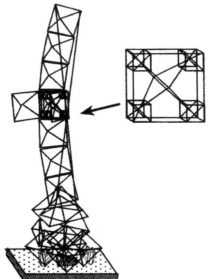

5. Choke is placed in the center of one Irradiator per System.

figure 35-2

**The irradi-
ators are
situated 52
degrees
apart —
the angle
of the
pyramid**

T-2 line from the center of the room, or 104 degrees from the first T-1 line, to the edge of the circle to establish T-3. Repeat this seven times total, until you have completed a circle of seven different positions. And in each position you place an Irradiator with a Mega Orb base lined to magnetic north, with the center of the Irradiator facing into the room. This arrangement for your seven Irradiators also defines pi, the radius of a circle (see figure 35-3).

Now you have set up Systems III, with seven Irradiators. Imagine looking down from your ceiling now. You'll see as big a circle as possible that you can fit inside this room (preferably the room is emptied out of all furnishings with the exception of a few plants and mirrors). And looking down from the top of the room you see this big circle and the top part of the circle points to magnetic north. And then 52 degrees around the circle is the first Irradiator, the Mega Orb pointing toward magnetic north, the Irradiator itself facing in. And another 52 degrees around you've got another Irradiator set up, the base of that Mega Orb also facing magnetic north, the Irradiator facing in, and so on all the way around. The seven Irradiators positioned exactly 52 degrees apart define the circle. (See Diagram of Systems III-2.)

Top View Systems III Placement

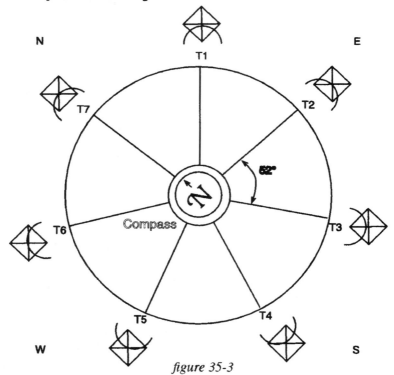

figure 35-3

Diagram of
Systems III-2

Creating a Virtual Pattern

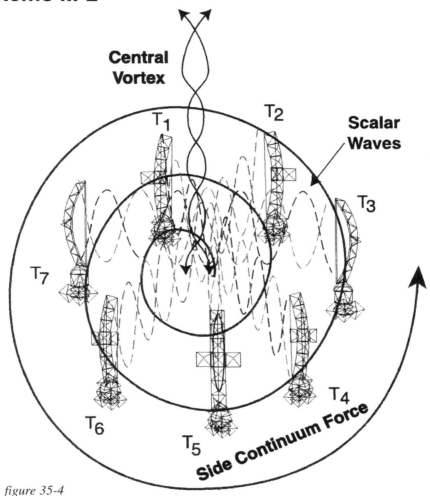

figure 35-4

In the configuration shown, all Irradiators are faced inward. This traps their energy, forcing open an interdimensional doorway. Shown here is the Systems III-2 and its energy patterns from the side. This system consists of seven Irradiators placed on top of seven Orbs.

The Pleiadean Systems III will react differently on each and every person but the change in each person is the same regarding energy balance.

In the center of the circle you would probably place your Master Crystal, and possibly your Omnion, with the Starr Orb fastened to the top of that, and any other kinds of crystals. What you've configured is a cosmic medicine wheel on one level, and it generates tremendous scalar frequencies. Connect all of the bases of the Mega Orbs together, with specially

341

Cosmic Medicine Wheel

insulated high voltage wire, and then connect them to one of our large Systems Power Supplies. Our System Power Supply is a must here because of the incredible amounts of energy that you're going to be running through the System. You need to have every cell in your body vitalized. Remember, in the bottom of each Irradiator you need two local stones and two pieces of small quartz points, approximately five to seven pounds, and so you'd have four crystals in the base of each Mega Orb. Then, up in the mixing chamber, which is the chamber up above the base of the Mega Orb, (see figure 35-4), place a gemstone that corresponds to that particular Irradiator's placement in the circle. Let me explain:

If you look at the Seven Rays Correspondences chart on page 217, you'll see the gemstone that correlates to each one of the chakras in the body. If you want to go forward in time and consciousness, you would start by moving energy from the base of the spine up to the crown chakra. The Earth is turning at 1,000 miles per hour, West to East, or counter-clockwise. So what you want to do is go clockwise, the opposite, with your energy field. Also, there are tremendous currents being generated inside the System because of the point in space where the Earth is. The Earth is moving 1,000 miles an hour in reference to where the Pleiades are positioned, where other planets are, where the sun is, where the moon is. **There's a tremendous velocity of vortex energy going on in the System.** That's why the moon appears to travel across the sky, as does the sun and other heavenly bodies. People aren't aware of the fact that even as they observe these movements, there's also an energy field that correlates to a turbulence which can be harnessed.

Pyradyne Mega Orb, Irradiator and Associated Components

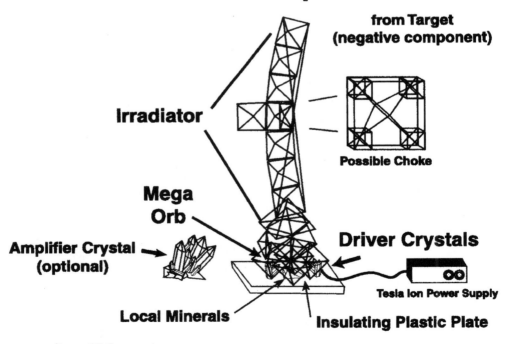

figure 35-5

Earlier we studied the "struck zone" energies, whereas spirit force moves into chakras on the **nadies** of the nerve and it strikes, creating a shock wave in the chakra or the nerve ending. It then explodes out through the etheric body, which enters the body cells through the minute holes of the nuclear membrane. **What we're doing is starting to utilize these forces!** This spiritual force strikes the body from the seven different levels, depending on where in the body it's picking up that consciousness to bring it into the bloodstream so the blood can circulate it through the body. Depending on where this is happening, certain amounts of energy are shocked, stunning you, causing you to be gravitated into time, and there are certain amounts of energies that you're escaping with, that free you of time. So, what we want to do is amplify the escaping energy, and transmute the gravitational forces to zero. When you do this, the Systems III is going to levitate you off the ground. That's one of the side effects that is often encountered. People who practice transcendental meditation have used this System and have been quite successful. A woman by the name of Rama Devi in Hawaii has been able to levitate almost 30 feet in the air. I do caution you, though. We did have one individual who floated high in the air eventually outside the circle. Once she floated as high as the ceiling would allow her go, she began to drift over to one side of the room, beyond the circle of Irradiators. And when she crossed the perimeter of the circle, the field broke, and she fell and did hurt herself severely. So I caution people about this possible side effect.

> The Sytems III can potentially levitate you off the ground

Now you have to **activate** this incredible energy. Put a gemstone corresponding to the base of the spine, which would be amethyst, in the mixing chamber of T-1, the Irradiator closest to magnetic north, which represents time zone 1. To activate time zone 2, T-2, use a gemstone like a citron, which would be a stomach area gemstone. Go clockwise to the third stationary Irradiator column, T-3, and use a stone related to the heart area of the body, something blue like sapphire, which is raising the frequency more. You can use Nuclear Receptors for this if you don't have a gemstone. The quality of the stones and their centers, whether it be synthetic or natural, doesn't matter — both work.

Address the throat chakra with T-4, possibly with emeralds, and for T-5 you access the pituitary body with a red stone, such as ruby. T-6 corresponds to the top of the head with a diamond, and finally T-7 should contain another diamond or some other white or light stone, or you could spiral the energy down with a gem such as lapis, which would then run the energy back to blue again, creating a spiraling effect.

As the Earth rotates through space and is struck with energy, your System has strike zones too. Spiritual energy comes from space also and strikes each Irradiator. Each Irradiator then releases its spiritual chakra/mantra energy field. This energy strikes the struck zones, the target zones, in the chakras of the human body of whoever is inside the center of the circle. It's being pushed by the big System with this powerful tesla power supply connected to it, plus all the power coming from the Irradiators, all in the form of scalar type energy which is a pure form of the energy. It's not being distorted now by ELF and radiation, and it's not being distorted by negative sound waves, because I would assume that you would be utilizing proper sound that has 4th-dimensional timbre characteristics, as we experienced during the sound session.

> Sometimes other beings materialize into the Systems III as they come into our 3-D world

Lasers are now added for their 4th dimensional energies into the System, and **the end result is your body will go into the 4th dimension.** It doesn't take much encouragement at this point in time. With a little bit of meditation to the point where you could probably not even think about going, you're on your way. And sometimes other beings materialize in the System as they are moved by it into our 3D world.

David Tickle is one of the producers of big bands such as U-2 and other celebrity musicians. He works a lot with Phil Collins and Rod Stewart, and he's had many world-class musicians in his Systems. They've experienced materializations in his Systems, which is a Quad System of four Irradiators. Also, when you're working with the Systems, they are firing all the chakras so fast that you may start vibrating. Don't be afraid if you get a tingling throughout your body, similar to your hand going to sleep. It's a form of astral projection. Just go with the feelings. Don't try to block it, don't be afraid of it. It will gradually consume your body. Some people feel a tremendous calm and then the tingling. Some people feel the tingling and then the calm. It varies. If you want to program the System as you would a Quad System, you could place a large meditation size Pyramid in the center of the System and program it just as though you were in a Quad System.

There are many things to do with the Irradiators positioned "facing in." If you're using the System throughout the new moon-full moon cycle, and you want to program it like the Quad System, you would face one Irradiator towards the center, one Irradiator towards the outside, one towards the center, one towards the outside and swing the Omnion up and down like you normally would in a Quad System (see figure 35-5).

What we've covered should give you a basic understanding of how the System works without getting caught up in the mechanical configuration. There are Systems specialists who can help you; you can network with other Systems users; there are a million different things you can do once you've gone to this point, and you've educated yourself, and you have an experience at this level. **This is one of the ultimate experiences that I feel you can have on this planet with Pleiadean technology as it exists for the general public at this point in time.**

There are also other things you can do with the System. For example, on Earth Day in 1987, we were conducting a seminar on top of the tower on top of the Old Cathedral Hill Hotel in San Francisco. I guess it's called Cathedral Hill now, formerly known as the Jack Tar Hotel, or vice-versa. We had rented the penthouse conference room and set up a group of seven Irradiators in about a 30-foot circle. Rather than put all of the Irradiators pointing in and out, we faced them all in one direction clockwise around the circle. Then we took the group of about 50 people, did a group meditation, and had them jog counter-clockwise around the Irradiator System. **People in the group began to levitate.** Instead of making 6-foot strides, they were making 8-foot strides, then 12-foot strides. The Tibetans call this phenomenon a "60-foot leap." The whole group was doing it. And, of course, when you're working with group energy, it's a lot easier and quicker to accomplish what I call "super physical feats." You can do it group-wise sometimes in one afternoon, whereas on an individual basis it might take two or three months, because your body has to be taught a lot of new things. In working with the System over a period of time, your body will be taught a lot of things, because gradually the hormone manufacturing and secreting in the body changes. As this change takes place, your body genetically changes in the direction that it should have genetically changed toward originally, toward higher beingness and high consciousness. And, unfortunately, mankind is not evolving this higher way, as I've said many times before, because of this polluted environment. **We're not even beginning to realize our super-physical capability.** What we do now is barely survive, and this is so stupid, because we should all be super-physical beings now. **That's what we are; we should be realizing this fact.**

So the Systems III helps you achieve many goals, and you can position the Irradiators in many different directions and do many different things. The sky is the limit. What I

Group meditation can produce super-physical feats

Systems III-2 — Top View

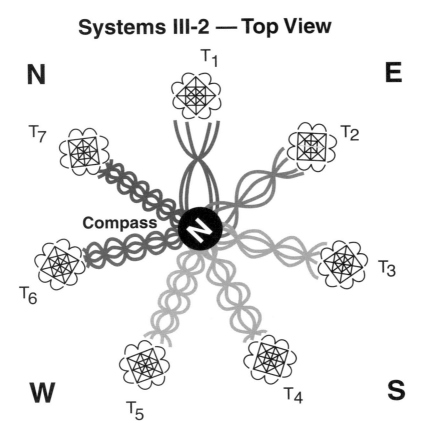

**Facing the Irradiators inward traps their
energy, forcing open an interdimensional doorway.**

This drawing of the seven column Systems III-2 shows the system's energy patterns from above. These patterns are mantric in shape, with T_1 being a root chakra energy, 4 petals, and T_7 being crown chakra energy (900 petals).

figure 35-6

usually do when people get this proficient is to network them with other Systems users, because I'm still a student of the System myself. There are successful Systems users all over the world. I have seen people do things far greater in the past, certainly, than I've been able to do, because I'm so busy I don't have the time to spend in my own System. I'm too busy developing this technology and educating people on how Systems work to really get in and enjoy them fully. Another problem that I have is my house isn't big enough to hold a Systems III. I only have a Quad System. Some day, when I have a larger house, I'm going to have a huge System, and I've even entertained the idea of stacking Systems in larger tiers.

What I mean when I mention tiers is that if I had a large enough room, I would set up seven Irradiators in the 1st circle and then I would set up more than seven on the next circle, and on the 3rd circle I would put even more Irradiators. I would have three rows of Irradiators and Mega Orbs all aligned to magnetic north, facing in or out. Or I could have them facing alternate directions, one circle facing in, the next one out, the next one against itself, and the other one counter-clockwise. Essentially, I would stack these Irradiators in the Fibonacci number series. Remember, the pine cone, for example, which might have 3 sections forming one inner circle, then 5 on the next, then 8 on the next, and 13 on the next. This can be done with several Irradiators.

You can construct a configuration that works with the chakras, and study the spokes on the chakras of what you want to accomplish. Every single chakra in your body has spokes, and what we're trying to do is to change the struck zone energy from what normally transforms, with gravity and bonding and spiritual energy in a 3D world — and shift it upwards to the 4th dimension. This shift will tune up the chakras by concentrating on where your blockages are the greatest in order to release energy. So there's no limit to what you could do with two or three of these Systems staggered together. That's just the beginning of what a Systems III can do.

Chapter 36

The FireStarr Orb

We have another type of System called the FireStarr, which can be just as exciting as the Systems III, but it occupies significantly less space. It is not designed to levitate you or move you through dimensions per se, but it's designed to develop your psychic resources so that you can become a contactee, or a channel, or a clairvoyant, or whatever you want. If you are one already, then what the FireStarr will do for you is make it a lot easier for you to perform these functions.

The FireStarr works with the auric field of the body. The Systems III performs with seven to ten chakras, but the FireStarr amplifies five chakras at one time. So it has five chambers for receiving the appropriate gemstones to work with the chakras that you want to address. In order to become a spiritual channeler, you wouldn't just work with any chakra, you would locate the ones that were blocking you and clear them. When you start channeling, you don't need to open up all your chakras. You may have a problem in your heart chakra, or in the gonad area. Any specific area may be blocking you from successfully channeling. Your crown chakra might be just fine, whereas someone else may have a problem with theirs. You've got to discover which area that you need to develop.

We have consultants that will help you through these transformations. In one experience, a singer was working on her singing career. She developed a blockage in her throat which impeded her upper octaves, like a gap in her octave range. We had a FireStarr built for her, tuned into the throat chakra and the pituitary area where she was blocked. When doing Receptor muscle testing, for example, on a person who is overweight, you would assume that they're going to test strong on thyroid, or emerald, because that is the area that governs weight control. Often they'll test strong on the pituitary, because the weight problem is a backup in the chain of command of endocrine instruction. The pituitary area is the tropic hormone center which regulates the thyroid gland. Well, this is the same problem that this vocalist had. She had pituitary problems which were affecting her throat, and so we tuned the FireStarr Orb to her throat frequency through the control center. In one session with the FireStarr her voice changed. She was very impressed with her improved vocal performance. As I explained earlier, when I was in Europe I met my wife because I was playing a concert where we had a FireStarr set up in Marnow, Germany, in the Bavarian Alps. While I was playing the frequencies of the Pleiadean sounds into the FireStarr, with 500 people concentrating, it invoked a myriad of flying saucers.

It takes about 3 months for this phenomenon to happen if you're tuning it to the extraterrestrial frequencies. I installed a FireStarr Orb in Oldenberg, Germany for a client named Werner. After 2-1/2 months he called me up and he said, "I haven't seen any extraterrestrials or had any sightings yet."

And I said, "Werner, how long have you had it now?"

He said, "2-1/2 months."

"You know," I said, "you Germans are a little impatient. Just wait a little longer." Exactly on the 90th day that he had that System he called me. I was in Munich at my distributor's office over there, and he said, "Fred, I don't know how to tell you this, but we had the sighting. Not only did we see it, but half the town of Oldenberg saw it. It made the front page of the newspaper. We videotaped it." It was really interesting because later on at a seminar when I saw the tape, he gave me copies of the actual videotapes of these flying saucers flying right down the Autobahn by his house.

In another instance, we were staying next door to Jack Nicholson at a friend's house in Aspen, Colorado, and we had a FireStarr Orb set up within the house at Aspen that attracted a ship; the whole town saw it. It was in the Aspen Times; this was around 1982. Then I went there with David Tickle in 1986, just to visit the place. We took a photograph by the old house, and even though the FireStarr wasn't there anymore, when we developed the photograph, four ships showed up in it. So the energy was still there. I put that picture in one of our catalogs. You'll see the four Pleiadean ships just coming out of a cloud screen. And I remember I had one of Billy Meiers' photos that showed a Semjase ship hiding in some clouds. You could see the outline of the ship very clearly. It wasn't like one of these reticular clouds at all. It was definitely the outline of a ship — I have that picture in my possession, too.

The FireStarr Orb can unblock several chakras at once

The FireStarr Orb is like the Receptor and the Irradiator combined. Let's say you had a blockage to five chakras; muscle testing on each told you what those five blockages were; and you tuned the FireStarr to remove the problem causing the five blockages. The problem vanished for six months, then suddenly you weren't getting results with the FireStarr that you thought you should be getting at that point in time. Re-tune the FireStarr to the next vibratory frequency up from where you were tuned last (more muscle testing and kinesiology), and move on again in the chakra experience.

My wife likes to teach classes on using the FireStarr Orb. Since we've done some more research with it, we've built up a back-up plate for the FireStarr. The back-up plate is called a shield. It focuses the energy into a concentrated point. The FireStarr is normally hung on the wall at a 40 to 50-degree angle. Depending on where you're positioning yourself on the ground, you direct the FireStarr at you so that it centers on you when you are in meditation or otherwise using it. Whenever you look up, you'll be looking directly into the focal point of the FireStarr. For those of you who haven't seen one, they're about 6' x 6', similar to a giant cross, except they're positioned at a 45-degree angle, like an "X", whereas a cross is vertical, like a "T."

The FireStarr also generates the same frequencies as the flower, as does the Systems III. All of these Systems generate the etheric frequencies of the flower. Cats like to lie in them. Sometimes friendly bees are attracted to them. An interesting note about the FireStarr is that lower form insects don't correspond to harmonic vibratory frequencies. Certain kinds of ants and moths, which don't fly, are repelled by the FireStarr and the Systems III (see figure 36-1).

The FireStarr Orb, although utilizing scalar waves within its functional mechanics, could be considered an aura-extending device. If you were aboard a Pleiadean spacecraft and you wanted to call someone up several light years away, radio-type communication would not be an adequate form of communication. The first problem would be that radio waves travel too slowly (the speed of light) and the second problem is that the amount of power required to send radiation across a vast distance would have to be generated by equipment as large as the ship itself. The Pleiadeans had to deal with this problem eons ago and solved it.

The first thing that they did was to realize that the human body, or Pleiadean body, which is with the exception of longer living cycles of DNA, the same as our bodies, was in itself a transmitter. I have always stated in my lectures that all inventions on earth are defined from internal body principles. They feel the same way. Not only can the human body, when trained, transmit and receive thoughts, but it can send these transmissions and receive transmissions interdimensionally and through time. The first step was to get more power out of the brain. Remember when we studied the brain in earlier chapters, we learned that the brain contains electrolytes and these electrolytes can be amplified by the herbs ginseng, fo ti and gotu kola? That's precisely what they did, added similarly functioning herbs from their home world as we have done here.

A lot of people do not realize that the Pleiadeans spend 60% of their time in the study of horticulture. They say that to be next to nature is to be next to God. They have pointed out that all of the technology on Earth can't produce one blade of grass.

> **Ayurvedic medicine is rooted in the Pleiadean civilization**

Obviously they are very advanced in the field of nutrition and energy. They have an average lifespan of over 1000 years in bodies the same as ours. Semjase has taught me a good portion of what I know about herbal and vitamin formulation. Our Ayurvedic medicine has its roots from their civilization, and our own texts on Earth date back almost 5000 years to 2500 B.C.!

Here are a few facts about terrestrial Ayurvedic principals:

1. The crown chakra is associated with the pineal gland and is helped by herbs gotu kola and nutmeg.

2. The brow chakra (pituitary gland) is supported by sandlewood and elecampane.

3. The throat chakra (thyroid gland) is strengthened by cloves and vervain.

4. The heart chakra (thymus gland) is strengthened by saffron and rose.

5. The solar plexus chakra (liver and adrenals) is supported by the herbs goldenseal and lemon balm.

6. The spleen chakra (testes and ovaries) is strengthened by coriander and fennel.

7. The root chakra (prostate and uterus) is strengthened by herbs ashwagandha and naritaki.

8. Ayurvedic medicine emphasizes a holistic approach treating the whole person with the appropriate remedies for the mind, body and spirit. This includes exercise and meditation. Also, I might add this is the medicine of old Tibet and as you can remember, the Rishis from the Pleiades brought science and medicine to Tibet.

THE FIRESTARR ORB

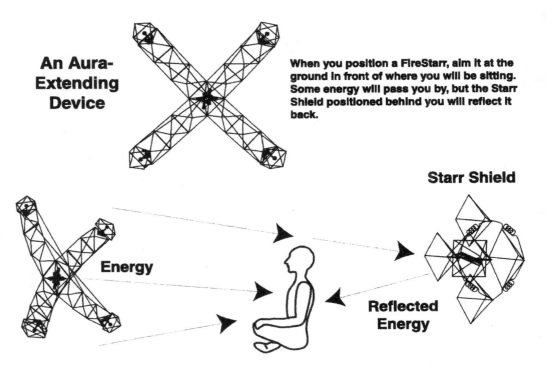

An Aura-Extending Device

When you position a FireStarr, aim it at the ground in front of where you will be sitting. Some energy will pass you by, but the Starr Shield positioned behind you will reflect it back.

Starr Shield

Energy

Reflected Energy

figure 36-1

Once the Pleiadeans raised their brain power, they then focused on the power outlets which distribute this increased energy. The first area, of course, is the nerves within the spinal cords. These are made more effective by the addition of trace minerals and vitamins such as vitamin E and lecithin, which increase the current-carrying capabilities of the nerves and sheaths themselves. Next, selenium and germanium were found to keep the currents flowing in one direction so that there is no feedback or stray oscillations that can block the flow of vital currents. Diseases such as epilepsy and muscular dystrophy here on Earth are the results of too little of the above nutrients within the central nervous system (CNS), causing feedback problems and blockages of vital electrical currents. Then larger amounts of sodium potassium and phosphorus are required to enhance the electrical signal as it is transmitted through the nerve passageways.

Once the important biochemistry is in place, the body, they found, had to be synchronized with the mind (brain) and consciousness.

This is accomplished by synchronizing what are called the Nodes of Ranvier, located along the nerve passageways themselves. So they developed their version of our FireStarr Orb. Devices like this teach our body to synchronize the Nodes of Ranvier so that there are no power losses when the body is asked to send conscious communication intelligence

350

(CCI) interdimensionally over long distances instantaneously. The following drawings will help explain this further.

I have worked on several projects in the past with the well-known author Brad Steiger. He is currently married to Sherry Hanson Steiger. The following quotation by his wife is taken from the book *The Fellowship*, written by Brad and published worldwide by Doubleday Publishers in 1988.

This incident took place shortly before they were married, when Sherry visited me to share a joint communication and contact that we had with Semjase. This was Sherry's first FireStarr experience!

When all rituals, preparations, and cleansings had been performed, she was instructed to sit in a meditative pose and to go within herself.

Sherry Steiger's experience in the FireStarr system

"I remember looking into the crystal, as instructed, feeling at peace, but also having to deal with the thought that perhaps nothing would happen." Sherry said. "I prayed, and almost in a 'poof,' I was gone. Somewhere.

"I have no earthly memories for nearly five hours. As I left for 'somewhere,' I was met by a being of light and escorted through the most mystically beautiful experience of my life. No words can ever come close to describing what occurred.

"As audacious as this may sound to many, I truly felt as if in some way I saw or touched the Divine Force. The Light Being, a facet of the divine Force, was so loving and caring and showed me so many things. The Being did not seem to have a gender, but I felt as though I knew him/her.

"It seemed as though we traveled through galaxies, making stops along the way. There was one place — maybe it was a planet...maybe it was the New Jerusalem — where the beauty was far above anything I've ever dreamed possible. It was like a crystal/diamond planet, reflecting and refracting the purest, most brilliant colors. The light all around was effervescent. As a 'living crystal' I became fused with the light...I became the Light.

"Blissful elation permeated every cell of my beingness. I longed to have others experience this powerful love...this perfect love.

"I remembered Fred...and I tried to call out to him, to ask if he could see it also. But I knew he could not hear me, because I couldn't use my 'body' mouth.

"Not long after that — or so it seemed—the Light Being told me that I had to go back. I was told that I would only remember a small part of what I had seen. More would be revealed to my conscious mind as I was able to share and to use the experience to help others."

With a jolt Sherry heard Fred firmly calling her name over and over. He had placed smelling salts under her nose.

Her body was numb. She felt disoriented, half in and half out of herself. Fred gave her some juice to ground her. She was not able to share much of the journey with him, but she remembers his sharing some of his observations.

"For three days I felt a little 'spacy' after the experience," Sherry stated. "Additional glimpses have gradually come back to me, and I know there is an absolute reality...a life beyond...a continuation of life...a perfect, all-encompassing power of love and peace, order and law. It is the love we are to be...it's the love we were...it's the love we are.

"More will be remembered by me when the time is right to share it. I bless and thank Semjase and Fred for this truly glorious gift."

The following is a statement from my wife, Frauke Bell. She has a "personally-tuned-to-her-frequencies" FireStarr System.

"The FireStarr System is a Pleiadean energy device which was first developed in the early 1980's. Like other devices such as the Irradiator, which works on the principle of the scalar wave to manifest thoughts instantaneously, the FireStarr Orb was given to Dr. Fred Bell to serve a specific purpose. The original function of this rather big device was to track Pleiadean spacecraft and to be able to establish contact with extraterrestrial beings. Only a frequency on the higher energy level will allow us to enter the energy field of extraterrestrials like the Pleiadeans. This means that we have to raise our frequency to attune to different levels of consciousness within the universe. Dr. Bell already spoke about the technical part of the FireStarr Orb and how it affects the human body and the full environment in which it is set up. I would like to share with you some of my own experiences I've had since I started working with this wonderful, very powerful Pleiadean device.

A Pleiadean energy device using scalar waves

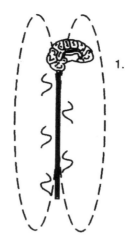

1. In a normal person, the auric radiation is very low. These thoughts can only be felt nearby such as within the confines of a small room. These individuals rely on spoken words and body language for communication

figure 36-2

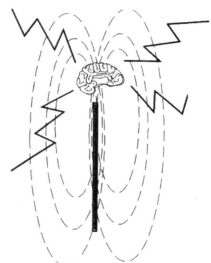

In a highly tuned person, thought waves can be felt great distances. With training, these individuals can transmit interdimensionally. This includes reaching the other side of the spirit world.

figure 36-3

"My personal system is set up in a room which is basically dedicated to the FireStarr Orb system. It is a place I come to in order to relax, be creative as a writer, or to experience higher states of consciousness. Most of our FireStarr Orb systems are custom-made and personalized. The energy chambers, which are the pyramid octahedrons in the four corners and in the center of the FireStarr Orb, are attuned to a person's needs at a given time. In each chamber we have a different gemstone depending on the color frequency we are trying to create. The octahedron will amplify the frequency of the color and also the properties of the particular gemstone. The octahedron in the center of the FireStarr Orb represents the heart of the device and is therefore of predominant significance. It becomes the focal point of our

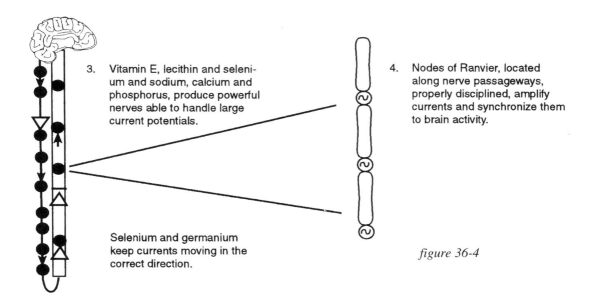

3. Vitamin E, lecithin and selenium and sodium, calcium and phosphorus, produce powerful nerves able to handle large current potentials.

Selenium and germanium keep currents moving in the correct direction.

4. Nodes of Ranvier, located along nerve passageways, properly disciplined, amplify currents and synchronize them to brain activity.

figure 36-4

meditation and will permit us to connect with our own higher consciousness.

"In the center of my personal FireStarr Orb I have three Fire Agates from Mexico. The Fire Agate is a gemstone which includes the colors of all seven rays of consciousness. Depending on the stone itself, one color or another will be predominating. Since we are dealing with a highly sensitive energy device which amplifies the given energies one hundred-fold, not only the color frequency and the characteristics of the stone, but also the place where it was found is extremely important. The installation of the gemstones is not meant to be of permanent nature.

"As we work with the FireStarr Orb, the vibratory rate of our body will change. Let's say we wanted to open up the third eye, the seat of the

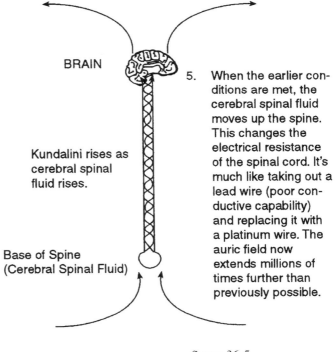

BRAIN

Kundalini rises as cerebral spinal fluid rises.

Base of Spine (Cerebral Spinal Fluid)

5. When the earlier conditions are met, the cerebral spinal fluid moves up the spine. This changes the electrical resistance of the spinal cord. It's much like taking out a lead wire (poor conductive capability) and replacing it with a platinum wire. The auric field now extends millions of times further than previously possible.

figure 36-5

pineal gland; in that case the possible stone would be smoky quartz. After a certain period of time the third eye is opened and we could concentrate on a different chakra. The crown chakra, located on the top of our head, is the main chakra. It affects the other nine chakras

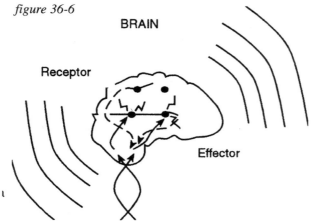

figure 36-6

6. When Ida and Pigala forces (positive EPCs) arrive at receptor sites, thoughts are turned into pure radiation.

This radiation is a form of communicative intelligence that is ready to go interdimensionally.

and is represented by the color white. The color white is not actually considered a color by itself, but a summation of our seven colors. It is represented by the diamond or other gemstones with equal properties, like for instance, the Herkimer diamond. The use of synthetic stones is possible since we are looking for the color frequency, but we recommend genuine gemstones, which would be more potent in the FireStarr Orb. It is also the energy of the gemstone itself we are looking for in our three-dimensional work with this device.

"The diamond affects all chakras at once. It becomes a very powerful energy within the FireStarr Orb system. Some people underestimate the potency of the diamond in conjunction with the FireStarr Orb or the super receptor. That's why we suggest you work with a specialist or somebody you know who would be competent and trustworthy for kinesiological testing. The selection of the wrong gemstones could be harmful to you and cause dysfunctional behaviors or even physical pain. I'm not stressing this to scare you, but I would like you to be aware of the FireStarr Orb's potency and to learn to respect it.

7. When a person is developed as in the foregoing explanation, the Pleiadean FireStarr becomes a potent communicative tool.

figure 36-7

FireStarr...
transmits to vast distances of space and time. It also receives intelligence from vast distances and times.

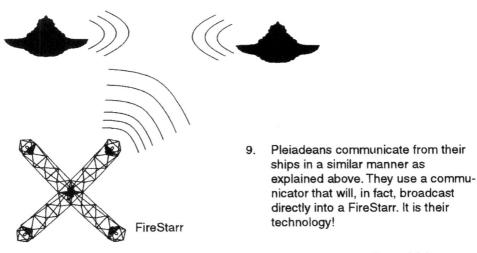

9. Pleiadeans communicate from their ships in a similar manner as explained above. They use a communicator that will, in fact, broadcast directly into a FireStarr. It is their technology!

figure 36-8

"The FireStarr by itself doesn't represent the complete FireStarr system. The second device, the Starr Shield, is a very important piece for the system's completion. The Starr Shield will receive from the FireStarr projected energy and reflect this energy back into the field where the meditating person is located. This unit has in its center two pyramids in the geometric forms of the Star of David and in the three-dimensional Star of David configuration you'll find double terminated crystals set in spirals of two different metals, each coming from the opposite direction of the pyramid star. The coils characterize the frequencies which create an exhilaration of thoughts, of feelings, and allow us to speed up time and to enter higher dimensions.

"In 1990, time sped up so dramatically that we all could physically feel it. Planet Earth is now making the transition from the 3rd into the 4th dimension. The FireStarr system will allow us to experience higher dimensions for moments at a time. This form of traveling in various dimensions is giving us the opportunity to gain knowledge we could not achieve with our limited minds. In all Pleiadean systems we are using a combination of sound, light, crystals, gems, and pyramid structures. Lasers are the light source for the FireStarr system. Red helium-neon or green and blue krypton-argon lasers or any other available colors can be used. The beam of the laser will enhance the energy field of the crystal or gemstone. For instance, we can use a green laser and a diamond so that the color green focuses on the female energy, the energy of the holy ghost in the Christian belief system. Green is a very harmonious soft energy with great healing abilities. It also will open up the realm of the 4th dimension and give us a deeper understanding of its reality. In conjunction with the diamond as a gemstone, the color green will affect all chakras simultaneously. The acceleration of time happens now in zero time, which means that our physical bodies have to be perfectly aligned in order to be prepared for this powerful boost of energies. The color red is a male energy representing the father energy in Christianity. Red focuses on the world power and brings us to the edge of the 4th dimension. It opens the first door of the next possible dimension, whereas the color green opens the second door, which brings us deeper into another dimension. These are the main colors I've been working with in conjunction with the FireStarr Orb.

"This interpretation of the colors is one way of experiencing it, but there are many other ways which are considered just as valid. Other colors, such as blue or yellow or violet, would also be wonderful colors to use with the FireStarr Orb. Lasers create a light in a crystal or gemstone which could never be reached with a simple colored ball. The laser beam brings out the energy of the crystal or gem and multiplies it a hundred-fold. This energy becomes visible around the crystal or gem and can even be seen more clearly when incense or a fog machine is used. **The longer we focus the laser beam on the crystal, the larger the energy field around it becomes.** Since the FireStarr Orb is a device which projects and reflects energies, it is a good idea to have a mirror behind the FireStarr Orb. In my personal system I created a mirror eye piece which represents the universe with its star systems of the Pleiades and Andromeda extraterrestrial civilizations. The mirror behind the FireStarr Orb will reflect our own thoughts and feelings, and therefore allow us to learn more about our own existence and purpose here on earth. And lastly, we are adding the element of sound to our multi-dimensional system. Pyradyne studios created special sound and music using quartz structures and timbres which alter our state of consciousness. The music affects our body cells to assist the pyramids, the crystals and the laser lights and help us tremendously on our journey in other dimensions. The unity of all these elements puts us into a state of consciousness where only beauty reigns. Oftentimes it is hard to readjust to our existing reality so that we have to give ourselves time to slowly come back into our daily lives.

"In our Intensive Seminars we give people the opportunity to experience the FireStarr system. We also teach all our FireStarr system users how to make the system work for themselves, and further, we connect them with other people who have personal experiences with the FireStarr system. The linkage of all the different systems and people who use them makes each one of the systems more powerful and gives us greater results on a personal level.

"I hope that you will have the opportunity one day to experience this wonderful multi-dimensional device on your own."

Chapter 37

Pleiadean Communications and Healing Technology

Another Pleiadean device that Semjase presented me with is called the Champagne Reflector. The story of this gift began in Herrsching, Germany, where Frauke and I had a lakefront apartment that we stayed in when we worked in Germany. It was located near Munich by two very old glacial lakes, Starnburg Lake and Ammersee Lake. Ammersee Lake where we lived, was less than 50 feet from our doorstep. The lake is probably 10 to 12 miles long and maybe two miles wide. I should mention that these lakes are old, probably formed back when the last Ice Age was spreading across the Earth. Many of the little lakes in Europe were formed during that time, so there are million-year-old, crater-type lakes.

Our apartment was located approximately five miles down on the shoreline that formed one of the longer sides of the roughly rectangular shape of the lake.

One autumn, in 1989, I was sitting by the shoreline looking out across the water. It was very unusual that evening, as the full moon was directly across the lake, slightly higher than the surface of the water. A thin fog crossed the center of the lake that gave the appearance of a drive-in movie theater screen placed directly in the center of the lake. Behind the screen was the moon. The way the moon appeared to me was similar to how it would appear if I was at a drive-in theater with a rear screen projector. As I sat there watching this interesting feat of nature, something moved suddenly across the center of the lake. Silhouetted against the fog was a medieval army of soldiers on horseback, with lances placed forward, and some soldiers holding those old flags that were predominant. Unfortunately, I could not read the insignias on the flags as they were too far away.

> An image seen due to a time shift

As this procession went by, I was flabbergasted by this obvious flashback into another time. Some famous battles were fought back in the medieval times around these lakes. So I figured it was some kind of a time shift that had taken place, an image of a battle that had taken place a long time ago (see figure 37-1).

Suddenly, Semjase began to talk to me by telepathy. I asked her what was going on and she explained that I was viewing an event from the past that was visible via the Akashic records in another continuum in the second ether.

I asked her for what purpose this was. She explained that this type of viewing was common back in olden days, before mankind instilled so much electronic pollution on the face of the Earth.

The radiation from TV screens, the character of billboard advertising, magazine

figure 37-1

advertising, the scanning rate of TV screens, all of these things programmed our consciousness away from our natural spiritual vision, and as a result we have lost our ability to see into the second etheric level of our own physical plane.

It seems that during the full moon period etheric veils can come down. The full moon period is not the best time to do programming and other metaphysical work, but it is really the best time to witness interesting etheric and astral phenomena. As more minds become illuminated, more of these incidents are going to become apparent, and those of us who are using devices like the Champagne Reflector are going to be leading the pack. We're going to be prepared for seeing phenomena long before others begin to. Soon many people will begin to have these experiences.

Etheric veils can come down and more will be

Back in King Arthur's time, approximately 400 B.C., there were legends surrounding Avalon that said if you were to go to the lake in one "state of mind," and cross the lake, you would arrive at a Benedictine Abbey, where medieval monks resided. If, however, you were in another "state of mind," you could cross the same lake and arrive at a village where white witches (probably a village of Druids) resided.

What caused two different locations to exist virtually one upon the other? The answer, she said, was in the second ether. The vibratory frequency is higher in the Druid village, closer to the frequency that a Pleiadean normally occupied.

This explained to me one reason that two people can look at an area in the sky during a UFO contact, and only one can see the ship. The person who can't see the ship does not have functioning etheric vision.

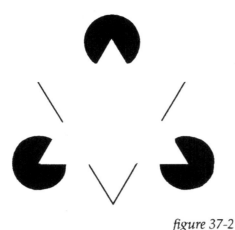

figure 37-2

Above is a drawing of a Kanisa triangle. What you should see is what I call three triangular lines and three "Pac" men. If you constantly see a white pyramid in the center, then your vision is severely programmed to the 3D world.

Semjase then gave us the design for the Champagne Reflector.

Basically, the Champagne Reflector is a device that will energize and sanctify a small area around it. It is placed in a high location in a room that you would spend time in but not a room that you would sleep in. Located in its octahedral chamber is a piece of quartz. As the sun sets daily, a timer is set to energize a laser that will send a red ray into the center of the crystal. Then at approximately 9:00 to 10:00 p.m., a second laser, this time a green one, goes on, and now the crystal is energized by two colors. At precisely midnight a third laser, gold, goes on. During the evening, sit nearby and look into the crystal as the different lasers come on. Gradually, over several evenings, the etheric/astral glow that is caused by the Champagne Reflector will change your vision and soften your aura so that you can begin to see and feel other aspects of the physical plane and acclimate yourself into the higher realms. At approximately 3:00 a.m. the green and gold lasers turn off, and at sunrise the red laser shuts down (see figures 37-3 and 37-4).

> Extreme low frequency fields have a definite biologocal action

This is probably one of the most unique of the Pleiadean devices, as its effects seem to grow on you over a period of time.

After I had used this device for a few years, Semjase came to me and told me to go to Aspen, Colorado. This was in the middle of winter, so off I went. She then had me drive to the end of a road that would normally be open during the summer, over the top of a mountain pass in an area known as "Pyramid Peak." I had to park and walk several miles through the snow on the now closed road. It was a moonlit journey, and I could hear white wolves howling in the woods beyond the open plain that I was sojourning upon.

> The etheric city near Aspen,CO

I knew instinctively that I was protected from these predators and when Semjase felt my thoughts, she told me that white wolves were the protectors of many hidden temples. When we reached the top of the peak, she told me to stop and look in a westerly direction. I turned my gaze to the west. Suddenly, about a mile away on a slightly higher peak, a beautiful city appeared. I asked her where this city came from, and she explained that it was an old Atlantean city that was quite modern by our times. She said that this city was not unlike Shamballa, located over the Gobi desert, and that it was a city that was "quite

Champagne Reflector

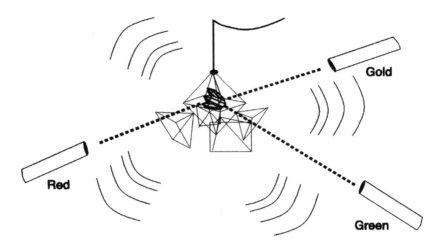

Lasers are positioned so that they send a pyramid-shaped beam from their three respective angles.

figure 37-3   Unit is positioned at the highest ceiling point in the building in which it is placed.

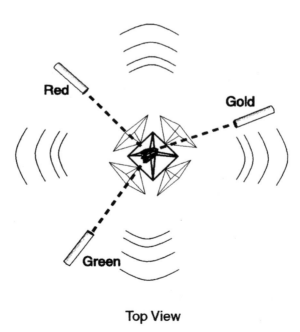

Top View

figure 37-4   The Champagne reflector creates a field that nullifies the day-to-day distortions that are inbred into our society's technologies.

physical" but located on the second ether. It was placed exactly in the vortex of the Aspen area of Colorado, but the city of Aspen was not centered in the vortex. This vortex, she explained, was the reason Aspen was there in the first place, that the original founders sensed, but did not see, the vortex when they settled in this area. She said that similar cities existed in other parts of the world where there were known power centers. But most occupants of the 3D reality could not see them because their etheric vision was clouded.

Certainly Pleiadean technology helps us get back to our esoteric roots. It's too bad our fossil fuel technology has led us so far astray. But it also helps the higher beings come down to our level without becoming contaminated by it. Here they can begin to assist us on our long journey home, back to our birthright among the stars.

We have seminars once a year in Laguna Beach, California. During these seminars, the attendees come to our home, perched upon this old, extinct volcano. When our Systems are fired up for a group demonstration, the Champagne Reflector is a popular form to gaze on. We have a beautiful group of slide photographs that show an angel present within the Champagne Reflector.

THE SOLAR ORB/ION SHOWER

When you position gold orgone-plated pyramids at different angles and in different groupings, a lot of different effects are created. If you reflect back on earlier chapters to the muscle test with an inverted pyramid and a normally positioned pyramid, you begin to see how energy scales between yin and yang or is able to balance EPCs (electrical precursing energy). This is precisely how the chakra system in the body triggers the endocrine system, thereby effectively controlling your energy levels and consciousness.

The pollution, toxins, drugs, ELFs and general man-made character projected into the world by mankind are detrimental to man's super-physical being. So the Pleiadean structures allow the body to correct itself by reintroducing the proper frequencies and waveforms.

Some of these structures operate on natural resonating frequencies induced by the character of the structure, and others are powered by tesla generators or lasers.

The Pleiadean Solar Orb is one device unique in that it can be unpowered as it is in its applications or normal usage, or powered as it is when it becomes an Ion Shower.

The Solar Orb was originally used to stimulate the creative process by placing a gemstone in its transmitting section and then placing it on your desk or in your workplace. We found it was further enhanced when it was powered by a small tesla negative ion generator, as the scalar energy behaves much like sunlight, and further enhanced by the negative ionization — it sped up healthy cellular reproduction.

One of the greater gifts was helping small drug-affected children recover (whose mothers were on hard drugs during pregnancy). I was amazed when we placed a Solar Orb over the crib of a three-month old baby who was having seizures because the child's mother was a cocaine user during her full term. The Solar Orb helped the infant's DNA change to a normal strand that excluded seizures and normalized the infant. Hopefully someday the world will realize how truly amazing this technology really is (see figure 37-5).

Did you ever get up in the morning and begin to write or play music or organize something important? Everything seemed to flow into a perfect idea or expression? Then you decided to take a short break, jump into your car, and take maybe a five-minute drive to the store and back — total time out and back 20 minutes?

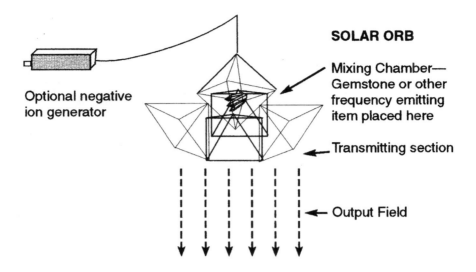

SOLAR ORB

Optional negative ion generator

Mixing Chamber— Gemstone or other frequency emitting item placed here

Transmitting section

Output Field

This unit may be placed over a crib, desk or bed when used as a Solar Orb.

figure 37-5

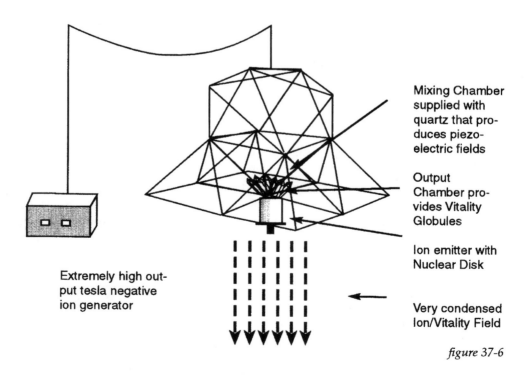

Mixing Chamber supplied with quartz that produces piezo-electric fields

Output Chamber provides Vitality Globules

Ion emitter with Nuclear Disk

Extremely high output tesla negative ion generator

Very condensed Ion/Vitality Field

figure 37-6

But, when you return, you go back to your project and guess what, ***no more creativity***. What happened?

The answer is simple carbon monoxide poisoning from other vehicles on the roads that you just imbibed on your short trip. Eight minutes in light traffic produces 24 hours of symptoms, and the first symptom is loss of creativity due to partial auric collapse caused by chemical poisoning of your bloodstream.

As I pointed out in earlier chapters, the aura is a sensitive field that needs to interface with the astral plane for full emotional body support. As soon as you lower the power of the emotional body, creativity is lowered and general health is also lowered, followed by vitality and attitude. If the source of poison is continuous, it can even lead to terminal diseases and loss of bodily form! (see figure 37-6)

> **8 minutes of auto exhaust cause 24 hours of symptoms**

This is why I think the Ion Shower is a vital tool for those who live in cities where the air is less than perfect. The Ion Shower utilizes an extremely high output tesla negative ion generator coupled to a highly modified Solar Orb. When you stand under it, it flushes the aura in a way that vitalizes the entire cell structure of the body, which then liberates the trapped poisonous gases that find a way into your system during your short mission out into the world of noxious fumes.

Chapter 38

The Pleiadean X-1 Healing Machine

I have, over the years, been involved with a number of research projects. At the very heart of Pleiadean technology is a machine called the X-1 Healing Machine. As you probably remember, I have emphasized throughout this treatise that the body has to heal itself and that technology can only create an environment wherein the body can heal itself at a more rapid rate than we are accustomed to.

Space science has demonstrated that in a zero gravity environment, the body can heal itself up to four times as fast as it would have on Earth with a one "G" gravity force. Astronauts that have been injured in space shuttle missions which were several days in progress, have had severe cuts completely heal, with no scarring, even before they return to Earth.

Burn victims can be hospitalized in space and will heal four times faster there, with no scarring, which under normal hospital conditions here on Earth would leave them scarred for life. The X-1 goes one step further—instantaneous healing, after proper diagnosis — while still being here on Earth. The key to this technology lies **in proper cellular repair frequencies being applied under altered time conditions.**

The original X-1 Healing Machine concept was given to Fred Hart and Thomas Colson back in the 1940s when they channeled it from a Venusian entity. It was originally called the "Depolar Ray." It had seven different transmitting output tubes, or ray transmitters. They originally worked up the concept for the first transmitting tube. In their interpretation of the concept, Hart and Colson built only a part of the original machine. The Depolar Ray resembled a large flood light with a black box power supply.

It transmitted a 44 megahertz modulated radio wave and when this wave was directed at a patient, it instigated an immediate remission of the conditions of arthritis. A few of these machines were successfully placed in health clinics around the United States.

Then the FDA stepped in about 1948 or 1949 and said that they couldn't manufacture this machine and sell it to the public because it was beyond their comprehension. So, as a result of that protest, Hart and Colson formed what is known today as the National Health Federation, which I've mentioned earlier. A lot of people aren't aware of the National Health Federation. It is a group of people that has a lobby in Congress and has long been representing people in the alternative health industry around the country, but it had extraterrestrial roots. So as a result of the earlier X-1 Depolar ray research, when I met Semjase, she began to educate me on the propulsion systems of the Pleiadean ships, and in the process of this propulsion educational series that I received from her, I began to understand more about the X-1. So we went ahead and developed the concept of what is known as the X-1 Healing Machine.

The X-1 sends energy into the body, photographs the energy while it is in the body, then reveals how the body distorts the energy as it passes through the cell and reaches the photograph. Next, it generates a report of the compensation that the body needs to augment the distortion that it has registered and projects the body energies back into the body with the proper corrections, which then enables the body to heal. Now, once again, this is not something that is going to heal you, but it's going to greatly enhance the body's ability to heal itself. It overcomes one of the dimensions of space that slows down the healing process, and that is time. It has the ability to emit coherent radiations in all different aspects of any three-dimensional energy requirement the body needs.

Remember that the color spectrum of light that falls on the hydrogen atom should be red at the nucleus and violet at the electron orbit during the morning hours, then rotate 180 degrees throughout the day so red is at the electron orbit and violet at the nucleus at sunset, then through the night rotate another 180 degrees. Of course, the hydrogen atom is part of the oxygen, hydrogen and nitrogen. These three elements and carbon combine themselves to create every cell in the body. So we work with basic building blocks.

The X-1's components

Before I explain the theory of the X-1, let us describe what it looks like.

The X-1 is basically three large components: the transmitter, the analyzer/controller, and the therapy tub or receiver. The transmitter is approximately six feet tall with seven different ray tubes, one for each basic color group. Within each of the seven tubes are seven subgroup transmitters, so that 49 frequencies of sound, light and color can be generated. These seven main tubes generate harmonious frequencies that correspond to one of the seven levels of consciousness, one of the seven endocrine glands, and likewise one of the seven colors and related frequencies of the hydrogen atom. (See figure 38-1)

The X-1 Transmitter Column

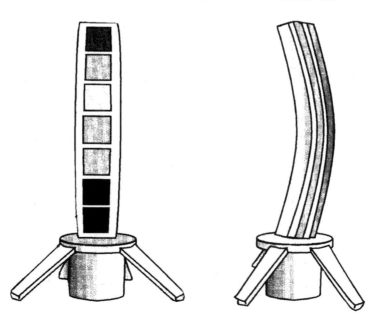

figure 38-1

The X-1 Analyzer Unit

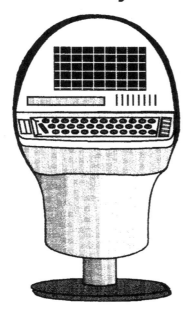

figure 38-2

When a patient is going to use the X-1, they sit in a chair and insert one hand into a small analyzing unit that basically is a mini darkroom with a Kirlian photography unit. But, instead of using a regular camera, the X-1 uses a specially designed television monitor. The TV monitor feeds data from the hand into a computer that analyzes the aurical information. (see figure 38-2)

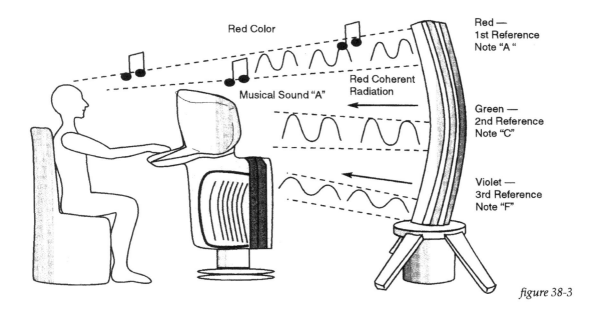

figure 38-3

While the patient's hand is still inserted into the analyzer, the person faces the transmitter column. The top radiation tube is activated in the center of the red spectrum (632 nm) and the sound generator sends a Pleiadean harmonic sound to the ears in the corresponding sound spectrum that, in this case, would be "A" major (see figure 38-3).

This procedure is then repeated with the center frequency green and note "C," and the last color to be transmitted is violet with the note "F" major.

While the person is looking at the first color, red, they may be color blind, or possibly slightly tone deaf, but this will not matter. The Kirlian camera will faithfully record auric phase shift from the sensory stimuli of the eyes and ears as it registers on all of the organs and cells in the body. As we have previously studied these ray pattern relationships in preceding chapters, you can begin to appreciate the technological advances of the X-1. By the time we have scanned through color and sounds from the X-1 via the five fingers of both hands, we have a complete analysis of every nerve, fiber, organ, cell and system in the entire body. This has been recorded in our database and is now ready for computation.

If there are any "grey" areas that need further analysis, we can take a blood sample, for example, and send it off for normal blood laboratory workups and do further Kirlian analysis in the X-1 Kirlian chamber.

Next, the patient gets into the therapy tub. The therapy tub is filled with warm water in a pleasant acid/alkaline pH balanced solution (see figure 38-4).

Therapy Tub

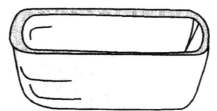

figure 38-4

Then the transmitter column is placed over the therapy tub. The analyzer will now adjust the parameter settings that are necessary to compensate for all blockages, fractures, nutritional deficiencies, heavy metal deposits and any other abnormalities that the patient may have.

As the transmitter column is activated, all of the sounds, colors and radiations are directed at the pathway in the tube. As the unit cycles through its healing spectrum, it begins with a slow repetition rate. The severity of the ailment determines how fast the unit will cycle and how much power will emit from each of the seven main transmitting tubes. Because of the sound harmonic, color frequency and radiation power being tightly coordinated, time augmentation is possible and necessary for severe injuries. Obviously someone with a pinched nerve would need a much lesser value of intensity than someone with a broken arm or cancerous organ.

When dealing with broken bones, the time augmentation mode must be relied upon for the body to heal itself instantaneously without the discomforts of a cast or support bandages.

Also, in the case of broken bones, the therapy tube is replaced with a special table that allows the bones to be physically "set" in place before they are fused back together in zero time.

What I feel that is unique about the X-1 is the transmitting tubes. Each tube has a small color dye laser built into it. The colored output of the laser is scanned electronically and the swept beam is projected through exotic gases from rare earths (noble gases) that are suspended in a vacuum. The beam is then accelerated to the output screen where it strikes colored phosphorus that enhances the photon output.

Sound is introduced up the current coils that move a large diaphragm at the rear of the transmitter tube. All of the light functions are in a vacuum within the tube. Each tube is capable of seven subfrequencies that correlate to cellular production. And, as there are seven major color tubes, there are a total of 49 organelle, cellular and atomic frequencies that correspond to the vedic text of the 49 fires of Agni and creation.

The analyzer unit also contains data compiled from biofeedback research, atomic and cellular science. It is virtually the brain of the transmitter column (see figures 38-5 and 38-6).

The analyzer unit contains the controller for all of the X-1 tube functions. In addition, it contains a very sensitive scanning photo diode tube that does the Kirlian analysis of the patient's hand. A detailed description of the full operational theories of the analyzer is not possible at this writing due to proprietary circuitry construction. In addition, if the X-1 were to fall into the wrong hands, it could be used as an ultimate beam weapon. As we approach closure of this book, the Pleiadeans will govern certain factual information, but not the concepts themselves. They feel that the world is entitled to know the full conceptual values of the technology herein disclosed. The details, they feel, are close at hand with existing technologies.

> **Each tube is capable of 7 subfrenquencies that correlate to cellular production**

Tube Operational Description

Unit utilizes dye laser (1) as multiple color source. Appropriately colored beam is diffused via diffusion optics and compressed acoustically via the sound pressure diaphragm. As the sound pressure is over 10 kilowatts, pressure is quite high. The vacuum tube controller regulator (2) controls the X-1 tube atmosphere pressure, which varies by sound octave. The exotic gas medium changes gas composition in accordance with optical frequency variation. As the beam gains mass from photon and sound pressure, it moves forward to the screen by accelerator anodes and the electrostatic beam scanner (3). As the beam is accelerated forward, it is compressed into a scalar medium and compressed or pinched by the torroidal field generators.

The timeless wave moves through the phosphor screens (4) which tints the beam for exact color octave definition. The output power can be varied between a few watts for healing purposes or several megawatts for propulsion purposes. The beam itself is similar to one of the seven life force rays of creation, thus giving it a potential for unlimited applications.

X-1 Tube 1 of 7 - Basic Light-Sound Function

(7 Tubes in X-1)

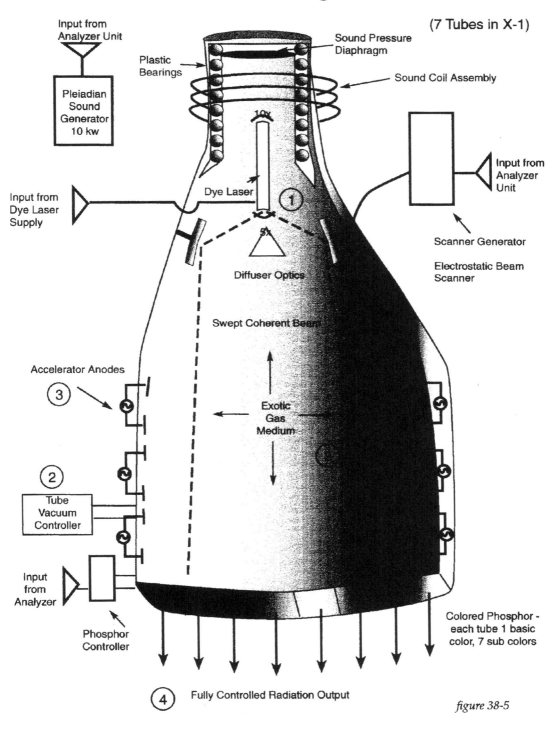

figure 38-5

371

X-1 Tube—Second View

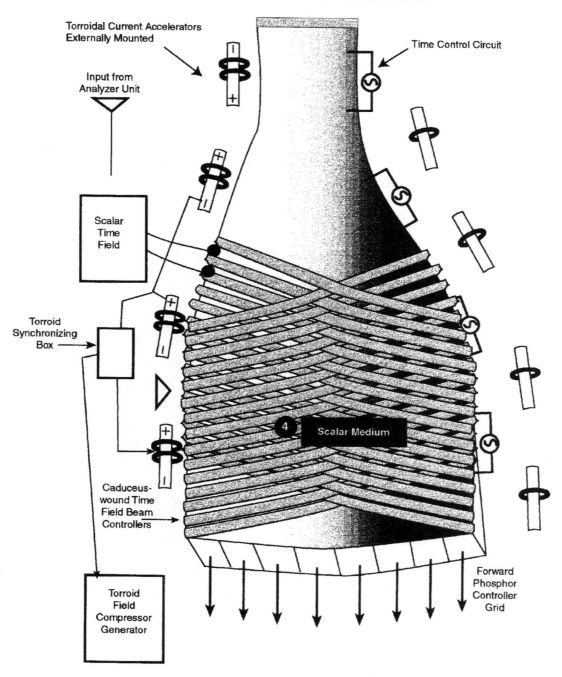

Torroidal Current Accelerators Externally Mounted

Time Control Circuit

Input from Analyzer Unit

Scalar Time Field

Torroid Synchronizing Box

Caduceus-wound Time Field Beam Controllers

Torroid Field Compressor Generator

4 Scalar Medium

Forward Phosphor Controller Grid

figure 38-6

Chapter 39

Actualizing Time, Space and Time Travel Transposition

"Time is a lady — treat her with respect," Semjase once told me. Later, as I began to realize that out of tradition came existence, I began to get the Pleiadean message. Repeating experiences over and over again gives a memory of the lessons of repetition, and the energy of this memory, as it builds up within the brain and gleans its essence of expression, builds the highways of existence that we eventually call our reality of this world and universe. Then the past becomes a collage of spent memory and the future, probabilities based upon our karmic potential. Throughout this book we have studied time related to science. But now, it's time to look upon the big picture.

From the view of our outer world, energies come together from the six other levels of consciousness, each with its own timeframe of inner space, and collide with the present here on the outer world, i.e., the physical plane, or seventh level of consciousness. This merging of times and energies is modulated by mind. Tradition could be said to be the modulating factor of the mind.

The first factor of motivation for mind is individual expression. Originating somewhere in the mineral kingdom, mind evolves through the plant and animal kingdoms until we reach the potential for expression through mankind. Of course, similar plateaus are reached on other worlds where the final expression is not always humanoid in appearance. But, whatever the physical result, there is a common factor, consciousness of consciousness, the breaking factor when entering the domain of immortality. When we become conscious of consciousness, we break the barrier between dimension and planes. The previous stop, the animal kingdom, is that of consciousness, but here perception is not yet a reality as consciousness is still growing upon itself.

So, now you finally incarnate as Adam or Eve. By himself, Adam has no real personality. Nor does Eve. But the two of them together begin to reflect their likenesses and differences, and karma begins between them.

Soon Eve has a child, and there are now three beings in the physical plane existence. This, of course, is the beginning of a race or nation. We have gone from singular time to dual time and graduated into tertiary or trinity time. This starts the dharmic clock and initiates probability upon the astral plane, from which, when individuals incarnate here on earth, will come the shape and outcome of the future. Because the summation of the human auric fields on the physical plane creates the astral plane, the karma and dharma from the physical plane activity seeds the probability for character expression in future incarnating souls, and as they form the present in future incarnations, they are in fact the future.

FROM KARMA TO DHARMA

As the Adam and Eve family perpetuates more and more offspring, and they create more and more of themselves, and bring individual souls out and express them into many other souls, then you end up with an entire "city" of beings, the only city on earth at this point in time. Now you form a religion so that you can contain your family energy field (racial dharma) within the city. You are traversing back and forth, to and from the astral plane. Now the funny thing about it is, when you move upon the astral plane and you're out of body and you're out of physical incarnation, you're still in time. You're in the time field that's created as a secondary field from the third dimension, so now the time relationship in the fourth dimension is a reaction, at this point in time, to the field that's created in the third dimension. So you have a third dimensional-fourth dimensional interchange. The astral plane, being the auspices for the beginning phase of the fourth dimension, is of a higher energy and frequency, therefore everything is self-illuminating. So when we bring physical science upon the astral plane, we realize we don't have the speed of light any more. Everything is instantaneous. So therefore on the astral plane everything is instantaneous in its energy form. So if everything is instantaneous, then we don't have anything in space. Space doesn't exist. **In between the third dimension and the fourth dimension is zero space. So if we could access this plane between the third dimension and fourth dimension as zero space, that means we could access anything in the universe instantly.** So now we have the ability to not only overcome time, we have the ability to overcome space. And when you have this understanding, then it's very simple to take the time problem and transpose and convert it into an interstellar flight machine. So now you begin to glimpse the horizon of Pleiadean technology or the principles of extraterrestrial technology.

> We have the ability to overcome time and space

THE ECHO OF TIME

So the first cause of time is like an echo. The only hard place that you're going to go in time travel is the past. If you go into the future, you go upon the astral planes and run into the "planning committee" that's planning to come back and reincarnate again here, and learn once again certain things that weren't learned in the previous incarnation. So for the sake of future time travel, just imagine that you're going to go meet the planning committee. The planning committee is always the group of individuals that has already incarnated here, made their mistakes, is in the astral plane within the religious phase, which is timeless in relation to the third dimension, and it is spaceless in relationship to the whole time continuum.

Because the energy is centered on the third dimension, not the fourth dimension, the "be here now" rule applies. I remember when I tried my second time travel experiment to go slightly ahead in time. I went right into a black void and found nothing there, because everything was timeless. So all the things that are going on that we're aware of, that are our reality, are being held together on this plane of consciousness in the third dimension by the summation of mental acuity that everyone contributes to. For example, if someone handed me a table, I would look at that table and I would immediately realize tradition. It took time to design this table, it took space to build it, it took time to realize the engineering of this table, meaning that if I put three legs on it, it would not have the same stability as four, or the strength. If I put two legs on it, it would fall over. And over a period of time tradition has taught me that four legs serves the best purpose for a table. And this would give the table some heritage.

Then I could look at this table and say, well, this was a Louis the XV or a Louis the XIV Dynasty table from France or England, or I could say this is an old German-built table, because it is very heavy and probably built during the times of the Crusades. And I would comfortably be able to relate to the existence of past human beings of a period that preceded me, because I'm looking at traditional things that have been put together scientifically and mechanically. The building concepts of tables have knowledgeably moved forward in time. If somebody says "I want to show you a future table," I would say okay fine. They more than likely are going to show me a drawing of a concept, because they haven't built it yet. So now you can see a precept of time.

Another thing that people ask me about time is: if you go into the past, what change on the present can you make? Well, usually very little, because mass mind is acclimated into being here at the present. For example, the entire consciousness is aware of and accepting today's date and time. And everybody in the three-dimensional world is attuned to that mass mind. Ask anybody anywhere in the world at this point in time what this moment in time represents to them, they're going to give you a date and a time and a place where they are, and we're going to have a correlation, which is going to give us three-dimensional world time zones, depending on whether they are in this longitude, or the next, or the next or the next or the next one.

Can we change the present via time travel?

Let's say somebody goes back and tries to stop Hitler from doing his evil tasks. The moment you jump to, say, 1937 or 1938, you're not in the real time. The real time is now; Hitler's dynamic, for example, has passed. But you could make a change in the group of energy that's forming the summation of that time and space field of 1938, because there still is a memory within people's thoughts of that time, and that memory, of what people's experiences were, is holding into the past dimension, the time of 1938. The number and power of imaginations affected in the present determines how much and how strong and how powerful the field is in the past — and what you can do to it.

CHANGING THE PAST

So let's say that you travel back through time and make a major change: the assassination of an evil figure, or maybe the institution of a positive humanitarian figure. The fact is that even though you made the change in that point in time, the chances are that it's going to echo and reverberate back and forth through existence, so by the time the effects arrive upon the present, that change has already faded out in people's minds, or in some cases, never registered in the first place. Changing a major figure like Hitler would be a large historic echo, but still the fact is the main mass of mind energy is in the present, so at some point the relocation of the past would cancel itself out. It would interfere with some of the interdimensional spaces between the present and the past, depending on how far in the past that you made this change. However, if you were to take every single person on the planet earth and say, all right, everybody, now we're all going back into 1938 and make changes, which would then make the present 1938! Then you would have had a monumental affect, and this is, of course, what civilization has to start to begin to deal with when you start encroaching upon the fact that, in reality, we are going into the fourth dimension. So some changes in the present will be possible at some time in the future, but they're not possible yet, because mass mind is till frozen in tradition.

The past is also used on this planet in another way. If you had a submarine, for example, moving through the Pacific Ocean, and, let's say, that you brought a reconnaissance plane out with infrared heat-sensing devices two weeks past or after the submarine had already gone on its path, through infrared sensing you would be able to detect a heat trail where the submarine was two weeks ago because of the way the heat affected the ocean and the currents of the ocean. So this is kind of like a residual echo.

THE BEGINNING OF TIME TRAVEL TECHNOLOGY

Particle experiments

How is time travel is achieved? I first got the idea when I was back at the University of Michigan working with the Wilson Cloud Chamber. We were able to look at particles that were moving at what we called "negative times." Science was giving these particles "half-life" periods, which is the rate of decay of radioactive particles, but that wasn't possible for some of the particles we were seeing.

Some of the particles only "appeared" during a small part of the experiments as the accelerated particles colliding with the larger mass, releasing new particles that did not exist in the normal reality that we were accustomed to. Basically, new at the time, particles came out of nowhere, lasted for a millionth or less of a second, and disappeared again. Today, of course, we call them leptons or quarks or hadrons, but this was back in the early 1950's.

We were often using particles called deutrons, which were manufactured within a cyclotron and accelerated down a long tube towards a target. As they traversed down the tube towards their target, which could be a simple substance such as a piece of calcium, these deutrons moved toward the speed of light, gaining tremendous mass. Upon impacting calcium, the energy created approached infinite, within a small confine, in this case a Wilson cloud chamber. The chamber was appropriately named because the secondary reaction created particles within its confines. *NOTE: the Wilson cloud chamber was originally invented by an English physicist, Charles T. R. Wilson (1869-1959) in 1915. In 1927, he won a Nobel Peace Prize for it.*

This tremendous impaction of nuclear forces penetrated the astral plane, about which we will learn more as we approach the final chapters in this book about gravity, and affected the nuclear binding forces of the target substance. When this happens, a sort of alchemy prevails, and a nuclear change takes place. The deutron is changed into something else, and so does the target (in this case, the calcium). The result is that we now have an isotope. An isotope can have similar characteristics of the original element it was, but now its mass number will have changed due to the rearrangement of the particles within its nucleus.

When you study the physics of a nuclear reaction, you will right away see that something is happening, not only with mass and energy, but also involving the transposition of the third dimension into the fourth. Thus we have stumbled onto the phenomenon of time travel. This phenomenon will prevail whether it be a small atomic change, or a large atomic structural change.

If it were possible to sustain the reaction obtained during the isotope transformation over a longer time, and keep the field energy more consistent, the half-life would appear to be a lot longer than it should have been. And so as a result I decided to build a Wilson Cloud Chamber as large as was necessary to take the human body inside of it and to excite the human body as we had excited particles inside of a nuclear reactor or cyclotron. Most of my earlier work was done in the cyclotron in Randolph Lab at the University of Michigan back in the 50's.

We began to do a study on the human body and how consciousness and time interacted. Review earlier portions of this text regarding spirit and the struck zone energies to better understand this point. So after reviewing the facts of how time began to work with consciousness, then we began to review the facts of how consciousness reacted to form and how form reacted to the cosmos. So having discovered that the basic spirit life force flows from the light ether to the reflective ether to the chemical ether, we decided that we had to work with the sub-atomic particles just after their transition through the astral plane from the other, higher interdimensional planes, and at the transition point whereby they arrived on the physical plane, and began to express themselves in some form of gravity. The laser was a good example of photons emitting from the astral planes, by the excitation of the orbiting electrons around a particular chemical or gas.

CREATING A TIME MACHINE

The first thing we needed to do was to examine time on a macro-level. The closest celestial representation I could think of was a comet. Imagine the present where we are now to be at the head of the comet. That is the present reality. Then, look out or back from your vantage point within the head towards the tail. While the head is made from dense matter, the tail is this same matter scattered in a wake trailing millions of miles in space behind, the farther back, the less dense, until there is only a few microns of comet occupying a small area of space.

Ahead of the comet lies nothing but empty space, a black void. The comet will travel ahead based on its passed inertia and be subject to other celestial objects and gravities it will encounter. Time is the same way. It leaves a trail or an echo, centers in the present, and relies on probability, calculated from tradition, to determine its future course of action. Both are centered in a black void, the comet in the blackness of space, void, and time in the black void of the infolute.

The next issue is that of light. A comet appears to be a bluish white light in the sky. In the first cause of creation, a white light fills the infolute in creating existence. Time separates the seven layers of existence, and the layers are made up of light. White light contains seven layers of colors, and each color is a level of consciousness in primal creation. So in order to travel in time, we must enter within the primal energy fields or layers of existence. We are ourselves light beings, drawing from the infolute (source of creation) the very energies that animate our atomic structures, our DNA, our cells, our organs and our organism. As we encounter each other, our karma creates a shadow across the path of existence we occupy, and our future shines from our ideals.

> To travel in time you must enter primal energy fields of existence

Within this concept of mind we have to start somewhere. That somewhere is the doorway between the fourth dimension, timelessness, and the physical plane, three-dimensional world. Here our atoms of the third dimension of creation receive their life from the higher light worlds within.

Everything that humans invent on the outer world is a perception of his inner workings. In order to conceive of any inventive notion, the conception comes from a principle of the working order of the human form. So we look around for a device or means that brings fourth dimensional energy onto the physical plane. Fortunately, we don't have to look too hard. If you studied Chapter 32 on lasers, then you are ahead of the game. The laser absorbs energy from the astral plane, and then in a coherent manner organizes photons (which are self-illuminating matter of astral origin) and sends them in perfect alignment through the three-dimensional world.

Basically, with this in mind, we need to accomplish the following for time travel:

A. Start an energy flow from the lower astral plane, which is the fourth dimension. (Don't confuse the higher astral plane with the lower—the higher astral plane contains beings and worlds, whereas the lower is only energy.) A further comparison to this would be that the lower physical plane is composed of atoms, forming matter.
B. Construct a reciprocating receptacle on the physical plane to receive and utilize this portal to timelessness.
C. Create a medium within the receiving receptacle that will allow our physical bodies to adapt to the disconnection of mass, mind and form, traditional values of the three-dimensional world.
D. Develop a means to track this time travel process in both directions, or in simple lay terms, don't get lost in time!

PHYSICAL CHANGES TO PREPARE FOR TIME TRAVEL

The first place we examine is what we already had. In Chapters 33 to 35 we describe in detail how our Pleiadean Systems create scalar waves and scale our consciousness into other time zones, both past, present and future. People using these systems have been quite successful over the years in performing feats of levitation, past life regression, astral time and space travel, changing or controlling future events and healing. But unless you are as realized as Sai Baba, your physical body usually remains where you initially put it when you entered the System. Utilizing the Systems definitely gets you ready for the physical transposition experience. But now we want a physical, "H.G. Wells" experience.

The first step is to change the physical body. That means rerouting orbital patterns of the electrons within our cells and then reversing the direction of the animating energies. This all has to happen within micro-nano seconds, or we will lose the life force, as it will separate or evaporate back to the source of creation in individual pieces, leaving a pile of dust in its wake. Also, during this sub-nano second of time ($1 \times 10^{-8} \times \infty$) we must tune our disconnected being into a previously unified past mass mind, wherein we make a perfect interface or connection. This, of course, is for traveling backwards in time. To go forward into the future, which is probability, we must first accelerate beyond the speed of light, then enter the probability factor of some potentials of where mass mind would be, based on its location in the present. This feat is a little more dangerous than traveling into the past, as in the past there are roads already paved, and in the future there are no roads, or even worlds, for that matter.

Moving forward or backward in time

Semjase always warned me that before trying interstellar travel into other dimensions, learn to travel the past first. Many a Pleiadean has gotten lost, not only in time, but also space. If you have to get lost, do it in time, not in time and space!

The first clue to reversing the physical atomic process lies in human digestion. In order to form cells, the body requires left spin amino acids (see previous chapters on digestion). However, as I pointed out earlier, during the absorption process into body amino acids, the body converts any incoming aminos to right spin aminos by using the already present eight essential aminos and introducing their frequencies via DNA and converting left spin new-comers to right spin, usable ingredients. If you study this process, you will find a pattern called a Mobius. Thus, in our cellular atomic structure, we must change our P orbital, S orbital, D orbital and F orbital patterns, etc., into another atomic model altogether in order to disconnect into time. This is done by introducing the Mobius curve into the quantum signature of the hydrogen atom.

Neils Bohr Orbit

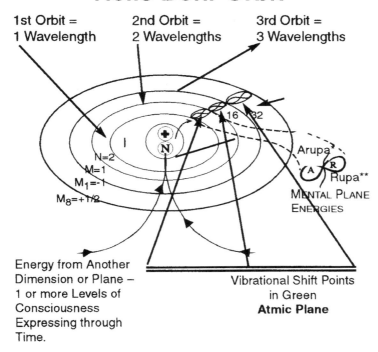

1st Orbit =
1 Wavelength

2nd Orbit =
2 Wavelengths

3rd Orbit =
3 Wavelengths

N=2
M=1
M_1=-1
M_8=+1/2

16   32

Arupa
(A) R
Rupa**
MENTAL PLANE
ENERGIES

Energy from Another
Dimension or Plane –
1 or more Levels of
Consciousness
Expressing through
Time.

Vibrational Shift Points
in Green
Atmic Plane

*Rupa is spontaneous thought and action.
**Arupa is logic and ordered thought.

figure 39-1

In figure 39-1 we are observing the quantum (energy) frequency shells around a theoretical atom. The heavier the element, the more shells or orbital rings of electrons will be found around the nucleus. If we subject a magnetic field to our atom, the electron clouds or patterns will change shape and frequency. These shapes and frequencies are called orbital patterns. In normal (orthodox) physics these patterns then form matter in the three-dimensional world.

If subjected to non- standard fields, i.e. Mobius, they form antimatter! If we oscillate atoms in a field between normal magnetic and Mobius, we obtain a momentary atomic on atomic movement that can be directed into another time altogether. This is done with scalar waves as a third ingredient.

Let's look at this a step at a time.

QUANTUM RELATIONSHIPS AND TIME TRAVEL

In the normal mode, the quantum numbers in figure 39-1 are mathematically related as particle wave functions. The principal number "N" corresponds to Bohr's single number, and can assume values $_{1, 2, 3}$, etc. The letter "I" is used to designate the azimuthal quantum number, and M_1 represents the magnetic quantum number. All three quantum numbers are mathematically related to one another.

The numbers in relationship to the letters are shown here at their lowest energy state. If we raised the energy within our atom, the numbers will increase.

Through the science of spectroscopic research we introduced a fourth quantum number, M_8. Called the spin quantum number, M_8 defines clockwise electron spin as $M_8 = +^1/2$, and counterclockwise spin as $M_8 = -^1/2$. Sometimes this is also designated as up ($\neq$) or down ($\emptyset$).

There are then a total of four quantum numbers N, I, M_1, and M_8. One of each together form a set which uniquely specifies the quantum state of an electron in an atom.

If we were to calculate the quantum numbers for our hydrogen atom (remember, the hydrogen atom moves consciousness in and out of the three-dimensional world), we would derive two quantum sets: $N = 1, I = 0, M_1 = 0, M_8 = + 1/2$; and $N = 1, I = 0, M_1 = 0, M_8 = - 1/2$.

As you can see, M_8 is showing a possible clockwise-counterclockwise potential. This is the first clue towards introducing a scalar-modulated, magnetic Mobius field into our equation. Quantum math leads us from the nucleus of the atom out, and Pleiadean science leads us from the outer energy levels towards the nucleus of the atom, inverting the field as it approaches the atomic core.

Now we have determined that the electrons move in "particle waves" around the nucleus, reversing direction. **The next thing we need to do is determine the shape of these waves, especially if we are to change orbital patterns.**

These waves are different orbital patterns. The waves within these patterns form different shapes with different densities. Also, as you move between the different shells, N = 2, M = 1, etc., the shape of the orbit differs. In other words, the atom has no resemblance to a solar system, as many people think, with the proton/neutrons as the central sun and the electrons symmetrically orbiting like good boys and girls. Look at figure 39-2 and you will see the shape of atoms. Within these shapes are sub shapes and these sub shapes are made of electron wave clouds in a variety of orbital (cloud) patterns.

Shown on the next page are a couple of sub shapes, consisting of P orbital and D orbital patterns. It is these shapes that compose the final atomic profile of an atom.

Although the P orbital is dumbbell shaped, it can be oriented in different directions. This is determined by the type of field the atom is subjected to. As small as the difference may be, these still can be determined spectroscopically. In quantum math the figure y or y^2 is used to represent the exact orientation or location of the densest part of the cloud or shell.

The P orbital would be located farther out from the nucleus. If we were to draw the next orbit, it then would be in the N = 4 level, (not shown in figure 39-1). It would begin to resemble, if drawn in three dimensions, the relationship, on a micro level, of our eight parallel universes as discussed earlier in the book. Herein lies the well-kept secret of time travel, subjugation of elements to "special" fields, without causing transmutation, in this case it would appear as destruction, within the element itself. Remember, we only want to

Secret of time travel: subjugate elements to special fields

change the location in time of an element, or in the core of the human body, several elements, **not the composition.** But, we have to deal with the heartbeat of the atomic structure we are attempting to transpose, and this is a delicate process.

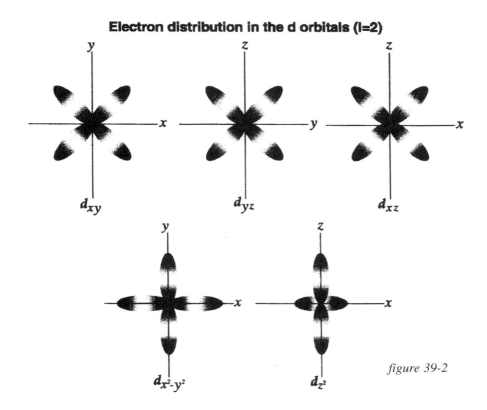

Electron distribution in the d orbitals (l=2)

d_{xy} d_{yz} d_{xz}

$d_{x^2-y^2}$ d_{z^2}

figure 39-2

SCALAR WAVES APPLIED TO A MOBIUS FIELD

Enter the Mobius field and the scalar wave. The Mobius field is our atom twister, and the scalar wave is our time locator. The two are all we need! The rest is easy. Look at the following diagram of a Mobius pattern (figure 39-3).

Originally conceived by a German mathematician, August F. Mobius, at the turn of the century, the Mobius pattern is one more mathematical theorem, that will eventually find its way into the physicist's laboratory, as all good theorems do. It's not uncommon for ideas such as this to sit on the shelves of science for many decades before someone finds a practical application in the three-dimensional world.

If we were to apply a magnetic field into the quantum field levels of the electrons that encircle an atom, in a Mobius pattern, then we would change the characteristics of the matter involved, but not the matter itself. The best way to describe the first step is that we selected a shirt to wear. But, rather than wear the shirt in a normal manner, we decided to turn the shirt inside out. The shirt is still a shirt, and if it had a pattern, now when worn, the pattern would appear backward to another observer. The same is true with time. Time still exists, but now it is traveling backwards. Just how far backward is determined by exactly where in

381

the Mobius field we injected our second component, the scalar wave. Let us look at our scalar wave a little more closely.

figure 39-3

Mobius Pattern

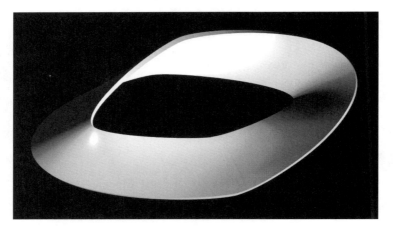

THE SCALAR WAVE, A CLOSER LOOK

Remember, as we discussed earlier, a scalar wave is in itself timeless but is a vehicle for time. Secondly, it becomes infinite in the amount of time it can contain. Because it is also of mind (remember, all reality is made of linked thoughts of mind), it can be controlled by mind. It originates in present mind and can be directed in past, present or future directions. However, if we direct it towards the future, we need an additional ingredient, acceleration, so that matter being transposed can enter upon multiples of the fourth dimension. Because the scalar wave is composed of energy, including that of the mind, it has mass, and will respond to the principles of acceleration, or $E = mc^2$.

A scalar wave is timeless but is a vehicle for time!

The scalar wave can be viewed as a reflection in the mirror (past), and the object being reflected, the present, and where the object could be reflected from, the future.

The scalar wave shown is of the simplest nature. When combined with, for example, a strong neutron source modulated in a Mobius electron field, it becomes a death ray as described by Nikola Tesla. Each one of the time zones, T_1 (right arrow) T_4, etc., represent a controlling factor for time travel. If the time gradient is directed into the fourth dimension momentarily and then back out to the present, we now have created a ray that will disassemble matter in the present. This is often referred to as a death ray.

In the death ray mode, the ray would always emerge after T_2 and before T_3. T_4 would never exist. Because of obvious reasons, I can't release more information on this subject. Our applications of scalar waves are for peaceful research and not destruction.

Now, to get a visual idea, imagine the Mobius field being created with the physical atomic structure of the object to be moved in time. As the Mobius field reaches its peak intensity, the electron clouds (orbital patterns) are then subjected to the time orientation by the scalar wave component as it is injected within the electrons, protons, neutrons, etc., of the structure. Then the structure is collapsed on a molecular level and moved into the fourth dimension window. From the window, it exits into the time reality thus programmed. If you review Chapter 35, you will get a visual picture of the way the carbon atom behaves during this process.

Anatomy of a Scalar Wave

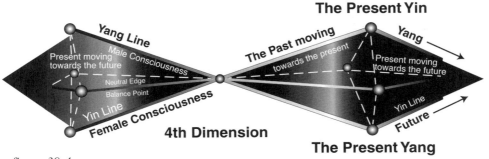

figure 39-4

Scalar Wave Time Zones

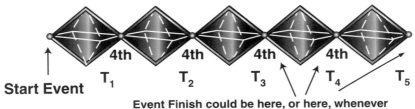

figure 39-5

Event Finish could be here, or here, whenever
the events of the programmed mind depict.

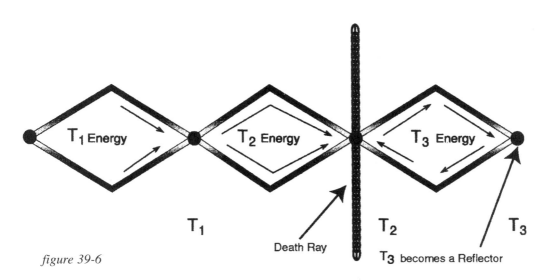

figure 39-6

TECHNOLOGY BEGINS A STEP INTO TIME

Back in the late 1960's and early 1970's, I had the honor of visiting over three thousand companies. My reason for so many visits was my expertise in the field of advanced instrumentation and measurement. Any company that manufactures technology has a research and development (R & D) department, and so I would find myself in the R & D departments of companies such as JPL, TRW, IBM, Burroughs, Hewlett-Packard, Hughes Aircraft, Bell Telephone - Murray Hill, EG & G, the Atomic Energy Commission, every Army, Navy and Air Force research facility you can name and many other research facilities that I still won't name. Even back then, there was a unified fascination for time travel and electromagnetic research projects.

One of the IBM groups was doing some interesting work at the Thomas J. Watson Research Center in collaboration with the University of California at Berkeley. Under the aegis of a sensing device, IBM researchers Mark B. Ketchen and Richard F. Voss developed a device called the Super Conduction Quantum Interface Device (SQUIDS) that could measure changes in a magnetic field as small as one millionth of a millionth of the field of the earth when these changes occurred at frequencies higher than 10 kilohertz. Electrogravity devices operated in a region that would be sensitive to SQUID's technology.

Key companies involved... and SQUIDS

This technology takes advantage of the fact that metals lose all electrical resistance in temperatures below absolute zero (-273°C).

SQUID technology has been admittedly used in earthquake prediction, gravity wave detection, searches for quarks and studies of magnetic materials.

Combined with the science of tunnel diodes (diodes that act like a receptor in the brain, that can turn on and off in a billionth of a second), SQUIDs are fabricated into what is called a "Josephson tunnel junction." In this form they can trigger feedback circuits and oscillators almost as fast as is observed in a Wilson cloud chamber during particle bombardment, wherein particles are observed originating from the astral plane. This sudden switching is necessary, not only to open the gateway into other dimensions, but also to maintain control of events occurring on the threshold of the speed of light.

When I was a young scientist, switching speed was critical in circuitry that bordered the twilight zone. A common factor to gauge switching speed is called "rise time," often

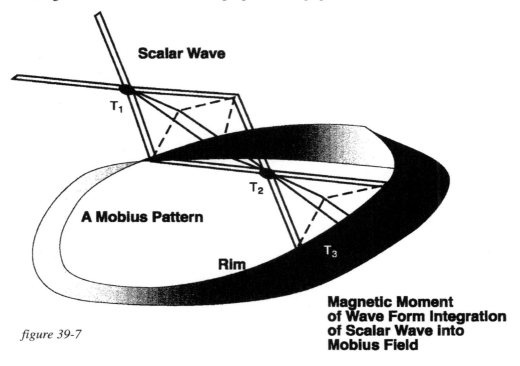

figure 39-7

Scalar Wave

T_1

A Mobius Pattern

T_2

Rim

T_3

Magnetic Moment of Wave Form Integration of Scalar Wave into Mobius Field

384

observed on high-speed oscilloscopes or sampling oscilloscopes. Rise time determines how fast something electronically switches and is the credibility factor that gauges a system's performance. Below are a few drawings enumerating what we saw (figure 39-8).

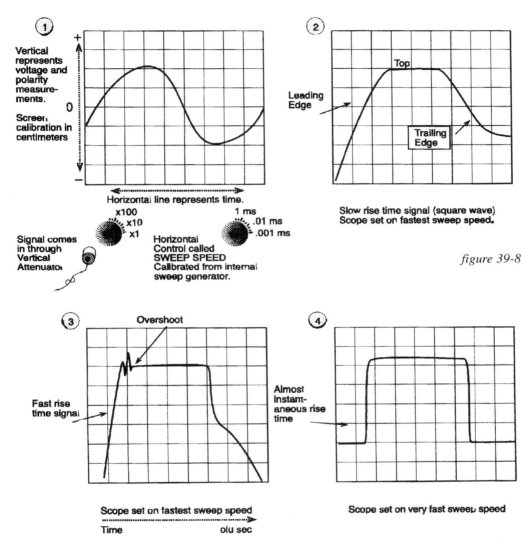

figure 39-8

Above are shown signals with progressively faster rise times. Overshoot, shown on screen number three, is usually undesirable, indicating electronic ringing or spurious oscillation within the circuitry. The faster electronic technology goes, the greater becomes the problem of impedance mismatch or circuitry problems. When switching at high speeds, the physical shape and size of a component becomes extremely critical. Remember, throughout this entire book shape energy has been a keynote factor.

Normal oscilloscope technology could not show a rise time greater than the speed of light, but if it could, the next screen would look like figure 39-9.

The reason I am now talking about rise time is that it will be used throughout the remainder of this book. Pleiadean technology deals with negative rise times, or with fourth-dimensional parameters (see figure 39-10.)

THEORETICAL WAVE

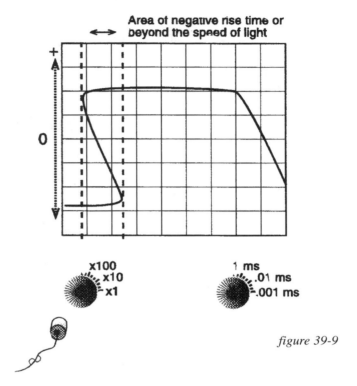

Area of negative rise time or
beyond the speed of light

figure 39-9

Rare earth metal alloys are also used in these advanced technical applications. In the Josephson tunnel junction, niobium is fabricated into metallic strips as small as eight nanometers, or billionths of a meter wide. The process to produce these strips is called "high-resolution electron beam lithography."

The SQUIDs consist of two Josephson elements connected together in a thin-film ring of superconducting metal. Each Josephson element has two superconducting electrodes that are separated by a "weak link"— either a very thin layer of insulator that is placed sandwich-like between the electrodes (to form a tunnel junction), or an ultra-small super-conduction stripe connected between coplanar electrodes (to form a nano bridge).

These weak links give rise to so-called Josephson coupling affects by allowing super-currents of electron pairs to "tunnel" or pass from one electrode to the other, up to some maximum supercurrent.

In a complete measurement system an input coil is used to extend the versatility of the SQUID for measurement of quantities such as voltage and current as well as to optimize magnetic-field measurements. Overall system performance, or sensitivity, thus depends on the input circuitry as well as the SQUID. Achievement of near-ultimate low noise levels in SQUIDS consequently increases the importance of optimizing the input circuit for the purpose of improving overall system measurement sensitivity.

Noise is the ultimate limit to the sensitivity of a SQUID sensing device. It can result, for example, from random motion of electrical charge produced by thermal agitation at elevated temperatures. But even at absolute zero, noise still exists as so-called zeropoint fluctuations, a manifestation of the uncertainty principle of quantum mechanics. Indeed, the IBM researchers showed that the noise in the niobium nanobridge SQUID is only somewhat greater than the limit set by fundamental physical theory (see figure 39-11).

Noise still exists even at absolute zero

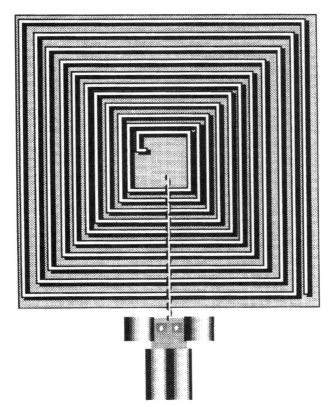

figure 39-10

FURTHER APPLICATIONS OF TIME TRAVEL TECHNOLOGY — EARTHQUAKE DETECTION

One other piece of equipment design given to us by Semjase was an earthquake detector. If you remember back in Chapters 26 through 28, we showed how humanity in conjunction with planetary alignment creates earthquakes. Earthquakes can be registered before they begin at the akashic record level. Since quartz has been shown to become heavier with age, in or out of the ground, it begins to swell before an earthquake. Most people are becoming aware that the Quartz Kingdom is the storehouse of the akashic records. As far back as the Atlantean times, quartz was accessed remotely for a variety of purposes, including record keeping and measurement functions. Unfortunately, at the present time the human race is mining quartz for its orthodox (semiconductor) and occult (meditation – psychic) functions. So, while the Atlanteans used quartz undisturbed in the ground, we physically have it in our possession, and so we should use it as constructively and conservatively as we can. One good application with present technology is earthquake prediction. Earthquake prediction can save the lives of many innocent families who fall victim to the errant parts of humanity that create earthquakes in the first place!

CONSTRUCTING AN EARTHQUAKE WARNING DEVICE

The first thing we need to understand is a Wheatstone bridge. Used for years in the field of metrology (the science of electrical measurement and calibration), the Wheatstone bridge measures minute electrical changes across its electronic arms with great accuracy and sensitivity. Wheatstone bridges are used to measure temperature variation on Mars probes and lunar landers, to control camera focusing on spy satellites and adjust the color on your TV set. They are found in automotive, aircraft and a myriad of different applications where critical measurements are required.

Once a differential is sensed, then it is amplified, compared to a reference, and as in our application, displayed on a voltmeter or strip chart recorder.

Below is a schematic drawing of a Wheatstone bridge. (figure 39-11)

Wheatstone Bridge Circuit

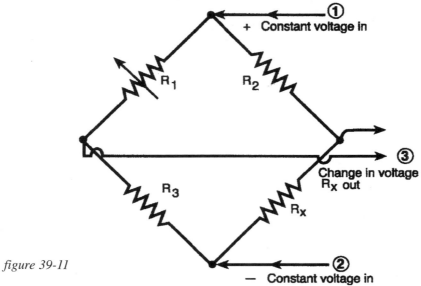

figure 39-11

Resistors, usually very stable over varied temperature changes, wirewound, R_1, R_2, balance the top of the bridge. Resistor R_3 is of the same value as R_1 and R_2, but resistor R_x is the unknown, subject to change. R_x could be a thermistor (temperature sensitive element used to detect metallic stress), or any element that could vary under changing conditions. The bridge receives electricity from points $_1$ and $_2$, from a highly regulated constant current and voltage power supply. Resistor R_1 is adjusted to balance R_x against R_3 and R_2.

A zero voltage and current is measured at point $_3$. This is called balancing the bridge. Once balanced, any change occurring at R_x will be observed at point $_3$. This change is then calibrated and becomes our intelligence information. For our application, we use a piece of quartz with two electrodes attached to each end for R_x and two SQUIDs for R_2 and R_3. The output at point $_3$ is amplified through a small low-noise amplifier and sent to a circuit that will interface it to a small voltmeter or strip chart recorder.

The drawing below is a simple depiction of the circuit (figure 39-12).

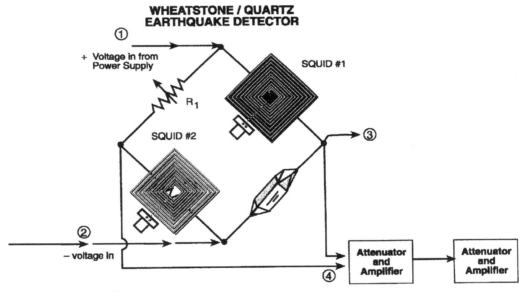

figure 39-12

In this application, electricity is delivered at points $_1$ and $_2$. Then, the voltage and current are balanced at points $_3$ and $_4$ to zero output. This is done by balancing both SQUIDs to zero against each other and R_1 against the quartz.

The quartz should be physically located in a small chamber large enough to hold a small specimen of mineral, taken from the region that is of seismic concern. The reason for this is covered in earlier chapters under the study of the Pleiadean Mega Orb. The completed unit could look like the following drawing (see figure 39-14).

So, now you can begin some practical applications to our Quantum Pleiadean Technologies.

EARTHQUAKE DETECTOR

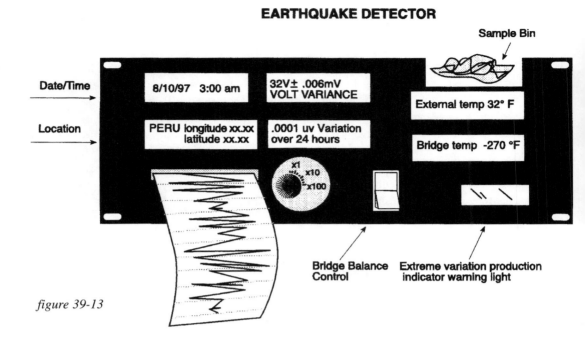

figure 39-13

T-700 Time Travel Transposer

Now let us look directly at the heart of a time machine.

Constructing a Working Time Machine
Note: in the following description, only the main operating systems are described.

In order to create a scalar wave and Mobius field, and merge them together, we need to combine the geometry of form and fields of electricity into one device. The outer structure is going to be octahedral in shape, surrounded at its diameter with two counter-rotating circular rings.

We begin with an octahedron that has a ten-foot base length. The basic octahedron has a total of eight sides. Triangular capacitor banks using mylar insulation are placed on each of the eight sides. The top capacitors have openings in them so that access can be granted to the inside of the octahedral structure.

Each capacitor has seven mylar plates capable of handling several million electron volts (mev). (See figure 39-15.) Mylar is a voltage amplifying dielectric. The basic octahedral is constructed of non-metallic carbon fiber. Because of the high intensity fields involved, most of the structure is non-metallic, high-dielectric material.

Around the outside center of the main structure are placed two large Whimhurst-type electrostatic rotors. One rotates clockwise, the other counter clockwise, generating through their counter-rotating action, a high voltage field that is distributed through the seven layers of the eight outer capacitors. In addition to generating a field, the rotors also act as a gyroscope to stabilize the vehicle when it is in motion.

Located along the inside edge of the two rotors are proximity switches. These switches move the positive and negative charges from the rings to the 56 plates located on the eight

390

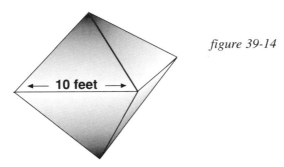

figure 39-14

10 feet

**Entry way openings in
Topside Capacitors**

**7 or more layers
of mylar**

Capacitor

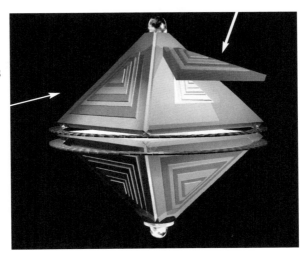

figure 39-15

capacitors (see figures 39-16 and 39-17). These charges arrive as electron clouds of controlled orbital character and produce the Mobius field across the time machine. The photodiodes (see figure 39-18) that are used with the proximity switches are controlled by an onboard computer that can adjust the rise time, current, voltage and duration of the signal that is sent to the 56 various locations of the capacitor plates (see figures 39-18 and 39-19). The plates are designated numbers and locations by the computer. As the machine gains momentum, the proximity switches send fast rise signals that have higher and higher current/voltage perimeters.

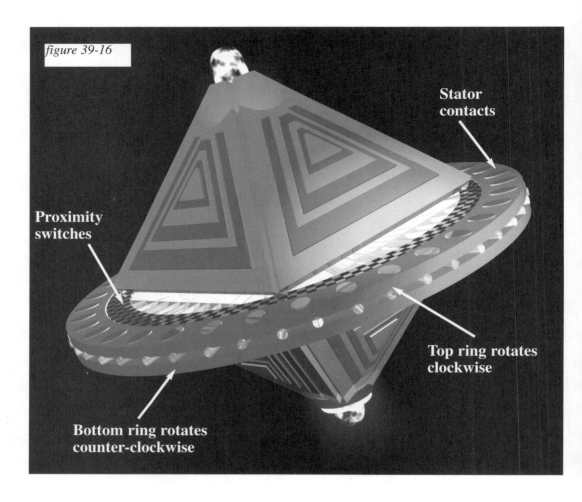

figure 39-16

Stator contacts

Proximity switches

Top ring rotates clockwise

Bottom ring rotates counter-clockwise

HV
Generator

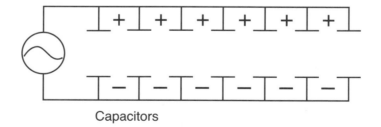

Capacitors

figure 39-17

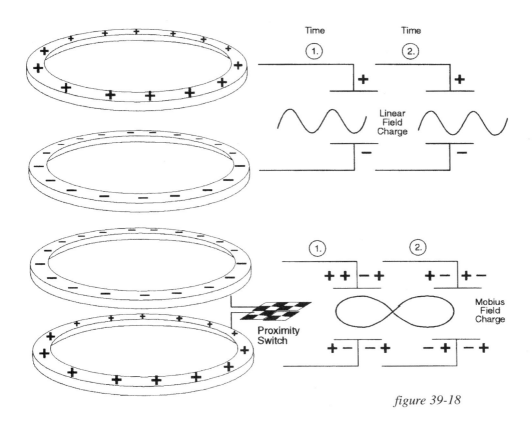

Time 1.) Time 2.)

Linear Field Charge

Proximity Switch

Mobius Field Charge

figure 39-18

This modulates electron clouds first in order to create a singular capacitive effect over the entire time machine (T-700 Time Travel Transposer). The effect of this is to put equal charges in a linear fashion upon the T-700 and its occupants. This would appear as a linear field. Then, once the field is established, the proximity switched alternating Mobius field gradually takes over. This action could be compared to the firing order for spark plugs on an automobile. Here the plates are the spark plugs and the proximity switches represent the distributor.

Now, let's look at the next section (see figure 39-19).

Starting at the top of the structure is a long, hollow column. It contains the next three components that further amplify the Mobius field and mix it with the scalar wave. The scalar wave itself is created by the geometry of the structure and the action of the vertical column containing a multifrequency laser, a linear accelerator and an electromagnetic field cancelling column.

Several things begin to happen simultaneously. As the Whimhurst begins building the Mobius field around the T-700, a separately synchronized Klystron oscillator begins to accelerate a field of particles from the anodes located at the top and bottom of the cancel column. The particles then are drawn in a synchronous (the Klystrons are timed with the

Whimhurst field and the pulsed multi-mode laser) manner down to the also oscillating cathode, located at the center of the cancel column. Located along the outer walls of the cancel column are caduceus-wound coils, similar to the ones located around the transmitter tubes on the X-1 Healing Machine. Note in the following drawings, the optical escape radiation vents (see figure 39-21).

Signal Path Showing Mobius Field
Application to Octahedral Core

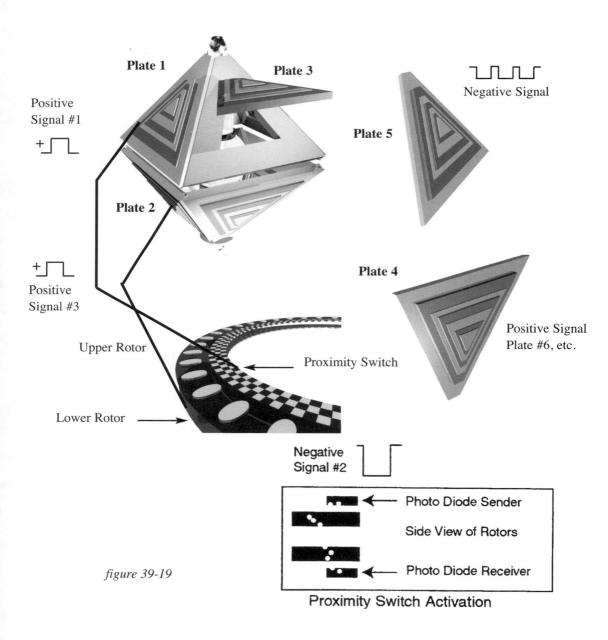

figure 39-19

CANCEL COLUMN

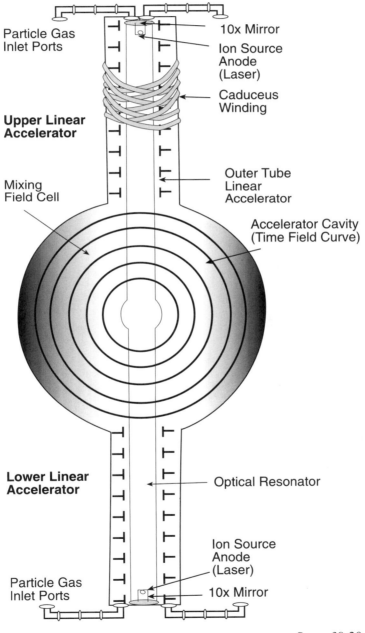

Particle Gas
Inlet Ports

10x Mirror

Ion Source
Anode
(Laser)

Caduceus
Winding

**Upper Linear
Accelerator**

Outer Tube
Linear
Accelerator

Mixing
Field Cell

Accelerator Cavity
(Time Field Curve)

**Lower Linear
Accelerator**

Optical Resonator

Ion Source
Anode
(Laser)

Particle Gas
Inlet Ports

10x Mirror

figure 39-20

Cancel Column Core

Located in Exact Center of T-700 Time Travel Transposer

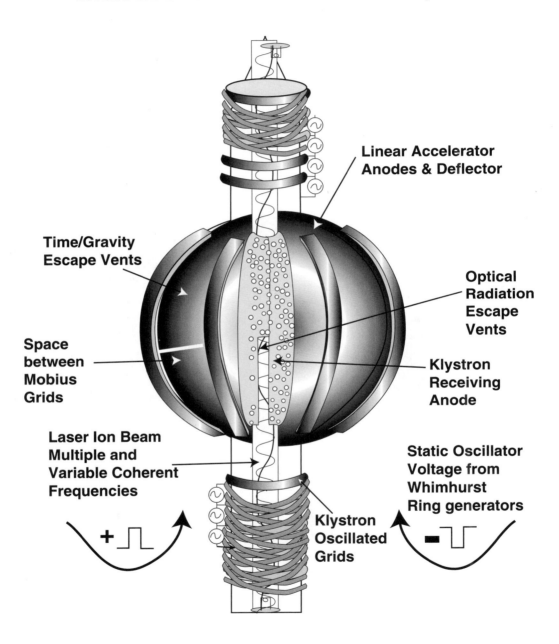

figure 39-21

Cancel Column Core

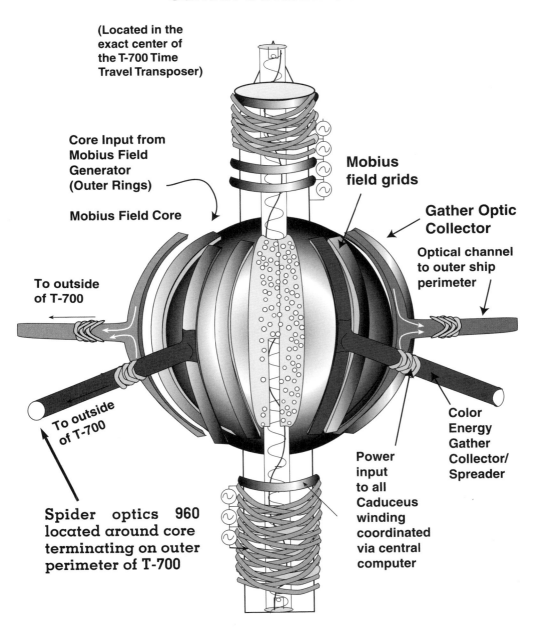

(Located in the exact center of the T-700 Time Travel Transposer)

Core Input from Mobius Field Generator (Outer Rings)

Mobius Field Core

Mobius field grids

Gather Optic Collector

Optical channel to outer ship perimeter

To outside of T-700

To outside of T-700

Color Energy Gather Collector/ Spreader

Power input to all Caduceus winding coordinated via central computer

Spider optics 960 located around core terminating on outer perimeter of T-700

figure 39-22

These are located within the cancel column's Klystron receiving anode, allowing the fourth dimensional collapsing laser sequences to escape from the cancel column core and into the spider optical system located between the Whimhurst charging discs. Looking at the cancel column core drawing (see figure 39-21) you will also notice the time/gravity escape vents. These are created by the spacing of the Mobius field grids.

It is here that the time field interacts with the laser field and linear accelerated particles, creating electro-gravity waves that allow the T-700 to lift above ground level during operation. Stabilized by the gyroscopic action of the rotating Whimhurst discs, the T-700 becomes a moveable craft. Although moveable, the T-700 is by no means a spacecraft. It is not pressurized, carries limited reserves of oxygen, and contains only minimal control parameters. Its lift system is electro-gravity, not anti-gravity, the difference is explained in the following chapter, and therefore could not be considered a source of transportation. The reason that the T-700 can fly in the first place is so that it can compensate for terrestrial changes over long geological time periods.

Shown on the previous page are the spider optics (see figure 39-22). Consisting of 960 pathways, this system delivers the core field potentials to the outer perimeter of the T-700, allowing it to become engulfed in a perfect lotus field of electro-gravity/time field waves.

In case you haven't noticed, the overall geometry of the T-700 is beginning to resemble the atomic structure of an atom. This is because we are duplicating on a macro level the inner (micro) workings of a semi-sophisticated atomic structure. Nature has always had a way of exposing her secrets within her beautiful forms. The structures of the rose, pine cone or snail give many hints of the operational mode, wherein spirit inter-penetrates the mammalian form of self-contained creatures.

The principals of spider optical systems in Pleiadean craft are quite similar. They distribute the electro/optical/time field/gravity/fields from their place of creation, usually somewhere within the confines of the craft, to the outside where expression (utilization) takes place (see figure 39-20). When these energies are created initially, within their central confines, their potency and radiation levels are quite lethal, such as the core of the sun. However, through the magic of spider optics, this lethal critical mass is delicately interwoven into the three-dimensional world with minimal exposure danger to people or objects that are nearby. However, I recommend that a distance of several hundred feet be maintained between observers of a T-700 Time Travel Transposer and any relative observers.

This is necessary because the electro-gravity waves are created and distributed slightly ahead of the time field waves. Any aluminum or other amphoteric objects are subjected to heating within a close perimeter. Watches, for example, often have aluminum parts and should positively not be worn within or near an active T-700.

The spider optical tubes also have smaller caduceus windings around them that are completely synchronized to the main cancel column. When the main cancel column field is energized, the fields around the spider optical systems are slightly delayed. This delay helps shape the arms of the the lotus field that is exhibited within and around the T-700 as it enters and exits its transporting modes.

Spider Optical Grid System

T-700 top view showing Spider Optics Locations

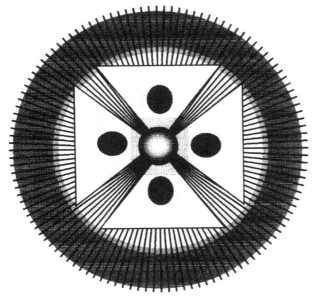

There are 960 different virtual time/gravity patterns exiting from the Cancel Column core to the outside perimeter of the T-700.

figure 39-23

The final and critical component left is the central column laser system. Its primary purpose is to behave like a normal laser and then reverse its field back upon itself. To accomplish this we use equally reflective mirror systems in the optical cavity that contain the coherent transmissions within the cancel column (see figure 39-24). The gases that we extract coherent light emissions from vary, much as they do in a multiple mode, multiple color dye laser. The laser power output is pulsed with a low duty cycle (duty cycle is the amount of time the laser is switched on and off during initial lasing stages) that still allows the peak power potential to reach several megawatts. When the lasing action reaches peak power, heavy hydrogen gases are allowed into the laser cavity, forcing the cavity out of ionization and into the acceleration of the highly charged protons (that were the core of the light emitting atoms), toward the doorway just opened by lasing action within the fourth dimension. In short, we created a lasing action with enough inertia to reverse upon itself. Thus, in concert with the linear accelerator, located directly outside of, and in tandem with, the laser, we have created a time wave field that is thus utilized precisely at the moment the T-700 transposes itself into another period in time.

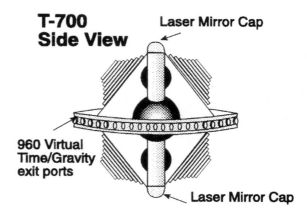

figure 39-24

T-700 BASIC THEORY OF OPERATION

The first part of the vehicle is the overall octahedral shape of the upper and lower sections. As pointed out in earlier chapters, the normal and inverted positions tend to create a scalar or mixed yin and yang field pattern. In the human body, management of these chi forces among disciplined individuals allows them to demonstrate great feats of strength, very quick speed, levitation and complete management of circulation, breath and pulse rate.

When we add the 56 triangular capacitor plate sections over the normal and inverted hull super-structure, we are creating a large Mobius field structure that is capable of affecting the orbital patterns of the atoms contained within its confines, as well as affecting those in the nearby vicinity. In addition, a variable Bloch Wall effect is also created (see Chapter 40).

As mentioned earlier, a very advanced Whimhurst design is used to provide a high-current, high-voltage DC source not only for the capacitors, but also for the caduceus-wound coils. Locating it amidship also lends gyroscopic stability under flight conditions.

If you refer back to the drawings, you will see that the caduceus coils are located over the optics (960 sections). In comparing a normal coil to a caduceus, the normal coil is series wound, which produces a linear field. The resonant frequency of a normal coil is determined by the size of the wire, the number of windings and the core composition.

If I take a normal coil "A" that has current moving through it and place another coil "B" nearby, the voltage and current of coil "A" will transform to the nearby coil "B." This action is called a transformer.

In the T-700 we use a caduceus coil. A caduceus coil is wound with each winding crossing its electrically opposite winding. This causes its field to cancel itself and creates a Bloch Wall effect that transfers energy into a null zone that it creates within its center. Therefore, a single caduceus coil is also a transformer.

Caduceus coils are wound on both vertical and torroidal forms. In addition, a caduceus field is always at infinite resonance, or it resonates at all frequencies.

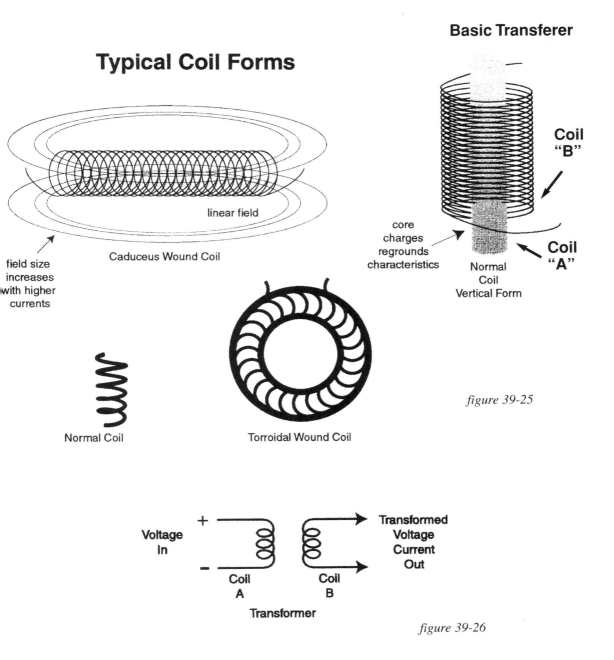

Typical Coil Forms

Basic Transferer

linear field

Caduceus Wound Coil

field size
increases
with higher
currents

Coil
"B"

core
charges
regrounds
characteristics

Normal
Coil
Vertical Form

Coil
"A"

figure 39-25

Normal Coil

Torroidal Wound Coil

Voltage
In

+

−

Coil
A

Coil
B

Transformed
Voltage
Current
Out

Transformer

figure 39-26

BEGINNING THE TIME SEQUENCE

Initially as the rotors come up to speed, the proximity switches, which are an integral part of the rotor, begin directing current in a pre-programmed manner onto the horizontal and vertical capacitor plates. The field is assembled in a Mobius fashion as **each capacitor charges and discharges at greater speeds.** This resulting field, as it gains momentum, begins to reshape the orbital patterns of all the occupants within the T-700, as well as the T-700 itself.

401

Typical Coil Forms (Continued)

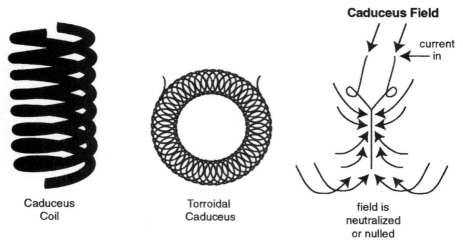

Caduceus
Coil

Torroidal
Caduceus

Caduceus Field

current
in

field is
neutralized
or nulled

figure 39-27

As the capacitor discharge current begins to reach a critical mass, it is phase directed down upon the linear accelerator plates located within the cancel column core. Solid state Klystron oscillators send signals to the accelerator rings on the column and direct the particle beam from both the top of the column and the bottom towards the center. It is as though you have two independent accelerators, one on top, one on the bottom, directing their particles at the same target, the center of the cancel column. Lighter or heavier particles are chosen to occupy the accelerator depending on the mission of the T-700. (See previous chapter on relativity discussions.) The capacitor section, due to its unique layout, creates electro-gravity waves in addition to its Mobius field characteristics. The linear accelerators are in concert (their charges being modulated from the capacitor discharge section), creating a Bloch Wall (defined in next chapter), along the vertical axis of the T-700. This field is now centered on the Klystron receiving anode.

Once the voltages upon the T-700 begin to reach peak potential, the contained variable ion laser, depending upon which gases are used within its optical cavity (also remember light is seven colors, seven levels of consciousness), is activated and the optical resonator begins to approach the appropriate lasing frequency.

As the laser is being brought up for its final discharge, the Whimhurst rotors are reaching peak RPMs (revolutions per minute). The 56 capacitor plates, 28 on top and 28 on the bottom, each have their own storage characteristics. The proximity switches are sending precise destination information data to each plate individually, and for every positive plate activated, a negative plate also is activated simultaneously.

Considering that millions of volts are being transferred at high rates of speed, literally megafarads of energy are being released, creating a high electrostatic field around the T-700. (A farad is the measurement of electrical capacity that a capacitor can store. Most capacitors are measured in microfarads: μfd.)

With the Mobius field now complete, the electro-gravity waves are centered along the vertical axis, and the scalar wave geometry of the entire machine is in complete focus. We are ready for the final phase.

402

All of the current within the entire ship is now released simultaneously into the optical resonator. When the laser fires, its entire energy is refocused into the caduceus coils located along the axis of the cancel column and the spider optical section. Basically, the lasing action is reversed into the canceling column mode, causing the vehicle to settle into its new time/frequency and time domain.

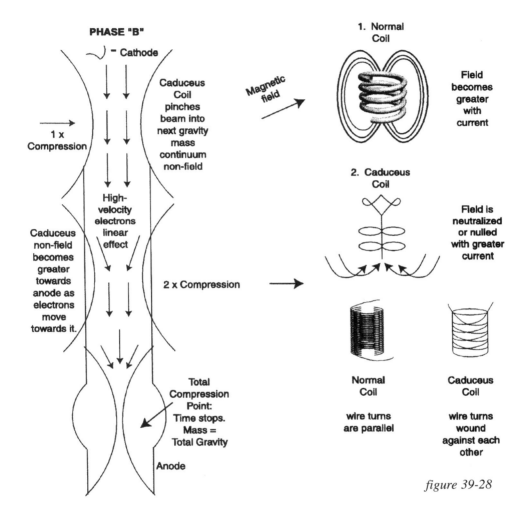

figure 39-28

So, as a result, you have made a time transposition. In effect, we have located a virtual time field in another dimension and created a matching virtual field with the T-700. The marriage of the two field creates the transposition. (See figure 39-29.)

Although the central field is along a vertical axis, the spider optics provide a balanced horizontal field. In addition, they relieve some of the quantum pressures that are experienced within the central core.

This safety valve balancing concept is quite prevalent in many of the Pleiadean transport vehicles, such as personal transports (cars), undersea craft, or deep space craft. More advanced races of beings, such as the Lyrians or Andromedans, use other methods, as their

**We do
not yet
assemble
in the 4th
dimension**

basic propulsion systems use less critical mass technologies and more resonant principles. Unfortunately, we do not possess yet the technologies for fourth dimensional assembly and construction practices. The Pleiadians are just beginning to approach these techniques as their wisdom in holographic concepts reaches new horizons. Our terrestrial assembly skills are just now reaching "0" gravity abilities, and until we build more space stations with "0" gravity factory manufacturing capabilities, we will remain somewhat stagnant.

T-700
The Final Moment as Core Reaches Time Travel

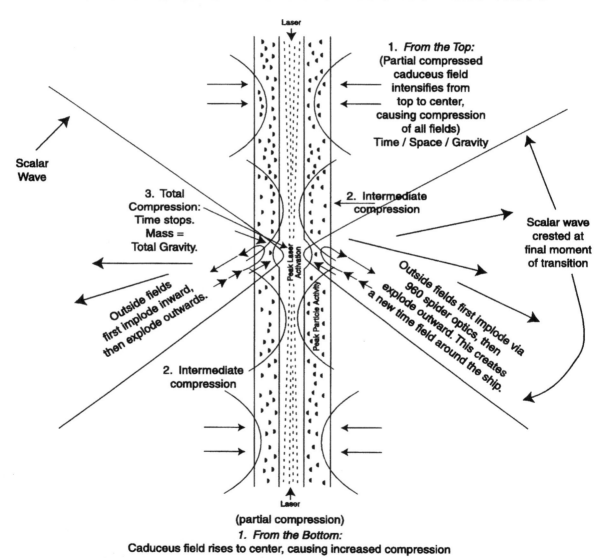

figure 39-29

Scalar Wave at Total Compression Time Zone 1 (T1)

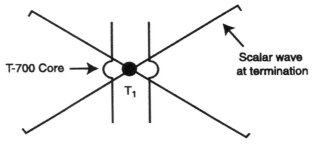

T-700 Core →

Scalar wave
at termination

T₁

figure 39-30

At total compression, point 3, a perfect scalar
wave has been created in the center of the
ship. The difference between this one and the
one created by an Irradiator is that you are IN
this one!

T-700 SCALAR/STELLAR ANALOGY

① 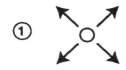 Star runs out of hydrogen fuel
and begins to cool off.

figure 39-31

② The star, now cool, becomes
smaller and denser.

③ 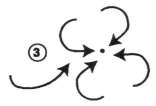 Now the very small star attracts
all gravity and light to itself.
Space becomes negatively curved.

④ Time also shifts around star
area, now called a space-time
singularity.

⑤ The compressed warped space captures/alters light, and singular time
creates a wormhole as matter enters the 4th dimension. The portal
itself is called a space-time singularity. The wormhole is formed as
matter evaporates into the 4th dimension. Time is singular in the 4th
dimension (no tradition).

405

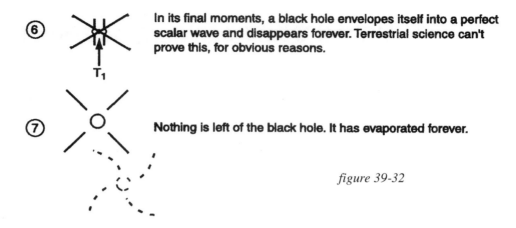

6 — In its final moments, a black hole envelopes itself into a perfect scalar wave and disappears forever. Terrestrial science can't prove this, for obvious reasons.

T_1

7 — Nothing is left of the black hole. It has evaporated forever.

figure 39-32

In the T-700 this phenomenon occurs exactly at the anode position of the cancel column, which is positioned at the exact center of the T-700, when the unit reaches critical mass and this mass is cancelled in its final moment by the caduceus coil. The result is a perfect scalar wave in which the T-700 is entirely enveloped.

T-700 Basic Details

Many people often ask me what is the raw power source for such a machine (see figure 39-33). You need power to drive the Whimhurst rotors, power for the Klystron oscillators, major power for the laser system, plus the onboard computer and cabin requirements.

T-700 Top View
(partial of interior)

figure 39-33

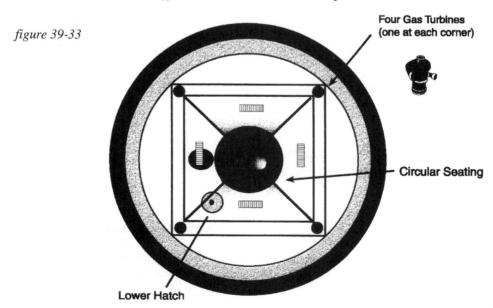

Four Gas Turbines
(one at each corner)

Circular Seating

Lower Hatch

Thanks to the refinements of today's micro-turbine/electric generators, there are a growing number of off-the-shelf generators becoming available. Companies such as Allied Signal are manufacturing small, lightweight turbines that are so compact that they have only one moving part, the turbine shaft, and furthermore, the generator section becomes the starter motor, thereby further decreasing weight vs. size. These turbines are inexpensive and use cheap fuels for their operation. Their high-velocity exhaust systems make them perfect candidates for air pressure that can be utilized to turn the rotors on the Whimhurst section of the T-700. The drawing on the next page shows some of the locations of the auxiliary equipment.

In addition to electricity for the electronic drive section, the turbines also provide current for the electro-hydraulic system that opens the access door and retracts the landing and support legs. The four support legs can be each individually adjusted to compensate for normal terrain conditions.

The outside of the T-700 has a strong, lightweight carbon fiber shell that serves as the outer skin. Parts of this skin are metalicized (extreme upper and lower portions). (See figure 39-36.)

T-700 Side View

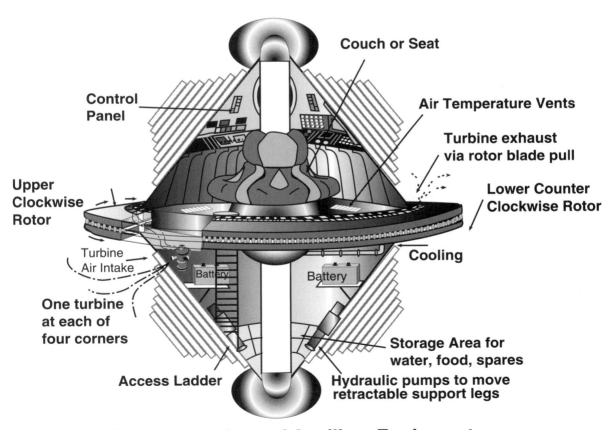

Partial Locations of Auxiliary Equipment

figure 39-34

T-700 Time Machine Without Outer Shell

Side View

Top View

figure 39-35

T-700 With Outer Shell

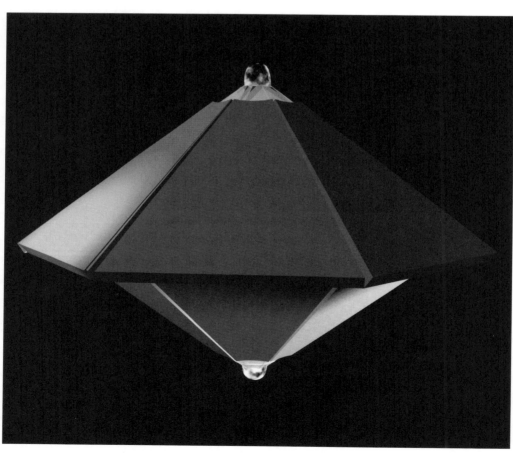

figure 39-36

The reason for this is that a small charge is bled off of the rotors to create a Bifield-Brown effect across the ship to lessen drag co-efficients and assist statically with lift. (See figure 39-35.)

I firmly believe that the time for time travel is upon us. Now that mankind is learning that we are basically beings of light clothed in matter made of protein, it is not a difficult process to examine and understand the underlying constituent forces that bind our oxygen, carbon, hydrogen, nitrogen make-up.

If you trace the relatively slow path of the historical, traditional progress of science, in relationship to the daily, monumental strides we are now taking, it doesn't take a visionary to see where we are going in short order. I feel that the greatest drawback at the present time is that the third ray has yet to balance with the seventh, or green into violet. In lay terms as applied to the establishment: the present reign of the orthodox scientific establishment lacks the basic spiritual knowledge of the order of matter into light and consciousness. But that will soon change. The old dogs won't learn; their shells are too crusted over with scars left upon them by insecurities buried in ego. The present mark of war will seal their tombs. This is the sign of the seventh ray.

Secondly, only a few of the financial moguls are beginning to see the light. This holds back the third ray. In 1997, a monumental step was taken when CNN's Ted Turner donated one billion dollars over a twelve-month period to a charity via the United Nations.

"Hell," he said. "This is less than a year's earnings. I can afford this! I hope others will follow suit." In that same year we lost two angels, both in one week. Princess Diana and Mother Teresa were called over to the other side to make preparation for a world stage of events that are soon to happen. The fusion of the rays is upon us now. The long wait is almost over.

When the curtain opens for the second act, so will the doorway to the second ether swing wide. This then allows human consciousness to look upon the astral plane, and time travel becomes a way of life.

Chapter 40

Gravity and Non-Gravity:
An Introduction to Advanced
Propulsion Systems

Extend your right arm straight out in front of you. Hold it there for two to three minutes. Does it feel as though it is getting heavier as it remains extended? Can you hold your arm extended for fifteen minutes? Is your arm actually getting heavier as it remains extended? No, it is not heaviness, it is an illusion. So is gravity.

Our reality of gravity is instilled into our DNA, beginning at birth. In our dreams we can travel the astral plane, flying free as a bird until we begin to think about gravity. The heaviness of an extended arm is only another program created within the confines of mass mind, from beings that have allowed themselves to be caught in the desire for freedom, rather than the will of aspiration.

Remove that thought of heaviness. Realize that you extended your arm because of my suggestion, and that it became heavy because others thought it would, and you allowed yourself to believe in their ignorance.

Now realize that these thoughts were a very powerful illusion, and that by holding them and allowing them to pass through your body and being, you are trapping your own self will within the illusion of heaviness, which in fact is **misusing** the energy of creation.

The longer you hold your arm forward, the more energy of creation you are misusing, as long as you believe it is getting heavier. And this, of course, creates the karmic acceptance that gravity holds things down and makes them heavy. Illusion. Knowledge and discipline carefully applied over time creates wisdom. Wisdom dispels illusion, freeing us from the bonds that bind us down into the earth.

WHAT IS GRAVITY?

Gravity does indeed exist. It is a bonding force holding atoms, molecules, cells and the universe into a tight moldable existence that contains powerful nuclear forces, ready at any moment's notice to be unleashed to perform unmeasurable tasks, of a wise man's bidding.

But gravity does not make things heavy.

THE TRUE NATURE OF GRAVITY

In order to understand its true nature and create the ability to fly effortlessly over a planet's surface, we need to revise our entire outlook on one of nature's most openly kept secrets.

Gravity is the auric field of the Logoic plane.

In nuclear fission, gravity begins to bend time out of our three-dimensional world within its core. In fusion, it will become free as it unites particles and releases energy. Cold fusion is the perfect example of gravity under control during a nuclear reaction.

Gravity is the glue of creation. It is a constant velocity of force. Gravity glues the atoms together as a universe, a galaxy, or a rock. Its greater attribute is its stability within its constant velocity as it moves from within the Logoic plane outwardly to the physical plane. Because it comes from the logic outward, it is not subject to the whims of mind, intellect, perception or any other characteristic created by the outward planes of consciousness and creation that it moves upon. Gravity is a karmic governor, regulator, stabilizer of all existence. It's no wonder why it has remained elusive to the many minds that have tried to conquer it over the many millennia. It is only now that our minds can begin to realize ways to overcome some of the effects of gravity and begin to move freely and effortlessly through space and time.

Not only does the quest for antigravity propulsion systems knowledge lies within the confines of gravity, but also free energy machines as well, because gravity seeks peace and balance and therefore creates inertia and friction which have long grounded many innovators from their idealistic goals.

First in our quest let us look at gravity and the world grid.

A PATTERN OF GRAVITIC ENERGY

As we have mentioned earlier, the earth is like a large crystal. The ancient civilizations of days gone by have known this fact and utilized this in their technologies. The Great Pyramid, Stonehenge and the knowledge of lay lines have been affiliated with the power transfer lines of the natural earth gravity grid all over the world. When you work within the physical localities of the various gravity grids, antigravity experiments are far more cooperative with the experimenter.

A good example of a nearby grid is around Lake Ontario near the Canadian border. In the 19th century a man named Daniel Home demonstrated levitation near Lake Ontario on a regular basis and obtained world prominence for his work. Later on in 1950, the Canadian National Research Council and the U.S. Navy began Project Magnet, an experiment in antigravity research.

Although this is the lone official U.S. government experiment into the earth grid system, the Naval Bureau of Ships still supplies the paycheck at the notorious Area 51. Called the "Marysburg Vortex," this grid area is called the "other Bermuda Triangle."

THE DISCOVERIES OF PROJECT MAGNET

Wilbur Smith was the director of Project Magnet. His team found, using very sensitive equipment, that large pillar-like columns extended several thousands of feet high above the lake. Anything within these columns had a loosening of the nuclear binding forces, in objects, especially along these stress lines. This, during certain astronomical conditions, could weaken the stress points, for example, in aircraft flying over the columns, that frequently led to crashes.

Similar anomalies occur in the Bermuda Triangle and often times missing aircraft and

412

ships have been found in deep space, orbiting the earth. This information, contained in many NASA files, suggests once again that under these same astronomical conditions the vertical energy grid columns levitated objects directly into space. Man, now knowing this, only has to study the forces and the conditions to achieve antigravity. This is precisely where many secret programs began.

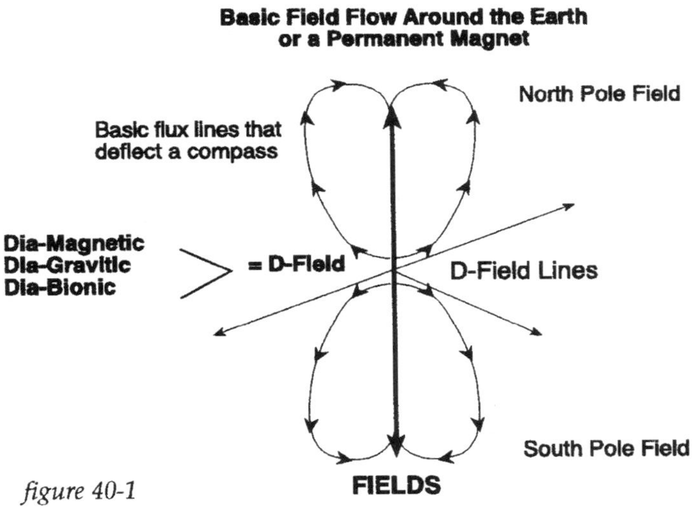

OUR MAGNETIC EQUATOR

Let us now study electro-gravity. Electro comes from electricity

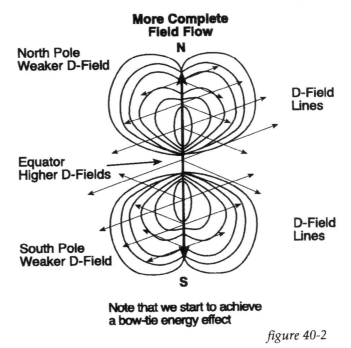

Basic Field Flow Around the Earth or a Permanent Magnet

North Pole Field

Basic flux lines that deflect a compass

Dia-Magnetic
Dia-Gravitic
Dia-Bionic

> = D-Field

D-Field Lines

South Pole Field

FIELDS

figure 40-1

which, as we observed earlier, is a byproduct of magnetism. Let us look at magnetism, the earth, and magnets. A permanent magnet has a north and south pole. Located midway between the north and south poles of a magnet is the magnetic equator. The earth also has a north and south pole with a magnetic equator. The magnetic equator is a place where the magnetic north and south poles meet. Located at this junction of poles is a third force that emanates at right angles from the other two. This third force could be called a dia-magnetic force, or a dia-gravitic force, or a dia-bionic force, depending upon the application. It would

be called dia-magnetic if we were studying the effects of electrical fields. It would be called dia-gravitic if we were studying the effects of weight changes and gravity, and it would be called dia-bionic if we were studying its effects on human or other bio systems. The Tibetans call it the anima mundi force when it is used to recharge the human aura during the sleep cycle.

In figure 40-1, we are showing the theoretical composition of the three fields. In figure 40-2, we are shown a more realistic location of the density of the d-field as it distributes itself across the entire proximity of magnetic parameters.

Now, if we increase the density of the three fields, we will observe a still different figure (see figure 40-3).

Because the earth has an

More Complete Field Flow

N

North Pole Weaker D-Field

D-Field Lines

Equator Higher D-Fields

South Pole Weaker D-Field

D-Field Lines

S

Note that we start to achieve a bow-tie energy effect

figure 40-2

413

uneven surface, the field patterns are less concentrated than those of a magnet. In addition, the earth is moving through space, past planetary bodies, also with D-fields, therefore there is a fourth field. This field is called time. When the earth D-fields interact with time, space time doors open and close, and antigravity phenomena become present displaying anomalies such as the vertical columns over Lake Ontario or the disappearances and teleportation phenomena within the Bermuda Triangle. Now, if we can grasp exactly what is happening here, we can begin to build an interstellar starship.

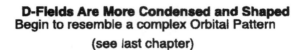

D-Fields Are More Condensed and Shaped
Begin to resemble a complex Orbital Pattern
(see last chapter)

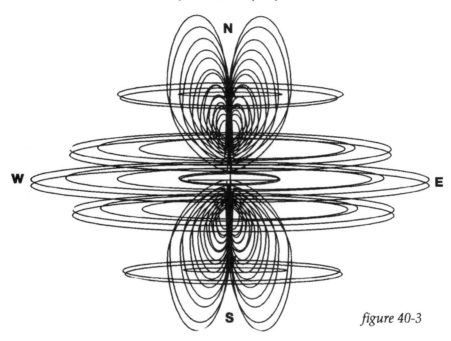

figure 40-3

Let's re-examine this. The magnet shown is a magnet with the spin directions of the magnetic fields.

Just as direct current in electricity moves from north to south through a wire, so do the forces of magnetism. However, in a magnet the electrons are held in a field circulating counterclockwise at the north and clockwise at the south. Where they meet in the center they reunite, constantly changing directions.

This meeting place in the center is called a Bloch Wall. From the magnetic resting point to the Bloch Wall comes a perpendicular D-field. In this case, we would call this D-field a dia-magnetic field.

The earth is the same way. It has a Bloch Wall, but the earth's Bloch Wall is not as concentric as the one shown on the magnet. Although centered on the magnetic equator, it bounces around, creating vortexes, lay lines and other assorted, unnamed phenomenon. These various Bloch Wall D-field points focus into a more even grid as they leave the uneven surface in vertical columns. So, if this is true, and you have your own portable

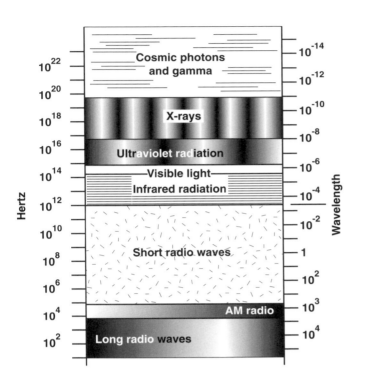

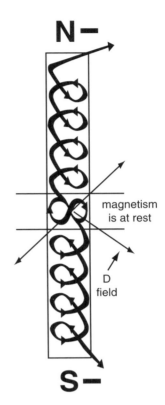

figure 40-4

anti-D-field generator, then you will have greater stability further away from the earth's surface, and greater stability means more focus, and more focus leads to greater acceleration. It's a known fact that UFOs and discs are seen to wobble and shake when they are low and slow, and when they move higher, they become fast and steady. Although graphically shown, the major and minor D-field lines appear isolated, these only represent the strong concentration as they are graphed in two rhombic triacontahedronal form. In reality, there is a smaller D-field haze occurring at any intersection of north and south pole magnetic lines. The more sensitive electro-gravity propulsion systems can maneuver almost anywhere above the planetary surface, whereas cruder systems are limited to low-level flight only over select areas. However, once you distance yourself from the immediate surface area, these lines begin to blend, making it possible for almost all electro-gravity craft to operate in a comfort zone. It is amazing how many types of electro-gravity systems have been developed by many different visiting civilizations. The Gray and Reptillian systems are very crude in comparison to Pleiadean electro-gravity systems. When you go into Lyrian or Andromedan systems, they no longer use electro-gravity; instead they use anti-gravity, which is far more efficient using more of the time component of a planetary field, rendering them immune to the pitfalls of planetary grids. These more advanced systems will be covered later on in this chapter.

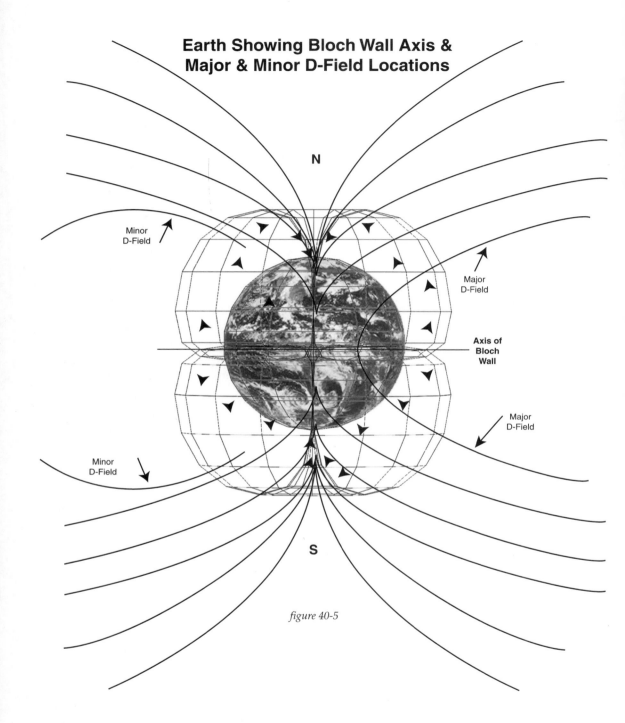

**Earth Showing Bloch Wall Axis &
Major & Minor D-Field Locations**

N

Minor
D-Field

Major
D-Field

**Axis of
Bloch
Wall**

Major
D-Field

Minor
D-Field

S

figure 40-5

GRAVITY AND WATER

As we had already discussed, if you live north of the Equator, when you take a bath and pull the drain plug, the water forms a counter clockwise whirlpool as it enters the drain. If you are south of the equator, a clockwise motion will be detected. Here clearly a relationship

416

between gravity and water is noticeable.

A well-known scientist from Austria, Viktor Schauberger (1885-1958), having constructed saucer craft for both the Third Reich (V-7) and our government in Texas after WWII, used his scientific observations as a naturalist and his electrical background to demonstrate levitation using air magnetism and water flows.

A waterfall's center is colder than its outside edges. Trout fish always swim upstream in waterfalls via the central area. Using gravity-sensing equipment, the area the trout swims to has a lighter gravity and therefore offers the least resistance to his upstream efforts. Schauberger copied this natural design of spiralling cold water flow, coupled to natural diamagnetic principles, for his work in building levitation systems. Would it not be funny to think that watching a fish inspired the first interplanetary drive systems!

Strangely enough, Schauberger named his water-implosion turbines "Trout Turbines."

GRAVITY AND SOUND

As I mentioned earlier on in this book, sound will also overcome gravity because sound is an electromagnetic wave of relatively low wavelength. Through the timber or pitch of sound, it can produce Bloch Wall D-field effects. I have been extremely successful at getting objects to levitate with sound. My earlier music album, entitled Fellowship the Sound, contains many such timbers. In levitating, however, we do away with speakers and substitute audio transducers that are capable of moving large amounts of power at very high bandwidths. In Chapter 23 figure 23-1 is an example of one such System that I developed in 1990. People often ask me why I don't market some of these systems. The answer is that we already do and I've been using these technologies in Pyradyne products for over 20 years. Our Systems III-2, when properly set up, has repeatedly demonstrated anti-gravity characteristics.

Levitating onjects with sound

Originally the powerful timber-carrying instruments such as the sitar occurred in Tibet as recently as 28,000 years ago. They were brought here by the Rishis, who originated on the Pleiades.

Today, in Tibet, their rituals continue.

A recent (1985) article appeared in a German magazine about current levitation in Tibet, written by a Swedish engineer, Olaf Alexanderson, in the publication Implosion number 13.

A Swedish doctor, Dr. Jarl, studied at Oxford with a young Tibetan student. A few years after the student graduated, he asked Dr. Jarl to come to Tibet to treat a High Lama.

One day, while in Tibet, Dr. Jarl was taken to a monastery that was high in the mountains and perched on a cliff. Just below the monastery was a cave that was accessible only by climbing up a 750 foot sheer wall. Apparently there was construction going on inside the cave that required some very heavy rocks that weighed several hundred pounds. The only way to get them up the sheer cliff to the cave opening was to use a crane (which would have been next to impossible to put in place high in these mountains in Tibet), or to levitate them into the cave opening.

Boulders levitated 750 feet using sound

The Tibetans chose levitation. By calculating some geometric launching positions 750 feet below on the floor of the plain that approached the cliff wall, the Tibetans used sound to move the rocks skyward to the cave opening. Their calculations accessed the world's D-field grid system. The stones to be moved were placed 750 feet away from the cliff and

417

directly below the cave's opening. Behind the stone to be lifted and facing the stone and the cliff were placed 19 musical instruments. The musicians were on a 90° arc behind the stone. Behind them were four rows of monks that provided chanting when the lifting ceremony started. The musical instruments consisted of eight three-foot-across-the-face drums, four drums that were two feet across and one small drum just one foot across. In addition were six trumpets called ragdons.

When a stone was in the correct launching position, the monk behind the smallest drum gave the signal to start with a sharp rap from his one-foot drum. The launching pad was a polished slab with a bowl-like cavity in the center. The large rocks were towed onto the pad by oxen, called yaks.

Once the small drum gave the sharp rap, the chanting began, along with the other instruments sounding away. After about three minutes the tempo increased and the rock gently lifted off the ground and on an approximately 1000-foot radius arc, traveled to the cave opening 750 feet high about the meadow floor. This procedure lifted about five to six large rocks per hour. Occasionally one would break and the pieces would have to be cleared before another could be launched.

Dr. Jarl filmed the incident, but when he returned to England with the films, the society for which Dr. Jarl was working confiscated his film and declared them classified. More information is available on these topics; see the bibliography.

D-Field Levitation Experiment

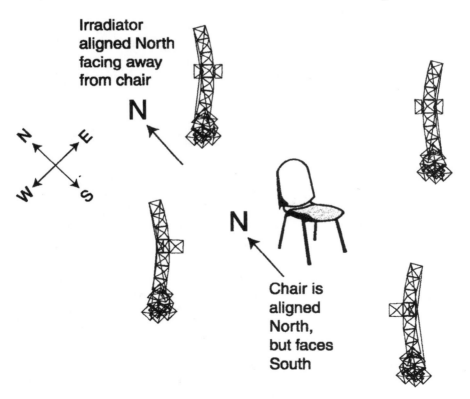

Irradiator aligned North facing away from chair

N

N

Chair is aligned North, but faces South

figure 40-6

SIMPLE PYRADYNE SYSTEMS —
DIA-BIONIC, DIA-GRAVITIC LEVITATION

You can demonstrate D-field activity with six people, a chair, four Irradiator/Mega Orb columns and a Fellowship music tape.

First, place the chair in the center of the room to be used. The area around the chair should be clear of all objects except maybe a carpet. Next, place four Irradiators facing out, equally a short distance from the chair. Make sure the first column is the farthest north from the chair. Below is a diagram showing proper location of the first components.

Face the Mega Orb bottoms and the chair to magnetic north. Face the Irradiators away from the chair in all directions. Next, select five other people to assist you with this experiment. The sex, weight or size of the different assistants is immaterial. Choose a person to be located in the chair (levitatee).

Have the levitatee sit in the chair facing south. Next, you and the other four stand around the chair, equidistant from each other, forming a circle, then breathe deeply and begin to rub your hands together. As you rub your hands together, become aware of the bio-magnetic, non-polarized magnetic field that exists in each and every one of us. Now open your hands, and as you open them, be aware of the tingling sensation that you feel between them. Surround the person sitting in the chair and in alternation place all ten of your hands above the levitatee's head. Then count to ten.

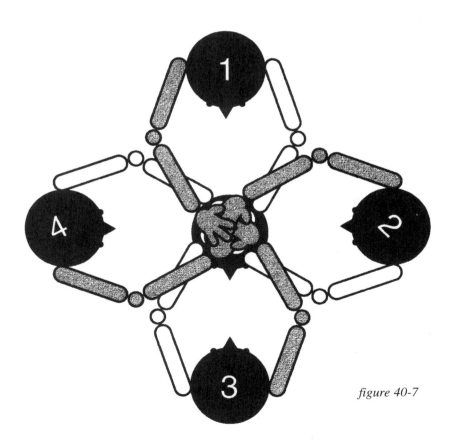

figure 40-7

Be sure that the levitatee is sitting in a straight-backed chair with his legs together, feet flat on the floor, and hands in his lap.

Now you step back and have the other four levitators equally surround the levitatee. Instruct all four to extend their arms and place their closed fists together, closed except for the forefingers, which should be extended and touching each other along their lengths as shown.

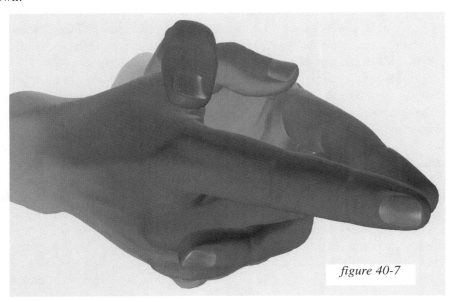

figure 40-7

The person nearest the levitatee's left shoulder is now asked to place his two extended fingers, palms downward, beneath the levitatee's left armpit. Likewise, his opposite number inserts his forefingers beneath the right armpit, and again the other two respectively beneath the levitatee's knees.

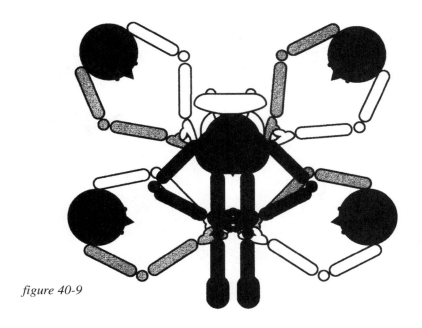

figure 40-9

When you reach the count of ten, using only your forefingers, have the four levitators lift the levitatee high above the chair. Their lift should be effortless.

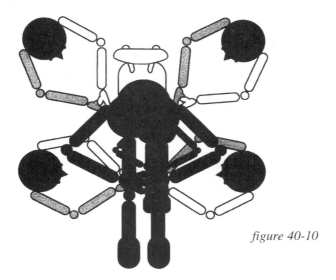

figure 40-10

Once the levitatee is high in the air, walk around to the back of the chair and, if you are right-handed, use your left arm, or if you are left-handed, use your right arm to remove the chair from under the levitatee. Open your hand and place it under the levitatee where the chair was.

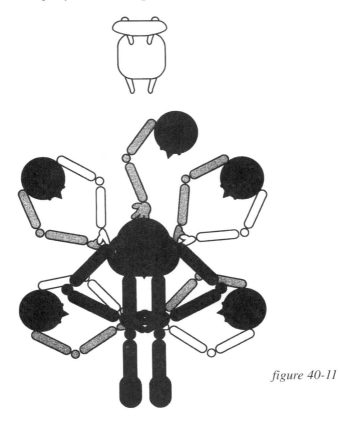

figure 40-11

Gradually push up on the levitatee with that hand. At the same time, have the four levitators lessen their pressure on the levitatee. As your energy D-fields come into balance, you alone, with one hand, can hold the levitatee in the air.

Whenever you are doing this use caution as the levitatee will be in a precarious position as the other four levitators relax their support.

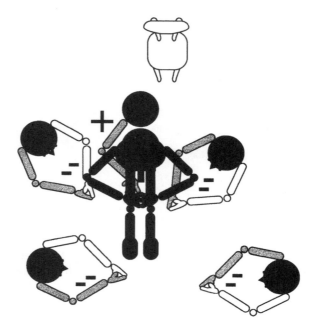

figure 40-12

Once you have held the levitatee yourself, have the other four levitators reassume their positions. Replace the chair and lower the levitatee back to his original grounded position.

If you were to diagram what happened, it would be explained this way:

Placing the Irradiators in all four corners, facing away from the chair, begins a four-pole field zone as the scalar waves emitting from the antennae are directed away from the center of the lifting anti-gravity area. Gravity is always affected behind a scalar wave, not in front of it. So by being behind the Irradiators you are starting a four-phase Bloch Wall potential. All you have to do is to energize it via your own non-polarized (SeeBeck effect) magnetic field. When you position yourselves around the levitatee, you consciously open up and direct your dia-bionic frequencies into a wavelength that corresponds to the earth's dia-magnetic Bloch Wall frequencies. The resulting resonance between the dia-bionic/dia-magnetic frequencies produces a heterodyning field (summation field) that you, as a group, can focus into an electro-gravity dia-magnetic field with the Bloch Wall centered right upon the levitatee.

The field actually comes into focus over the levitatee at the end of the ten count. You, as the coach, should move slowly and stay close to the levitatee when you finish the ten count and go to the back of the levitatee in preparation to remove the chair and support him or her alone. If anyone moves out of position after the ten count, it will de-focus the field. If this happens and someone begins to experience weight on their forefingers, go back to the ten count and repeat the entire procedure from that point.

Side View of D-Field Focus

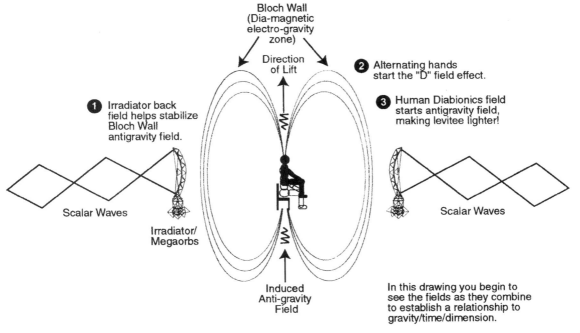

Bloch Wall
(Dia-magnetic
electro-gravity
zone)

Direction
of Lift

2 Alternating hands
start the "D" field effect.

1 Irradiator back
field helps stabilize
Bloch Wall
antigravity field.

3 Human Diabionics field
starts antigravity field,
making levitee lighter!

Scalar Waves

Irradiator/
Megaorbs

Scalar Waves

Induced
Anti-gravity
Field

In this drawing you begin to
see the fields as they combine
to establish a relationship to
gravity/time/dimension.

figure 40-13

The next logical step is to create the Bloch Wall effect using only one person. That's exactly what happened in Coral Castle, Florida. Edward Leedskalnin, a Latvian immigrant, located the dia-magnetic anomalies in that region and constructed an entire castle of huge rocks by himself, using the D-field levitation. He was able to focus electro-gravity waves, but instead of requiring other helpers to start the fields, he did it all himself. He may have constructed something such as the Pyradyne Irradiators to establish a balance of forces to make his lifting areas stable. Among his accomplishments, he constructed a castle/residence, with stone furniture, a moon pond, a sundial and a North star telescope. Today his accomplishments are well respected and no one knows how one man could do so much.

If we reflect back on the drawing on pages 418-420 and study the energy configuration of our six-person D-field lift, a lot of clues begin to become apparent. In the central area with the levitatee and four lifting humans that, with practice, shifts to one human lifter or levitator and one levitatee coupled to four Irradiators, one for each initial levitator, we begin to see a familiar energy pattern—an electro-gravitic central field with a multi-sided scalar/time wave field, very similar to the relationship of the vertical accelerator column surrounded by the 960 spider optical network located amidship on the T-700 time travel transposer.

So, what we need to do now is to create a full-blown machine that can mimic what the combined effect of six humans and four Irradiators did in a simple demonstration of partially overcoming gravity. Except now we need to go all the way. The following drawing leads us in that direction.

figure 40-14

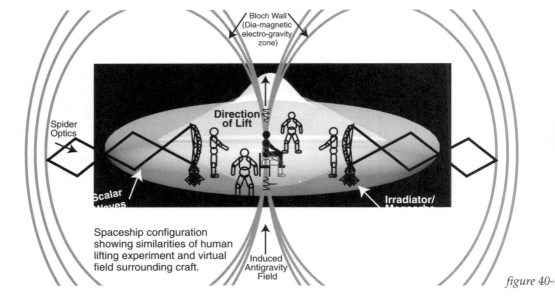

figure 40-

Here we are superimposing a saucer craft design over our lifting experiment for the simple purpose of allowing you to begin to focus on the relationships of various wave/energy functions. We know that Victor Schauberger's trout turbine saucer craft flew from Leonstein, Germany in the early 1940s to an altitude of eight miles in 3.12 minutes and reached a horizontal speed of 1,200 miles per hour. Also, an Austrian-born scientist, Rudolf Schriever, and a Dr. Miethe also had success in this field. Later on names such as John R. Searle (Searle Disk), T. Townsend Brown and Charles Bifield (Bifield-Brown propulsion system), Norman Dean (Dean Drive), John Frost (Auro-Car), Henry Coanda (Coanda Effect Lifting Devices) all became associated with anti-electro-gravity flying machines. Hundreds of patents such as Bifield-Brown #2,949,550, and Guerrero #3,432,120, or Barr #3,067,967 and Constantin Lent #2,801,058 were filed beginning with Nikola Tesla's turn-of-the-century patents and up to the present day. Then, in the late 1940s, alien ships began to be recovered and the science of reverse engineering began to merge with our already aggressive research. That brings us to the present.

Existing anti-gravity patents

THE PARTICLES WITHIN GRAVITY'S DOMAIN

Part of understanding gravity lies in the manner in which subnuclear particles convert consciousness, especially within the hydrogen atom, into tremendous binding nuclear and electromagnetic forces. Science is working very hard to reverse these forces and produce "counterbary." (Counterbary is a term used when a man-made force is created that overcomes gravity in such an amount that the mechanism creating the antigravitic force is also lifted in the process.) As this proceeds into a flight condition, the term changes to "lofting." The area around such a levitating craft is called the "Barycentric" control area.

As I mentioned in Chapter 39, Bevatrons are one of the linear particle accelerations of choice for this research. When I was at the University of Michigan, I spent a lot of time around the Bevatron. However, the Bevatron located there was in no way comparable to the one in Berkeley, California, which is 6.2 Bev (billion electron volts).

Dr. Chamberlain at U.C. Berkeley has led a group using the Bevatron to find an anti-neutron (remember, a neutron has a large mass such as a proton, with the exception that it is neutral in charge, and thereby making it a candidate for lofting kinetic energy), and to identify more of the characteristics of the already discovered anti-proton.

In this quest protons are accelerated toward the speed of light with a force of 6.2 Bev and hit a target made of copper. When the proton projectile strikes a neutron in one of the copper atoms, the following emerge: the two original particles (the projectile proton and struck neutron) and a new pair of particles, a proton and anti-proton. The anti-proton continues briefly until it hits another proton, then both disappear and decay into mesons.

Mesons, discovered in 1939, are hadrons with integral (mathematically integrating) spin and zero Baryon number. (A Baryon is a group of subatomic particles, such as nucleons, that undergo strong interactions and are held to be a combination of three quarks. In this case, a zero Baryon would not have an orbital quantum number. If a particle has an additive quantum number (see Chapter 39), this number would not be an "M", "O", "N" number, but a "B" number such as B=1 for protons and neutrons. A hadron is a particle exhibiting strong interactions with other subatomic particles.

If we were to track a particle as it is directed by mind arriving from the astral plane, the first plane, the particle would become visible on the physical plane within the Light ether. Here it would drop down from the speed of light and acquire mass on this dimension. Particles on the Logoic Plane, or first plane of consciousness, are called "ultimate physical atoms" or UPAs. As they move through the lower dimensions and approach the physical planes, they begin to acquire the lower characteristics of the respectfully-approaching plane.

After they move through the Monadic plane, they come through the Atmic plane or third plane, or third ray, which we also refer to as the female or the Holy Ghost plane.

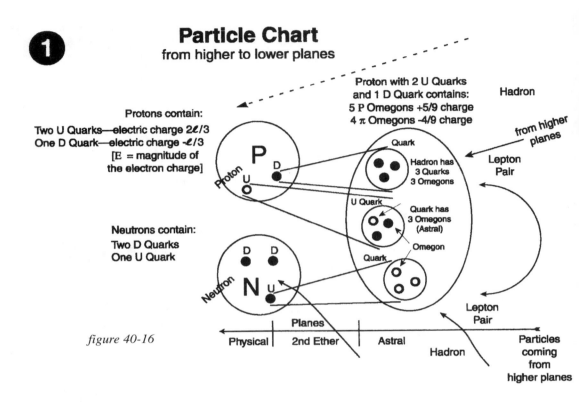

Particle Chart
from higher to lower planes

Protons contain:
Two U Quarks—electric charge 2ℓ/3
One D Quark—electric charge -ℓ/3
[E = magnitude of the electron charge]

Proton with 2 U Quarks and 1 D Quark contains:
5 P Omegons +5/9 charge
4 π Omegons -4/9 charge

Hadron

Neutrons contain:
Two D Quarks
One U Quark

Hadron has 3 Quarks 3 Omegons

Quark has 3 Omegons (Astral)

from higher planes

Lepton Pair

Quark

Omegon

Lepton Pair

Planes

Physical | 2nd Ether | Astral

Hadron

Particles coming from higher planes

figure 40-16

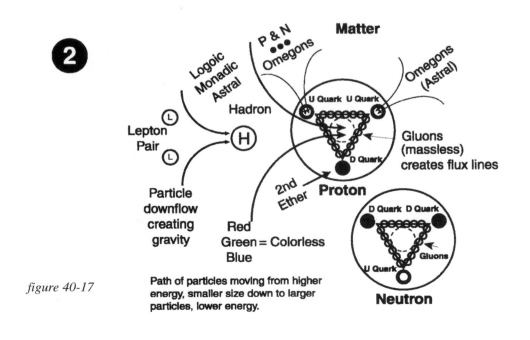

Matter

P & N Omegons

Logoic Monadic Astral

Omegons (Astral)

Lepton Pair

Hadron

U Quark U Quark

Gluons (massless) creates flux lines

Particle downflow creating gravity

2nd Ether

Proton

D Quark

Red Green = Colorless Blue

D Quark D Quark

Gluons

U Quark

Neutron

figure 40-17

Path of particles moving from higher energy, smaller size down to larger particles, lower energy.

It is interesting that the third ray is called the Holy Ghost, because it is here that matter, in the becoming, gains polarity, genders and **ghosts itself**. By this I mean that the **particles themselves are anti-matter** and here on the Atmic level they clothe themselves with physical characteristics that later become matter.

Science here on the physical plane looks at matter as physical first, then searches for anti-matter or its equal particle opposite. From the higher view, the anti-matter is first. An anomaly to this is human digestion. Proteins are left-spin going into the body. Right-spin proteins are considered poisons going into thebody. However, once proteins are in the body, left-spin proteins have to be converted to right-spin by the electronic digestion process spoken about in earlier chapters, in order to become part of DNA. Herein lies the secret to gravity and anti-gravity as once you grasp the dualities involved, then reverse the concept of dualism.

When we go into subatomic physics, it is like going into a fruit and produce store. If we were to go into a store and pick up some cherries, strawberries, apples and bananas, and take them home and mix them into various puddings, we would have a blend of "flavours" that we could taste.

However, if we were asked to formulate each pudding and what it contained fruitwise, it would be difficult because so many combinations of fruit would be similar. Some would have stronger flavours, thereby masking the weaker flavours. Basically, to figure out what each pudding contained would take some time while we experimented with all of the possible "tastes" fruit blending could produce.

The high-energy physicist who examines and identifies the debris scattered in all directions by the collisions of very fast-moving particles, finds himself in an analogous situation. Over the last forty years, more than two hundred different types of particles have been discovered, although they possess only a few "flavours." The nature of the fundamental relationship among them has not been easy for the physicist to uncover, but he is aided by various experimental facts and laws that he has inferred from them. Some of these are now summarized. A particle flavour is assigned a number that can assume only certain discrete values. These distinguish different particles with the same flavour. Examples are isospin, strangeness, and charm. A particle with a certain flavour and its antiparticle have flavour quantum numbers of the same numerical value but of opposite sign. A particle has a flavour quantum number of value zero if it does not have the appropriate flavour. These quantum numbers are additive: the flavour quantum number of a group of particles with different flavours is the sum of the values taken by the number for each particle. There are two classes of particles: THE HADRON, WHICH INTERACTS WITH OTHER HADRONS THROUGH THE "STRONG" FORCE (RESPONSIBLE FOR THE BINDING TOGETHER OF PROTONS AND NEUTRONS IN NUCLEI), AND THE LEPTON, WHICH INTERACTS WITH HADRONS AND OTHER LEPTONS THROUGH A MUCH WEAKER FORCE —the "weak" interaction (responsible for the decay of radioactive nuclei). Hadrons weakly interact with one another, but leptons do not strongly interact with one another or with hadrons (as far as is as yet known). The flavour quantum numbers of hadrons are unchanged by their strong interaction but are altered by their weak interaction. Electrically charged hadrons and leptons share the "electromagnetic interaction" (a force of intermediate strength that is responsible, for example, for the binding of electrons in atoms). Each class of particles is assigned another quantum number that is unchanged by all three types of force. This is the "baryon number" for hadrons and the "lepton number" for leptons. Hadrons have a lepton number of zero, and leptons have a baryon number of zero.

All hadrons detected up to 1974 could be grouped in certain families or "multiplets" according to their flavours and baryon numbers. The latter were found to be just those allowed if all hadrons were asembled from a set of three fundamental particles called "quarks" (u, d, and s) with different flavours, taken either three at a time or as a quark-antiquark pair. Despite intensive research, no particles have been found that are other combinations of quarks — for example, single quarks, pairs of quarks ("diquarks"), or three quarks and an antiquark. Since hadrons differ widely in mass, one quark (the s quark with the "strangeness" flavor) has to be heavier than the other two. Other quarks have been found to exist. Some are called B (Bottom) and T (Top). Quarks are usually found in pairs because as the lepton pairs draw the hadrons into quarks, quarks can exist at first as triads. Leptons and hadrons have weak electromagnetic properties because they are closer to the astral plane, and as we studied earlier, magnetism is only a physical plane property, as gravity, being the glue of creation existing on all planes. When high-energy particle physicists create artificial nuclear radiation in Bevatrons or cyclatrons, for example, as soon as the acceleration process or nuclear bombardment of the target is finished, nuclear decay begins and lepton pairs are briefly seen. This is the reverse process of creation and as higher particles escape back to their source (antimatter decay), the situation of true neutralization of gravity begins to take shape.

Quarks are assigned colours, which is natural because they are made of smaller particles that are characteristic of the first three rays which are red, blue and green. Quarks change colour (as a result of nuclear acceleration-deceleration), as they absorb or emit zero mass particles called "gluons." Gluons are particles among quarks, coupling them together to form systems of either three different coloured quarks or a quark of a certain colour and an antiquark, whose colour is a mixture of two colors. Since red, blue and green make white quarks, thus bound are converted to hadrons. This colour theory is an emerging process in physics called "quantum chromodynamics" (QCD). The colouring aspect of the quarks is composed of "omegons" and omegons are particles from the fourth dimension or the astral plane. Remember, the astral plane is self-illuminating.

Quarks and some of their binding particles such as hadrons are also called "magnetic monopoles" and it is their characteristics that allow them to be virtualized within the confines of super-conducting magnetic fields. A normal magnet would not have enough flux density to effect them in stronger anti-gravitic virtual fields.

PARALLEL UNIVERSES

Parallel universes exist because they started their existence in different time references. They create antimatter between themselves because they want to balance upon the seven rays or levels of consciousness.

The common bond between them is acceleration. This is why antimatter is detected in high-energy particle physics. Quarks, hadrons, omegons, and leptons become predictable as particles such as protons and neutrons are accelerated toward the speed of light. The larger the particle, the easier the detection. Remember, light is seven colours, each representing a level of consciousness. So light becomes the common denominator for any of the eight parallel universes co-existing in one sector of our universe. Because the astral plane (4th dimension) is the first real gate to connect time, it also compares particles in different times. One particle in one time compared to another is an antiparticle. Hence, a physicist in another parallel universe would see matter from our universe as antimatter, and vice versa, as he accelerated toward the speed of light and approached the window of time (remember, gravity is the glue of creation — gluons).

So in our virtual machines, we are going to approach weightlessness under acceleration. Our mass will increase and as we feel the potential pull of gravity from another universe, we are lifted in that direction. The illusion from our 3-D world reference is anti-gravity, not electro-gravity. Herein lies the difference. Electro-gravity will indeed lift a spacecraft, but the lift cannot pull the vehicle into another time continuum. A separate system is needed for this purpose. The anti-gravity such as utilized by the Pleiadeans has interdimensional capabilities and is an easy tie-in for their hyperspace drive.

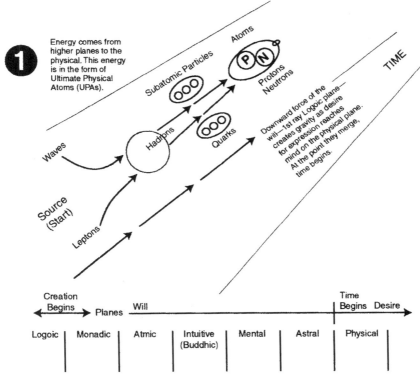

figure 40-18

Each of the four directions is a universe. Each of the four directions has an anti-direction. This creates eight directions. Matter moves away from the center (core) of the cross. However, in time and evolution, the cores or centers of the two crosses become only one core for both crosses. Then consciousness has double-crossed into one and the universe ceases to exist. As we move closer to this fact, beings in other dimensions become aware of their coexistence. Then science and religion in all planes of existence begin to come together. As this process nears completion, all of God's universal secrets become known to mankind. Eventually — usually in the latter part of the eleventh hour — humankind begins to their power and work in harmony with creation.

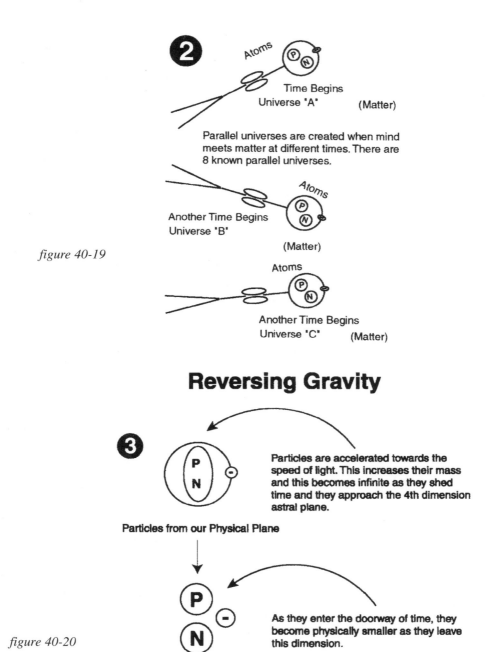

figure 40-19

2 Atoms
P N
Time Begins
Universe "A"　　(Matter)

Parallel universes are created when mind
meets matter at different times. There are
8 known parallel universes.

Atoms
P N
Another Time Begins
Universe "B"
(Matter)

Atoms
P N
Another Time Begins
Universe "C"　　(Matter)

Reversing Gravity

3
P N −

Particles are accelerated towards the
speed of light. This increases their mass
and this becomes infinite as they shed
time and they approach the 4th dimension
astral plane.

Particles from our Physical Plane

P − N

As they enter the doorway of time, they
become physically smaller as they leave
this dimension.

figure 40-20

Matter　　　**Antimatter**

Particles
from
parallel
universe

− P N
Quark Hadron

Matter

Then particles are attracted from the closest
beginning time-referencing parallel universe.
These particles are pulled from their co-existing
universe by virtual simularities and form
antimatter to our matter. If they initiated the
acceleration first, they would be drawn to us
and we would become antimatter.

4

Mass Push / Pull

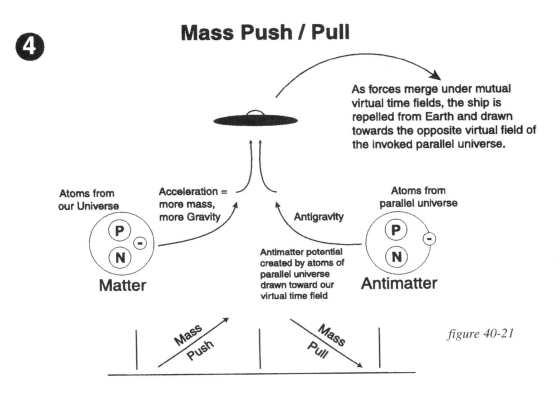

As forces merge under mutual virtual time fields, the ship is repelled from Earth and drawn towards the opposite virtual field of the invoked parallel universe.

Atoms from our Universe

Acceleration = more mass, more Gravity

Antigravity

Atoms from parallel universe

Antimatter potential created by atoms of parallel universe drawn toward our virtual time field

Matter

P **N** -

P **N** -

Antimatter

Mass Push

Mass Pull

figure 40-21

5  → # To Andromeda

If ship decides not to go to a parallel universe, but rather move a vast distance across ours, then the time mergence is only partial and the antigravity reaction is partial enough to move away from our planet's gravity and into free space. Then the ship disengages the virtual pattern of parallel universes' virtual patterns and simultaneously, while still in time (the 4th dimension), engages a new virtual pattern that is composed of energies pertinent to *our* universe's specific locational destination. This pattern is a beam connected from the trip origin to the final destination. A comparison would be a spider traveling in the wind from point "A" to point "B", leaving a single strand of its fibrous web material behind it so that it can retrace its original path at a later time. It is also analogous to a human experiencing astral travel with the astral body connected to the physical body by a silver cord.

figure 40-22

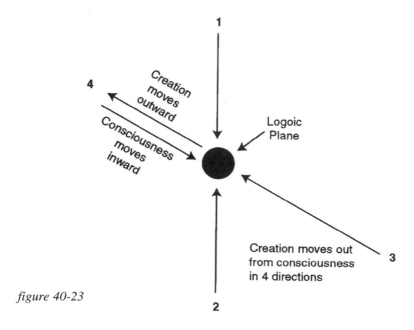

figure 40-23

The cross is also representative of parallel universes. There are four directions in the physical universe. Consciousness is constantly expanding towards the Creator (Logoic plane, home of the ultimate physical atom). As consciousness moves inward, it pushes (the universe) outward. This is why the universe is constantly expanding on the physical level.

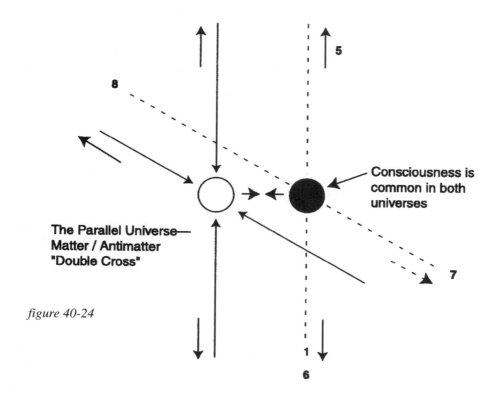

figure 40-24

432

ENTER SUPER-CONDUCTING MAGNETS

In 1933 two scientists, Meissner and Ochsenfeld, discovered that when a magnetic field was applied to a super-conductive material such as copper, gold or titanium, and that the material was cooled to such a low (sub zero) temperature for it to exhibit no electrical resistance, the magnetic flux lines were almost completely expelled from its interior.

This was called the "Meissner" effect and gave birth to the science of superconductivity. Under this condition large numbers of electrons formed "Cooper Pairs" (electrons bound in pairs). Cooper Pairs are alternately creating an attractive and repulsive force in the core of the superconducting material that cancels the field out in the core and intensifies it at the outer surface. This process only achieves cancellation of core magnetism during the super-conduction phase when there are ample amounts of Cooper Pairs.

Normal Wire vs. Superconductor

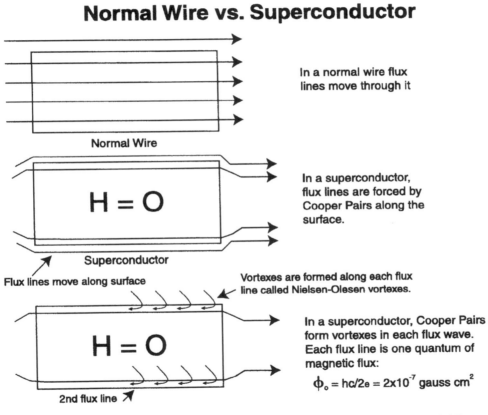

In a normal wire flux lines move through it

Normal Wire

$H = O$

In a superconductor, flux lines are forced by Cooper Pairs along the surface.

Superconductor

Flux lines move along surface

Vortexes are formed along each flux line called Nielsen-Olesen vortexes.

$H = O$

In a superconductor, Cooper Pairs form vortexes in each flux wave. Each flux line is one quantum of magnetic flux:

$$\phi_o = hc/2e = 2 \times 10^{-7} \text{ gauss cm}^2$$

2nd flux line

figure 40-25

What is extremely unique about this process is the fact that the magnetic lines of force are squeezed out of the core and onto the surface causing a compression of flux lines. In addition to this compression, the currents moving along the surface form whirlpool vortexes (Alblian vortexes) which compress coexisting photons which are normally massless (Yang-Mills gauge fields) into a short-range physical plane condition whereby photons now achieve mass. In particle physics, this process is called the "Higgs mechanism." This, as

433

you will shortly see, becomes, in part, an important step in creating virtual fields around an object, necessary to move it across space and into time.

As we have explained earlier, photons come from the astral plane and within them are magnetic monopoles (quarks) and mesons, as monopole-antimonopole pairs. This superconducting compression of magnetic flux creates a super fluid which is bound by particles called baryons, mentioned earlier in this chapter.

The core of a virtual propulsion kinetic thruster is the exact timing of the Alblian magnetic flux lines moving across the superconductor, merging with the non-Alblian forces created within the core of the wire (Higgs vacuum) and gaining mass as they merge particle-wise — quark — meson — baryon — or magnetic monopoles to monopole within what are called by physicists "Nielson-Oleson vortices". Depending on how the monopoles join each other, gives a "character" charge and the combining flux densities either get denser (source) or lighter (sink). It is the harnessing of these forces that creates the true antigravitic force.

THE BEGINNING — ELECTRO GRAVITY

When I was very young living in Ann Arbor, Michigan, I began to experiment with electrostatics. At the University of Michigan we had a Van de Graaff generator that put a very high D.C. (direct current) potential on a large round dome perched high upon a tower. Normally if you take a piece of tissue paper and drop it on the floor, it will gradually fall very slowly to the ground. But if you take the same piece of paper and place it on top of a Van de Graaff generator, it will fly 20 feet or more to the nearest object so fast that you can't see it move. What ever happened to air resistance, I wondered?

Soon I began to experiment with round capacitors and I noticed that the higher the dielectric (insulation) between the positive and negative high-voltage plates that made up the capacitor, the stronger the force around the capacitor became. By charging a capacitor and hanging it on a string, the capacitor produced measurable thrust and would move suspended through the air.

Later on as I began to study Townsend Brown's work, I learned there were two critical elements to building a condenser motor.

The first was the core dielectric number which determined the ability of the capacitor to hold its charge. This is called the "K" number. With air as "1", current dielectric materials can yield 6. Milar, barium aluminate, and barium titanium oxide (a baked ceramic) can yield considerably higher K numbers approaching 30,000. This would produce an electrostatic field that could produce supersonic speed.

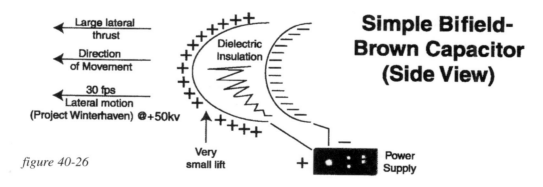

figure 40-26

The second factor is voltage across the plates. The magic beginning number is 50,000 volts. Remember, the T-700 time travel transposer produces over 1 million volts as it reaches flight speed.

Project Winterhaven was Brown's original flight experiment. He was able to produce 30 feet per second thrust on 50,000 volts of charge in a lateral direction. Now gravity is a downward force of 32.174 feet per second. So while Project Winterhaven (circa 1952) produced a force, it still had to be held up by a rope, as gravity still has a higher force, but this was the beginning. As we discussed, it's the marriage of particle dualisms — matter — anti-matter — that is true anti-gravity, but here we are issuing streams of electrons from an electrostatic energy source and producing a small amount of Counterbary. In this manner we are looking at a partial attempt for propulsion which considers gravity as a small-scale departure from Euclidean space in the general theory of relativity. The gravitational constant is one of four dimensionless constants: first, the mass relation of the nucleon (center of the atom) and the electron; second, $1^2/hc$; third, the Compton wavelength of the proton; and fourth is the gravitational constant, which is the ratio of the electrostatic to the gravitational attraction between the electron and the proton. With dimensionless constants, science at that time was limited. Our previous study of anti-gravity is that of the Unified Field Theory and far more substantial.

But that did not slow science.

As more research continued, people such as Englishman John Searl went a little further by adding higher dielectric super-light magnets to the picture, incorporating the Bloch Wall effect to the electrostatics. This now gave birth to faster lateral motion with a magnetic assist in the "O", "G" field than is partially achieved by electrostatics alone.

So now we had this:

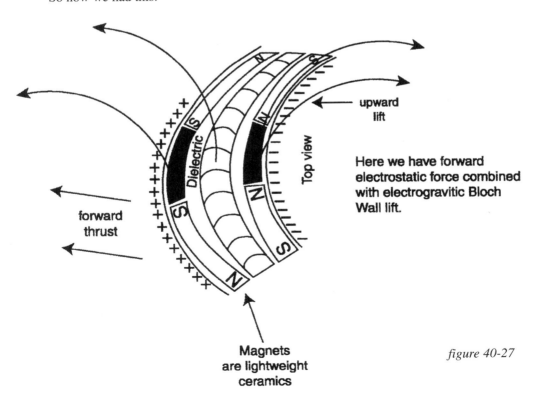

upward lift

forward thrust

Top view

Here we have forward electrostatic force combined with electrogravitic Bloch Wall lift.

Magnets are lightweight ceramics

figure 40-27

435

As you will see later on in this chapter with Mark McCandlish's Area 51 A.R.V. craft, this technology is very advanced and in place.

Now let us backtrack a little.

A few years ago I was contacted by the research department at NASA Ames Research Group, Moffett Field. They knew of my earlier work in this field and asked if I would entertain a small research grant in the field of application of electrostatics for the purpose of partially eliminating the forward air resistance in commercial jetliners, thereby reducing fuel costs. I submitted a written proposal and a crude drawing.

What I envisioned was to insulate the forward surfaces of the aircraft with a positively-charged magnetic dielectric and a negatively-charged magnetic dielectric across the trailing surfaces. As a logic choice for the high-voltage negative and positive charges, the hot-cold airstream of the jet's engines was more than adequate.

Here is a drawing of my proposal:

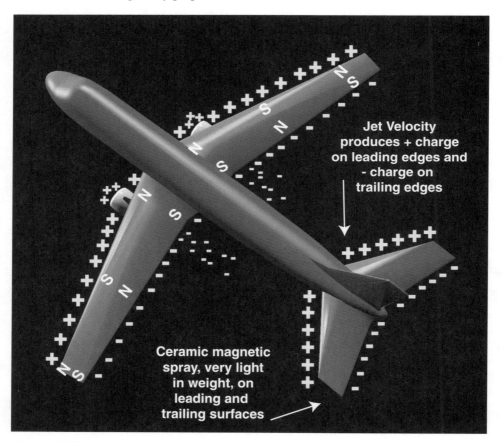

figure 40-28

My theory was this system would not only produce partial thrust as it overcame air resistance, but by using a slightly magnetic, sprayed-on ceramic magnetic coating on the leading edge surfaces, it would cause a partial lift as well. Although not very useful at take-off, once airborn and approaching flight speed, the system becomes very effective, greatly increasing the plane's normal airspeed by more than 50%, greatly reducing the load stress on the support members, such as the wings and tail.

When I presented my ideas, they basically freaked out. Later on I found out why.

A little while later, Aviation Week magazine released an article on the B-2 Bomber. It seems that the B-2 is 69 feet from front to back with a wingspan of 172 feet. Cowlings on either side of the cockpit feed large amounts of air into the jet engines mixed with negative ions. This makes the engine a high-voltage flame jet, pushing a higher negative charge out of the back. By insulating critical parts of the engine with high dielectric substances such as asbestos ceramics, the engine becomes electrically insulated from the craft and positive charges are created as a result of the opposite negative cloud that is behind, and by insulated wires are thereby conveyed to the leading edges of the wings. The faster the craft goes, the larger the forward positive charge and rearward negative charge. By adding an opposing magnetic field slightly behind the leading and trailing surfaces, we can now add in the Bloch Wall lift as well as the electrostatic thrust, which in itself also produces a small lift at supersonic speeds. At this point I now realized why NASA suddenly became nervous!

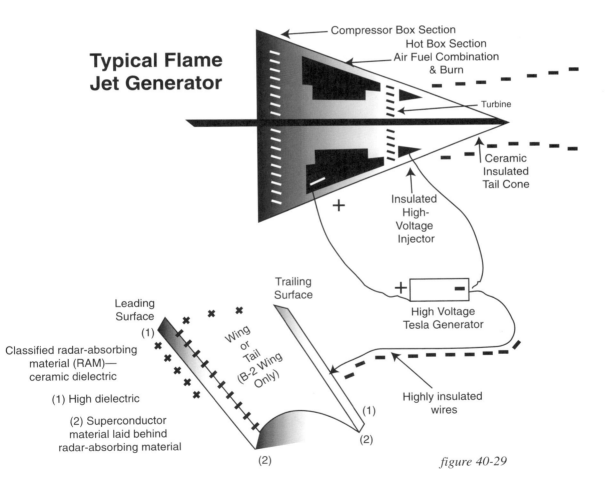

figure 40-29

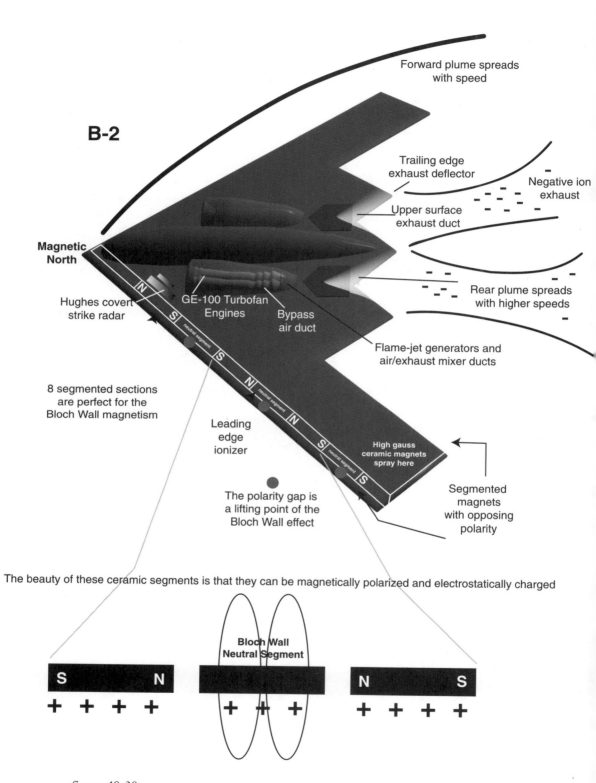

B-2

Forward plume spreads
with speed

Trailing edge
exhaust deflector

Negative ion
exhaust

Upper surface
exhaust duct

**Magnetic
North**

Hughes covert
strike radar

GE-100 Turbofan
Engines

Bypass
air duct

Rear plume spreads
with higher speeds

Flame-jet generators and
air/exhaust mixer ducts

8 segmented sections
are perfect for the
Bloch Wall magnetism

Leading
edge
ionizer

High gauss
ceramic magnets
spray here

The polarity gap is
a lifting point of the
Bloch Wall effect

Segmented
magnets
with opposing
polarity

The beauty of these ceramic segments is that they can be magnetically polarized and electrostatically charged

S   N

Bloch Wall
Neutral Segment

N   S

+ + + +   + + +   + + + +

figure 40-30

B-2 Showing Partial Field Cloud

figure 40-31

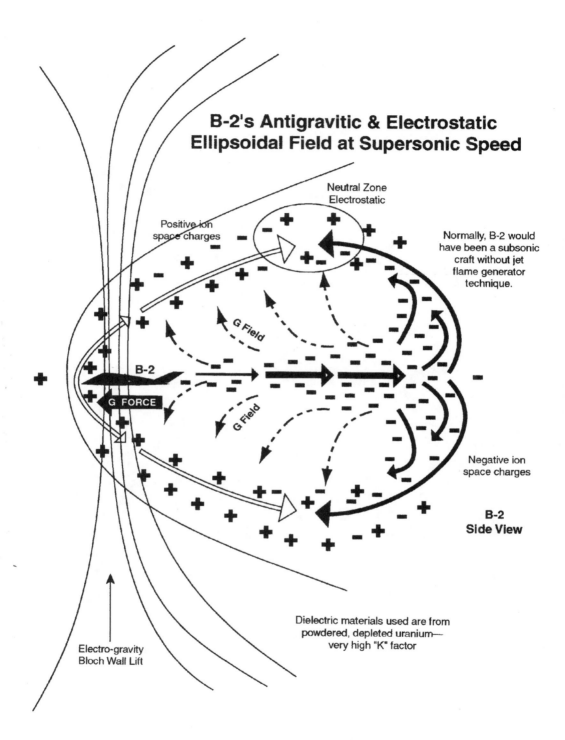

**B-2's Antigravitic & Electrostatic
Ellipsoidal Field at Supersonic Speed**

Neutral Zone
Electrostatic

Positive ion
space charges

Normally, B-2 would
have been a subsonic
craft without jet
flame generator
technique.

G Field

B-2

G FORCE

G Field

Negative ion
space charges

**B-2
Side View**

Dielectric materials used are from
powdered, depleted uranium—
very high "K" factor

Electro-gravity
Bloch Wall Lift

figure 40-30

440

Companies known to be engaged in antigravitic work and research are:

Hiller Aviation
Glen L. Martin Aircraft
Sikorsky
Douglas Aircraft
Boeing Aircraft
Lockheed Aircraft
Rockwell International
Clarke Electronics
General Electric
Curtis-Wright
MIT
Cal Tech
Gravity Research Foundation of New Boston
Princeton University
University of North Carolina

and others.

Countries

Canada
England
France
Germany
Russia
Sweden
USA

and others.

A VIEW INTO OTHER ADVANCED PROPULSION SYSTEMS

One of my former friends, Alan C. Holt, came up with some very interesting ideas that begin to approach the systems currently used by my Pleiadean brothers and sisters. Alan is a former director of NASA Skylab project, which was our first endeavor into a space station.

He presented some very good ideas in a paper entitled *Prospects for a Breakthrough in Field Dependent Propulsion*, #A1AA-80-1233. The group that heard his proposal in 1980, called the American Institute of Aeronautics and Astronautics (AIAA), is also sponsored by the Society of Automotive Engineers (SAE) and the American Society of Mechanical Engineers (ASME).

The following is a brief summary of Alan's ideas, some of which are becoming a reality now, almost twenty years later.

Field-dependent propulsion systems entirely rely on internally generated electromagnetic patterns (electro-gravity) to alter the gravitational forces that act on the craft as it navigates through space/time.

In addition to being anti-gravitic, Alan's proposed craft would also incorporate a field resonant system that would create an artificial virtual space/time structure that would be in harmony with a distant space/time point. When this virtual asymmetric system, as it is called, creates its field patterns that attract and repel other virtual space patterns, it would be able to move the craft great distances without the linear effect of time needed to cover vast spatial distance that the three dimensional world experiences in stellar and interstellar space.

In Alan's theory, he defines interactive forces observed over long distances, gravitational forces, and forces dominating intermedial or micro-distances as electro-magnetic and strong and weak nuclear forces.

These attraction and repulsion forces are described in Einstein's General Theory of Relativity as the nonlinear coordinate transformation properties of space/time.

In an asymmetric propulsion system, the energy which goes into the virtual pattern generators can be recycled and thereby these systems are highly energy efficient.

The first system Alan describes is the gravimetric system. This system is very close in operation to the system that Mark McCandlish and I described in "AREA 51, ARV Vehicle" later on in this chapter.

In earlier parts of this chapter I mention the Bloch wall effect and magnetic waves. What we now need to look at is not just the creation of a field, but the individual lines of force of the field itself.

In physics laboratories, we experiment with very high megagauss (gauss is a unit of magnetic flux density) fields that we created by linear acceleration of particles, such as the one in the T-700, cyclotrons, synchrotrons, bevatrons, super conduction magnetics (fields created by high conduction mediums in a super cold environment), and laser field generators. When I was a young researcher we created pinched fields that created laboratory fusion with temperatures approaching that of the sun. The "pinch effect," as it was called in the 1950's, continued on to the 1990's with great sophistication. When we work today with these fields we engage them, merge them coherently with other megagauss fields, and literally shape new types of very high energy fields.

By controlling wave frequency, wave amplitude (size) and wave orientation with respect to the individual field lines, and incorporating high current line pulses with extremely short rise times, we can create virtual field patterns that contain plasmas that can be accelerated into controllable kinetic energy. When you have manageable kinetic energy, the virtual field that it is contained in now can be mixed and matched to surrounding space/time fields. Because of the tremendous attractive and repulsive forces in motion during this process of creation, space/time three-dimensional world forces are muted to the larger picture that starts to emerge.

As these waves move into a phasable orientation from their creation in a machine, to their in-phase matching of universal space time/space locations, we now create a **hydro-magnetic wave.**

The field of force behind the hydro-magnetic wave can be conceptually identified with Einstein's generalized tensor field which Einstein strived to develop to unify gravitational and electro-magnetic forces in a single mathematical formalism (Unified Field theory, never completed by Einstein). The Unified field was a marriage of forces created by particles, planets, stars, comets, magnetic fields and theoretical virtual patterns which emerge as an underlying structure of flat, negatively-positively curved space and the mass/time relationships, thus forming the underlying structure of space/time.

If you have carefully followed the previous chapters, starting with DNA formation into the evaporation of a black hole into a wormhole, you will now begin to see the Unified Field, which also takes into consideration consciousness, and with consciousness in consideration, the missing link in Einstein's theory is now in place.

Before looking indepth at Alan's design, let us look at yet another propulsion system.

AREA 51 ARV VEHICLE

The following drawing is an ARV (Alien Reproduction Vehicle). This craft has been seen many times at Area "51", located at Tonapah, Nevada.

Photographed by Gary Schultz on December 19, 1990 at the "mailbox" in Area 51, Dr. Bell shows this photograph at his seminars. Mark McCandlish who presents this outstanding ARV Vehicle is a graphic contractor for the U.S. Government in various military branches. Mark had direct contact with eyewitnesses whom had seen this vehicle in an Air Force hangar at Norton AFB, November 12, 1988 during an Air Force Open House conducted by the local Governor and military officials. Among these dignitaries were George E. Brown, Jr., who was chairman of the House Subcommittee on Space, Science and Advanced Technology. Senator Alan Cranston was also present. Also included was the Lockheed Aurora (CP-140). There were 3 ARVs on display, one of which was 24 feet in diameter. The next one was approximately 60 feet in diameter, and the largest was 130 feet in diameter. All three vehicles were hovering silently with no landing gear protruded. The smallest of the three vehicles was partially dissassembled with the panels open as shown in this drawing.

Next to the smallest vehicle was a cutaway illustration similar to the one shown on the following pages.

The following text was written by Mark E. McCandlish, © by Mark E. McCandlish, March, 1989.

"The cutaway illustration shown on the next page represents details witnessed directly by three civilians and corroborated by four military officials.A photograph taken in 1967, available from retired Lt. Col. Wendell Steven's UFO photo archives, matches the external details of this craft in most respects except in the size of the clear, hemispherical covers for the "synthetic vision system", which appear larger, (2-3 feet in diameter in the 1967 photo). A 1988 witness, who provided the greatest amount of information regarding the internal details, stated that many of the components used were "off the shelf" items and that the closed-circuit cameras and their clear covers were "just like the kind used for surveillance in the Las Vegas casinos." During a November 12th, 1988 Norton Air Force Base exhibit, a four-star general making a presentation regarding the A.R.V. stated that this type of craft was capable of "light speed or better." Three such craft were on display in the exhibit, being 24, 60 and 360 feet in diameter. The smallest craft was partially disassembled to reveal some internal components. General proportions of the three craft were identical." The following text (A — T) is illustrated on the next two drawings.

A. The central column supports a nine-foot diameter disc at its center, four ejection seats above the disc and approximately eighteen oxygen/air tanks below the disc.

B. The nine-foot diameter disc may be either a "flywheel" for stabilization, or an enclosed Wimhurst generator, consisting of two counter-rotating plexiglas discs with numerous radially-mounted strips of gold foil bonded to the two inner, opposing faces. A static-electrical charge is created during rotation, and may be used to drive a motor in the central column operating off of the "corona discharge" of the Wimhurst generator. Such an arrangement, if used with magnetic bearings and a power "feedback loop", may comprise an "over-unity" energy device, if tapping the local zero-point fluctuations in the environment by the entire system reduces the mass of its components; most particularly in the weightlessness of outer space.

C. Four MK-H7 ejection seats are mounted back-to-back on the upper half of the central column, each having a set of guide-rails. The "headrest" consists of a parachute enclosure and two face-shield pull-down loops similar to the navy version of this seat. It is known that the upper half of the crew compartment sphere jettisons with explosive bolts during the ejection sequence, possibly pulling the outer sheath of the top half of the central column, and the four ejection seats with it, to provide some limited protection for the crew from the ionizing radiation surrounding the craft during flight. After clearing this hazard, the outer hull may also function as a rudimentary "re-entry shield" if ejection occurs in low earth orbit, with the ejection seats being deployed sequentially below 15,000 feet in altitude.

D. Inside the central column, the construction of the so-called "amplifier section" is a closely guarded secret. It is known that this section of the A.R.V. uses "condensed charge technology" or CCT, and its operation relates entirely to the science of "scalar physics." It is known that this device makes use of "noble gases" or vaporized metals, such as mercury vapor, and is similar to the device described in U.S. Patent No. 5,018,180, issued May 21, 1991, which also uses mercury vapor, (a fact that is not disclosed in the patent itself). It is

444

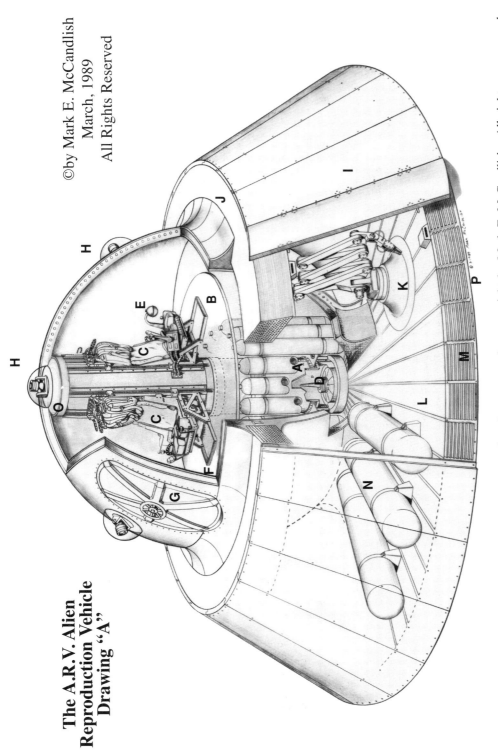

**The A.R.V. Alien
Reproduction Vehicle
Drawing "A"**

known that this vapor is maintained in a partial vacuum state, and that the energy produced by the central column is 10 to the 26th power joules per cubic meter of vacuum in the column. At the base of the column is a high-frequency, solid-state power distribution mechanism for shunting electrical current to the individual capacitor sections in the bottom of the craft. It is believed that within the outer sheath of the central column there are numerous coils that may gather energy from an electrical discharge within the central core through induction and which function as the primary windings of a tesla coil which steps up the voltage from the "amplifier section."

E. Controls on the pilot seat are a high-voltage potentiometer on the right and directional control mechanism on the left. The directional control device is a metallic sphere that is suspended on a curved metal "arm" with a metallic "bowl," slightly larger in diameter, magnetically held to its bottom. The witness at Norton AFB in 1988 noted that while in the "hover" mode, completely unmanned, this control device was influenced by the Earth's gravity to the extent that whenever the craft began listing in a particular direction, the "bowl" would swing in the same direction, and correct the attitude of the craft. The movements of the craft, while hovering, were described as similar to the listing to and fro of a large ship at harbor, as though the craft were quite literally floating on a "sea" of energy.

F. Each seat is equipped with a supplementary oxygen supply, a retractable foot rest tray and leg restraints.

G. The crew compartment hatch is similar in appearance to a submarine door, with six raised braces radiating from the center where the latch/lock mechanism is a manually rotated wheel, with "dead-bolt" rods that extend into the metal door frame and seal.

H. The "synthetic vision system" uses closed-circuit, ccd cameras, one on top, with six others around the upper circumference of the crew compartment sphere. each is covered by a glass or plexiglas bubble about twelve to fourteen inches in diameter. Cameras are paired off to produce a 3-D image that is projected inside the visor of the pilot and the other crew members, slewing to match the head and eye movements of the specific user.

I. The outer panels of the "skirt" of the fuselage are made of a composite material laminate such as fiberglass, kevlar or carbon fiber. The sides slope at approximately 35° from the vertical. Each is attached by dzus fasteners, with a slight overlap along the vertical seams.

J. The "antenna section" is held in place between the flanges on the upper and lower halves of the crew compartment sphere, and appears to be the secondary windings of a large tesla coil, with an inner diameter of about twelve feet. It is eighteen inches wide on the top surface and is nine inches in total thickness. Inside this section are copper-colored "bands or cables" about one quarter of an inch thick, separated by three-eighths of an inch in a green, translucent, dielectric material, possibly "g-10" glass. The outer edge of this section is "milled" at about a 35° degree angle from the vertical. Note the similarities to Tesla U.S. patent no. 593,138, issued 2 november, 1897.

446

The A.R.V. "Fluxliner" Alien Reproduction Vehicle Drawing "B"

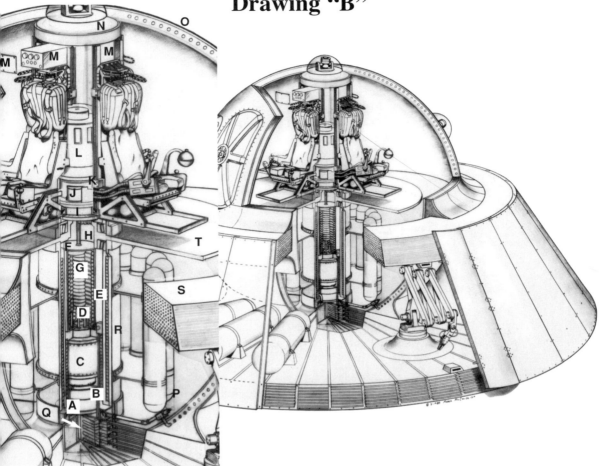

A. Voltage Distributor / Flight Control
B. Distributor Motor and Power Slip Ring
C. Plutonium Reactor / Heat Source
D. Control Rod Actuator Mechanism
E. Control Rods
F. Liquid Sodium Heat Exchange Chamber
G. Steam Generator Coils
H. Steam Line to Turbine through Transmission
I. Transmission — for Turbine and Flywheel Drive and Electrical Generator
J. Phase-Shift Transmission Control (when power lever causes mass cancellation, transmission torque is reduced)

K. Steam Turbine and Exaust Manifold Generator
L. Generator
M. Avionics Compartment and Electronics
N. Steam Manifold Ducting System to Hull of Crew Compartment (to warm interior and cool steam back into water)
O. Steam Ducts in Hull Exchange Heat to Cold of Space
P. Return Valve and Control
Q. Water Collector Manifold
R. Secondary Coils
S. Primary Coils
T. Flywheel

K. This articulated, robotic arm is capable of extending outward through two hinged panels on the "skirt" of the A.R.V. with a "reach" of about ten to fifteen feet. A flanged pedestal is bonded to the upper surface of the "capacitor section."

L. The "capacitor section" is about twenty-four feet in diameter, twelve to fourteen inches thick, and divided into forty-eight narrow, wedge-shaped sections, approximately 7.5° in arc-width, with eight copper-colored plates, one-half of an inch thick, stacked up in each section. The plates and each capacitor section are separated by three-quarters of an inch of a green, translucent, dielectric material, possibly "G-10" glass or a similar material. None of the plates is exposed to the air. The outer rim of the capacitor section appeared to have been milled off at a 35° angle from the vertical, as if by a huge lathe.

M. Individual capacitor plates are made of billions of compressed, 15 micron copper spheres to dramatically increase the surface area for conducting of electrical current. Flight of this craft is achieved through a combination of casimir force and the "Biefield-Brown effect." (See U.S. Patent No. 3,187,206, issued June 1, 1965; two years before the Wendell Stevens photo was taken.) Directional changes are executed by varying the amount of current delivered to individual capacitor sections, producing the effect of yaw and pitch. Current is distributed at an extremely high frequency, possibly as high as 30 to 150 kHz (thousands of cycles per second). Charge distribution is divided into two, counter-rotating "channels," each having 24 sections, and using every other section, with the opposing channel using those in between. Adjacent sections have individual plates stacked in laterally opposed order, where the plates of one section align with the gaps between the plates in the sections of either side of it.

N. Approximately 24 oxygen/air tanks are mounted around the circumference of the craft, strapped into two saddles constructed of a composite material that is bonded to the upper surface of the "capacitor section." These tanks are of a "pultruded" construction, using composite materials and are twelve to fourteen inches in diameter, and about six feet in length.

O. Initial power-up of the system is performed by two 24-volt marine batteries, possibly located in the upper section of the crew compartment. Actual location is unknown.

P. It is believed that the two counter-rotating electrostatic fields interfere with the interaction between the atomic structure of the craft and the zero-point fluctuation force responsible for creating the mass of all matter. This causes the structure of the craft, and a portion of the surrounding space to become mass-depleted or mass-cancelled. The amplifier section may further deplete the local zero-point energy [ZPE] during operation, when the powerful electrical discharge inside drives the random energy of the ZPE out of equilibrium "cohering" the energy into a rotating, torroidal field, (much like blowing a smoke ring), which transfers some of its energy, by induction as this torroidal field travels up through the core, passing the primary windings of the tesla coil which encircle this section. This feature may act as a kind of feedback loop, adding more power to the system with each new discharge in the core. Progressive mass-cancellation would also reduce the mass of electrons pulsing through the system, creating the ultimate high-temperature super-conducting circuit.

448

In addition was a motion picture video showing the vehicle hovering over a dry lakebed, presumably at Groom Lake. In the video the craft was shown making three side-long hopping motions, where it quickly rose, moved laterally, and descended again three times. Immediately thereafter, the vehicle shot straight up as the camera followed and disappeared from view within 2.5 to 3 seconds on a very clear day.

The other witness was a crew chief working on an experimental aircraft flown by Bill Scott, currently of Aviation Week and Space Technology (AWST). Bill Scott was a test pilot back in 1973 when this event was photographed.

The crew chief's discovery of this caused him to have 18 hours of debriefing in 1973 when his presence was detected by security teams. The crew chief walked by a hangar where the vehicle was hovering and the hanger door was accidentally left partially open, allowing him to witness the ARV vehicle being tested inside the hangar.

FIELD RESONANCE PROPULSION

Now let us look at Alan's model with a few additions to the original 1980 proposal, and compare it to some previous text.

He further defines a virtual structure as a many dimensional structure, which transcends and permeates the four dimensions of space and time.

A virtual pattern can be described if it is assumed that the pattern manifests as a space/time form. Alan further states that these virtual patterns can be energized by patterns created by pulsating spheroids and ellipsoids, and dipole, quadrapole and octapole forms, and these virtual patterns might result in projection of the energizing object into different space/time locations throughout the universe. Although the T-700 was not designed to travel in deep space, its systems employ all of the above-described patterns. The T-700 basically creates a virtual time model of some location in the past, present or future.

FIELD LINE RECONNECTION PROCESS

In our field resonance model of Alan Holt's original concept, let us look at some physical examples. Alan suggests a laser system that divides the main beam into twelve different sub-beams. These beams originate in the center of a circle and diverge into a central rim. The rim itself is a magnetic field line wave, toroidal wave guide. Surrounding the twelve spokes that converge into the center are super-conducting magnets that pulse the newly created magnetic plasma and direct it towards the outer ring wave shape wave guide. As they converge from the spokes, there is a 90° phase shift that takes place. The plasma that comes from the spokes is the plasma field, and as it connects to the rotating magnetic field in the toroidal circular rim structure, the 90° mergence creates the hydro-magnetic waves that then set up the virtual fields in the reconnection (plasma/magnetism) process. This is called the field line reconnection process.

Now, in order to increase the mass and density of our new virtual field, we need to increase the energy of our virtual fields so that they overcome the effects of local gravity, holding the vehicle earth-bound, and space/time that holds our craft within the limited confines of line-of-sight travel, i.e., within the bounds of the three-dimensional world speed of light.

This is accomplished with the following steps to our initial model.

Initial Model Virtual Field Generator

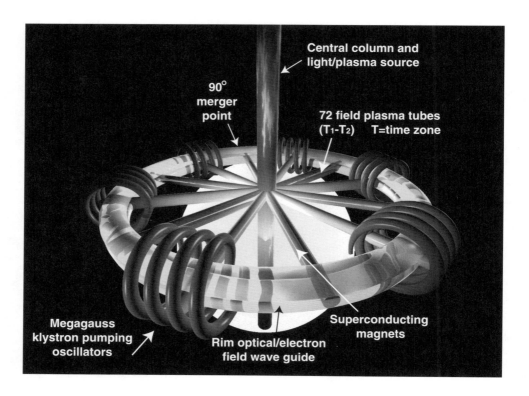

figure 40-33   Alan Holt's 12-spoke model

Winged Disc
Field resonance propulsion system in Winged Disc

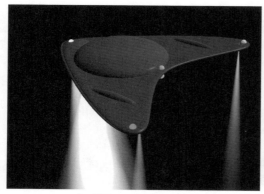

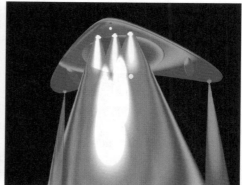

Top View

Underside View

figure 40-34

First, we divide our 12 plasma tubes into T_1 through T_{12} (T=time zone). Right away you can see the comparison to our Systems III-2 setup with time zones T_1 to T_7!

Between each spoke we place a megagauss klystron oscillator, not unlike the ones in the T-700. When the hydro-magnetic waves are created at each 90° spoke intersection as previously discussed, they now are accelerated in phase in a clockwise manner. As they move from T_1 to T_{12} they are pulsed through the klystron oscillators, with a very fast rise-time pulse, and each time the hydro-magnetic waves cross T_1, they gain mass and energy that, when focused by fine tuning of all of the above-mentioned parameters, creates a denser, higher mass virtual pattern that by natural law will force the object (the ship) to balance itself against a similar pattern somewhere else in the universe.

Virtual Field Hydromagnetic Generator Showing Synchronized Current Injection

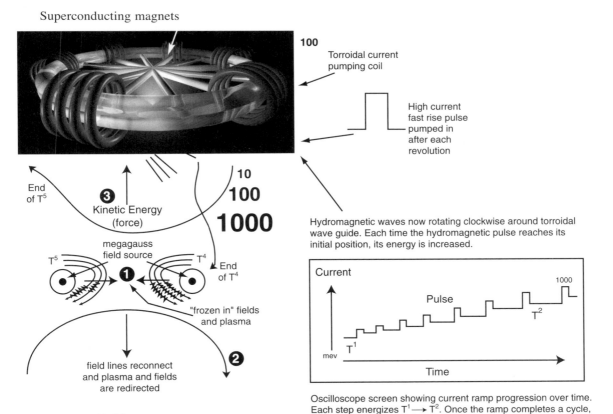

Superconducting magnets

100
Torroidal current pumping coil

High current fast rise pulse pumped in after each revolution

10
100
1000

End of T^5

③ Kinetic Energy (force)

megagauss field source

T^5 T^4

①

End of T^4

"frozen in" fields and plasma

②

field lines reconnect and plasma and fields are redirected

figure 40-35

Hydromagnetic waves now rotating clockwise around torroidal wave guide. Each time the hydromagnetic pulse reaches its initial position, its energy is increased.

Current

Pulse

1000

T^2

mev T^1

Time

Oscilloscope screen showing current ramp progression over time. Each step energizes $T^1 \longrightarrow T^2$. Once the ramp completes a cycle, it steps up to a higher beginning current pulse until a virtual field is created that is usable.

When you study what is happening here, you can begin to see a correlation to our Systems III-2 configuration with time zones T_1 through T_7.

This can be fine-tuned to create a space jump anywhere in the galaxy or beyond. This tuning will be discussed later on in this chapter. Due to the extreme pressure created by the system, kinetic energy in abundance is generated. Kinetic energy is the force that moves all objects, including cars, planes and spaceships.

Side View

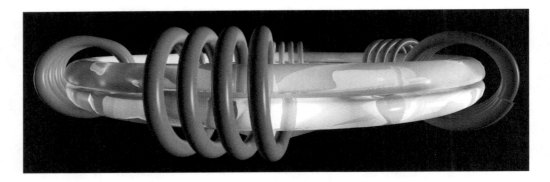

figure 40-36

As you can see, there is a direct parallel in Alan Holt's system to the T-700 time travel transposer. His 12 different spokes are similar to the 12 spokes of a Pleiadean spider optical system. In the areas between the spokes of the spider optics a kinetically energized fourth-dimensional virtual field is created, allowing the ship to slip into the virtual pattern it has itself created. In the T-700, the virtual field is created at its core and enveloped through the 960 optical wave guides that compose its overall system. Bottom line — same principle, different mechanics.

Now, as you have probably wondered, how is the occupant protected from acceleration in such a system?

Since the source of the initial signal originates within the immediate confines of the ship, the occupants are part of the virtual signal. In short, if you create your own virtual gravity, that's what you will feel. If the ship appears to make 90° high-speed turns to the outside world, it's only an illusion to the observer.

This is because there is no conflict to the merging of virtual patterns. Inside, the crew feels nothing, because the kinetic energy created is a constant acceleration that we now know to be a constant gravity. Gravity, as you remember from the first part of this chapter, is a constant acceleration from the physical plane (three-dimensional world) onto the Logoic plane. This force you will feel normally.

POWER SOURCES FOR FIELD RESONANCE SYSTEMS

Initially, to start the system we can use plutonium steam turbines or nuclear wafers (a secret sandwich device that provides an electron source based on nuclear decay). Once the system starts and reaches the potential to develop its own kinetic energy, the system will gain energy for its three-dimensional world fourth-dimensional world transition directly from the transform itself. The main focus is to focus the reconnection process while the process engages. Once engaged, there is more than enough energy coming from the stars that creates virtual fields to provide the continual kinetic transform of high magnetic energy necessary to complete a space/time jump.

Virtual Pattern Forming as Ship Enters Hyperspace

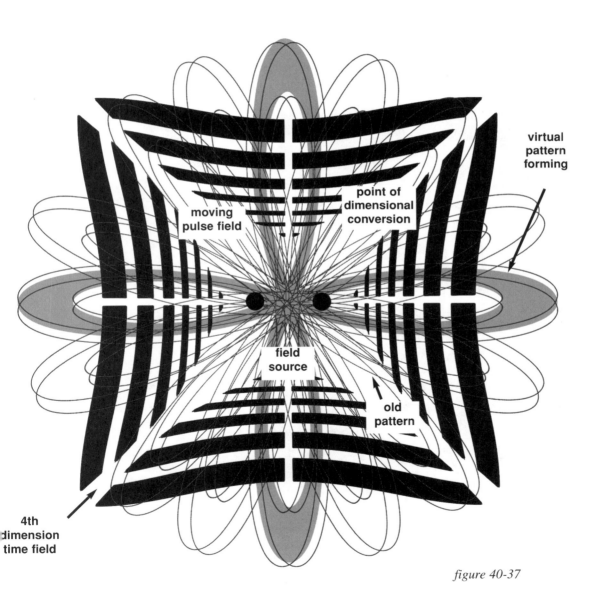

figure 40-37

453

Virtual Pattern Forming —
Jumping Between 3rd and 4th Dimensions

Origination Field

Destination Field

figure 40-38

A Comparison to Systems III-2

If you go back to the Systems III-2 diagrams and study the similarities of the time zones T_1 to T_7 created by charging the frequencies of the gemstones located in the Mega Orb bases below the Irradiators, you will see a similar path of a "pulse" of consciousness move either forward from T_1 to T_7 or backward from T_7 to T_1 depending upon the order of color and corresponding level of consciousness. The Systems III-2 creates a virtual pattern similar to Alan's field-dependent resonant system, the big difference being the amount of power created and some of the nuclear technology.

However, because of the similarity of the two systems, astral body travel can be accomplished by people using the Irradiator System by allowing the System to be programmed for actual virtual locations throughout space and time. This is done by using a specially developed computer laser scanner.

The location destination is programmed into the computer being used, (our current system is IBM compatible), then downloaded into the System III-2's master crystal via a special laser scanner. Also present within the system are various gemstones, meteorites and other artifacts that contain traces of the energy patterns that are similar in characteristics of the virtual pattern of our astral destinations. The primary gemstones start with the top of the rainbow, white (diamond, located in T_1), and continue through red (ruby) and terminate in violet (amethyst, T_7). This, of course, is a forward direction so that the system pulse velocity moves forward clockwise from T_1 to T_7, gaining inertia and creating a kinetic energy within the human body (located at the center of the Systems III-2). When the human kinetic potential reaches its peak window for virtual expression, the pattern is then amplified by the Systems' pulsed DC ion supply, which supercharges the human aura and body in the Systems' center. The key to this type of travel is extreme mental focus as the System changes energy potential as it begins to resonate with its virtual target objective. The nice thing about working with a Systems III-2 in this manner is that it is a lot safer if the Systems virtual pattern does not exactly match the pattern of the target. No one gets hurt or lost in space and time. As I mentioned in earlier chapters, it is better to get lost in time than space, but to get lost in both, as earlier Pleiadean spaceships did, is pure disaster. I always encourage astral time travel in our Systems III-2 before you attempt acceleration into space/time locations. Secondly, the Systems III-2 prepares us for the time when we actually construct and utilize a physical body transport device. The more "practice" we do prepares our body DNA for the big game.

The DNA of a space travelling Pleiadean is different from the DNA of a Pleiadean who only maintains a location on their homeworld. Any time you accelerate the atomic structure of a body through the portal of the speed of light into the fourth dimension and beyond, the DNA remembers the virtual energy patterns it is being put through. This memory aids the secondarily created cells in adapting to these space/time changes, without the suffering (inability to adapt to vast location change, similar to sea sickness, car sickness, air sickness, etc.), and discomfort that often befalls new voyagers. Remember that the body reproduces cells at the rate of 50 million per second!

Pleiadean Spacecraft Systems

In order to understand the sophistication of a time and proven hyperspace system, we need to examine the culture of the creators themselves.

The Pleiadeans have over 250 stars in their system, and are located 400-500 light years from earth. Their culture is much older than ours as we are descendants of their system. Their science was brought here 28,000 years ago by the Rishis (Pleiadean voyagers) and deposited in the care of the original Brahmans in Tibet. They don't have a fear of death and the unknown as our society does, so their culture is more stable than ours. Their technologies are based upon the complexities of the unlimited potential of the human form.

Their genetic research has taken them into the realm of devices such as bio computers.

Several years ago a book here on Earth was published, entitled The *Secret Life of Plants,* by Peter Tomkins. In it, Peter talks about plants sensing stress from their owners when the owners themselves were several miles away. My old friend Quentin McConnel and I were both friends of Peter Tomkins. Quentin had also researched plant communication, but instead of using biofeedback equipment as had many researchers before him, instead he used spectrum analyzers. Spectrum analyzers look for radio transmitted signals (RF energy) and compute the frequency range that the RF signals occur in. Quentin found that plants transmitted intelligence via subtle RF signals amongst themselves, and that they also gathered intelligence from the astral plane via the second ether.

Today, this science is making headway as people can now transmit signals from beyond the grave here, and the intelligence is received in the form of white noise on the 56 to 256 megahertz band albeit about half the central receiving frequency of human DNA. Also making news now is that the mental telepathy is growing more prominent between families that have close ties. This communication is still elusive to our mainstream science, although quite within reach as full spectrum research is still difficult because it requires a very low noise environment and some spiritual understanding of the relationship of and between electronic signals and subtle matter.

The Pleiadeans, however, are very versed in these areas. To the Pleiadean, horticulture is 60% of their time and energy. They believe that to be next to God is to be next to nature, whereas here on earth, nature is destroyed on a daily basis.

Our science looks, for example, at fingerprints as a form of identification. Human fingerprints are like six-sided snowflakes; no two are ever the same. The Pleaidians know that no two souls are the same. Each soul has its own karmic signature, thereby proclaiming true freedom of expression and individuality. Once the group oversoul individualizes itself into five seed atoms, those same seed atoms go on through every incarnation. When a mother is pregnant, the incarnating soul overshadows the expectant mother, sometimes even before she is pregnant. As the fetus forms the brain, the nervous system, then the heart and circulatory system, blood begins to pump from the newly created heart. As we studied earlier, at the center of the hemoglobin in blood is an octahedral-shaped center of four iron atoms. Blood, with magnetic iron at its core, becomes galvanized by the overshadowing soul, much in the same way that plants communicate. This galvanized blood now bends the DNA tissue controlling the hand and footprints into the familiar patterns we see when the child is born.

The Pleiadeans intercept the process of galvanization before the baby is born, and because their culture is older and more stable than ours, they can identify the newborn from its past lives with absolute certainty. This ability makes their culture stronger as now they can stay in touch with their loved ones.

These teachings were brought to Tibet. When the Dalai Lama gets old, he tells the monks that he is going to pass on. After his passing, a few years go by, and the remaining monks go to a forecasted local village and begin looking for a very bright child. The villagers also know the routine and happily produce their prodigy. The child identifies himself as the reincarnation of the past Lama to the monks by personality and various artifacts.

The Pleiadean educational system is about 120 years long. Early on the children are given the data on whom their last biological ties were with. Then they are given absolute freedom to re-establish old ties if they feel it is necessary. Likewise, the previous relatives are also notified, but no one feels pressured, as they all live over 1000 years, thereby creating a powerful family infrastructure. Semjases' husband was killed when she was only about 325 years old (27 years old by our standards.)

Today, she is about 360 years old. I am sure that by now she could find her previous husband in a child's body. I know that she was distressed at his passing, but she got over it and as far as I know, never pursued his whereabouts.

Anyway, you begin to get the picture. Pleiadeans are different, more settled, more scientific, more real in their views. They do have quarrels, tempers, disagreements, but they are not toxic enough to let Reptillian energies control their chi forces and commit heinous crimes.

Around Alcyone and Taygata are a number of stars that are a light year or slightly more apart. That allowed their scientists to use symmetrical propulsion systems to go between them easily within a lifetime. Utilizing slower-than-light-speed propulsion, they began mapping the virtual energy patterns into their bio computers, so that by the time they had developed their asymmetrical systems, they had raw data to begin their experimentation with.

In a nutshell, which we will open shortly, the way a Pleiadean ship makes hyperspace leaps (nearly instantaneous jumps across light-year distances in space) is to take a virtual photograph of where it is presently located, Point "A," and have in its bio-computer an impression of the virtual photography of where it wants to go, Point "B." It then gathers in the virtual data, mixes it with the destination data, and transmits this new virtual information to the outside parameters of the ship via a series of beams (giving their ships the title of "beam ships"). Once these transmissions encompass the ship, it arrives in virtual time at the destination that it was programmed for.

I remember back in 1980 when asking Semjase about how virtual information is obtained for traveling vast light-year distances when no one from this group had been there before in order to gain virtual data. This is a direct quote as of February 26, 1980:

Semjase had said that some Pleiadean stars were a light year or so apart, so they were able to develop the space drive systems that allow them to move around very easily and conveniently by conventional means to map out the energy to make the photographic transmissions possible. The beam ship is sound powered and light separated, and the question was, "Well, what about the trailblazers that travel the cosmos where you have never been before? I'm sure there's always an unknown regardless of how old your race is. The universe is infinite, and because of that there's always going to be an unknown." And Semjase said, "Yes," and she explained further:

"The beam ship is sound powered and light separated. It's mantrams change with each engineer who designs the particular ship. His mate is the pilot, he is the power source, she is the director of power. Each ship lives only with the crew and when the crew dies, so does the ship. These ships are their signatures of a life purpose, and are a karmic debt on their lifespan. They are creations only of the captain and his soul-mate. The crew is on a journey to the creator and this is only one path. Someday they, too, will find their soul-mates. It is a purpose and dedication to a life of service, just like ours."

When I heard that it made a lot of sense, and it sounded very, very familiar.

THE PLEIADEAN VARIATION CRAFT — "THE BEAM SHIPS"

When Semjase commented on the fact that Pleaidean ships were sound-powered and light-separated, it helped me get a few facts straight about the universe.

A. As we studied earlier, out of the black void came the white light. The white light contained the seven colours which are, we now know, directly linked to the seven levels of consciousness. This could be the center of the cross in our discussion on parallel universes.

B. The white light is the Godhead or the Logoic plane, home of the ultimate physical atom (UPA).

C. After the white light was created, consciousness manifested itself and thus gave birth to individuality, Ray II and the Monadic plane.

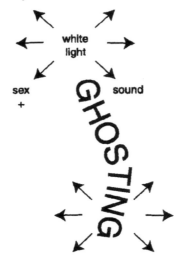

figure 40-39

D. Then came the Third ray, the Atmic plane, and here began physicality, starting with sound. The sound chant "AUM" used by the Tibetans represents polarity duality and the beginning of sex—separateness, thus creating the desire for reunion attraction. Here on the plane of the Holy Ghost, true ghosting (parallel comparisons) begins. Sound, as we studied earlier, is a positive sinasodial wave connected to a negative sinasodial wave. Sound harmonics and timbres permeate every atom of every living creature, fixed object or material substance that possess form! It can create or destroy matter in an instant. Its power is infinite in material creation. *There by sound* is what the Pleiadians chose for their power source!

458

How does that work? Simple. Back to horticulture. Have you ever eaten a psyloscybin mushroom? If you have, you might have hallucinated or imagined yourself out of your body moving through the stars. Why did you do this with a mushroom? Why not a potato or a peach?

The answer is simple. A mushroom is a spore with third ray DNA intelligence. When "its" DNA enters your body, it opens your DNA via serotonin (pineal gland) displacement. This unlocks consciousness of the higher planes into your awaking mind and displaces your daily survival on the physical plane — memories, limitations, and mundane gravity-locking, binding thoughts. You on a mental level temporarily can become free and soar wildly, without constraint into the freedom of your own imagination. Remember what Einstein said. The wisest mind is truly dead unless it posses an unlimited imagination.

That is what a Pleiadean ship is — a controllable imagination!

Let's look at a magic mushroom. If we remove the stalk, and slice the crown in a vertical slice, we have this, a small mini spacecraft with miniature cavities on its underside. These are sound chambers each tuned by the air as it vibrates via sound around the mushroom, as it grew from an infant. These are chordal chambers. If they were large enough for you to put your ear next to like we do with a snail shell, we would hear the music of the stars, the same as you hear the music of the sea in a seashell! Another thing in common with seashells and mushrooms is that the order of their chordal chamber is that of the familiar Fibonacci series.

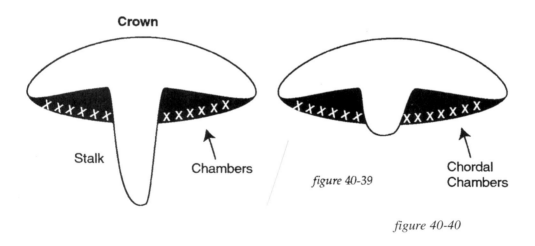

figure 40-39

figure 40-40

When the outer and inner linings of the outer hull are constructed for containers of the inner cabin, the hull is grown in a special greenhouse. A special spore is planted in a hydroponic environment which can become the equivalent of a twenty-one foot mushroom.

As this plant grows, it is bathed in special light and is showered with multi-timbral sound presented to it by a holographic sound system which is an integral part of the greenhouse. When the "hull plant" reaches maturity, its stem is injected with a special resin hardener that circulates through the entire plant and hardens the plant to a hardness greater than that of steel, with greater flexibility and strength than carbon fiber composite, and once cured, the hull plant is lighter than magnesium. These hull plants have a complete

459

chambering system that amplifies sound into a power source that literally **virtualizes light into beams.**

Ship Side View

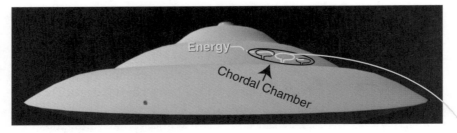

**Because of their different sizes and shapes, these units are called "cells."
There are many cells in one chamber. As cells are expanded or
made larger, the power increases and begins to tranmit outwards.
The sound transmisssions create virtual light.**

Grown Chordal Chamber

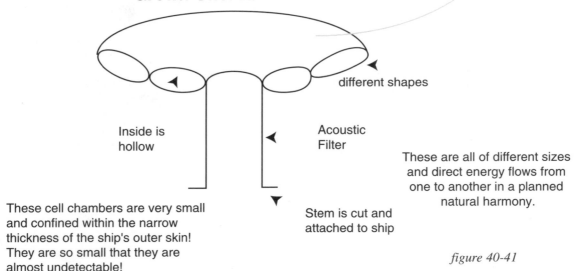

figure 40-41

Expansion Chamber — Inner Skin of the Ship Top View—Variation III

This section covers a large area but is very thin and is concealed within the outer skin on the inner layer.

Inlets conduct sound or exaust sound. Inlets are often hidden within ship.

Inlets

figure 40-42

This Expansion Chamber is located on the inner skin of the upper part of the ship. Its actual thickness is far less than 1 inch.

Some control of the sound is from "thoughts." These "thoughts" increase through natural resonance-sensitive portals in a moulded control device and their output is filtered and amplified into what we would call a harmonic sensitive "fluid" amplifier.

461

Pleiadean Variation IV
Ship Top View

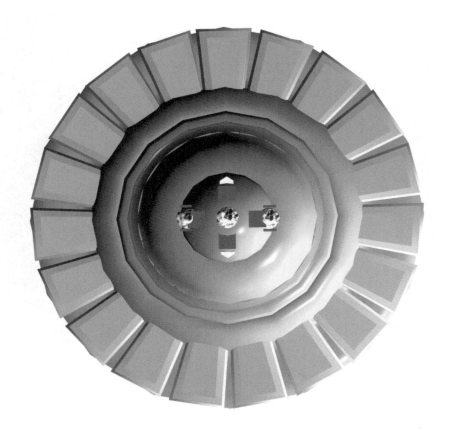

figure 40-43

Variation IV

figure 40-44

But as the frequency of transmissions increases, the overall resonance of the ship increases, and it becomes "At-tuned" to its surroundings.

THE "S" CURVED FLUTE

I remember Semjase mentioning something about liquid light. If sound is produced in such a manner as to excite the air, luminous light can be produced. Having heard the sound of a Pleiadean ship several times myself, I know what kind of excitement that meant.

One of the things we dealt in my early days with the Tibetans was called a trespasso. This is a Tibetan exercise where two people sit in a lotus position and look into each other's left eye. Usually a candle is placed between them as they sit facing each other. We both do what is called a breath of fire, which is between one hundred to ten thousand fire breaths, with left eye fixation.

After the last breath, you both can easily teleport into the astral plane. The more intense

463

and repetitious the breaths, the farther you go. I remember doing this exercise with a group underground in an ashram in total darkness. One of the first things that happened was that we all could see each other in total darkness, long after we stopped the fire breathing ceremony! So there is a direct link between fire breathing — prana (oxygen in body) — and the light illumination principles of the astral plane. So when I was informed of the S curved flute, it was another confirmation of sound vs. light.

Basically what happened is that the flute is another member of the consciousness-raising sound instruments, whose timbres, discussed in earlier chapters, raise consciousness. Normally only one person plays a flute, but this Pleiadean instrument is shaped like an S. What happens is two people sit or stand facing each other and do an equivalent of a trespasso. As they gain left eye contact, their souls begin to connect on many levels.

Then this connection is transposed into sound as the "S" curve flute is placed between them, and air is harmonized as they synchronize their breaths into one instrument. I myself am a clarinet player and have never been able to produce a decent sound out of a flute. It is a difficult instrument. Imagine the sound of two people playing one flute. The sound is so melodic that light liquifies as the surrounding ethers receive this multitimbral sound. I can't wait for the Earth's vibratory frequency to increase, so that this is possible here!

SIGNATURES

All of the Pleiadean ships have signatures of the pilots who are assigned to operate them. Similar in design to a locking code for an automobile ignition, these signatures are coded from the auric biofield of the ship's pilot. When a ship is to be flown, the pilot stands on a grid and holds his or her hand over a raised pedestal, and by moving her hand into various positions over the top of the pedestal, the ship moves in coordination to the respective hand location. Of course, this is for localized surface navigation. In the hyperspace mode, once the signature is actuated, the ship onboard computer takes over. One of the more interesting things about this system is that if the ship is captured by hostile beings, the signature system self-destructs and along the path of destruction, several key components that make the ship spaceworthy are also destroyed. This seems to be the problem with what appears to be Pleiadean ships captured by our government and stored at Area 51. Our government can get them to "hover", but beyond that, they don't seem to be able to do anything else with them.

INITIAL LIFT

There are several types of initial lift systems used on the different variation craft. One system uses two large rings that encircle the ship just inside of the central part of largest circumferance of the disk craft. Earlier in our studies we mentioned the SeeBeck effect, whereby the human body creates a nonpolarized magnetic field which, of course, in our levitation section we utilize the Bloch Wall effect for levitating a person on a chair. In this case, a similar effect is obtained by suspending two different materials in a colloidal solution, and rotating them in opposite directions in close proximity to one another.

Here on Earth the SeeBeck effect is accomplished by winding coils with dissimilar metals such as copper and nickel.

Pleiadean Ship Control Mechanism

Palm sensors for pilot's hand signature

This system "reads" 2 or more parts of the pilot's biofield. If the signature detects a mismatch, parts of the ship's propulsion system self-destruct.

Foot sensitive biofield stand

figure 40-45

However, when using dissimilar metals in a colloidal solution, you can shape gravity waves, by molding the Bloch fields with high-power torroidal fields, which are a part of a process that creates the virtual patterns, that are necessary for cancellation of gravity in the immediate area around the ship. Once airborn, a series of electrostatic fields are utilized to assist the antigravitic fields and the combination of the two are capable of getting the ship out into space quite quickly. Once in space, the hyperdrive part of the system engages and the ship goes inter-dimensional. Although the ships appear to leap and blink in and out of dimensions when they are close to the earth's surface, they usually are moving in a straight course, but appear to blink and stop because the lifting mechanism pulls light photons around it.

Variation IV Dome Beam
Outgoing Sweep Into Phase Changes

figure 40-46

Majority of critical components located in dome section of the ship.

When the antigravity section is in operation, it creates an equal number of electrons and positrons (electrons with a positive charge that neutralize negative elctrons creating photons), as it goes through phase changes. The phase changes are ony enough to partially engage the ship into time (the fourth dimension), long enough to create a small amount of antimatter. (See earlier part of chapter.) In the hover mode and in close proximity to large gravitational objects such as Earth, it is dangerous to go into full 4D transition as utilized in hyperdrive.

One of the dangers of this is that it creates a rent in the veil between dimensions and times. Other races visiting here are not as cautious and, as a result, doorways have been opened and astral vampires have moved upon our dimension. The "chupa cabra" is one creature of late that has been found roaming around in Mexico and South America. Other creatures end up here also as a result of this errant practice.

Initially, solutions are ionized in opposite manner to create fluid motion. this creates a gyroscopic effect and a cold fusion process where colloids are made into a plasma. The plasma then is pulsed in a circular manner, creating hydrodynamic fields that mature into virtual antigravity waves. These are focused around the ship, bending external light waves and creating lift. This system can be focused during hover and slow movements so that only select people on the ground or in an observational aircraft are able to see it.

Pleiadean Initial Lift System in Early Variation Craft

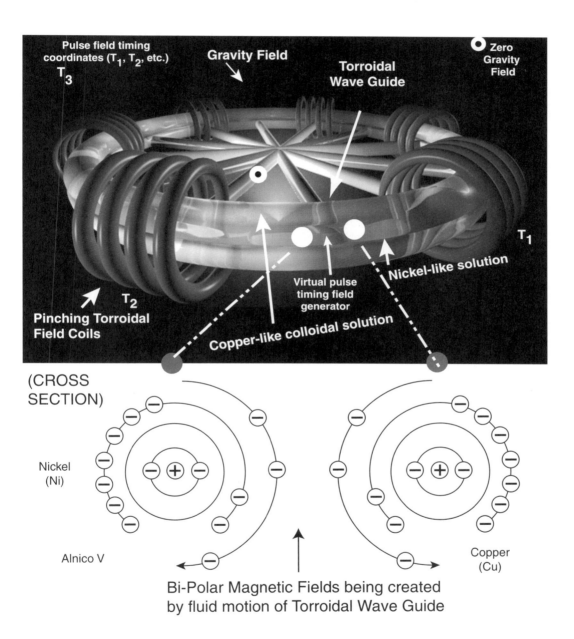

figure 40-47

467

THE FOURSQUARE PRINCIPLE

This message was given to me by Semjase on November 14, 1981:

"Dual dynamics are the force majeur of the old cubit system. They were lost to the secrets they held in time during the precession of the equinoxes 12,000 years ago. Then intellect was not fostered by true experience, only desire bred intuitive response (superstition) and the human race lost self-control to the natural backlash of basic elemental laws. I give you this knowledge now, Fred, to free our cause to Spirit.

These simple facts can only be felt by those who, like yourself, seek freedom in the unmanifest.

Manifest seekers who read these pages, will know too, where comes the source of this knowledge, as time has no favorites.

When the vehicles are again constructed on Earth as they have been in the past, the federations will govern their purpose. The council elders know well the rules of the forces herein explained and live the wisdom of the ages.

Force relationship is, of course, as important as family relationship, being the root of the cause. Biological formations are expressions of these divine essences. Your own Essenes procured their original doctorates by the natural laws we are now sharing.

Our own beamship technology cornerstones upon the foursquare principle I shared with you. As you grow more into this lifetime, I will share greater intellect and clarify many details that you yet comprehend not."

Looking back at this statement now in the late '90s and knowing what is already written about starship technology, made that statement absolutely correct!

When I designed the choke accessory for the Irradiator (mentioned in earlier chapters), I was learning how the carbon atom behaves as it is approaching the speed of light, gaining mass and changing form. Acceleration is a missing link in alchemy. Because the carbon atom is the binding, directing figure in the addition of oxygen, hydrogen and nitrogen in cellular reproduction, the geometry changes it goes through when cells are moved up to and beyond the speed of light are very important.

The Atlanteans knew this and based the old cubit system (one cubit = 25.092 British inches), later adopted by the Egyptians, on all of their measurements. The cubit system is very close to our standard one inch, one foot, one yard, one pound system.

This system takes into consideration the weights, lengths and sizes of planetary bodies, whereas the metric system which started in France, is based on greed, not fact, so that the units are higher over a measured volume, making things appear to be larger and longer than they really are. For example, one U.S. gallon of gas is maybe $1.60, whereas a liter is one quarter of a gallon and is also priced at $1.60 in other countries that predominate with the greedier metric system.

If you remember from earlier chapters, the Great Pyramid's circumference measured in pyramid inches defines the precision of the equinox. Another noted fact of the Great Pyramid is the exact placement of four cornerstones, each located at the corners of the base of the Great Pyramid of Cheops.

Sir John Herschel, one of Britain's most eminent astronomers at the beginning of the 19th Century, suggested that the regular British inch (which was compiled as the length of three grains of barley taken from the middle and placed end to end), be arbitrarily lengthened

468

by a mere one thousandth part in order to obtain a truly scientific, Earth-commensurable unit exactly one fifty millionth part of the polar axis of the Earth. He further stated that the French meter, derived from a curved meridian of the Earth, was erratic and variable from country to country because the Earth is not a true sphere and each meridian would, therefore, be different. Furthermore, the French had erred and produced a meter that was .0002 too short. Fifty such inches said Herschel would make a yard that was one ten-millionth the polar axis, and half that measure or 25 inches would make a very useful cubit. These measurements of Herschel of the cubit and the inch were the same as the cubit and inch which were found in the pyramid in multiples of 366.

In addition, the sacred cubit was used by Moses to build the tabernacle and Noah to construct his Ark.

The four cornerstones of the Great Pyramid were instrumental not only in showing accuracy, stability and conformity, but also highlighted Semjase's statement.

The pyramid inch furthermore depicted our revolution around the Pleiades or precession of the equinoxes. The solar year is obtained by observing the exact time between two successive vernal or autumnal equinoxes, when the day is exactly as long as the night. It is now 365 days, 5 hours, 8 minutes and 49.7 seconds, or in decimals, 365.2242, the sidereal year from Latin "sidus" for star, is the time it takes a star to reappear in the same space in the sky, as seen by an Earth observer. It is about 20 minutes longer than a solar year or 365.25636 days. This 20-minute lag causes what is known as the precession of the equinoxes, which comes 20 minutes earlier each year in relation to the equinoxes behind the equinoctial point. The anomalistic or orbital year is the time it takes the Earth to return to the point in its elliptical orbit nearest the sun, or perihelion. This is about 4.75 minutes longer than the sidereal year. The pyramid not only gives this value, but it gives the number of solar years it takes for the perihelion to complete a full circle of 360°, or one rotation about the Pleiades.

Looking at the pyramid and measuring one side between the cornerstones we find 9,141 inches. If we divide them by 4 we have 366. When the sum of the base diagonals is computed, we come up with 25,826.68, which is rounded off to 25,827 years — again, the precession of the equinoxes. Place that geometry onto the carbon atom, and you begin to see the foursquare principle of Semjase.

Note: This is a contact note. It should be interpreted only on an individual level — not as any particular scientific fact! The foursquare principle has four dynamics:

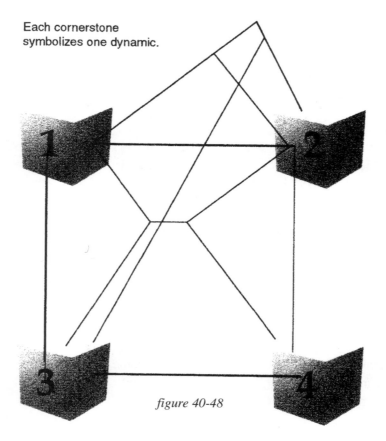

Each cornerstone symbolizes one dynamic.

Note: All drawings are from contact notes.These drawings are simple and will be interpreted by your own inner understanding.

Cornerstones measured by cubits. There are 4.

figure 40-48

OLD CUBIT SYSTEM
1st Dynamic

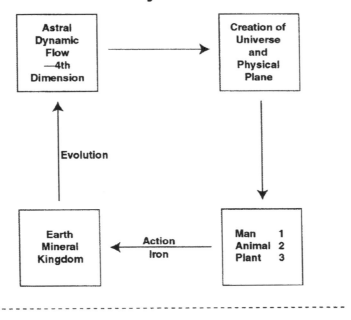

2nd Dynamic

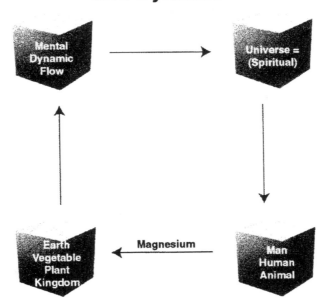

figure 40-49

3rd Dynamic

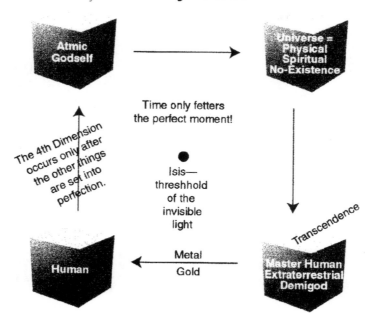

Intuitive → 3rd Universal Divine Order

Motion

Feedback

Physical Reality in Dimension

Light Gains Hue

Animal Kingdom Human ← Copper / 1st Order ← Superhuman Human Man

4th Dynamic

Atmic Godself → Universe = Physical Spiritual No-Existence

Time only fetters the perfect moment!

The 4th Dimension occurs only after the other things are set into perfection.

Isis— threshhold of the invisible light

Transcendence

Human ← Metal / Gold ← Master Human Extraterrestrial Demigod

figure 40-50

Contact Note (continued)

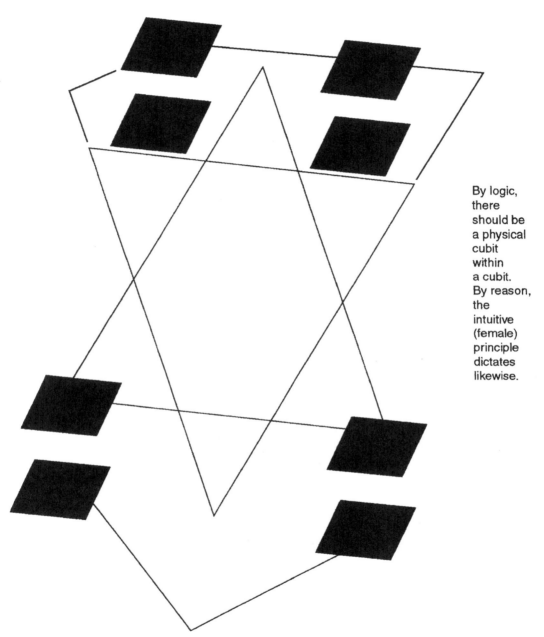

By logic, there should be a physical cubit within a cubit. By reason, the intuitive (female) principle dictates likewise.

Writer's Note:
It appears by this drawing that the carbon atom and consciousness are experiencing acceleration and 4th-dimensional separation increases beyond light speeds.

figure 40-51

Then Semjase gave me this:

"**Scalar Wave** — A moment of energy that comes from infinity — the past, present and future that can be felt and realized now, in this moment, which is, of course, what will always be for you and me.

The word "scalar" means to scale or climb in separate moments of time, long enough to realize the progression of unity.

To be called "Christ", the scalar principle, once realized and accepted, will lead to the ultimate light, love and sound of perfect balance. Then one is freed from all causes. Remember, a cause is only a moment where goal and purpose meet. Before a goal ends, a purpose, whether it be self-esteem or service to mankind, must discern itself. Then time will engage itself and the inaugural consciousness will uplift itself to a form."

When I heard all of these statements over the years, and saw the science that linked them with reality, it became apparent to me that there was a great metaphysical coverup of extraterrestrial science. Obviously the builders of the Great Pyramid knew the secrets to interstellar flight, but very carefully concealed great statements in geometrical constructions. The foursquare principle simply defined evolution and consciousness as the ability to travel vast distances, through consciousness, while still maintaining individuality and form, upon arriving at a specific far distant destination, sometimes even in another time or space — and then still being able to return to your point of origin with the precision of a highly-trained celestial navigator.

During these early interviews that took place between Semjase and myself during the late 1970s and early 80s, I once asked her, "Semjase, when you fly into a new universe or civilization and meet new beings, how do you initially know whether they are good or evil?" Her answer given on February 29, 1980, was rather prophetic:

"Our spaceships, though physical, become living flames in flight. When you fly the astral plane, both sides are pure. Both good and evil dwell as deep space denizens. Only purpose is a sign of progress. We fly with purpose and when we lose it as in old age, it is immediately regained by the super soul of the Universe. Our individuality is never lost. Whether we work for God or against God, it matters not, for we all are of God and our forms preserve our karmic quest in search of the unmanifest.

The Dark Powers of the Universe are easily discerned. They are in search of the manifest. Through spirit, gained in purity, we see (both sides) the divine game of Shiva and Shakti played not only in 108 civilizations, not only in 1008 different civilizations, but all civilizations throughout space and throughout time, for time here is only temporal for those caught in it to gain the essence of its message. Space separates the various times into individualizations known to us as men, demi-gods, archetypes, ancients of the days, grandmen of the heavens and so on! The higher the intellect, the greater the rationale of the acceptance that we are all of one God."

I really could not reply to that. Her reference to living flames is exactly what happens as you move beyond high speeds, causing mass to become infinite. The only thing that can happen so that mass doesn't become so infinite that it creates a black hole, is to become a subatomic structure that moves through virtual fields in the form of a self-contained flame of consciousness. The physics stated earlier on in this chapter are the roadmap through that great door of the unknown!

STELLAR OPTICS

Now that we have lifted our spaceship off of the ground, we can study the Pleiadean system of converting us and our ship into a living flame and thus moving through space and time.

We move our ship out away from the immediate overwhelming influence of the Earth's various fields. Our ship is equipped with a precision-beam receiving and transmitting optical system. I am going to show three different systems that, due to technological advances, are different in physicality, but the same in operation.

The first one is a system that is possible with present Earth technologies. The other two would be difficult. Remember, this part of the system is not the anti-gravity propulsion, but the virtual field apparatus used for the great hyperspace leaps.

OLD SHIP VARIATION ONE

Located on the top of the ship is an optical/matter field gathering lens called an Upper Capture Lens. It reads all of the data of the ship's location from the center of the ship to the top. (See next page)

Located on the bottom of the ship is the Lower Capture Lens. It reads all of the data from the center of the ship to the bottom. Just behind both lenses are the focusing lenses called Downsend lenses, that project all data from the ship's top to bottom directly through the cancel column to a central point located in the center of the ship called the Stellar Orb.

Also located with both the upper and lower Capture Lenses are the upper and lower Gather Lenses. They focus the captured fields and direct them with great precision into the Stellar Orb. As the fields are moving towards the outer of the ship, they travel through a tube called the Cancel Column which behaves very much like the cancel column in the T-700. The main difference here is that the laser in the T-700 is replaced with the field information collected by the Capture/Gather lenses. Once this information is received in the Stellar Orb, it is fed into the Curtain Countdown Virtual Data System. Adjacent to the curtain countdown system is a biocomputer that has a complete virtual databank of virtual images of what the Stellar Orb would see in the ship's Gather/Capture system, somewhere else in the galaxy.

This is, of course, called "target information." The data that is presently being viewed externally is called the Locale information.

Next, the Locale information and the target information are sent into a TIME/SEND converter. The TIME/SEND converter looks at the data and makes a time measurement between the two datas. This is then transmitted to Andromeda where it is processed by the Council Elders for dispatch. The reason for this step is so that two ships will not teleport simultaneously into the same space at the same time. I call it a "step in cosmic air control." Semjase said over a given time in the infancy of hyperleap technology, a lot of travelers were killed in this very manner.

Older Model Concept Engine

Data in

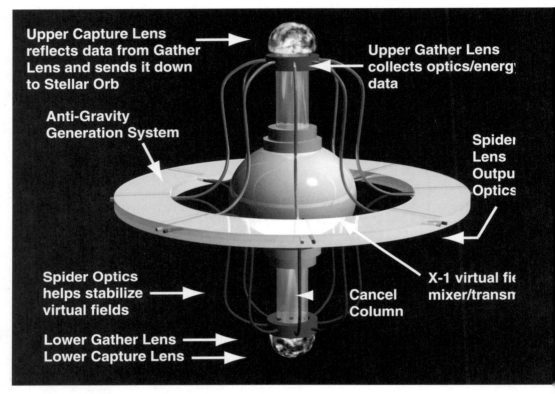

Upper Capture Lens reflects data from Gather Lens and sends it down to Stellar Orb

Upper Gather Lens collects optics/energy data

Anti-Gravity Generation System

Spider Lens Outpu Optics

Spider Optics helps stabilize virtual fields

X-1 virtual fie mixer/transn

Cancel Column

Lower Gather Lens
Lower Capture Lens

figure 40-52

This unit was discontinued due to radiation leaks.

Once the clearance is given, a device located alongside the Stellar Orb begins to feed a summation signal of the target/Locale information into the Stellar Orb.

The feeding device is none other than our own X-1 healing machine.

Remember, the X-1 allows the body to heal itself instantaneously by removing time from the consciousness of the individual cell and thus the chromosome of the DNA is fed energy directly from the decay of a black hole via a space-time singularity and followed by a wormhole. This wormhole is exactly what the X-1 feeds into when used in this manner. **The virtual resonation of an active wormhole is an excellent source of energy and is a map through consciousness when the ship leaves the 3rd dimension and travels through the 4th.** At the precise moment that the 4th is entered, the foursquare dual dynamic system goes into effect. (Review Chapter 35 on the Irradiator choke.)

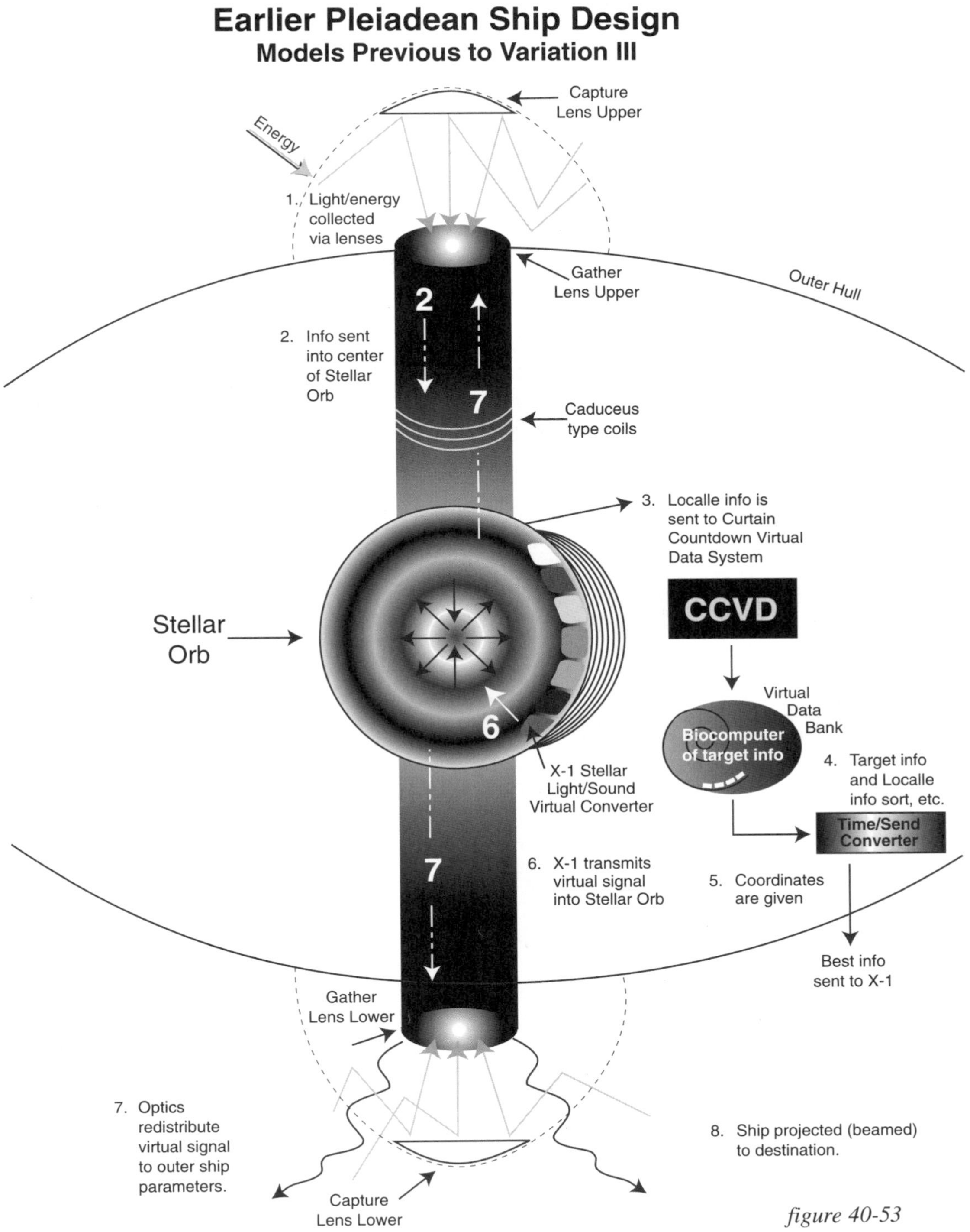

Earlier Pleiadean Ship Design
Models Previous to Variation III

Energy

Capture
Lens Upper

1. Light/energy
collected
via lenses

Gather
Lens Upper

Outer Hull

2

2. Info sent
into center
of Stellar
Orb

7

Caduceus
type coils

3. Locale info is
sent to Curtain
Countdown Virtual
Data System

CCVD

Virtual
Data
Bank

**Biocomputer
of target info**

Stellar
Orb

4. Target info
and Locale
info sort, etc.

6

**Time/Send
Converter**

X-1 Stellar
Light/Sound
Virtual Converter

6. X-1 transmits
virtual signal
into Stellar Orb

5. Coordinates
are given

7

Best info
sent to X-1

Gather
Lens Lower

7. Optics
redistribute
virtual signal
to outer ship
parameters.

8. Ship projected (beamed)
to destination.

Capture
Lens Lower

figure 40-53

477

Now the X-1 projects virtual destination imagery into the Stellar Orb. The new image moves back up the Cancel Column and is projected around the ship by the original data gathering optics. Just as they gather and capture, they also focus and transmit.

In addition to the system just described is an adjacent spider optical system. The mechanical arrangement varies in different ships, but its main purpose is to stabilize virtual subfields. When the main optics are engaged, the spider optics act as a virtual gyroscope, insuring that small subfields are stabilized. If they are not, the ship will be in a limited capacity in its hyperleap mode. Also, during slow-speed operation, they control Veil Curtains which manage gravity waves.

Variation III Craft showing Relocated Components

The term "variation" refers to similar components performing similar functions more efficiently because they are placed in different locations.

figure 40-54

478

View of Variation IV as it Approaches Erra

figure 40-55

As the ship moves closer, it is apparent that the planet is greener than Earth.

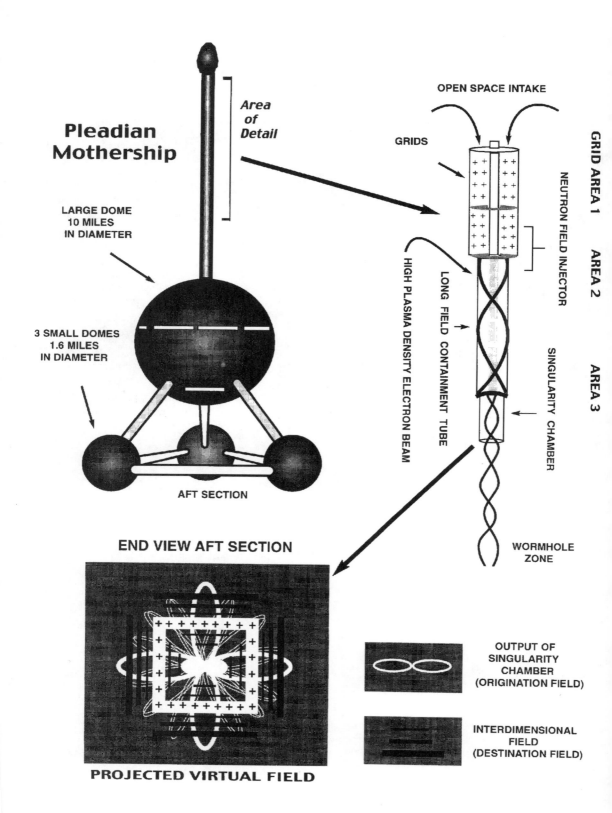

Pleadian Mothership

Area of Detail

LARGE DOME 10 MILES IN DIAMETER

3 SMALL DOMES 1.6 MILES IN DIAMETER

AFT SECTION

OPEN SPACE INTAKE

GRIDS

GRID AREA 1   AREA 2   AREA 3

NEUTRON FIELD INJECTOR

HIGH PLASMA DENSITY ELECTRON BEAM

LONG FIELD CONTAINMENT TUBE

SINGULARITY CHAMBER

WORMHOLE ZONE

END VIEW AFT SECTION

PROJECTED VIRTUAL FIELD

OUTPUT OF SINGULARITY CHAMBER (ORIGINATION FIELD)

INTERDIMENSIONAL FIELD (DESTINATION FIELD)

Theory of Operation: Large Object Transport System

This system is used in mother ships. The outside geometry of the ship varies from the one illustrated, to the more popular large cigar craft. When not in the highly excited mode but a low frequency mode, the unit produces and artificial gravity which emanates from the singularity chamber section of the long field containment tube. As you can see this system is best suited to a cylindrical shaped craft.

The unit projects a proton field into nearby space. Space itself although thought of as a void, is actually active with hydrogen atoms and other atomic debris. This debris is too small to cause physical damage to third dimensional traveling craft. But when excited at grid area #1 and bombarded with slow neutrons of area #2 creates a plasma that when focused into area #3 begins building, a black hole, because of the high gravitic density of the point of origin of the singularity field.

Those thusly created gravity waves are directed from the center of the large sphere into the center of the small spheres. This in turn creates a comfortable gravity for the occupants. If a heavy object needs to be moved within the structure, gravity around the object is lowered and object becomes manageable by a small labor force.

As a propulsion system the wormhole field is increased in the aft direction (bottom section) of the ship and it moves in the aft direction onto hyper speed.

Again for slow speed manipulation the gravity field is subtly oriented against nearby planetary bodies such as mining operations on objects as small as asteroids. In addition by increasing the proton field around the +grids area #1 and extending this field, a protective field is produced that protects the ships from stray meteorites or intruding weaponry from hostile invaders.

Bibliography

Antigravity & The World Grid, edited by David Hatcher, Childress Adventures Unlimited Press, Stelle, IL ISBN 0-932813-03-8, c-1987

Biochemistry, Second Edition, N.V. Bhagvan, Ph.D., J.B. Lippincott Co., ISBN 0-397-52086-7, c-1974

Biological Effects of Electric and Magnetic Fields of Extremely Low Frequency, Merril Eisenbud, Sc.D., Asher Sheppard, Ph.D. Institute of Environmental Medicine, New York University, ISBN 0-8147-2562-7, c-1977

Chemistry — Third Edition, J.V. Quagliano & L.M. Vollarino, Prentice-Hall, Englewood Cliffs, NJ, ISBN 69-10012, c-1958

Chemistry — Imagination and Implication, A. Truman, Schwartz Academic Press, NYC-London, ISBN 72-84366, c-1923

Conversations Byond the Light, Dr. Pat Kubis, Mark Macy Griffin Publishing, Boulder, CO, ISBN 1-882180-47-X, c-1995

Death of Ignorance, Frederick Bell, Ph.D., Pyradyne Press, Laguna Beach, CA ISBN 714-499-2603, c-1979

Diseases/Causes Diagnosis, Current Therapy Nursing Management Patient Education, (manual), Inter-Med Communications, Spring House, PA, ISBN 0-916730-19-0, c-1983

Electro Gravitics, edited by Thomas Valone, M.D., P.E., Integrity Research Institute, Washington, D.C., ISBN 0-9641070-0-7, c-1993

Enter the Zone, Barry Sears, Ph.D., Harper Collins, NYC, ISBN 0-06-039150-2, c-1995

Extra-Sensory Perception of Quarks, Stephen M. Phillips, Ph.D., Theosophical Publishing House, Madras India/London, England/Wheaton, IL, USA, ISBN 0-8356-0227-3, c-1980

Fats & Oils, Udo Erasmus, Alive/Vancouver, Canada BC, ISBN 0-920470-10-6, c-1995

Flax Oil as a True Aid Against Arthritis, Heart Infarction, Cancer and Other Diseases, Dr. Johanus Budwig, Apple Publishing, Vancouver, BC, ISBN 0-09695272-1-7, c-1992

Gem Elixers & Vibrational Healing, Volume One, Guru Das, Cassandra Press, Boulder, CO, ISBN 0-961-58750-4, c-1985

Lasers: Theory & Applications, K. Thyagarajan & A.K. Ghatak, Plenum Press, NYC-London, ISBN 0-306-40598-9, c-1981

Life Extension & Life Extension Companion, Durk Pearson, Sandy Shaw, Warner Books, NYC, ISBN 0-446-51272-9, c- 1982

Nuclear Evolution, Christopher Hills, University of the Trees Press, Boulder Creek, CA, ISBN 0-916438-09-0, c-1968

Outlines of Biochemistry, Second Edition, Eric E. Conn, P.K. Stumpf, John Wiley & Sons, NYC/London/Sydney, Australia, ISBN 66-22836, c-1973

Prescription for Nutritional Healing, James F. Balch, M.D., Phyllis A. Balch, C.N.C. Avery Publishing Group, Garden Park City, NY, ISBN 089529-7272, c-1997

The Antigravity Handbook, compiled by David Hatcher, Childress Adventures Unlimited Press, Stelle, IL, ISBN 0-932813-01-2, c-1985

The Complete Medicinal Herbal, Penelope Ody, Dorling Kindersley, London, NYC, Stuttgart, ISBN 1-56458-187-X, c-1993

The Encyclopedia of Common Diseases, Staff of Prevention Magazine, Rodale Press, ISBN 0-87857-113-2, c-1976

The Fellowship, Brad Steiger, Doubleday, NYC, ISBN 0-385-24304-9, c-1988

The Ion Effect, Fred Soyka, Alan Edmunds, E.P. Dutton & Co., NYC, ISBN 0-525-13480-8, c-1977

The Promise, Brad Steiger, Frederick Bell, Ph.D., Inner Light Publications, NYC, ISBN 0-938294-07-5, c-1991

The World of Biology, P. William Davis, Eldra Pearl Solomon, McGraw-Hill, NYC, ISBN 0-07-015548-8, c-1974

UFO Crash at Aztec, William S. Steinman, Wendelle C. Stevens, Privately published by Wendelle Stevens, ISBN 0-934269-05X, c-1984

About the Author

Dr. Fred Bell was born in Ann Arbor, Michigan. At nine years old he was working at the university of Michigan on projects such as early Stealth (later known as the Philadelphia experiment) and the "Pinch effect," the predecessor to nuclear fusion (H bomb). At sixteen years old, he entered the United States Air Force (he could not wear a uniform until his seventeenth birthday because that was the legal age of admission with parental consent.) During his Air Force days he worked on SAGE radar tracking UFOs in northern California. The sister SAGE site to Dr. Bell's was later known as the Montauk in upstate New York, notorious for UFO sightings.

After he left the USAF he worked for Rockwell International on projects such as the Eyeglass, a predecessor to President Reagan's Star Wars. During his tenure at Rockwell, he worked along side Dr. Werner Von Braun on the Apollo Saturn lunar landing projects. He left Rockwell and went into the private sector. Here he visited over 3000 companies as a consultant on many top secret projects. Some of these companies were IBM — Univac, EG&G, Lockhead, Boeing, Hughs, TRW, Bell Telephone Research, Murray Hill, CIA R&D department Langely, FBI, all Naval-Airforce and AEC (Atomic Energy Commision) labs in the continental United States and many, many more. He retired from commercial science in the 1970's and studied with many Himalayan masters. During this time he became a world famous contactee with Pleiadian scientists. After obtaining a medical degree he began lecturing with the National Health Federation worldwide.

His work is the subject of many author's books, including Brad Steiger, who wrote 2 bestsellers about his life. The first, called *The Fellowship*, published by Doubleday and Bertelsman in Europe, and the second called *The Promise*, is still a running bestseller in Japan.

He is an international inventor and has patented the Nuclear Receptor. He is the father of "Negative Ionization" and his inventions are used worldwide. Some of his clients include Queen Elizabeth, the Dalai Lama, TM of America, Andrew Young, Ray Bradbury, Mohammed Ali, Ken Norton, James Brown, George Winston and many holistic institutions worldwide.

Dr. Bell also works with world renowned bands and has composed 4 musical albums to raise consciousness. He has remained anonymous until now due to reasons of privacy but now he is here to enlighten you into the true values of the new millennium.

Dr. Bell is currently a state chairman serving on the business advising counsel under House majority leader congressman Tom Delay in the 106th Congress. He is currently traveling the world conducting seminars and concerts. Watch for his appearance in your area.